Public Service Ethics

The study and practice of ethics, in all its exemplary and execrable forms, matter now more than ever. It deals with one of the most gripping questions in life: "What is the right thing to do?"

Public Service Ethics: Individual and Institutional Responsibilities, Third Edition, introduces readers to this personally relevant and professionally challenging field of study. No matter the topic—the necessity of ethics, intriguing human behavior experiments, provocative approaches to decision-making, new theories to understand ethical actions, the role of ethics codes, whistleblowing incidents, corruption exposés, and the grandeur as well as decay of morality—there is no shortage of controversy. This book discusses these issues, explains how they arise, and suggests what can be done about them. The authors make the narrative user-friendly and accessible by highlighting dilemmas, challenging readers to resolve them, and enticing them to go beyond the text to discover and confront new issues. New to this Third Edition:

- Exploration of fascinating and important new topics such as the Green New Deal, Black Lives Matter, oaths of office, classroom dishonesty, state corruption, the Biden administration, and the ethical challenges of the COVID-19 pandemic and response.
- In-depth profiles of newsworthy figures, including Michael Flynn, Alexander Vindman, Anthony Fauci, and John Lewis.
- All new case studies drawing on actual and hypothetical events to give students an opportunity to apply concepts and analytical frameworks.
- All new end-of-chapter discussion questions and exercises to encourage students to think more deeply about ethical issues.

The authors' conversational writing style invites readers to annotate pages with their own ideas, experiences, comparisons, and insights, bolstering students' confidence and ultimately preparing them for the ethical problems they will face in their own careers. This lively and thorough new edition is required reading for all public administration and public policy students.

James S. Bowman is Professor Emeritus of Public Administration at the Askew School of Public Administration and Policy, Florida State University, USA.

Jonathan P. West is Professor of Political Science and Director of the graduate public administration and policy program at the University of Miami, USA.

"In this new edition of *Public Service Ethics*, Bowman and West drive home the point that ethical behavior requires much more than following the rules and that ethics belongs at the center of effective and democratic governance. Up-to-date and comprehensive at the individual, organizational, and policy levels, they provide a guidebook for navigating the challenging ethical landscape of contemporary public service that can be used in both the classroom and the workplace."

Danny L. Balfour, *Grand Valley State University, USA*

"In this excellent contribution to the field, Bowman and West's third edition continues their tradition of sweeping, cutting-edge analysis of public administration ethics. They provide a broad sweep of normative issues, emerging questions confronting the field, and one of the few in-depth treatments of institutional ethics programs."

Stuart C. Gilman, *United Nations Program against Corruption (Retired), USA*

"At a time of immense public challenges, this updated classic masterfully coaches the next generation of public servants in ethics. The authors present balanced and thorough assessments of current ethical issues facing individuals and organizations, as well as creative case studies. This is a first-rate textbook for public affairs courses."

Rosemary O'Leary, *University of Kansas, USA*

"Bowman and West's third edition brings ethics alive and up to date with examples relevant to government agencies, nonprofits, and the private sector. Current ethical dilemmas include mask wearing, societal and governmental responses to COVID, economic inequality as an ethical issue, social impact investing, the Green New Deal, and the climate crisis as ethical issues, Black Lives Matter calling attention to the disparate impact on Black men's lives of criminal justice policies, and an update of the horrific Grenfell Tower disaster. Bowman and West remind us that ethics is not for the fainthearted."

Sharon Mastracci, *University of Utah, USA*

"*Public Service Ethics: Individual and Institutional Responsibilities* is an excellent foundation for the study of public service ethics, providing a clear explanation of the major approaches, useful discussion topics for students, and excellent examples of ethical dilemmas in practical administration. A valuable and comprehensive text and an impressive achievement!"

Ian Scott, *Murdoch University, Australia*

Public Service Ethics

Individual and Institutional Responsibilities

Third Edition

James S. Bowman and Jonathan P. West

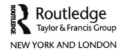

Routledge
Taylor & Francis Group

NEW YORK AND LONDON

Third edition published 2022
by Routledge
605 Third Avenue, New York, NY 10158

and by Routledge
2 Park Square, Milton Park, Abingdon, Oxon, OX14 4RN

Routledge is an imprint of the Taylor & Francis Group, an informa business

First edition published by CQ Press 2014
Second edition published by Routledge 2018

Library of Congress Cataloging-in-Publication Data
A catalog record has been requested for this book

ISBN: 978-1-032-06632-5 (hbk)
ISBN: 978-1-032-06631-8 (pbk)
ISBN: 978-1-003-20314-8 (ebk)

DOI: 10.4324/9781003203148

Typeset in Minion
by Apex CoVantage, LLC

Access the Support Material: www.routledge.com/9781032066318

In Memorandum:

Phyllis J. Bowman
Everett R. Bowman
JSB

For Colleen
JPW

Contents

List of Figures, Tables, and Exhibits

EXHIBITS

About the Authors

James S. Bowman is Professor Emeritus of Public Administration at the Askew School of Public Administration and Policy, Florida State University. Noted for his work in ethics and human resource management, Dr. Bowman is the author of nearly 150 journal articles and book chapters, as well as the editor of six anthologies. He is a coauthor of the prize-winning *Human Resource Management in Public Service: Paradoxes, Processes and Problems* (7th ed., in press). He is the former editor-in-chief of *Public Integrity*, a journal owned by the American Society for Public Administration. A past Network of Schools of Public Affairs and Administration Fellow, as well as a Kellogg Foundation Fellow, he has experience in the military, civil service, and business. Bowman was elected to the National Academy of Public Administration in 2017.

Jonathan P. West is Professor of Political Science and Director of the graduate public administration and policy program at the University of Miami. His research interests include ethics, public administration, and human resource management. He has published more than 150 peer-reviewed articles and book chapters as well as nine books. In addition to the books mentioned here, coauthored with Bowman and others, he has coauthored *American Politics and the Environment* (2nd ed., 2016) and coedited *American Public Service: Radical Reform and the Merit System* (2007) and *The Ethics Edge* (2nd ed., 2006). For 16 years he was the managing editor of *Public Integrity* journal. He was a captain in the U.S. Army serving as a management analyst in the Office of the Surgeon General.

Preface to the Third Edition

Compared to earlier editions, there remains an even more pressing need to address this vital area of study. Ethics—in all its exemplary and execrable, exhilarating and exhausting forms—*matters*. It deals with the most gripping question in life: "What is the right thing to do?" As important as it may be to "do things right," it is essential to "do right things." Indeed, regardless of how many things a person does in life, what will be remembered is how he or she responded to ethical challenges. The imperative nature of the topic, then, invites investigation. Since most existing public service ethics books do not report recent research or bring other material up to date, we have expanded our treatment of the subject. The aim is to capture reader interest by featuring in each chapter learning objectives, essential knowledge, skill-building material, telling endnotes, discussion questions, exercises, and appendices.

The intent is to make the narrative user-friendly and accessible by highlighting dilemmas, challenging readers to resolve them, and enticing them to go beyond the text to discover and confront new issues. In so doing, we trust that readers will contact us with their suggestions for improvement in the book (jbowman@fsu.edu; jwest@miami.edu). The ultimate goal is to contribute to student confidence as he or she confronts ethical issues in the future. In so doing, truly "own" this publication by annotating these pages with *your* ideas, disputes, satisfactions, discomforts, experiences, comparisons, applications, and insights. Then interact with others in a live or virtual classroom to stretch your thinking about the management of ethics and ethics of management.

As in the second edition, *Public Service Ethics: Individual and Institutional Responsibilities*, Third Edition, introduces readers to this personally relevant and professionally challenging field of study. No matter the topic—the necessity of ethics, intriguing human behavior experiments, provocative approaches to decision-making, new theories to understand ethical actions, the role of ethics codes, whistleblowing incidents, corruption exposés, and the grandeur as well as decay of morality—there is no shortage of controversy. This book discusses these issues, explains how they arise, and suggests what can be done about them. Be advised, however, that it will not, and cannot, provide answers for every case; the study of ethics is not like a cookbook full of recipes.

We have crafted a volume that

- assumes that readers are or will be line managers or technical experts,
- presents a comprehensive range of topics and issues,
- illustrates these discussions with a blend of current events from business, government, and the not-for-profit sectors, and
- encourages students not merely to peruse the material but also to apply it.

As members of the American Society of Public Administration, who have widely published in the field (see "About the Authors"), we believe that while no one is perfect, most people care deeply about ethics and are willing to think about basic issues when given the opportunity. To that extent, all of us are ethicists. Professionals, it follows, need to have not only technical and leadership competencies but also well-honed ethical skills to effectively conduct the public's business. That belief also motivated us to write the type of text described here.

The initial chapter—the first of three in Part I that explores the foundations of public service ethics—discusses the multiple rationales for examining ethics. Knowing why one is undertaking an activity is the first step to understanding. New material includes further discussion of the relationship between technical and ethical competence; selected updates on the nature of the market economy, journal-writing guidance, and further documentation; discussion questions; and exercises in this chapter as well as all others.

The second chapter probes multiple frames of reference in comprehending how to study the subject area. This is now augmented with scientific, critical thinking, moral clarity, and moral grandstanding concepts. Additionally, the Green New Deal and Black Lives Matter are referenced, case analysis of the 2017 London Grenfell Towers fire and the Penn State scandal are updated, and pandemic information is provided. The third exploratory chapter defines values and ethics. Fresh information includes references to oaths of office and profiles of Michael Flynn and Alexander Vindman.

With foundations in mind, Part II investigates approaches to ethics. These strategies emphasize individual-centered (cognitive and virtue) schools of thought. To gain a perspective on this material, Chapter 4 focuses on an inclusive and hierarchical theory of moral development that can be applied to individuals and organizations. It also introduces a recent contrasting theory from behavioral ethics that relies on psychological tendencies to explain human conduct. Among the revisions are further analysis of Milgram and Zimbardo experiments, updates on "trolley-ology," as well as discussion of morality pills. Since people do not necessarily make ethically sound choices, Chapter 5 presents a problem-solving strategy that showcases two cognitive decision-making methods: results and rule. More information on moral courage is provided using John Lewis as a compelling illustration. Chapter 6, the third and final individual-premised approach to ethics, turns the discussion from results and rule cognitive philosophies to virtue theory, from "head" to "heart." The theory is further defined in the context of role morality. One exemplary public servant profile, Donna Shalala, is brought up to date and another—Anthony Fauci—replaces an earlier one. As noted, and like other chapters, this one contains new discussion questions, exercises, and/or references for further reading.

Chapter 7 then consolidates the three individual-centered methods to ethics into a tripartite framework—the ethics triad—that provides a comprehensive tool to analyze difficult work issues. This framework is used to examine selected cases throughout the balance of the book. The chapter also introduces further elaboration of the field of behavioral ethics, which directly challenges the usefulness of traditional views of ethical decision-making such as those found in the triad. This school of thought argues that the prescriptive character of cognitive and virtue ethics does not adequately explain how people really act in ethical situations. Based on experimental and experiential evidence, the claim is that emotion is at least as important as logic—indeed, may be the basis of rationality—in decision-making. This in-depth discussion has been revised and expanded by furnishing discussion of the 2019 Business Roundtable Declaration and behavioral science nudges, plus a new case study and exhibit on the corona virus challenges.

Part III, beginning with Chapter 8, shifts from individual cognitive ("head") and virtue ("heart") ethics to organization-centered (physique or "body") approaches. That is, while the mastery of personally focused ethics explored in Part II is necessary, it is not sufficient for understanding the full scope of ethics, as individual conduct is affected by the environment within which it occurs. The chapter scrutinizes the ethical infrastructure in organizations and is followed by subsequent chapters dealing with corruption control and whistleblowing in institutions. Changes include discussion of inspectors general (IGs), oaths of office, and classroom dishonesty. Chapter 9's revisions on corruption control introduce new material on fraud in government, the roots of corruption, COVID as well as "the other COVID," "drain the swamp," systemically dangerous institutions, gift-giving, plus scandals containing updates on the Flint, Michigan water disaster, the Wells Fargo case, and the Olympic swimming scandal. Chapter 10 on whistleblowing supplies updates as well as new material on normalization of fraud, the importance of how whistleblowing incidents are framed, elaboration on resignations in protest, and a United Nations peacekeeping case.

Selected issues in public service ethics constitute Part IV of the book, with separate chapters on ethics of elected officials, organizational gaming and performance measurement, at-will employment doctrine, and the Hatch Act. These discussions represent a diverse set of topics that illustrate the all-encompassing character of topic area. Chapters 11 and 12, respectively, examine behaviors of political figures and an important dimension of improper institutional conduct, gaming the system. Added are congressional conflicts of interest, alternatives to lying, incivility, further discussion of "dirty hands," presidential falsehoods, the 2020 elections, the Temple University ranking disgrace, the college admission scandal, and new cases.

Chapters 13 and 14 explore, in depth, two different issues using the ethic triad. The first is the analysis of employment at-will, which is updated to include Donald Trump's 2020 effort to politicize large parts of the civil service. The second is new to this book and examines a related issue, the potential amending of the 1939 Hatch Act.

Part V consists of the closing chapter that serves as a capstone for the text. It emphasizes that all people are ethical agents who have the choice between moral grandeur and decay, and provides guidelines for honorable action in the years ahead. In addition to updates, especially on white-collar crime, coverage of the governmental response to the pandemic, state corruption and anti-corruption measures, democratic governance, the Biden administration, and the American experiment in light of catastrophic climate change are new to this edition.

Each chapter, then, includes case studies drawing on actual and hypothetical events that give students the opportunity to apply the concepts and analytical frameworks in the chapters. Some cases present scenarios that are then followed by questions to consider; others are applied case studies in which we guide the reader through the application of a decision-making framework to show the thought process behind how a decision might be made. Chapters 13 and 14 are the exception, in that the entirety of the chapter is essentially a case analysis. In addition, end-of-chapter discussion questions and exercises give students further opportunity to think more deeply about ethical issues, as well as apply what they have learned.

Welcome to public service ethics in a book whose subject will affect the future of all readers in their careers. And now for the adventure!

James S. Bowman and *Jonathan P. West*
Spring, 2021

Acknowledgments

We take pleasure in acknowledging the contributions and assistance of Qian Huang, Yi Fang, Karen Cinkus, Stephanie M. Belaustegui, Jasmine Atkinson and the anonymous referees. In addition, our past students, both on campus and online, have helped us clarify thinking about ethics.

Routledge, as well as the authors, would also like to thank the reviewers for their time and insights.

Finally, appreciation is due to M. E. Sharpe Publishers, SAGE Publications, Routledge, and Elsevier for granting permission to adapt some of our previous work to this book.

PART I

Foundations of Public Service Ethics

1 Pertinence, Practicality, and Poppycock

Always do right. This will gratify some people and astonish the rest.

—Mark Twain

This chapter—the first of three that explore the foundations of public service ethics—explores the multiple rationales for examining ethics as well as reasons behind the reluctance to discuss ethics in policy and administration. Knowing why one is undertaking an activity is the first step to understanding any situation. The chapter objectives are to

- appreciate personal reasons for studying ethics;
- recognize the pervasiveness of ethics;
- acknowledge that professional public service has never been solely a technical enterprise;
- understand that the exercise of power is immediate, real, and vital;
- distinguish the costs associated with ethical pitfalls; and
- evaluate credulous poppycock that claims ethics is impossible, unnecessary, and simple.

PERTINENCE: REASONS TO STUDY ETHICS

There is no guarantee that anyone will make more effective choices by studying ethics. But such study helps to contemplate them on your own and to speak intelligently about ethical matters with others. Reflecting on ethics issues encourages the recognition of moral duty and obligations. Ideally, it serves to make prudent judgments that can be publicly justified. This understanding is the basis for at least five reasons to explore ethics: It is personal, pervasive, professional, powerful, and full of pitfalls where the costs of ethical failure are high.

Personal

While the word "ethics" may provoke fear and loathing as a dull topic, or one that takes people out of their comfort zone, in fact, it stimulates thinking on life's most compelling questions—those that deal with what is right and wrong, good and bad. As Thomas Schelling (1984, 38) writes, "Often the question is not 'Do I want to do the right thing?' but rather 'What is the right thing to want

DOI: 10.4324/9781003203148-2

to do?'" The initial observation, then, is that humans are the only creatures that are struck by the difference between *is* and *ought*, and wonder about what sort of creatures they are and could be. *Homo sapiens* are, in other words, unique moral agents because they have the capacity to think about thinking, to ponder about what is "right" and "proper" and "fair" (Wilson, 1993).

In public service, the "what is" question seeks to discern what is actually occurring in a particular setting. This seemingly obvious factual or descriptive question aims to better recognize or make judgments about ethical behavior. However, describing "what is" is complicated by the varying perceptions, beliefs, values, and biases found at the individual, organizational, and societal levels. The "ought to be" question is normative and focuses on what should be done in a given situation (e.g., how to treat a long-time employee when downsizing). The issue for managers and leaders is how to get from "what is" to "what ought to be" in practice. It is challenging because it requires weighing what can be done with what ought to be done. This is where you come in.

You count, and you can make a difference in the movement from "what is" to "what ought to be" by adding to—or subtracting from—excellence and joy in the workplace. What you do matters. This book is aimed squarely at readers, inviting everyone to actively engage ethics—to take it personally. It will help prepare for the day when you are called upon to juggle these considerations and then decide: "This is what should be done, this is why it should be done, and this is how it will be done." When that time comes, it will be important to be confident that the action taken is ethically feasible and desirable.

This leads to a second observation: People unabashedly make decisions about what is best. Henry Ford said, "Believe in your best, think your best, study your best, have a goal for your best, never be satisfied with less than your best, try your best—and in the long run, things will work out for the best." You need to know what is right and that the choices you make are good. If an unexamined life is not worth living, following Socrates, then, an examined life is lived for a good reason. Every act of every person is a moral act, to be tested by moral criteria; to study ethics is to learn not only how people make good judgments but also why they make bad ones. Readers are bid to probe the empowering, if inherently controversial, choices about meaning and value in public service. Administrators and employees without a carefully considered set of public service values are likely to be poor decision makers; they are inclined to dither when confronted with decisions presenting ethical implications.

The third observation of a personal nature is that individual values are the final standard, as there are many, sometimes conflicting, determinants of action. "To the question of your life," wrote Jo Coudert in *Advice from a Failure*, "you are the only answer. To the problems of your life, you are the only solution." Individual responsibility and accountability, therefore, are inescapable (notice the "i" in "ethical"). But note that people typically perceive themselves as more ethical than others and that consensus regarding proper behavior diminishes when proceeding from abstract to specific circumstances. Actual human contact can change everything, clarifying some issues while confounding others. Black and white can, in fact, look like two shades of gray.

The implications of the personal reason for studying ethics are that they can be both enabling (it is not mere sentimentality) and debilitating (being questioned about ethics can strike at the core of one's moral being). Either way, how you handle an ethical dilemma may be the only thing remembered about you ("The decision of a moment," it has been said, "lasts a lifetime"). The question, in short, is not whether we will die but how we will *live*. Existence is defined by choices, as French philosopher Albert Camus asked, "Should I kill myself, or have a cup of coffee?"

Pervasiveness

Not only is ethics a highly personal concern, but it is also a pervasive one. It is part and parcel of the activities of everyday life, encompassing and affecting almost everything that happens. Indeed, as technology has further interconnected with others around the globe, it has also made us more ethically interdependent. Ethics is a fundamental, familiar component of all walks of life: business, government, religion, sports, academe, and nonprofit organizations. Newspaper headlines, television and radio broadcasts, and Internet coverage provide story after story of wrongdoing in business, government, and nonprofit sector organizations. Heroes and heroines plummet from their exalted status by making poor choices. Likewise, organizational brands are tarnished by immoral actions. In both, citizen trust is lost and financial resources are squandered for short-term gain. Ethical leadership is lacking and sorely needed, particularly in the civil service where public-regarding ethics is so central to the core of democracy: government by, for, and of the people.

And ethical concern is probably greater than ever before as ethical issues have a tendency to be magnified and expanded today for three interrelated reasons:

- The *scale effect:* Modern technologies make it possible to do misdeeds on a massive scale.
- The *display effect:* Communications systems (particularly the advent of social media) can dramatically package, instantly distribute, and repeat incidents.
- The *PR effect:* Public communication has become professionalized public relations as a result of polling, focus group research, image management, news event "spin," "damage control," "spontaneous" grassroots mobilization, and related marketing techniques.

(Adapted from Heclo, 2008, 26–28)

Velocity, in short, can readily trump veracity. As Mark Twain said, "A lie can travel halfway round the world while the truth is putting on its shoes."

Additionally, as the postindustrial service economy shifts emphasis from products to people, higher moral standards are expected. People have learned to become sensitive to the natural environment, and today they are also becoming sensitive to the ethical environment. Yet while a broader range of activities are seen as unethical today, conditions for employee abuse continue to grow, exacerbated by rapid societal change.

Professional

Public servants, accordingly, must not only do technical things right but also do ethically right things. Professional work is value intensive as it focuses on goals, synthesis, and priorities; leaders take responsibility for what is done as they serve as models and represent others. Someone without basic ethics skills is professionally illiterate. Indeed, ethical competence encompasses technical competence. The classic definition—and often oath—of a *professional* is someone who shows leadership in technical ability and ethical character. A professional is not a professional merely because of her expertise but also because of her adherence to ethical standards. The ability to contemplate, enhance, and act on these faculties is the essence of professional life. It is unthinkable for a professional not to do her best; it is her duty (consult Appendix 1.2, Book Chapters and NASPAA Professional Competencies in Public Administration).

This is what makes scandals so devastating. Scandals result when professionals in a variety of fields have demonstrated a lack of understanding of this basic precept—namely, the question "Management for what?" seems to have been misunderstood. Management is not an end; rather, it is a means to an end. Thus, while process and policy often overlap, the ethics of process—regardless of the policy issues involved—is key. If process is ably done, policy is likely to be ethical as well. A focus on "why" when making decisions may lead to recognition of ignorance, followed by the acquisition of knowledge, resulting in expansion of moral imagination. The aptitude for critical judgment is the sine qua non of a professional. Those who treat management and ethics apart will never understand either one.

One attempt to keep management focused on ethics is the appointment of a chief ethics and compliance officer in an organization. Criticized by some as window dressing, while praised by others as a way to highlight ethical issues and promote right behavior, these officials have become commonplace in large firms, nonprofit organizations, and governments (see Exhibit 1.1 on a week in the life of Marisol Lopez, an ethics and compliance officer). A critical question is whether these positions have the power and resources to make a difference (see Chapter 8).

EXHIBIT 1.1   A Week in the Life of Ethics Officer Marisol Lopez

Marisol Lopez is an ethics and compliance officer for XYZ, a large nonprofit organization in a big southeastern city. Like most nonprofit ethics officers, Lopez faces a thorny set of issues that creates challenges, threats, and opportunities for her and for her charitable organization. Her work is complicated by the coronavirus, the downturn in the economy, declining charitable donations, a rapidly changing workforce, an increasingly cumbersome legal and regulatory environment, pressures for higher productivity, and pending layoffs. Lopez earned her MPA degree with a concentration in law and ethics more than 20 years ago. She has been working in the nonprofit arena since that time, progressing up the ranks to become the organization's first ethics and compliance officer, a position she has held since its creation ten years ago. She is a strong communicator, politically savvy, and able to assimilate information quickly.

After arriving at the office on Monday morning, Lopez is told about a breaking news story on a financial scandal involving another major employer in the city. She is aware that any large organization, whether in business, a nonprofit, or government, can have its reputation tarnished by the unethical actions of managers or employees. She is grateful to be working for an organization that has long recognized the importance of ethics and proactively created her office to reduce the risk of any scandal or wrongdoing. Other nonprofits, such as the American Cancer Society, American Red Cross, and American Arbitration Association, have created ethics officer positions to supplement their ongoing ethics programs. She feels fortunate that she reports directly to the CEO and makes regular presentations to the board of directors, unlike some chief ethics officers in her professional association (the Ethics and Compliance Officer Association), who report indirectly through the general counsel. Her direct reporting channel helps her to be strategically relevant and independent, a key to her effectiveness.

As she reviews her schedule for the week, she notes several important matters that must be attended to:

- *Today*—She needs to put the finishing touches on an article for her organization's newsletter, a Q&A-style piece regarding hypothetical ethical situations and how to deal with them. Then she is giving a briefing to a small group of board members at lunch highlighting several good examples of ethical behavior by organization members. In the afternoon, she is meeting with staff to review final revisions of their "no-gifts" policy. She also has a conference call scheduled with her counterparts in three other local not-for-profits to discuss common challenges.

- *Tuesday*—She is working with staff to complete a risk assessment study of the organization's fund-raising effort; in the afternoon, she is overseeing with the HR director an internal investigation of charges involving unfair hiring practices; later that day, she will participate in a new-employee orientation using Zoom, where she will be speaking about standards of behavior and the code of ethics.
- *Wednesday*—She is briefing the CEO and his staff regarding the implications of a compliance initiative affecting international operations. That afternoon, she is scheduled to attend an outside consultant's briefing on an assessment of program effectiveness in the budget office. Lopez closes the day with a one-hour meeting with key stakeholders to discuss the city's COVID-19 measures as the economy recovers.
- *Thursday*—She is planning to review revisions to the policies and procedures manual; later, she will convene an ethics committee composed of representatives from human resources, finance, fund-raising, and operations. They will be discussing ways in which the organizational culture creates risks and how to mitigate them to stay out of trouble. The committee is trying to get away from the "one-and-done" checklist mentality for improving ethics, which simply tallies how many people certify that they've read the code of conduct or participated in mandatory ethics training.
- *Friday*—She is scheduled to examine ethics hotline messages that report misconduct to see if there are any red flags needing attention. After that, she is meeting with a group of mid-level supervisors to discuss how to make people feel comfortable in reporting problems. Lopez remembered how impressed she was by a recent article written by another ethics officer that said, "If employees believe reporting bad news equates to failure, that organization is building a toxic culture." She wants to avoid spending all of her time and her staff's "firefighting" in response to compliance problems and instead focus on building a culture that promotes ethics. She will encourage the committee to benchmark their practices against peer group nonprofits with similar histories.

Lopez's schedule shows the broad range of issues and events that might be encountered by ethics and compliance officers. In the corporate arena, chief ethics officers emerged in the early 1990s when the Federal Sentencing Guidelines for corporations were implemented. Under this legislation, firms with effective compliance and ethics programs receive preferential treatment during prosecutions for white-collar crime. The 2002 Sarbanes–Oxley Act and the 2010 Dodd–Frank Act further accelerated this trend to help identify potential problems. Nonprofit organizations and governments have taken a similar path by establishing ethics officer positions as part of their ethics program.

Power

A fourth reason for interest in ethics is found in the capacity of government and its agents to exercise power. The study and practice of public administration has never been regarded as only a technical matter. Moral reform is the impetus of modern public administration as values are at its soul (Frederickson, 1996). Governance is both a democratic and a moral endeavor. The argument for democracy is not that it is efficient but that it is the right form of government. If questions of right and wrong are answered by the state, those decisions are the immediate, real, and vital official allocation of values. When citizens, advocacy groups, and lobbyists demand government intervention, they seek an authoritative resolution of a conflict of values. This distribution of values—promoting particular values while minimizing others—is significant because it has far-reaching ethical consequences. The results range from human health to social and corporate welfare to government regulation. Democracy provides accountability mechanisms for such value allocations, which can permit careful consideration of competing interests by decision makers.

Social control of ethical behavior in public service can be assessed by considering the types of power exercised, the source of the power within or outside the organization, and the locus of social control mechanisms applied to individuals and organizations. Table 1.1 shows social influence exercised through three types of power: symbolic, economic, or coercive. Symbolic power is linked to values and beliefs, and it invokes emotional reactions (e.g., internal: praise; external: publicity), which can be used by an organization to appeal to its members, the media, and other stakeholders and to incentivize action on ethical issues.

TABLE 1.1	Social Control of Ethical Behavior in Organizations: Type, Source, and Focus of Power		
Source of Power	**Type of Power Used**	**Applied to the Individual**	**Applied to the Organization**
Internal to the Organization (Organization Culture and Structure)	• Symbolic Power • Economic Power • Coercive Power	• Letter of commendation, award, praise, criticism, humiliation, storytelling • Bonus, raise, promotion, firing, pay freeze • Not legally available (But: kidnapping, forceful threat, beating, forced exposure to toxins, etc.)	• Code of ethics, policies and processes that generate behavioral norms • Mission, strategy • Not relevant (unless organization is "suicidal")
External to the Organization (Nongovernmental Stakeholders)	• Symbolic Power • Economic Power • Coercive Power	• Minority proxy resolution to remove firm's officers • Bribe, kickback, award, reward • Not legally available (But: disruptive picketing of executive homes, terrorist attacks, vandalism)	• Publicity, news • Purchase, boycott, strike, slowdown • Not legally available (But: violence accompanying strike, vandalism, sabotage, terrorism)
External to the Organization (Legal and Government Pressures)	• Symbolic Power • Economic Power • Coercive Power	• Jawboning, warning, use of social networks • Fine, tax • Jail, execution	• Warning, citation, testimony at congressional hearing • Fine, tax, contract, quota, tax credit, tariff, regulatory barriers to entry • Forced shutdown

Source: Wood (1994, 305). Reprinted by permission of Pearson Education, Inc., Upper Saddle River, NJ.

Economic power involves material rewards or sanctions to achieve ethical objectives. It is exercised by those inside or outside the organization in the form of pay raises or adverse personnel actions, in the case of the former, and budget cuts, in the case of the latter. Coercive power entails the use of force or threat (e.g., incarceration) to control behavior. Internal social controls seek to generate behavior norms (e.g., mission statements); external social controls are applied by government regulations or stakeholders who seek to influence policy.

Price of Ethical Pitfalls

A final consideration in studying ethics is the substantial costs that ethical problems can incur. It is difficult to put a dollar figure on the costs of such failures because they are not reported on a balance sheet. However, the expenses can be considerable and, as Thomas, Schermerhorn, and Dienhart (2004, 58–59) demonstrate, they can occur at three levels (Figure 1.1). Level 1 costs are less problematic to calculate and are often overemphasized by leaders. They include fines and penalties occurring as a consequence of ethical breakdown. These levies may be significant but are often bearable, even nominal, notably for those organizations that are well insured. Level 2 costs are "clean-up" expenditures (audit, attorney, investigator fees) that are usually as high as, or higher than, Level 1 costs. Level 3 outlays are typically underappreciated by executives and harder to quantify but often devastating. They can take the greatest toll because the costs include multiple adverse effects: loss of reputation and morale, and increase of cynicism and regulation. Given the high price of ethical failure, preventive strategies are a wise investment.

| FIGURE **1.1** | **Price of Ethical Failure** |

Source: Adapted from Thomas et al. (2004).

EXHIBIT 1.2	Crossing the Line . . . With Costly Consequences

The Houston Astros sign-stealing scandal is costly to careers and pocketbooks. Throughout their 2017 World Series title run and part of the 2018 season the Astros stole signs that signaled to the hitter what pitch to expect. The scheme was revealed by Evan Drellick and Ken Rosenthal of *The Athletic* and confirmed by people working for the team, including pitcher Mike Fiers. The genesis of the sign-stealing process was a player and a coach, the hitter hoping to benefit at the plate from advance knowledge of the sign and the coach trying to help (Calcaterra, 2019).

The rule breaking took place despite warnings of severe penalties for violators. The sign-swiping involved the use of electronics to capture catcher-to-pitcher signs and relay them to the hitter by loud whistling, clapping, and eventually thumping on a garbage can. The penalties included suspensions of the Astros manager, general manager, and assistant manager; forfeiting the Astros draft picks (first- and second-round) for two years; and paying the maximum fine allowed of $5 million. Lawsuits, subsequent firing of the Astros manager and general manager, tainted pennants, and tarnished reputations were longer-range consequences of the infractions.

Sources: Anderson and Axisa (2020), Calcaterra (2019), ESPN (2020), Vigdor (2020).

In short, all of these reasons—with their personal, pervasiveness, professional, power, and pitfall implications—account for the salience of issues such as business fraud, alleged misuse of National Rifle Association assets by its own executives, questionable Red Cross management and accounting practices, corporate profiteering during the pandemic, the Federal Bureau of Investigation (FBI) not heeding terrorist warnings, firefighters setting fires, clergymen and coaches and scout masters abusing children (and their superiors covering up the problem), Olympic judges and school teachers rigging scores, baseball sign stealing (Exhibit 1.2), players taking steroids, Wall Street insider trading, document shredding, off-shore tax havens, media moguls sexually harassing coworkers, Wells Fargo creating fake customer accounts, automakers cheating on emission standards, cyber bullying, businesses dumping toxic waste, and hundreds of financial officers "restating" misleading company audits. Ethics and violations of ethics, in short, are based on the actions of people.

PRACTICALITY: COMMITMENT AS A PRIVILEGE AND OBLIGATION

Accordingly, ethics cannot be achieved unless all people in the organization practice it at a personal level. A personal commitment to honorable behavior is both a privilege and an obligation (see Newell, 2015). Most people want to be ethical and to follow through on personal and professional commitments. They intend to do the right thing but sometimes make wrong choices or remain uncertain about which course of action is the right one. Success ultimately depends on what we know, what we do, and what we become as a result. To live well is to cultivate virtues and avoid vices (see Chapter 6 as well as Hall, 2018). As Robert Byrne observed, "the purpose of life is to live a life of purpose."

Excellence, as Aristotle saw, cannot be attained without studying and mastering the art of achievement. As a manager or future manager, you cannot delegate that responsibility; you must show the way by example. This requires careful thought, clarification of one's values, and a willingness to do what it takes to achieve ethical competency. An ounce of practice, Gandhi observed, is worth more than tons of preaching. It is in this spirit that we challenge readers to develop an "ethics journal" that includes the creation of a customized checklist to help supply material for the journal. (See Exercise 4 at the end of the chapter.)

POPPYCOCK: MYTHS ABOUT ETHICS

Despite the compelling reasons to study ethics and its practicality, there is often a reluctance to discuss ethics in policy and administration. This hesitation—or outright rejection of ethics—rests on three contentions: that ethics is impossible, unnecessary, and simple. Recognize that nonsense may be more common than common sense.

Ethics as Impossible

It is contended that ethics is unattainable. Relativism maintains that all judgments are subjective and private, a matter of taste and opinion. Yet casual support for relativism, with the desire to be tolerant and respectful of others, is clearly deficient and misleading. "Relativity applies to physics," as Einstein saw, "not to ethics." Yes, different people have different codes and norms, but this truism proves little. There may be, for instance, different views about science (e.g., flat earth, evil spirits cause disease, global warming). Most people, however, do not therefore conclude that there is no truth in geography, medicine, or meteorology. Similarly, why assume that for an ethical truth to exist everyone must know it (Rachels & Rachels, 2019). People are fallible and cultures change; making reasoned, ethical judgments is not only appropriate but also a moral responsibility.

William J. Bennett (1978, 22), former U.S. Secretary of Education, tells of his visit to a classroom where his colleague encounters a student who is skeptical of a class on ethics. The dialogue illustrates that ethics is inescapable:

> *Student:* Mr. Jones, I don't think you can teach ethics, because there really aren't any in any real sense. Each person's values are as good as anybody else's. Values are subjective.
>
> *Instructor:* No, that's not true. Some people's values are better than others.
>
> *Student:* No, they're subjective. No one can impose his values on somebody else.
>
> *Instructor:* That's not true.
>
> *Student:* Yes, it is.
>
> *Instructor:* No, it isn't.
>
> *Student:* Well, that's your opinion and I have mine and it's just like I'm saying we disagree and you can't impose your viewpoint on me.
>
> *Instructor:* Well, I'm the teacher here and I say values are not subjective.
>
> *Student:* So what? I'm a student and I say they are.
>
> *Instructor:* Well, what do you think of this? I say values are not subjective and if you don't agree with me then I'll flunk you.
>
> *Student:* (gasp) What? What? You can't do that! Are you crazy?

Instructor: No, I can do that. Why not?

Student: Well, (sputtering) because it's not fair.

Instructor: "Fair," "fair," what do you mean "fair"? Don't impose your values and sense of right and wrong on me.

Student: (pause, and eventually) I see your point.

The instructor was able to parry back and forth with his student effectively to make a point, namely, suggesting that all values are equally valid because they are personal is simply not tenable. Adolph Hitler and Martin Luther King are not moral equivalents.

It also may be that some values are relative to culture but others are not. It is a mistake to say that if some values are relative, all must be. Why? It would mean that there are no cultural practices that are wrong (torture and slavery are widely accepted as wrong independent of culture). As Nietzsche famously wrote, "Nothing is true, all is permitted." To assert that no reasons need be given for one's beliefs is self-defeating—that is, to defend such a view requires giving reasons for it. If norms are impossible, then how does one defend her own standpoint (Rachels & Rachels, 2019)? If everything is relative, then, reductio ad absurdum, relativism has no foundation; everything loses meaning—including relativism.

Aristotle summarized the situation in this manner: Differences between traditions have enough in common—by virtue of shared humanity—to make the achievement of common norms a realistic goal. With relativism, however, there is no basis to condemn evil, no hope that people can work together to address humanity's problems. The goal in thinking about ethics is to generate progress, tolerate diversity without moral recklessness, and encourage moral imagination to find common ground between disparate views. Nonetheless, the relativity debate continues because rights are normative aims, not descriptive facts—a vision for a better world will always be contested (Boghossian, 2017).

It is, of course, true that many arguments—scientific and moral—cannot be definitively proved by logic or evidence. They can, however, be rational. Short of finality, there is ample scope for rationality in discussions. Decisions are objective in the sense that they can be defended and criticized by logical arguments. The irony today is that people often have strong convictions about minor issues (sports, fashions, weather), while holding weak convictions about major issues (what is right and wrong).

While personal preferences in food and drink may be the ultimate point as they require no public justification ("I like *nachos*" is inconsequential), an official's attitude toward whistleblowers does matter. If an opinion has no basis in reason, then it is unlikely to be very persuasive. And if ethical arguments cannot be conclusively resolved, this only indicates how fundamental they are.

Ethics as Unnecessary

In addition to the claim that ethics is impossible, a second contention is that ethics is simply unnecessary. The proposition is that society is a market system in which participants have only to look out for themselves and let the "invisible hand" handle all conflicts. Oblivious to ethical concerns, morality has nothing to do with anything. This self-operating, "automatic," nonjudgmental approach explains the appeal of commercial reasoning. Even arch global capitalist George Soros, however, points out that "[W]e can have a market economy, but we cannot have a market society" (Sandon, 2002). The embrace of the marketplace, along with the reluctance to engage moral issues, enfeebles discourse in the public square (Sandel, 2012, 14).

Former U.S. Secretary of Labor Robert Reich (2012) provocatively recounts abuses of public trust seen on Wall Street and in corporate suites, concluding that these "are not matters of private morality. They're violations of public morality. They undermine the integrity of our economy and democracy. They've led millions of Americans to conclude the game is rigged." Markets, stated differently, are at least as susceptible to erratic performance and emotional reaction as those in politics and government. To combat declining trust and rising cynicism in all sectors of the economy, moral imperatives must not be obscured.

The market, left on its own, is an arena of antagonistic, autonomous, isolated, selfish figures; ethics is irrelevant, impractical, and inappropriate. The idea of public life, in contrast, encourages citizens to see themselves as living with others in common purpose and to see leading an ethical life as contribution to a just polity. In a democratic society, value differences are resolved by the political process. The economy serves society; society does not serve the economy. If society exists to serve the market, then any moral limits that introduce market inefficiencies should be eliminated. Adam Smith, who after all was a professor of moral philosophy, knew this. Capitalism may make the world a better place, but only when it is a servant, not a master of human needs.

When economists talk about self-regulating markets, what they mean is that markets reach an equilibrium between supply and demand. This says nothing about whether this equilibrium is good for society. Unfortunately, morality is not built into markets; they are fine, for instance, with child labor and slavery. Ethics is not only optional but also vulnerable to a variation of Gresham's Law—like counterfeit currency, bad ethics drives out good ethics. This is why markets must be subject to other forces such as ethics and government. The "invisible hand" operates for the public good only if directed by the social values the political system enacts by its laws. Governments do not intrude on free markets; they organize and maintain them. As Peter Drucker (1977) famously wrote, "Free enterprise cannot be justified as being good for business. It can be justified only as being good for society."

Perhaps the first two contentions—that ethics is impossible and unnecessary—can best be countered in this way: Be bold in what you stand for and careful for what you fall for. The next justification to avoid ethics is that it is a clear-cut matter like the difference between day and night, so that discussing it is not worth the effort.

Ethics as Simple

Ethical decision-making is difficult and multifaceted, not as obvious and easy as concluding that everything is either black or white. Such judgments are often

- troublesome (conflicting standards may apply when confronting situations),
- hard to recognize (crucial information may be unavailable or deliberately withheld), and
- submerged in everyday workplace behavior (harassment and intimidation).

Many moral problems in institutions involve individuals, groups, or organizations, some of whom will be helped and others hurt as a result of factors beyond their control. Some may have their rights recognized, respected, and expanded; others may have their rights denied or ignored. Ethical resolution of issues related to benefits and harms, rights and wrongs, for different stakeholders are complex and require careful deliberation.

There are five reasons why ethical decision-making is not a straightforward process, as these decisions have

1. extended consequences—there is often a ripple effect, noted previously, as first-level consequences have multiple impacts both within and outside the organization (e.g., downsizing),

2. multiple alternatives—they are not usually just dichotomous options such as A versus B decisions (tell the truth or lie?) but involve more complex choices,

3. mixed outcomes—results are seldom clear, unambiguous, and "win-win," but frequently knotty and murky, with winners and losers,

4. uncertain impacts—unanticipated outcomes (greater costs, lower benefits) are not unusual, and

5. personal implications—decision makers often face real disadvantages and advantages (job loss, reputation enhancement).

(Adapted from Hosmer, 1987, 12–14)

As suggested by the first two statements, leaders should seriously ponder the possible second- and third-order consequences of all available alternatives. In doing so, they need to garner the advice from those who have relevant knowledge and experience to anticipate the likely differing reasons given the uncertain consequences. However, even the best-intentioned leaders often encounter two potentially dangerous pressures when facing decision deadlines: the need to craft timely solutions before all of the facts are in and the temptation to be more confident than circumstances warrant (see also Chapters 5 and 10). In these situations, Jean Lipman-Blumen (2005, 95) suggests following the old dictum "make haste slowly" and cites Steven Sample's recommendation to "think gray, see double, never completely trust an expert."

Studies of well-regarded "high reliability" organizations have examined the concept of "mindfulness." Weick, Sutcliffe, and Obstfeld (1999), for example, refer to this as enriched awareness among those in an organization concerned about the potential for a catastrophe. This awareness results in heightened consciousness and a sense of personal responsibility to prevent its occurrence. Such reflective conduct linking ethical thinking with action should promote "right-doing" and avoid wrongdoing. It requires open lines of communication from the bottom up, not just the top down. Sears, Roebuck & Company, for instance, had as part of its ethics program an employee survey called "My Opinion Counts." Among the questions were "Do you believe unethical issues are tolerated or not tolerated here?" and "Do you know how to report an ethical issue?" The program enabled the reporting of problems without fear of reprisal (subsequent chapters, especially Chapter 5, describe some additional tools to use when confronting thorny ethical choices).

A final reason people mistake ethics as elementary is that they fail to distinguish between what ethics is and what it is not. Ethics is not only complying with the letter of the law, religious beliefs, our feelings, and prevailing social norms or scientific formulas. While ethics is related to each of these claims, it is not as simple as they suggest. If ethics is not derived solely from feelings, law, religion, social norms, or science, where do we derive standards of behavior to act in the many situations encountered in personal and professional lives? The chapters that follow explore this question as the many facets of ethics and ethical decision-making are examined.

CONCLUSION

The observations on pertinence, practicality, and poppycock in this chapter can produce personal discomfort because ethics exists in the sphere of aspiration where one's reach exceeds one's grasp—the gap between the "is" and the "ought." Ethical quandaries are both hauntingly unavoidable and maddeningly intractable. Creating this awareness produces some anxiety, and thoughtful people already have plenty of that. Yet, for Aristotle, public service is not merely one calling among others but rather essential for the good life, to form good character and cultivate responsible communities. Moral excellence does not consist of maximizing pleasure over pain but rather is the result of taking pleasure and pain in the right things (Sandel, 2009).

Although ethical problems cannot be easily "solved" (Aristotle's admonition not to demand greater clarity than a subject permits is relevant here), their importance remains. The fact that decisions are hard to make does not stop them from being made. Striving for excellence, if not perfection, is essential. It is better to be aware of troubling arguments that bear on workplace issues than to act on simplistic generalizations and unexamined premises.

It should not go unnoticed that no definition of the term *ethics* has been offered in this chapter, a task deliberately delayed for later discussion. The goal here has been to engage, enrich, and elevate an essential inquiry into the self. "Goodness without knowledge is weak and feeble," according to John Phillips, the founder of Exeter Academy, "but knowledge without goodness is dangerous."

***

Since most of us spend our lives doing ordinary tasks, the most important thing is to carry them out extraordinarily well.

—Henry David Thoreau

DISCUSSION

1. Critically examine the reasons for studying ethics discussed in this chapter, modify as needed, and offer additional ones.

2. Critique these statements:

   - A technically incompetent manager is as unprofessional as an ethically incompetent one.
   - An ethically competent manager will be working on technical competence; the opposite may not be true.
   - Ethical competence may be more important, harder to come by, and more difficult to recognize than technical competence.
   - "A professional is someone who can do his best work when he doesn't feel like it."—Alistair Cooke

3. The chapter rebutted claims that ethics is impossible, unnecessary, and simple. Refute the rebuttal.

4. Contest this claim: Relativism is a toxic combination of intellectual inferiority and moral superiority.

5. Draw upon the concepts presented in this chapter to discuss "Life: some assembly required."

6. Identify a headline scandal or an incident in an organization you are personally familiar with. Discuss how the problem is being handled. Ensure that some context for the case is briefly provided, such as the type of organization and its size (the organization does not have to be named), when the problem occurred, and the exact nature of the issue.

EXERCISES

1. Develop a *very* brief, easily remembered, personally meaningful course mission statement. It will be the "Admission Ticket" to the next class.

   Avoid Dilbert's admonition that such a statement is "a long, awkward sentence that demonstrates the inability to think clearly." If the statement or slogan is more than a short sentence, then it may be difficult to remember—especially if it is vague. If it cannot be recalled, then it is not effective. You may be asked to repeat your statement from memory. Keep a copy—in your notebook, as a bookmark in the text, and/or in your cell phone—for your continuous use of this term.
   The Greek proverb "Before you can score, you must have a goal" is important because its underlying principles can be a great motivator. One possible source for your statement then could be why you signed up for this class. Knowing what you want is the first step in getting it—in the long run, we hit only what we aim at. So, there must be a sense of purpose before there is going to be any seriousness in learning. Paradoxically, begin with the end in mind. As one wise pundit observed, "Sooner or later, those who win are those who think they can."

   My mission in this course is (if more than a simple sentence, you may not remember it):

   How will I be able to remember my statement?
   What needs to happen so that I can achieve my mission?
   How can I align my mission with course goals?
   Remember, there is honor in doing your best.

2. Complete at least two sentence stems. For instance:

   - "I disagree with___."
   - "I wonder about___."
   - "I was surprised by___."
   - "I re-learned that___."
   - "I did not understand___."

   A completed stem, then, would be, "I think that there is at least one other reason to study this subject; this additional reason is___." Next, add a one- or two-sentence explanation to the stem so that others can ascertain your reasoning. Another example would be, "I doubt that the contention in the chapter about topic X is accurate. Instead,___."

3. There are a number of websites that attempt to verify the truth claims surrounding current event controversies, such as

- www.factcheck.org
- www.politifact.com/truth-o-meter
- http://snope.com
- www.truthorfiction.com

Identify at least one other site as well as two sites dedicated to the study of ethics. Be sure to provide the complete URL, the purpose of the organization, and the range of issues it covers.

4. The 21st century began with the Enron Era that set off a wave of corporate scandals involving scores of flagship corporations in many sectors of the economy and leading banks that facilitated the dubious transactions for them and many other less well-known businesses. In fact, many of the debacles implicated not just individual firms but entire industries. The widening scandal involved illegal manipulation of company stock options at the expense of investors (among the charges were racketeering, fraud, obstruction of justice, money laundering, tax evasion, insider trading, grand larceny, destruction of evidence, and misuse of company funds). For some commentators, the things that were done that were legal were just as troubling (Labaton, 2006).

By 2007, the worst home mortgage crisis since the Great Depression (the subprime crisis) emerged as a result of deregulation, predatory lending, and risky investments that undermined the housing sector and the nation's financial institutions. The shockwaves impacted the entire U.S. economy and the world banking system. Indeed, the $65 billion involved in the Bernie Madoff Ponzi scheme would be dwarfed by the over $2.5 trillion paid by citizens to bail out Wall Street firms deemed "too big to fail." As the nation entered the second decade of the new century, it experienced the deepest recession since the 1930s—one of the weakest on record. Indeed, budget cuts, hiring freezes, and sequestration (across-the-board spending reductions) would later reveal the lack of preparation for the pandemic at the outset of the next decade. Preventive measures and responses to crises will continue to fail so long as government devalued.

Nonprofits (such as the United Way and the Red Cross) as well as chronically under-staffed government entities (e.g., the Securities and Exchange Commission, Internal Revenue Service (IRS)) also did not go uncriticized during these episodes. In fact, these sectors are often led by former business executives—some of whom engaged in dubious practices.

To prepare for class participation, include, as needed, information from the previous commentary and consider the claim that Americans are socialized to believe that their economic system is inherently superior, which leads to little consideration of its morality.

5. The book began with four reasons—personal, pervasiveness, professional, and power—to study ethics. Apply these factors to the following case in order to help understand what is at stake here. What would you do? Why? Hints: Is your participation actually needed? What is in the best interest of your supervisor with whom you wish to maintain a good relationship?

> A work colleague has been able to succeed despite a pattern of poor performance. She does not seek feedback or take it well when received; the result is that projects are regularly submitted late and contain problems that others must fix. She has also been dishonest about relationships with coworkers and their duties. She is able to retain her position because she reports to an executive who has not held her accountable.
>
> Recently, she terminated a competent subordinate who had attempted to assist in correcting her mistakes. This upset other employees as they felt the individual was treated unfairly: the low-level worker was in an impossible situation of trying to ensure that the work was done competently, while her boss wanted it done in an inferior manner that would require rework by others. The discharged employee has retained an attorney to show that the adverse action was retaliatory. The lawyer has asked me to tell what I know of the situation (and I may be required to testify under oath); my employer will tell me that I am not authorized to discuss personnel matters. I feel as though I should speak up for "the little guy," but am concerned that I will just hurt myself. (Adapted from Appiah, 2017, June 21)

6. Ethics Checklist and Journal:

> The most important thing in life is knowing the most important things in life.—David Jakielo

> Although at the start I thought the journal and checklist exercise was going to be a waste of time, I have found that they have proved to be one of the most useful tools I have ever used. They have taught me more about both the material and myself than I ever could have hoped to learn just by reading.

> *When we were given the personal checklist and journal assignment, my first thought was, "How on earth is this supposed to help? I know how to stay ontrack with what I need to do; I don't need this checklist to help me do it." Oh, how wrong I was!*

> *The checklist serves as a guide; I learned early on that procrastination decreases any time allotted to perform at my greatest ability. The journal served to assist in application of the material. Understanding the text became easier once I began to write in my journal and apply the literature to current events and personal experiences. Considering these tools, there is no reason why an individual should neglect to perform at his/her best.*

These comments demonstrate how past students, who may once have been skeptical, profited from the checklist and journal assignments. The checklist, once customized as desired, becomes a useful way to track activities that you identified as important. Accordingly, make the reading material personally meaningful by launching the ethics journal (Exhibit 1.3). An initial entry might be a challenging case you have experienced; it should identify the dilemma in one sentence, describe it in several paragraphs, analyze the outcome, and indicate what was learned. If the readings shed light on the case, then that might be noted.

EXHIBIT 1.3 **Ethics Journal**

In addition to reflections on current events, personal experiences, your work or school habits, course readings, and class discussions, here are more prompts that may be helpful as you journal:

- How did you plan your activities for today? What values underlie your plan?
- Draft a message that describes your favorite moral exemplar.
- Describe the way you solve problems.
- What is the most important thing you did today? Why?
- Develop and complete several sentence stems (see Exercise 1) and then supply a short explanation or commentary to elaborate on your stems.

Like a new physical exercise, keeping a journal and checklist may seem a bit awkward and uncomfortable at first; if so, this feeling is likely to diminish as you continue to practice and benefit from the activity. Remember the Rule of the Trumpet: You get out what you put in.

The positive outcomes of this exercise include

- ownership (taking responsibility for your own learning),
- enhanced awareness of personal growth,
- self-confidence,
- good study habits,
- focusing on the subject area as a whole, and
- "reflectivity" (digging deeper to examine meanings rather than taking things at face value).

As one student revealed, "It is surprising how easy it is *not* to do my best." If you are not having fun doing this project, then start anew!

Throughout the term, illustrate the journal with a current events file based on a search of ethics websites, newspaper stories, blog reports, magazine articles, scholarly publications, and television reports (this material likely will help inform your contributions to discussions with colleagues). As well, include your reactions to this book and emphasize interesting, surprising reflections about what you (dis)agreed with. Complete a copy of the Personal Checklist form (Appendix 1.1) as part of the journal each week. Note that the sample checklist should be modified as needed.

Journaling is straightforward: Simply put words on a page. Because this is your personal log, there is no right or wrong way to keep it. While there are no rules or limits in this assignment, you can seek a comfortable place for sketching your entries, talk about what was significant today, write from the heart, and, if you like, pretend you are scribbling a note to your best friend.

Write what you know, and think of your diary as an old buddy you are having coffee with. Just ask, "What's up?" and start recording your thoughts (www.journalingsaves. com/how-to-journal/). The value of this exercise is in the process, not necessarily the product. Frequent entries help gain perspective. Get to know yourself. To do good things in the world, you must know who you are and what gives meaning to your life. Your journal might include such issues as how you exercise integrity and courage, deal with pressures to compromise your principles, and/or take personal responsibility for your actions. There is power in the written word, sorting through the events, recognizing patterns, generating energy for change, and seeking control over your environment. A journal is a gift we give to ourselves.

7. Access and watch the 60-minute video, "Do Unto Others" (1989) from the Ethics in America series as part of the Annenberg/CPB Collection at www.learner.org/series/ethics-in-america//do-unto-others/

REFERENCES

Anderson, R., & Axisa, M. (2020, January 18). *Astros sign-stealing scandal: What to know about MLB's penalties against Houston.* Retrieved from www.cbssports.com/mlb/news/astros-sign-stealing-scandal-what-to-know-about-mlbspenalties-against-houston/

Appiah, K. (2017, June 21). Should I help an unjustly fired co-worker? *New York Times Sunday Magazine*, pp. 22–23.

Bennett, W. J. (1978, July 25). What values are substituted for truth? *Wall Street Journal*, p. 22.

Boghossian, P. (2017). The moral maze of relativism. In P. Catapano & S. Critchley (Eds.), *Modern ethics in 77 arguments: A stone reader*. New York: Liveright Publishing Corporation.

Calcaterra, C. (2019, November 12). *Astros stole signs electronically in 2017.* Retrieved from https://mlb.nbcsports.com/2019/11/12/astros-stole-signselectrnically-in-2017/

Drucker, P. (1977). *People and performance* (p. 29). New York: Routledge.

ESPN. (2020). *Everything you need to know about MLB'S sign-stealing scandal.* Retrieved from www.espn.com/mlb/story/_/id/28476282/everything-need-know-mlb-signstealing-scandal

Frederickson, H. (1996). *The spirit of public administration*. San Francisco: Jossey-Bass.

Hall, E. (2018). *Aristotle's way: How ancient wisdom can change your life*. New York: Penguin Press.

Heclo, H. (2008). *On thinking institutionally (on politics)*. Chicago: Paradigm.

Hosmer, L. (1987). *The ethics of management*. Boston, MA: Richard D. Irwin.

Labaton, S. (2006, December 17). A push to fix the fix on Wall Street. *New York Times*. Retrieved from www.nytimes.com/2006/12/17/weekinreview/171abaton.html

Lipman-Blumen, J. (2005). *The allure of toxic leaders*. Oxford: Oxford University Press.

Newell, T. (2015). *To serve with honor: Doing the right thing in government*. Crozet, VA: Loftland Press.

Rachels, J., & Rachels, S. (2019). *Elements of moral philosophy* (9th ed.). New York: McGraw-Hill.

Reich, R. (2012, March 14). The difference between private and public morality. *Huffington Post*. Retrieved from www.huffingtonpost.com/robert-reich/the-difference-between-pr_b_1344690.html

Sandel, M. (2009). *Justice: What's the right thing to do?* New York: Farrar, Straus & Giroux.

Sandel, M. (2012). *What money can't buy: The moral limits to markets*. New York: Farrar, Straus & Giroux.

Sandon, L. (2002, September 10). Common or excessive, greed is a sin. *Tallahassee Democrat*, p. 1D.

Schelling, T. (1984). *Choice and consequence*. Cambridge, MA: Harvard University Press.

Thomas, T., Schermerhorn, J., & Dienhart, J. (2004). Strategic leadership of ethical behavior in business. *Academy of Management Executive, 18*, 56–66.

Vigdor, N. (2020, July 16). The Houston Astros cheating scandal: Sign-stealing, buzzer intrigue and tainted pennants. *New York Times*. Retrieved from www.nytimes.com/article/astros-cheating.html

Weick, K., Sutcliffe, K., & Obstfeld, D. (1999). Organizing for high reliability: Processes of collective mindfulness. *Research in Organizational Behavior, 21*, 81–123.

Wilson, J. (1993). *The moral sense*. New York: Free Press.

Wood, D. (1994). *Business and society*. New York: HarperCollins.

Appendix 1.1
Personal Checklist

The premises of this exercise include the following:

- People want to do a good job; one way to know if someone is doing a good job is *to find out* by keeping records ("the strongest memory is weaker than the palest ink").
- Problems are opportunities to improve quality (check marks on the accompanying checklist are facts, and facts *are* friends).
- It is more effective to fix the process that is the cause of the problem rather than to fix blame on a person.

Benefits of the checklist:

- Its mere presence on your desk not only is a continuing reminder of your commitment but also may actually prevent problems from arising in the first place.
- Properly constructed (see next), the list should have a "calming effect" as it is a way to bring order to personal activities, thereby harnessing initiative and motivation.

Tips for developing and using the list:

- Use the KISS principle (keep it sweet and simple), since a complex, lengthy list will likely lead to frustration.
- Seek a balance between new standards that may result in less time wasted and those that may expand time commitments.
- Recognize that not all specific problems can be dealt with by a checklist (e.g., a frustrating experience with a checklist may reveal for the first time an over-commitment to activities that may lead to a general cutback in responsibilities).
- Note that the list is subject to change and continuous improvement.
- Watch for synergy (e.g., being on time for an activity [in]directly contributes to a state of mind that leads to improved participation).
- Know that analyzing "why" something happens leads to "how" to improve.

Sample Checklist

Instructions: Modify the checklist as needed and use regularly.

Checklist, Week of _____

Problem Category	M	T	W	Th	F	Sa	Su	Total
Complete reading on a timely basis								
Review notes at the end of the week								
Keep up with current events								
Study at least ___ hours/day								
Devote significant time to projects								
Spend so much time improving own activities that none is left for griping or blaming others								
Exercise and maintain a balanced diet								
Refer to this checklist								
Customized entry here								
Customized entry here								

Appendix 1.2
Book Chapters and NASPAA Professional Competencies in Public Administration

The Network of Schools of Public Policy, Affairs and Administration (NASPAA) requires MPA programs to identify learning outcomes and competencies for all courses and program objectives. The aim is to provide students with concepts and techniques needed to think through ethical issues and to understand the kinds of questions that should be asked in decision-making. The following table shows chapters of the book that introduce material to help develop the five managerial competencies of public service professionalism.

Chapter	NASPAA Competencies				
	To Lead and Manage in Public Governance	To Participate in the Policy Process	To Analyze, Synthesize, Think Critically, Solve Problems, and Make Decisions	To Articulate and Apply a Public Service Perspective	To Communicate and Interact Productively with a Diverse and Changing Workforce and Citizenry
1	✗		✗	✗	
2	✗		✗	✗	
3	✗		✗	✗	
4	✗	✗	✗	✗	
5	✗	✗	✗	✗	✗
6	✗		✗	✗	✗
7	✗		✗	✗	
8	✗	✗	✗	✗	✗
9	✗	✗	✗	✗	
10	✗	✗	✗	✗	
11	✗	✗	✗	✗	✗
12	✗	✗	✗	✗	✗
13	✗		✗	✗	
14	✗		✗	✗	
15	✗	✗	✗	✗	

2 Perspectives on Ethics

Macro, Meso, Micro

Successful leaders see the opportunities in every difficulty rather than the difficulty in every opportunity.

Reed Markham

LEVELS OF ANALYSIS

Since ethics is personal, pervasive, professionally significant, powerful, practical, and full of pitfalls (Chapter 1), it is not about to go away. It is important, therefore, to move beyond the consciousness raising in the initial chapter to an understanding of ethics. This second foundational chapter examines the three levels of analysis in ethics: macro (intellectual and historical societal concerns), meso (organizational), and micro (individual). Gaining an appreciation for multiple frames of reference is helpful in comprehending the nature of the subject area. The chapter objectives are to

- understand different levels of analysis and their implications,
- analyze interactions at the macro, meso, and micro dimensions on ethics,
- recognize the need for integration of the three levels in promoting ethics,
- appreciate factors that influence admirable behavior,
- know that ethical inquiry can be explored as readily as any other type of management analysis,
- embrace ethics as both the easiest and the hardest topic anyone encounters, and
- apply chapter concepts to real cases.

This chapter shows how developments at the macro level (society, markets, government) interact with those at the micro (individual) and meso (organizational) levels. At each point, conflicts may be encountered, and people must decide how to resolve them. In some cases, societal and organizational ethical climates will be compatible with individual ethics, reducing the likelihood of discord.

Conflicts, however, may occur when there is a clash of societal, organizational, and individual ethics. One of the most common issues is conflicts of interest, where an employee has to weigh personal interests against the public good. Such dilemmas raise the question, "How should I handle

DOI: 10.4324/9781003203148-3

this situation?" When interest compatibility is absent, cynicism may result, especially if the employee wants to make right choices but the organization demands wrong choices. The dynamic interaction that exists among the three levels adds complexity to decision-making (Figure 2.1). Specific issues that can arise at each level are shown in Table 2.1.

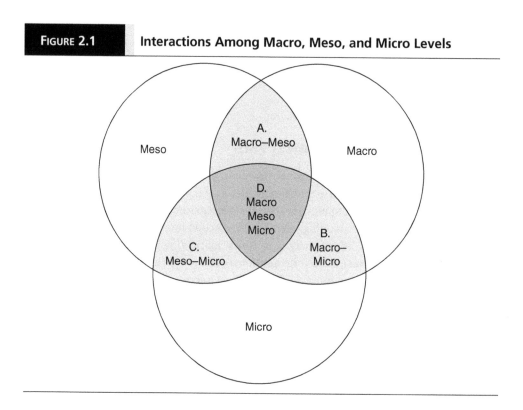

FIGURE 2.1   **Interactions Among Macro, Meso, and Micro Levels**

An application of the macro, meso, and micro framework is revealed by how people understand risk-taking in public health. Humans simply are not very good at assessing risk (Carroll, 2020, August 28; Horenstein & Grabiszewski, 2020, July 20; Shilton, 2020, June 30; Yong, 2020, May 20). Accordingly, planning for the next pandemic now is prudent due to the short attention span of the public and the marginal political support for preparedness. To learn lessons from the most recent contagion, it is critical to avoid the self-defeating behaviors noted here.

At the micro level, as people get used to living with a viral pestilence many lower their guard. Thus, while mask wearing, social distancing, and handwashing clearly decrease the chance of infection, the apparent effectiveness of safety measures paradoxically produces a false sense of security and allows people to take more risk: As conditions get safer, the temptation to act more recklessly increases. Not being infected was the condition prior to taking precautions, suggesting that sacrifices made were not really necessary.

Adherence to protective protocols wanes overtime, especially without policies to sustain them. Indeed at the meso level, the record of successful public health departments can

TABLE 2.1	Levels of Ethical Issues

Profession-Wide/Public Sector–Wide (Macro) Level
- Is the established public hearing process really fair to citizens and truly democratic in nature?
- Is the procurement process sufficiently insulated from political concerns and undue influence?
- Are unelected bureaucrats sufficiently responsive to the needs of the citizenry?
- Are the viewpoints of all affected parties (i.e., stakeholders) considered in the course of decision-making?

Organizational (Meso) Level
- What kinds of values am I communicating to my peers and subordinates by my behavior? And do these values cohere with my organization's values? Are they supportive of the public welfare/common good?
- Should I deploy standards of evaluation stricter than those required by law because I know that the legal standard is grossly inadequate?
- Should I overlook the misdeeds of my colleagues in the interest of organizational cohesion?
- Should I blow the whistle on the wrongdoings in my organization, knowing that there will be detrimental political consequences for the organization?
- Is my use of organizational resources mainly for the benefit of the public or for personal gain?
- Should I give the promotion to my sister's husband because I know they are having financial troubles even though someone else deserves it more?
- Should I use my work car on family road trips because I don't want to pay for the expensive gas and put miles on my personal leased car?
- Should I tell my supervisor the project is almost finished when in reality I haven't begun?
- Should I hire the person I like or the person who is most qualified?
- Should I tell my manager that my coworker has been taking confidential financial statements home?

Individual (Micro) Level
- Should I leave or wait until the person whose car I hit in the store parking lot comes back?
- Should I run the stop sign because nobody is around?
- Should I tell the waitress she forgot to charge me for my meal?
- Should I return the sunglasses I accidentally left the store with even though no one noticed?
- Should I leave a restaurant without paying because the service was poor?
- Should I cheat on my taxes by overstating my charitable contributions?
- Should I tell the cashier that she gave me change for a $20 when I paid with a $10?
- Should I tell my bank that they deposited someone else's money in my account?
- Should I lie to a friend or family member to avoid hurting their feelings?

Source: Adapted from Carroll and Buchholtz (2000). Reproduced by permission, www.cengage.com/permissions end box

actually be used to argue that such preventive investments are no longer needed. The failure of success is that the more effective preventive programs are, the greater the pressure to cut them back; public health departments tragically make the case for their own decline. Thus, not only are citizens vulnerable, but they may also ignore warnings.

At the macro level, some countries may get overconfident, prematurely relax restrictions, and experience another wave of infections, making them susceptible to predictable deaths. It follows that if nations properly prepare, provide key programs (i.e., universal health care, paid sick leave, child care) and adequately fund the World Health Organization, they will rank highly in the Global Health Security Index. Such initiatives will complement organizational and individual actions and help make preventive behavior habitual.

While each level is analyzed separately, it is important to appreciate that the levels cross over in a way that is not quite as black and white as a sequential narrative may suggest. Overlapping ethical situations may arise as well as those that conform to a macro, meso, or micro level (Figure 2.1, intersection D). A further application of the three-level framework comes from human resource management: A local human resource manager is confronted with a dilemma resulting from the termination of a high-performing employee who failed a random drug test (micro). The worker previously obtained a state-level medical marijuana license to cope with his condition. The HR department has merit system guidelines specifying criteria for adverse actions against a staff member (meso). The state court holds that there is no exception for medical marijuana under federal law (macro). However, the local HR official considering the consequences of the decision wonders, "What sort of employer would terminate a good employee for such an absurd reason?" The cross-cutting policies over the three levels clearly add layers of decision complexity with ethical implications.

The discussion continues with a brief intellectual and historical perspective on the large-scale, macro level of analysis: the study of knowledge and political history. This is followed by an examination of contemporary research on the three analytical levels, bolstered by focusing on societal, organizational, and individual ethics.

MACRO LEVEL OF ANALYSIS: HISTORICAL DIMENSIONS

The Study of Knowledge

Until the end of the 19th century, ethics was integral to higher education; its purpose was to develop mind and soul, to cultivate character and morality. Teddy Roosevelt's observation, "To educate a man in mind, but not morals is to create a menace to society," captures the spirit of this perspective. Universities were cathedrals of learning devoted to probing the meaning of life. Character formation was at the center of education. The academy, using the Oxford/Cambridge model, was where morality and philosophy were taught: The supreme end of education was to distinguish right from wrong, to seek the good life, and to become model citizens.

This classical organic view—that the world was an enchanted garden and people an integral part of it—would be confronted with the modern mechanistic view that nature can be understood and controlled through experimental manipulation; God created the universe and science would define it (Table 2.2). A positivist theory of knowledge based on the Newtonian paradigm denied attention to the moral and social nature of knowledge. The Enlightenment created an intellectual world of skepticism, reason, and evidence-based change. The central lesson of the Enlightenment was that facts matter, especially when they conflict with dogma. The result was C. P. Snow's (1959/1993) "two cultures"; science (with its emphasis on questions of "how") superseded the humanities (forever fascinated by questions of "why"). Since, historically, religion had provided moral guidance in institutions of higher learning, the study of ethics was relegated to philosophy and religion departments as an afterthought. Mandatory attendance at chapel services was dropped. Academic research and teaching replaced character formation and civic education at the core of the university's mission. Virtue was divorced from knowledge as an essential contribution to the common good (Sandel, 2020).

TABLE 2.2	Classical and Modern Worldviews

Classical World View

Religious belief
God exists
Future-world orientation
World as a mysterious garden
Centralized authority
Intuition
Sense of community
Charity
Justice
Routine
Just price

Modern worldview

Religious skepticism
God may or may not exist
This-world orientation
World as scientific project
Diverse moral authorities
Rationality
Sense of individualism
Self-interest
Liberty
Innovation
Market price

Source: Adapted from an anonymous source.

As David Brooks (2020, May 29) writes:

Right now, science and the humanities should be in lock step: sciences producing vaccines, with the humanities stocking leader and citizens with the capacities of resilience, care, and collaboration until they outcome. But instead, the humanities are in crisis at the exact moment history is revealing how vital moral formation really is.

The modern mystique of science would eventually fade as it became evident that scientists were often effective in addressing questions of how but not why (e.g., see Kuhn, 1962; Watson, 1969). People realized that scientism—science as the only way to discover truth—could not deal with the most fundamental aspects of reality: its values, meaning, and purpose. Scientific inquiry never produced standards to adjudicate moral claims. Science and religion simply ask different questions with the former emphasizing the "is" and the latter focusing on the "ought." "Science without religion is lame," said Einstein, and "religion without science is blind."

What is important is metacognition: reflection on what to believe, its meaning and significance, sometimes alluded to as "thinking about thinking." Such critical thinking is the processes of reasoned consideration of ideas, methods, evidence, the capacity to understand and take up positions in intellectual debate, and to discern the difference between sense and nonsense. Activities central to critical thinking are identifying and challenging assumptions and exploring alternative ways of thinking about phenomena.

This approach fosters "moral clarity," the ability to think clearly about good and bad based on truths held to be self-evident. The idea is to strike a balance between both oversimplifying and overcomplicating ideas in problem-solving. What is to be avoided in today's toxic, polarized politics is "moral grandstanding" (Tosi & Warmke, 2020): the self-aggrandizing posturing, righteous declarations, and bitter outrage that poisons public discourse at the expense of deliberation and evidence-based decisions.

Political History

Arthur Schlesinger (1986/1999) analyzed 20th-century America in terms of two types of alternating periods. *Public purpose eras* were times of high idealism, commitment to the public good, new programs to benefit others, reform movements (provoked by issues that the market could not resolve), and a relative absence of corruption (the early 1900s, 1930s, 1960s). *Private interest eras* were times when people became exhausted by intense public action, displeased with its consequences, and pursued their own interests. Materialism, personal satisfaction, privatization, cult of the market, and sanctity of private property were the watchwords; there was a priority of wealth over commonwealth that nourished a propensity for corruption (the 1920s, 1950s, 1980s—present). Each phase flows out of the conditions and contradictions of the phase before it, as there is always a desire to better the sociopolitical condition. Citizens are never fulfilled for long with either cycle—eventually, a time for a change emerges.

Whether one is operating in the public interest or private interest era, the insights gleaned from both the humanities and science—from asking questions about "why" and "how" and about "what ought" and "what is"—are important in understanding ethics. From a historical perspective, the analysis now moves to the contemporary period and summarizes selected studies germane to the three levels of ethics.

Contemporary Research on Levels of Ethics

While macro-level influences obviously affect meso and micro ethics, Applebaum et al. (2009) stress that critical interactions and integration occur at the macro–meso upper boundary (dyad A) and at the meso–micro lower boundary (dyad C) (Figure 2.2) depicted as a triangle of bent arrows. Here, law and ethics policy interact with organizational responses, such as conduct codes and ethics training, and ethical leadership seeks to cultivate "individual and organizational ethical congruence" (528).

Appelbaum et al. (2009) emphasize that the meso level is pivotal in creating and sustaining an organization's ethical culture because it is a critical link between macro and micro levels. However, by stressing the organization–individual relationship (i.e., meso–micro; Figure 2.1, dyad C) as the most important one in building a shared and lasting ethic with its employees, the authors neglect the influence of the macro level, particularly the impact it has on the micro level (the "Macro–Micro Interface" in Figure 2.2 fills in this gap in their model). For example, they maintain that the strategic significance of the macro level is difficult to verify empirically as having positive and observable behavioral effects on individuals.

Nielsen and Massa (2012), in their examination of the ineluctable pull of societal factors, provide support for the crucial influence of macro forces. They point out that macro-level developments can influence meso- and micro-level ethics; they can be both the cause of problems and the locus of solutions. This is exemplified in blowing the whistle and the Great Recession.

FIGURE 2.2	Integration of the Three Levels

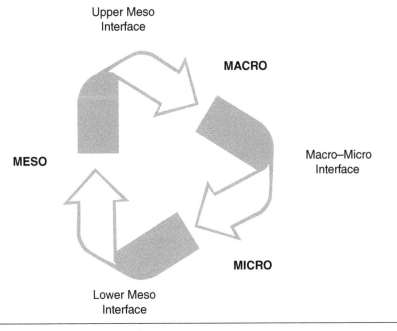

Source: Adapted from Applebaum et al. (2009).

Whistleblowing (see Chapter 10) shows the relationship between macro and micro ethical issues. Nielsen and Massa (2012, 142) contend that the structure of macro "U.S. finance capitalism" creates barriers for whistleblowers: First, regulatory agencies are understaffed due to "the logic of minimal regulation"; second, junior regulators have financial incentives "to learn on the job and then leave . . . to work in lobbying firms"; third, lobbyists contribute considerable amounts of money to the politicians who appoint regulators.

The COVID-19 pandemic economic crisis and the 2008 recession illustrate how organizational ethics problems can originate at the macro level. Specifically, the central cause of the macro financial crisis is the system of today's capitalism and its emphasis on short-term profit maximization. If organizational ethics problems are caused primarily by the macro level, then long-range solutions may necessitate systemic reforms. As these cases suggest, macro developments should not be discounted and understanding the interfaces at each of the three levels is essential.

An example of macro–meso–micro relationships (Figure 2.1, intersection D) is changes in the global economy (resulting from competition, technological innovation, pricing mechanisms, and public health crises) that impact the meso level (layoffs, contingent workers, privatization) with repercussions at the micro level for employees (modification of the "psychological contract," the unwritten understanding about mutual goals and expectations). When individuals see a breach in their psychological contract—which heretofore led them to expect a reciprocal relationship between hard work and loyalty—this can lead to detrimental repercussions in job satisfaction, performance, commitment, and retention (Berman et al., 2021; Rigotti, 2009; West, 2012; Zhao et al., 2007). Coupled with the risk shifting of costs from employers to employees (health co-pays, higher deductibles, replacement of defined benefit pensions to defined contribution pensions), this departure from the hard work–loyalty norm can further affect employee attitudes and behaviors.

What can be done in response to these trends? At the meso level, cost cutting does not have to take the form of layoffs. There are many alternative strategies that can be used before resorting to more drastic measures that depress employee satisfaction and commitment (West & Condrey, 2011). Indeed, it is possible to increase productivity by establishing closer employee–management relationships and competency-development options (Matzler & Renzl, 2006; Mayfield & Mayfield, 2002; Olson-Buchanan & Boswell, 2002). Using economic and nonmonetary incentives also may bring about a decline in opportunistic behavior and augment employee effort due to a mutual desire to see the organization flourish (Brown et al., 2011; Green, 2008; Pfeffer, 1994).

At the micro level, another response to recent trends involves micro changes affecting macro level (Figure 2.1, dyad B). One illustration is ethical investing in which investors decide where to put their money by considering the social impacts created by the businesses. Human rights, the environment, and arms production have become important considerations by investors when supporting socially responsible mutual funds (which are generally competitive with other funds). Consumers could be motivated as well to examine the record of producers before deciding to purchase their products. The assumption is that businesses will have to respond to ethical investors and critical customers who seek to hold firms accountable (Jeurissen, 1997, 249). Organizations such as Greenpeace, Corporate International Accountability, and Amnesty International, for instance, have pressured multinational corporations to be more socially responsible. However, Robert Reich (2007, 181), former U.S. Secretary of Labor, is skeptical about the extent to which business will pursue social goals:

> Making companies more "socially responsible" is a worthy goal, but it would be better served by making democracy work better. Pressuring companies to be more virtuous is an unaccountable mechanism for deciding complex social issues better left to legislators . . . the democratic process and courts at least provide means for weighing and balancing claims. Not so in the private sector.

Government is often slow to act on social problems, but it would be more likely to respond if citizens and service recipients aggressively made their wishes known. The Tea Party, Occupy Wall Street, the Green New Deal, and Black Lives Matter movements showed the potential impact of an aroused citizenry as they have been effective in electing candidates to Congress and/or changing the national conversation about who actually benefits in today's society. In short, the macro-level developments both affect and are affected by meso and micro behaviors, including relationships depicted in Figure 2.1, vectors A, B, and D. Attention now shifts to meso-level analysis.

MESO LEVEL OF ANALYSIS: THE ORGANIZATION

In thinking about ethics in the world of work, it is possible to rely on everyday morality. Yet the workplace has features that limit the applicability of ordinary ethics. The most obvious example is the mission of the military in dealing with enemies when under fire. What people ought to do on the job depends to some extent on the organizational roles that they occupy, as Miles's Law states, "Where you stand depends upon where you sit." Ethical dilemmas confronting soldiers are likely to differ considerably from those facing journalists, professors, physicians, attorneys, and people in other occupations. And those in public service have important, specialized ethical issues to deal with as well.

Integrating meso- and micro-level ethics (Figure 2.1, dyad C) in public service is challenging. While designing and implementing ethics codes and offering training are not easy tasks (see Chapters 3, 4, 8), it is critical to undertake them as codes and training promote integrity at work. They are especially important in the public sector from which citizens expect accountability and transparency.

Yet while internalizing ethics is a key component to an organization's success, it is often underemphasized, a problem that frequently results in questionable activities. For example, the behavior of some police forces in recent years has resulted from officers abusing their roles (see, e.g., Mclean & Poisson, 2015). By wearing their uniforms when shopping off-duty to get reduced prices or, more importantly, using deadly force for minor traffic violations, these personnel taint the character of civil servants and consequently public trust. Transgressions among employees occur elsewhere as well: college admissions officers who lower standards for the children of wealthy donors, charity fundraisers who allocate gift moneys to projects that violate the donor's intent, and social service providers who fudge the data from evaluation studies to make their program appear more successful than it is (see Chapter 12).

To mend deterioration of standards, organizations must take action. It is not enough for managers to devise codes and offer training for an ethics program to be effective, just as it is not sufficient for those charged with serving the public to decide whose interests should be privileged. Rather, both meso and micro strategies must be employed in unison to combat unethical behavior. The agency should promote ethical awareness and responsibility while, simultaneously, the public servants themselves must internalize moral consciousness.

What can be done to avoid improper behavior? Two strategies, one micro level and one meso, are needed. At the micro level, employees should be encouraged to discuss integrity issues. More open lines of communication among coworkers about ethical dilemmas and personal responsibilities at work should occur in an atmosphere not of recrimination but of continuous improvement. In turn, at the meso level, the department should clarify norms of proper behavior and provide guidance. Thus, action is required, as Jeurissen (1997, 251) suggests, by "a combination of responsible autonomy from below, and control from above." Communicative process and norm clarification throughout the organization necessitate meso and micro integration of ethics, whereby individuals internalize institutional values, making them a part of their moral consciousness.

Meso strategies such as codes, training, audits, and ombudspersons can be useful aids in promoting moral sensitivity (the ability to recognize ethical issues), moral analysis skills (the capacity to analyze moral problems), and moral creativity (the talent to weigh decision options in light of conflicting values). Clearly, there are actions organizations can take to cultivate an ethical environment, but employees have a responsibility as well to uphold ethics and avoid wrongdoing, as discussed later.

MICRO LEVEL OF ANALYSIS: THE INDIVIDUAL

The question is, "How does one apply his values, learned as a child, in the workplace?" The quip, "I learned ethics at my mother's knee, but she did not tell me about highly leveraged derivative transactions," illustrates that basic intuitions developed in the family may not be easily applied to many issues. Stated differently, while there are important affective forces in value formation, there is also a significant cognitive component that depends on analysis and reflection.

The good news is that most people want to be ethical, most organizations want to be ethical, and most employees and organizations want to be treated ethically—indeed, they demand it. The bad news is that many individuals and institutions just are not very good at applying shared values to decision-making. The glory of the human story is that the capacity for good makes ethics possible. The tragedy is that the propensity for evil makes ethics necessary (Preston, 1994).

Does a good ethical match between individuals and organizations make a difference in the life of both? Research by Ambrose, Amaud, and Schminke (2008, 329) examines "ethical fit," or congruence, between the individual and the institution. By adopting a phenomenological approach—that is, focusing on the unique perspectives encapsulated in each of the three levels of analysis—they find that this "fit" does make a difference: Ethical congruence strengthens employees' and employers' commitment. Why? An ethical climate that creates a sense of community—a "corporate family" working together for the common good—coheres with employees who exhibit conventional levels of moral reasoning, focusing on mutual benefits and obligations (see Kohlberg's theory of moral development in Chapters 4 and 8). The effect is an increase in commitment to the agency and job satisfaction, and reduced turnover. The practical implication from this work is that ethical person–organization (P-O) congruence deserves attention from managers when crafting learning, development, and selection strategies (Ambrose et al., 2008, 330–331).

Training and development efforts coupled with judicious hiring are crucial. For ethics to become a predominant factor in organizational life means gaining ethics skills as one would develop other management skills. The goal is to manage, not moralize. Ethical analysis can be learned as readily as other forms of policy analysis. As in policy decisions, conceptual tools to examine the ethical dimension of decisions are needed. The objective, consistent with the Aristotelian notion of human flourishing, is to explore how one could act by increasing resources for decision-making and not reducing ethics to nonethical criteria (Chapter 5).

Without ethics education, new members of the profession will likely rely on values such as unthinking organizational loyalty, technical competence (untempered by moral judgment), or passive obedience to authority. Professionals bring both idealism and cynicism to their work; the hope here is to reinforce the former and minimize the latter. In our efforts, let us seek the middle ground between

- naïve utopianism ("we can change the world," a morality model that is unrealistically optimistic and ineffectual), and
- cynical pessimism ("we can't change anything," a fatalistic model that permits the worst to prevail).

It is between these two poles—optimistic realism—where progress is made: The Arab saying, "Trust in Allah, but tie your camel," demonstrates the utility of this approach. Trust is fine, but being informed is also prudent. Consider the following case (Exhibit 2.1).

Ethical Dilemma: Macro, Meso, Micro Ethics in Action

I support the Other 98, 99% Power, and Occupy Wall Street movement, and I am aghast at the predatory behavior of corporate banking. Although I do not work on Wall Street, I own stock in a mutual fund that includes these firms. Am I a hypocrite?

Taking offense at a dilemma and doing nothing about it defines a hypocrite. But a hard look at the situation suggests that you do not qualify. Your conduct, so far, may not be up to your convictions, a very common human condition. "In the real world, ethical standards have to accommodate some degree of ambivalence" (Kaminer, 2011). No one can do everything. If there were no room for hesitation, no one would ever meet ethical ideals or have much reason to try. The movement itself has no qualifications for membership, as it tolerates contradictions and welcomes everyone; it definitely does not demand that people sell their stock.

The first obligation, then, is to determine if stock ownership is actually part of the problem or part of the solution. Is it preferable to stay with the mutual fund and learn what policy, if any, it has toward diversification and support for reform? If it is decided that the situation is untenable, then change is mandated. But even such an action will not stop investment bankers from enriching themselves off you: The financial sector is so entwined in every aspect of the economy that it is difficult for any individual to be isolated from it. Some form of compromise is inevitable. Its precise nature depends on the economy, the firm's investments, and personal values.

Source: Adapted from Kaminer (2011).

What are some factors that can influence ethics at the meso and micro levels? That is the topic of the next section.

FACTORS INFLUENCING MESO–MICRO ETHICS

Narrowing the focus to interactions at the meso–micro level (Figure 2.1, intersection C), there are four meso forces that can promote or impede individual behavior (Figure 2.3): leadership, strategic policies, organizational culture, and individual characteristics. These forces often influence whether ethical performance is high, mediocre, or low.

Meso Forces Shaping Ethical Behavior

Source: Adapted from Steiner and Steiner (2006, 196).

Leadership

The importance of top leadership in setting the tone and providing role models in public service settings is well documented (Dobel, 2018; Johnson, 2012; Kaptein et al., 2005; Van Wart, 2005; West & Berman, 2006). A study charting ethics in six Asia-Pacific countries and four U.S. states stresses the important role of senior managers in setting high performance expectations and displaying exemplary leadership (West, Beh, & Sabharwal, 2013). People look to leaders to signal, through their actions and words, the values that are important to the organization. Unethical signals or unclear standards of behavior can lead to employee distrust and compromised performance standards. If leaders engage in ethically dubious behavior, it becomes easier for personnel to rationalize doing the same thing.

Most managers, as noted, want to do a good job. The grandfather of one of the authors of this book used the words "right" and "good" in a redundant way by saying things such as "That was a right-good idea" or "You did a right-good job." He meant to convey "very good" by using this phrase, but it is helpful to keep the relationship and distinction of the double adjectives in mind between ethics and economics. Government managers have a job to do as stewards of public monies and administrators of public projects, and they need to do these things ethically to uphold citizen trust. They want to produce good, not bad, economic results and to do so in ways that are ethically right, not wrong (Bowman, 1995, 65).

Strategic Policies

Managers are responsible for implementing the goals and objectives of their organizations. They want to aggressively pursue performance targets, without pushing so hard that their efforts erode standards. Organizations should encourage employees to perform, while simultaneously articulating and implementing policies about appropriate behavior (e.g., conduct codes, ethics training, ethics audits). By promoting strategies that put too much stress on performance and too little on ethics, the results could compromise both. This is a way of reiterating Dennis Thompson's (1992, 255) caution, "[B]ecause other issues are more important than ethics, ethics are more important than any issue." Ethics, in other words, is a precondition for good government.

Unwelcome compromises can also result from reward and pay policies. Setting inflexible numerical quotas for performance and allocating rewards based on attaining the quota can lead to perverse outcomes (see Chapter 12). For example, compensating solid-waste collectors for the weight of their load can lead them to water down the garbage to add weight to the truck. Incentivizing police for the number of traffic tickets issued can result in questionable traffic stops and justified citizen complaints. Penalizing, instead of rewarding, teachers for accurately grading students can result in compromised standards, dishonest grades, and grade inflation.

Organizational Culture

The culture of an organization—the third meso-level factor affecting micro behavior—encompasses its values, norms, rules, and rituals. Culture, like leadership and strategic policies, communicates what is important, often through informal and subtle ways. If the accepted practice is that "anything goes, so long as it is not illegal" or "get it done, no matter what," then dishonorable behavior is likely to occur. Under such circumstances, employees will be fearful and unwilling to sound the alarm on dubious behavior. Manipulating figures to make performance look good could be one consequence; failing to recognize the ethical dimension of one's actions could be another. In both instances, "culture eats strategy for breakfast": The action could be framed as a "good" economic decision, discounting any "wrong" ethical implications. The actions of one local government to positively influence the ethical culture in its jurisdiction are exemplified by Miami-Dade County (Exhibit 2.2).

EXHIBIT 2.2   Miami-Dade Commission on Ethics and Public Trust

On March 12, 1996, the voters of Miami-Dade County, Florida, opted to amend the county's Home Rule Charter to create an ethics commission. Following the amendment, the county created the Commission on Ethics and Public Trust to help guarantee the honesty of both the electoral process and the governmental decision-making. Acting as a safeguard for county residents, the commission's purpose is to educate the citizenry on the standards of conduct and to impose them on public officials.

Its unique membership comprises five people appointed by different stakeholders in the community. The Chief Judge of the Eleventh Judicial Circuit appoints two members: one former federal or state court judge and one past U.S., state, or county attorney or assistant. Next, the deans of the University of Miami Law School and St. Thomas School of Law alternately select a third member from his or her law school. Additionally, the director of Florida International University's Center for Labor Research and Studies designates the fourth representative. Finally, the Miami-Dade County League of Cities, Inc., names a fifth individual who has held elected office at the local level in the past.

Among the powers and duties outlined in the Code of Metropolitan Miami-Dade County, the commission is authorized to review, interpret, and render advisory opinions regarding the Citizens' Bill of Rights. In addition, it is empowered to appoint and remove the inspector general and conduct both preliminary investigations and public hearings. By a two-thirds vote of all members, it can subpoena witnesses, take evidence, compel attendance, and administer oaths.

In 2019, the Commission wielded its power of investigation and quasi-judicially conducted hearings and delivered opinions on a variety of issues and complaints. During that year there were 46 complaints filed on a multitude of topics. A few examples include

- a manager publicly announcing candidacy for city council before the seat was publicly advertised,
- fire chief charged to have falsified performance record,
- city attorney alleged to have executed his own severance package,
- city human resource director accused of pressuring other employees to make personnel decision they are not authorized to make,
- a public hospital physician claiming he was terminated for whistleblowing,
- a city mayor's failure to make proper financial disclosures,
- noncompliance with a public records request.

In addition, the Ethics Commission has investigated an issue sweeping across the entire county. As reported by *The Miami Herald*, local politicians and public officials in several Miami-Dade County municipalities had been using free tickets to sporting events, concerts, and festivals for their personal benefit, tickets meant to be set aside for underprivileged children, the elderly, and the needy. The commission decided to call a public discussion on the issue and established guidelines prohibiting officials from using these tickets in their self-interest.

Since its creation in 1996, the Commission on Ethics and Public Trust has proved its essential and central role in local government. Acting as an independent agency, it has provided opinions and answered questions on various ethical issues regarding public officials, elections, and ethical standards.

Sources: Smiley (2012); Miami-Dade Ethics Commission; Code of Metropolitan Dade County.

Individual Characteristics

Employee and managerial behavior is related to both incentives in the meso environment and personal internal dispositions at the micro level. When working in an ethically troubling environment with incentive systems that unintentionally encourage wrongdoing (e.g., amoral or corrupt leaders, unrealistic deadlines or pressures to "achieve your numbers," overly permissive departmental culture), employees might succumb to temptations to violate their ethical code. Personal characteristics (age, experience, gender, education, religion) may have a bearing on their willingness to engage in unethical behavior, but researchers have found mixed results when exploring these relationships. A final example showing the interactions of the three levels and their impacts is the 2011 Pennsylvania State University sexual abuse case (Case Study 2.1) and the 2017 London fire disaster (Case Study 2.2).

CASE STUDY 2.1

The Pennsylvania State University Athletic Sex Abuse Scandal

On June 22, 2012, former Penn State assistant football coach Gerald "Jerry" A. Sandusky was found guilty of 45 criminal charges, including nine counts of unlawful conduct with minors, ten counts of corruption of minors, ten counts of endangering the welfare of children, and eight counts of involuntary deviant sexual intercourse. For some university employees—ranging from locker room janitors to high-ranking administrators, and all the way up to the university's president—it was hardly a shock. In 1998, the first incident was reported to university officials, and they swept it under the rug. As the years went on, more reports came in, and still nothing was done. For over a decade, officials were aware of Sandusky's crimes and yet continued to give him the very access to university facilities and football events he needed to groom young boys for sexual abuse. If rank-and-file workers at the bottom of the university hierarchy had come forward, or if those at the top had taken action, the childhoods of almost a dozen boys would have been unsullied and the integrity of an institution would still be intact.

Although, at first glance, it seems inconceivable that such heinous negligence and blatant disregard for the welfare of children could have persisted for so long, a closer look reveals a situation that is entirely understandable, though nevertheless inexcusable. It is the age-old story of the corrupting influence of organizational dynamics but in an unexpected setting and with devastating consequences. As the details of who knew what and when, and failed to act on it, became evident, the picture that emerged is less one of malicious individuals engaged in a conspiracy and more of a tragic tale of the pernicious effects of an insulated, hierarchical, and publicity-minded organization, which enabled the key actors to make the wrong decisions at each step. While the failures of Penn State illustrate how an unscrupulous organizational infrastructure (meso) can mislead individual decision-making (micro) and overwhelm cultural factors (macro), it also suggests what measures should be taken to ensure that meso-level factors exert a positive ethical influence both above and below.

Zooming in on the micro-level decision-making of the actors involved, it can be seen how a rotten organizational infrastructure not only encouraged individuals to shirk their sense of responsibility but also, more fundamentally, clouded their very perception of ethical issues. This was evident in the 2001 incident, when assistant coach Mike McQueary witnessed Sandusky molesting a boy in the shower. Although McQueary reported what he saw to head football coach Joe Paterno the next day, things went awry from then on. McQueary said that the encounter between Sandusky and the boy was "extremely sexual in nature" and he "thought that some kind of intercourse was going on."

Yet according to Athletic Director Timothy Curley and Senior Vice President Gary Schultz, when Paterno conveyed the account to them, details were lacking, and they were under the impression that the encounter was disturbing but not criminal. And even though Curley and Schultz later met with McQueary directly, by the time they informed University President Graham Spanier, the account had morphed into "horsing around" in the shower. Moreover, Spanier himself described the situation of an employee showering with a child as "unique," even though he was well aware of Sandusky's shower room behavior with another boy in 1998.

What can account for such a blatant disregard for the truth and such an egregious failure to identify the situation as an ethical issue? Loyalty plays a big part here, for, as J. Patrick Dobel observes, "the mind will often perform surgery and reinterpret what they see into a frame compatible with their respect and trust for the person." Moreover, to admit that Sandusky, a man they trusted and admired for so long, was a child molester would force them to confront their own moral failures for befriending him and, in the case of Schultz, Curley, and Spanier, for continuing to trust him after the 1998 incident. Predictably, the failure to properly categorize the situation as ethical allowed these men to rationalize their decision not to report Sandusky, opting instead to offer him "professional help," which they framed as the more "humane" approach.

Yet even those who did perceive the ethical issue at hand found their ethical duty hindered by organizational factors. McQueary himself was wrongfully absolved of his responsibilities by the strict hierarchy of the football team, since he was told by Paterno, "[Y]ou did what you had to do. It's my job now to figure out what we want to do" (quoted in Freeh Sporkin, & Sullivan, LLP, 2012, 65). Likewise, the dominant status of the coaches discouraged a janitor from reporting a similar incident he witnessed a year earlier. The janitor feared he would be fired if he came forward because, as he explained, "football runs this University" (65). If any of these individuals had spoken up at the time, at least two more assaults of young boys could have been prevented.

Nevertheless, if macro-level safeguards had been functioning properly, the ethical lapses at the meso and micro levels, although regrettable, would not have been so disastrous. As an insulated and highly prized part of the university, the football program existed outside the boundaries of standard operating procedure. Although the Office of Human Resources is regularly notified of incidents involving employees, officials like Vice President Schultz failed to report the 1998 incident so they could handle it themselves and keep it from getting out. Moreover, from 2000 to 2008, even though he was retired, Sandusky was allowed to operate summer youth football camps on campus without a Memorandum of Agreement, which is required of all third parties using university facilities.

Far more notable than these infractions, however, is the fact that, for nearly two decades, the university had failed to implement the federal Clery Act, which requires all institutions of higher learning to collect and report crime statistics and warn the community of ongoing threats to safety. Thus, as athletic staff falling under the purview of the statute, Paterno, Curley, and McQueary were obligated by federal law to report the 2001 incident to the University Police. But since the university was not in compliance with the act until 2012, institutional checks that could have averted future abuses were not in place. Indeed, Schultz and Spanier should have been concerned with guaranteeing compliance with the Clery Act, rather than with protecting Penn State's image.

Had individuals displayed greater moral courage at the micro level, or had institution-wide, macro-level policies been more strictly enforced, the tragedy might never have happened. In the final analysis, however, it becomes clear that the situation did not call for supererogatory behavior or a perfectly functioning bureaucracy but rather accountability, transparency, and integration at the meso level. According to the report of the investigation by former FBI Director Louis Freeh, the key is to have a "values- and ethics-centered community where everyone is engaged in placing the needs of children above the needs of adults; and . . . an environment where everyone who sees or suspects child abuse will feel empowered to report the abuse" (129). A more ethically aware organizational culture, paired with institutionalized training and guidelines—as well as the integration of the athletic program into the broader university administrative and human resource structure—can help ensure that, in the future, organizational factors do not lead otherwise good people astray.

Six years after the Sandusky scandal, leadership at Penn State was still divided into two camps over the case with "Paterno deniers" supporting the former coach who are not persuaded by the evidence and those who think the facts are clear that top officials at Penn State covered up the convicted child molester (Hobson, 2017)

Questions to Consider

1. How can you relate the material in this chapter to the Pennsylvania State scandal?

2. How do macro, meso, and micro ethics come into play in this case?

Sources: Freeh Sporkin and Sullivan, LLP (2012); Dobel (2011).

CASE STUDY 2.2

Ethical Dilemmas During the Grenfell Tower Fire

Introduction. In 2017, a freezer malfunctioned and caught fire in a West London apartment building (Malkin & Siddique, 2017). The fire spread rapidly due to a layer of very flammable insulation that enveloped the entire high rise. It took more than 200 firefighters over 12 hours to extinguish the resulting blaze (London Fire Brigade, 2017). It was so dangerous that nearby buildings were evacuated, and riot police units, using their ballistic shields, were called to protect firefighters and victims from falling debris (Towers, 2017). At least 71 people died; more than 70 were injured (Yeginsu, 2017). The BBC reported that the fire was the worst single loss of life since the end of World War II (Rushton, 2017, June 6).

The building had been renovated in 2016, but a resident action group had been calling for a full safety overhaul since 2013. Not only was the polyethylene material flammable, but hundreds of fire doors did not meet code (Booth & Wahlquist, 2017). In the aftermath, one firefighter wrote an anonymous letter to the press, describing his or her experiences (Anonymous, 2017). It detailed the life-altering choices that this individual made, decisions that would have irrevocable repercussions.

Micro Dilemmas. The letter particularly highlights dilemmas that factor into the decision encountered in trying to evacuate victims from the building. The firefighter faced a nearly impossible decision after reaching the 19th floor with their partner and locating two victims. The victims were delirious, but said that there were five more people trapped four floors above. The firefighter had to weigh the situation and explain every thought that he or she had before deciding what to do. The decision had to be made in seconds as is typical in so many life-threatening situations, and the firefighter reveals the high level of stress experienced in choice making:

> Micro dilemmas each have consequences: Was there enough air left in the breathing apparatuses to reach the 23rd floor? Since the victims are delirious from smoke inhalation, is their report accurate? If we let them carry on down the stairs alone, could they find their way out? If we went up another floor, would we actually find five? If we found them, what state would they be in? Could the two of us get that many out, especially if one or more were unconscious? How would we decide who to take? Did we have enough air to make it back down to safety ourselves from where we were? Could I live with the thought that saving two lives is better than taking the risk to go up and potentially save no one?
>
> (Anonymous, 2017)

The letter writer expressed the difficulty of suppressing growing panic as the situation obviously became dire. Although never explicitly stated, the firefighter seems to have made the decision to save the two people and called for another team to go up and attempt to retrieve the remaining victims on the 23rd floor.

The rescuer describes a second dilemma that occurred once outside the building, as a saved victim was talking on a phone with her friend and her child on the 11th floor, and begged the first responder to save them. She was told to stay on the line with her friend, while another team was dispatched to get her and her child (Anonymous, 2017). There were scores of these dilemmas over the 12-hour period. The firefighter teams went back again and again despite exhaustion and pain, retrieving as many people as was possible before the building was too unsafe to enter. This experience gives credence to why ethical dilemmas are studied: No one ever wants to believe they will have to make a decision about someone's life, but people may have to do just that.

The situation faced here compares to the trolley dilemma (Chapter 4): the concern of exchanging some lives for others, the factor of direct action versus indirect action, and the intervention of a third party that must make the decision. But more like the MIT moral machine (Chapter 4, Exercise 8), there are numerous factors beyond the number of people who came into play for the London fire case. Although the firefighter does not describe the final decision, it is clear that the two people on the 19th floor were rescued. The caveat is that the decision was made once another team was called to retrieve the other five people on the 23rd floor, but it is never made clear if that team makes it up there or what they found. The mayor of London issued a statement that the full report will not be available for quite some time. It may take months just to determine the identity of all the victims and the status of all of the missing people.

The initial dilemma is apparently decided, but unlike the trolley dilemma, no final outcome is ever described. Regardless, the firefighter who authored the letter weighed the options and evidently determined the risk was too great to himself, to his partner, and to the two victims they were already attending to. All the markers would indicate that this decision was arrived at through utilitarian means, but that assumption rests on the lack of details provided in the letter. In short, the author might have felt other emotions that affected the decision which were not defined as bluntly as the quantifiable risks of attempting to retrieve the other people.

It is difficult to determine whether this decision was an adequate response. As with all first responders and soldiers, it was made in the heat of battle; to judge such a choice in hindsight—without overwhelming evidence that the decision was incorrect—may be unjust. Based on the letter, the utilitarian approach would dictate that—while the greatest good needs to be achieved—the firefighters did exactly that. They guaranteed two lives over the seemingly remote possibility of saving five lives. The unknown condition of the other five people might have been the most influential factor. If all five were no longer conscious, the firefighters would have had to choose whom to save. They made a prudent decision that guaranteed the lives of the two people they knew were still alive.

Micro, Meso, and Macro Implications and Consequences. As mentioned, the implications are difficult to discern since the letter writer did not provide further notation regarding the fate of the other five or even the fate of the two that he or she brought out. When considering the three levels of ethical influence, the immediate dilemma and subsequent decision executed on a micro level in that the firefighter had to make the decision for him- or herself. There were, however, significant meso- and macro-level decisions occurring as well.

Most intriguing was an unusual interaction between micro- and macro-level ethical decision-making. This can be seen through the scale and display effects (Chapter 1). The letter provided to the media allowed thousands to experience the visceral nature of the firefighter's decision-making process. Importantly, it acted as further ammunition for citizen groups calling for responsible parties to face consequences for allowing this building to become a death trap.

A meso-level result might be revising how the London Fire Brigade handles large-scale vertical fires, although it is unclear that they could have done any more than what was done. Months after the disaster, the medical examiners are still working through the site and investigators have warned the public not to even look at the site as it could cause psychological trauma, a reminder to the populace of how horrendous this event was (Hardy & Cooper, 2017). This grim reality could be interpreted as a meso- or macro-level interaction.

This could explain the mounting pressure on local leadership and the community to hold the responsible parties accountable. Initially, the building designers and material manufacturers were thought to be accountable, but as the weeks passed, the community's desire for justice shifted focus to community leadership, predominantly at the meso level, the "Royal Borough of Kensington and Chelsea and the Kensington and Chelsea Tenent Management Organization." The police have stated that these two organizations are being investigated for "corporate manslaughter," which is punishable by fines but not imprisonment (Dodd & Sherwood, 2017). While this may not constitute justice in the eyes of victims' families, the ripple effect to other communities and their leaders has been undeniable. Here, the connection between meso- and macro-level ethics, and how they interact, is on display. Fire safety had been an ongoing concern for this community for some time. Now, pressure to test and prepare for fire safety is a focus for many communities across the UK and abroad.

This effect may not be long-lasting, but if it reduces the risks of large-scale fire incidents like this one, then the benefits are tangible. Naturally, it would be ideal for community leaders to be more proactive, seeking solutions without external pressure, but ethics does not exist in a vacuum. Behavioral factors play a significant role. Meso- and macro-level decisions are influenced by events and public outcry. The two levels impact each other as meso-level decisions can lead to national lawmakers changing their position. Macro-level changes can lead to meso-level changes in communities that might not have otherwise given consideration to this issue.

Testing for fire safety has become a top priority for local councils and members of Parliament. By late July, the BBC reported that at least 82 buildings failed their fire safety inspections; more than half are owned and managed by housing authorities like the one at Grenfell (2017). A new test is more comprehensive, consisting of three parts—all of which must be passed. Members of Parliament worked with fire fighters to devise the new tests, while councils struggled with the immense costs to complete the upgrades necessary to safeguard thousands of homes (BBC, 2017). A full public report on Grenfell Tower is pending.

While top-down political pressure on councils has been significant, fire safety experts and community organizers are already concerned that the fervor will cool and that local governments will not act. Indeed, as Dame Judith Hackitt of the Manufacturers Organization explained, upgrades for Grenfell were on a two-year schedule, a completely unacceptable timetable (BBC, 2017). Hackitt welcomes all recommendations to improve the situation, but already, councils in outlying areas of London and beyond are losing awareness of the issue. The meso-level impact cannot affect independent organizational meso-level actors absent continuous macro-level support when new issues dominate the news.

A 1,000-page preliminary report was issued in 2019 after the Grenfell disaster shed new light on some of the macro and meso problems. At the macro level it found that Britain had lax construction standards, insufficient testing of whether materials met fire safety rules, and inadequate inspections of building fire-code compliance. It also found ineffective oversight of contractors and overreliance on self-policing by builders and owners. While the government said it would remove and replace flammable cladding (protective material) and insulation in similar high-rise buildings, two years later it had not been done (Perez-Pefia, 2019; Booth, 2020). Accusations of corporate manipulation in materials testing (to get approval from privatized regulatory bodies) help to explain the cladding crisis (Strether, 2020).

Grenfell United, a group representing bereaved families and survivors, summarized their critique of the macro institutions in a letter to the national housing secretary, "We have witnessed shocking dereliction of care and professionalism . . . a total lack of empathy towards our loss and a focus on greed and profit at the expense of the wellbeing of residents" (cited in Booth, 2020). More broadly, the fire sparked "a national conversation about the gap between the country's haves and have-nots" (Adam, 2018).

Among the meso-level systemic and operational issues discussed in the report were several dealing with the fire brigade, including the instructions to firefighters and emergency operators to tell residents to stay in their apartments with the doors closed, their "gravely inadequate" preparation and training, lack of an evacuation plan, failure to instruct first responders of risks created by cladding and insulation, and delay in deploying crews with breathing apparatuses (Booth, 2020; Perez-Pefia, 2019). The report did not include an in-depth examination of the tower's renovation and the materials used in it, but the next phase of the investigation will explore that. A police investigation into the disaster continues, but criminal charges will not be made until the public inquiry process ends, likely in 2022 (Shirbon, 2019).

Upshot. The micro-level impact, however, could remain strong among homeowners, residents, and first responders who will not soon forget what occurred. Grenfell teaches the lesson that some catastrophes are too difficult to overcome without the necessary resources and support, but proper preparation could reduce the chance of such occurrences. Conveying and sustaining that message at the meso and macro levels is difficult with so many other issues competing for the attention of decision makers. Still, the choices of fire fighters will have long-lasting impacts on the lives they touched, a quality that cannot be measured.

Questions to Consider

1. How can you relate the material in this chapter to the Grenfell Tower fire?

2. How do macro, meso, and micro ethics come into play in this case?

CONCLUSION

As this chapter has shown, ethics is exalting and eviscerating; it is both the easiest and the most difficult of subjects: People want to praise good actions and condemn bad ones, but there often is no one best way, no bottom line. The questions are easy, the answers are hard. This book makes the topic easier but not easy.

Moral issues are encountered at each of the three analytical levels discussed here. Contrasting the historical and modern worldviews shows the shift in emphasis over time from morality to reason, from questions of "why" to "how," and from a focus on "ought" to "is." Nonetheless, normative questions of morality and ethics continue to be compelling. The macro–meso–micro interfaces are significant, complex, and dynamic, as actions between and within these levels affect ethics in myriad ways.

As demonstrated, macro-socioeconomic forces influence meso-level actions (e.g., regulators) and micro-level actions of individuals (e.g., whistleblowers), with implications for ethics. Macro-level change also can have a cascading effect on organizational response strategies (cost cutting) and individual job prospects (job insecurity), ultimately raising ethical concerns. However, micro- and meso-level activism (e.g., the Black Lives Matter movement) can impact the macro level (local and state governments affecting the national government). It is at the personal and organizational level, in fact, where much of the action on ethics is played out in the workplace, with institutions seeking to clarify norms of right behavior and individuals grappling with issues of personal responsibility. Exemplary leadership, strategic policies, organizational culture, and individual characteristics are important factors influencing ethical behavior. The fit between the ethical values of agencies and their members affects desired policy outcomes and employee well-being.

***

The simplest truths often meet the sternest resistance and are slowest in getting general acceptance.

—Frederick Douglass

DISCUSSION

1. The question "Can ethics be taught?" is a conceptually confused one. Ethics and values are taught—the urgent questions are "Which ones?" and "How can the lessons be sustained?"

2. Metacognition nurtures inquisitive, informed, and open-minded students to use critical thinking tools such as paradoxes, category error, Ockham's Razor, reframing, the inferential fallacy, and the "wrong-problem problem." Teams should define these terms, then select at least one of them and/or identify another one, and provide an example for the entire class.

3. Different incentives drive organizations in each sector of the economy: economic self-interest in business, power in government, virtue in nonprofit agencies. Be ready to identify some ethical implications at each of the three analytical levels of this statement.

4. Analyze these topics:

   • Teddy Roosevelt's quote near the start of this chapter
   • C. P. Snow's "two cultures" discussed early in the chapter as illustrated by Newton's observation that "Gravity explains the motions of planets, but it cannot explain who put the planets in motion."
   • Knowledge is knowing what; perspective is knowing why
   • Ethics as the easiest and hardest topic in management

5. Today, the tension between Snow's "two cultures" (classical view versus the modern view of education) has morphed into a disdain for science and for education in general. Belief trumps reason and ideology overwhelms politics, with the result that the findings of nonpartisan research organizations (e.g., the Government Accountability Office, the Congressional Budget Office) are ignored and draconian budget cuts are levied on departments that rely on science (such as the National Institutes of Health, the National Oceanographic and Atmospheric Administration, the Department of Energy, the Environmental Protection Agency). Discuss.

6. If Schlesinger is correct in finding a cyclical pattern in the arc of American history, a new public purpose era should have emerged by now. Speculate about the reasons why this has not happened.

7. During the pandemic, many people yearned to eat inside a restaurant again—and some did. Like many decisions, dining affects go beyond individual risk-tolerance. Explain the micro, meso, and macro dimensions of eating at a restaurant in the midst of a contagious disease.

8. Comment on the Douglass quote found at the end of the chapter, and invite others to respond to your views.

EXERCISES

1. Norman Bowie, professor of philosophy at the University of Delaware, makes the following comparison of management philosophies:

   • Boss in organization A says to employees, "You will never be fired without cause, but if the economy turns sour, some of you will have to be let go."
   • Boss in organization B says to employees, "You will never be terminated without cause neither will you be fired in the event of an economic downturn. If the company should go under because of circumstances beyond our control, we will all go under together."

   (Adapted from Bowie, 1988, 111)

   If you were an employee, which employer would you prefer? Why? If you were an investor, which firm would you choose? Why? Which management philosophy is closer to the classical view of a corporation's purpose? Explain.

2. Summarize your notes (made in the page margins of this text, a notebook, or your journal), and establish links between this chapter and the overall book objectives. Continue to do this as self-study exercise throughout your work. While doing so, create sentence stems (see Chapter 1) for discussion.

REFERENCES

Adam, K. (2018, October 30). *London fire brigade failed in new report on Grenfell tower tragedy*. Retrieved from https://linkgale.com.access.library.miamiedu/apps/doc/A604173550/AONE?u=miami_richter&sid=AONE*xid=580f1f4e.

Ambrose, M., Amaud, A., & Schminke, M. (2008). Individual moral development and ethical climate: The influence of person-organization fit on job attitudes. *Journal of Business Ethics, 77*, 323–333.

Anonymous. (2017, June 20). *"I was a firefighter at Grenfell Tower—and this is what it was really like." Independent*. Retrieved from www.independent.co.uk/voices/grenfell-tower-fire-fighter-what-it-was-like-a7798766.html

Appelbaum, S., Vigneault, L., Walker, E., & Shapiro, B. (2009). (Good) corporate governance and the strategic integration of meso ethics. *Social Responsibility Journal, 5*, 525–533.

Berman, E., Bowman, J., West, J., & Van Wart, M. (2021). *Human resource management in public service* (7th ed.). Thousand Oaks, CA: Sage.

Booth, R. (2020, September 6). Grenfell tower inquiry: What we have learned since July. *The Guardian*. Retrieved from www.theguardian.com/uk-news/2020/sep/06/grenfell-tower-inquiry-what-we-have-learned-since-july

Booth, R., & Wahlquist, C. (2017, June 14). Grenfell Tower residents say managers 'brushed away' fire safety concerns. *The Guardian*. Retrieved from theguardian.com

Bowie, N. (1988). The paradox of profit. In N. D. Wright (Ed.), *Papers on the ethics of administration* (pp. 97–120). New York: State University of New York Press.

Bowman, J. (1995). Ethics and quality: A "right-good" combination. In J. West (Ed.), *Quality management today* (pp. 64–72). Washington, DC: International City/County Management Association.

Brooks, D. (2020, May 28). If we had a real leader. *New York Times*. Retrieved from www.nytimes.com/2020/05/28/opinion/coronavirus-trump.html

Brown, S., McHardy, J., McNabb, R., & Taylor, K. (2011). Workplace performance, worker commitment, and loyalty. *Journal of Economics & Management Strategy, 20*, 925–955.

Carroll, A. (2020 August 28). When it comes to COVID-19, most of us have risk exactly backward. *New York Times*. Retrieved from www.nytimes.com/2020/08/28/opinion/coronavirus-schools-tradeoffs.html

Carroll, A., & Buchholtz, A. (2000). *Business and society: Ethics and stakeholder management* (4th ed.). Cincinnati, OH: South-Western College.Code of Metropolitan Dade County, *Florida*, Chapter 2: Administration Article LXXVI Commission on Ethics and Public Trust.

Dobel, J. P. (1998). Political prudence and the ethics of leadership. *Public Administration Review, 58*, 74–81.

Dobel, J. P. (2011, November 11). *The Penn State scandal: How good men become moral failures* [Web log post]. Retrieved from http://pointofthegame.blogspot.com/2011/11/penn-state-scandal-how-good-men-become.html

Dobel, J. P. (2018). *Public Leadership Ethics: A management approach*. New York: Routledge.

Dodd, V., & Sherwood, H. (2017, July 28). Grenfell council "may have committed corporate manslaughter"—Met police. *The Guardian*. Retrieved from theguardian.comFreeh Sporkin, & Sullivan, LLP. (2012, July 12). *Report of the Special Investigative Counsel regarding the actions of the Pennsylvania State University related to the child sexual abuse committed by Gerald A. Sandusky*. Retrieved from http://progress.psu.edu/assets/content/REPORT_FINAL_071212.pdf

Green, F. (2008). Leeway for the loyal: A model of employee discretion. *British Journal of Industrial Relations, 46*, 1–32.

Grenfell Tower: 82 buildings fail new fire safety test. (2017, July 28). *BBC*. Retrieved from bbc.com

Hardy, J., & Cooper, G. (2017, October 15). Grenfell Tower fire: Work begins to screen stricken high rise. *getwestlondon*. Retrieved from getwestlondon.co.uk

Hobson, W. (2017, December 28). Six years later Penn State is still at war over the Sandusky scandal. *Washington Post*. Retrieved from *Gale Academic OneFile*. https://gale.com/apps/doc/A520615596/AONE?u=miami_richter&sid=AONE&xid=e169476d.

Horenstein, A., & Grabiszewski, K. (2020, July 20). Mandatory face masks might lull people into taking more coronavirus risks. *The Conversation*. Retrieved from https://theconversation.com/mandatory-face-masks-might-lull-people-into-taking-more-coronavirus-risks-142951

Jeurissen, R. (1997). Integrating micro, meso and macro levels in business ethics. *Ethical Perspectives, 4*, 246–253.

Johnson, C. (2012). *Meeting the ethical challenge of leadership: Casting light or shadow* (3rd ed.). Thousand Oaks, CA: Sage.

Kaminer, A. (2011, October 28). Occupational hazard. *New York Times Sunday Magazine*. Retrieved from www.nytimes.com/2011/10/30/magazine/the-ethicist-occupational-hazard.html?_r=0

Kaptein, M., Huberts, L., Avelino, S., & Lasthuizen, K. (2005). Demonstrating ethical leadership by measuring ethics: A survey of U.S. public servants. *Public Integrity, 7*, 299–311.

Kuhn, T. (1962). *The structure of scientific revolutions*. Chicago: University of Chicago Press.

London Fire Brigade. (2017, June 19). *Grenfell Tower fire update*. Retrieved from london-fire.gov.uk

Malkin, B., & Siddique, H. (2017, June 14). What we know so far about the London tower block fire. *The Guardian*. Retrieved from theguardian.com

Matzler, K., & Renzl, B. (2006). The relationship between interpersonal trust, employee satisfaction, and employee loyalty. *Total Quality Management & Business Excellence, 17*, 1261–1271.

Mayfield, J., & Mayfield, M. (2002). Leader communication strategies critical paths to improving employee commitment. *American Business Review, 20*(2), 89–94.

Mclean, J., & Poisson, J. (2015, September 21). Police officers caught using their position for personal gain in recent years. *The Toronto Star*. Retrieved from www.thestar.com/news/canada/2015/09/21/police-officers-caught-using-their-positon-for-personal-gain-in-recent-yers.htmlMiami-Dade Ethics Commission. (2012). *Ethics opinions*. Retrieved from http://ethics.miamidade.gov/opinions.asp

Nielsen, R., & Massa, F. (2012). Reintegrating ethics and institutional theories. *Journal of Business Ethics, 115*, 135–147.

Olson-Buchanan, J. B., & Boswell, W. R. (2002). The role of employee loyalty and formality in voicing discontent. *Journal of Applied Psychology, 87*, 1167–1174.

Perez-Pefia, R. (2019, October 29). Grenfell tower report faults fire brigade's response. *New York Times*. Retrieved from www.nytimes.com/2019/10/29/world/europe/grenfell-tower-fire-report.html

Pfeffer, J. (1994). *Competitive advantage through people*. Boston, MA: Harvard Business School Press.

Preston, N. (Ed.). (1994). *Ethics for the public sector*. Leichhardt, Australia: Federation Press.

Reich, R. (2007). *Supercapitalism: The transformation of business, democracy and everyday life*. New York: Vintage Books.

Rigotti, T. (2009). Enough is enough? Threshold models for the relationship between psychological contract breach and job-related attitudes. *European Journal of Work and Organizational Psychology*, *18*, 442–463.

Rushton, S. (2017, June 6). Greed caused London's worst fire since WWII. *occupy.com*. Retrieved from www.occupy.com/article/greed-caused-london-s-worst-fire-wwii#sthash.e4T6xwPR.qRAYuNPx.dpbs

Sandel, M. (2020). *The tyranny of merit: What's become of the common good?* New York: Farrar, Straus, and Giroux.

Schlesinger, A. (1986/1999). *Cycles of American history*. New York: Mariner.

Shilton, A. (2020, June 30). Why you're probably not so great at risk assessment. *New York Times*. Retrieved from www.nytimes.com/2020/06/30/smarter-living/why-youre-probably-not-so-great-at-risk-assessment.html

Shirbon, E. (2019, October 29). London fire brigade failings worsened Grenfell tower death toll: report. *Reuters*. Retrieved from www.reuters.com/article/us-britain-fire-grenfell/london-fire-brigade-failings-worsened-grenfell-tower-death-toll-report-idUSKBN1X80X4

Smiley, D. (2012, February 21). Miami-Dade ethics report rips ticket freebies. *Miami Herald*. Retrieved from http://ethics.miamidade.gov/library/Publications/no-more-freebies_herald.pdfSnow, C. P. (1959/1993). *The two cultures*. Cambridge: Cambridge University Press.

Steiner, G., & Steiner, J. (2006). *Business, government and society* (11th ed.). New York: McGraw-Hill.

Strether, L. (2020). Privatized regulators and corrupt corporations caused deadly Grenfell tower fire and now threaten the collapse of UK housing market through cladding-crisis. Retrieved from https://www.nakedcapitalism.com/2020/12/privatized-regulators-corrupt-corporations-caused-deadly-grenfell-tower-fire-now-threaten-collapse-of-uk-housing-market-through-cladding-crisis.html

Thompson, D. (1992). Paradoxes of government ethics. *Public Administration Review*, *52*, 255–256.

Tosi, J., & Warmke, B. (2020). *Grandstanding: The use and abuse of moral talk*. New York: Oxford University Press.

Towers, T. (2017, June 14). Riot police protect firefighters from falling debris: Grenfell Tower block fire. *Metro News*. Retrieved from metro.co.uk

Van Wart, M. (2005). *Dynamics of leadership in public service: Theory and practice*. Armonk, NY: M. E. Sharpe.

Watson, J. (1969). *The double helix*. New York: Mentor.

West, J. (2012). Employee-friendly policies and development benefits for millennials. In R. Sims & W. Sauser (Eds.), *Managing human resources from the millennial generation* (pp. 201–228). Charlotte, NC: Information Age Press.

West, J., Beh, L., & Sabharwal, M. (2013). Charting ethics in Asia-Pacific: Does East meet West, ethically? *Review of Public Personnel Administration*, *33*, 185–204.

West, J., & Berman, E. (Eds.). (2006). *The ethics edge*. Washington, DC: International City/County Management Association.

West, J., & Condrey, S. (2011). Local government strategies for controlling personnel costs. *Journal of Public Budgeting, Accounting and Financial Management*, *23*, 423–454.

Yeginsu, C. (2017, November 17). British authorities put final death toll of Grenfell Tower at 71. *New York Times*. Retrieved from www.nytimes.com/.../europe/uk-grenfell-tower-death-toll.html

Yong, E. (2020, May 20). America's patchwork pandemic is fraying even further. *The Atlantic*. Retrieved from www.theatlantic.com/health/archive/2020/05/patchwork-pandemic-states-reopening-inequalities/611866/

Zhao, H., Wayne, S., Glibkowski, B., & Bravo, J. (2007). The impact of psychological contract breach on work-related outcomes: A meta-analysis. *Personnel Psychology*, *60*, 647–680.

3 Values, Ethics, and Dilemmas

The time is always right to do what is right.

—Martin Luther King, Jr.

This third chapter in Part I defines values, ethics, and dilemmas. Understanding these terms is a prerequisite to the rest of the book. Indeed, as Socrates believed, "The beginning of wisdom is the definition of terms." The chapter objectives include:

- identifying values and outlining them as found in American culture,
- applying values in public service,
- defining ethics,
- discerning when an issue is an ethical one,
- differentiating an ethical problem from an ethical dilemma,
- analyzing the domains of human action, and
- recognizing factors that endanger a concern for ethics.

As with so much of Western civilization, it is helpful to go back to ancient Greece to gain a perspective on contemporary times. The Greek root word for ethics is *ethos*, which includes an emphasis on individual character as well as on the citizen as part of the city-state. The moral development of a person and group is a mutual responsibility in the community; the good life (*eudaimonia*, flourishing or living well as a human being) is achieved in the environment of the polity. "Without civic morality communities perish," wrote philosopher Bertrand Russell, "without personal morality their survival has no value." Given this essential perspective, ethics is nonetheless hard to define. The attempt can be initiated by first understanding values, then ethics.

DEFINING VALUES

It is said the most important thing in life is to decide what is important, to decide how to live our lives. Values are what matter. They determine who a person is and what gives meaning to life. Everything that is done is influenced by values. They are core beliefs that shape one's worldview and impact the character of an individual and the community; a shared value is a kind of "cement" that brings and holds people together. Such norms can be found at three levels: culture, the workplace, and public

DOI: 10.4324/9781003203148-4

service. First, values—latent and espoused—distinctive to American culture as a whole include

- enterprise and hard work (challenges rooted in the pioneer experience emphasized competitiveness and achievement),
- independence or love of freedom (derived from the founders and immigrants),
- humanitarianism or concern for others (a belief that few people in history are as sensitive to appeals on behalf of the needy as Americans),
- cooperation (teamwork by individuals, e.g., sports), and
- honesty (the number-one value in most public opinion surveys). (Manning, Curtis, & McMillen, 1996, 202–203)

Second, contemporary American values at work include recognition of competence, individual respect and dignity, personal choice and freedom, employee involvement, pride in one's work, individual lifestyles, financial security, self-improvement, and wellness (Jamieson & O'Mara, 1991). Third, key values for public service ethics are (a) regime values (constitutional foundations as repositories of values), (b) organizational culture (consistent with regime values, which is not the case, as most organizations are not run by democratic principles), and (c) personal values (in the Western tradition, the individual should not be submerged by the organization) (Cooper, 2000).

Additional values composing the traditional public service ethos include transparency, accountability, responsiveness, humility, compassion, fairness, integrity, caring, social trust, altruism, equality, democratic participation, and civic duty that ennoble daily civil service (Houston & Cartwright, 2007, 91; McConkie, 2008; Newell, 2015, 14). These concepts are widely considered to be the source of ethics codes that can guide "right behavior." Public service norms, grounded in a wider moral context, can create a strong foundation on which to make ethical judgments by developing expertise, offering continuity, and speaking truth to power. The motivation to "do the right thing" emanates from deeply held beliefs that are part of a larger orientation to work toward a common good:

Judgments about right behavior must be rooted in a "vision of the good," . . . from which our moral intuitions flow. Public-service values are the means by which we articulate this vision of the good. . . . Taken as a whole, they describe not just what it is right to do but—which comes first—who public servants are: what a public service is for, what it stands for, what it means, what it wants to be. . . . Public-service values reawaken our sense of public service as a "special calling. (Heintzman, 2007, 594–595)

As one former counterterrorism civil servant said, "I worked with tens of thousands of individuals who took seriously the oath to the Constitution, generally shunned the limelight, and wanted only to work on behalf of the United States" (Travers, 2020, July 14). Yet today democratic norms and the public's faith in the purpose of government are challenged by the pandemic, economic collapse, racial injustice, and election controversies to the point that the very idea of America may be at risk.

APPLYING VALUES IN PUBLIC SERVICE

Conflicts among these value sets are inevitable. Ideally, the function of government is to maintain conditions of life in which morality is possible. Recall Thompson's (1992) ethics paradox from the last chapter: Because other issues are more important than ethics, ethics is more important than any issue—that is, ethics provides the preconditions for the making and implementing of a sound public policy. It is to be expected that high-level public servants should be socialized to the core values of honor, benevolence, and justice in exercising their bureaucratic responsibilities. These internal controls—personal beliefs and professional values—are buttressed by external controls—legislative oversight, citizen participation, judicial review, law and legal traditions—to help ensure promotion of the public interest.

Indeed, Dwight Waldo (1980) lists no fewer than 12 features of ethics terrain for the public servant, with obligations to the constitution, the law, the country, the democracy, public agency norms, professionalism, family and friends, self, other institutions and interests (e.g., party, church, class, race, union), the public interest, human rights, and religion or God. In any case, bureaucratic pathologies promoting maladministration can and do occur when these controls and obligations break down or conflict, resulting in actions that are undemocratic, unfair, unethical, and illegal. Political expediency and short-term goals are not worth undermining basic American values.

Two contrasting examples are provided here: The first shows how a public servant, Michael Flynn, made false statements to the FBI and Vice President Mike Pence and other wrongful behavior sacrificing values of ethics and honesty in the process; the second demonstrates how another official, Alexander Vindman, used ethical values as a consistent guide to action in his responsibilities.

Exemplar Profile: Michael Flynn Compromising Values

Michael Flynn, former national security advisor and a senior member of President Trump's administration, was indicted in 2016 on charges that he lied to the FBI concerning his contacts with Russia. He pled guilty in 2017. Special Counsel Robert Mueller brought the charges in connection with his probe of Russian meddling in the 2016 American election. The allegations specifically involved his phone conversation with the Russian ambassador Sergey Kislyak discussing lessening U.S. sanctions on Russia in advance of Trump's inauguration and that he was not truthful in communicating with the U.S. vice president Mike Pence about that matter. The Logan Act prohibits private parties from conducting American foreign policy. As a consequence, Flynn was forced out of his White House position after little more than three weeks in the job.

Other revelations of wrongdoing were investigated, including his failure to disclose monies received from presentations and consulting fees from Russian and Turkey lobbyists, and lying about the source of funds used in a trip to Russia that involved interaction with Vladimir Putin. In 2020, Flynn sought immunity from congressional inquiries about Russian interference with the 2016 election, in a negotiated deal for his testimony. He admitted his guilt in lying to the FBI, and the court agreed to his plea deal. Later, the government reversed its position and sought to dismiss the charges (BBC, 2020; Ethics Unwrapped, n.d.; Graham, 2020; Lederman, 2020).

Before considering the basis for the government's effort to dismiss charges, a closer look at the personal background of Flynn is needed. His 33-year military career included numerous decorations, awards, and honors. He was involved in operations in Grenada, Haiti, Afghanistan, and Iraq. He earned promotion to Lieutenant General in 2011, and a year later he was nominated by President Obama to become Director of the Defense Intelligence Agency. After two years he retired under pressure due to an unpredictable management style and conflict with his superiors and subordinates.

In retirement, he was publicly critical of Obama initiatives in Afghanistan and Iraq and, despite his Democratic Party affiliation, he supported Trump's candidacy for president in 2016, going so far as to lead chants of "lock her up" about Hillary Clinton, Trump's election opponent, at the Republican National Convention (Ethics Unwrapped, n.d.). He was quick to identify the faults in others but showed blind spots when it came to his own questionable ethical behavior, including his communications with Sergey Kislyak and lying to Vice President Pence.[1]

As noted, the Justice Department, in a surprise initiative in May 2020, moved to drop the case against Flynn, leading to a twisting legal and political journey for the case that was not yet concluded. President Trump and his allies reviewed the evidence against Flynn and concluded that actions by the "deep state" were bent on destroying the incoming administration from its beginning. Allegations of Bureau misconduct were levied, stating they failed to warn Flynn during questioning that lying is a crime and that the goal of entrapment was guiding the questioning. FBI notes on the Flynn interviews provide examples of dubious behavior, such as the statement by one FBI employee, "What is our goal? Truth/admission or to get him to lie, so we can prosecute him or get him fired?" (Graham, 2020; Eisen, 2020). This line of reasoning was echoed by Attorney General Bill Barr, who more broadly said the Russian investigation "was one of the greatest travesties in American history" (cited in Eisen, 2020). Barr had powers to support a motion that would set aside a guilty plea and dismiss charges against Flynn. If this strategy was unsuccessful, President Trump hinted he was "strongly considering" a pardon (Eisen, 2020).

Flynn petitioned the DC Circuit Court to issue a writ of mandamus against district court judge Emmet Sullivan to direct him to end the inquiry and dismiss the case against Flynn (McCarthy, 2020; Eisen, 2020; Gleason, O'Neal, & Miller, 2020); however, the Circuit Court ruled in August that Sullivan could hold hearings about the request to dismiss the case before he rules on it (Savage, 2020; Lederman, 2020). Trump supporters and Flynn hoped to undo his guilty plea; many Justice Department employees saw efforts to dismiss the case as a troubling instance of the Department succumbing to political pressures and presidential interests (Marimow, 2020). President Trump on November 25 ended the three-year legal saga by granting a full pardon to Michael Flynn. The *Washington Post* editorial board referred to Trump's pardon prior to leaving office as "the last official degradation of his office" (Editorial Board, 2020). The Trump pardon cut short Sullivan's ongoing review (Helderman &Dawsey, 2020), and the case was dismissed on December 9, 2020.

In contrast to these events, Alexander Vindman provides an example of uncompromising ethical values in action as a public servant.

Exemplar Profile: Alexander Vindman Embodying Values of Honor, Respect, Duty

A critical piece of evidence in the Congressional impeachment hearings involved a phone call on July 25, 2019, between President Trump and Ukrainian President Zelenskly. Army Lieutenant Colonel Alexander Vindman testified at the hearings in response to a subpoena expressing his alarm over the president's "inappropriate" attempt to get Ukraine to attack his political rivals and his concern about the actions of others working for the president who did similar things. He twice reported his misgivings to his superiors. His disclosures were made to White House lawyers following the chain of command and conforming to established procedural requirements.

He was in the White House situation room when the July 25 phone call occurred. He was agitated by what he characterized as "outside influences" that fashioned a "false narrative" about Ukraine. He did not think it was proper to request that Ukraine investigate a U.S. citizen, Hunter Biden, son of Democratic presidential contender Joe Biden, about Hunter's work with a Ukrainian natural gas company called Burisma. He felt duty-bound to disclose what he heard and defend the country "irrespective of party or politics." He took pains to clarify that he was not the whistleblower but acknowledged he was involved in discussions about Ukraine for several months (Stolberg, 2019; Harnik, 2020; Myre, 2019).

Understanding Vindman's actions requires more information about his personal history. Vindman and his identical twin were born in 1975 in Ukraine, which at the time was part of the Soviet Union. Following the death of their mother, their father brought the twins and a brother to New York when the twins were four. The Vindmans lived in a community with other Russian/Ukrainian immigrants, many of whom shared the Vindmans's Jewish background. Following college, Alexander began his career in the military in 1999 as an infantry officer. Five years later he was injured in a roadside bomb attack and received a Purple Heart for this, and numerous performance-related awards and decorations followed. He speaks Russian and Ukrainian, served in embassies in both countries, earned a master's degree from Harvard, worked at the Pentagon as a Russian-East European expert, and advanced to the rank of Lieutenant Colonel. In 2018 he joined the National Security Council (NSC), where he worked alongside his twin brother, a lawyer, in the West Wing of the White House.

Following his testimony in the impeachment proceedings, Vindman was subjected to smear and insinuation, notwithstanding his 21-year impeccable record of military service. Among the allegations were that he had split loyalties to the United States and Ukraine, was advising two governments, and was "simpatico" with Ukraine. President Trump referred to him as "very insubordinate" and a "Never Trumper." Trump-friendly commentators questioned his patriotism, loyalty, and character, hinting in one instance that he might be guilty of espionage for talking to Ukrainian officials and in another that he was "apparently acting against the president's interests" (McFall, 2019; Bershidsky, 2019). Trump claimed Vindman had "problems with judgment" and was "leaking information" (Harnik, 2020; Carleen, 2020). In February 2020, President Trump fired Vindman as the top Ukraine expert on the National Security Council and dismissed his twin brother from the White House staff as an NSC attorney. Vindman retired from the Army once he concluded that "his future in the armed forces will be forever limited" due to political retaliation (Sciutto, 2020; Carleen, 2020). Vindman's attorney, David Pressman, alleged that a "campaign of bullying, intimidation and retaliation" linked to the president forced Vindman to choose between following the law and honoring his oath or pleasing a president and protecting his career, choices Pressman thought no one should have to make (Sciutto, 2020).

John Kelly, retired Army general and former chief of staff to President Trump, found no fault in Vindman's disclosing what he had heard, stating, "He did exactly what we teach them to do from cradle to grave. He went and told his boss what he just heard" (cited in Carleen, 2020). Vindman supporters think he exhibited the best characteristics of public servants: a willingness to sacrifice their career if necessary to do their duty. He did not waver in his conviction that what he witnessed was wrong and required disclosure. Failure to do so would have been a dereliction of duty,

In an op-ed piece published by the *Washington Post*, Vindman (2020) concluded his essay by saying:

> When I was asked why I had the confidence to tell my father not to worry about my testimony, my response was, "Congressman, because this is America, this is the country I have served and defended, that all my brothers have served, and here, right matters."

At the close of 2020, Vindman was a doctoral student at Johns Hopkins, a fellow at Lawfare, and doing some consulting work (Howell, 2020).

As a thought experiment, suppose that two people with very different values—Flynn and Vindman—are close friends. Should Vindman break off the friendship? Being friends with others does not condone everything they do; so long as he does nothing to contradict his values (e.g., lying, covering up), the relationship is valid. Ending the relationship is unlikely to have much impact; remaining friends holds the potential that Flynn could be influenced by a different way of thinking. Part of being a good person is being open to others; indeed, a person cannot be sure who he is until he interacts with others (see discussion of the Milgram experiment in the next chapter). If someone associates only with those who share similar views, the scope of life experience has been significantly reduced (commentary is based on a parallel case in Klosterman, 2013, 16).

In short, Albert Einstein said, "Try not to become a man of success, but rather try to become a man of value." Public service is noble work, but ensuring that public servants serve in a worthy manner requires an individual internal moral compass, an organizational culture that cherishes honor, and a nation that confers respect for those who live up to the ideals of democracy (Newell, 2015, 177). For example, while the response to the pandemic left a lot to be desired (see Chapters 2 and 15), there were personnel working behind the scenes who sounded the alarm early on, labored 24/7 to develop a vaccine, and blew the whistle on unsafe practices (Shoop, 2020, August 5).

DEFINING ETHICS, ISSUES, AND DILEMMAS

Ethics in theory is grounded in values that are general, constant, and internally derived. In contrast, ethics in practice is specific, changing, and situationally determined. Stated differently, ethics translates values into action. A leader like Admiral Loy must understand and internalize a definition of management before he can begin to manage effectively. Unlike Scooter Libby, an administrator needs to adopt a definition of ethics to make effective, defensible, value-based decisions and to stand by those judgments in times of difficulty.

Ethics might be defined as the way values are practiced, the way "business is done around here." It is both a process of inquiry (deciding how to decide) and a code of conduct (a set of standards that govern action). It is a system of right and wrong and a means to live accordingly. It is a quest for the good life. "Sometimes," as Wayne Heinrichs wrote, "all it takes for you to start making right choices is the spark of realization that your life was meant for something better." Ethics, then, studies how one ought to live, principles of right and wrong, and what it is to live a fulfilled life.[2]

Ethics begins with care, namely, caring about human and natural life, the welfare of others, honest and trustworthy communication, and fundamental individual and group freedoms. Relevant performance standards are to do no harm, enable informed choice, solve problems, seek the common good, and engage in continuous improvement (DiNorcia, 1998). An issue is an ethical one when it is genuinely important, conflicting rights are at stake, and harms and benefits are involved. Yet ethics is not always, or even often, about problems that involve choosing between right and wrong. Rather, it is frequently about genuine ethical dilemmas: choosing between two different rights or between two different wrongs. Thus, advice to "do the right thing" may not be very helpful. While ethical problems may have a straightforward answer, ethical dilemmas are complex moral mazes with no easy answers. That is, decisions are distinguished from one another based on the premises on which they are made.

Ethics asks us to think mindfully, and challenges emotions by asking why we feel the way we do and if that feeling is fair. It demands that we not only feel but *think* through the situation. Ethics, then, is about creating strength (to turn a phrase, "right makes might"). It is not primarily about staying out of trouble, although avoiding misdoing is often a beneficial side effect of worthy behavior. A person need not be an angel or a hero to behave ethically. The only moral requirement is to do good and avoid doing evil. Ethics does not demand sainthood, just ordinary decency, a readiness to wrestle with fundamental issues in human relations and to learn enough to make informed decisions. Put another way, Justice Potter Stewart noted that ethics is knowing the difference between what you have the right to do and what is right to do (Caccese, 1997, 14).

Case Study 3.1 portrays an issue in everyday organizational life (what should you do?) that calls for sound judgment—knowing what ethics is and what it is not. Case Study 3.2 offers a compelling look at what might constitute hypocrisy. End-of-chapter Exercise 5 takes into account the importance of the decision makers' obligations and role constraints in addressing an ethical scenario.

CASE STUDY 3.1

Challenge the Leader

I worked for a nonprofit organization that ran an international leadership program for high school students. I had access to the president's contact list, which included many names from an escort service. I feel that the parents of the students would want to know this about a man who will be with their children overseas. What should I do?

Parents likely would want to know this fact; indeed, they might want his medical history, credit rating, and other personal information. But those things, including his choice of whom to have sex with, are not job related. Breaking the law, however, is a different matter. Someone who routinely does that has an appetite for risk, which is not a desirable qualification for this position. Still, it is unknown if he gets a thrill from perusing the list but goes no further. Likewise, perhaps the people on the list are volunteers at an AIDS community program. Since he gave you access to the file, why not just ask him, "Did you mean for me to see it? I am concerned that you might be putting children at risk."

Questions to Consider

1. What do you think? Why? Remember, you can judge his answer for yourself, but "judge carefully: chaperoning children is a scary business, but so is endangering someone's career."

2. Is easing the worker's conscience in revealing the list (individual, micro ethics) what is best for the organization (meso)—and ultimately for students who benefit from the program?

Source: Adapted from Kaminer (2011).

CASE STUDY 3.2

Hypocrisy or Humanity?

In 2017, Amazon sent governmental officials across the nation scrambling to respond to its announcement to build a headquarters, promising tens of thousands of jobs and billions in investment to the winning location. Governments are mobilizing to devise lucrative incentive packages. I know how this works, because I spent eight years supporting these types of incentive as the governor of Delaware from 2009 to 2017.

The bidding war highlights a competition that state and local governments engage in every day. But it's a self-defeating war that should stop. A *New York Times* investigation in 2012 found that states, counties, and cities were handing out more than $80 billion a year in incentives to attract and retain companies—money better spent on education, roads, and parks.

The result is a market failure in which neither side is motivated to fix the problem. State and local policymakers can't unilaterally opt out without potentially negative consequences for their constituents, while businesses have a fiduciary obligation to pursue these short-term incentives.

There's a better way to compete for business: a federal tax of 100 percent on every dollar a business receives in state or local incentives. This tax would end payouts that go to a corporation's bottom line and would eliminate the pressure these companies are under to divert tax monies to themselves. States would still compete for these jobs, but they would do so in a way that better aligns with the long-term interests of taxpayers and the businesses themselves. This approach would provide a significant victory for taxpayers. Instead of making payments to businesses, states and municipalities would invest in and compete based on factors that make the most difference for an area's economic potential and for a company's ultimate success: the abilities of the workforce, the excellence of schools, the physical infrastructure, and the quality of life. That is a competition worth having.

Discussion Questions

1. What do you think of desirability of such a tax (is it a good idea)? Why? Is the tax feasible (given political realities, could it be approved)? Explain.

2. Join this conversation:

   - Bob: "The governor is being a hypocrite for advocating change that he could have fought for while he was in office."
   - Sally: "Just because someone made a mistake and belatedly admits it, that does not mean we cannot learn from him; indeed, if humans lived by that rule, there would be a lot of silence."

Source: Narrative adapted and condensed from Markell (2017, September 21).

DOMAINS OF HUMAN ACTION: LAW VERSUS FREE CHOICE

Law is one domain of action (the obedience to the enforceable), and free choice (the complete freedom for spontaneity, originality, and energy) is the other. But the cardinal question remains, "How is free will used?" Between the two domains lies ethics. Where law is silent, ethics should speak. Ethics is self-enforced obedience to the unenforceable obligation. Simplified, ethics is what one does when no one is watching. Law is external, mandatory, and objective (what we can do), whereas ethics is internal, voluntary, and subjective (what we should do). Law is imposed, ethics is inspired. Table 3.1 shows the distinctions between law, ethics, and values.

Ethics is at risk of destruction from both law ("regulate everything") and free choice ("anything not illegal is permissible"). The greatness of a nation is measured not by mere obedience to law (timorous people) and not by "letting it all hang out" (resulting in anarchy). Rather, the true test of distinction is the extent to which citizens can be entrusted to obey self-imposed law, for without ethics civilization perishes (Kidder, 1994, 67). Another test for citizens is the ability to puzzle through myths to discern reality. Which of these statements is a "myth" or a "reality"?

- Ethical people are always ethical no matter what happens.
- Ethics cannot be learned or taught.
- Ethical values are personal and are not expressed within the organization.
- Focusing on ethics does little to improve productivity, morale, or problem-solving.
- When an ethics code is written and distributed, there is no need to do anything else.
- The appearance of wrongdoing and actually doing wrong are two entirely different things.
- An ethical organization can be created quickly.
- Morality cannot be legislated. Law is judged by ethics.

Some of these claims represent "common sense"—which itself may be a myth. In short, a heavy burden rests on the shoulders of the populace as they ponder law, ethics, and values.

TABLE 3.1	Distinctions Between Law, Ethics, and Values	
Law	**Ethics**	**Values**
• Defined as a rule established in a community by authority or custom	• Defined as the determinant of morality	• Defined as an individual's driving force
• Exists to remedy wrongs	• Focused on right and wrong	• Used in individual decision-making
• Based on Common Law	• Maintains that every profession has its own code	• Are subject to change
• Defines community standards	• Upholds peer and professional oversight	
• Can conflict with ethics	• Can be incongruent with law	
• Maintains that ignorance is not a defense		

Source: Adapted from DeChello (2003, 4).

SOCIAL FORCES ENDANGERING ETHICS

Ethics is not just about definitions and distinctions, information and insight. It is about transformation: It requires performance and expects responsibility. As such, ethics is endangered not only by relativism (Chapter 1) but also by at least five other phenomena.

First, sensational scandals typically pit right against wrong. Seductively, they distract attention from important daily ethical issues which may not have ready answers. Second, grasping the best solution can be the enemy of the good (Aristotle wisely warns against setting impossible standards, a caution consistent with the recommendation to aim for the "middle ground," as discussed in Chapter 2). Ongoing improvement of character development and decision-making is the objective as ethical problems can be progressively managed, if not solved, provided ideals are kept in mind. Third, the topic of ethics can be easily trivialized (e.g., worrying excessively about accidentally taking pencils home from work). Fourth, cherished myths can act as a powerful deterrent to thinking about ethics: The capacity of self-deception and moral illusion should not be overlooked (Chapter 7).

A fifth factor menacing public service ethics is the increasing importance of private-sector values, including the advent of the New Public Management (NPM), and its growing emphasis on market norms. As Turo Vertanen (2000, 338) notes, "Self-interest is the key coordination mechanism of markets and the basis of performance-related pay, privatization and consumer choice." Under NPM-inspired managerialism (and its assumptions that people are money-driven rather than value-driven), he cautions, there is a weakening of the commitment to the public interest and egalitarian principles that have long been associated with public service. These changes also require different competencies of managers. While there is some evidence that managerial commitments to public and business-like values are complementary (cf. Berman & West, 2012), concerns that government administrators may be overly responsive to and influenced by private interests dominate. The shift of values under NPM and the resulting tensions—specifically, the greater weight increasingly given to "a lean state, citizen activism and markets" at the expense of long-standing commitments to "public service ethics and the specificity of the public sector"—demand attention (Vertanen, 2000, 340–341). The commitment to public service as a vocation serving the common good is at risk by deference to an unquestioning faith in markets and instrumental values.

Yet the appeal of market values is understandable: The market system does not judge the ethical quality of decisions. Instead, the legitimacy of an exchange is based on its efficiency in the broad framework of the marketplace. The problem is that such market "imperialism"— the reduction of every activity and value to a corporate commodity—tends to erode non-market ethical norms, thereby impoverishing moral and civic life. The manner in which a society structures its institutions affects how people behave; corporatization usually means centralization, consolidation, and homogenization at the expense of public participation and democratic governance. In the decision to commercialize and commodify a good or service, intrinsic commitments—not just extrinsic motivation—warrant consideration. Michael Sandel's (2012) *What Money Can't Buy: The Moral Limits of Markets* examines, inter alia, blood collection systems and life insurance policies.

Despite the assumed efficiency of markets, they "not only lead to chronic shortages, wasted blood, high costs, and significant risks of contamination" (Sandel, 2012, 123) but also the exploitation of the poor by for-profit blood banks and the decline in the sense of obligation to donate blood. Blood collected for transfusion in the United States is given by volunteer blood donors. In contrast to the hybrid commercial and nonprofit American system, the highly effective British blood collection is based on unpaid volunteers.

In the second case example, dead peasant or janitor's insurance (formally known as corporate-owned life insurance) companies secretly insure the lives of their employees so that they profit from their deaths. Sandel writes that this creates "conditions where workers are worth more dead than alive" and treats them as commodities, not people "whose value to the company lies in the work they do" (136). These policies, which constitute approximately a quarter of all life insurance sold, have become a strategy for tax-free, windfall corporate finance. After 9/11, for instance, some of the first insurance payouts went to the victims' employers, not their families. In spite of some recent changes, "it is hard to see why," Sandel continues, "the tax system should encourage companies to invest billions in the mortality of their workers rather than in the production of goods and services" (136).

There has been a shift, Sandel believes, "from *having* a market economy to *being* a market society" (10, original empahsis). In both the blood supply and life insurance cases, what was once largely an endeavor that had public benefits increasingly has become an instrument of private gain. Commodification is seen as good in itself, irrespective of its effectiveness or its impact on the daily lives of people. In the process, the moral meaning of blood collection and life insurance systems has been eroded. Since these transformed activities serve little social good beyond profit, their corrosive nature suggests the need for decommodification, the reclaiming of certain goods—water, genes, seeds, education, health care, and politicians—from market logic and failure. Inevitably, tradeoffs will be made in any such decisions. Figure 3.1 poses tradeoffs between competing values of economic imperatives versus ethical principles (further discussion of such tradeoffs is found in West & Bowman, 2008; see Exercise 4 to apply this matrix of tradeoffs to different scenarios).

| FIGURE 3.1 | **Ethical Principles Versus Economic Imperatives** |

Ethical Contribution

	Right	Wrong	
Economic Contribution	A. Ethically correct and economically efficient	B. Ethically deficient but economically efficient	Good
	C. Ethically correct but economically inefficient	D. Ethically incorrect and economically inefficient	Bad

Source: Adapted from West and Bowman (2008, 32).

CONCLUSION

Terms such as "values," "ethics," "dilemmas," and "law" are fundamental concepts examined here and explored further in the chapters to follow. Public service provides the opportunity to act on American values in advancing the commonwealth. Especially challenging for administrators is the management of norms in an increasingly diverse world and an ever-changing public service where value conflicts are inevitable (Case Study 3.3). Some public servants like Alexander Vindman make core values the singular focus; others such as Michael Flynn lose their value moorings and succumb to pressures that compromise public values. Between the arenas of law and free choice lies ethics. Officials can choose to be obedient to the enforceable (law) or the unenforceable (ethics). Flynn failed to obey either, and Vindman was guided by both. But adherence to ethics is challenging given the social forces that provide seductive distractions. Nonmarket norms are sometimes subverted by the encroachment of market values, resulting in the degradation and devaluation of the public good.

CASE STUDY 3.3

Value Conflicts in World Affairs

Ethical dilemmas arise out of value conflicts—instances when the courses of action open to a decision maker support equally legitimate but opposing or incompatible goals. In the chapters that follow, you will be exposed to different resources to draw on when mediating challenging dilemmas. But, for these tools to be useful, it is necessary to first be familiar with the contours of value conflicts as they occur in the practice of public management. Examining two high-profile incidents—the run-up to the U.S. invasion of Iraq and the Danish cartoon controversy—will help to understand how to identify value conflicts as well as the sometimes dire consequences of failing to acknowledge such conflicts when they occur.

The Bush administration's decision to invade Iraq in 2003 provoked public uproar when it was later discovered that the primary justification for the invasion—Saddam Hussein's stockpile of weapons of mass destruction (WMDs)—was never proved to exist. According to Fredrik Bynander (2011), the fraudulence of the justification renders the decision an ethical failure, not just because it constituted an act of deception, but also because it neglected the multiplicity of values at stake (see Chapter 11 for more on presidential deception and foreign policy).

In Bynander's analysis, the leveraging of a tenuous WMD claim as incontrovertible reflects how the administration "overemphasized internal values domestically and internationally (how to sell the war, rather than establish a cause for war that would hold up across time)" (46). While this tactic was nevertheless successful in mobilizing domestic support, its use displayed a disregard for a core international affairs value: multilateral action grounded in international law (clearly present due to Iraq's noncompliance with UN weapons inspection requirements). The interplay of domestic and international values requires a tactful balancing act, but this was eschewed by the administration's steadfast resolve to unseat a tyrant. Thus, its justification proved to be unsustainable, as "the state-centric value of standing up to challengers came out as grossly over privileged (and dishonestly so) to audiences in arenas that support other values" (Svedin, 2011, 221).

While both cases presented here entail diplomatic crises, unlike the domestic–international hybrid WMD incident, the Danish cartoon incident is largely a domestic ethical dilemma. It illustrates how a values conflict can spiral out of control if not handled with discretion. In October 2005, the Danish newspaper *Jyllands-Posten* published political cartoons of the Prophet Muhammad, the representation of whom in any manner (let alone wearing a turban in the shape of a bomb) is forbidden by Islamic law. When Muslim organizations sought a meeting with the country's prime minister to address their outrage, he dismissed their request, citing Denmark's long-standing commitment to freedom of expression (Olsson, 2011, 146–148).

After months of demonstrations by religious leaders throughout the Muslim world, the prime minister realized the issue was not simply one of freedom of speech but also of freedom of religion. By that point it was too late. Calls for boycotts of Danish products were already circulating around the Internet. The burning of Danish flags gave way to the burning of Denmark's embassy in Lebanon. The prime minister resorted to hiding behind the efforts of the European Union and Danish Imams to appease the Muslim community and eventually defused the crisis (Olsson, 2011, 151–154).

These two incidents demonstrate failure to take the crucial first steps in tackling an ethical dilemma: identifying the value conflict and isolating those values that clash. Evident in these cases, the stakes in ethical dilemmas are high: Failure to recognize a collusion of values in a timely manner can be disastrous.

Questions to Consider

1. What ethics principles were violated in the run-up to the U.S. invasion of Iraq?

2. How does the Danish cartoon incident illustrate Dennis Thompson's observation, made earlier, "Because other issues are more important than ethics, ethics are more important than any issue"?

Sources: Bynander (2011); Olsson (2011); Svedin (2011).

Both sets of values have their place. Each can contribute to social betterment, but, as shown, excessive reliance on commercial premises can undermine the civic goods that should not be on sale. In short, values and ethics are of paramount importance: Almost anything a manager does has ethical implications, as he or she is regularly confronted with asking, "What should I do?" Ethics is much like tennis: Those who fail to master the basics of serving well usually lose. And like good tennis playing, ethics takes practice. Take this opportunity to *carpe diem*.

***

Ethical managers must know what's right, value what's right, and do what's right.

—Carl Skoogland

NOTES

1. Winston Churchill once said of a colleague: "He has all the virtues I dislike and none of the vices I admire."
2. Ethics are principles by which one is guided in relationships with others (what people do in society), while morals have to do with principles that guide the behavior of individuals with respect to their own integrity. The two inform one another, although their focus is different.

The terms, following their classical origins (Latin: morality; Greek: ethics) whose definitions are synonymous, are frequently used interchangeably since both have to do with right conduct and good character. It may also be useful to indicate what ethics is not (Markkula Center for Applied Ethics, n.d.). It is not the same as feelings (emotions are important, but people can feel good when doing wrong), religion (religions advocate high standards but may not address all problems confronted), law (statutes, as the lowest common dominator, may or may not be ethical), culture (culture can be blind to some ethical problems), and science (it cannot tell people what they ought to do).

3. Business etiquette and ethics may overlap, but the former emphasizes manners and customs (e.g., shaking hands, dress, courtesy), while the latter focuses on moral standards of right and wrong.

DISCUSSION

1. Every organization has values, but they may not be the dominant purpose of business or government. Nonprofits, however, arose to meet societal needs not addressed by the other sectors (indeed, they were often created to right a societal wrong). Explore this statement.

2. Dennis Thompson's belief that ethics is more important than any other issue is discussed in this chapter. Do you agree or disagree? Why?

3. If ethics is defined as a system of right and wrong, and as a means to live accordingly, how does etiquette differ from ethics?[3]

4. Comment on these observations:
    *   "Are you taking responsibility for taking responsibility?"
    *   "Everyone knows right from wrong." Right?
    *   "The habit of not thinking something is wrong, gives it the appearance of being right." Thomas Paine
    *   "Values are critical guides for making decisions. When in doubt, they cut through the fog like a beacon in the night." Robert Townsend
    *   "Educating the mind without educating the heart is no education at all." Aristotle

5. Traditional public administration values emphasize consensus, shared ideals, democracy, and social equality. An emergent anti-government paradigm advocates self-interest, individualism, competition, Machiavellianism, and survival of the fittest (Abels, 2017, July 17). Discuss.

6. Is it ethical for a student to cut her ethics class?

7. Select one of the following observations and prepare a response, with examples, for class:
    (a) Why is it so hard to live up to one's own standards?
    (b) We can't expect our leaders to be perfect is to ignore what can be achieved by recognizing both the ideal and the limits of the real.
    (c) The function of government is to maintain conditions of life in which morality is possible.

8. In 2018, a store employee returned a million-dollar lottery ticket to a customer who left it on a counter has no regrets. He knew the neighborhood where the customer lived,

and drove around until he found the customer as he was driving away from his home. The clerk did not want to live with the guilt of keeping the money: "Good deeds come back to help you and bad deeds come back to haunt you," he said (Associated Press, 2018, June 6). A law firm gave the clerk a $1,200 check to reward him for doing the right thing.

What would you have done if you were the clerk, the customer, or a resident of the city where this occurred? Why? (Hint: What values are at stake in this situation?)

9. In 2019, Robert Kraft, owner of the New England Patriots football team, was among hundreds of "johns" (including other billionaires), snared in a Florida human trafficking investigation. Why would these ultra-wealthy men go to a strip mall sex spa? According to one of the officials involved, "it has a lot to do with the danger of it, the excitement of getting away with it" (Smart, 2019, February 20). In addition, scholarly studies have documented that the rich cheat more on taxes and their wives as well as are more likely to shoplift and bilk others in games of chance (e.g., Piff, 2014).

So perhaps the question is not, "Why would they do it," but rather, "Why wouldn't they?" To become wealthy can require risk, so why should risk-taking be limited to finances? The more power and money people have, the more freedom they feel to take chances; in so doing, their values and true nature are revealed. For example, power and money can reduce empathy and undermine ethical behavior. It follows that the public "should care a great deal about our leaders' personalities, because no position is prestigious enough to make a person of questionable character behave themselves" (Kraus, 2016, October 14).

Recognizing that the tendencies noted here do not necessarily infect all well-to-do individuals, ponder why some well-off people engage in the types of behavior noted.

EXERCISES

1. Complete the following sentence: "Ethics is like. . ." and explain your sentence in a one-page paper. This assignment is intended to help you think about ethics in a metaphorical sense. Ethics might be seen as an icy street, with people slipping and sliding on the verge of falling. It could be like an apple—bright and shiny and full of promise on the outside but rotten to the core. Perhaps ethics is like the Golden Rule "Do unto others as you would have them do unto you," a guiding principle for life, or "He who has the gold rules," a cynical, if insightful, commentary on contemporary human affairs. However you see ethics, be creative with your metaphor and enjoy discussing it with others (Courtesy of Professor Ramona Ortega-Liston, University of Akron).

2. What are some of your most important values? What is the basis of them (did they derive from family, religious, or school experiences)? Record your thinking in your journal.

3. Use the following topics as catalysts for journal entries:

   • Your personal definition of ethics
   • At least three values you value and describe one professional experience when one of those values was realized or tested

- How dramatic news stories may distract from genuine ethical dilemmas
- How "the best can be the enemy of the good"
- How ethics can be trivialized
- How economic imperatives can compromise ethical principles

4. Read the following scenarios and decide which quadrant in Figure 3.1 is the best fit. Put the appropriate letter (A–D) next to each of the following items:

- Paying an extra fee to skip security lines at the airport
- Freeways creating special lanes that allow those willing to pay to skip rush hour traffic
- A university accepting donations from a donor who has strong public feelings against interracial and interreligious marriages
- A lobbyist paying in excess of $1,000 to a line-stander to arrive minutes before a congressional hearing that is open to the public free of charge with limited capacity
- Paying someone to stand in line for you to get otherwise free tickets to a performance held by New York City's Public Theater with limited capacity
- Hiring someone to camp out in front of the Supreme Court days before the Affordable Care Act arguments begin, although the hearing is free to the public (with limited capacity)
- A business that does not discriminate against customers belonging to a racial/ethnic minority group
- Rejecting a lucrative contract with Chick-Fil-A because their anti-gay contributions offend your university's student and faculty population
- A business that does discriminate against customers belonging to a racial/ethnic minority group
- The City of Miami allowing community redevelopment agencies to redraw lines to include both affluent and slum-and-blight areas, and then only improve the already affluent areas
- Paying $200 to receive seven football tickets at the beginning of the season rather than wait in line for free student tickets the day before games
- Paying $15,000 a year to a concierge doctor who is available around the clock, doesn't make you wait, and has only 600 patients rather than 3,000
- Prisoners paying a fee for an upgrade to a cleaner, nicer jail cell
- An employee telling a supervisor that progress has been made on a project when none has
- States selling naming rights to state parks

(Note: Some items are adapted from Sandel (2012).)

5. Every year a private media group sponsors the Theodore Roosevelt Government Leadership Awards (www.govexec.com/feature/government-hall-fame/), honoring 12 exemplary federal employees in a variety of categories. Consult the latest list of winners and report on one of them to the class.

6. Bad Actor Exercises
Instructions: The tabletop exercises serve to provide students with a framework for the application of ethical decision-making in real-world scenarios. For the following

scenario (and those that follow in Chapters 5, 9, 11, and 12), you will be assigned a role to assume. After reviewing the scenario and the role, form a response outlining your decision and the reasoning behind it. Be sure to consider ethical theories and principles and answer in earnest. Your decision may not always be the most ethical choice; however, you should explain the constraints in your decision-making and state relevant reasons for your response.

Tabletop Exercise 1: The Bad Parent

Jane Weber is a single mother of five children. She is currently raising one teenager, two preteens, and two children under the age of nine. None of the children's fathers is involved financially or otherwise. Jane is on welfare and has a tendency to bounce between several minimum wage jobs, including bartending and housekeeping. She often works odd hours and is forced to leave the children home alone. With little income, Jane struggles to provide the essentials for her family, and they often have to go without simple amenities. Jane is on the verge of eviction and was recently laid off from her housekeeping job.

Role 1: Teacher

You are a teacher for one of Jane's oldest children. You have noticed that the child is often wearing clothes that do not fit and appears distraught and distracted in class. The child is teased for his appearance regularly. After talking to the child, you learn that his free lunch at school is often his only meal, and he stays awake watching his siblings most nights. The child's grades are slipping and he is now at risk academically. Do you feel obligated to act in this situation? How would you respond? Consider your obligations, ethical and otherwise. To whom are you accountable as an educator? What factors impact your decision?

Role 2: Friend

You are Jane's friend and former coworker, and you have intimate knowledge of her financial situation. Having met her children, you are aware of the struggle that they face on a daily basis. You know that Jane does not intend to endanger her children, but she is irresponsible and often neglectful in her duties as a mother. You do not have the capacity to help Jane yourself, but you know that she needs assistance. What do you do? Do you report Jane to family services? Consider your obligations, ethical and otherwise. To whom are you accountable as a friend? What factors impact your decision?

Role 3: Close Relative

You are Jane's only living relative and have become aware of her escalating situation. You have offered your help in the past, but Jane has refused out of pride. In your last conversation, Jane reveals that she is nearing eviction, and she again refuses your help. You know about the children's issues at school and feel the situation is worsening. What do you do? Consider your obligations, ethical and otherwise. To whom are you accountable as a family member? What factors impact your decision?

Role 4: Neighbor

You have been Jane's neighbor for the past year. You often see Jane coming and going at odd hours and know that she has five children at home. You notice the children often leave for school late and are dressed poorly; sometimes the children don't go to school at all. Your children are friends of Jane's kids, and they admit they sometimes sneak food to the neighbors when they don't have enough. You saw an eviction notice on Jane's door last week and know that the family needs more help than you can offer. What do you do? Consider your obligations, ethical and otherwise. To whom are you accountable? What factors impact your decision?

7. View the YouTube video by Damon Horowitz, "Moral Operating Systems" (16 minutes), and Ted Talk by Monica Lewinsky: "The Price of Shame" (22 minutes).

References

Abels, M. (2017, July 17). A new public administration paradigm is emerging. *PA Times*. Retrieved from https://patimes.org/public-administration-paradigm-emerging

Associated Press. (2018, June 6). Kansas man doesn't regret giving up $1million ticket. *The Salina Journal*. Retrieved from www.usatoday.com/story/news/nation/2018/06/06/kansas-man-doesnt-regret-giving-up-1-million-lottery-ticket/679002002/

BBC. (2020). *Michael Flynn: Former US national security advisor*. Retrieved from www.bbc.com/news/world-us-canada-38025057

Berman, E., & West, J. (2012). Public values in special districts: A survey of managerial commitment. *Public Administration Review*, *72*, 43–54.

Bershidsky, L. (2019, November 1). *Commentary: Why accusing Lt. Col. Vindman of divided loyalties makes no sense*. Retrieved from www.mcall.com/opinion/mc-opi-vindman-ukraine-loyalty-immigrants-20191101-3wymnqkgkncj7a6euuwbzwgokq-story.html

Bynander, F. (2011). Value conflicts in foreign policy crises: How the United States and the U.K. wrestled with the ethical dilemma of going to war in Iraq. In L. Svedin (Ed.), *Ethics and crisis management* (pp. 37–56). Charlotte, NC: Information Age.

Caccese, M. S. (1997). Ethics and the financial analyst. *Financial Analysts Journal*, *53*(1), 9–14.

Carleen, A. (2020, July 10). *Alexander Vindman told the truth. If only more Republics were tolling to do the same*. Retrieved from www.wbur.org/cognoscenti/2020/07/10/alexander-vindman-retires-andrew-carleen

Cooper, T. (2000). *Handbook of administrative ethics*. New York: Marcel Dekker.

DeChello, P. (2003). *Law and ethics: A clinician's guide to legal and ethical practice*. Middlefield, CT: D&S Associates.

DiNorcia, V. (1998). *Hard like water: Ethics in business*. New York: Oxford University Press.

Editorial Board. (2020, November 25). Trump's pardon of Michael Flynn is a parting disgrace. *The Washington Post*. Retrieved from www.washingtonpost.com/opinions/trumps-pardon-of-michael-flynn-is-a-parting-disgrace/2020/11/25/12817de2-2f7c-11eb-bae0–50bb17126614_story.html

Eisen, N. (2020, May 1). Why Trump is obsessed with the Flynn case. *New York Times*. Retrieved from www.nytimes.com/2020/05/01/opinion/trump-flynn-fbi.html

Ethics Unwrapped. (n.d.). *Michael Flynn: Under investigation*. Retrieved from https://ethicsunwrapped.utexas.edu/video/michael-flynn-under-investigation

Gleason, J., O'Neal, J., & Miller, M. (2020, May 11). The Flynn case isn't over until the judge says it's over. *The Washington Post*. Retrieved from www.washingtonpost.com/opinions/2020/05/11/flynn-case-isnt-over-until-judge-says-its-over/www.washingtonpost.com/opinions/2020/05/11/the-flynn-case-isn't-over-until-the-judge-says-it's-over/

Graham, D. (2020, May 9). Viewpoint: Why Michael Flynn is walking free. *The Atlantic*. Retrieved from justicesecurityorg/7043/understanding-the-michael-flynn-case-separating-the-wheat-from-the-chaff-and-the-proper-from-the-improper

Harnik, A. (2020, July 8). *Lt. Col. Vindman, fired by White House after testifying in Trump impeachment, will retire from Army*. Retrieved from www.stripes.com/news/army/lt-col-vindman-fired-by-white-house-after-testifying-in-trump-impeachment-will-retire-from-army-1.636781

Heintzman, R. (2007). Public-service values and ethics: Dead end or strong foundation? *Canadian Public Administration*, *50*, 573–602.

Helderman, R., & Dawsey, J. (2020, November 25). Trump pardons former national security advisor Michael Flynn who pleaded guilty to lying to the FBI. *Washington Post*. Retrieved from www.washingtonpost.com/politics/michael-flynn-trump-pardon/2020/11/25/3cd79198-2e65-11eb-bae0-50bg17126614_storyhtml

Houston, D. J., & Cartwright, K. E. (2007). Spirituality and public service. *Public Administration Review*, *67*, 88–102.

Howell, J. (2020, November 23). A conversation with Alexander Vindman. *The Lawfare*. Retrieved from www.lawfareblog.com/lawfare.podcast.conversation-aexander-vindman

Jamieson, D., & O'Mara, J. (1991). *Managing workforce 2000: Gaining the diversity advantage*. San Francisco: Jossey-Bass.

Kaminer, A. (2011, June 14). Challenge the leader. *New York Times Sunday Magazine*. Retrieved from www.nytimes.com/2011/06/12/magazine/the-ethicist-challenge-the-leader.html

Kidder, R. (1994). *Shared values in a troubled world*. San Francisco: Jossey-Bass.

Klosterman, C. (2013, March 17). My cheating friend. *New York Times Sunday Magazine*, p. 16.

Kraus, M. (2016, October 13). Psychology suggests that power doesn't make people bad—it just reveals their true nature. *Quartz*. Retrieved from https://qz.com/809580/psychology-shows-that-the-more-power-we-give-to-people-like-donald-trump-the-worse-they-get/

Lederman, M. (2020, May 29). *Understanding the Michael Flynn case: Separating the wheat from the chaff, and the proper from the improper*. Retrieved from www.justsecurity.org/70431/understanding-the-michael-flynn-case-separating-the-wheat-from-the-chaff-and-the-proper-from-the-improper/

Manning, G., Curtis, K., & McMillen, S. (1996). *Building community: The human side of work*. Duluth, MN: Whole Person Associates.

Marimow, A. (2020, August 31). Michael Flynn case does not have to be immediately dismissed, appeals court rules. *The Washington Post*. Retrieved from www.washingtonpost.com/opinions/2020/05/11/flynn-case-isnt-over-until-judge-says-its-over/

Markell, J. (2017, September 21). Let's stop government giveaways to corporations. *New York Times*. Retrieved from www.nytimes.com/2017/09/21/opinion/incentives-businesses-corporations-giveaways.html?emc=edit_th_20170921&nl=todaysheadlines&nlid=63449989

Markkula Center for Applied Ethics. (n.d.). *A framework for ethical decision making*. Retrieved from www.scu.edu/ethics/ethics-resources/ethical-decision-making/a-framework-for-ethical-decision-making/

McCarthy, A. (2020). Andrew McCarthy: Michael Flynn will lose battle but win war to end his persecution. *Fox News*. Retrieved from www.foxnews.com/opinion/michael-flynn-appeal-decision-andrew-mccarthy

McConkie, M. (2008). Spirituality and the public sector. *International Journal of Public Administration*, *31*, 337–341.

McFall, M. (2019, October 30). *Alexander Vindman should be celebrated, not smeared.* Retrieved from www.washingtonpost.com/opinions/alexander-vindman-should-be-celebrated-not-smeared/2019/10/30/f4781d86-fb44-11e9-8906-ab6b60de9124_story.html

Myre, G. (2019, October 29). *Who is Lt. Col. Alexander Vindman?* Retrieved from www.wyso.org/2019-10-29/who-is-lt-col-alexander-vindman

Newell, T. (2015). *To serve with honor.* Crozet, VA: Loftlands Press.

Olsson, E. (2011). Communication in crises of public diplomacy: The quest for ethical capital. In L. Svedin (Ed.), *Ethics and crisis management* (pp. 141–162). Charlotte, NC: Information Age.

Piff, P. (2014). Wealth and the inflated self-class, entitlement, and narcissism. *Personality and Social Psychology Bulletin, 40*(1), 34–43.

Sandel, M. (2012). *What money can't buy: The moral limits of markets.* New York: Farrar, Straus & Giroux.

Savage, C. (2020, September 1). Court denies Flynn's bid to end case and renews fight over McGahn subpoena1. *New York Times.* Retrieved from www.nytimes.com/2020/08/31/us/politics/michael-flynn-appeals-court.html

Sciutto, J. (2020, July 8). *Exclusive: Vindman to retire from military. His lawyer lames White House 'campaign of bullying, intimidation and retaliation'.* Retrieved from www.cnn.com/2020/07/08/politics/vindman-retiring-alleged-white-house-retaliation/index.html

Shoop, T. (2020, August 5). They Sounded the alarm, evacuated Americans and started working on a vaccine. *Government Executive.* Retrieved from www.govexec.com/management/2020/08/they-sounded-alarm-evacuated-americans-and-started-working-vaccine/167453/

Smart, G. (2019, February 26). Why would a billionaire go to a strip mall sex spa? *Treasure Coast Newspapers.* Retrieved from www.tcpalm.com/story/opinion/columnists/gil-smart/2019/02/25/why-would-wealthy-johns-risk-sex-spa-bust/2977936002/

Stolberg, S. G. (2019, October 29). Meet Alexander Vindman, the colonel who testified on Trump's phone call. *The New York Times.* Retrieved from www.nytimes.com/2019/10/29/us/politics/who-is-alexandervindman.html

Svedin, L. (2011). Conclusions. In L. Svedin (Ed.), *Ethics and crisis management* (pp. 217–246). Charlotte, NC: Information Age.

Thompson, D. (1992). The paradoxes of government ethics. *Public Administration Review, 52,* 254–259.

Travers, R. (2020, July 14). I'm a former civil servant. We are professionals, not a 'deep state'. *Washington Post.* Retrieved from www.washingtonpost.com/opinions/im-a-former-civil-servant-we-are-professionals-not-a-deep-state/2020/07/14/119b1280-c5f0–11ea-b037-f9711f89ee46_story.html

Vertanen, T. (2000). Changing competences of public managers: Tensions in commitment. *International Journal of Public Sector Management, 13,* 333–341.

Vindman, A. (2020, August 1). Alexander Vindman: Coming forward ended my career, I still believe doing what's right matters. *The Washington Post.* Retrieved from www.washingtonpost.com/opinions/2020/08/01/alexander-vindman-retiring-oped/

Waldo, D. (1980). *The enterprise of public administration: A summary view.* Novato, CA: Chandler & Sharp.

West, J., & Bowman, J. (2008). Employee benefits: Weighing ethical principles and economic imperatives. In C. Reddick & J. Coggburn (Eds.), *Handbook of employee benefits and administration* (pp. 29–54). Boca Raton, FL: CRC Press.

PART II

Individual-Centered Approaches to Ethics

4 Moral Development Theory

The perfecting of one's self is the fundamental base of all progress and all moral development.

—Confucius

This chapter initiates Part II of the book, "Individual-Centered Approaches to Ethics." The chapters included in this part present philosophically based approaches to ethics (cognitive and social intuition) as well as psychologically based ethics. To gain perspective on this material, this chapter focuses on an inclusive and hierarchical theory of moral development that can be applied to both individuals and institutions. It also offers a critique of this theory. The chapter objectives are to

- comprehend Kohlberg's theory of moral development,
- apply moral development theory,
- relate the theory to professionalism,
- explore the implications of two classical laboratory experiments,
- understand Haidt's critique of Kohlberg, and
- distinguish between utilitarian and deontological approaches.

KOHLBERG'S MORAL DEVELOPMENT THEORY: A RATIONAL APPROACH

The leading theory of moral development was formulated by Lawrence Kohlberg, shown in Table 4.1. Kohlberg posited that people may mature morally by moving from stage to stage in each of three levels, although they may stop at any time. He argued that most people reason at the "conventional" level.

The levels and stages of Kohlberg's theory are hierarchically ordered: Level 1, Stages 1 and 2 constitute preconventional morality. Stage 1 is characterized by a punishment and obedience orientation, wherein obedience is linked to externally imposed punishment, deference to power, and fear of pain or loss of love. Here, morality is determined by avoiding punishment and receiving rewards. Stage 2 is characterized by instrumentalism and deal making with negotiated exchanges of favors for personal benefit ("you scratch my back and I'll scratch yours"). Morality is seen as advancing self-interest and honoring agreements.

DOI: 10.4324/9781003203148-6

TABLE 4.1		Kohlberg's Stages of Moral Development With Behavioral Orientation		

Level	Self-Perception	Stage Orientation	"Right" Behavior	Reference Frame
Level 1: Preconventional	Outside Group	1. Punishment and obedience 2. Instrumental–relativistic	1. Avoid punishment, defer to power 2. Satisfaction of own needs	1. Physical consequence of actions 2. Human relations are like a marketplace
Level 2: Conventional	Inside Group	3. Good boy–nice girl 4. Law and order	3. That which pleases/helps others 4. Duty, maintenance of social order	3. Majority or "natural" behavior 4. Authority and fixed rules of society
Level 3: Postconventional	Above Group	5. Social contract 6. Universal–ethical	5. In terms of individual rights, free agreement 6. Choice of conscience, ethical principles	5. Constitutional/democratic agreement, social utility 6. Universal imperatives, justice, human rights

Source: Adapted from Kohlberg (1971).

Level 2, Stages 3 and 4 reflect conventional morality. Stage 3 highlights the approval of others (family, friends, coworkers) as a determinant of behavior. Living up to the expectations of others (the childhood desire to be a "good boy/nice girl") and winning the acceptance and approval of one's social group is a primary value. Stage 4 emphasizes compliance with laws, policies, and proper authorities. Orientations focus on complying with authority, doing one's duty, and maintaining social order. Reasoning at Level 2 is conventional and not critical—responding to pressures to conform to accepted expectations, standards, and rules.

Level 3, Stages 5 and 6 represent postconventional morality. Stage 5 gives emphasis to due process, individual rights, and social consensus. Cognition at the fifth stage can lead to challenges to legitimate authority. Critical reflection, independence of mind, and a more impartial view are evident. Stage 6 is grounded in universal ethical principles, wherein right actions are determined based on individual conscience and commitments to abstract concepts such as justice, care, and freedom.

Kohlberg built on the work of Jean Piaget, developing an empirically based moral development theory premised solely on moral reasoning. For Kohlberg, the levels at which people operate when confronting moral issues vary as they pass through different phases of their lives. Children, adolescents, and some adults dominate the preconventional level, while most of the population operates at the conventional level and a much smaller percentage reaches the postconventional level. Upward movement from lower to higher stages in the hierarchy can occur through a maturation process that leads to a more sophisticated and complex understanding of ethical problems and solutions.

Kohlberg posed case dilemmas to his research subjects, asking them what they would do in such situations. However, he was less concerned with their answers than in their response to a second question: "Why?" He was interested in the moral *reasoning* subjects used in addressing the issue. Kohlberg's question was why do people behave in certain ways at each level of moral development? A well-known case used by Kohlberg involved a man, Heinz, who had to decide whether to steal a drug he couldn't afford to buy but that would save the life of his ailing wife. Kohlberg observed variation in the way people reacted to, interpreted, and dealt with Heinz's and other dilemmas. The theory of cognitive moral development grew out of the recorded responses to such hypotheticals posed to different respondent groups. Analysis of the contemporary hypothetical case in Case Study 4.1 illustrates the thought processes using Kohlberg's three-level, six-stage model that might be provoked by an ethically challenging situation confronting military Private X.

Twenty years in the making, Kohlberg's theory presumes that careful moral reasoning can—and should—affect one's ethical perspective and that moral judgment has cognitive features. His theory, while extraordinarily influential, has been challenged on many fronts. Among the criticisms are the narrow focus on moral judgment, inattention to issues of conflict of interest or confidentiality, insufficient evidence of postconventional thinking, overemphasis on macro and underemphasis on micro morality, a hard "staircase" approach to stage development, undue reliance on verbal responses, an implication that higher stages are morally preferable to lower stages, the restriction of samples to males, and its inclusion of certain ethical approaches while excluding others (Rest & Narrvaez, 1994; Rest et al., 1999; Swisher, Rizzo, & Marley, 2005; Velasquez, 1998). Other researchers refer to "schemas" and "orientations" rather than stages in describing moral development.

Carol Gilligan, a student of Kohlberg's, finds that while men may pass through the developmental stages as described, the moral thinking patterns of women are not the same. The "male" perspective on ethics addresses issues using "impersonal, impartial, and abstract moral rules," relying on principles of justice and rights that Kohlberg associates with postconventional thinking. Gilligan's research identifies an alternative "female" viewpoint wherein subjects see themselves as "part of a 'web' of relationships with family and friends," which gives emphasis to addressing moral issues stressing "sustaining these relationships, avoiding hurt to others . . . and caring for their well being." Caring and being responsible are more important in the "female" approach while "adhering to impartial and impersonal rules" is closer to the "male" perspective (Velasquez, 1998, 28). As Gilligan notes, for women, "morality is conceived in interpersonal terms and goodness is equated with helping and pleasing others" (quoted in Singer, 1994, 55–56). Gilligan's work suggests the need to be cautious in making blanket generalizations about moral development.

CASE STUDY 4.1

Applying Kohlberg's Stages of Moral Development

A low-ranking military serviceman (Private X) is ordered to kill innocent civilians by his superior (albeit crazed) officer. How might the private analyze his ethical requirements?

In the early stages of development, a *punishment/obedience orientation* (similar to that of a young child) compels Private X to comply with stated rules (in this case, the requirements to unquestioningly follow the orders of his superior). This imperative is reinforced through a fear of consequences of noncompliance. In this case, the private believes that disobedience will result in a range of unpleasant consequences, ranging from physical harm to court martial.

He may feel that it is necessary to conform to the norms of his peer group soldiers, who, he believes, will also follow such orders, soldiers who have been trained to use violence without prejudice. In doing so, the soldier affirms his loyalty to his group of peers and is thus gratified by his sense of belonging. Here, he has traded his feelings of concern for the value of belonging. This dynamic illustrates the second stage in Kohlberg's development: the *self-gratification orientation*.

Private X has likely (up to this point) developed a substantial level of trust and loyalty toward his leader. Further, a similar level of trust and loyalty has no doubt developed among the soldiers—whose lives depend on it. An orientation toward Stage 3, *approval of others*, directs him to do the "right thing"; do what the lieutenant and the other men "expect"; do what the others would presumably do. He is compelled by this need for the support of his leader and of his friends. In this approval, he may find adequate justification for questionable actions.

Having been indoctrinated into the military culture, Private X is ever aware of the chain of command. The hierarchy of rank within this community and the authority that stems from it are at the very foundation of this military culture. The laws, rules, and customs of the organization are necessarily inflexible; they are constant and demand compliance. This compliance is essential for the efficient function and stability of its culture. It may be that, regardless of other judgments, Private X is compelled by this Stage 4 orientation that prioritizes *law and order* above all else. In this context, obedience to the directives of his superior (regardless of reservation) is given the greater moral weight.

Approaching the later stages of moral development, the private may begin to loosen his previous commitment to the expectations of his lieutenant and platoon, and the authority of military protocol and convention. Oriented in this way, toward a greater social contract, he relies more on his own personal standards of social responsibility; he recognizes that it is not moral to follow a directive (such as killing innocent civilians) that lacks legitimacy. Here, the values of his platoon and perhaps of the military are judged with relativity. Outside these organizations, perhaps, there exists an overriding social consensus on his own personal standards; Stage 5—*consensus/social contract*—allows him to more appropriately judge the validity of the order.

If, however, Private X had developed to the last stage of moral development, he would apply a set of *universal ethical principles* to his analysis. His principles are not simple laws that map a course of action but rather represent a host of abstract ideas that address the concepts of justice, reciprocity, equality, and respect for others. Based on his personal morality, these tenets provide guidance beyond the dictates of the conventions of the military establishment. He understands the rights of the innocent civilians and places value on their lives. His principles provide a compass that guides his questioning.

The hypothetical in Case Study 4.1 reveals different reactions Private X might have experienced at each stage of moral development when confronted with an extraordinarily stressful situation. Now, two classical laboratory trials—Stanley Milgram's "shock" experiment and Philip Zimbardo's Stanford prison experiment—further illustrate Kohlberg's theory of moral development. They both suggest the importance of "getting in touch with your inner psychopath" (see Exhibit 4.1).

EXHIBIT 4.1   Getting in Touch With Your Inner Psychopath

We all loathe the psychopaths of the business world. They use others, they see themselves as deserving more and better than everyone else, and they feel entitled to do things the way they want rather than doing as they really should. Sometimes impulsively and sometimes planfully, they're looking out for "Number 1" above all else. Psychopathy can look like all kinds of things, but we just hate it when we see it.

Here's the problem with that loathing of ours: Every one of us carries around those very same wishes and impulses. All that makes us different from the psychopaths we read about, or perhaps see each day a few offices down from us, is really just a matter of degree and our personal level of self-control—pretty thin tethers to both our ethics and much-loved feelings of virtue.

Here's the other problem with that loathing: The more we refuse to see those impulses and desires in ourselves, the less control we actually have over them. Shunning them because "I could never be like that" is simply a combination of wishful thinking and blind faith. A far more effective way to prevent ethical lapses is to look hard and deep at yourself and see what your particular wishes and impulses actually are, however unsavory some of them may sometimes feel to you. That will then allow you to begin to see the places where you might have previously unseen risks for loosening your self-control or needed attention to ethics.

Lest it need to be said, the goal is not to befriend those inner psychopathic impulses—they obviously need to not be encouraged! However, to acknowledge their presence is the foundation for actually controlling them as opposed to simply choosing to assume that your behavior is—and will somehow always magically be—appropriate. As Ralph Waldo Emerson observed, "the only person you are destined to become is the person you decide to be."

Source: ethicsthought@aweber.com. Used with permission.

MILGRAM'S SHOCK AND ZIMBARDO'S PRISON EXPERIMENTS: ETHICS UNDER PRESSURE

Milgram: Situation Ethics

The objective of Milgram's work was to discover conditions under which people would defy authority to honor the moral imperative not to inflict harm on a helpless individual. Two individuals are taken to a room where one (the "learner") is strapped in a chair and an electrode is placed on his arm. The other (the "teacher") is taken to an adjoining room where she reads word pairs and asks the learner to read them back. If the learner gets the answer correct, then they move on to the next word pair. If the answer is incorrect, the teacher shocks the learner, starting at 15 volts and gradually going up to 450 volts in 15-volt increments. Although the teachers believed they were administering shocks, the learners were Milgram's confederates and were not harmed.[1]

The key micro relationship, then, was not between the teacher and the learner but between the teacher and the experimenter—that is, whether or not the teacher would obey Milgram, who relied solely on verbal commands for persuasion. The experiment is oceanic because it extends beyond mere speculation and written tests; it is one thing to discuss in the abstract individual rights and authority, and quite another to examine moral choice in an actual situation.

Psychiatrists, students, and middle-class adults interviewed by Milgram prior to the experiment all predicted that only a lunatic fringe, perhaps one in 1,000 people, would go all the way and administer 450 volts. The experiment was conducted with hundreds of individuals aged 20–50 from various walks of life, and there were few demographic variables associated with obedience (Milgram, 1974; see also Blass, 2000 and McLeod, 2007, which include video excerpts of the experiment). The subjects were not blindly obedient (although many seemed more concerned about their own stress than that of the learner).

But they were obedient as nearly two-thirds of "teachers" went to 450 volts; in fact, none of the participants who refused to administer the final shocks (everyone went to at least 300 volts) insisted that the experiment itself be stopped. Consider too what might have happened if the learner, on meeting the teacher prior to the beginning of the experiment, had been unpleasant to him. Here the teacher's personal microethics were subverted by the permissive ethics of the meso, Milgram-led organization. Predictions about what would happen in the experiment were so far off because they focused on the autonomous individual rather than the situation in which he or she finds himself or herself. Ethics is a question not only of belief but also of action. The problem is not knowing right from wrong, but doing it.

Unwelcome insights into human behavior derived from the experiment include the following:

- It is not so much the kind of person one is as it is the type of situation he or she is confronted with that determines how one will act.
- Those in the experiment who carried out their tasks were dominated by an administrative, rather than a moral, outlook; they were a component of a system ("just doing my job"), not autonomous individuals.

- People can become an instrument of organizational authority in the presence of an authority and may be unable to free themselves from it (the superior–subordinate relationship—and the control panel itself—overwhelms any other consideration).
- It is psychologically easy to ignore responsibility when one is only an intermediate link in a chain of action.

The results of Milgram's work, one of the best-known psychological experiments in history, are disquieting, so much so that some researchers believe that he manipulated and mistreated subjects and misinterpreted or exaggerated the findings. In reviewing the experiment's archives, the records of all 24 variations of the experiment (each with a different protocol), one scholar found that in over one-half of them 60 percent of the teachers *disobeyed* the authority figure. "The high percentage rate compliance results was made famous since it was the initial interaction that Milgram reported . . . that involved only 40 subjects" (Perry, 2013).

Nonetheless, what is disconcerting about the experiment is that many of the subjects were not perverted or sadistic but rather terrifyingly normal. As one analyst noted, they were nothing more—and nothing less—than "desk murderers," as they were unable to balance the two components of being a professional: technical and ethical competence (see Chapters 1 and 3). It is befitting that professionals make moral decisions at Kohlberg's Level 3 of moral development. A professional cannot make moral decisions solely from the self-interested Level 1 perspective. The Level 2 perspective may be inadequate because some social roles are unjust (e.g., police in the Jim Crow American South, Nazi doctors, U.S. intelligence officials torturing prisoners during the Iraq War). Level 3 reasoning, however, checks abuse of one's skills for either one's own advantage or the advantage of one's social group.

The task of professionalism is not to eliminate self- and group interest but to balance them in light of a higher claim of human dignity. Advancing from Level 1 to Level 2 is a common psychological development requiring little deliberate decision. Professional life, however, requires a conscious commitment to both the technical and the moral standards of excellence. It is unthinkable for a professional to do otherwise (Snell, 1993).

Zimbardo: The Stanford Prison Experiment

In another well-known experiment, Philip Zimbardo, like Milgram, investigated the pressures of social conformity, arguing that situations can induce unexpected responses to the extent that nearly any deed may be committed by anyone. The infamous "Stanford Prison Experiment" that placed students in a mock jail can be viewed at http://prisonexp.org. One difference between the two classic experiments is that Milgram's work emphasized short, one-on-one sessions, whereas Zimbardo's work involved the "total immersion" of multiple subjects for six days and nights.

In August 1971, Zimbardo turned the basement of the Stanford psychology department into a mock prison. Twenty-four college students were arbitrarily assigned to roles as either prisoner or guard by the flip of a coin. Once they had been arrested and processed, the prisoners were stripped of all their clothing and given uniforms and an identification number. With three small cells each housing three of the nine total prisoners and a two-by-two closet representing solitary confinement, the inmates experienced harsh and dehumanizing conditions.

The guards began exerting their power by forcing prisoners to endure physical activity when they believed the convicts misbehaved. The inmates began showing signs of emotional distress to the point that one of them had to be released. Soon the prisoners believed that they could never leave the institution and that it was no longer just an experiment. Educated young men were transformed into cruel prison guards or emotionally tortured inmates. Astonishingly, even Zimbardo lost himself in his role as superintendent, forgetting his position as experimenter. After only six days, Zimbardo had to call off his two-week experiment because both the guards and the prisoners had completely fallen into their roles, having forgotten reality and their personal identities. Participants subverted their ethics—and even their identities—in pursuit of a task.

Like the Milgram experiment, the authenticity and value of Zimbardo's work have been questioned (Blum, 2018, June 7; Haslam, Reicher, & Van Bavel, 2018, June 6). In a detailed response Zimbardo addressed criticisms one by one, arguing that the main message:

> Is not that a psychological simulation of prison life is the same as the real thing, or that prisoners and guards always or even usually behave the way that they did in the SPE. Rather, the SPE serves as a precautionary tale of what *might* happen to any of us if we underestimate the extent to which the power of social roles and external pressures can influence our actions. (Statement from Philip Zimbardo (c. 2018), original emphasis)

Analysis

Both Milgram's and Zimbardo's findings have withstood the test of time, as evidenced by compelling documentaries, popular movies (*The Experiment* [2010] with Adrian Brody and Forrest Whitaker and *Experimenter* [2015] with Peter Sarsgaard and Winona Ryder as well as *The Stanford Prison Experiment* [2015] drama), and continuations of their research. In 2006, Court TV's "Human Behavior Experiments" (45-minute) program demonstrated the relevance of obedience experiments today. It involved cases including a criminally malicious "telephone strip search" of a restaurant employee by a person claiming to be a police officer (also portrayed in the 2012 movie *Compliance*), actions of a fraternity resulting in a hazing death, and torture at Iraqi prisons.[2]

Primetime's "The Science of Evil" (www.youtube.com/watch?v=HwqNP9HRy7Y) was a rare replication of Milgram's experiments conducted in cooperation with Santa Clara University (see also Rushton, 2004). Even though participants were advised that deception was involved (the only way the experiment could be legally redone), the findings were similar to the original trials. There have also been recent virtual replications of the experiments where human participants "shocked" virtual beings with comparable results (teachers had to be reminded that the virtual representations of people were not actually real). In popular culture, reality shows, video games, and hidden camera scenarios in ABC's "What Would You Do?" program often involve wrongdoing and how people respond to it. More scholarly updates of Milgram's work include Blass (2000) as well as Zimbardo (2007).

There are at least three undeniable themes common to all these materials. One is that while people think that they know how they would react to a given scenario, they are often bewildered once they find themselves confronted with an actual situation and submit to authority figures. The power of self-deception—when confidence is confused with competence—can be compelling. Indeed, thinking about moral dilemmas in World War II, Preston (2001) asks, how can I know that "I would not have deceived myself to avoid moral responsibility had I worked in Nazi Germany, just as I may presently deceive myself about my responsibility to victims of systemic poverty and oppression in our world?" (95).

The second commonality is "willful blindness" to problems in plain sight (Hefferman, 2012), such as Bernie Madoff's Ponzi scheme, British Petroleum's safety record, the pedophile scandal in the Catholic Church and the Boy Scouts of America, the misbegotten Iraq War, subprime mortgages, Volkswagen's emissions-cheating scandal, safety issues with Boeing's 737 Max jetliner, or the effectiveness of mask-wearing during a pandemic. In every instance, and many more, why were repeated warnings not heeded? The impulse to obey and conform—as well as the fear and futility involved in challenging authority—makes people blind to personal, organizational, and national tragedies. It takes considerable intestinal fortitude to doubt the official view. As in Hans Christian Andersen's *The Emperor's New Clothes*, few people are willing to appear unfit for their positions or ignorant by asking questions—even if the emperor *does* have no clothes. The results from the Milgram and Zimbardo protocols run counter to Kohlberg's findings that moral judgments are settled upon by moral reasoning. Clearly, contextual factors influence behavior in ethical dilemmas. Evil is done not only by monsters but also, at least as frequently, by normal people put in trying circumstances.

The final common theme is a set of psychological mechanisms that summarize why the experiment participants acted as they did (Mueller, 2019, 126ff.): authorization (acceptance, and acting as agents, of authority) along with routinization (amoral adoption of work tasks and dehumanization of victims). These mechanisms of obedience can be found in many scandals and assist in understanding the behavior of individuals and organizations.

HAIDT'S SOCIAL INTUITIONALIST APPROACH

In contrast to Kohlberg's moral development theory, which emphasized reasoning and not emotion, stands the work of Jonathan Haidt (2012). There are two central differences between Haidt's and Kohlberg's theories: One is process, the other substance.

Regarding process, Kohlberg finds that moral judgments are settled on by moral reasoning, which progresses from lesser to greater complexity in stages. Kohlberg's rationalism links morality to individual autonomy, rights, and justice, while paying comparatively little attention to authority, hierarchy, and tradition—factors important in the Milgram and Zimbardo experiments. Haidt sees things differently, apparent in his assessment of the Heinz case. Haidt views the dilemma ("Should Heinz steal a drug to save his wife's life?") as one constructed by Kohlberg to achieve an inevitable response: rational moral thinking that involves weighing "concerns about harm and life against concerns about law and property rights" (36). He found that 30 University of Virginia students were not dumbfounded by the Heinz case. They offered sound reasons for their assessment: Saving a life overrules property concerns. Instead, Haidt (2012, 45) chose a brother–sister scenario involving a "taboo violation" that would elicit a "gut reaction."

> Julie and Mark, who are sister and brother, are traveling together in France. They are both on summer vacation from college. One night they are staying alone in a cabin near the beach. They decide that it would be interesting and fun if they tried making love. At the very least, it would be a new experience for each of them. Julie is already taking birth control pills, but

Mark uses a condom too, just to be safe. They both enjoy it, but they decide not to do it again. They keep that night as a special secret between them, which makes them feel even closer to each other. So what do you think about this? Was it wrong for them to have sex?

Haidt used a second scenario involving another "taboo violation": A family's dog is killed by a car in front of their house. The students have heard that dog meat is delicious, so they cut up the dog's body, cook it, and eat it for dinner. Haidt expected immediate moral condemnation from the same students in each case. He was right. The participants viewed sex between siblings and consumption of dogs as wrong, but when they were asked to explain why, they were flummoxed, responding with explanations like "I don't know, I can't explain it, I just know." When those vague explanations are challenged by researchers, the participants flounder, grasping for reason after reason to justify their moral judgments (see Chapter 7). Haidt concluded that emotional reactions precede moral judgments. The participants made their moral judgment quickly and emotionally, then sought to develop a rational explanation for their decision. He maintains that morality does not come primarily from moral logic, but rather reasoning in these cases was simply an ex post facto search for ideas to justify the judgments they had already made. As Haidt has observed, "The emotional tail wags the rational dog" (quoted in Kahneman, 2011, 40).

Social Intuitionalism

Haidt contends that two separate processes are at work in thinking about (a) ethics judgment (seeing that) and (b) reasoning why (describing how one reaches the judgment). According to Haidt, while Kohlberg studied the "reasoning why," he neglected the "seeing that." Haidt, along with others (Margolis, 1987; Wason, 1960), maintains that rapid intuitive moral judgments precede carefully reasoned justifications. In the Heinz dilemma, it is contended that subjects can intuitively "see that" stealing the drug to save his wife's life was the preferred act and that the case was constructed to enable good arguments on both sides of the issue. In contrast, in the brother–sister and dog consumption cases, strong gut feelings about right and wrong influence a snap judgment that is later justified through moral reasoning. His rule: "[I]ntuitions come first, strategic reasoning second" (Haidt, 2012, 52). Reasoning does not seem to play a decisive role in formulating ethical judgments.

Haidt's model is referred to as the social intuitionist approach. His findings may cast doubt on the cognitive approaches to ethics (Chapter 5) or may just suggest that ethical reasoning is largely interpersonal. Presenting someone with a different perspective can trigger them to question their own beliefs. This reversal is less likely to happen, although still possible, on private reflection.

In a return to Milgram, the shock experiment has been replicated with a significant change. There are three teachers who are working together to administer shocks; two of the teachers are confederates of the experimenter. As the shocks become more intense, the confederates express concern for the welfare of the learner. This concern increases as the shocks continue to be administered. Eventually, the confederates, at different voltage levels, can take it no more and decide to leave the room with comments indicating their unhappiness with the actions taking place. Expressed disapproval ultimately influences the third teacher to question his own behavior—an example of the important influence of social context on ethical behavior.

Moral Foundations Theory

Haidt's work also can be contrasted with Kohlberg's on substantive grounds. Haidt finds the six stages of moral development to be deficient because they reflect only a portion of a broader domain of moral values (Haidt & Graham, 2007). Kohlberg's rationalism was "oversystematized and underempathized" (121). Haidt's ideas were influenced by Richard Shweder, a cultural psychologist whose work criticized rationalist thinking, on the grounds that Kohlberg's theories were valid only for individualistic cultures and not for others. Shweder's rival three ethics—autonomy, community, and divinity—were found to have cross-cultural applicability. Subsequent studies (Graham et al., 2011; Graham, Haidt, & Nosek, 2009; Iyer et al., 2011) confirmed the same, ultimately leading to the six foundations or intuitions of moral foundations theory (MFT).

Two exemplary foundations are care/harm and liberty/oppression, which support ideals of social justice emphasizing compassion for the poor and the political equality of population subgroups. Care/harm empathizes with suffering and despises cruelty; liberty/oppression opposes abuse of power, abhors tyranny, and supports powerless groups. The third premise is fairness/cheating, which focuses on proportionality and people getting their just deserts. It seeks to punish cheaters and foster cooperation while avoiding exploitation. The remaining elements are

- loyalty/betrayal (helps us discern whether someone is or isn't a team player and to reward loyal members of the team while punishing those who betray us or others),
- authority/subversion (helps us discern rank or status and whether people are behaving appropriately), and
- sanctity/degradation (makes us sensitive to symbolic objects or threats and makes it possible to give objects irrational values).

These pillars round out the list of psychological systems that compose what Haidt (2012, 154, 181–184) refers to as "the universal foundations of the world's many moral matrices" (see data on the Moral Foundations Questionnaire at www.YourMorals.org). It is possible that MFT is simply the next step in what can be viewed as a gradual process of settling on a definition of morality by enlarging its frontiers.[3]

Two specific examples further indicate the importance of both rationality and emotion in moral decision-making: the trolley and footbridge dilemmas (Exhibit 4.2).

EXHIBIT 4.2   **The Trolley and Footbridge Dilemmas**

Psychologists are fond of discussing the famous "trolley dilemma" and a variation of it referred to as the "footbridge dilemma" (see Bazerman & Tenbrunsel, 2011; Haidt, 2012). In the footbridge scenario, a runaway trolley can only be stopped from killing five people by a bystander pushing a heavy person with a large backpack off a footbridge onto the tracks below. Would it be acceptable to cause the death of one person to save many? The dilemma is often used to contrast two cognitive schools of thought regarding ethics: a utilitarian (consequentialist) approach and a deontological (rules or duties) approach (see Chapter 5). Utilitarian theory seeks the greatest total good, which in this case would lead to the conclusion that it was ethically justifiable to heave the man off the bridge in order to save the lives of the five others, assuming there was no other way to save them. Deontological theory, by contrast, focuses on the duties to respect individual lives and avoid harming others, and views shoving someone off the bridge to be immoral and as violating the victim's rights.

Most people respond to this dilemma by judging the act of throwing the man as ethically unacceptable, justifying their decision using such deontological arguments as that it would be breaching the victim's rights or that the ends do not justify the means. Bazerman and Tenbrunsel (2011) compare this response with the utilitarian strategy, which includes totaling up the costs and benefits for all involved and opting to save the lives of many even if it meant sacrificing one.

The second related scenario, discussed by Bazerman and Tenbrunsel (2011), also involves a runaway trolley racing toward five workmen who are standing on the tracks and likely to die if it continues to race forward. In this instance, the five men could be saved if a switch were pulled to turn the trolley to a side track where it would kill one person rather than five. Is it ethically justifiable to pull the switch, killing one to save five? The response of most people is that it is morally justifiable, believing that causing the death of five is worse than one: a consequentialist rationale focusing on consequences.

But do people actually do what they say they will do? In 2003, a Union Pacific employee faced a trolley-like decision: a runaway train was headed toward downtown Los Angeles. Should the train be diverted to a sidetrack to go to a less populated community knowing it would derail causing death and destruction? Consistent with utilitarian calculus, the switch was thrown, and 13 people were injured (including three children who were hospitalized) in the small suburb (Keysar & Costa, 2014, June 20).

As might be expected, sacrificial hypotheticals like those here have been subjected to criticism (e.g., Engber, 2018, June 18) as being absurd, inane, and useless. Yet, as Engber points out, they might not predict real-world actions, but they are useful in understanding "real-word reactions" as they tease out aspects of cognition that are difficult to discern in actual settings.

For an update on "trolley-ology," using self-driving cars, consult Kaplan (2015, October 28): namely, what if your self-driving car decides one death is better than two—and that one is you? See also the moral dilemmas depicted in MIT Moral Machine (moralmachine.mit.edu), a platform for gathering a human perspective on moral decisions made by machine intelligence, such as self-driving cars. You will be presented with random dilemmas that a self-driving car is facing, and you can select the outcome you feel is most acceptable.

For some, it is troubling to observe the contradiction between responses to the two cases. Haidt cites the work of Greene et al. (2001), who thought the two trolley cases were not morally equivalent. Greene and his colleagues suspected that gut feelings led people to make deontological judgments, while utilitarian judgments relied more on rationality (see Chapter 5 for definitions of these two approaches). Absent the "bare-handed push" found in the first case, Greene contends, it was possible in the second instance to weigh the costs and benefits and select the one that saved the five men. A portion of Greene's research involved presenting participants with these cases while they were undergoing an MRI brain scan. He found that the portions of the brain involved in emotional processing were immediately activated, demonstrating a correlation between emotion and moral decision-making, thereby offering support to the position of social intuitionists about the central role of emotion. The views of both rationalists like Kohlberg and social intuitionists such as Haidt provide valuable and competing insights on the nature of moral decision-making.

Before leaving the discussion of moral development foundations, it would be remiss not to include the work of Paul Bloom (2014). On the basis of experimental data, he argues that babies can judge the goodness or badness of others' actions, feel compassion, and exhibit a sense of justice. Using puppet shows (see "60 Minutes" segment at www.youtube.com/watch?v=FRvVFW85IcU), he discovered that babies have the capacity for moral judgment: They see who they want to interact with and who they want to reward and punish. Babies are moral animals. To teach a child ethics, it is not necessary to start from scratch; they already know the basics. A complete theory of morality, then, consists of both innate capacities that humans are born with and cultural influences that affect individual development.

CONCLUSION

Kohlberg's emphasis on psychological rationalism led to his six-stage progression in moral reasoning. The rational approach suggests that sound reasoning about ethics causes morally upright behavior. Accordingly, Kohlberg had no interest in unconscious inferences or intuition. Haidt, in contrast, suggests that emotion—not rationality—is the key to understanding moral judgments. In his view, social intuition provides a quick response to moral dilemmas and rational justifications are then conceived. On substantive grounds, Haidt's work differs from Kohlberg's as well. Haidt finds Kohlberg's emphasis on individual autonomy to be culture-bound, and the focus on justice, fairness, and harm to be too limited. He maintains that his MFT is more comprehensive and valid cross-culturally. Paradoxically, remember that "only those who understand their own potential for unethical behavior can become the decision makers that they aspire to be" (Banaji, Bazerman, & Chugh, 2003, 64). The important roles of rationality and emotion as explanations for moral judgments are explored more fully in subsequent chapters.

***

The omission of good is no less reprehensible than the commission of evil.

—Plutarch

NOTES

1. The preceding two paragraphs are adapted from an essay by Heather Miller (1997).
2. "Ghosts of Abu Ghraib" (HBO, 2007; 100 minutes) is available from Netflix or other vendors. It begins and ends with excerpts from the original black-and-white films taken during the experiments.
3. Whether or not the conventional/postconventional distinction remains valid in spite of the contributions of MFT remains a matter of debate. Indeed, there is a clear similarity between Kohlberg's justice-centered picture of morality and the fairness/reciprocity and care/harm foundations. Prioritizing fairness and harm over the other three foundations (excluding the liberty/oppression foundation) is positively related to postconventional reasoning on the Kohlbergian Defining Issues Test (Baril & Wright, 2012). Thus, if the Kohlbergian narrative of moral development is true, then the authority, loyalty, and sanctity foundations would not be proper foundations at all but rather relics of conventional reasoning. Haidt also observes that care and fairness are valued by liberals far more than the loyalty, authority, and sanctity foundations, whereas conservatives are more or less equal in their valuations of all the MFT foundations (Graham, Haidt, & Nosek, 2009; Haidt, 2012; Haidt & Graham, 2007). Indeed, debates over political issues such as abortion, gun ownership, and gay rights are less about policy than underlying core values, which makes political compromise difficult.

DISCUSSION

1. What were the key lesson(s) of the Milgram experiment?

2. Comment:

   - "The experiment was completely contrived and is therefore irrelevant and has nothing to do with real life."
   - "Only those who understand their own potential for unethical behavior can become the ethical decision-makers that they aspire to be. Simple conviction or sincere intentions are not enough" (Banaji et al., 2003, 64).

3. There are many similarities that the Milgram and Zimbardo experiments share as well as significant differences. Identify and critique. Hint: Consider such factors as the nature of participation by the subjects, the duration of the experiments, the importance of role-prescribed behavior, infliction of physical and psychological pain, and so forth.

4. Participate in discussion of these cases:

   (a) In 2017, Miami teenager Naika Venant hanged herself live on Facebook. The *Miami Herald* reported that 1,000 people watched for nearly an hour as she prepared herself and another hour as she dangled from the noose. They mocked her, called her names, posted laughing emoji, and produced parody videos pretending to hang themselves. Then they clicked their browsers to see what else was on (Pitts, 2017, January 30).

   The same year, a Florida man drowned in a pool while a group of teens laughed and recorded the death; one of them yelled, "Ain't nobody going to help you." See Fifield (2017, September 19) for an insightful analysis of the ethics and legality in such incidents.

   Comment using moral development concepts and/or referencing the Kew Gardens case, discussed in Chapter 5.

   (b) It is well known that the Nazis operated death camps during World War II. One ethicist was recently asked by a colleague how many camps the Nazis had; he thought that is was about "three." At the beginning of this century, the U.S. Holocaust Museum began cataloging all killing centers—ghettos, slave labor sites, brothels with sex slaves, prisoner-of-war camps, and concentration camps (Lichtblau, 2013, March 13). Based on postwar estimates, researchers believed that there might be about 7,000 sites. Over 42,500 throughout Europe, from France to Russia, have now been documented. Discuss.

5. It is claimed that the vast majority of evil is not done by bad people. It is committed by ordinary men and women under certain circumstances; evil is knowing better but doing worse. Agree or disagree? Defend your view.

6. Klein (2008) recounts a scenario in "strategic ignorance:" You can earn money to buy a new flat-screen by selling a homeless child to a business that will harvest his organs for transplants. It can be suggested that any time you buy a new TV instead of sending

money to a homeless children's charity, you are doing essentially the same thing. Discuss.

7. In the future, one's moral development could be enhanced by "morality pills"—pyscho-active substances that act upon the ability to do the right thing (Crutchfield, 2020, August 10). Chemicals such as oxytocin and psilocybin may cause empathy and altruism as well as lower aggressive behavior. The science and use of these drugs are in its infancy and are not without their challenges and dangers, but the military has used "uppers" on soldiers for a long time.

8. One ethics class syllabus states that "ethics as practiced by the individual is the founda-tion upon which this course is built." A student indicated:

[I]f one of us is not doing our best, then that destabilizes the discussion for the rest of the class. Without authentic discussion, we cannot benefit from the deep thought required to have meaningful exploration of important issues. One strong effort can position us for the next success, as one builds upon another. The effectiveness of one student's contribution leads to the success of others. Our micro-level effort as scholars contributes to our meso-level success as a class.

Comment.

EXERCISES

1. Summarize your notes (made in the page margins of the readings or a notebook) and establish links between chapter and course objectives. Continue to do this as self-study exercise. While doing this, create sentence stems (see Chapter 1) for possible use.

2. Watch the following brief videos and write a one-page essay describing the insights gained:

   "Marc Hauser"
   "Human Morality, Part 1": www.youtube.com/watch?v=KiUqBKGHp8o
   "Human Morality, Part 2": www.youtube.com/watch?v=KiUqBKGHp8o feature=related; approximately five minutes each

   "Massimo Pigliucci"
   "Neuroethics and the Trolley Dilemma": www.youtube.com/ watch?v=NOfKyjy-WiU0&feature=related (five minutes)

3. The plot of the movie *Unthinkable* (2010) is summarized here:

An American Muslim man, Yusuf, made a videotape in which he threatens to detonate three nuclear bombs in separate U.S. cities if his demands are not met. A special interro-gator, H, is brought in to force Yusuf to reveal the locations of the bombs. He tortures the suspect, escalating his methods over time, justifying his acts by indicating that potentially disastrous consequences necessitate the extreme measures. Yusuf demands that the U.S. president announce a cessation of support for "puppet governments" and dictatorships in Islamic countries and a withdrawal of American troops from all Muslim countries. The demand is dismissed. When Yusuf is accused of faking the threat to make a point about the moral character of the U.S. government, he breaks down and admits that it was all a ruse. He provides an address to prove it. Investigators find a room that matches the scene in the video and locate evidence on the roof. A soldier removes a picture from an electrical switch, which triggers a tremendous explosion at a nearby shopping mall, killing 53 people. Yusuf justifies the deaths, stating that the Americans kill that many people every day.

H questions whether Yusef will reveal the bombs' locations unless Yusuf's wife is found. With some difficulty, she is found and detained. H brings her in front of her husband and threatens to mutilate her in front of him. H slashes her throat and she bleeds to death in front of Yusuf. Still without cooperation, H brings in Yusuf's two children. H makes it clear that he will torture them if the locations of the bombs are not divulged. Yusuf breaks and gives three addresses (in New York, Los Angeles, and Dallas), but H does not stop. Citing the amount of missing nuclear material Yusuf potentially had at his disposal, H insists that Yusuf has not admitted anything about a likely *fourth* bomb. H points out that everything Yusuf has done so far has been planned meticulously. He knew the torture would most likely break him, and he would have been certain to plant a fourth bomb, just in case. H makes it clear to Yusuf what would happen to his children if he did not cooperate.

H asks for the children to be brought back in for further interrogation. H then demands that the heretofore most ethically sensitive person, Brody, bring the children back in, because her decency will give him the moral approval that he needs to do the "unthinkable." When she refuses to retrieve the children for H, he unstraps Yusuf, sarcastically setting him free. An officer draws his pistol and aims it at H to coerce him into further interrogation. Yusuf grabs the officer's gun. He asks Brody to take care of his children and kills himself. In the final scene, Brody walks out of the building with Yusuf's children.

Analyze the situation depicted in the film as follows:

- Use one of the theories described in this chapter to analyze the plot from the perspective of (a) Yusef, (b) H, or (c) Brody.
- What moral justification might Yusuf have offered for his actions? What moral justification might H have offered for his actions? What moral justification might Brody, the female official, offer for her actions?

4. In the early 1980s, conferees at the International City/County Management Association (ICMA) national convention turned in a questionnaire that contained ten cases. While many of the results demonstrated a high degree of consensus, several did not ("Ethics," 1982), including the following. Select at least two of these scenarios for analysis. Do you believe that the lack of agreement then would still be the same today? Why or why not?

   - The chamber of commerce in a nearby city is hosting work panels at a resort, and you as the city manager are invited to go, all expenses paid. Do you accept?
   - A physician friend asks you (the city manager) if you are interested in investing with him in a building in the city. Do you agree to do so?

- A highly valued employee recently told you that she borrowed money from the petty cash fund during the past year, wrote false receipts, and later returned the money. Under the personnel rules of the city, her behavior warrants an adverse personnel action against her. What would you do? Why?

5. The ICMA offers several ethics self-assessments and quizzes (http://icma.org). Take at least one and record the results in your journal and/or allude to them in class discussion.

6. Do you usually decide an ethical issue based on possible consequences of an action or on an ethical belief? Provide an example in your journal.

7. "Trolley-ology" (Exhibit 4.2) has fascinated philosophers for nearly 50 years and continues to do so (Cathcart, 2013; Edmonds, 2013). Do you agree that ethical responses are contingent depending upon circumstances and that basic instincts are fickle and readily manipulated?

8. The psychological mechanisms of obedience evident in the Milgram and Zimbardo experiments can be found in many scandals and assist in understanding the behavior of individuals as well as organizations. Select a recent scandal and report whether or not these mechanisms shed light on what happened.

9. Access MIT Moral Machine dilemmas at moralmachine.mit.edu. Choose between the two different options in 13 situations and then at the end compare your decisions based on others who took the test. Think about and be prepared to discuss the reasoning behind your choices.

10. View the following videos available on YouTube: "Philip Zimbardo: The Psychology of Evil" (23 minutes); "Marc Hauser-Human Morality Parts 1 & 2" (five minutes each); "Neuroethics and the Trolley Dilemma"; "Jonathan Haidt, Moral Roots of Liberals and Conservatives" (19 minutes); Dan Ariely, "Our Buggy Moral Code" (16 minutes).

11. As a capstone to this chapter, discuss this observation by John le Carre: "The fact that you can only do a little is no excuse for doing nothing."

REFERENCES

Banaji, M. R., Bazerman, M. H., & Chugh, D. (2003). How (un)ethical are you? *Harvard Business Review*, *81*, 56–65.

Baril, G., & Wright, C. (2012). Different types of moral cognition: Moral stages versus moral foundations. *Personality and Individual Differences*, *53*, 468–473.

Bazerman, M., & Tenbrunsel, A. (2011). *Blind spots: Why we fail to do what's right and what to do about it*. Princeton, NJ: Princeton University Press.

Blass, T. (Ed.) (2000). *Obedience to authority: current perspectives on the Milgram paradigm*. Mahwah, NJ: Elbaum.

Bloom, P. (2014). *Just babies: The origins of good and evil*. New York: Broadway Books.

Blum, B. (2018, June 7). The Lifespan of a Lie: The most famous psychology study of all time was a sham. *Medium*. Retrieved from https://gen.medium.com/the-lifespan-of-a-lie-d869212b1f62

Cathcart, T. (2013). *The trolley problem, or would you throw the fat guy off the bridge?* New York: Workman Publishing.

Crutchfield, P. (2020, August 10). 'Morality pills' may be the US's best short at ending the coronavirus pandemic, according to one ethicist. *The Conversation*. Retrieved from https://theconversation.com/morality-pills-may-be-the-uss-best-shot-at-ending-the-coronavirus-pandemic-according-to-one-ethicist-142601

Edmonds, D. (2013). *Would you kill the fat man? The trolley problem and what your answer tells us about right and wrong*. Princeton, NJ: Princeton University Press.

Engber, D. (2018, June 18). Does the trolley problem have a problem? *Slate*. Retrieved from https://slate.com/technology/2018/06/psychologys-trolley-problem-might-have-a-problem.html

Ethics. (1982). *Public Management*, 20–21.

Fifield, J. (2017, September 19). Why it is hard to punish "bad Samaritans". *Stateline*. Retrieved from www.pewtrusts.org/en/research-and-analysis/blogsstateline/2017/09/19/why-its-hard-to-punish-bad-samaritans

Graham, J., Haidt, J., & Nosek, B. (2009). Liberals and conservatives rely on different sets of moral foundations. *Journal of Personality and Social Psychology*, *96*, 1029–1046.

Graham, J., Nosek, B., Haidt, J., Iyer, R., Koleva, S., & Ditto, P. (2011). Mapping the moral domain. *Journal of Personality and Social Psychology*, *101*, 366–385.

Greene, J., Sommerville, R., Nystrom, L., Darley, J., & Cohen, J. (2001). An fMRI study of emotional engagement in moral judgment. *Science*, *293*, 2105–2108.

Haidt, J. (2012). *The righteous mind: Why good people are divided by politics and religion*. New York: Pantheon Books.

Haidt, J., & Graham, J. (2007). When morality opposes justice: Conservatives have moral intuitions that liberals may not recognize. *Social Justice Research*, *20*, 98–116.

Haslam, A., Reicher, S., & Van Bavel, J. (2018, June 6). Doing ill for 'the greater good': Understanding what really went on in the Stanford Prison Experiment. *InMind*. Retrieved from www.in-mind.org/blog/post/doing-ill-for-the-greater-good-unde rstanding-what-really-went-on-in-the-stanford-prison#:~:text=Doing%20ill%20for%20%E2%80%98the%20greater%20good%E2%80%99%3A%20Understanding%20what,extensive%20coverage%20of%20Zimbardo%E2%80%99s%20Stanford%20Prison%20Experiment%20%28SPE%29.

Hefferman, M. (2012). *Willful blindness: Why we ignore the obvious at our peril*. New York: Walker.

Iyer, R., Koleva, S., Graham, J., Ditto, P., & Haidt, J. (2011). Understanding libertarian morality: The psychological roots of individual ideology. *Unpublished manuscript*, Department of Psychology, University of Southern California. Available at http://papers.ssrn.com/sol3/papers.cfm?abstract_id=1665934

Kahneman, D. (2011). *Thinking, fast and slow*. New York: Random House.

Kaplan, S. (2015, October 29). What if your self-driving car decides one death is better than two—and that one is you? *Washington Post*. Retrieved from www.washingtonpost.com/news/morning-mix/wp/2015/10/28/what-if-your-self-driving-car-decides-one-death-is-better-than-two-and-that-one-is-you/

Keysar, B., & Costa, A. (2014, June 20). Our moral tongue. *New York Times*. Retrieved from http://nytimes.com/2014/06/22/opinion/sunday/moraljudgement

Klein, D. (2008). *Plato and a platypus walk into a bar*. New York: Penguin.

Kohlberg, L. (1971). From is to ought: How to commit the naturalistic fallacy and get away with it in the study of moral development. In T. Mischel (Ed.), *Cognitive development and psychology* (pp. 151–235). New York: Academic Press.

Lichtblau, E. (2013, March 13). The Holocaust just got more shocking. *New York Times*. Retrieved from www.nytimes.com/2013/03/03/sunday-review/the-holocaust-just-got-more-shocking.html?nl=todaysheadlines&emc=edit_th_20130303

Margolis, H. (1987). *Patterns, thinking and cognition*. Chicago: University of Chicago Press.

McLeod, S. (2007). *The Milgram experiment*. Retrieved from www.simplypsychology.org/milgram.html

Milgram, S. (1974). *Obedience to authority: An experimental view*. New York: McGraw-Hill.

Miller, H. (1997, May). *Stanley Milgram (1933–1984)*. Retrieved from http://muskingum.edu/~psych/psycweb/history/milgram.htm

Mueller, T. (2019). *Crisis of confidence: Whistleblowing in an age of fraud*. New York: Penguin.

Perry, G. (2013). *Behind the shock machine*. New York: New Press.

Pitts, L. (2017, January 30). The lonely death of Nakia Venant and what it says about us. *Tallahassee Democrat*. Retrieved from www.tallahassee.com/.../01/29/pitts-death-lonely-naika-venant/97196020

Preston, N. (2001). *Understanding ethics* (2nd ed.). Leichhardt: Federation Press.

Rest, J., & Narrvaez, D. (Eds.). (1994). *Moral development in the professions: Psychology and applied ethics*. Hillsdale, NJ: Erlbaum.

Rest, J., Narrvaez, D., Bebeau, M., & Thoma, S. (1999). *Postconventional moral thinking: A neo-Kohlbergian approach*. Mahwah, NJ: Erlbaum.

Rushton, S. (Ed.). (2004). *The Milgram re-enactment: Essays on Rod Dickinson's re-enactment of Stanley Milgram's obedience to authority experiment in collaboration with Graeme Edler*. Maastricht: Eyck Academie.

Singer, P. (1994). *Ethics*. New York: Oxford University Press.

Snell, R. (1993). *Developing skills for ethical management*. London: Chapman & Hall.

Statement from Philip Zimbardo (c. 2018). Retrieved from www.prisonexp.org/response

Swisher, L., Rizzo, A., & Marley, M. (2005). Update on moral reasoning research and theory in public administration: A new-Kohlbergian perspective. In H. G. Frederickson & R. Ghere (Eds.), *Ethics in management* (pp. 70–94). Armonk, NY: M. E. Sharpe.

Velasquez, M. (1998). *Business ethics: Concepts and cases*. Upper Saddle River, NJ: Prentice Hall.

Wason, P. C. (1960). On the failure to eliminate hypotheses in a conceptual task. *Quarterly Journal of Experimental Psychology*, *12*, 129–140.

Zimbardo, P. (2007). *The Lucifer effect: Understanding how good people turn evil*. New York: Random House.

5 Cognitive Ethics Methods

Result and Rule Problem-Solving Approaches

We make our decisions, and then our decisions turn around and make us.
—F. W. Boreham

The personal, pervasive, professional, and powerful motivation (Chapter 1) behind much of ethics is the search for the good life, one well-lived. There are many different conceptions of the good life, and it is not necessarily obvious which is superior. Since life is about making choices, and people do not necessarily make ethically sound decisions (Chapter 4), this chapter highlights cognitive decision-making approaches to aid in making choices. A problem cannot be solved if it is not understood.

While the first question of philosophy is "How do I know?" the fundamental issue of ethics is, as Socrates said, "What ought one to do?" No single theory exists that will resolve ethical dilemmas. There is no unified theory, no secular "one best way" that tells someone what it is to be moral. Accordingly, the chapter objectives are to

- recognize different approaches to ethics,
- understand a five-stage method to analyze issues,
- comprehend the role of moral courage in decision-making,
- show the utility of several complementary decision-making strategies, and
- apply ethical philosophies to cases.

APPROACHES TO ETHICS

Approaches to ethics depend upon the "head," "heart," and physique or "body." The first concerns the right decision, the kind of act one performs by identifying psychological and social cognitive factors that affect a choice. This cognitive school of thought includes two well-known philosophies (discussed further in Chapter 7). If one expects a theory to solve tough problems, then these strategies may be helpful. The second, "heart" perspective (Chapter 6), emphasizes the "right person," the kind of individual one is, by recognizing and nurturing personal virtues of character that enable people to live an exemplary life. If a theory is expected to help people

DOI: 10.4324/9781003203148-7

in their daily activities, then this viewpoint may be useful. Finally, the physique strategy (Chapters 8–10) focuses on institutional circumstances, by discerning ways to structure organizations to enhance honorable behavior and combat corruption. If a theory is expected to help understand the impact of the environment on individuals, then this method may be appropriate.

These philosophies are quite different, but they are not wholly incompatible, as hybrid systems are possible. The idea is to strive for balance: Ethics is not geometry but the art of the possible. In ethics, as in the rest of life, there are no magic answers. In addition, differences between theories should not lead one to despair or to the conclusion that one is as good as another. In this imperfect world, the best that can be done is to fully analyze the issues, develop the most complete arguments possible, and make a defensible choice. Administrators must be able to give credible reasons for their decisions. A five-stage model is presented next; this will be complemented by introducing several "shortcut" approaches, as well as additional decision-making aids for the key step—action—in the five-stage model.

A FIVE-STAGE METHOD FOR ANALYZING ETHICAL ISSUES

"I'm trying to figure out if I have an ethical conflict," a man said. "If you have to ask, then you do," replied his wife.

Consider this five-step method to deal with ethical issues: (1) attention, (2) perception, (3) processing, (4) action, (5) evaluation (Exhibit 5.1; see also Figure 5.1). The focus of this strategy is on the head, or cognitive ethics.

EXHIBIT 5.1	Five-Stage Problem-Solving Method for Confronting Ethical Situations

ATTENTION →	PERCEPTION →	PROCESSING →	ACTION →	EVALUATION
Must "see" problem	See problem (i.e., who, when, where), but is it my responsibility?	How should I think about the problem? **Levels of Analysis:** 1. Expressive 2. Simple rule 3. Ethical reflection	OK to think about ethics, but do I need to act? **Kew Gardens Principles:** 1. Need 2. Proximity 3. Capability 4. Last resort (results/ethical rules)	What did I learn?

Source: Adapted from McDanield (1985).

Attention and Perception

One must initially "see," recognize, or attend to a problem, something some of Milgram's "teachers" failed to do in shocking the "learners" (Chapter 4). Indeed, this initial phase may well, by definition, be the most important one. Once—or if—the person's attention is gained, then it is up to the individual to perceive the underlying ethical issues (if any) and determine whether it is her responsibility, an obligation that many of the shock experiment subjects did not understand.

Processing

The third step is processing, or how one should cope with the problem. Responses include impulsive reaction ("just do it"), simple rule ("I just work here"), and ethical reflection (cognitive theories). The last reaction defers to philosophies that contend matters of right and wrong are a function of either (a) the weighing of expected results or consequences of an action (teleology, also known as *consequentialism*) or (b) the application of a universal rule (deontology or duty/rule ethics). Thus, deontology emphasizes doing one's duty or adherence to a moral imperative, whereas teleology emphasizes the results of an action. For instance, a deontologist would claim an absolute duty to abstain from murder, whereas a teleologist would contend people usually should not commit murder because it can cause undesirable consequences.

While these two strategies—deontology and teleology—are hardly perfect, their claimed strength is that rational calculus is superior to impulse, a simple rule, or an intuitive understanding of right or wrong—to say nothing of sheer expediency. However, the cardinal drawback in teleology is that predicting consequences is hazardous. "What we anticipate seldom occurs," Disraeli observed, "what we least expect generally happens." As for deontology, "ought" implies "can," but deciding what to do when duties conflict is no mean task. An undue emphasis on duty, with its "all or nothing" approach, also may deprive the individual of responsibility. Either way, very little in the world is exactly what it at first seems to be. As the old oracle said, "All things have two handles: beware of the wrong one."

Action

The fourth step is action. After processing the problem, the immediate question becomes, "Does the decision maker need to act?" The Kew Gardens principles (named after an infamous 1964 murder in Kew Gardens, New York, in which 38 people purportedly witnessed a street killing from the safety of their apartments and did nothing)[1] may be helpful in answering the question (see, e.g., Cook, 2014). Together, they offer assistance in determining action:

1. Need—is there a genuine requirement for action?

2. Proximity—is the actor nearby or in proximity?

3. Capability—does the person have some capacity to change the situation?

4. Last resort—if no one else is going to act, then the individual must decide to act and develop an action plan to execute the decision.

A moral agent, in short, is only responsible for problems he can do something about.

Depending on the issue under consideration, several additional methods—flowcharting and line drawing—might be useful as complements or substitutes for these Kew Gardens principles to assist in deciding whether action should be taken (Exhibit 5.2).

FIGURE 5.1   **Application of Flowcharting**

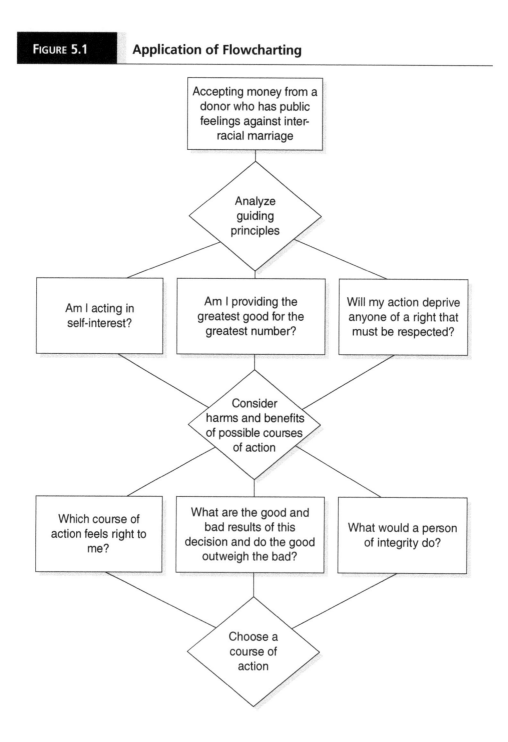

EXHIBIT 5.2	**Flowcharting and Line Drawing**

Engineers use flowcharts in their projects to outline possible courses of action and to clearly view each of their effects. For instance, assume the president of a public university has just received a donation from a donor who is well known for her opposition to interracial marriage. Figure 5.1 analyzes a dilemma using the flowchart method. This involves considering principles—such as the decision maker's motivations for action (self-interest, greatest good, individual rights, harms, and benefits) as well as whether the action feels right. It assesses whether the positive consequences outweigh the negatives, and whether a virtuous person would act in this way. After careful deliberation, the decision maker may conclude that declining this donation is a prudent course. Such a thorough analysis may require more time than available in a fast-moving, time-pressed workplace; however, where a manager does have the luxury to ruminate at length over a dilemma, flowcharting is a useful method.

A second technique to consider when facing a decision is line drawing. This involves a process whereby a test case is placed along a continuum between an ethical action ("positive paradigm") and an unethical action ("negative paradigm") (Gotterbarn, 2007, 56; Harris, Pritchard, & Rabins, 2009, 80–84). The positive paradigm (PP, clearly acceptable) and the negative paradigm (NP, clearly unacceptable) are the outliers in the scenario, while the test case is the action under scrutiny. The individual confronted with a challenge, after brainstorming about the features of the paradigms, can draw a line for each feature and locate its positive and negative descriptions at either end of the continuum. The relevant aspects of the situation can then be plotted along the PP–NP continuum. This enables the decision maker to circle the features with the most ethical relevance and determine where the case falls on those scales.

Line drawing has both benefits and drawbacks. Gotterbarn (2007, 55) notes that, unlike approaches that examine the overall context and the broad ethical issues of the situation, line drawing examines the specific elements that help determine the ethical or unethical aspects of a decision. By plotting the significant aspects of the case and placing them on the continuum, then identifying the most relevant features and where they stand in relation to the polar points on the scale, policymakers can evaluate an action on a variety of levels and balance the positive and negative features in making a decision. It is especially useful when dealing with ethically "gray areas" where there is uncertainty about "where to 'draw the line' between permissible and impermissible actions" (Harris & Rabins, 1993, 412).

There are limitations of line drawing: It is necessary to know the details of the case, it is subjective and can be arbitrary, and factors under consideration may vary in weight. Nonetheless, since there is not always a bright line differentiating ethical from unethical actions, exercising prudent judgment through drawing lines can be useful. As Harris and his colleagues (2009) observe, "[S]ometimes arbitrary conventions to separate acceptable from wrong actions are in order" (84; see Appendix 5.3, Case Study 5.3 for an application of line drawing).

Evaluation

The final stage in the five-step model is evaluation. That is, the policymaker considers what happened and what was learned. Evaluation is important because it provides a test of the utility of the analytical approach used, the reasoning behind the judgment, and a catalyst of change. For example, in Maria's situation (Case Study 5.1), she may have decided not to take action regarding harassment charges against her former employer as a result of reasoning guided by the Kew Gardens principles. While she satisfied the first three criteria in assessing her moral obligation to act—need, proximity, and capability—she may have concluded that she was not the last resort and thus declined to pursue the matter. A post-decision assessment (evaluation) may have validated her judgment as other affected parties could have stepped up to resolve the problem. Alternatively, the harassment could have persisted or intensified, harming her former coworkers, leading her to question or regret her decision not to act. Lessons learned from evaluation provide valuable data—whether confirming one's judgment or refuting it—prompting continuous improvement that informs future decisions and actions.

While the five-stage model is useful for its comprehensive nature, Exhibit 5.3 offers three shortcut approaches that may be handy in some circumstances and may be regarded as a starting point in decision-making. (Two other guides to decision-making and action are described with applications in Appendices 5.1 and 5.2.) Exercise 3 provides another framework for the application of ethical decision-making in real-world scenarios that takes into account the policymaker's role.

CASE STUDY 5.1

Utilization of the Kew Gardens Principles

This scenario describes Maria's previous employment at an unnamed agency.

During her three years of employment at the agency, Maria experienced and witnessed acts of sexual and racial harassment. Having gained employment elsewhere, she now enjoys freedom from fears of termination by her past employer. Knowing that others continue to be the target of such abuses, she wonders if she has a micro-level ethical obligation to undertake actions against the meso-level organizational ethics of her former agency.

Maria seeks an answer; she reaches one by applying the Kew Gardens principles:

1. Given the well-known psychological and moral consequences of harassment, it is clear that it will result in social injury. As the severity of that injury is difficult to assess, it is also hard to determine whether need is increasing or decreasing. Increasing need will add to Maria's responsibility. Regardless, the potential—if not the certainty—of social injury exists. As such, a *need* for action exists.

2. Over a period of three years, harassment of both a sexual and racial nature was observed. Despite relocation to other employment, a responsibility may remain. According to the Kew

Gardens principles, such knowledge is defined as *proximity*. Further, having been immersed in such a hostile environment, it is safe to assume that knowledge of resulting risk and social injury exists.

3. Having established that need and proximity are present, it must be determined if there are actions available that might be expected to provide relief. In other words, "Is there a capability to purse such a remedy?" Appropriate legal channels exist for such grievances, and, since these procedures may not produce substantial hardship, reasonable strategies are available. Therefore, the necessary *capability* is present.

4. Those employees who remain in the department feel helpless as fears of reprisal (including termination) prevent the filing of formal complaints. With this decreased likelihood comes greater obligation on an individual level. Although such determination is complex, and many variables exist, the level of responsibility grows as it becomes more and more likely that an individual is the last resort. In this case, however, it is difficult to imagine that there are no other possibilities. Other options may be complicated or unpleasant, but they likely exist. Here, the case may not adequately meet the criterion of *last resort*.

In short, by using the Kew Gardens principles to think through the dilemma, Maria may conclude that she is not obligated to take action against her former employer.

EXHIBIT 5.3   **Selected Decision-Making Tools**

Blanchard and Peale's (1988) "Ethics Check"

1. Is it "legal"? Will I be violating either civil law or agency policy?

2. Is it balanced? Is it fair to all concerned in the short term as well as the long term? Does it promote win-win relationships?

3. How will it make me feel about myself? Will it make me proud? Would I feel good if my decision was published in the newspaper? Would I feel good if my family knew about it?

Josephson's (1992) Code

1. Ethical people treat others the way they want to be treated.

2. Ethical values (honesty, fidelity, tolerance, self-discipline, integrity, promise keeping, and so forth) should always take precedence over nonethical ones (wealth, comfort, success).

3. It is proper to violate an ethical principle only to advance a more valid ethical principle (e.g., lying to a terrorist to save an innocent life).

Stone's (2009) Guidelines to Use When Contemplating Violation of Ethical Rules

1. Will you gain a personal benefit?

2. Is the decision simply taking the easy way out?

3. Does it serve the cause of justice?

Sources: Blanchard and Peale (1988); Joseph and Edna Josephson's Institute of Ethics (1992); Stone (2009).

MORAL COURAGE OF CONVICTION: JOHN LEWIS

Success is not final, failure is not fatal. It is the courage to continue that counts.

—Winston Churchill

Carefully proceeding through the five-step method—putting principles into practice—requires courage: "the readiness to endure danger for the sake of principle"; "knowing the right thing to do is not the same as doing the right thing" (Comer & Vega, 2011, xv, 4). Moral courage consists of moral principle, danger in adhering to principle, and endurance in service to principle despite danger (Kidder, 2006). Newell (2017, March 7) maintains:

> All three are required: principle and danger without endurance is timidity. Principle and endurance without awareness of the danger is foolhardiness. Danger and endurance with no moral principle at stake may be physical courage), but it is not moral courage.

The classical Greek concept of manliness emphasizes the virtue of courage: assertiveness, competitiveness, and confidence to be the best. He not only knows what to do and when to do it but also is brave enough to follow through. Courage does not always roar, according to Mary Anne Radmacher; it may be that little voice at the end of the day that says, "I'll try again tomorrow."

Public service, when viewed as a calling, demands moral courage. Newell (2017, December 4) continues:

> Ensuring government works is not for the faint of heart. It requires persistence and humility. It means paying more attention to doing the right thing than doing things right. It requires the ability to speak up for those without a voice and to speak against those, inside government, who would deny the value of that voice. You won't find moral courage—including the character and ability to establish justice—on lists of competencies for public servants or on job vacancy announcements. You won't see it referred to in performance appraisals. Yet without it, the public service is a vastly diminished institution, and America suffers as a result.

In a divided and partisan nation, people are not used to honesty and courage. Seeing a leader stand up for what he or she believes is right has been increasingly rare.

John Robert Lewis (1940–2020) was a civil rights leader and 17-term Georgia Congressman. Dedicated to the philosophy of nonviolence, he was a founding member of the Student Nonviolent Coordinating Committee in 1960; one of the original 1961 Freedom Riders to protest segregated buses; a member of the Big Six representing leaders of groups who organized the March, 1963, on Washington; an organizer of restaurant customer sit-ins as well as consumer boycotts; and a leader in the 1965 "Bloody Sunday" march across the Edmund Pettus Bridge in Selma, Alabama, and beaten, arrested, and jailed many times.

Taking an unyielding stance against social injustice, his stubborn spirit of moral commitment represented moral clarity: the capacity to make distinctions between good and evil and to take principled action accordingly (Gan, 2019, June 2). "If you see something that is not right, not fair, not just," Lewis wrote, "you have a moral obligation to do something about it." Vincent Van Gogh asked, "What would life be if we had no courage to attempt anything?" Democracy is an act, something that cannot be limited to voting; it must be lived and practiced to make democracy real (Bouie, 2020, August 2). Constitutional rights do not exist unless they are practiced.

Lewis remained active in the civil rights movement, most notably as the director of the Voter Education Project. In 1977, President Jimmy Carter put Lewis in charge of ACTION, the umbrella federal volunteer agency that included the Peace Corps and Volunteers in Service to America (VISTA). Lewis entered elective office as an Atlanta city councilman in 1981 and in 1986 began representing a district that included Atlanta in the U.S. House of Representatives. When confronting legislative bills, he would apply a moral filter when deciding how to vote on them. Among his other activities in the House, in 2016, Lewis and a colleague led a sit-in demanding the Speaker to allow a vote on gun-safety legislation in the aftermath of the Pulse nightclub shooting. The House was ordered into recess, but Democrats refused to leave the chamber for nearly 26 hours.

Lewis was the recipient of over 50 honorary degrees, awarded the Presidential Medal of Freedom in 2011, and known as the "Conscience of the Congress." He challenged the country to do better; who can now speak with the same moral urgency? (Porter, 2020, July 20). For a record of his legislative achievements, see www.govtrack.us/congress/members/john_lewis/400240/report-card/2019/. Lewis would lie in state in the United States Capitol Rotunda, the first African-American to be so honored. He will be remembered as saying, "Never, ever be afraid to make some noise and get in good, trouble, necessary trouble."

As John Lewis's life demonstrated, it takes courage to believe that things can and will change, and that they can get better. Yet many people avoid challenges and obstacles and miss the chance to grow and learn. Knowing what to do is often clear; what is needed is the bravery to do it. Kets de Vries (2009) believes courage can be developed by starting with small acts of assertiveness, imagining the best and worse outcomes, discovering what can be controlled, and practicing going beyond one's comfort zone. Being technically competent and ethically upright erodes fear and feeds bravery. There is peace of mind in doing the right thing.

As evident during the athletic sex scandals (Chapters 2 and 10), organizational pressures overcame personal courage and inhibited individuals from taking the action they knew was ethically required. Those who wish to do good are frequently called on to exhibit moral valor: the resolve "to do what . . . is right, despite fear of social or economic consequences" (Peterson & Seligman, 2004, 216). Those who kept quiet were certainly lacking in moral boldness.

Comer and Vega's (2011, 25) personal threshold concept—"what it takes for us to cross our proverbial moral line to act in a way that violates our standards and values"—explains how unethical outcomes persist in the face of sound ethical reasoning. Decision-maker thresholds were low: Their need to do what was right was easily overwhelmed by their narrower desire to promote the interests of the athletic program. For those with higher thresholds, the consequences of putting principles into practice can be significant (see Chapter 10 on whistleblowing). By constantly attuning one's self to elements of an organizational setting that can distract from doing the right thing, one's threshold can be heightened. And as it rises, moral bravery is nurtured to the benefit of professional and organizational development (Comer & Vega, 2011, 34). Moral competence, understanding how to address quandaries, likely will lead to greater levels of courage; if the issue is fully understood, then it is easier to address it with confidence. You are braver than you believe, stronger than you seem, and smarter than you think.

APPLYING THE FIVE-STAGE METHOD: A PERSONAL AND PROFESSIONAL CONFLICT

Having examined the five-stage problem-solving strategy and the central role of moral courage, this section offers an application of the approach. As noted in the last chapter, officials at an ICMA national convention turned in a questionnaire that contained ten cases ("Ethics," 1982). While many of the responses demonstrated a high degree of consensus, several did not, including the following scenario:

> For years, you and a lifelong friend have celebrated your birthday with your families at an expensive restaurant, and she has always insisted on paying. This year, you have been elected to serve on the county commission. Your birthday is next week, and your friend has made reservations. Do you go?

Discussions through the years with in-service and pre-service students reveal the following findings, arrived at using the step method:

Step 1: *Attention.* The initial impulse of some students is to object to the case on the grounds that their personal life—their birthday for heaven's sake!—should not be a matter of public debate.

Step 2: *Perception.* In a similar vein, classmates reluctantly concede that perhaps there could be an issue here but regard it to be sufficiently trivial as to be inconsequential.

Step 3: *Processing.* For those who attend to the issue and perceive it to be one that requires deliberation, robust argumentation often takes place based on results- and rule-oriented ethics.

Step 4: *Action.* Satisfaction of all four factors in the Kew Gardens principles is evident. The action taken, depending on the outcome of the discussion, could range considerably: to keep the custom "as is," to keep the tradition but split the check, to have the dinner at a private home, to suspend the party while in public service, to reject the invitation.

Step 5: *Evaluation.* Based on the aforementioned, this step reveals errors in analysis and judgment and suggests the need for an enhanced sensitivity to ethical matters.

Consider this: Would the responses differ if the research were replicated today? Why?

The sexual harassment case study (5.1) also demonstrates how application of the Kew Gardens factors can help in determining the responsibility to act. The same hypothetical case shows the utility of the five-step approach to analyzing ethical issues. The flagrant instances of sexual and racial misconduct surely captured Maria's *attention*; indeed, it was undoubtedly one of the factors pushing her to seek other employment. She *perceived* that this inappropriate, demeaning, and destructive behavior created a hostile work environment. The *processing* of this situation involved assessing the four criteria associated with Kew Gardens principles—need, proximity, capability, and last-resort criteria—and could have involved the consideration of results and rules. Her *action* alternatives—doing nothing or intervening in an attempt to correct the situation—were mulled over before making a decision. Finally, she would likely *evaluate* in retrospect whether she made the right decision in light of subsequent events. Although not all four criteria are met in this case, it is important to remember that the principles foster awareness of legitimate need and ways to remedy a situation in a manner that compels a person to right conduct.

CONCLUSION

Chance favors the prepared mind.

—Louis Pasteur

Milgram found that untutored human nature cannot be trusted to protect people from inhumane treatment at the direction of malevolent authority. James Baldwin wrote that people do not wish to be worse. Rather, "they really wish to become better, but they often do not know how." An exploration of cognitive ethics suggests that selected strategies can assist decision makers. The theories are analogous to rules of grammar—precise, accurate, and indispensable—while their application to—knowledge of—good writing may be loose, vague, and indeterminate.

Accordingly, it is best to use approaches to ethics to expand one's imagination: far better an imprecise answer to the right question than a precise answer to the wrong question—or not to even recognize the existence of a problem. If a situation is considered outside its original context (a "figure–ground" reversal), then a coffee cup suddenly becomes a paperweight, pencil holder, or a planter. Moral imagination, then, encompasses thinking anew, recognizing ethical problems, asking difficult questions about one's actions, and finding alternatives when those available are unacceptable.[2]

In other words, seek different viewpoints, a changed basis for choices, and new assumptions by making unusual friends, engaging in new activities, and reading things that you do not normally read (see also Jacobs, 2018, January 12). It is no surprise that leading Japanese organizations encourage employees to learn flower arranging, practice the highly ritualized tea ceremony, and play team sports in order to appreciate the value of beauty, precision, and cooperation.

In short, the diverse forms of ethical reflection in Step 3 of the five-stage model are powerful ways to reframe problems, an ability lacking in many of Milgram's subjects. While such approaches have limitations, the objective is to clarify issues, enlarge one's vision, and seek enriched understanding. Like good maps, various theories offer choices, not a formula. Just as a map outlines a journey, a theory offers guidelines—landmarks, dangers, possible routes—but leaves the traveling to the travelers. These objective ethical belief systems provide help in making inevitable compromises. They do not eliminate the need for judgment but emphasize the significance of independent thinking.

These strategies are not mutually exclusive but, rather, are complementary. Used in combination, they can result in improved decision-making. It is also entirely possible that contradictory guidance may result when analyzing a dilemma from multiple perspectives (see Chapter 7). Yet each encourages careful sifting of facts, thoughtful weighing of alternatives, and a willingness to exercise moral imagination by applying different lenses when exploring solutions to wicked problems. Expertise may be necessary, but it is not sufficient. As Einstein noted, "Logic will get you from A to Z; imagination will get you everywhere." Dilemmas raise crucial questions that demand answers. The cases included here show the range of ethical issues confronting public servants. These approaches provide a toolbox of strategies for dealing with these perplexing workplace issues.

***

The hardest task is not to do what is right, but to know what is right.

—Lyndon Baines Johnson

NOTES

1. The Kitty Genovese murder in 1964 is one of the most infamous in history; it inspired the creation of the 911 emergency call number, numerous story lines in television serials, a book (Cook, 2014), and a 2016 documentary. The event is evidence of bystander apathy and the diffusion of responsibility. While initial newspaper stories may have been misleading, a powerful cultural parable resulted. The incident, in any case, illustrates the stories that people tell themselves to justify their (in)action (Merry, 2016, June 29). For more on bystanders in the George Floyd case see Eastman (2021).
2. If you believe that you lack imaginative powers, reawaken the skill you had as a child when you used your imagination to play and daydream. This skill declined in school, which emphasized the logical, reasoning left side of the brain at the expense of the imaginative, creative right side. Visualizing interesting, outlandish scenarios (daydreaming) is one way to nurture your creativity. Another is to ask yourself, "What would I attempt to do if I knew I could not fail," or "If the obvious ways to deal with a problem did not exist, then what would I do?"

DISCUSSION

1. "The five-stage decision-making method purports to be a comprehensive model, with most other approaches either part of, or supplementary to, it." It may be useful because nothing is worse than a right problem but a wrong answer or a right answer to the wrong problem. Critique this statement.

2. The Moral Minimum is a negative injunction to avoid and correct social injury. This principle is not unlike a physician's obligation to do no harm. While helpful, it is vague and lacks the specificity needed to be a precise guide to action. Brainstorm some circumstances in which social injury cannot be avoided or corrected. Identify an ethical problem and analyze it using the Moral Minimum in combination with the Kew Gardens principles. In what ways do the Kew Gardens principles become useful corollaries of the Moral Minimum?

3. Activist and politician Jeanette Rankin (1880–1973) said, "You don't do the right thing because of the consequences. If you're wise, you do it regardless of the consequences." Why or why not?

4. When asked about one of Saul Alinsky's controversial community-organizing tactics— does the end justify the means?—he replied, "That is never the question, but rather do these particular ends justify these particular means?" Discuss.

EXERCISES

1. This chapter focuses on "deciding how to decide." Select any one of the scenarios in this chapter and examine it using a different analytical approach than the one provided in the chapter. For example, the harassment case was analyzed using the Kew Gardens principles and the five-step approach, but it could be examined using another strategy such as flowcharting, line drawing, the sensitivity–intensity matrix, or the ethical principles approach.

2. Complete an unethical performance appraisal?

   Your supervisor has asked you to inflate the annual review of one of your staff members. To exercise moral courage and imagination, stand up for what is right without jeopardizing the relationship with your supervisor. To accomplish both goals, consider some of the following options and then provide a better one:

   • Calmly explain why you believe the assignment is wrong and it is just bad business (it is possible that he does not know it is imprudent or he may think that, because others have done it, it is acceptable). Agree that you wish to help your employee, but the evaluation will hurt both him and the agency in the long run. Importantly, provide some win-win solutions such as training or mentoring to enhance the subordinate's performance. Find a way to accomplish the objective without compromising personal integrity by consulting privately with those whom you respect.
   • Keep in mind that you may be wrong (seek a "reality check" with a trusted colleague; perhaps the employee's work is not as disastrous as you think it is).
   • Pick your battles. Refuse to fake the appraisal (if your boss is reasonable, he will rethink his approach, but if not, do not participate in the charade). However, take a hard line if convinced the issue is worth fighting for; it is a sign of integrity to stand firm, but for only truly egregious tasks should you prepare to walk away or suffer an adverse personnel action. (Adapted from Weinstein, 2011, 110–111)

3. Review Appendix 5.1, Figures 5.2 and 5.3, and Table 5.1 on the sensitivity–intensity matrix and complete the assignments described there.

4. Examine Appendix 5.2, Table 5.2, and the example provided on the ethical principles approach and complete the assignment at the end.

5. Read Appendix 5.3 illustrating the line drawing method. Identify an ethical scenario that might be appropriately analyzed using the line drawing approach and then identify the dimensions of the case and the negative and positive paradigms. How useful is this strategy in analyzing the scenario and arriving at a decision? Why?

TABLE 5.1	**Ethical Dilemmas and Possible Solutions**	
Ethical Dilemma	**Solution 1**	**Solution 2**
1. Allowing a toxic culture to exist	Adapt to environment and follow own ethical standards	Follow conscience and protect the team as much as possible
2. Incivility	Require training courses on diversity	Open discussion to resolve differences
3. Harassment	Make changes to management style	Seek help from human resources
4. Violation of privacy	Find out circumstances and procedures to be followed	Seek assistance from human resources
5. Retaliation	Report any retaliation	Avoid retaliating against an individual
6. Coercion	Engender accountability	Apply participative management
7. Not respecting values	Respect cultural values	Do not alienate different values
8. Not providing honest feedback	Question remarks and assumptions	Publish reliable and frequent metrics on performance
9. Treating people inequitably	Ensure everyone has opportunity to speak and participate	Task and responsibilities can be assigned
10. Lacking personal responsibility	Offer opportunities to participate in planning and execution	Assign roles and responsibilities
11. Spreading malicious rumors	Hold meetings to confront and communicate	Collect facts and data that substantiate or counter
12. Misusing power and position	Obtain participation by key stakeholders	Ask stakeholders for feedback on performance
13. Discriminating	Encourage team member interaction	Provide diversity training
14. Encouraging or not dealing with infighting	Maintain independence and credibility	Apply conflict management
15. Not treating everyone fairly and respectfully	Give fair opportunity to participate	Ask for volunteers
16. Not stopping hidden agendas	Remove person from project	Call out agenda in meeting to uncover and verify or discredit
17. Exploiting people	Reemphasize vision of project	Ask what is best interest of the project
18. Deliberately and maliciously damaging reputations	Address comments up front	Get human resources involved

Source: Adapted from Kleim (2012, 130–138).

TABLE 5.2	The Ethical Principles Approach
Ethical Principle	**Ethical Reasoning**
Consequences	*What course of action will do the most good and the least harm?*
Utilitarian ethics	What course of action brings the greatest good for the greatest number of people?
Proportionality ethic	What are the good and bad results of this decision, and do the good outweigh the bad?
Theory of justice	Does this action apply impartially to each employee and organizational unit?
Golden rule	If I were in the position of another person affected by my decision, would my actions be considered fair by that person?
Reversibility rule	Would you be willing to change places with the person affected by my contemplated action?
Protect health, safety, welfare	What course of action will best protect the health, safety, and welfare of others?
Integrity	*What plan can I live with, which is considered with the basic values and commitments in my organization?*
Virtuous character	Would this action be undertaken by someone of exemplary or virtuous character?
Disclosure rule	What course of action would I be comfortable with if it was examined by my friends, family, and associates?
Professional ethic	Can my action be explained before a committee of peers?
Intuition ethic	Which course of action feels right to me?
Rights	*Which alternative best serves others' rights, including stakeholders' rights?*
Principle of equal freedom	Will my contemplated action restrict others from actions that they have legitimate right to undertake?
Rights ethic	Will my action deprive any person affected by it of a right that must be respected?
Practicality	*Which course of action is feasible in the world as it is?*
Conventionalist ethic	What action will further my self-interest without violating the law?
Darwinian ethic	What course of action will enable me to succeed and survive in this organization?
Organizational versus personal ethic	Is this action consistent with both organizational ethics and personal ethics and do organizational considerations override personal ones?
Organizational loyalty	What are the organizational goals, and what can I do that is good for the organization?

Source: Cava, West, and Berman (1995).

6. Critique Klosterman's criticism of the Golden Rule (www.nytimes.com/2013/10/27/magazine/does-the-golden-rule-hold-up-in-modern-society.html?_r=0).

7. Ethics is like a muscle: The more it is used, the more it develops. Intentionally exercising it may seem strange at first, but with practice results it will become second nature. Start with small daily issues to strengthen your muscles; if you wait for a major event you may not be ready. Record efforts at exercising your ethics muscles in your journal and share at least one of them in class.

8. **Tabletop Exercise 2:** The Bad Cop. Instructions (see Chapter 3, Exercise 6).

Officer Bleakman has been on the police force in his city for five years. In that time, dozens of complaints have been lodged against him for harassing members of the community, particularly minorities. With the rise of the Black Lives Matter movement, the public has begun to record interactions with officers, and a video of Bleakman harassing a young Black man has surfaced on the Internet. In the video, Bleakman is clearly abusing his power and uses a racial slur when referring to the young man. Ultimately, Officer Bleakman lets him go after shoving and roughly restraining him. There appears to be no cause for the hostile interaction, and there was no report filed by Bleakman regarding the incident.

Role 1: Police Chief
You are the Chief of Police in Officer Bleakman's force. You are aware of his history of complaints and have seen the video of his interaction with the young Black man. How do you react? Do you take punitive action against Bleakman? If so, to what extent? Consider your obligations, ethical and otherwise. To whom are you accountable as the Chief of Police? What factors impact your decision?

Role 2: City Official
 are a city official in the same city as Officer Bleakman. After seeing the video of his interaction with the young Black man, you are made aware of his history of complaints. The public has not been informed of his background, and community members are demanding answers. Do you feel obligated to react in this situation? What would be your reaction, if any? Consider your obligations, ethical and otherwise. To whom are you accountable as a city official? What factors impact your decision?

Role 3: Partner
You have been Bleakman's partner on the force for the last year. In that time, you have witnessed several inappropriate acts, including the situation from the video. Bleakman often speaks in a derogatory manner about minorities, especially Blacks, and you have firsthand knowledge of his improper behavior while on duty. Do you blow the whistle on Bleakman? Why or why not? Consider your obligations, ethical and otherwise. To whom are you accountable as an officer of the law? What factors impact your decision?

Role 4: Community Member
You are a member of the community in which Officer Bleakman often patrols. You have heard about his abuse from fellow community members. You are a close family friend

of the young man Bleakman assaulted in the video. Are you compelled to take action in this situation? If so, what action would you take? Consider your obligations, ethical and otherwise. To whom are you accountable as a member of the community? What factors impact your decision?

Role 5: Local News Reporter
You are a local news anchor and journalist reporting on the incident from the video recording. After working your sources, you have discovered that Officer Bleakman has a history of complaints from minorities within the community. What angle do you report in your story? Do you protect Bleakman's past? Why or why not? Consider your obligations, ethical and otherwise. To whom are you accountable as a reporter and journalist? What factors impact your decision?

REFERENCES

Blanchard, K., & Peale, N. (1988). *The power of ethical management.* New York: Morrow.
Bouie, J. (2020, August 20). John Lewis was the Anti-Trump. *New York Times*, p. SR9.
Cava, A., West, J., & Berman, E. (1995). Ethical decision-making in business and government: An analysis of formal and informal strategies. *Spectrum: The Journal of State Government, 68*, 28–36.
Comer, D. R., & Vega, G. (2011). The personal ethical threshold. In D. R. Comer & G. Vega (Eds.), *Moral courage in organizations: Doing the right thing at work* (pp. 25–34). Armonk, NY: M. E. Sharpe.
Cook, K. (2014). *Kitty Genovese: The murder, the bystanders, the crime that changed America.* New York: Norton.
Ethics. (1982). *Public Management*, 20–21.
Eastman, W. (2021, April 30). *Why onlookers didn't stop Derek Chauvin? The Conversation.* Retrieved from https://www.msn.com/en-us/news/us/why-didn-t-onlookers-stop-derek-chauvin-here-s-what-research-really-shows-about-bystanders-getting-involved/ar-BB1gdL99
Gan, F. (2019, June 2). What could be wrong with a little 'moral clarity'? *New York Times Magazine.* Retrieved from www.nytimes.com/2019/01/02/magazine/what-could-be-wrong-with-a-little-moral-clarity.html
Gotterbarn, D. (2007). Enhancing ethical decision support methods: Clarifying the solution space with line drawing. *SIGCAS Computers and Society, 37*, 53–63.
Harris, C., Pritchard, M., & Rabins, M. (2009). *Engineering ethics: Concepts and cases* (4th ed.). Belmont, CA: Wadsworth.
Harris, C., & Rabins, M. (1993, November). *Two methods for ethical case analysis.* Paper presented at Frontiers in Education Conference, Washington, DC.
Jacobs, R. (2018, January 12). Ethical curiosity: An essential dimension of ethical leadership. *PA Times.* Retrieved from https://patimes.org/ethical-curiosity-essential-dimension-ethical
Joseph and Edna Josephson's Institute of Ethics. (1992). *Survey of employee opinions, values, and behavior.* Los Angeles: Author.
Josephson, M. (1992). *Making ethical decisions.* Marina Del Ray, CA: Josephson Institute.
Kets de Vries, M. (2009). *Reflections on character and leadership.* New York: John Wiley & Sons.
Kidder, R. (2006). *Moral courage.* New York: Morrow.
Kleim, R. (2012). *Ethics of project management.* Boca Raton, FL: CRC Press.
McDanield, M. (1985). *Lecture, Ethics and Public Administration.* Florida State University, Fall Semester.

Merry, S. (2016, June 29). Her shocking murder became the stuff of legend. But everyone got the story wrong. *Washington Post*. Retrieved from https://hiwihhi.com/washingtonpost/status/748198366350278656

Newell, T. (2017, March 7). Abraham Lincoln's second inaugural: Moral courage in public life. *PA Times*. Retrieved from https://patimes.org/abraham-lincolns-inaugural-moral-courage.

Newell, T. (2017, December 4). Moral courage in public service: Lessons from the life of Susan B. Anthony. *PA Times*. Retrieved from https://patimes.org/moral-courage-public-service-lessons-life-susan-b-anthony/

Peterson, C., & Seligman, M. E. P. (2004). *Character strengths and virtues: A handbook and classification*. Washington, DC: American Psychological Association.

Porter, D. (2020, July 20). Who will be our conscience now that John Lewis is gone? *Washington Post*. Retrieved from www.washingtonpost.com/opinions/2020/07/20/who-will-be-our-conscience-now-that-john-lewis-is-gone/?arc404=true

Stone, B. (2009, November 4). Go ahead, break a rule. *Governing*. Retrieved from www.governing.com/columns/mgmt-insights/Go-Ahead-Break-a.html

Weinstein, B. (2011). *Ethical intelligence*. Novato, CA: New World Library.

Appendix 5.1
Sensitivity–Intensity Matrix Approach

The sensitivity–intensity matrix, like the Kew Gardens principles and the Moral Minimum, helps answer the question of what action should be taken (i.e., following the five-step method, they focus on Step 4). For Ralph Kleim (2012), there are two signal considerations to be made when confronting an ethical dilemma: the sensitivity of the issue and the intensity of the response. Some transgressions will capture the immediate attention of decision makers because of their sensitivity (e.g., a pattern of racial discrimination), while others may not warrant immediate attention (a few instances of occasional tardiness) because of their relatively lesser intensity. These considerations assist to determine the suitable response. For instance, the need to act promptly in dealing with a late employee is not as compelling as the need to confront the person responsible for repeated instances of discrimination.

Kleim (2012, 36–37) specifies 12 factors in assessing the sensitivity of an ethical situation and gauging the intensity of the managerial reaction: the magnitude of the issue, scalability of the issue, context of occurrence, ramification of actions, control over the situation, accident or design, facts and data, impact on decision makers, consequences, assumptions, and the causes and the impact of response. Taking these elements into account will aid managers to determine both the issue sensitivity and the response intensity, and whether the circumstances require action.

APPLYING THE SENSITIVITY–INTENSITY MATRIX

Figure 5.2 shows four situations, appropriate responses, and questions to consider in assessing the sensitivity of the issue and the intensity of the reaction. The second matrix (Figure 5.3) is purposefully blank. Identify two issues that can be classified in cells A, B, C, and D and devise two answers for each issue.

Questions to ask in determining the sensitivity of the issue and the intensity of the response to an ethical dilemma include the following:

- Is this an important or unimportant issue?
- What were the circumstances when this occurred?

FIGURE 5.2	Sensitivity–Intensity Matrix

Sensitivity of Ethics

		Low	High
Intensity of Response	**High**	A. Issue: Spread a rumor about a co-worker Response: Removal from project	B. Issue: Teacher altering student responses on standardized test Response: Investigation and termination
	Low	C. Issue: Taking paper and pencils home from work Response: Verbal warning	D. Issue: Government official revealing identity of CIA agent Response: Presidential discretion used to mitigate prison sentence

Source: Kleim (2012).

FIGURE 5.3	Sensitivity–Intensity Matrix (blank)

Sensitivity of Ethics

		Low	High
Intensity of Response	**High**	A. Issue: Response:	B. Issue: Response:
	Low	C. Issue: Response:	D. Issue: Response:

- How much control does the actor have?
- What facts and data are relevant?
- Is the situation severe enough to warrant attention?
- What caused the situation or transgression?
- What are the likely impacts of the response?
- What is the likely effect of the action?
- Does it affect one person or a larger group?
- Did the event occur by accident or by design?
- In what ways are stakeholders impacted?
- Can the assumptions be treated as facts?

The next application of the matrix approach (Table 5.1) also invites your decision-making. Consider the scenarios facing administrators in dealing with employees. Two solutions are provided for each ethical problem. Furnish additional answers to the following 18 problems by considering the sensitivity of ethics and the intensity of the response. Assessing how to act can also be illuminated by flowcharting and line drawing strategies.

Directions: After reading and analyzing Table 5.1, offer two additional solutions for each ethical dilemma:

1.

2.

3.

4.

5.

6.

7.

8.

9.

10.

11.

12.

13.

14.

15.

16.

17.

18.

Appendix 5.2
The Ethical Principles Approach

Cava et al. (1995) used this "series of questions" approach as shown in Appendix 5.1. These are categorized into groups focusing on principles of consequences, integrity, rights, and practicality, each of which is significant and sometimes conflicting when deciding how to resolve a dilemma.

To illustrate the application of this approach, consider the situation described in Case Study 5.2. The decision maker uses the ethical principles listed (along with the question prompts) to reason through the dilemma.

 CASE STUDY 5.2

Applying the Ethical Principles Approach: Playing Poker With a Vendor

Consider the following case.

> Mario Rodriguez is a state-level purchasing agent who plays poker. He meets a vendor, Jay Roberts, who also enjoys poker. Jay gets Mario access to a prestigious private country club where Saturday night poker games are routinely played. Over time, stakes keep getting higher and higher. Money exchanges hands with Mario frequently winning. A membership to the country club and continued access to the poker game is also arranged by the vendor for the purchasing agent in the course of their relationship. As time goes on, Mario realizes that he is a much better poker player than Jay and that he has won quite a lot of money from him. He is also aware that he has a business relationship with the vendor on a daily basis. Should Mario continue socializing with Jay or not?

Mario can decide what action he wants to take, if any, by making assessments based on several different ethical principles from the list in Table 5.2:

> Conventionalist ethic: "What action will further my self-interest without violating the law?"

Mario and Jay's relationship does not violate any law, and the relationship certainly benefits Mario: He has received membership at an exclusive club, money from Jay in the form of wagers, and new acquaintances and relations. This rather conventional principle supports Mario's continued social relationship with Jay:

> Intuition ethic: "Which course of action feels right to me?"

Mario's awareness that he has a business relationship with Jay on a daily basis inevitably raises some questions in his mind about whether or not he should be allowing it to happen. His concern reveals that he knows that other vendors may argue that it is no longer a fair market and that his employer may believe he has stepped out of line. The application of this principle may not satisfy the "butterflies in the stomach" test:

> Professional ethic: "Can my action be explained before a committee of peers?"

While Mario believes that he can explain that the relationship was harmless and consisted of just two new friends sharing a game they love, in reality, his peers may look at the relationship from another perspective. They may see the money and benefits being given to Mario, a state purchaser, from Jay, a vendor. Using this principle, it appears clear that continuing this relationship may compromise his professional standing, despite explanations that reveal no evil intent:

> Proportionality ethic: "What are the good and bad results of this decision and do the good outweigh the bad?"

The good results revolve around Mario's self-interest. He receives membership at a country club, a group to play poker with, and the money from winning wagers. However, the bad results connect to his professional life. Mario may possibly lose his job, taint the integrity of his employer, and lose respect at work. On balance, it appears that the possible negative effects of continuing the relationship with Jay deserve greater weight than the beneficial results of continuing the relationship under these conditions:

> Rights ethic: "Will my action deprive any person affected by it of a right that must be respected?"

Mario's relationship with Jay may deprive other vendors of their right to fair and free market trade. With money being exchanged and their relationship growing, Mario may feel indebted to Jay and the other contractors may unfairly lose out on business with Mario's company. The relationship is not advisable. Mario's decision is ultimately a personal one; guidance is obtained by using the principles of ethical decision-making, cultivating critical thinking, and, as a consequence, improving decision-making.

Exercise
Choose two other ethical principles from the list of 15 in Table 5.2 and use them to analyze Mario's decision.

Appendix 5.3
Line Drawing

To illustrate line drawing (Exercise 5), consider this government contracting case.

 CASE STUDY 5.3

Applying the Line Drawing Method: A Questionable Gift

You work for the XYZ Agency and are in charge of awarding a government contract for the production of solar panels to be installed on federal buildings. After a thorough review process, you decide that GREEN, Inc., can provide the highest quality panels for the best price and will therefore be receiving the contract. Shortly after placing the order for the panels, a sales representative from GREEN, Inc., visits you and offers an all-expenses-paid trip to their factory in Hawaii, which includes a tour of their facilities as well as recreational excursions. Is this a bribe? Should you accept? (adapted from Harris et al., 2009, 81).

Case analysis includes identification of the NP and PP dimensions:

- Negative Paradigm: Bribery
    - Gift size: large
    - Timing: before decision
    - Reason: personal gain
    - Responsibility: sole
    - Product quality: worst in industry
    - Product cost: highest in market
- Positive Paradigm: Not Bribery
    - Gift size: small
    - Timing: after decision
    - Reason: educational
    - Responsibility: none
- Product quality: best in industry
- Product cost: lowest in market

Line plotting the features of the case result in this diagram:

Feature	Negative Paradigm (Bribery)	Test Case	Positive Paradigm (Not Bribery)
Gift size	Large	---X———-----	Small
Timing	Before decision	--------X---	After decision
Reason	Personal gain	—X———-----	Educational
Responsibility	Sole	--X---------	None
Product quality	Worst	--------X--	Best
Product cost	Highest	---------X--	Lowest

Although two out of the three most important factors (in bold) are closer to the NP, the timing criterion is close to the PP, and perhaps the fact that both product quality and cost fall closer to the PP outweighs the gift size and responsibility. Or maybe the fact that the decision maker bears sole responsibility for awarding contracts generates an overwhelming perception of impropriety, outweighing other factors. An important caution: Those who use this tool must consider all of the relevant factors, for failure to do so could distort the results.

6 Virtue Theory

An honest heart being the first blessing, a knowing head is the second.
—Thomas Jefferson

Cognitive ethics approaches, paradoxically, are both too precise in logic and too abstract to be easily applied. Importantly, an emphasis on results or rules can be seen as a cold rationalistic way to make decisions that ignore the person. The third and final individual-centered approach to ethics, accordingly, shifts the focus from cognitive philosophies to virtue theory— from "head" to "heart." The objectives of this chapter are to

- contrast cognitive and virtue ethics,
- define key virtue ethics terms,
- understand how character is formed,
- apply virtue theory,
- assess the strengths and weakness of the theory, and
- determine the utility of virtue ethics for public managers.

COMPARING COGNITIVE AND VIRTUE ETHICS

Cognitive ethics holds that rationality can supply morality with a foundation by relying on a logical process to determine what to do in a given situation.[1] While helpful and illuminating, growing disillusionment with modernity leads to the realization that life is too complex to conform to a simple equation; cognitive ethics has undue confidence in the power of reason to recognize and pursue the good. Ethics involves more than following general norms like results or duty—the strength of cognitive ethics is its weakness. A preoccupation with the process of decisions cannot produce understanding about the actual content of an individual's morality. Indeed, a focus on process can be at the expense of substance.

Virtue ethics, then, is an alternative to endless debates between results and rules in cognitive ethics. Reason may be essential in carrying out moral decisions, but the source of morality is human sentiment. To wit, "The heart of the problem is the problem of the heart." That is, the formulation of a problem can never be a purely technical procedure; reason is usually greeted with indifference by the heart. Virtue theory is a framework, not a formula. As shown in earlier chapters, ethics can include questions about consequences and duties, but it also entails questions about what kind of person someone is. It concerns being considerate, helpful, and honest: being a good individual and taking responsibility for living a meaningful life. Ethics is about developing the right character more than following the right procedure. Behind every action is a person. This does not mean that results and rules are irrelevant, but rather that they are most effectively considered

DOI: 10.4324/9781003203148-8

in the context of individual character. Stated differently, we cannot control circumstances, but we *can* control character. Virtue ethics is a branch of moral philosophy that emphasizes character rather than rules or results found in the rival cognitive strategies.

Virtue theory, accordingly, is more personal in approach than cognitive ethics. One's answer to "What to do?" has less to do with results and rules, and everything to do with what kind of person one is. Every action is measured in terms of character, one's internal moral compass. We must *be* before we can *do*; one must be good before one can do good (we are human beings, not human doings). Virtue ethics, it follows, is a way of life, not a mere method of analysis.

The primary moral faculty is intuition and not intellect, because reason more easily leads to error. Many do not have the capacity or training for discursive reasoning. Cleopatra is said to have persuaded her people that twilight was dawn (consider, too, the convincing—and opposing—jury closings in television courtroom dramas such as "Law and Order" reruns). The intended role of theory in virtue ethics is not to get the decision maker out of a jam but to help build her character. "Being virtuous is no precise science, (but) it is nonetheless a demanding art, whose mastery is vital to achieve human potential. Unfortunately . . . moral decision-making lacks the conceptual clarity and compelling certainty of Euclidean geometry" (Anderson, 1996, 7).

THE VOCABULARY OF VIRTUE

If Socrates was right in saying that "the beginning of wisdom is the definition of terms," critical concepts—character, virtue, integrity, practical wisdom—require examination to comprehend the range of virtue ethics. As these terms are unpacked, beware that they are much more easily recognized than defined. *Character*, according to Anderson (1996, 5), is the sum of enduring dispositions—good or bad—that define the individual and are cultivated over a lifetime. Comprising a person's pattern of behavior, character is related to the moral qualities of individual self-discipline and collective social responsibility. An individual cannot be understood apart from the larger community in which he participates. "There is no such thing as a 'self-made man,'" asserts George Matthew Adams:

> We are made up of thousands of others. Everyone who has ever done a kind deed for us, or spoken one word of encouragement to us, has entered in the make-up of our character and of our thoughts, as well as our success. (www.quoteworld.org/quotes/65)

Indeed, the polis is about learning how to live the good life. Character is developed experientially in communal relations through modeling significant others and by reflecting on important encounters (Preston, 2001). The strength of the community is each individual member; the strength of each member is the community.

Good character is not arrived at by chance. Developing strong moral fiber is a continuous process of self-discovery requiring commitment to ethical values and the cultivation of virtuous habits. Many people are clearer about how to build an external career than on how to build internal character. External success is gained through competition with others, while internal development occurs by confrontation with one's self. Character is one's moral center or "naked soul." What matters is not so much how long one lives but how one lives.

Franz (1998, 65) emphasizes the importance of personal identity, the willingness to take responsibility for one's life:

> By character, I mean the internal resources, knowledge, and discipline to know one's own mind and the resolve to pursue its direction. Character is based on beliefs, nourished by knowledge, forged in experience, and committed to values. A person of character has the ability to make things happen, persevere through adversity, forgo alternatives, and alter course. Character implies a mastery over one's own will. Someone without such mastery would hardly be characterized as responsible ... or a person of integrity. ... This mastery is no accident. It is learned.

It is evident that citizens should care a great deal about their leaders' personality traits, apart from their policies, because no position is sufficiently prestigious to make a person of dubious character conduct themselves with dignity, grace, and veracity. Indeed, many voters do not pick candidates based on policy details. Rather, they care about the person's convictions and temperament, her capacity to place duty and honor above partisan advantage and personal interest, as well as an unwavering devotion to put the nation's interest above self-interest.

One test of character is what one would do if one were invisible. Does the invisible person, in the modern vernacular, have the "right stuff" to do the right thing? Recall the Milgram experiments. Good people make moral choices. For them, the reply to "What is a good life for a human being?" is to create an ethical character, to achieve excellence in all aspects of life, to live virtuously with others—in brief, to become a "virtuoso." *Leadership*, in fact, can be defined as the practical application of character. In reciprocal fashion, virtuous citizens build moral communities that, in turn, encourage further character formation.

Virtue is a trait or excellence of individual and societal character. Virtues are principles of goodness and rightness in character and conduct that lead toward nobility and away from depravity. Common examples include justice, courage, truthfulness, and temperance. Woven into character, they are ingrained dispositions to act rightly, developed by practice, just as vices are tendencies to act wrongly. Not easily honed, virtues make people sensitive to ethical issues and shape how they think and act. One becomes prudent, for example, by repeatedly behaving in a prudent manner. Per the three perspectives on ethics (Chapter 2), an individual may be virtuous (micro-level ethics) through her personal character development, as can an organization (meso level) through integrity-based practices and a society (macro level) through upholding a pervasive culture of virtue.

Virtue (Greek: *arête*) is found between the vicious extremes of excess and deficiency—Aristotle's "golden mean" is between two vices (Confucius and the Buddha also endorse a concept of equilibrium). In every situation, a person of character will determine the mean—neither excessive nor deficient—based on reason and experience appropriate for that circumstance. Courage, to take one example, is the mean between the vices of foolhardiness and cowardice, an awareness of what to fear and what not to fear. Prudence, to offer another example, is the considered position between being overly cautious, on the one hand, and rash, on the other. What is reasonable in one situation may not be in another. Individuals of character are guided by their principles, not popularity or expedience.

Virtues, then, are more than habitual skills enabling right action—they promote the attainment of what it means to be human, to function well, to be moral. Virtues are character traits needed to live a flourishing life (*eudaimonia*). They are valuable for intrinsic, not instrumental, reasons. A happy life is one spent in pursuit of virtuous excellence, of living up to one's potential, of learning and doing the right thing,. While there is no one definitive list of virtues, seven cardinal virtues can be noted: prudence (wisdom), courage (fortitude), temperance (moderation, self-mastery), justice (rightness) (the "natural" virtues of ancient Greece philosophers), faith, hope, and love (from Christianity).[2] These virtues are cardinal in the sense that all other moral virtues can be derived from them. Humility, kindness, patience, diligence, generosity, abstinence, and chastity are the opposite of the "seven deadly sins" of pride, envy, wrath, sloth, greed, gluttony, and lust. Likewise, prudence (wisdom stemming from disciplined, reasoned judgment) is the converse of negligence.

Integrity, a product or synthesis of virtues, is a predisposition to maintain one's virtues and act in accordance to character. In today's parlance, this consistency between belief and conduct, to make actions congruent with values, is to "walk the talk," to "have it all together." If a building has structural integrity, a person with integrity has "gravitas"—a sure sense of right from wrong; he or she knows what his or her core beliefs are, and what he or she will or will not do, no matter what. Integrity grows from internal values, experiences, and the ability to act thoughtfully. The individual must have a strong commitment to principles and self-discipline while continually striving to meet high ethical standards. Serving as one's "moral identity," integrity is the aptitude to contemplate one's roles and obligations, to nurture an ethical soundness both as an individual and as a member of the community. Compromising one's integrity is a profound mistake, as evidenced by officials when they are embroiled in scandal (Chapter 11).

To act thoughtfully requires *practical wisdom*. Such prudence, what Aristotle calls *phronesis*, is the capacity to distinguish right from wrong and take sensible action.[3] It is the ability to consider competing claims and to tolerate moral ambiguity. The reflective person recognizes the distinction between knowing and doing. Moral virtue directs one to the right end; practical wisdom directs one to the right means. It is not always enough to act with sincere intentions; behaving effectively demands discerning all the relevant factors leading to a fitting decision. Good judgment comes from the integrity of a well-developed character.

Practical wisdom enables one to grasp the golden mean in particular situations, a quality requiring experience that cannot be reduced to rules or consequences. The use of practical wisdom differs from analytical reasoning because formulating a judgment is circumstantial, personal, and steeped in wise counsel to do right for each member of one's community. It involves an understanding of what it means to be human and the capacity to deliberate thoughtfully (thereby realizing virtuous ends) when confronted with dilemmas. For example, prudent rule following includes discerning the purpose of the measure and when rule departure more effectively meets responsibilities than adhering to the rule.

Essential for an ethical life, practical wisdom engages and unifies the intellectual and the moral: Right action requires intellectual judgment, which itself requires virtue. Right action has no standard external to itself—to act rightly is to do what a good person would do in a particular circumstance. No pedestrian average, temperance is Greek for "the middle way," moderation, and balancing competing interests. One deliberates as long as necessary and then acts decisively with compassion, precision, and speed. One must see his or her duty and perform it. Virtuous action, founded on arduous practice, may be nearly spontaneous. A person cannot claim to be kind unless he or she is habitually kind—kindness is shown automatically, without thought of its being kind.

To summarize briefly, character (personal behavior patterns) is enriched by virtues (disposition to act). The synthesis of character and virtues constitutes integrity, something that can be achieved through the exercise of practical wisdom, a preeminent virtue. A good tree bears good fruit; good people make good decisions. As tennis champion Arthur Ashe observed, "You are really never playing an opponent. You are playing yourself, your own highest standards, and when you reach your limits; that is real joy."

Two sterling public officials, who display many of the virtues discussed in this chapter, are now profiled. The first shows how an appointed public servant, Donna Shalala, former secretary of Health and Human Service (HHS), university president, and member of Congress has managed large organizations and governed with honesty and integrity. The second demonstrates how a senior public servant, Dr. Anthony Fauci, long-time Director of the National Institute of Allergy and Infectious Diseases, serves the public interest with integrity with a hands-on approach to addressing human problems. Both of these exemplary people have a blend of ethical, technical, and leadership competencies grounded in a virtue-based public service ethos.

Exemplar Profile: Donna Shalala

Dr. Donna Shalala is no stranger to major organizations: She holds the distinction of being the longest-serving secretary of the Department of Health and Human Services, served as president of both Hunter College and the University of Wisconsin–Madison, and continued to make headlines as president of the University of Miami, which steadily ascended in academic ranking under her leadership. In 2015, she moved to New York to become chief executive officer of the Clinton Foundation. A few years later, she returned to the University of Miami to resume her status as a tenured faculty member. She has served on several corporate and civic boards of directors, and is the recipient of numerous awards, including the Medal of Freedom, the Nelson Mandela Award for Health and Human Rights, and more than 50 honorary degrees.

While she is clearly a paragon of effective management, she is also an exemplar of the sort of virtue-oriented action that is the subject of this chapter. In fact, she is more than just a testament to virtuous leadership—she is also an outspoken advocate for it. In an article in *Public Integrity*, Shalala (2004, 350) shares 12 tips for "managing a large public sector organization with honesty and integrity," for she learned from experience that it is the cultivation of these virtues that makes an effective and ethical organization a reality. It is no coincidence that each of the 12 pointers is matched by an anecdote from her time at HHS. Examining some of these instructive snapshots of the career of a distinguished public servant should help you understand both why virtues are vital to an organization and how they can be attained in practice.

One of Shalala's lessons speaks directly to the importance of character—but not simply the leader's character. Her advice is to "[c]hoose people based on both the content of their resume and their character" (351). She relates how it was crucial to resist pressure from the White House to appoint senior campaign officials to her HHS team, because the values of the staff were tantamount to favors owed: Without a team that shares your values and your vision, which is committed to "serv[ing] the public interest ethically" (355), the goal of an ethical organization could never be reached. Yet the resume is just as important as the individual's character, "because you can't make the right [ethical] decision if you don't have the necessary competence" (351). Thus, Shalala believes that competence and character feed into each other, and took care in selecting whom to work with.

Shalala also found that at the core of leading with integrity is "the courage of your convictions," which, in a government department, translates into refusing to "subordinate policy to politics." And the temptation to let politics take the wheel is always looming in the field of public health: While scientific facts cannot be disputed, unfavorable data can be swept under the rug and favorable information can be blown out of proportion. Yet when confronted with either, Shalala refused to yield to temptation. When HHS received a report from the nation's leading health officials indicating that a program to provide clean needles to drug addicts could reduce the rate of HIV infection, the department stood behind it, in spite of fierce opposition to needle-exchange programs. Likewise, "the White House was told 'no' if they wanted to over-emphasize or distort the significance of a scientific finding" (353).

Integrity can also mean going above and beyond the merely required. At the meso-organizational level, this can mean being "concerned not just with the legal imperatives but the moral ones," as when the HHS inspector general issued criticism of the department's policy on the protection of human subjects in research. The report triggered an overhaul of the research-oversight process that went far beyond closing the gaps in legal compliance and properly reflected the importance of guaranteeing the safety of subjects (351).

Another more personal lesson of Shalala's is "It is your friends, not your enemies, who will often get you in trouble." She observes how even the most experienced official can unknowingly fall sway to the influence of a personal relationship or simply be perceived as acting out of favoritism. As such, it is imperative to own up to the fact of one's own fallibility and accept the need to avoid any signs of impropriety, real or imagined. It was for this reason that instead of self-righteously assuming that her actions were always beyond reproach, Shalala made sure there was always a witness to any meetings she had with individuals outside HHS (354).

While most of Shalala's career has been as an appointed public administrator, in 2018 she became an elected official winning a seat in the U.S. House of Representatives, running in Florida's 27th district. Congresswoman Shalala is a vigorous advocate for women's rights, civil rights, increased access to health care, better education and public schools, and a clean and sustainable environment. She leads by example in the organizations she has managed and in the policies she promotes. Virtues, while lofty, are not to be placed high up on a pedestal out of reach. They are, in conjunction with technical skills, the fuel that powers successful organizations and policymaking. As Donna Shalala has proved in the course of a long career, demonstrating integrity, prudence, and humility in leadership "will never be easy, but it will always be right . . . it will never be effortless, but it will always be rewarding" (355).

Exemplar Profile: Anthony Fauci

Dr. Anthony Fauci, the Director of the National Institute of Allergy and Infectious Diseases since 1984, is a widely respected and trusted public health expert with more than five decades of experience in the field. His role at the National Institutes of Health began in 1968, and since then he has worked with six U.S. presidents, starting with Ronald Reagan (Vazquez, 2020; CNN, 2020). Well known for his pioneering HIV/AIDS research, Fauci has been lauded as "an American hero" (Smith, 2020). He was awarded the Presidential Medal of Freedom by George W. Bush in 2008. He worked on Ebola, the Zika virus, SARS, Swine flu, anthrax scares, and the COVID-19 pandemic. He recently received a $1 million Israeli prize for "speaking truth to power" on Covid-19 (Papenfuss, 2021). A recent poll identified Fauci, along with Governor Mario Cuomo, as the most trusted leaders in America when it comes to the coronavirus response (Panetta, 2020). Fauci was named by *Time* magazine as the 2020 guardian of the year and portrayed by Brad Pitt on "Saturday Night Live."

His principle-based leadership and finely honed communication skills help to explain his success as a public service professional. William Meehan (2020) has identified the seven principles of Fauci's leadership: He has carved out a career based on service to others, he uses wise discernment in making decisions, he relies on critical analytical thinking, he follows a disciplined regimen to ensure fitness, he shows compassion and empathy to those he encounters, he uses ethics-based decision-making, and he evinces loving concern for all. He is a perpetual learner, a willing collaborator, a proud mentor who seeks solutions rather than credit for his accomplishments. As a leader he would not ask his staff to do anything that he would not do himself. Guided by principles, good character, and core values, it is not surprising that he is among the most trusted medical experts in the country (Kiley, 2020).

As a communicator it is not only what he says but how he says it that sets him apart from those less adept at conveying crucial information in uncertain times. Nick Westergaard (2020) notes his multiple skills as a communicator: He has a slow, deliberate speaking style, pausing frequently and using hand gestures effectively to emphasize main points. He is not pedantic, avoids scientific jargon, and is able to address complex subjects in clear understandable terms. In doing so, he conveys both competence and warmth. As one astute observer noted, Dr. Fauci "learned how to speak truth to, but to do so in a way that did not threaten those big political egos" (cited in Leibovich, 2020). Joe McLeod's (2020) analysis of Fauci's success as a communicator links his credibility to his approach at stating what he knows using current data, acknowledging what he does not, and admitting when he is wrong. His authentic, calm, and soothing manner is reassuring to an anxious public. As a spokesperson for the White House Coronavirus Task Force, Fauci's communication skills "inspire, lead and comfort" those seeking information.

Fauci is a highly successful and highly visible scientist. Barbara Gastel (2020) has highlighted ten reasons that have contributed to his success, summarized by these words: smart, integrity, empathy, flexibility, energy, trustworthiness, connections, communication, recognizability, and teamwork. He is a prolific author, having published more than 1,000 articles, more than half of these about AIDS, and is among the most highly cited living researchers, having been referenced more than 50,000 times by other publications (Gastel, 2020), not to mention even more cites in social media.

Despite his professional accomplishments, leadership attributes, and communication competencies, Fauci has not avoided criticism and attempts to undermine his position. This occurred in part because his growing popularity did threaten "big political egos." During the COVID-19 pandemic the president twice called for Fauci to be fired, mocked him, and attempted to discredit Fauci. Peter Navarro, White House trade advisor, wrote a hyper-critical op-ed piece in *USA Today* targeting Fauci, arguing that he was "wrong about everything" (Leibovich, 2020; Mazza, 2020). Critics asserted that he was trying to subvert the economy and force vaccines on Americans. Fauci's desire to ramp up testing and be cautious on opening the economy was perceived by some in the Oval Office to be at cross purposes with the Trump administration (Downie, 2020).

At the same time, Fauci's absence at task force briefings led people to ask, "What's happening to Dr. Fauci?" (Leibovich, 2020; Alba, Welker, & Lee, 2020). Supporters defended him against the attacks from the Trump administration, arguing that his opponents undermined science, scientists, and public health professionals. One physician following a Fauci presentation said, "Saying Dr. Fauci is a bad doctor is like saying Michael Jordan is terrible at basketball" (cited by Kiley, 2020). Fauci came to his own defense: "You can trust respected medical authorities. . . . I believe I am one of them, so I think you can trust me" (Leibovich, 2020). Nonetheless, by mid-2021 the former president and his allies sought to revise history casting Fauci as "public enemy no 1" (Viser & Abutaleb, 2021).

Both Shalala and Fauci exemplify good character where right action became second nature based on habits cultivated over a lifetime of service. Ability may get someone to the top, but it takes character to stay there. The Good Men Project (https://goodmenproject.com) and Bruce Weinstein's weekly high-character leadership column in *Forbes* magazine offer regular profiles of praiseworthy individuals.

HABITUATION: THE FORMATION OF CHARACTER

How is character formed? Through habit. There are no instant habits—they must be repeatedly practiced. "Excellence," Aristotle believed:

> [I]s an act won by training and habituation. We do not act rightly because we have virtue or excellence, but rather we have those qualities because we have acted rightly. We are what we repeatedly do. Excellence, then, is not an act, but a habit. (in Durant, 1926/1991, 76)

Indeed, "we first make our habits," writes John Dryden, "and then our habits make us." Good habits (virtues) can be hard to form and easy to lose; cruelly, bad habits (vices) can be easy to form and hard to lose (Exhibit 6.1).

EXHIBIT 6.1   **Managerial Work Habits**

Since ethics is central to the professional identities of public officials (Chapter 1), they are responsible not only for acquainting themselves with the theories associated with a cognitive approach to ethics but also for cultivating exemplary character traits. Thus, as habits (both good and bad) shape character, it is vital to understand how workplace habits are attained or lost, transformed or solidified. While developing an admirable character must take place at the individual level, the climate at the top sets the tone for those at the bottom and everywhere in between. It therefore behooves us to explore the work habits of managers.

West and Berman (2011) do just that, discussing the results of a national survey of senior officials in city governments with populations over 50,000 about the work habits of their subordinate managers. The reporting of managers on their employees and themselves represents the organizational or meso-level ethic. The institutional culture promoted by managers through the policies they implement is a feature of meso-level ethics. While managers are individuals with emotions and values, this may lead one to think they operate at the micro-personal level, but the role of the manager is typically to put the needs of the organization (meso) first. Although close to 90 percent of senior administrators report that their subordinates "regularly demonstrate civility, courtesy and decency," as well as "take a stand where issues of ethics are at stake" (69), the authors nevertheless stress the necessity of constant vigilance because of two unexpected discoveries.

First, 45 percent of those surveyed reported that one or more negative managerial habits (such as being overly judgmental, aggressive, passive, or defensive) were present alongside good habits (71). Second, while poor management habits can crowd out good habits, the converse relationship does not hold. "Managers cannot rely on the presence of good management work habits in order to reduce the presence of bad management work habits" (77). Officials must first work to elevate awareness of the presence of bad habits for training and incentives to be effective. Nevertheless, the findings also indicate that top management is least likely to concentrate on work practices when there are high levels of good managerial habits (and thus organizational performance). This contributes to a vicious cycle whereby "when things are going well, the possibility exists of giving insufficient attention to bad management work habits which, however minimal, sow the seeds of subsequent performance problems," and, it should be added, ethical problems, when ethical habits are at stake (79).

While these conclusions may seem discouraging, they only confirm that cultivating a virtuous professional character (where virtues of both competence and ethics converge) is a never-ending process of habituation. At the individual level, this development requires engaging in "a difficult process that typically requires persistence, practice and, hence, considerable time" (67). However, employees do not have to set off alone on the long and winding road to virtue. Organizational policies can complement individual efforts by including certain positive behaviors as criteria in performance reviews or by establishing training, mentoring, and on-the-job coaching to help individuals identify good and bad work habits and strive toward reinforcing the former while weaning them off the latter (67).

Alternatively, and more in accordance with the personal nature of character development, Chun (2005, 281) sees the role of the manager as "to make sure the strategic virtues are . . . embedded in [a] member's cognition in everyday organizational life." Although this directive entails a cognitive component of identifying (with help from a manager) the virtues to be pursued, virtue ethics is still very much about the heart: It entails gaining, through experience, a practical knowledge of which actions lead one to virtue and performing them routinely until they become second nature.

Habit shapes character, as improvement comes from repeatedly making good decisions that avoid extremes and aim at moderation. Like physical fitness, no one can transmute character to someone else; it cannot be bought, as it must be earned. "The highest reward for man's toil," writes John Ruskin, "is not what he gets for it but what he becomes by it." Moral behavior, rather than a product of cognition, is a product of habituation to virtuous conduct. It is quicker to act your way into right thinking than to think your way into right acting. Answers to life's questions are found not "in the back of the book" but rather inside one's self. You are the only person who can decide where you want to go in life and how you are going to get there. Cultivating virtues is required for the good life, the achievement of human purpose. As Eric Fromm said, "Man's main task in life is to give birth to himself." Every day and everything counts. Character is destiny. Success in life ultimately depends on what an individual knows, what he or she does, and what he or she becomes as a result. Your character will be what you yourself choose to make it.

Excellences of character find expression in action. The practice of virtues may not require deliberation; instead, it becomes ingrained in one's stature after years of performance. Benjamin Franklin describes in his autobiography how he consciously nurtured some dozen virtues he thought important to a meaningful life. A modern-day approach to such habituation is found in Stephen Covey's (1991) *Principle-Centered Leadership*. As a result of deliberate practice, virtue becomes natural, such that lying is not thought of as an option when confronted with a difficult issue. What we do will likely depend on what we already are, and what we will be in the future will be the result of ongoing self-discipline.

Because individuals and circumstances vary, no complete catalogue of virtues exists. More useful than a recitable slate is possession of the capacity (practical wisdom) to know when and how to exhibit the appropriate virtue. An individual with good character "knows" how to feel and act. Indeed, compiling a list misses the point, which is to get away from a formulaic way of thinking about ethics and emphasize its personal nature and context sensitivity.

"The true test of character," according to John Holt, "is not how much we know how to do, but how we behave when we don't know what to do." Does the problem challenge or defeat us? While virtue ethics does not rely on methodical approaches to issues, some aids to thinking about the personal nature of decision-making may nonetheless be helpful. Michael Rion (1996, 13–14) encourages managers to mull over the following questions when faced with a dilemma. Note that most of them directly or indirectly focus on the person as a decision maker:

1. Why is this bothering me? Is it really an issue? Am I genuinely perplexed, or am I afraid to do what I know is right?

2. Who else matters? Who are the stakeholders who may be affected by my decisions?

3. Is it my problem? Have I caused the problem, or has someone else? How far should I go in resolving the issue?

4. What is the ethical concern—legal obligation, fairness, promise keeping, honesty, doing good work, and/or avoiding harm?

5. What do others think? Can I learn from those who disagree with my judgment?

6. Am I being true to myself? What kind of person or company would do what I am contemplating? Could I share my decision "in good conscience" with my family? With colleagues? With public officials?

A "defining moment" (Badaracco, 1997), one that reveals, tests, and shapes character, is portrayed in Case Study 6.1. A human being with good character, Aristotle believed, likely would be wise, temperate, courageous, and generous. The Greek admonition "know thyself" remains central to the study and practice of ethics in the 21st century.

To know one's self includes the significance of context when making a decision— namely, there may not be a single version of you; as virtue ethics recognizes, circumstances matter. While people prefer to believe that they are inherently moral, "role morality" is well-documented: "[W]here you stand depends upon where you sit." That is, people wear "different hats" and play different roles as behavioral norms and expectations vary depending upon the environment. Thus, during the pandemic telecommuters working from home exhibited more honest behavior than when they worked at the office (Abeler, Becker, & Falk, 2012; Kaplan, 2020, April 27).

Further, your role as an employee (at home or office) is likely to be quite different from you as a churchgoers, neighbor, and community volunteer. Given people's vulnerability to role morality, the need for understanding practical wisdom is essential. In fact, although it is important to nurture character independent of circumstances, it is also critical to understand that the environment influences behavior (recall the Milgram experiments in Chapter 4; see also Chapter 7 and the Tabletop Exercises in Chapters 3, 5, 9, 11, and 12).

VIRTUE THEORY STRENGTHS AND WEAKNESSES

Virtue theory attends realistically to the actual dynamics of moral life—what one feels comfortable with or what an admired person would do. Understanding virtue ethics is more intuitive than cognitive ethics. People cultivate ethics by living ethically and making everyday choices—not by studying isolated, dramatic cases of decision-making. Blaise Pascal captures this distinction by saying, "The power of a man's virtue should not be measured by his special efforts, but by his ordinary doing." Indeed, developing virtues keeps us from finding ourselves in moral quandaries in the first place. We are moral not because of rules but because of what we demand of ourselves in character—the capacity to recognize challenges and respond appropriately.

Knowing the difference between right and wrong is necessary but not sufficient; we must also care about the difference. If we ask the questions, "What is a moral life?" and "What is the right thing to do?" then cognitive ethics is a minimalist approach with an instrumental focus ("ethics without virtue"). Virtue ethics is a maximalist approach that demands ethics with virtue, deep reflection, and high ideals.

CASE STUDY 6.1

Applying Rion's Ethical Decision-Making Framework: Probing the Conscience

The following case concerns an ethical dilemma confronting an academic executive.

You are the president of an elite public university and very much committed to fostering diversity within the student body. You have championed an affirmative action program that is widely popular throughout the university and has set an example for other high-ranking institutions. A wealthy alumnus has made a very generous donation, and the funds are desperately needed by the university. However, the alum is an outspoken opponent of affirmative action. (He attended the university when it was an all-white, male institution.) Should you accept the donation?

Rion's questions can be used as a guide to help the president in deciding whether or not to accept the donation:

1. *Why is this bothering me?* After a career spent supporting affirmative action programs and fostering diversity on campus, this decision has caused me many sleepless nights. In the short term, the funds are desperately needed, but I fear that in the long run, I will be tainting the school's character and my own. The face and integrity of the school, its financial stability, and its present and future students all play key roles in weighing this decision. I also must think of the colleges that have followed in our footsteps and view us as a role model. Making a prudent decision will require due diligence and the courage to explain my action to the wealthy alumnus.

2. *Is it my problem?* Yes, I cannot see how it is not my problem. After years of progress since the days of all-white, male graduating classes, I fear that my singular decision could eliminate that progress and take the university back decades. My own conscience and the well-being of the school I lead are on the line.

3. *What do others think?* This decision will certainly be accompanied by backlash either way: I will make headlines for ruining the school's progress or for denying it of essential funds. I risk losing major programs or polluting its character.

4. *Am I being true to myself?* To retain integrity, only one answer makes that possible. After defending and promoting student diversity, which I firmly believe in, I cannot be true to myself and accept a donation, no matter the size, from an opponent of everything we have stood for.

Yet virtue ethics lacks universality, as no general theory of human virtue exists. So-called cardinal virtues vary from time to time and place to place, and the same virtues may not apply to all individuals in a society. To illustrate, for centuries, a virtuous woman was considered to be quiet, servile, and industrious. Further, virtue ethics lacks a theory of action. Cognitive approaches have fewer problems precisely because they force decision, but virtue theory does not offer much direction about what people should do. Virtues may generate instructions for action (the virtue of justice, for instance, provides the motivation to act justly), but what does a just person do in a given dilemma? Finally, the theory—ironically—lacks integrity due to its ambiguity. One may be good, but may not know how to do good. Indeed, confusing being with doing can easily lead to self-righteousness—if one believes he is good, it is not hard for him to believe that what he does is good, even when it is not. To conclude, the revival of virtue ethics in contemporary times, despite its limitations, has resulted in a more complete portrait of morality in public affairs. The contemporary renaissance of virtue theory has both encouraged a scrutiny of other approaches and led to disagreements about the applicability of virtue theory for managers. This dichotomy is addressed below.

UTILITY OF VIRTUE ETHICS FOR MANAGERS: CHALLENGE AND RESPONSE

The literature on virtue theory includes critiques and rebuttals regarding its applicability to public administration. Alasdair MacIntyre (1985), among others, questions whether it can be imported into public administration because he sees the bureaucrat as a figure devoid of virtue: "[T]he bureaucratic manager relies on a system of knowledge that promotes efficiency and effectiveness—looks at controlling means rather than ends—and therefore leaves no room for moral debate" (in Macaulay & Lawton, 2006, 704). MacIntyre views administrators as operating solely within "the realms in which rational agreement is possible—that is, of course . . . to the realm of fact, the realm of means, the realm of measurable effectiveness" (30). If so, technical competence is the proper concern of bureaucrats, not perfection of character.

Bowman, West, and Beck (2010) contend, however, that technical skill is not the only element of good administration, as it must be complemented by ethical and leadership competence. Together, these three competencies provide the "edge" necessary for successful public service. Bowman et al. demonstrate that ethics is personally as well as professionally relevant. Officials encounter ethical issues at every level of bureaucracy—identifying and dealing with them are core responsibilities. The professional—whether in government, business, or nonprofit sector—must rely on ethical resources, including what constitutes a virtue, for guidance in addressing professionally perilous dilemmas.

Thus, technical, ethical, and leadership competencies are integrated and mutually reinforcing, evidenced by these observations:

- The competent administrator is technically adroit and ethically concerned, and takes the lead in performing his or her tasks with excellence.
- "[S]uch questions as 'What should I do?' and 'What kind of person am I?' are not separate questions, but come together to allow for individual flourishing."
- Competence is valued as a virtue, an excellence, of public service by employers. (Macaulay & Lawton, 2006, 709)

Macaulay and Lawton studied compliance officers in the UK and found no sharp distinction between competence and virtue in the perceptions of their knowledge, skills, and abilities (KSAs). Not only did officers cite a variety of virtue-based and competence-based KSAs, they also interpreted many in terms of both virtue and competence. The KSA of "ethical awareness," for instance, can be seen as invoking virtue (understanding morality and abiding by its dictates), as well as competence in terms of "transparency, accountability, and the rights and wrongs of local authority systems and practices" (707–708). In so doing, trust in government can be nourished when it is demonstrated that it has the ability to do the job, the benevolence to care about people, and the integrity to do the right thing (Brooks, 2020, May 16).

Gilbert Harman (2003) and Miguel Alzola (2007) also contribute to the virtue ethics and public administration debate. Harman contends that "Aristotelian style virtue ethics [has] . . . a commitment to broad-based character traits of a sort that people simply do not have" (92). The argument maintains that although it may be possible to come to a conclusion about what characteristics constitute a virtuous person, individuals typically lack the "broad and stable dispositions corresponding to the sorts of character and personality traits" needed for virtue (92). Harman subscribes to the consensus of social psychology that the understanding of character presupposed by virtue ethics simply does not exist in human behavior. If he is correct, virtue ethics is misguided and cannot serve as a basis for bureaucratic ethics.

Harman's view is rooted in fundamental attribution error (Chapter 7), the erroneous tendency to attribute individual behavior to a person's character, not situational factors. Thus, he maintains that it is people's situation, and not just their character traits, that best explains what they do. It is a mistake to neglect the high susceptibility of public administrators to "subtle situational effects"—"minor and seemingly irrelevant differences in the perceived situation sometimes make significant differences to what people do" (90). Thus, even a morally upright person may make objectionable decisions under the pressures of the workplace to perform. Failure to do the so-called right thing does not mean an administrator is morally depraved and that ethics therefore has no role at work—just as failure to obey street signs while in a rush to the hospital does not make one an inherently dangerous driver, or warrant the removal of street signs since "no one obeys them anyway." Circumstances matter.

For example, consider an experiment in which test subjects making a phone call in a telephone booth witness a passerby (a confederate of the experimenters) drop a folder full of papers, which scatter across the ground. Callers who found a coin planted in the return slot were far more likely to help than those who did not find a coin (Isen & Levin, 1972, cited in Harman, 2003). Just as the coins encouraged the subjects enough to perform an altruistic act (one that, ideally, they would have performed without the incentive), an administrator's willingness to do the "right thing" may vary with external factors—securing a grant or an argument at home—that make her more or less likely to ascribe to ethical behavior. The Milgram experiments (Chapter 4) also show the importance of situational factors in affecting ethical judgments. Although it is an oversimplification to impugn the character of those who (a) did not help pick up the papers (subject to subtle situational effects) or (b) administered shocks (the influence of authoritative figures), this is nevertheless what often happens because of the fundamental attribution error (i.e., the tendency to attribute events to individuals rather than situations).

Through rigorous analysis, Miguel Alzola (2007) demonstrates that the psychological studies cited by "situationalists" such as Harman are actually inconclusive: Many of the experimental conditions are unrealistic, and the evidence itself is inconsistent with the claim that situational factors determine behavior. Moreover, Alzola suggests that Harman draws the wrong conclusions from the psychological evidence, whether the evidence is accurate or not.

Alzola observes that the key lesson for virtue ethics from experimental psychology "is that human beings are morally weak," especially when confronted with an authority figure, a unanimous group, or an intense situation. He maintains that this pessimistic conclusion presents not just a cognitive weakness, in which the bearings of one's moral compass are lost to situational pressures, but also a motivational weakness. Most of humanity displays the unfortunate tendency, whether consciously or unconsciously, to subordinate the desire to be ethical to competing desires such as self-interest or obedience. Thus, "virtue ethics must account for the experimental evidence, but that does not lead to the abandonment of character and virtue" (354). To the contrary, this evidence that virtue is subverted to self-interest should compel people to strive harder to overcome the natural tendency toward vice that hinders, but does not foreclose, the attainment of a virtuous character.

The debate between Harman (the situationalist) and Alzola (the dispositionist)—as well as the controversy between MacIntyre (a partitionist, who sees a division between competence and virtue) and Macaulay and Lawton (integrationists, who reject the division)—over the contribution of virtue ethics to public administration testifies to the vibrancy of virtue ethics discourse.

CONCLUSION

Former U.S. secretary of HSS and past president of the University of Miami, Donna Shalala's resistance to efforts by others to put politics ahead of policy provides a concrete example of integrity. Anthony Fauci's speaking truth to power during the COVID-19 pandemic is an ethical act because it shows courage, especially when the message contradicts the perspective of the person with power. Integrity and courage are virtuous character traits reflected in the actions of these exemplary public servants. But it is not just the details of an event that are consequential—it is the virtuous life of the whole person over time that will be determinant of ethical evaluations. Ethical decision-making skills, as noted earlier, are nourished by consistently exercising practical wisdom. Aristotle makes the point, "We are what we repeatedly do. Excellence, then, is not an act, but a habit."

Virtue theory is both an alternative and a complement to other decision-making approaches. Unlike cognitive theories, virtue theory provides a more personal lens or basis for evaluating an ethical act by putting intuition and character front and center. Public servants have their character routinely tested, making prudent reflection, high ideals, and virtuous behavior essential to effective public service. While virtue theory does not come with precise instructions for right action, like cognitive theory, it can be helpful by raising questions to be considered when tested by a dilemma or judging the ethics of a decision.

As discussed, virtue theory has its advantages and disadvantages. It is not always clear why certain virtues are good or whether they are good in *all* situations. Anyone who has ever said "Yes, that outfit does make you look fat" has learned honesty is not always the best policy. It is critical to consider why certain virtues are good given the circumstances. In public service, however, honesty is a requirement, often legally, as on tax filings. It is also useful to ponder ways to cultivate virtues. One creative effort to nurture courage, for example, is the Seattle-based Giraffe Project, which has developed a character education curriculum that invites students to become "giraffes" who "stick their necks out for the common good" (Medlock, 2004, 338). This book provides examples of seasoned public servants who have displayed "giraffe-like" traits to advance the public interest. It also offers cases of rather ungiraffe-like employees who ran afoul of conflict-of-interest requirements, succumbed to bribery, deliberately misled citizens and coworkers, and tarnished the image of public service by their actions.

The debates between situationalists and dispositionists, and partitionists and integrationists, raise the question of the role of circumstance and character as well as competence and virtue in public administration. The contention here is that elements of both sides of the arguments are crucial components of a professional. As the Shalala profile shows, "competence and character can feed into each other," providing a useful guide to dealing with thorny moral quandaries and helping ensure a successful professional career as a leader in public service.

***

"I don't know what the best thing to do is" is a common statement, but rarely will someone say, "I don't know what the right thing to do is."[4]

—Laura Schlessinger

NOTES

1. This chapter is adapted from Bowman (2003). Used with permission.
2. Peterson and Seligman (2004) empirically analyzed lists of virtues from cultures around the world to develop a set of character strengths.
3. In an insightful analysis, Kane and Patapan (2006) examine the loss of prudence as a result of the different values embodied by the New Public Management approach to government.
4. The distinction between knowing and doing can be illustrated by former Texas Governor Ann Richards, former Senator George Mitchell, and one-time Reagan White House Chief of Staff and former Senator Howard Baker. In 1997, the tobacco industry hired them to lobby Congress. Each widely known for integrity, Richards (a recovering alcoholic familiar with the problem of addiction), Mitchell (a peace negotiator, could work for life in Ireland and death in America), and Baker (whose sister died of lung cancer) earned huge sums of money for their efforts

supporting an industry they knew to be harmful to the health of Americans. Unlike the elected officials-turned-lobbyists, Reagan's surgeon general, C. Everett Koop, on leaving office in 1989, refused millions of dollars in offers to endorse breakfast cereals and condoms—actions that were at least consistent with good health—because he did not want to erode the impartiality of his office by endorsing commercial products.

DISCUSSION

1. Define virtue theory and evaluate its strengths and weaknesses.

2. In thinking about virtue theory, comment on these statements:

   - "You may find the worst enemy or best friend in yourself."—English aphorism
   - "Thoughts become words, words become actions, actions become character, and character is everything."—Anonymous.
   - "If you have integrity, nothing else matters. If you don't have integrity, nothing else matters."—Alan Simpson
   - "When you look for the good in others, you discover the best in yourself."—Martin Walsh
   - "Courage is required for every other virtue; in your moments of courage, you meet your true self."—Shelly L. Francis
   - "Sometimes the heart sees what is invisible to the eye."—H. Jackson Browne
   - "Virtue is hard to define, but easy to recognize."—Anonymous
   - "You don't realize how important character is in the highest office in the land until you don't have it."—Adam Schiff

3. Discuss these quotations in the context of role morality:

   - "The greatest of minds are capable of the greatest vices as well as the greatest virtues."—Rene Descrates
   - "People are good or half good or a quarter good, and it changes all the time—but even on the best day nobody's perfect."—Colum McCann
   - "Hard times reveal and test character."—Anon.

4. Produce a pithy, provocative proverb or submit an existing one to class discussion.

5. React to these claims:

   (a) "Since virtues are the heart and soul of human existence, they must be cultivated. When people fail to do this, the results of the Milgram shock experiment (Chapter 4) should not be surprising."

   (b) Milgram's and Zimbardo's experiments suggest that character does not matter as otherwise "good" people commit bad acts under certain circumstances.

6. "A leader of a value-intensive organization (especially, a nonprofit) is expected not only to adhere to, but also to create, morality in her unit by example." Examine this statement.

7. Select a well-known elected official and discuss his or her career in light of these insights:

   - "A great man is always willing to be little."—Ralph Waldo Emerson
   - "Integrity has no need for rules."—Albert Camus

- "The quality of one's work is directly related to the quality of a person's character."—Orrin Woodward
- "You don't realize how important character is in the highest office of the land until you don't have it."—Adam Schiff

8. Widely respected Pennsylvania State University football coach Joe Paterno had his contract terminated in the wake of a sex scandal involving one of his assistant coaches (Chapter 2). In a provocative article, "The Devil and Joe Paterno," *New York Times* columnist Ross Douthat (2011) argued that a life of virtue became an excuse for extraordinary vice—good people, by their very goodness, their many duties and accomplishments, may overlook important responsibilities and duties. Discuss.

9. Explain this statement in light of virtue theory: "Learn the rules, so you know how to break them properly."

10. Weiner (2017, December 8) writes:

    Public and private virtue are not identical. Machiavelli showed that what is virtuous for the individual may be vicious in the prince. But that is fundamentally different from saying character does not matter at all or that policies may stand alone, disembodied from the human being who pursues them. Public virtue exists and is separable from the character of the person who exercises it.

    Discuss.

11. Regarding the debate between Harman (the situationalist) and Alzola (the dispositionist) on the contribution of virtue ethics to public administration, as well as the debate between MacIntyre (a partitionist who sees a division between competence and virtue) and Macaulay and Lawton (integrationists who reject the division), which point of view do you find most compelling? Why?

12. John Lennon said,

    - When I was five years old, my mother always told me that happiness was the key to life.
    - When I went to school, they asked me what I wanted to be when I grew up. I wrote down "happy." They told me that I didn't understand the assignment, and I told them that they did not understand life.
    - What would Aristotle say about this contention?

13. It is often indicated that "character is destiny." According to Tom Morris, in an ever-changing world, it is the foundation for dealing with uncertainty and securing success and excellence in what we do best. Do you agree or disagree? Why?

EXERCISES

1. Continue the journal/personal checklist assignment. As Michael Novak (1996, 159) notes, "Ethics . . . calls us to . . . ground ourselves in new habits . . . building our character, building up ourselves." It is never too late to make the most of your journal and checklist.

2. Vivian Buchan (1997) offers ideas about how to develop character:

   - Identify qualities you aspire to and admire in others; think of ways you can emulate those traits.
   - Recognize those qualities in other people and let them know how much you admire them.
   - Analyze and observe the actions of those individuals; let them serve as your guide.
   - Review your actions daily to ascertain if you are developing such qualities.
   - Visualize the virtuous person you want to be every day; if you can see that person, then others will start to see you in that manner too.

   Consider these suggestions in your journal with the goal of developing specific initiatives as part of your ethical effectiveness plan (Chapter 15, Exercise 2).

3. In a similar manner, Jacobs (2015, September 4) suggests that public administrators ask themselves, "do I" or "how to I do"

   - exercise integrity, courage, benevolence, and optimism?
   - maintain honesty and protect against the use of office for personal gain?
   - resist political, organizational, and personal pressures to compromise integrity—and support others subject to such pressures?
   - accept responsibility for my actions?
   - guard against the appearance and reality of conflict of interest?
   - conduct business without partisanship or favoritism?
   - ensure that others get credit for their contributions?

   During the next week, record in your journal answers to as many of these questions as possible.

4. Plagiarized Poem

   - *My daughter shared with me instances in which one of her peers had plagiarized papers and cheated on exams. One afternoon she came home upset because the cheater read aloud a supposedly original poem that my daughter recognized as written by a former student. She quietly pointed out to the cheater that she recognized the work. The student shrugged. I suggested that she photocopy the original poem and give it to the teacher and allow the teacher to reach her own conclusions.*
   - *My daughter's friends independently became aware of the student's behavior and urged my daughter to "rat" on her. It seems unlikely that the friends are willing or able to join together to talk to a teacher. But I really want my daughter to take a stand here.*
   - Young people belong to a world of group norms, and a central one favors loyalty to their peers over the authority of elders. "Ratting out" a peer violates that norm. A member of the group, however, can get away with it if others regard the wrong in question as a serious violation that constitutes betrayal of the group.
   - You want your daughter to take sole responsibility for seeing that this wrong is recognized. Upholding the value of honesty would make sense if she were the only person in a position to do so. But she isn't. A better solution: A group of those who know what's going on should come forward. You doubt that they'll do this. But has anyone asked them?

- I am suggesting this approach because the collective affirmation of honesty would be a better outcome for her peer group. Nothing fixes a value in your mind better than having stood up for it with your friends.
- Condensed and adapted from Appiah, K. (2019, April 2). Should My Daughter Speak Up About a Classmate's Plagiarized Poem? *New York Times Magazine*. Retrieved from www.nytimes.com/2019/04/02/magazine/ethicist-plagiarism-cheating-classmate.html

5. Should I Resign in Protest?

- *I work at a nonprofit that advocates for consumer rights and financial literacy, a mission I have been proud to serve. We recently suffered a financial crisis of our own. Due to changing federal policies, among other factors, we lost a chunk of our annual budget. Management decided to cut about a quarter of the staff to protect our long-term future.*
- *I was of course saddened by what happened, but I understood that there were no good options. Then a staff member who was laid off told me that senior managers' salaries made up nearly a quarter of the budget and that we were paying for a "company car" for our president.*
- *Our leaders sacrificed dozens of direct-service jobs that impact our clients' lives but seemingly not their own relatively large salaries and fringe benefits. I am considering quitting in protest.*
- Your organization is obliged to serve its mission with the resources it can muster. To do so, it needs good staff and good management, which requires it to be mindful of the market rate for people it needs. At the same time, income is just one factor that draws employees; often staff members will work for less when they find the work genuinely rewarding.
- Especially given the mission of your nonprofit, the situation sounds worrisome, and it might indeed have been a good idea to appeal to those at the top to accept cuts in salary in order to reduce the number of frontline employees who were let go.
- Suppose cutting your president's perks or pay would incline her to take a job elsewhere. The cost to your organization of finding a new one might mean that it wasn't worth the risk. A fixed, across-the-board reduction in salary, defined in percentage terms, might simply produce an organization full of disgruntled people. It's conceivable, too, that the core competences of the organization lie in the best-paid people and that the less well paid would be easier to replace if and when funds return.
- The inequality in rewards between top and bottom is ultimately a structural problem that requires structural solutions. Several countries in Europe have chosen to deal with it by having higher taxes and more generous transfers to the less well off than we do, ensuring that their income inequality is much less than ours. If we want to do something about them, resigning in protest from your nonprofit probably isn't the answer.
- Adapted and condensed from Appiah, K. (2018, December 4). Should a nonprofit splurge on management? *New York Times Sunday Magazine*. Retrieved from www.nytimes.com/2018/12/04/magazine/should-a-nonprofit-splurge-on-management.html

REFERENCES

Abeler, J., Becker, A., & Falk, A. (2012). Truth telling: A representative assessment. *Institute for Labor Economics*. Retrieved from http://ftp.iza.org/dp6919.pdf

Alba, M., Welker, K., & Lee, C. (2020, April 25). *Fauci's absence at recent coronavirus briefings draws notice*. Retrieved from www.abcnewscom/politics/white-house/fauci-s-absence-recent-coronavirus-briefings-draws-notice-n1192421

Alzola, M. (2007). Character and environment: The status of virtues in organizations. *Journal of Business Ethics, 78,* 343–357.

Anderson, A. (1996). *Ethics for fundraisers*. Bloomington: University of Indiana Press.

Badaracco, J. L., Jr. (1997). *Defining moments: When managers must choose between right and right*. Boston, MA: Harvard Business School Press.

Bowman, J. (2003). Virtue ethics. In J. Rabin (Ed.), *Encyclopedia of public administration and policy* (pp. 1259–1263). New York: Marcel Dekker.

Bowman, J., West, J., & Beck, M. (2010). *Achieving competencies in public service: The professional edge* (2nd ed.). Armonk, NY: M. E. Sharpe.

Brooks, C. (2020, May 16). Trust isn't simple when it comes to government. *Futurity*. Retrieved from www.futurity.org/political-trust-2064132/

Buchan, V. (1997). *Presentations with confidence* (2nd ed.). Hauppauge, NY: Barron's Educational Series.

Chun, R. (2005). Ethical character and virtue of organizations: An empirical assessment and strategic implications. *Journal of Business Ethics, 57,* 269–284.

CNN. (2020, May 28). *Dr. Anthony Fauci's career under six presidents*. Retrieved from www.cnn.com/2020/04/02/health/gallery/anthony-fauci/index.html

Covey, S. (1991). *Principle-centered leadership*. New York: Summit Books.

Douthat, R. (2011, November 11). The devil and Joe Paterno. *New York Times*. Retrieved from http://newyorktime.com/2011/11/13/opinon/sunday/douthat-the-devel-and-joe-paterno.htm

Downie, J. (2020, July 5). No wonder the Trump administration doesn't want Anthony Fauci on TV. *Washington Post*. Retrieved from www.washingtonpost.com/opinions/2020/07/05/no-wonder-trump-administration-doesnt-want-anthony-fauci-tv/

Durant, W. (1991). *The story of philosophy: The lives and opinions of the world's greatest philosophers*. New York: Simon & Schuster/Pocket Books. [Original work published 1926]

Franz, R. (1998). Don't treat students like customers. *Journal of Management Education, 22,* 63–69.

Gastel, B. (2020). 10 reasons why Anthony Fauci was ready to be the face of the US pandemic response. *The Conversation*. Retrieved from the conversation.com/10-reasons-why-anthony-fauci-was-ready-to-be-the-face-of-the-us-pandemic-response-150596

Harman, G. (2003). No character or personality. *Business Ethics Quarterly, 13,* 87–94.

Isen, A. M., & Levin, P. F. (1972). Effect of feeling good on helping: Cookies and kindness. *Journal of Personality and Social Psychology, 21,* 384–388.

Jacobs, R. (2015, September 4). Leading by doing: Conducting a personal ethics audit. *PA Times*. Retrieved from http://patimes.org/leading-doing-conducting-personal-ethics-audit/

Kane, J., & Patapan, H. (2006). In search of prudence: The hidden problem of managerial reform. *Public Administration Review, 66,* 711–724.

Kaplan, J. (2020, April 27). Will working at home make us more ethical? *Ethical Systems*. Retrieved from www.ethicalsystems.org/will-working-at-home-make-us-more-ethical/

Kiley, R. (2020, July). Stories of Dr Fauci's leadership and legacy circulate as White House Continues attempt to discredit him. *God.Dailydot.com*. Retrieved from https://god.dailydot.com/brave-dr-fauci/

Leibovich, M. (2020, July 17). Treacherous times for Dr. Fauci in the SacredCow Business. *The New York Times*. Retrieved from www.nytimes.com/2020/07/17/us/fauci-trump.html

Macaulay, M., & Lawton, A. (2006). From virtue to competence: Changing the principles of public service. *Public Administration Review, 66*, 702–710.

MacIntyre, A. (1985). *After virtue: A study in moral theory*. London: Duckworth.

Mazza, E. (2020, July 16). What leadership looks like: Old Fauci pic resurfaces amid White House attacks. *Huffpost*. Retrieved from www.huffpost.com/entry/anthony-fauci-ebola-suitleadership_n_5f0fdce6c5b6d14c3362dc4c

McLeod, J. (2020, April 9). 5 Communication lessons from Dr. Anthony Fauci. *PRdaily*. Retrieved from www.prdaily.com/5-communication-lessons-from-dranthony-fauci/

Medlock, A. (2004). The courage to stick your neck out. In M. Josephson & W. Hanson (Eds.), *The power of character* (pp. 336–346, 2nd ed.). San Francisco: Jossey-Bass.

Meehan, W. (2020, April 30). Anthony S. Fauci, M.D. Part III: The 7 principles of Faucian leadership. *Forbes*. Retrieved from www.forbes.com/sites/williammeehan/2020/04/30/anthony-s-fauci-md-part-iii-the-7-principles-of-faucian-leadership/#704e8d29313d

Novak, M. (1996). *Business as a calling: Work and the examined life*. New York: Free Press.

Panetta, G. (2020, May 26). *Dr. Anthony Fauci and Gov. Andrew Cuomo are the most trusted leaders in America on the coronavirus right now. Trump is not*. Retrieved from www.businessinsider.com/americans-most-trust-fauci-cuomo-on-coronavirus-response-insider-poll-2020-3

Papenfuss, M. (2021, February 16). Dr. Anthony Fauci wins $1 million prize for 'speaking truth to power' on COVID-19. *Huffington Post*. Retrieved from https://www.huffpost.com/entry/dan-david-prize-anthony-fauci_n_602b59bec5b6741597e44980?ncid=engmodushpmg00000006

Peterson, C., & Seligman, M. (2004). *Character strengths and virtues: A handbook and classification*. Washington, DC: American Psychological Association.

Preston, N. (2001). *Understanding ethics* (2nd ed.). Leichhardt: Federation Press.

Rion, M. (1996). *The responsible manager: Practical strategies for ethical decision making*. West Harford, CT: Resources for Ethics and Management.

Shalala, D. (2004). Managing large organizations with honesty and integrity. *Public Integrity, 6*, 349–356.

Smith, V. K. (2020, April 4). 5 Reasons Gov. Cuomo and Dr. Fauci are America's de facto leaders during the coronavirus pandemic. *MarketWatch*. Retrieved from www.marketwatch.com/story/5-reasons-gov-cuomo-and-dr-fauci-areamericas-de-facto-leaders-during-the-coronavirus-pandemic-2020–03–30

Vazquez, M. (2020, March 14). *How Dr. Anthony Fauci became Trump's coronavirus truth teller*. Retrieved from https://www.cnn.com/2020/03/14/politics/anthony-fauci-trump-coronavirus/index.html

Weiner, G. (2017, December 8). The scoundrel theory of American politics. *New York Times*. Retrieved from https://nyt.com/.../roy-moore-scoundrel-politics-theory-politics.html

West, J. P., & Berman, E. M. (2011). The impact of management work habits on public sector performance: A study of local government managers. *Public Personnel Management, 40*, 63–86.

Westergaard, N. (2020, April 19). What Dr. Fauci can teach you about leadership communication. *Nickwestergaard*. Retrieved from www.nickwestergaard.com/what-dr-fauci-can-teach-you-aboutleadership-communication/

7 Conscious Deliberation and Subconscious Action

The Dishonesty of Honest People

Some folks are wise, and some are otherwise.

—T. Smollett

Consider this statement: Managers should be virtuous, but not only virtuous. If philosophers cannot agree on competing models, then why should managers? The reason is that professionals must be able to defend their decisions—they are obligated to develop virtues, predict results, and adhere to rules. Unless a course of action can be justified on ethical grounds, it is not a responsible act. As a "knowledge worker" in today's economy, the duty of a professional is to provide her best thinking. While a good sense of right and wrong may be necessary, it is hardly sufficient in ethical decision-making—a process that can be complex and complicated. If judgments are to be intentional and rational, then the procedure by which they are made must be more systematic.

There is little doubt that the use of various decision-making models can considerably enhance ethical discernment.[1] These approaches typically focus on step-by-step techniques, stages in decision-making, or sets of principles (see Chapter 5). In so doing, the ethical dimensions of an issue can be explored and potential solutions identified. The seductiveness of such tools is evident—their use is superior to rigid rules, self-interest, and sheer opportunism. Indeed, this chapter employs one of these techniques, an ethics triad, to examine a case. Accordingly, the discussion encourages readers to embrace the complementarity and interdependence of both cognitive and virtue ethics. In so doing, it emphasizes that cognition without virtue is as insufficient as virtue without cognition. No single perspective is adequate, and no perspective should be neglected.

DOI: 10.4324/9781003203148-9

This same approach, however, is not without significant limitations. Philosophical ethics explains how rational people should act at the expense of how real human beings actually behave. Implicit in the traditional philosophical approach is the assumption that people will recognize ethical dilemmas and know how they should then act. Yet, if the goal of decision theory is to predict conduct, it is not always useful to ask people, or offer prescriptions about, what they might do. Instead, behavioral ethics, drawing from psychology, is less interested in prescriptions and more focused on descriptions of how individuals really act. With that knowledge, researchers will be better positioned to suggest ways to encourage ethical conduct.

This chapter, then, (1) consolidates the three individual-centered approaches to ethics into a tripartite framework and (2) examines the findings in the field of behavioral ethics, with its focus on human conduct. Its objectives are to

- understand that ethics requires not just the rectitude to refuse wrongdoing, but the resourcefulness to create a worthy alternative,
- analyze the strengths and weaknesses of the triad strategy and apply it to cases, and
- examine the behavioral ethics approach to understanding how people act.

The discussion begins by describing a comprehensive tool that encompasses results-based utilitarian ethics, rule-based duty ethics, and virtue-based character ethics. The technique is applied to a case to demonstrate its decision-making utility. A corresponding set of insights from behavioral ethics is then used to suggest that such models are problematic. The discussion and conclusion explore the implications of the findings derived from decision scientists.

RESULTS, RULE, RECTITUDE: DECISION-MAKING WITH THE ETHICS TRIAD

While various frameworks shed light on how ethical issues might be considered, one is particularly helpful because its broad scope reduces the chances of an incomplete—and therefore potentially flawed—decision.[2] This tool, the ethics triad, triumvirate, or "triangle" (Svara, 1997, 2007), recognizes the value and utility of the imperatives in three schools of thought based on

- results of an action (consequentialism or teleology),
- pertinent rules (duty ethics or deontology), and
- personal rectitude, integrity, or character (virtue ethics).

When considering results in decision-making, the question is, "Which policy produces the greatest good for the greatest number?" (e.g., "Would I want my decision to be in the newspapers tomorrow?"). In contemplating rules, the issue is, "Would I want everyone else to make the same decision that I did?" (e.g., "What is good for one is good for all."). From the virtue ethics vantage point, one might ask, "What would a person of integrity do?" (e.g., seek the "golden mean" between the extremes of excess and deficiency). Although the synthesis developed from the analysis may not provide definitive solutions to an ethical dilemma, it offers guidance by teasing out the underlying logic by which decisions are justified. Importantly, an overreaching application of a single perspective, at the expense of the others, holds considerable dangers—expediency (results-based ethics), rigid rule application (rule-based ethics), and self-justification (virtue-based ethics). In light of the shortcomings of the individual vantage points, it is evident that this amalgamated technique can be helpful.

UTILIZING THE ETHICS TRIAD

Professionals should consider results, respect rules, and develop virtues to justify their decisions. Indeed, each philosophy represented in the trinity is attractive to policymakers:

- The results-based approach is useful for administrators seeking the common good for the majority of citizens.
- A rule-based strategy is appealing to managers obligated to follow the principles found in the Constitution, court cases, and laws and regulations.
- Virtue-based ethics is compelling for officials because it is a personal approach informed by one's character that nurtures individual and collective well-being.

Because credible arguments can be developed in support of each philosophy, deliberations stimulated by the ethics triad could provoke moral imagination in searching for a solution.

The triad is especially helpful in examining issues wherein there is no clear sense of right and wrong. Public administrators may want to be good at what they do but may not know how. Sincere intent and simple conviction are not enough. They may not recognize ethical concerns or be able to articulate what is at stake in ethical terms. Whatever the situation might be, the strategy demands that it be examined in three different ways by using formal, abstract thinking to advance understanding of results, rules, and rectitude. It is not, however, a definitive tool; rather, it is a means to assess a policy from distinctive vantage points—impact (results), conduct (duty), and effort (virtue). Given the human genius for rationalization, a certain humility is necessary when employing the technique.

Note that each of the three components of the triumvirate does not necessarily attempt to argue what actions should be moral but rather describes the underlying logic by which decisions are justified. Decisions are distinguished from one another based on the premises from which they are made. A better understanding of how judgments are made can produce ethically acceptable choices.

Each component of the tool provides a distinctive filter to reveal different aspects that clarify and reframe a situation. However, unduly emphasizing one component above others spells trouble. Full examination of all three viewpoints helps prevent the shortcomings of each one, since each acts as a limit on the others. Thus, the three perspectives may reinforce and inform one another. When they do not, the decision should be guided by benevolence and the admonition "do no harm" (see also May, 2019). The policymaker should exercise moral imagination and promote the public interest using an ethic of compromise and social integration—a moral tenet of democracy. However, do not assume there is some "objective reality" on which everyone agrees and a set of evaluation criteria that all use. It is an imperfect world where no one gets all that one wants.

Encountering ethical issues—in both appearance and reality—is part of being a public servant.[3] To take a simple example of how the triad can be used, consider whether or not to run a red stop light when driving. From the results viewpoint, "the greatest good for the greatest number" is almost always achieved by not doing so (the ill consequences of not stopping are hard to justify in the short and long run). Using a rules interpretation, the duty to honor an ethical law is also the right thing to do. To justify ignoring the rule would imply it is acceptable for everyone to run a red light ("what is good for one is good for all"), a behavior difficult to defend. When an organizational policy or societal law conflicts with a universal ethical rule, the ethical rule predominates. Under virtue ethics—the third member of the trinity—excellence in individual and community character may be nourished by avoiding reckless driving (knowingly endangering one's self and others usually does not build good character).

Recognize that while the red light scenario is an elementary example, the findings do not suggest that running the light is never justified (Aristotle's "practical wisdom" could be carefully employed in specific circumstances; see Chapter 6). Ethics demands consideration of the social context, directing empathy with other people to ask, "What circumstances would account for his behavior?" Try the same three-part analysis for going considerably over—or under—the speed limit (e.g., for virtue ethics, to nurture character would be to avoid extremes of too fast or too slow driving).

Complex issues can be analyzed using the triad as well, producing more interesting—and often conflicting—findings. Unlike the stop light scenario, examining each school of thought in the approach may advise a different course of action (Case Studies 7.1 and 7.2). In such circumstances, the policymaker at least has the satisfaction that the problem has been fully examined, balance has been sought, and the decision can be rationally defended.[4] He or she self-consciously weighed consequences, is familiar with ethical rules, and has considered what a virtuous person would do. Tough judgments, thereby, become easier (but not easy) than they might otherwise be. There are situations where "right-reason/wrong-action" and "wrong-reason/right-action" choices occur; using the triad may enhance the chances that "right-reason/right-action" decisions are made (see Case Studies 7.1 and 7.2).

CASE STUDY 7.1

The Ethics Triad: Applying the Rational Approach to a Birthday Invitation

Consider this case, a reprise from one in Chapter 5.

Mark and Frank Jordan have been close friends for years. They went to high school together and were college classmates. Each was the best man at the other's wedding. Their wives are good friends. For the past ten years, Frank and his wife have taken Mark and his wife to dinner on Mark's birthday. It is something he insists on doing and has become something of a tradition. Frank can well afford it—he owns the largest plumbing supply business in the state and does more than $1,000,000 in business each year with the city.

Mark was recently hired as an aide to a councilman who chairs the committee that oversees procurement contracts, including plumbing supplies. His birthday is coming up in a couple of weeks. Frank has called to remind Mark that he and Mrs. Jordan have a special treat for his birthday dinner this year. Frank has made reservations at a fancy new restaurant that everyone is talking about. Does Mark accept?

Results-Based Analysis. Thinking about the results part of the ethics triad, what is the greatest good for the greatest number? On the one hand, the most happiness and the least amount of harm may be achieved by accepting the invitation. After all, most people do not trade their integrity for gifts. There is no valid reason to avoid the party; indeed, the friendship may be put at risk if the invitation is declined—Frank may be insulted.

On the other hand, the greatest good could also be achieved by preventing erosion of public trust in governmental decision-making. A key utilitarian guideline is "Would I feel comfortable if my action were on the front page tomorrow?" Clearly. the greatest good extends well beyond personal acquaintances. Most individuals do not impugn their honor for gifts.

But while the premise may be correct, the conclusion does not follow. As Paul Brest (2012, 490) suggests, "[W]e tend to accede to requests from people who have done favors for us—even when the favors were uninvited and trivial and the subsequent requests substantial." Thus, the counterargument takes the form of a challenge: Name one good reason why an official should accept a gift presenting a conflict of interest. Corruption demands nothing as vulgar as a quid pro quo, because "business courtesies" introduce the potential for favoritism.

Bribery is not the point. The value of dinner is not enough to sway a favor. Rather, the dinner secures access to the recipient and influence. Wariness of inducements includes an understanding that individual presents can give rise to institutional corruption—the creation of a system that fosters decisions based not on the substance of issues but on favoritism (see also Chapter 9).

Rule-Based Analysis. From the rules ethics angle, Mark asks, "Would I want everyone else to make the same decision that I did?" Rules ethics dictates Mark's duty in this case is to cultivate friendship, something Aristotle believed should be universal practice in human relations to encourage ethical behavior. Rigidly applying rules when they are not germane is overreaching. So long as existing laws are followed, there is no basis for rejecting the invitation. Yet it is not clear that it would be acceptable if every civil servant routinely accepted such arrangements. One's responsibility as a public official is to help nurture citizen confidence in government. Participating in activities that arguably raise suspicions about decision-making should not be a common practice.

Virtue-Based Analysis. From the virtue ethics vantage point, Mark asks, "What would a person of integrity do?" In this system, each person must continuously fortify his character and the character of the polity. By going to the dinner, deep friendships are maintained and enhanced. This helps nourish individual character and the strength of community ties. Turning down the invitation demonstrates pointless self-righteousness. Yet because it is not reasonable to expect citizens to delve into the particulars of specific cases, Mark should not attend. Taxpayers, after all, are more likely to be concerned that government employees use public monies effectively than whether they have friends. Thoughtlessly accepting the invitation—and ignoring other viewpoints—is simply expedient, hardly an ethical standard of decision-making.

Summary. This case is based on a scenario presented to attendees at an ICMA convention in the early 1980s. There was no consensus among conferees, as they split almost evenly on whether or not to attend the party. ICMA's answer, in advising its membership on how to deal with the situation, does not directly allude to results, rules, or virtues. It does, however, indicate that "yes" the manager should go based on the following reasoning:

> Public service does not require that you give up previous acquaintances and friendships. What is required is that at any point in the future in which your friend's business is involved, i.e., contract negotiations, you disqualify yourself from influencing the decision in any way. If you decide not to go with Frank, you are still ethical, but probably overzealous.
>
> ("Ethics," 1982, p.122)

By interpolation, the association does not think that everyone should attend the dinner, because it does not automatically serve the greatest good and it would be unwise to universalize such practice. Also, and more directly, the case reveals sensitivity to the virtue of care and friendship. The golden mean would be to find a prudent course of action that lies between extremes of blissfully accepting and self-righteously rejecting the invitation—that is, Mark could pay his own way or recuse himself from any future committee actions involving Frank's business. A true friend would, after listening to Mark explain his new role in government, understand the situation and not take the decision personally.

CASE STUDY 7.2

Reopening Schools: A Nurse's Decision to Quit

For the past four years, I worked as a school nurse in Georgia. I loved my job: My days were spent helping kids with special needs, kids who had seizures several times a day, or kids who needed help with medications or tube feedings. I made my clinic a place where students and staff felt safe. I knew that the shutdowns were necessary to stop the coronavirus, but they still made my heart ache for the kids who got at school the regular meals and affection they didn't get at home.

But as the school board finalized its reopening plan, it seemed obvious that leadership wasn't taking the pandemic seriously. When I read the instructions for faculty and staff, I knew I couldn't carry them out and sleep well at night. They make no sense—and won't keep people safe. I quit.

Of course, I was afraid of catching the coronavirus but my bigger fear was that I'd unknowingly spread it to students and their families, or to my colleagues. I refuse to be complicit in endangering the health or the life of a child. I refuse to act as a prop, making people feel secure when, in reality, we're putting their health at risk.

The district makes no provision to check temperatures and mask-wearing is optional. From personal experience. I know that when a child feels under the weather, it's tempting to give them a fever-reducer and send them to school anyway. That instinct will be catastrophic in a community where many people have been vocally skeptical about the severity or even the existence of the pandemic. Our county's case count had been rising. It seems inevitable that someone will come to school carrying the virus and we'll have an outbreak.

In the past, our schools have found it challenging to contain outbreaks of lice, scabies or fifth disease, and the coronavirus is much more serious. It's also difficult to detect: Its symptoms can easily be mistaken for those of many common childhood illnesses. But even if every family swore to be vigilant, young children often don't speak up about not feeling well. If and when a child complains, they don't always know how to describe their symptoms.

Our schools do have a plan if a teacher spots a potential COVID-19 case. We nurses would split our clinics into a "well" side and a "sick" side. The student would be sent to the "sick" side, and, if their symptoms were confirmed, they would be isolated until their parent could pick them up. (T)his isn't workable. At my school, serving over 1,300 students, there's only me. I'd be passing back and forth among "sick" and "well" and "isolation" constantly, and I wouldn't have time for following elaborate hygiene routines or putting on and removing protective equipment. (That is, if we even have the budget for gowns, gloves and masks; the district said it would provide us each with only a plastic face shield.)

On a typical day before the pandemic, I might be wrapping up a possible wrist fracture when a teacher comes running in with a student who's bleeding and needs a compress immediately.

There's no way I could safely tend to these kinds of emergencies and to possible coronavirus cases in what's essentially a shared space—yet my colleagues and I were expected to be the school's first line of defense should someone fall ill.

The district also decided that the nursing staff would act as ad hoc contact tracers. We keep flu logs every year, and for the upcoming year, they told us to note everyone with COVID-19, what spaces they were in and whom they were with. Our supervisors would then send out the appropriate notifications. Paperwork comes with the job, and I was perfectly willing to do any work that would actually help, but this made no sense. Adults have a hard enough time remembering the details of the past 14 days; try interrogating a kid about all the places they've been and people they've seen.

These new procedures don't seem to be designed to stop viral spread and promote public health. They seem like products of magical thinking. Now that the county's schools have been open for a couple of weeks, it's become even more obvious that the district is more concerned about the appearance of safety than with actual safety. Two high-schoolers posted photos and videos of their crowded hallways online and were initially suspended; then, after nine people later tested positive for the virus, the school decided to shut down its building for a week. An hour away, in Cherokee County, schools had to close within days of reopening after a second-grader tested positive. The same story has been playing out in Indiana, Mississippi, and Louisiana.

Schools and families want badly to resume normal, stable routines. But without the virus under control, and lacking any support from the government so people can stay home, we're left to muddle through the chaos.

Using the format in Case Study 7.1, analyze the nurse's decision using the ethics triad. For more on the ethics and disasters (e.g., pandemics, plane crashes, hurricanes) using the triad, see Zach (2009). It is also employed in assessing how to respond to cyberattacks (Shackelford & Wade, 2021).

Source: Condensed from Westmoreland (2020, August 14). A physician's perspective on serving during a pandemic can be found at Jauhar (2020, April 2). For a discussion of the lack of nurses in many schools, and for those that have them only 40 percent meet CDC guidelines of one nurse per 750 students, refer to Sorg (2020, August 25).

The triad approach discussed here cannot produce a final, perfect decision for all seasons. Instead, it attempts to reconcile conflicting values and highlights a key function of decision-making: generating alternative viewpoints, systemically evaluating them, and crafting a considered judgment. The technique enables the management of ethical ambiguity and provides help in making the inevitable compromises. This eclectic, pluralistic method to adjudicate difficult ethical issues can be demanding, as it requires considerable discernment. Be it results, rule, or rectitude, it is challenging to live up to their standards. However cogent abstract theories of right and wrong may be, they can fail as practical guides to decision-making between what is desirable and possible under concrete circumstances of time and place. Yet in light of the limitations of each part of the triad, there is little option given the complexity of the human condition. The approach enables the user to learn to be ethical by developing well-rounded and well-grounded decisions.

Lessons from cases like those discussed here include an understanding that the manager is a moral agent responsible for her actions, doing right things is likely to be interpreted differently by others, appearances matter, ethical awareness may be accompanied by self-delusion, exemplary behavior is important, and ethics means engagement. The implications of these lessons include the need to have knowledge of ethical principles and codes, respect the rule of law, serve the public interest, and use ethical reasoning tools (Menzel, 2010, 225–231).

BEHAVIORAL ETHICS

What people do versus what they say they do are entirely different things.

—Margaret Mead

While rational decision-making models are certainly valuable, a relatively new school of thought—behavioral ethics—identifies significant shortcomings. One key criticism is the frequent failure to delineate a relationship between moral theorizing and ethical action. As Gazzaniga (2008, 148) observes, "It has been hard to find any correlation between moral reasoning and proactive moral behavior. In fact, in most studies, none has been found." Similarly, Haidt (2001, 817) contends that "moral reasoning is rarely the direct cause of moral judgment." This suggests that other factors—unconscious biases, moral emotions, personal intuitions—are likely to affect what one does (Shao, Aquino, & Freeman, 2008; see also Chapter 4). As Elder Shafir (2012, 2) observes, "People do not respond to objective experience; rather, stimuli are mentally construed, interpreted, and understood or misunderstood." Stated differently, behavioral findings offer an alternative view of the individual as a moral agent by demystifying the idea of classical rationality.

Behavioral ethics draws on work in psychology and focuses on the actual conduct of the individual. By examining psychological tendencies to explain human actions, this school of thought attempts to apply ethics to the real world. Not only does the rational model place considerable cognitive demands on people, it also devalues unconscious, emotional, and tacit elements in making judgments, elements that can subsume—or even be the basis of—reason. Moral claims motivate in ways that factual claims do not; factoring emotions into judgments explains much about them. The traditional approach is incomplete because it "fails to acknowledge our innate psychological responses when faced with ethical dilemmas" (Bazerman & Tenbrunsel, 2011, 4). Both the potency of passion and the limits of reason tend to be overlooked. We are not as good as we think we are, and we are apt to act unethically without being consciously aware of such behavior (Banaji, Bazerman, & Chugh, 2003; Bazerman & Banaji, 2004), as the Milgram and Zimbardo experiments demonstrated (Chapter 4). Further, people tend to overestimate how ethical they are and can fall into behavioral blind spots as a result.

This section identifies key propositions from behavioral ethics research.[5] Together, they highlight the underlying psychology behind unethical conduct, actions that may be unintentional and based on inadequate information, improper application of ethical principles, or lack of awareness of the moral dimension of problems. While these ideas are not necessarily new, what is new is the growing evidence that individual conduct is less under conscious control than believed. Even decisions that are conscious are affected by nonconscious factors in unknown ways (see Kahneman, Sibony, & Sunstein, 2021 on how judgements are affected by "noise"). For instance, behavioral ethics helps explain why judges give out more lenient sentences after lunch, why people feel more politically conservative when bottles of hand sanitizer are available, and why employees who have photos of their family on their desks are less likely to misbehave (Parramore, 2020, February 11; Miller-Washington, 2020, August 21). Instead of supposing people are rational, behavioral ethics investigates whether or not they act rationally in experimental or actual situations. The data suggest that humans are far less rational than assumed.[6]

Rather than "Star Trek's" hyper-rational Mr. Spock, they can be more like "The Simpsons' " emotional and prejudiced Homer (Ariely, 2008; Bazerman & Tenbrunsel, 2011; Brooks, 2011). Feelings, intuition, and perception are at least as significant in affecting behavior as logic, rationality, and calculation. Indeed, emotion can be the foundation of reason. Modern neuroscience suggests that people process information automatically and emotionally without reflection or even awareness—which leads them to misinterpret or dismiss objective evidence. The mind tends to refuse to engage the prefrontal cortex, the part of the brain needed to make sense of unfamiliar ideas (Ropeik, 2012, September 30, p. 12).

Emotions, then, discolor what people otherwise see as their dispassionate, logical views. Reasoning is confused with rationalization. This does not mean that people are uninterested in accurate perception but rather that there are objectives other than accuracy (Mooney, 2011). Humans prefer to believe that they are like judges, conscientiously deliberating over the issues and arriving at reasoned conclusions after examining all the evidence. Instead, people are more like lawyers, looking for anything that might help make their case (Seawright, 2013).

The field of behavioral economics employs controlled laboratory and field experiments in cognitive science, social psychology, and neuroimaging, and these have repeatedly shown how policymakers, average citizens, and students can be wrong about their motivations, justifications for their beliefs, and the accuracy of their memories. The choices they make may be unconscious because the brain is set on automatic pilot: Most of the stimuli it receives is processed instinctively, as a mere fraction of that information makes it into consciousness. This makes brains efficient (not everything need be attended to at once), but the effect is that judgments are made based on information of which there is not full awareness (Bennett, 2014, November 5).

Investigators have developed a set of complementary principles that help explain decision-making. The resulting insights into systematic errors found in concealed biases, brain quirks, and behavioral traps highlight the underlying science behind dishonorable acts. Actions may be unintentional and based on inadequate knowledge, involve improper application of moral tenets, and/or simply miss the ethical dimension of issues. Just as people are tricked by visual illusions, they are fooled by illusions about how they make choices. The problem is that most individuals are often not rational actors (Ariely, 2008); they are fallible, normal human beings.

Pervasive and overlapping behavioral science claims are examined later. Primarily descriptive, rather than normative, the propositions show how cognitive heuristics, psychological tendencies, social and organizational pressures, and seemingly irrelevant situational factors can account for the dishonesty of otherwise honest people. These ubiquitous phenomena have serious consequences as they distort knowledge, corrupt public discourse, and conceal solutions to problems. The question may not be so much whether a decision maker is moral but rather in what circumstances and to what degree (review role morality discussed in Chapter 6). It is not only a matter of knowing what is right but also about thinking of the meaning and relevance of rectitude in a given situation (Kaptein, 2013). Ethical issues are often embedded in decisions that appear to lack moral ramifications. Due to space limitations, the list of comparable behavioral science focal points that follows is simply illustrative of some of the most compelling ones (see Samson, 2017 for a fuller discussion). These include (1) principles (bounded rationality/ethicality, System 1/System 2 thinking, motivated reasoning, and a set of biases), (2) monitoring and sanctions, (3) organizational context, and (4) debiasing techniques.

PRINCIPLES

Bounded Rationality/Bounded Ethicality

Bounded rationality, a term coined by Herbert Simon, describes a "behavioral model [in which] human rationality is very limited, very much bounded by the situation and by homo sapien computational powers" (1983, 34). The idea that if people just had information they would make the logical choice is simply incorrect. Individuals often do not have complete and accurate information, and, even if they did, they have a less-than-perfect capacity for information processing to reach an optimal choice. Ethicality can be bounded by human cognitive processes. Such sub-optimization overlooks significant facts, omits stakeholders, or gives insufficient attention to long-term consequences.

Decision-maker rationality also may be affected by self-interest, false assumptions, subliminal inclinations, innate responses to ethical circumstances, and failures in problem definition (Bazerman & Chugh, 2006). People can be blind to the obvious and blind to their blindness (Bazerman & Tenbrunsel, 2011; Kahneman, 2011). Bounded ethicality results in virtuous men and women making questionable decisions. The pressures and demands facing managers, for example, can cause them to depend on habit, instead of deliberation (Chugh, 2004), leading to a related principle: fast and slow thinking.

System 1/System 2 Thinking

System 1 is a rapid, intuitive way to process information and yields an instinctive response, or gut reaction, which can be a useful guide for many decisions. Indeed, Hoomans (2015, March 20) reports that adults make an incredible 35,000 conscious and nonconscious choices every day. In most situations there is just not enough time for another approach. System 1 is an effortless, decision-without-thought default process for arriving at routine judgments in a quick, visceral, and easy way.[7] Generally, the fast system is efficient and good enough—the immediate, obvious answer feels right—but it is also prone to prejudice and error. System 2 is a slow paced, thoughtful strategy that weighs the merits and demerits of an issue. Judgments made under stress might rely on System 1 when System 2 is warranted, because the linkages from emotional brain circuits to cognitive brain components are stronger than those from cognitive circuits to emotional systems. As Harvard's David Ropeik observes, the "architecture of the brain ensures that we feel first and think second" (2012, September 30, p. 12).

Haidt (2001) finds that intuitions like hunches are the primary source of moral judgments, as rational arguments are commonly used post hoc to justify determinations. And compromising those moral positions, unlike "split-the-difference" economic issues, is often unimaginable. Moreover, detecting error does not necessarily lead to change: The slow system's reasoning ability, in fact, may be invoked to generate rationalizations for decisions already made. Initial views are also strengthened by "confirmation bias," as people focus on data that reinforce their preexisting opinions. Political scientist Emily Thorson (2016, January 8) points out that these "belief echoes" persist even when misinformation is corrected. Individuals have a built-in tendency to expect and see what they want to expect and see, so that fact-checkers with their unwelcome facts are perceived as prejudiced. Falsehoods like the pandemic is a "hoax," masks are ineffective, tax cuts increase public revenue, estate taxes are a "death tax," widespread voter fraud exists, Obama is a Muslim and/or is not a citizen, Iraq–Al Qaeda collaborated on 9/11, and denial of global warming exemplify how System 1 thinking interacts with "motivated reasoning," a related supposition.

Motivated Reasoning

Facts mean little if someone ascribes to a belief different from what the facts dictate. Motivated reasoning indicates that individuals are psychologically geared to maintain their existing evaluations, independent of facts (Redlawsk, Civettini, & Emmerson, 2010). Opinions are based on beliefs. People feel what they think, as "emotion assigns value to things and reason can only make choices on the basis of those valuations" (Brooks, 2011, 21). As they become more informed, such viewpoints—despite their utter implausibility—make them more likely to be wrong, resulting in a kind of invincible ignorance. No amount of evidence will change the belief held by some citizens that the 2020 presidential election was stolen.

This "smart idiot effect" explains why corrections to false information have a "backfire effect": When presented with documented facts, some people become *less* likely to believe them (Mooney, 2012; Mercier & Sperber, 2017; Sloman & Fernbach, 2017). Thus, if something or someone is disliked by the "true believer," contradictory information can be discounted to the point that the object of dislike will be loathed as much or more than before. When faith meets evidence, evidence does not have a chance.

The use of this defense mechanism is psychologically easier than to change beliefs and admit error. Once something is accepted as true, it is difficult to falsify the belief. If confidence is lost in society's institutions and its experts, then that may explain why many Americans are not affected by facts. This repudiation dangerously undermines the very idea of objective reality should truth and reality become nothing more than what one happens to believe. The illogical denial of real existence, for example, puts both unvaccinated children and the community at risk. Motivated reasoning, like many behavioral principles, operates at the subconscious level. Sincere claims can be made that one is not influenced by prejudice, even though their "unbiased opinion" [*sic*] is self-serving—a process facilitated by decision framing.

Framing Effects

How issues are cast impact how people react to them (Kern & Chugh, 2009).[8] Many workplace decisions, for instance, have both a business and an ethical dimension, and people often do not recognize when they are making an ethical decision (Roddel, 2019, November 21). If the situation is seen as a business matter, it could lead to "ethical fading" and allow the emotional, impulsive "want" self to be dominant—especially since people tend to accept the frame that is provided. Improper behavior may occur instinctively without deliberation, as moral concerns are set aside in pursuit of other goals like efficiency. Tenbrunsel and Messick (2004, 22) use the term "ethical cleansing" to describe how individuals "unconsciously transform ethical decisions into ones that are ethically clean."

Further, "want" choices are made in the present, while "should" choices take place before and after the decision. Ironically, this "want–should theory" separation of the two selves—

paralleling fast and slow thinking—can allow people to believe they are more virtuous than is actually the case. There is also a tendency to choose and then engage in faded, faux moral reasoning to justify the determination. Because human beings value morality, they are motivated to forget the details of their unjust actions in a kind of "ethical amnesia." In contrast, when the situation is interpreted primarily in ethical terms, the thoughtful, deliberative "should" self emerges, and fading and cleansing would not occur. Recognizing both the business side and the ethical side of judgments is crucial, then, if one seeks to do things right and do right things. In short, how a problem is framed affects susceptibility to the effects already noted as well as those discussed next.

Bias and Decision-Making Errors

In considering additional cognitive distortions, mental short cuts, and unconscious presumptions, it is important to recognize that the brain interprets all experiences based on its model of the world. People hold certain beliefs because they fit the sense they have made of their environment. As already seen, this process can be inaccurate—and convincing—in part, because of unacknowledged competing emotions and conflicting intuitions. Subliminal predispositions, described later, materialize in differing circumstances, appear in many guises, interact in pernicious ways to impair judgment, and are not readily susceptible to reasoned debate and negotiation.

First, "status quo bias" takes place when someone is faced with choices, and the default option operates (deciding not to decide) to live in the moment. This occurs (a) by taking the path of least resistance ("effort aversion"), (b) by valuing what one has ("present preference") because she owns it ("endowment effect" or "loss aversion"), and (c) by staying the course, the person can hope to capitalize on "sunk costs" (Schmidt, 2016). It would be a serious error to underestimate the difficulty in changing lifetime habits: The 600,000 patients who have heart bypasses each year are told their lifestyle (diet, exercise, smoking) must change because surgery is a temporary fix. Change or die? The answer is not a question of awareness or knowledge. Instead, the reaction is the "deaf effect": Over 90 percent of patients choose death, as immediate pleasures override long-term survival (Rainer & Geiger, 2011; see also Cotteleer & Murphy, 2015). It can be even more difficult to make changes for the health of others, the basis of the field of public health, which helps explain resistance to mask-wearing. Applied to management of organizational change, employees who are likely losers will fight a lot harder against reforms than potential winners, due to loss aversion. Cognitive rigidity (the "competency trap") disables the capacity to deal effectively with new ideas.

Second, "preference falsification" happens when someone suppresses what they think to agree with what others think—"private truths, but public lies" (Kuran, 1997). This phenomenon may prop up social stability; however, when norms erode, otherwise puzzling events occur, such as the widespread surprise endorsement of gay marriage, abrupt condemnation of the Confederate battle flag and monuments, protests to defund police departments, and unexpected enthusiasm for nativism in recent years.

Third, "overconfidence bias" assumes comprehension when comprehension does not exist. This well-documented tendency shows individuals believe that they know far more than they actually do. In fact, the least proficient often overestimate their abilities, as cupidity begets confidence. The greatest enemy of knowledge is not ignorance but the illusion of knowledge (Sloman & Fernbach, 2017). Overstating one's talents, for instance, famously clouds drivers' judgments: Most rate themselves better than average (the "Lake Wobegon effect"). The vast majority of the population believes that it cannot multitask well enough to drive safely, yet many drivers admit to regular texting (Hogan Assessment Systems, 2017). It is not just that they do not know what they do not know but that they do not factor their limitations into their decisions: They are quite certain about uncertainty. The problem is that the incompetent cannot know they are incompetent—a dangerous phenomenon in management decision-making.

Fourth, when faced with a dilemma, people may predict that they will make an honorable choice, but when actually faced with the dilemma, they do not. Overestimating their moral capacity, they nonetheless still consider themselves to be ethical ("ethicality bias") (Bazerman & Tenbrunsel, 2011). They are not only wrong but confident that they are right. In fact, humans recall their unethical action with less-than-vivid clarity—increasing the likelihood of similar decisions in the future. Those who set aside moral concerns in pursuit of other goals can be quite creative in the rationalization of behavior and may not even be aware that this process is occurring.

Professionals, for instance, tend to believe in their work and to view themselves as persons of integrity in control of their lives. However, overconfidence in one's own ability (and the arrogance that can accompany it) affects decisions. Eventually a "new normal," an adjustment of what is defined as proper, emerges. These cognitive distortions help justify and forget questionable behavior, and reconcile it with the self-image as a righteous person. Eisenberger and Lieberman (2009) suggest that high intelligence often corresponds with low self-awareness: Neural networks involved in cognitive problem-solving reside in the lateral portions of the brain, whereas the middle regions support self-awareness. These individuals may have ill-contrived views, but they are seldom in doubt (see Jones-Lee & Aven, 2017, for data on this point).

Fifth, a similar phenomenon is the "moral equilibrium scorecard," wherein individuals keep a mental ledger that compares the type of person they believe themselves to be with their actual behavior (Prentice, 2015, 45). If they do something worthwhile, the account is then in surplus, giving them license to do something dubious. If they then make a poor judgment, they may compensate by doing something positive to balance the record. This kind of "moral licensing" makes it possible for moral actors to do bad things, while thinking of themselves as good. To take one example, the Business Roundtable issued a declaration in 2019 stating that a corporation's purpose is not just to make a profit for shareholders but instead to create value for all stakeholders (employees, customers, suppliers, communities). Declaration signatories committed more violations of the spirit and letter of the statement than non-signatories (Appelbaum, 2020, September 18),

Among the many other tendencies (see Samson, 2017, 82–114), "naïve idealism" is the belief that one's own views reflect reality and that they are shared by neutral parties. The "availability effect" bases a decision simply on immediately available information. "Anchoring bias" occurs when people emphasize the first piece of information they learned about an issue, so that all future arguments are discussed in relation to the anchor to the point that new, more accurate information may be rejected. "Action bias" is the felt pressure to do something, anything to reduce anxiety. The "forbidden fruit" effect is the temptation to react to rules and regulations by breaking them (see also "reactance bias"). Thus, desiring to maintain control, employees rebel against being distrusted and told what to do. An organization that focuses on controls and sanctions may very well result in lower compliance with procedures than one that encourages personal integrity and responsibility (Bowles, 2017; Bhanot, 2020, March 20).

As already seen, these cognitive dispositions (and scores of others not discussed here due to page constraints) can combine in powerful ways. They can also culminate in a self-limiting manner; no one knows less than the individual who knows it all. Once someone begins to feel that they have mastered their biases, they may be experiencing the "bias blind spot": seeing shortcomings in other people but not in their own (Bradberry & Greaves, 2012), as they consider others to be more unreasonable than themselves.

The product of all these stubborn biases—as well as bounded ethicality, System 1 thinking, motivated reasoning, and decision framing—can be unethical behavior that may occur slowly, incrementally, and unconsciously, rather than in an abrupt shift. Ariely (2008) finds that individuals have an inclination to cheat a little (a "personal fudge factor") without the inconvenience of changing their honest self-image. This erosion of ethics might begin as a trivial infraction (the "peanuts effect") with the seriousness of the wrongdoing growing as time passes, leading the wrongdoer to alter her definition of appropriate standards. Moral seduction theory (Moore et al., 2006) posits that decision makers can become compromised over time, a development facilitated by nonconscious habits, ingrained motives, and deeply seated thought patterns.

In short, behavioral science concepts, both obvious and subtle, are not necessarily new, but they are important and interesting. What is new is the mounting evidence that ethical conduct is less under conscious control than commonly believed. The science of decisions has demonstrated that the faith in the power of pure reason is unwarranted; people are susceptible to subliminal beliefs, emotional reactions, and mental shortcuts that help explain deviations from a rational norm. Questionable behavior is not necessarily a function of bad character but a consequence of shared *homo sapien* cognitive inheritance.

Preconceived ideas, to summarize, can trump better judgment and good intention; the brain relies on personal convictions over hard fact. These relatively unacknowledged predilections are often so strong that they are inconsistent with logic and reason and personal motives and ethics. Intuition tends to involve certainty about uncertainty, and it is usually followed by an inability to accept one's determination as wrong (Hogan Assessment Systems, 2017). Like the allegory of Plato's cave, humans are bound by the images received through the senses. Men and women have, accordingly, a distorted view of reality because they cannot observe reality objectively (Kaptein, 2013). "Decisions are not based on the objective state of the world," according to Rogerson et al. (2011, 616), "but rather on our subjective experience with it." Such cognitive distortions help justify questionable behavior and reconcile it with her self-image as a praiseworthy person. As Elder Shafir (2012, 5) argues, it is difficult to know when to expect bias as well as when to anticipate clear judgment: "Things that ought not to matter . . . often do, and things that ought to matter often fail to have an impact." Yet while there may be no sure way to take into account biases, they can be identified and techniques can be employed to limit their impact.

Monitoring and Sanctions

This behavioral ethics tenet includes the counterintuitive role of sanctions and the nature of those sanctions. "Common sense" approaches to monitoring and penalties intended to promote exemplary conduct may be ineffective or dysfunctional. "There is a charm," Mark

Twain said, "about the forbidden that makes it unspeakably desirable." Compliance systems, then, can have a reactance effect—that is, noncompliance may become attractive simply because it is prohibited (Bazerman & Tenbrunsel, 2011, 113). As discussed, when decisions are framed in business terms (rather than ethical terms)—and the existence of a sanctioning system notwithstanding—the decision maker might view wrongdoing as a cost of doing business, allowing ethical concerns to recede from consideration.

Implementing sanctions can lead to calculations of the likelihood of being caught or punished—rather than reflective thought questioning whether the action is the proper thing to do. By relabeling situations as "business decisions," ethical implications may be hidden, discounted, or disregarded, making it more likely that dubious behavior will result. In the dinner case, it would be expedient to downplay the importance of appearance. Mark calculated the risk of being caught out to dinner to be low and accepted, rather than ask himself if accepting were a violation of a professional ethic. Similarly, with both principals and teachers involved in erasing answers, rationalizing what they did may have been relatively easy. A teacher could figure the risk of being caught by his principal to be low, given that the principal was on the scheme, too!

Gneezy and Rustichini (2000) confirmed the connection between framing, sanctions, and behavior with a practical case evaluating a new fine imposed on parents by a daycare center when they arrived late to pick up their children. Unexpectedly, the number of parents arriving late increased rather than decreased. The explanation is that the payment led parents to view the matter as a business calculation. A harried parent determined the cost of arriving late and decided to pay the money—rather than viewing on-time arrival as right behavior. A sanctioning system can produce less cooperative participation if intrinsic motivation to cooperate is replaced by extrinsic motivation to respond to penalties. Tenbrunsel and Messick (1999) suggest that when a no-punishment procedure exists, people are more likely to see the decision as a moral one.

Organizational Context and Ethical Infrastructure

The penultimate behavioral ethics tenet, organizational context, can influence performance in many ways: job pressures to act unethically, unrealistic organizational goals, rewards or incentives to act improperly, and weak sanctions for questionable deeds and organizational cultures that normalize unethical conduct (Treviño, Weaver, & Reynolds, 2006). The ethical infrastructure, designed to counteract these factors and encourage right behavior in the workplace, includes robust formal and informal systems (Tenbrunsel, Smith-Crowe, & Umphress, 2003; see also Chapter 8).

The formal infrastructure includes communication (codes, mission statements, performance standards, training), surveillance (performance monitoring, hotlines, ethics ombudspersons), and management systems (evaluations, salaries, promotions, bonuses). Informal information systems also include communication (hallway conversations, unofficial training, stories), surveillance (personal observation and relationships, extra-organizational sources), and sanctions (group pressure, whistleblowing). Together with the organizational climate, formal and informal systems can influence conduct. The "morning moral" effect (Kouchaki & Smith, 2013) suggests that ethical awareness and self-control decline during the day; accordingly, important meetings and decisions should be scheduled before noon. Thus, while systems and organizational climate may foster proper behavior, under certain circumstances, they can be counterproductive. In both the dinner and school cases, weak formal penalties and a permissive informal ethical climate could easily suggest that dubious actions would be tolerated.

Given the findings from the behavioral ethics literature summarized here, what strategies might be used to mitigate the dishonesty of otherwise honest people? While there may be no sure way to take into account biases, they can be identified and techniques can be employed to limit their impact; if the causes of behavior are known, then cures may be found. "De-biasing" requires determination to deal with unconscious biases and to make an effort to correct them, as discussed next.

Countering Biases

In recognizing that more information alone is insufficient to solve problems, decision science looks for ways to help the prefrontal cortex make better choices. After all, as the epigram in the chapter implies, people have the ability to change by thinking about thinking. In point of fact, the same psychological tendencies that induce irrational behavior can be used to encourage better choices. It is better to work with human nature than against it, and using "nudges" is one way to do that (Exhibit 7.1), to focus on changing behavior instead of trying to change belief. Indeed, insights from behavioral ethics discussed earlier can be used to support life-saving pandemic policies by making them easy (e.g., free masks, home testing kits), understood (emphasizing positive nudges and informed consent), and expected (adherence to social norms) (see Anthes, 2021; Soofi, Najan, & Karami-Matin, 2020; and Duckworth, Ungar, & Emanuel, 2020). What a classical philosopher and neoclassical economist might regard as an irrelevant situational factor, a behaviorist might see as a useful tool. But do not underestimate the mind's ability to sabotage good intentions.

EXHIBIT 7.1	**Behavioral Science Nudges**

Behavioral science has shown that decision makers routinely violate the assumptions of the rational agent model. As a result, its application to societal problems, by practitioners, "pract-a-demics," and consultants at all levels of government around the world have devised new processes to improve public public service (see, e.g., Organization for Economic Cooperation and Development, 2017; Social and Behavioral Sciences Team, 2016; World Bank, 2016, February 23).

More than two dozen countries have decision science teams to enhance the efficiency and effectiveness of programs in consumer protection, education, energy, and the environment. Acknowledging that governments inevitably set prompts ("nudges"), consciously or unconsciously, behavioral research also has been utilized (by making changes in how messages are framed) on issues like the accuracy of eyewitness identification, improving school attendance, stimulating voter turnout, and valuing environmental goods (Fox & Sitkin, 2015). Among the well-known examples of changes at little or no expense are (a) retirement savings and organ donation programs (if the default is set to "opt in" rather than "opt out," dramatic enrollment gains occur), (b) tax compliance (switching the signature box on forms from the bottom to the top commits the filer to personal honesty at the outset, thereby increasing accurate reporting), and (c) water consumption (conservation is reinforced when a "social proof," peer comparison message is enclosed with the bill indicating how much water others save).

Behavioral principles have been implemented in areas such as readable financial disclosure information for consumers (2009 Credit Card Accountability and Disclosure Act), automatic registration in health plans (2010 Affordable Care Act), and simplification of choices available under Medicare Part D. As well, over 25 cost-effective projects in U.S. cities have promoted citizen enrollment in services, municipal workforces, and compliance with legal notices (Behavioral Insights Team, 2016). O'Leary and Murphy (2017) compiled successful initiatives that incorporated behavioral sciences insights to improve outcomes in good citizenship behavior (voting, carpools, recycling), program compliance (unemployment insurance, permits, licenses), and benefit program participation (prenatal visits, job training classes).

Interventions can be especially efficacious when (a) there are good reasons to believe that there will benefits from change, (b) citizens agree that reform is, in fact, desirable, and (c) the innovation is nearly effortless and cost-free (Thayer, 2017, 341). Even nudges that have small impact are still cost-effective because they are inexpensive to implement. When innovations are easy, attractive, social, and timely (EAST), people can be motivated to make selections consistent with their own value preferences.

The New Zealand Prime Minister, for instance, made pandemic masks a fashion statement by matching colors of her masks with her outfits. Likewise, testing and vaccination centers should be convenient, free, and fun by being readily accessible and visible (with "I Voted"-like stickers reading "I got the COVID-19 vaccine"), having local celebrities present, and giving away candy and ice cream (also see Anthes, 2021). Doing no harm, the emphasis is on helping people help themselves. Smart nudges, in fact, can be more successful in prompting good decisions than conventional techniques like public hearings, public service announcements, and tax incentives. In 2021 the Biden administration committed to evidence-based policy and reinstated Obamacare behavioral initiatives (cancelled by president Trump); this was done by instructing the Office of Management and Budget to build upon president Obama's order.

Although behavioral sciences offer helpful ideas, some commentators suggest that they foster the belief that "minor tweaks," "tinkering at the margins," can be a substitute for major reform. This kind of nudge does not change the service provided (e.g., making it easier to enroll in college does not affect course content). Indeed, economists Loewenstein and Urel (2010, July 14) indicate that soft-touch behavioral techniques might be used as a political expedient, allowing officials to avoid controversial, but more productive, policies. Skeptics also point out that most successes remain small and suspect that they erode with the passage of time.

To illustrate, energy-saving programs that rely on behavioral innovation may not be successful long term in promoting large-scale alteration in personal habits (Sussman, Gifford, & Abrahamse, 2016). Barreto (2017), however, claims that "by and large those doubts have been allayed. Even if specific results turn out to be mistaken, an experimental, iterative, data-driven approach to policymaking is gaining ground . . . throughout government" (see also Sunstein, 2015).

Further, critics have expressed concern about the possibility of misuse. The White House's Social and Behavioral Science Team (2016), for instance, documented success in improving the lives of citizens and saving money during the Obama years by using evidence-based policies. A different administration, however, could use the skills developed by the now-defunct Team in a less benevolent, more deceptive, manner (Jachimowiz, 2017, February 2). Akerlof and Shiller (2015), as matter of fact, offer numerous, suggestive cases of manipulation and deception in the private sector. To help guard against abuse, nudges should be transparent, based on empirical data, preserve freedom of choice and personal autonomy, provide for knowledgeable choices, be easy to opt out of, do no harm, and in the end enhance self-government in the public interest (Sunstein, 2016).

Source: adapted from Bowman (2018).

Using behaviorally informed activities and prompts, organizations and their employees can change the "choice environment" to override blind spots and improve decisions, by

1. practicing narratives to plan ahead, and write out, how to respond to issues (role play exercises, for example; Gentile, 2010) in order to narrow the intention-action gap,

2. setting self-binding pledges in advance to specific courses of action with an implementation procedure to overcome bounded will power (bank vacation savings clubs, predetermined stock price buying/selling plans, advanced medical directives),

3. utilizing checklists, fact-checks, and moral reminders ("priming" per Gawande, 2011) to encourage awareness and foster compliance with best practices by exposing employees to ethics stimuli such as placing a conduct code, a mirror, or surveillance cameras in strategic places, enclosing citizen-comparison, moral-appeal letters with tax bills (Bott et al., 2017), or making a pandemic vaccination appointment (with timely reminders),

4. forming diverse teams to reach a fuller understanding (by taking advantage of knowledge aggregation and error reduction) to counter "group think,"

5. implementing training programs showing how vulnerable employees are to mental shortcuts and how simple tactics such as those here can reduce their influence (for a discussion of empirical evidence that training impacts subsequent behavior; reviewing this chapter, for instance, may help readers increase awareness of pandemic-related ideas leading them to healthier decisions),

6. engaging in critical reflection to legitimize and incentivize doubt (e.g., by challenging assumptions and prevailing norms, developing alternatives, employing dialectical problem-solving, dialoguing between System 1 and 2, playing "devil's advocate," referring to one's self in the third person to gain psychological distance from the issue, holding a "pre-mortem" by imagining the plan failed and seeking to understand why),

7. creating "cooling off" time (anxiety and fatigue—cognitive depletion—impede thoughtful decisions) to monitor emotions, encourage self-reflection, and consult with disinterested parties,

8. being wary of rationalizations ("it's legal," "I had no choice," "everyone does it"),

9. considering if the pending option was posted to social media tomorrow, and

10. contemplating one's own eulogy.

Techniques like these—especially when reinforced by a meso-level organizational infrastructure (Chapter 8) such as psychological contracts, oaths, value statements, and compliance strategies—should help overcome disaster-ignoring biases that interpret low probability events like a global disease outbreak as having practically zero chance of happening (Khazan, 2020, April 28). There are many obstacles in behavior; individuals and organizations should not allow themselves to become one of them. Indeed, there is evidence that social biases also may be reduced when sleeping, through subliminal reinforcement and brain training (Varazzani, 2017, June 20).

The toolset here can encourage decision makers to thoughtfully consider dilemmas by developing methods that enhance the ability to make sound decisions. Behavioral researchers have come to several overall conclusions: People are not really very good at understanding how their brains work, they have a strong tendency to fall short of their own standards, and most bad behavior is done by regular folks (Di Miceli, 2020, March 16). It should also be recalled that heuristics can be efficient; accordingly, the use of cognitive expedients resulting in seemingly irrational decisions can actually be quite sensible under select circumstances. In any case, the behavioral approach offers insights to understand conduct, counterfactuals to mitigate error, and evidence-based management strategies.

In brief, it is simply not sufficient to assume that men and women are good, and that the ethical issues they encounter will take care of themselves. First impressions—*prima facie* obligations— upon further reflection may not be self-evident. Behavioral science cannot tell individuals what they ought to do. However, as this review of its components suggests, it can help explain how and why people act, something of great value to practitioners and academicians alike. As Varazzani (2017, June 20) reports, for example, "neuroscience can lend insight into when a bias will manifest and how to design an effective intervention to counteract it." When it is understood why mistakes are made, steps can be taken to minimize them by using behaviorally informed policies.

The shift in approach from philosophical to psychological decision-making portends an important implication for thinking about ethics: The focus should be understanding psychological factors that lead to unethical acts rather than just emphasizing how people should behave. Because good people unwittingly contribute to unethical action, change in the practice of ethics needs to emphasize hidden, unconscious influences on behavior. For Bazerman and Tenbrunsel (2011), the goal is to become prepared for unrecognized psychological forces that occur during decision-making—that is, to learn to think in a thoughtful manner to help ensure that self-interest does not smother self-integrity. This usually involves correcting System 1 intuitions with System 2 analysis by becoming aware of biases and using formal procedures that require consideration of opposing viewpoints.

In addition, creating time for reflection in the face of a superior's demand for a quick decision may be helpful, as shown in Exhibit 7.2. Finally, because fatigue and sleep deprivation reduce clear thinking and moral engagement, organizational cultures that demand overwork and long hours need reexamination.

| **EXHIBIT 7.2** | **Avoiding Poor Judgments With Confidence** |

In the crush of everyday business, managers confront demands to respond to difficult questions without delay. If pressured to make a quick decision, consider these guidelines:

- Request time to think it over. Most decisions do not, in fact, have to be made immediately. Bargaining for time ("Let me think about it, and I'll get back to you by 2:00 today") should provide space to confer with others and to use systematic decision-making techniques.
- Ask if your organization has a policy relevant to the situation.
- Turn the demand around and ask your boss for advice, or ask if you and she can take a minute to consult with the department's legal staff or her superior.
- Use the disclosure test—that is, if you would be embarrassed to have the decision reported in the newspaper, then defer until a proper judgment can be rendered.

- Trust yourself and value intuition. If your "heart" suggests that something is not quite right, then consider it a warning siren (adapted from Treviño & Nelson, 1995, 77; see also Zhang, et al. 2020).

Impatience breeds anxiety, fear, and failure. Patience creates confidence, deliberation, and decisiveness.

Prudent decision makers prepare for uncertainty by having premeditated processes and behavioral ethics frameworks for finding answers. The response, then, to challenges becomes not to provide solutions immediately but to use reliable procedures in the pursuit of answers.

Skilled decision makers know that confidence and certainty are not synonymous—the latter emphasizes outcomes that can seldom be predicted and the former focuses on known procedures to deal with the issue. Confidence comes not from always being right but from not fearing mistakes—a deliberate, rational decision-making process, including consulting with others, will limit the magnitude of error. Throughout an ethical crisis, the confident administrator remains calm, asks hard questions, and rejects an elusive perfect result for the quest for the good. Such managers act as a morally conscious person would act in any setting and set the example for the workplace. Slow down and engage System 2 thinking discussed earlier. It is more important to make the right decision than to make a fast one. No one is in a hurry for a bad outcome.

Queries like those listed in Exhibit 7.2 can assist in problem framing, interfering with the "want" self and System 1 thinking, and moderating biases and errors (see also Banaji et al., 2003, esp. 61–63). In the dinner case, the "front page" caution may have been useful to Mark; in the test-tampering case, a precommitment by teachers and school administrators to hold independent audits would likely have identified problems. Thus, a variety of concerns that are examples of decision mistakes (e.g., action bias, self-serving bias) can be exploited to help individuals accomplish their ethical objectives.

CONCLUSION

Obviously, people make decisions deviant from the classical rational model and its prescriptions. Often the expression "I'm only human" is offered as a tenuous defense of a less-than-rational decision. Many factors, including situational context, can help explain the dishonesty of honest people. The heroic assumptions made by the traditional approach—that individuals are ostensibly and universally logical, possess full information, have the will-power to use it, and act in their self-interest—often do not hold in real life.

Thus, for instance, if the goal is to persuade someone to change his or her views, then do not lead with evidence and facts that are likely to provoke defense mechanisms such as the backfire effect discussed earlier. Rather, ethical thinkers from Plato to St. Augustine to Thomas Hobbes understand "that human beings are fundamentally passionate creatures and that reason alone is too weak to contain their drives" (Lilla, 2010, December 17). Political controversies are often really debates about values, not facts. Seeking common ground, lead with values in a context within which he or she is familiar to engage emotions; introducing new information in that psychologically safe environment may be effective.

The various irrational behaviors explored in this chapter must be taken into account when choices are made. Hypocrisy is part of the human comedy. In so doing, behavioral ethics is transforming the way conduct is understood when ethics matters most—individuals actually making judgments. The limited applicability of traditional ethics does not warrant casting it off altogether—upholding ideals under stress is the very reason for the classical study of ethics. One is unlikely to carry out an action in pursuit of a principle to which he or she has never given thought. As Paul Moloney (2011) observes, "What gives meaning to behavior is purpose." For this reason philosophy examines thought, not behavior.

Tools like the ethics triad nudge decision makers to thoughtfully consider perplexing moral dilemmas. Accordingly, each of the chapters that follow will include one or more cases that are briefly analyzed using the lens of the trinity. Readers should keep in mind, however, the insights from behavioral ethics when relying on such cognitive approaches. If the prescriptions characteristic of the orthodox triune decision-making model and the descriptions of conduct in the behavioral model are viewed as mutually reinforcing, rather than inimical, a more complete understanding of the human condition may result in the workplace. They both ask to think about thinking. The incorporation of such a synthesis into organizational cultures promises that the quality of ethical decision-making will improve in the future. Indeed, humans have great potential: Most people want to make a positive contribution to society.

***

One way to find out if a man is honest is to ask him. If he says "yes," you know he is crooked.

—Groucho Marx

NOTES

1. With permission, the following discussion draws on Bowman and West (2013). Copyright © 2013 by M. E. Sharpe, Inc., Used by permission. All Rights Reserved. Not for reproduction.
2. Parts of this and the next section are drawn from Bowman, West, and Beck (2010). Copyright © M. E. Sharpe, Inc. Used by permission. All Rights Reserved. Not for reproduction.
3. Some decision situations may be "easy" to analyze since they are right versus wrong "problems" (there is a clear ethically correct answer), and others more convoluted, as in right versus right dilemmas (there may be several "right" solutions, all of which nonetheless may be problematic). Simplicity does not imply ease of solution—even in dilemmas wherein the right answer is evident, for nonethical reasons, the dilemma may remain difficult to resolve.

   In both simple and complex cases, ethics requires not just the fortitude to support the proper decision and refuse wrongdoing but also the resourcefulness to devise honorable ways to deal with the issue. Scores of public sphere cases providing testimony from administrators have been gathered by Menzel (2010). Among the many issues discussed are those dealing with the ethics of commercializing a city's website (139–142) and the hiring of a supervisor's highly qualified friend (193–194).
4. Beware the pitfalls risked when just one school of thought is emphasized at the expense of the others. For example, reliance on the results approach alone may be problematic because it is difficult to anticipate all possible consequences of a decision and because limiting the focus to results may lead to imprudent, expedient action.
5. Parts of this section are adapted from Bowman (2018).
6. Similarly, exclusive use of rule-based ethics may lack compassion (Svara, 1997), as when truth telling produces cold and inconsiderate behaviors. The benevolence of virtue ethics, combined with the greater good—emphasis of results-oriented ethics, might humanize the hard objectivity of a rule-based approach. Last, the potential of virtue theory to be self-serving can be counterbalanced with results and rules ethics thinking. An integrated approach produces

a defensible decision that takes into account results, rules, and virtues. To battle a dilemma, an administrator must choose wisely from the armory of ethics and choose more than one weapon. An important tool is used in behavioral ethics: human subject laboratory experiments. Although college students are often participants in these trials, some experiments are conducted using business professionals with similar results (e.g., Bazerman & Tenbrunsel, 2011).

7. Joshua Greene (2010) employs a camera metaphor (recounted in Brooks, 2011, 290) that helps to explain the role of intuition in System 1. Automatic settings on the camera quickly and efficiently regulate the focus and shutter speed, but sometimes the settings need to be overridden to allow for manual adjustment. While manual adjustment is more time-consuming, it enables the photographer to accomplish things that could not otherwise be done. Similarly, a person may experience automatic ethical concerns but then override them and fine-tune them through a slower, in-depth reasoning.

8. Also see Thaler and Sunstein (2009), who argue that people's behavior can be influenced in predictable ways without their realizing it. The key is the "architecture" of a decision.

DISCUSSION

1. It is said the biggest problem is not ignorance but the illusion of knowledge. Examine this claim in the context of the assumptions of rational ethical decision-making.

2. Considering C. S. Lewis's comment that "We are what we believe," identify the strengths and weaknesses of the classical rationalism and psychological realism approaches to understanding ethics.

3. Examine at least one of the major findings of behavioral ethics. Critique it.

4. Thomas Jefferson wrote, "In matters of style, swim with the current. In matters of principle, stand like a rock." Consider how this insight is germane to both the classical and psychological schools of ethical decision-making. Discuss.

5. It is said that morality both binds and blinds: As someone's wealth and power increases indifference toward others, rule-rule breaking, exploitation, and cheating also increases (Mueller, 2019, 162ff.). Comment.

6. Ponder this observation by Oscar Wilde: "[T]he only difference between a saint and a sinner is that all saints have a past and all sinners have a future."

7. Use behavioral insights to explain:
   - Eighty-seven percent of Americans believed that they would go to Heaven, while just 70 percent thought that Mother Teresa of Calcutta would also make it.
   - People whose names begin with the letter C (like Carl) tend to drink Coke while those whose name start with P (such as Peter) like Pepsi.
   - A clear conscience is a sign of a bad memory.

8. Select biases that might help explain these actions during the pandemic: (a) many states prematurely reopened their economies and (b) some citizens objected to mask mandates.

9. A manager was interviewing a new graduate, and he asked if the student had taken a professional ethics course. The interviewee said "yes," and the manager asked what he had learned. The candidate explained that he learned about results, rule, and virtue ethics and their behavioral ethics implications. He continued saying that whenever he would encounter a dilemma, he would decide what to do and then select a model of ethics that would best support his choice. Is the student's response sensible or not? Why?

10. After studying different approaches to decision-making in this chapter, unpack this recommendation: "Why not make a decision that you can be proud of?"

EXERCISES

1. Several cases (Bowman & Knox, 2008; Svara, 1997) can be used to illustrate the interactive nature of the threefold decision-making approach described in this chapter; for each one that follows, examine the decision using the three viewpoints and explain what the individual should do. (Note: There is always incomplete information; if there were complete information, the case would be a foregone conclusion, not a dilemma.) Recognize that some of the "ethical pickles" here should be fairly easy to analyze since they are right versus wrong "problems," not right versus right "dilemmas." For both problems and dilemmas, the best way out is through. Note that ethics requires not just the rectitude to support the proper decision and refuse wrongdoing but also the resourcefulness to devise possible noble ways to deal with the problem:

The Candidate. A candidate for a city manager position is asked by the city council to agree to fire the public works director and is told that the other finalist for the job has agreed, if hired, to fire the public works director.

The Sting. A properly conducted law enforcement sting operation nets some criminals.

The Analyst. A data analyst for a community college finds that enrollment figures are being padded to increase state funding.

The Boss. Your boss tells you your organization may be downsized next month and pledges you to secrecy. One of your subordinates, about to purchase a house with his expecting wife, later asks you about downsizing rumors that are going around.

Each school of thought is represented by a shorthand question that corresponds to results, rules, or rectitude. Some illustrative prompts may be helpful in puzzling through what to do:

- Results approach: "What's the greatest good for the greatest number of people?" "What are the short- and long-run consequences of the proposed decision?
- Duty-based approach: "Is what's right for one, right for all?" "What if everyone did that?" "Is this action universally acceptable?" (Note: Assume that specific organizational rules are trumped by universal ethical rules reflected in the prompts presented previously)
- Virtue ethics: "Does the proposed decision make me a better person in my community?" "Which choice is most true to my character?"

For each case, answer the question raised by each school of thought. Then explain what would you do and why. Be alert to the human capacity (yours!) for self-deception.

Avoid talking about results, rules, and virtues without a clear reference point. Discuss each philosophy separately using the prompts as a starting point. Resist the temptation to let other philosophies obstruct the analysis as illustrated here. They will get their turn; the overall assessment at the end will provide a synthesis. For a critique of some student case analyses, see Appendix 7.1, which shows (a) how students reacted, using the threefold decision-making procedure, to a complex classroom dishonesty case and (b) why their responses were understandable but an incorrect application of the procedure.

2. Continue condensing your notes (made in the page margins of the text or a notebook) after reading each chapter to establish links between chapter and course objectives. While doing this, create sentence stems (see Chapter 1) to identify insights and questions.

3. In light of bias and common decision-making errors, do facts actually work to change minds—or do inertia and denial predominate? Provide examples.

4. Examine criticisms of behavioral ethics (e.g., Bubb & Pildes, 2014) and assess their validity.

5. Retrieve David Brooks' (2015, January 13), "Child in the Basement" in the *New York Times* at www.nytimes.com/2015/01/13/opinion/david-brooks-the-child-in-the-basement.html. This riveting story compels readers to confront the tragic compromises that are built into society (don't miss it!).

6. View Michael Sandel's "Justice," Episode 01 (15 minutes)" in YouTube to further enrich this chapter's discussion by reinforcing the distinction between utilitarian and deontological arguments (include the trolley case and organ replacement).

A link between the want/should self-theory and ethical fading (as well as bounded ethicality) is evident. As Tenbrunsel et al. (2009) point out, when the ethical dimensions of a decision fade away, it enables the "want" self to appear.

REFERENCES

Appelbaum, B. (2020, September 18). 50 years of blaming Milton Friedman. Here's another idea. *New York Times*. Retrieved from www.nytimes.com/2020/09/18/opinion/milton-friedman-essay.html

Ariely, D. (2008). *Predictably irrational*. New York: HarperCollins.

Anthes, E. (2021, April 2). How to nudge people into getting tested for the coronavirus. *New York Times*. Retrieved from https://www.nytimes.com/2021/04/02/health/coronavirus-testing-behavior-hesitancy.html

Banaji, M., Bazerman, M., & Chugh, D. (2003). How (un)ethical are you? *Harvard Business Review*, *81*, 56–63.

Bazerman, M., & Banaji, M. R. (2004). The social psychology of ordinary ethical failures. *Social Justice Research*, *17*(2), 111–115.

Bazerman, M., & Chugh, D. (2006). Bounded awareness: Focusing failures in negotiation. In L. L. Thompson (Ed.), *Negotiation theory and research* (pp. 7–26). New York: Psychology Press.

Bazerman, M., & Tenbrunsel, A. (2011). *Blind spots: Why we fail to do what's right and what to do about it*. Princeton, NJ: Princeton University Press.

Bennett, D. (2014, November 5). How to take control of your brain and make better decisions. *Washington Post*. Retrieved from www.washingtonpost.com/posteverything/wp/2014/11/05/how-to-take-control-of-your-brain-and-make-better-decisions/?utm_term=.344e25176145

Bhanot, S. (2020, March 20). Why are people ignoring experts warning? Psychological reactance. *Behavioral Scientist*. Retrieved from https://behavioralscientist.org/why-are-people-ignoring-expert-warnings-psychological-reactance-coronavirus-covid-19/

Bott, K., Cappelen, A., Sorensen, E., & Tungodden, B. (2017). Research: Moral appeals can help reduce tax evasion. *Harvard Business Review*. Retrieved from https://hbr.org/2017/07/research-moral-appeals-can-help-reduce-tax-evasion

Bowles, S. (2017). *Moral economy: Why good incentives are no substitute for good citizens*. New Haven, CT: Yale University Press.

Bowman, J. (2018). Thinking about thinking. Beyond decision-making rationalism and the emergence of behavioral ethics. *Public Integrity*, *20*(S), S89–105.

Bowman, J., & Knox, C. (2008). Ethics in government: No matter how long and dark the night. *Public Administration Review*, *68*, 625–637.

Bowman, J., & West, J. (2013). From classical rationalism to psychological realism in ethical decision-making. In R. Ghere & H. G. Frederickson (Eds.), *Ethics and public management* (pp. 155–171, 2nd ed.). Armonk, NY: M. E. Sharpe.

Bowman, J., West, J., & Beck, M. (2010). *Competencies in public service: The professional edge* (2nd ed.). Armonk, NY: M. E. Sharpe.

Bradberry, T., & Greaves, J. (2012). *Emotional intelligence 2.0*. San Diego, CA: Talent Smart.

Brest, P. (2012). Quis custodiet ipsos custodes? In E. Shafir (Ed.), *Behavioral foundations of public policy* (pp. 481–493). Princeton, NJ: Princeton University Press.

Brooks, D. (2011). *The social animal: The hidden sources of love, character, and achievement*. New York: Random House.

Bubb, R., & Pildes, R. (2014). How behavioral economics trims its sails and why. *Harvard Law Review*, *127*, 1593–1678.

Chugh, D. (2004). Why milliseconds matter: Societal and managerial implications of implicit social cognition. *Social Justice Research*, *17*, 203–222.

Cotteleer, M., & Murphy, T. (2015). *Ignoring bad news* (Paper, Series on Behavioral Economics and Management). West Lake, TX: DeLoitte Consulting, LLP.

Di Miceli, A. (2020, March 16). What is behavioral ethics? Why is it important for all companies? *The Virtuous Barrel*. Retrieved from https://alexdimiceli.medium.com/what-is-behavioral-ethics-why-is-it-important-for-all-companies-146432dbaf1f

Duckworth, A., Ungar, L., & Emanuel, E. (2020, May 27). There are three things we have to do to get people wearing masks. *New York Times*. Retrieved from www.nytimes.com/2020/05/27/opinion/coronavirus-masks.html

Ethics. (1982). *Public Management*, 20–21.

Eisenberger, N., & Lieberman, M. (2009). The pains and pleasures of social life. *Science*, *323*(*5916*), 890–891.

Gawande, A. (2011). *Checklist manifesto*. New York: Picador.

Gazzaniga, M. (2008). *Human: The science behind what makes us unique*. New York: Harper Perennial.

Gentile, M. (2010). *Giving voice to values*. New Haven, CT: Yale University Press.

Gneezy, U., & Rustichini, A. (2000). A fine is a price. *Journal of Legal Studies*, *29*, 1–17.

Greene, J. (2010). *Does moral action depend on reasoning? Less than it should*. Retrieved from www.ethics-based-on-science.com/uploads/2/8/5/1/28516163/mjm-notes-moral-reasoning_bq_spring_2010.pdf

Haidt, J. (2001). The emotional dog and its rational tail: A social intuitionist approach to moral judgment. *Psychological Review*, *108*, 814–834.

Hogan Assessment Systems. (2017). *Hey, your biases are showing*. Tulsa, OK: Author.

Hoomans, J. (2015, March 20). 35,000 decisions: The great choices of strategic leaders. *Leading Edge Journal*. Retrieved from https://go.roberts.edu/leadingedge/the-great-choices-of-strategic-leaders

Jauhar, S. (2020, April 2). In a pandemic, do doctors still have duty to treat? *New York Times*. Retrieved from www.nytimes.com/2020/04/02/opinion/sunday/coronavirus-doctors-duty.html

Jones-Lee, M., & Aven, T. (2017). Weighing private preferences in public sector safety decisions. *Behavioral Public Policy*, *1*(*1*), 122–142.

Kahneman, D. (2011). *Thinking, fast and slow*. New York: Farrer, Straus, & Giroux.

Kahneman, D., Sibony,O. & Sunstein, C. (2021). *Noise: A flaw in human judgment*. Little Brown.

Kaptein, M. (2013). *Workplace morality: Behavioral ethics in organizations*. Bingley: Emerald.

Kern, M., & Chugh, D. (2009). Bounded ethicality: The perils of loss framing. *Psychological Science*, 20, 378–384.

Khazan, O. (2020, April 28). Humans are too optimistic to the comprehend coronavirus. *The Atlantic*. Retrieved from www.theatlantic.com/health/archive/2020/04/why-was-coronavirus-hard-predict/610432/

Kouchaki, M., & Smith, I. (2013). The morning effect: The influence of time of day on unethical behavior. *Psychological Science*, 25(1), 95–102.

Kuran, T. (1997). *Private truth, public lies*. Cambridge, MA: Harvard University Press.

Lilla, M. (2010, December 17). The president and the passions. *New York Times*. Retrieved from www.nytimes.com/2010/12/19/magazine/19Fob-WWLN-t.html.

May, T. (2019). *A decent life: Morality for the rest of us*. Chicago: University of Chicago Press.

Menzel, D. (2010). *Ethics moments in government: Cases and controversies*. Boca Raton, FL: CRC Press.

Mercier, H., & Sperber, D. (2017). *Enigma of reason*. Cambridge, MA: Harvard University Press.

Miller-Washington, J. (2020, August 21). Family photos at work curb fraud and unethical activity. *Futurity*. Retrieved from www.futurity.org/family-photos-work-fraud-2426632-2/

Moloney, P. (2011, April 2). Comments. *Philosophy on the Mesa*. Retrieved from http://philosophyonthemesa.com/2011/03/30/behavioral-ethics-explanation-or-excuse/

Mooney, C. (2011, April 18). The science of why we don't believe in science. *Mother Jones*. Retrieved from www.motherjones.com/politics/2011/03/denial-science-chris-mooney

Mooney, C. (2012). *The republican brain*. Hoboken, NJ: Wiley.

Moore, D., Tetlock, P., Tanlu, L., & Bazerman, M. (2006). Conflict of interest and the case of auditor independence: Moral seduction and strategic issue cycling. *Academy of Management Review, 31*, 10–49.

Mueller, T. (2019). *Crisis of confidence: Whistleblowing in an age of fraud*. New York: Riverhead Books.

Parramore, L. (2020, February 11). Psychologist explains why economists—and liberals—get human nature wrong. *Institute for New Economic Thinking*. Retrieved from www.ineteconomics.org/perspectives/blog/psychologist-explains-why-economists-and-liberals-get-human-nature-wrong

Prentice, R. (2015). Behavioral ethics. *Notre Dame Journal of Law, Ethics, and Public Policy, 29*(1), 36–85.

Rainer, T., & Geiger, E. (2011). *Simple church*. Nashville, TN: B&H Publishing.

Redlawsk, D. P., Civettini, A. W., & Emmerson, K. M. (2010). The affective tipping point: Do motivated reasoners ever "get it"? *Political Psychology, 31*, 563–593.

Roddel, S. (2019, November 21). Study offers first large sample evidence of the effects of ethics training on financial sector behaviour. *Phys.org*. Retrieved from https://phys.org/news/2019-11-large-sample-evidence-effect-ethics-financial.html

Rogerson, M., Gottlieb, M., Handelsman, M., Knapp, S., & Younggren, J. (2011). Nonrational processes in ethical decision making. *American Psychologist*, 66(7), 614–623.

Ropeik, D. (2012, September 30). Inside the mind of worry. *New York Times*, p. SR12.

Samson, A. (Ed.). (2017). *The behavioural economics guide*. London: Behavioral Science Solutions Ltd. Retrieved from www.behavioraleconomics.com

Schmidt, R. (2016). *Frozen: Using behavioral design to overcome decision making paralysis*. (Paper, Series on Behavioral Economics and Management). West Lake, TX: DeLoitte Consulting, LLP.

Seawright, R. (2013, March 10). *The narrative opportunity* [Web log comment]. Retrieved from http://rpseawright.wordpress.com/2013/03/10/the-narrative-opportunity/

Shafir, E. (2012). Introduction. In E. Shafir (Ed.), *Behavioral foundations of public policy* (pp. 1–12). Princeton, NJ: Princeton University Press.

Shao, R., Aquino, K., & Freeman, D. (2008). Beyond moral reasoning: A review of moral identity research and its implications for business research. *Business Ethics Quarterly*, *18*, 513–540.

Simon, H. (1983). *Reason in human affairs*. Stanford, CA: Stanford University Press.

Shackelford, S. & Wade, M. (2021, May 26). Colonial Pipeline forked over $4.4M to end cyberattack—but is paying a ransom ever the ethical thing to do?

The Conversation. https://theconversation.com/colonial-pipeline-forked-over-4-4m-to-end-cyberattack-but-is-paying-a-ransom-ever-the-ethical-thing-to-do-161383

Sloman, S., & Fernbach, P. (2017). *The knowledge illusion*. New York: Riverhead.

Soofi, M., Najan, F., & Karami-Matin, B. (2020). Using insights from behavioral economics to mitigate the spread of COVID-19. *Applied Health Economics and Health Policy*, *18*, 345–350.

Sorg, M. (2020, August 25). School nurses should be leading the COVID-19 response, but any schools don't have one. *The Conversation*. Retrieved from https://theconversation.com/school-nurses-should-be-leading-the-covid-19-response-but-many-schools-dont-have-one-144793

Svara, J. (1997). The ethical triangle: Synthesizing the bases of administrative ethics. In J. Bowman (Ed.), *Public Integrity Annual* (pp. 33–41). Lexington, KY: Council of State Governments.

Svara, J. (2007). *The ethics primer for public administrators in government and nonprofit organizations*. Sudbury, MA: Jones & Bartlett.

Tenbrunsel, A., Diekmann, K., Wade-Benzoni, K., & Bazerman, M. (2009). The ethical mirage: A temporal explanation as to why we aren't as ethical as we think we are. *Research in Organizational Behavior*, *30*, 153–173.

Tenbrunsel, A., & Messick, D. (1999). Sanctioning systems, decision frames, and cooperation. *Administrative Science Quarterly*, *44*, 684–707.

Tenbrunsel, A., & Messick, D. (2004). Ethical fading: The role of self deception in unethical behavior. *Social Justice Research*, *17*, 223–236.

Tenbrunsel, A., Smith-Crowe, K., & Umphress, E. (2003). Building houses on rocks: The role of ethical infrastructure in the ethical effectiveness of organizations. *Social Justice Research*, *16*, 285–307.

Thaler, R., & Sunstein, C. (2009). *Nudge*. Delmar, NY: Caravan Books.

Thorson, E. (2016, January 8). Debunking Donald Trump won't work if you repeat what he got wrong. *Washington Post*. Retrieved from www.washingtonpost.com/opinions/why-correcting-donald-trump--or-anyone-else--doesnt-work/2016/01/08/9e5ef5d4-b57d-11e5-a842-0feb51d1d124_story.html?utm_term=.57f7bd2d35f7

Treviño, L., & Nelson, K. (1995). *Managing business ethics*. New York: Wiley.

Treviño, L., Weaver, G., & Reynolds, S. (2006). Behavioral ethics in organizations: A review. *Journal of Management*, *32*, 951–990.

Varazzani, C. (2017, June 20). The risks of ignoring the brain. *Behavioral Scientist*. Retrieved from http://behavioralscientist.org/risks-ignoring-brain/

Viser, M. & Abutaleb, Y. (2021, June 6). Trump and his allied try to rewrite, distort history of pandemic while casting Fauci as public enemy no. 1. Washington Post. Retrieved from https://www.msn.com/en-us/news/politics/trump-and-his-allies-try-to-rewrite-history-of-pandemic-while-casting-fauci-as-public-enemy-no-1/ar-AAKKeFW?ocid=se

Westmoreland, A. (2020, August 14). My county wanted school nurses to justify its unsafe reopening plan. So I quit. *Washington Post*. Retrieved from www.washingtonpost.com/outlook/school-nurse-unsafe-reopening/2020/08/14/92011c48-dd84-11ea-8051-d5f887d73381_story.html

Zach, N. (2009). *Ethics for disaster*. Rowman & Littlefield.

Zhang, Y., Yam, K., Kouchaki, M., & Zhang, J. (2020). Why bosses cut some employees slack for unethical behavior. *Kellogg Insights*. Retrieved from https://insight.kellogg.northwestern.edu/article/why-bosses-cut-some-employees-slack-for-unethical-behavior

Appendix 7.1
Critiquing Student Case Analyses

The following are responses from graduate students in a professional ethics course to a complex classroom dishonesty case. The reactions show how they tried to apply the decision-making procedure discussed in this chapter. The italicized sentences note the shortcomings in their analyses. The argument offered may function logically but does not address the issue at hand (Aristotle's *ignoratio elenchi*, or ignoring the issue).

"In this cheating case, the ethics trinity may not lead to an easy determination."

This is a reasonable statement, as that is to be expected when dealing with true dilemmas; the tool is not likely to produce facile answers; it will provide a comprehensive analysis of the issue.

"From the rules viewpoint, it would clearly be determined that academic dishonesty is against school policy and any moral code that lists honesty is an essential value."

This comment does not speak to the rules prompt: What is good for one is good for all. School rules are secondary to ethical rules.

"The results perspective may point to either the results the accused is aiming for in getting a good grade, which would say cheating is alright to achieve the best results, or it may say that the activity is still wrong because it does not make him a better person."

This view misconstrues the results prompt by converting the greatest good for the greatest number to the best result for one person by emphasizing the short run. It then focuses on virtue theory, which, by definition, cannot be part of the results theory.

"The virtue approach is likely to disallow disgraceful behavior because it does nothing productive for society as a whole and does not contribute to the greater good."

This response includes results thinking ("does nothing productive" and the "greater good"), ignoring the virtue prompt: How does the decision affect my character and that of my community?

As noted in the chapter, the case should be examined by each of the three philosophies, one by one, using their respective question prompt. When searching for insights from one approach, the other approaches should not interfere with the one under analysis. When all three philosophies are considered, it will provide a synthesis, or at least a conclusion, of sorts. Don't jump to confusions(!). Indeed, recall the behavioral ethics tenets that might be useful in formulating a final judgment. Beware anyone, including yourself, who seems to know all the answers but none of the right questions.

PART III

Institutional
Approaches
to Ethics

8 Organizational Ethics

Nothing is possible without individuals; nothing is lasting without institutions.
—Jean Monnet

Mastery of individual-centered, micro-level ethics is necessary, but not sufficient, for understanding the full scope of ethics, as it revolves around both individuals and organizations (recall the Greek perspective on ethics in Chapter 1). Cognitive and virtue ethics by themselves may not produce ethical behavior, as people remain susceptible to meso-level workplace influences. Recall from Chapter 2 that the organizational level of ethics interacts with both the narrower and broader levels of ethics—micro (individual) and macro (societal), respectively. As Milgram demonstrated so shockingly with his laboratory experiments (Chapter 4), it is faulty to assume that people are ethical no matter what the context, because ethics is revealed in social situations. Good intentions may not be enough when employees are overwhelmed by pressures to conform to improper organizational behaviors that conflict with their good intentions.

As observed in earlier chapters, individual ethical judgment is an ability to be developed through practice. People must be given opportunity, autonomy, power, and encouragement to gain a new skill. In the workplace, some kind of collective basis for professional conduct is necessary. Employees may make decisions based on personal standards, but institutions define and govern the situations in which decisions are made. Individual responsibility is often discharged through organizations. Consider the possibilities if Milgram had designed an experiment to encourage praiseworthy behavior. Stated differently, the ethical health of a society and its members is significantly affected by the institutions that employ them.

Organizations represent major agencies of social control. Ethical behavior is not only an individual psychological phenomenon but also collective and sociological. Disreputable conduct is committed not just by a few "bad apples" but also by ordinary people doing extraordinary things under certain circumstances. Some people refuse to acknowledge organizational factors contributing to wrong behavior for fear of diluting personal moral responsibility. Yet this concern is based on a false dichotomy—recognizing the role of organization does not exculpate individual wrongdoers. Personal responsibility is by no means identical to sole responsibility. Individual blame (the "rotten apple") and institutional innocence ("the barrel") is an unwarranted double standard.

DOI: 10.4324/9781003203148-11

This chapter—which commences Part III of the book—begins the shift from cognitive ("head") and virtue ("heart") individual-centered ethics to organization-centered (physique or "body") approaches. An examination of organizational ethics will be undertaken in subsequent chapters on corruption control and whistleblowing. The discussion here encompasses:

- the recognition that individual-centered cognitive and virtue ethics is an important but inadequate basis for a comprehensive understanding of management ethics,
- the delineation of types of organization and the strategies that they use to nurture ethics,
- a critique of compliance-based and integrity-based ethics strategies, and
- the elements of an ethical infrastructure.

Organizations put people in environments where they have discretion, and it may be difficult to ascertain what appropriate behavior is. Employers are responsible, therefore, for the conduct of employees, as it would be imprudent to leave this important management function to chance. Creating an admirable institution is no mean task, yet it is easier—and more controllable—than attempting to directly affect individual behavior.

TYPES OF ORGANIZATIONAL STRATEGY

Approaches to ethics—immoral, amoral, moral—that may be used by organizations (Carroll, 1987, 12) are shown in Table 8.1. For the immoral unit, the norms, motives, goals, orientation toward law, and overall ethical strategy emphasize doing whatever is necessary to achieve its goals. Amoral institutions, by definition, are neither unethical nor ethical, as a minimalist stance toward ethical behaviors and laws prevails so as to avoid unnecessary trouble and do what needs to be done. Moral management defines success within professional (ethical) and legal standards of conduct.

Recall Kohlberg's stages of individual moral development (Chapter 4), a framework that also can be applied to organizations. Thus, Stage 1 organizations focus on financial survival as their moral beacon. A characteristic of this simplest level is preservation—any strategy is employed to protect against extinction. Stage 2 institutions stress the exclusive pursuit of self-interest, success justifying the tactics used. The two stages are not unlike Carroll's immoral organizations. Stage 3 companies, nonprofits, and public agencies conform to the practices of peer institutions—the vogue of rival organizations dictates what is right and wrong. This stage corresponds to Carroll's amoral organization, especially if the nature of the sister organizations is amoral. Stage 4 organizations take direction from institutional authority to determine their standards. Their moral compass is based on society's legal structure. This stage, and the following one, characterizes moral management in increasing degrees of substance. Stage 5 departments rely on participatory management and democratic decision-making—the majority rule becomes the standard. Stage 6 businesses, not-for-profits, and governmental offices value moral ideals such as justice and individual rights, balancing judgment among competing interests, based on universal principles, to determine right behavior.

TABLE 8.1	**Approaches to Management Ethics**		
	Immoral Management	**Amoral Management**	**Moral Management**
Ethical Norms	Management decisions, actions, and behavior imply a positive and active opposition to what is moral (ethical)	Management is neither moral nor immoral, but decisions lie outside the sphere to which moral judgments apply Management activity is outside or beyond the moral order of a particular code	Management activity conforms to a standard of ethical, or right, behavior. Conforms to accepted professional standards of conduct Ethical leadership is commonplace on the part of management
Motives	Selfish Management cares only about its or the organization's gains	Well-intentioned but selfish (impact on others is not considered)	Good Management wants to succeed but only within the confines of sound ethical precepts (fairness, justice, due process) Success within the confines of legal obedience and ethical standards
Goals	Organizational success at any price	Success; other goals are not considered	Success within the confines of legal obedience and ethical standards
Orientation toward Law	Legal standards are barriers that management must overcome to accomplish what it wants	Law is the ethical guide, preferably the letter of the law The central question is what can be done legally	Obedience toward letter and spirit of the law Law is a minimal ethical behavior Prefer to operate well above what law mandates
Strategy	Exploit opportunities for organizational gain Cut corners when it appears useful	Give managers free reign Personal ethics may apply but only if managers choose Respond to legal mandates if caught and required to do so	Live by sound ethical standards Assume leadership position when ethical dilemmas arise Enlightened self-interest

Source: Carroll (1987, 12).

With these types of approaches to moral management and organizational development, what is the best way to manage a diversity of values that emphasizes service to the commonweal? The aim of an ethically grounded system of management is to build and sustain a set of shared values that will be beneficial to the organization, its members, and the public (Berman & West, 1994). Maintaining the health of the system requires continuous communication and education that reaches beyond mere compliance with laws and rules, and involves communicating a vision of the organization and cultivating trust among its members and stakeholders.

Achieving consensus on values raises this puzzle: Do top officials designate a set of values that determine subordinate behavior and performance, or do the values of employees determine outcomes? The two directions of causality can be described as two institutional models of ethics (Table 8.2). The personal, negative, punitive, "low-road" compliance strategy is clearly important, for without it an ethics program may lack credibility. Yet it focuses on individuals, defines ethics as avoiding problems, emphasizes "symptom solving," fosters the view that ethical practices are best regulated from the outside rather than from within, and often uses ethics to control behavior instead of encouraging reflection. Heavy on proscription and light on prescription, the approach demands ethical compliance, not ethical competence.

TABLE 8.2	Comparing Low- and High-Road Compliance Strategies	
	Low-Road Compliance	**High-Road Compliance**
Ethos	Conformity with external standards	Self-governance according to chosen standards
Objective	Prevent criminal conduct	Enable responsible conduct
Leadership	Lawyer driven	Management driven
Methods	Training, limited discretion, controls, penalties	Education, leadership, accountability
Assumption	People driven by material self-interest	People guided by humanistic ideals

Source: Adapted from Paine (1994, 113).

The structural, affirmative, "high-road," integrity commitment system is aimed at deterring—rather than merely detecting—problems by emphasizing right behavior. Rather than blame and punishment, it focuses on reform and improvement. It is easy to manipulate an organization's policies and procedures relative to trying to change individual behavior. The challenge is to create systems that enable honesty. Programs focused on inspiring positive conduct are more effective than those limited to requiring compliance with minimal legal standards (Anechiarico & Jacobs, 1996; Clark, 2020; Hoekstra, Belling, & van der Heide, 2008; Rohr, 1988). Yet to the extent that the high road relies on the more mature levels of moral development theory, the approach, while laudable, may not be readily attainable.

The Organization for Economic Cooperation and Development (OECD) (1996) examined values management systems in nine countries and plotted them using a two-dimensional classification scheme with an integrity–compliance dimension and a public administration–managerialism dimension (Figure 8.1). The report concluded that a balance is needed, avoiding too much control (where nothing gets done) and too little control (where wrong things occur), and recognizes that each nation's ethics infrastructure must be based on local political and bureaucratic traditions.

| FIGURE 8.1 | **Classification by Integrity–Compliance Dimension and Public Administration–Managerialism Dimension** |

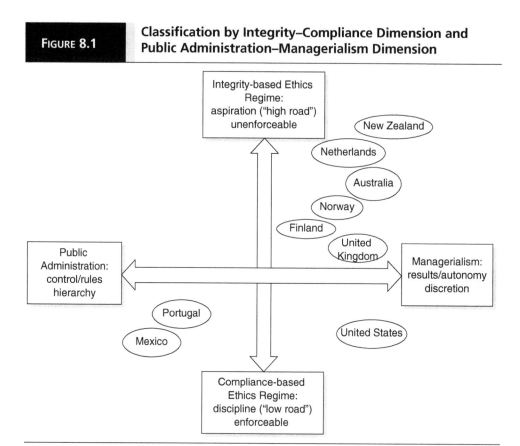

Source: Adapted from OECD (1996).

One dimension, a low-road strategy based on strict centralized compliance, emphasizes staying out of trouble; a high-road integrity approach relies on self-governance and personal responsibility for engaging in ethical behavior (Bowman, West, & Beck, 2010; Paine, 1994). The other dimension—a rule-based system built on hierarchy and control—differs from the results-oriented, flexible managerialist system. Tradeoffs must be finely calibrated for both dimensions between decentralization and control. In like measure, values management strategies must weigh the diverse values public servants bring to their work against the unity of purpose in government organizations needed to realize common goals.

A complete ethics strategy, then, should include all elements and involve a plan for what to do when something goes wrong. Overall, such programs are intended not mainly to prevent crimes (the purpose of law) and not simply to promote favorable public relations (the goal of public affairs staff). Their objective, instead, is to create and sustain confidence in government, nonprofit, and business arenas (Thompson, 2009). Precisely because people are not saints, ethical institutions, standards, and programs seek to channel human behavior in productive ways (Heclo, 2008, 25). That is, organizations have an opportunity to affect the moral agency of their employees, to reinforce their ethical identity. Although an effective system will not produce perfect people, an inadequate system will produce wrongdoers. Many of the organizations mired in scandal had rules in place and even won ethics awards. What they lacked was a proactive strategy—an ethical infrastructure—that relied more heavily on commitment than compliance.

Challenges arise when individual ethics clash with organizational ethics. The organizational ethos is often reflected in policies and procedures. An employee who possesses an affirmative, high-road personal ethic will resist a low-road compliance strategy he or she finds demeaning. The employee may express his or her concerns to management or resist the approach by ignoring it or meeting the minimum compliance requirement. Even a policy that reflects the high-road method may cause internal disagreements, because of differing positions on the appropriateness of implementing a policy. Someone who objects to a policy may recognize its ethics "on paper" but still feel the policy will produce unethical results in practice. The ethics triad presented in the previous chapter can be applied to resolve tensions between individual and organization ethics, and help decide whether the individual ought to resist a policy (see Case Study 8.1).

ETHICAL INFRASTRUCTURE: BUILDING BLOCKS IN ETHICS MANAGEMENT

Managers, as moral custodians of collective goals, are strategically placed to recognize factors that promote and inhibit laudatory behavior. Accordingly, they are responsible for providing a foundation for professional conduct. An ethical infrastructure includes the building blocks discussed in the next section: organizational structure, values statements, psychological contracts, oaths and codes, managing institutional ethics, and creating ethical competency. In developing this approach to ethical action, the following assumptions are made:

- The maintenance of a high level of trust and confidence between the public and its government is essential in democracy.
- Since each group in society is governed by a written or unwritten code of behavior, effort to encourage ethical action must be "culture based" and germane to the performance of public service.
- Humans are at least partially knowing beings, and while knowing is not an automatic process, the potential for learning exists. Modifying behavior, however, is a difficult task, and transformations should not be expected in the short run.
- Any significant organizational activity must be integrated into the mainstream of operations or it does not get done; ethical programs must be infused into the everyday life of the agency.

- In an institution where ethics is taken seriously, an atmosphere of trust, mutuality, and credibility will exist.
- Under appropriate circumstances, ethical programs can result in a different standard of conduct than would be achieved by the spontaneous development of group norms. (Bowman, 1983)

Stated differently, public confidence cannot be left to chance. The citizenry deserves assurance that government can be depended on to conduct the people's business according to high standards. Likewise, the public is entitled to socially responsible practices in the nonprofit and business areas.

CASE STUDY 8.1

Applying Philosophical and Behavioral Ethics Approaches: To Follow or Not to Follow Government Hiring Policy

The Human Resource Management Department of Metropolitan County government receives background checks on job applicants from the State Bureau of Investigation. The job in question is a supervisory position in a politically popular preschool summer program operated by the Parks and Recreation Department. Public policies state that hiring should not be biased against those with arrest (not conviction) records, because consideration of arrests may adversely affect some minority groups with higher-than-average arrest rates. Even convicted felons could be hired under certain circumstances, such as the nature of the offense and rehabilitation efforts. Patricia Cobb, a county human resource specialist, is concerned about two applicants. One has a deferred sentence for child molestation, the other a suspended sentence for domestic violence. While there was no legal conviction in either case, Patricia decided not to pass these files to the hiring authority in the Parks and Recreation Department and indicated instead that the other candidates "were a better fit" for the job. Now she is having second thoughts and wonders if she behaved unethically.

Both philosophical rationalism and psychological realism approaches, discussed in the last chapter, provide insight into thinking about this case.

Results-Based Analysis. Classical philosophy prescribes how people should act using the three schools of thought here. From a results perspective, Patricia believes she has minimized any risk to the student participants in the program by excluding the two applicants: the greatest good for the greatest number. She knows that any harm that may come to a child while in the care of the county would put the program in jeopardy. She realizes that a deferred or suspended sentence does not necessarily mean that the applicant would be technically "unqualified," but she did not want to take a chance that could result in danger to children.

Patricia is also aware that employees who disregard policy may be putting themselves at risk. If the two applicants learned that their files were not seriously considered, they might challenge the hiring process and question the grounds for their exclusion. The prior deferred and suspended sentences should not have been the basis for any action regarding their application. An appeal on these grounds would put the spotlight on Patricia and force her to explain actions difficult to justify.

Rule-Based Analysis. From a rules or principles perspective, Patricia's decision can be both supported and criticized. She violated organizational policy, which clearly states that the deferred and suspended sentences are not relevant criteria in hiring decisions. Employees who disregard policy can face adverse personnel actions. Patricia normally complies with policy; she views this as an exceptional circumstance. The Moral Minimum to "avoid and correct social injury" could be used in her defense. However, the "what is good for one is good for all" triad guideline mandates that applicants be reviewed according to the same screening standards.

All public employees should consider law and policy when making a decision. Substituting one's own judgment for policies that have been approved by legitimate bodies is typically ill-advised. Patricia could have consulted with her superiors before excluding the two candidates from the applicant pool. She failed to do so and violated the rights of the applicants by excluding them, putting them at an unfair disadvantage in the selection process. This is inconsistent with her role as a human resource management specialist. Any bias in the selection process is a breach of the merit system. Her professional obligation is to minimize any preferential treatment of applicants and to rule out criteria that are not strictly job related.

Virtue-Based Analysis. Considering virtue ethics, she must ask, "Does this decision represent what a virtuous person would do?" Honesty, integrity, and fairness are important virtues, and when Patricia indicates that other applicants were a "better fit for the job," she is not being entirely honest with the preschool's hiring department about her motivation in passing over these two candidates. While she may initially believe that she is preserving the preschool's integrity by excluding these applicants, she is also compromising integrity by rejecting two qualified individuals, denying them a chance at a job even though neither of them was legally convicted. This violates the preschool's integrity because the program has pledged not to consider arrest reports in its hiring process. Denying these two persons was unfair to them when they did not legally do anything wrong, and organizational policy says arrest records are not legitimate grounds for such denials.

Caring, prudence, and empathy are three other important virtues that help her to see another side of the dilemma. Patricia did mull over her decision and did not act in an arbitrary and capricious manner. She prides herself on her character traits of empathy and commitment to the best interests of children. She could not live with herself if harm were to come to a child because of a decision she made. It would violate her personal code to put children at risk. However, she also sees virtue in evenhanded treatment and policy compliance, recognizing that willingness to substitute one's personal judgment for established standard operating procedures can become a character flaw if taken too far or too often. She values her good judgment and believes she displayed practical wisdom, but she also knows of cases of wrongdoing when public administrators disregard organizational norms and act in any way they see fit.

Behavioral Ethics-Based Analysis. While the cognitive and virtue theories focusing on results, rules, and virtues help Patricia reason through her decision, the psychological realism approach embodied in behavioral ethics suggests that something else is needed for a complete analysis. The case, accordingly, can also be considered drawing on concepts such as bounded rationality, inadequate information, and ethical fading (Chapter 7). Recall that reason may be well intended—but also unreliable—due to unacknowledged, emotional effects on conduct (e.g., people tend to believe what they want to believe).

Bounded rationality suggests that decision makers often lack complete and accurate information, and even when they have it, they may not process it in a way that yields the best decision. Patricia did not discuss this issue with the appointing authority, neither did she dig deeper through fact-finding beyond what was on the applications.

She did not conduct an interview with the two excluded applicants to determine the details about prior arrests and whether they were just misunderstandings with no bearing on the position. Her focal concern on protecting the children might have blinded her to the unfairness to the two unsuccessful applicants. This is a framing issue indicating that ethical fading may have occurred. Clearly, Patricia must be alert to the possibilities of various irrational, unconscious influences by, for instance, consulting with others, setting aside time for reflection, and considering what might happen if her decision was posted in social media tomorrow.

Source: Case adapted from Sharp, Aguirre, and Kickham (2010, Case 48).

ORGANIZATIONAL STRUCTURE

The evolution from the "old" to the "new" public service in recent years has resulted in flatter organizational structures that are increasingly modifying or replacing hierarchical models. The former public service emerged from industrial-era government typified by centralized bureaucracies, routine standard operating procedures, and limited decision-making discretion. The new public service is defined as a postindustrial model typified by horizontal networks rather than vertical hierarchy, "flattened" agencies, cross-sector service delivery, and shared leadership structures. These changes bring managers into closer contact with employees, thereby potentially facilitating the communication of values. Networked organizations can enhance communication among different sections of the enterprise and foster employee interaction, even if they are not part of the same team. The resulting interactions should help managers and leaders align organizational values with diverse employee values and encourage personnel to develop behaviors integral to the organizational mission that may not flow from their existing value orientations.

Only by understanding the motivations and behavior of colleagues, and the different norms on which these are based, can values be synthesized or prioritized in ways that correspond to the agency's overall goals. Decentralization measures used to enhance organizational performance also can be used to produce a culture that helps translate varied values into a unified public service mission (Barrett, 2006, 199–200).

An organization can complement the new public service by encouraging honorable public service as compared to traditional civil service administration. As shown in Table 8.3, such a shift is animated by citizen-like commitments instead of bureaucratic administration.

	Public Service as Responsible Citizenship	Civil Service as Program Administration
TABLE 8.3 — Comparing Honorable Public Service With Civil Service Administration		
Guiding Documents	Declaration of Independence and the U.S. Constitution	Agency-specific law and regulation
Ethical Touchstone	Oath of Office (moral obligation)	Code of Ethics (regulatory and legal observance)
Orientation to Public Service	Public service as a calling Public servant as trustee	Government employment as a job Government employee as a delegate
Orientation to the U.S. Constitution	A work in progress, toward the achievement of the Preamble's promise	A rulebook and a guide to permissible action
Goal	The success of the "American experiment" in Republican government	Program effectiveness/efficiency
Justice Achieved Through	Benevolence, charity, love	Adherence to law and program success
Key Metaphor	The public as a commons	Government as a business
Time Orientation	Past, present and future	The short-term present
Key Audience	Citizens	Customers
Key Expectation of the Public	Responsible and engaged citizenship	Consumer of government goods and services
Approach to the Public	Engage and learn	Serve and guide
Engagement in Political Management	High—in service to the common good and regime values	Low—in service to neutral competence
Focus for Education of the Public Servant	Constitutional thinking, regime values, ethical behavior	Professional expertise and administrative excellence
Risk From Failure	Shame	Loss of power, pay, and perquisites

Source: Adapted from Newell (2016).

VALUES STATEMENTS

Kenneth Kernaghan (2003) identifies the values statement as the centerpiece for integrating values into public service. His analysis focuses on ways to embed values into organizational structures, processes, and systems. Statements alone do not promote value integration—efforts must be made to align values with actions—but they can furnish general guidance to aid in the creation of ethics codes and more detailed provisions customized to particular units. The challenge begins with identifying public service values and then assimilating them into the institutional culture, management processes, and practices. Christopher Bauer (2016) suggests six essentials when creating a values statement: make it organization-wide, keep it brief (four to eight values), write it with as few words as possible, identify only the most important values, vet the statement with everyone in the organization, and take the time to do it right. Thus, human resource management strategies can be designed to implement agency values through hiring, promotion, performance appraisal, training, and termination (West, 2016). During a job interview, commitment to the value of "meeting citizen needs," for instance, can be strengthened by asking applicants to provide examples of how their past actions support the goal of responding effectively to the general public (Berman & West, 2012).

Values integration requires leaders to set the tone in the organization and promote, protect, and manage the desired norms. Managers can hone moral insight and teach personnel how to translate values into praiseworthy behavior by emphasizing priorities, highlighting the role and importance of ethics, and providing feedback (e.g., "I appreciate your telling me that you are related to a candidate for the job we are seeking to fill"). Dynamic interaction between leaders and employees is central to the process of aligning values with the organizational mission.

OATHS AND CODES

An oath of office may share similarities with codes of ethics, a core element of a profession and a key component in an ethics program. Both raise the question of what difference such promises or commitments might make when taken seriously. An example of a government oath follows:

> Federal Oath of Office
> I, [name], do solemnly swear (or affirm) that I will support and defend the Constitution of the United States against all enemies, foreign and domestic; that I will bear true faith and allegiance to the same; that I take this obligation freely, without any mental reservation or purpose of evasion; and that I will well and faithfully discharge the duties of office on which I am about to enter. So help me God.
>
> (5 U.S.C. & 3331)

No shallow legalism, the pledge is profound moral commitment that "binds the conscience" and appeals to a higher authority (Rohr, 1986, Chapter 4; see also Bowman & West, 2020). Crises like a pandemic or war serve to magnify this unequivocal duty to protect and defend the constitution; the primary duty is to American institutors and ideals, not to elected officials. It is what distinguishes the public servant from those in other organizations.

Are oaths often dismissed because they are ineffective, or are they ineffective because they are dismissed? Scott Eblin (2010) answers, "Who knows? One thing I do know, however, is what doesn't get said, doesn't get heard." While it may be valid to question the efficacy of such commitments, it is also fair to ask if circumstances can be created in which they are effective. Indeed, Miller (2020) argues that college honor pledges—when taken seriously and not used as public relations stunts—not only promote honesty but also reduce cheating. Moral reminders—a commitment ceremony at the beginning of the term followed by affirming the honor code on assignments—can embed ethical behavior in the student culture. That is, an oath is one way organizations instill and reinforce core values in their members, and serves as a useful reminder of obligations such as faithful discharge of duties.

There are two types of code: conduct codes (Exhibit 8.1) and ethics codes (Exhibit 8.2). The former delineates—often in considerable detail—legislative and executive legal restraints placed on employees that typically prohibit the use of public position for private gain, gifts, conflicts of interest, nepotism, and political activity. Sanctions are levied for violations of conduct codes. Ethics codes, in contrast, may be promulgated by governments or professional associations and, typically, are aspirational in nature (Bruce, 1996). These codes, relatively brief and general, represent a collective recognition of professional responsibilities to nurture an environment wherein ethical behavior is the norm. Such canons are controversial, as opinions of them range from pointless and unnecessary to useful and important. What might be said is that codes are more likely to have indirect, rather than direct, effects. They can serve as a "signpost," leading employees to consult other employees and organizational policies; a "shield," allowing personnel to better challenge dubious actions; and an "alarm," encouraging individuals to report wrongdoing (Schwartz, 2011, 280). While codes cannot "solve" ethical conundrums, they do set standards, identify duties, and provide principles against which to assess behavior.

EXHIBIT 8.1	**Code of Conduct Sample**

United Nations (1996) Principles of the International Code for Public Officials

I. General Principles

1. A public office, as defined by national law, is a position of trust, implying a duty to act in the public interest. Therefore, the ultimate loyalty of public officials shall be to the public interests of their country as expressed through democratic institutions of government.

2. Public officials shall ensure that they perform their duties and functions efficiently, effectively and with integrity, in accordance with laws or administrative practices. They shall at all times seek to ensure that the public resources for which they are responsible are administered in the most effective and efficient manner.

3. Public officials shall be attentive, fair, and impartial in the performance of their functions and, in particular, in their relations with the public. They shall at no time afford any undue preferential treatment to any group or individual or improperly discriminate against any group or individual, or otherwise abuse the power and authority vested in them.

II. Conflict of Interest and Disqualification

1. Public officials shall not use their official authority for the improper advancement of their own or their family's personal or financial interest. They shall not engage

in any transaction, acquire any position or function or have any financial, commercial or other comparable interest that is incompatible with their office, functions and duties or the discharge thereof.

2. Public officials, to the extent required by their position, shall, in accordance with laws or administrative policies, declare business, commercial and financial interests or activities undertaken for financial gain that may raise a possible conflict of interest. In situations of possible or perceived conflict of interest between the duties and private interests of public officials, they shall comply with the measures established to reduce or eliminate such conflict of interest.

3. Public officials shall at no time improperly use public moneys, property, services or information that is acquired in the performance of, or as a result of, their official duties for activities not related to their official work.

4. Public officials shall comply with measures established by law or by administrative policies in order that after leaving their official positions they will not take improper advantage of their previous office.

III. Disclosure of Assets

1. Public officials shall, in accord with their position and as permitted or required by law and administrative policies, comply with requirements to declare or to disclose personal assets and liabilities, as well as, if possible, those of their spouses and/or dependants.

IV. Acceptance of Gifts or Other Favours

1. Public officials shall not solicit or receive directly or indirectly any gift or other favour that may influence the exercise of their functions, the performance of their duties or their judgment.

V. Confidential Information

1. Matters of a confidential nature in the possession of public officials shall be kept confidential unless national legislation, the performance of duty or the needs of justice strictly require otherwise. Such restrictions shall also apply after separation from service.

VI. Political Activity

1. The political or other activity of public officials outside the scope of their office shall, in accordance with laws and administrative policies, not be such as to impair public confidence in the impartial performance of their functions and duties.

Source: United Nations (1996).

EXHIBIT 8.2	**Code of Ethics Sample**

Code of Ethics for U.S. Government Service

Adopted July 11, 1958 Resolved by the House of Representatives {the Senate concurring}, that it is the sense of the Congress that the following Code of Ethics should be adhered to by all Government employees, including officeholders.

Code of Ethics for Government Service

Any person in Government service should:

1. Put loyalty to the highest moral principles and to country above loyalty to Government persons, party, or department.
2. Uphold the Constitution, laws, and legal regulations of the United States and of all governments therein and never be a party to their evasion.
3. Give a full day's labor for a full day's pay; giving to the performance of his duties his earnest effort and best thought.
4. Seek to find and employ more efficient and economical ways of getting tasks accomplished.
5. Never discriminate unfairly by the dispensing of special favors or privileges to anyone, whether for remuneration or not; and never accept for himself or his family, favors or benefits under circumstances which might be construed by reasonable persons as influencing the performance of his governmental duties.
6. Make no private promises of any kind binding upon the duties of office, since a Government employee has no private word which can be binding on public duty.
7. Engage in no business with the Government, either directly or indirectly which is inconsistent with the conscientious performance of his governmental duties.
8. Never use any information coming to him confidentially in the performance of governmental duties as a means for making private profit.
9. Expose corruption wherever discovered.
10. Uphold these principles, ever conscious that public office is a public trust.

Source: *House Ethics Manual* (n.d.).

To be taken seriously, managers need to translate code generalities into guidance for specific situations. Codes in government agencies, nonprofit and philanthropic organizations, and professional organizations, such as the American Society of Public Administration (ASPA) and the ICMA, all state that it is essential to be impartial, not to unfairly favor (or appear to favor) anyone in the performance of duties, and to avoid conflicts of interest or their appearance. These provisions, however, are often vague and open to interpretation. The ICMA code, to illustrate, states, "Members should disclose any personal relationship to the governing body in any instance where there could be the appearance of a conflict of interest." The language leaves the types ("instances") and nature ("appearance of conflict of interest") of specific encounters vulnerable to a variety of meanings. Other expressed values, such as loyalty, honesty, promise keeping, and privacy, are also susceptible to different definitions. Exhibit 8.3 compares the theory and practice of codes in the auditing profession. Ironically, the power of large accounting firms has been reinforced, not diminished by the accounting scandals in recent years, calling into question the effectiveness of regulatory oversight (Brooks, 2019).

While less than everything, oaths and codes are more than nothing, as they provide a standard against which behavior can be assessed. Indeed, arguments against them fail when asked for the grounds for rejection and for practical alternatives. Few observers suffer from the delusion that oaths and codes will dramatically improve conduct. These documents do, however, function as enabling devices to strive for high ideals and as record of professional consensus.

EXHIBIT 8.3 **Organizational Ethics and the Case of Auditing**

Auditing standards and procedures, George Lowenstein believes, virtually guarantee unethical behavior:

> Left justify In theory, auditors are supposed to represent the interests of external users of financial statements. They are paid by the company they audit . . . who can hire or fire them. . . . Moreover, auditors often socialize with company management. The American Institute of Certified Public Accountants acknowledges the pressures on auditors, but argues that personal integrity is sufficient for objectivity, . . . maintaining that "members should accept the obligation to act in a way that will serve the public interest . . . and demonstrate commitment to professionalism."
>
> (1996, 225–226)

Lowenstein thinks this standard is entirely unattainable for most auditors because those affected by misrepresentation are statistical in contrast to organization executives who would be personally impacted by a negative opinion, and such an opinion would likely mean immediate loss of business. Further, financial records are inherently ambiguous, so it is easy to rationalize departures from standards.

Sam McCall, the past national president of the Association of Government Accountants, recognized by the AICPA as Outstanding CPA in Government for Career Contributions, and member of the Institute of Internal Auditor's American Hall of Distinguished Audit Practitioners responded:

> The public's desire for reliable financial statements is the reason an independent auditing profession exists. It is made up of dedicated individuals, who have demonstrated their knowledge of accounting and auditing standards by passing the national Certified Public Accountant examination and who are licensed by state Boards of Accountancy. There is additional oversight audit by the Securities and Exchange Commission, the Public Company Accounting Oversight Board, the Government Accountability Office, the U.S. Department of Labor, and other federal, state, and local authorities.
>
> As to Lowenstein's assertions, it is true that an auditor is unlikely to issue a qualified opinion when minor monetary losses occur. The auditor's opinion is based on whether the financial statements are "fairly stated" and presented in accordance with Generally Accepted Accounting Principles (GAAP). The auditor is responsible for providing reasonable, not absolute, assurance that the statements are free of material misstatement, whether caused by error or fraud.
>
> As to loss of friendship, a contract, or unemployment, no auditor would knowingly jeopardize their license and career because of such factors. The profession is clear that auditors should honor the public trust, perform work with integrity, and be independent in fact and appearance.

The author also states that auditors may adapt to gradual changes in the company's financial condition and arrive at judgments consistent with self-interest rather than actual figures. The profession provides guidance when there are threats to independence caused by familiarity, undue influence, and self-interest. When these occur, the auditor is required to address and document them in the working papers by identifying safeguards (actions to eliminate or reduce the threat) or consider resignation from the audit.

Nonetheless, there have been audit failures that have tarnished the profession. These incidents lend support to the view that it is difficult for the auditor to be independent and think of the public interest at the same time the auditor is paid by the organization they audit.

For internal auditors, maintaining integrity and objectivity is challenging because the Chief Audit Executive (CAE) often has a dual reporting responsibility to both the Chief Executive Officer (CEO) and to the Board of Trustees. Since the CEO is the one that normally recommends raises and promotions, some have asserted the CAE may be less likely to report issues that cast the CEO in a bad light. A 2015 IIA survey found that 49 percent of CAE's were told not to perform work in high-risk areas and 32 percent were told to work in low-risk areas. Should the auditor succumb to such direction and undue influence, that would be a reflection on the auditor and not on the standards the auditor is professionally bound to follow. A company's Board of Trustees and audit committee should want to know about unacceptable risk posing a threat to operations and should fully expect the auditor to report those risks.

Most audit failures occur because the auditors lacked independence, placed firm profit ahead of their responsibility, or did not follow GAAS (Generally Accepted Auditing Standards). When company and auditor actions have been determined to be egregious, there have been significant consequences. Companies of note include Enron, WorldCom, and Bernard L. Madoff Investment Securities. Affected audit firms include Arthur Andersen (Enron and WorldCom) and Friehling & Horowitz (Madoff Securities). Firms convicted of wrongdoing lost their ability to file financial statements with the SEC and the privilege to practice. Individual independent auditors associated with the firms were sanctioned by their respective State Boards of Accountancy.

What is clear is that government cannot regulate greed or prevent persons or companies from committing fraud. Yet, Lowenstein offered little in the way of a better system of independent auditing. To be fair, since Lowenstein's comments, there has been a movement toward establishing Board appointed audit committees made up of financially literate members, requiring audit committee charters, and tasking the committee with selecting the external audit firm. Audit Committees have also addressed auditor independence when an audit firm has a multiple year contract by requiring a change in audit partners at least once every five years.

CPAs do not produce tangible products such as manufacturing goods. They provide a service which is an independent opinion on the accuracy of financial statements. The acceptance of the opinion is dependent on the public trusting the audit was conducted with integrity. For an auditor or firm to commit dishonorable acts is to jeopardize the accountants' license, public confidence, and the profession itself. That is why the word "Public" is so prominent in the CPA, Certified Public Accountant, designation.

(McCall, personal communication, November 24, 2017)

Behavioral ethics research (Chapter 7) demonstrates that people tend to be overconfident in their ethicality; indeed, there is some evidence that the mere exposure to money increases unethical activity. Unaware of or doubting the effect of blind spots, such as motivated reasoning and ethical fading, those exposed to such phenomena usually believe they are immune to their influence. When there is a conflict of interest, it is especially difficult for well-meaning individuals to see things objectively. This was poignantly noted by Upton Sinclair, who observed, "It is difficult to get a man to understand something, when his salary depends on his not understanding it."

In the end, do you think Lowenstein's or McCall's claims are the more illuminating? Why?

Source: Lowenstein (1996).

PSYCHOLOGICAL CONTRACTS

The psychological contract is another device that helps both parties in the employment relationship—the agency leadership and the individual employee—to understand reciprocal obligations. These contracts are typically informal agreements that seek to increase commitment to the organization and its mission by clarifying expectations, addressing ambiguity, and establishing a balance between expectations and contributions (Berman & West, 2003; Guest, 2000). Once consensus is reached on core organizational values, managers work with individuals to develop a contract that translates values into performance-specific obligations (e.g., more timely response to citizens' service requests).

Psychological contracts enhance personal well-being by fostering a sense of security through "mutual commitment on the part of managers and employees to shared ideals and values, and shared organizational identity" (Bruce, 2000, 136). By emphasizing the multifaceted components of spiritual and professional development, these agreements help employees "bring their whole selves" to work, while concurrently communicating departmental values and reinforcing organizational culture in daily work (Selden, 2009, 63–64, 87). These contracts promote ethical behavior and prevent devolution into "anti-ethics" while also making personnel accountable to each other, as well as to management (Barrett, 2006, 114; Bruce, 2000).

INSTITUTIONALIZING ETHICS CULTURAL COMPETENCY

A valuable question is how oaths and codes are created, and what developmental activities accompany them. Oaths and codes should be a part of a larger effort to nourish the organizational culture by offering incentives, reducing opportunities for corruption, and increasing the risk of unethical behavior. The strategy, designed and implemented by a representative task force of employees, is to conduct a self-generated needs assessment. Depending on the results of the task force efforts, initiatives could include

- decision-making mechanisms (e.g., the use of an ethics board, an "angel's" advocate, or an ombudsperson),
- promotional activities (e.g., posting the code and reprinting it in agency reports; establishing an awards program), and
- personnel system changes (e.g., recruitment, training (see later), performance evaluation processes including a specification of the ethical dimensions of tasks in job descriptions, independent grievance processes, whistleblower protections, and sanctions).

Periodic ethics audits—document reviews, interviews, vulnerability assessments, survey data, and evaluation of existing systems—provide an ongoing appraisal of the effectiveness of the program. Indeed, the Program Effectiveness Index could be used to assess ethical decision-making, organizational justice, and freedom of expression (Jacobs, 2017). In addition, the use of Ethical Impact Statements, modeled after environmental impact statements (prepared prior to major federal decisions affecting the natural environment), can "assist in setting priorities and realistic objectives, identify early on the problems and needed corrections in policy or regulation, pinpoint unsettled issues and unanticipated effects . . . and inform decision makers and the public" (Lewis & Gilman, 2012, 267–268).

Stated differently, leaders should "ask for trouble." If the old rule was never surprise the boss, then the new rule should be to tell her about the problem to foster learning and accountability. The focus, then, is on prevention and solutions, not blame and consequences. When dealing with issues is a natural part of daily work, not something to be feared or avoided, people become more confident and competent (Mabry, 2017, September 6). To address small problems before they become big ones, the "bad-news-never-travels-up" norm should be discarded; instead, agency leadership should clearly support those identifying issues, ensure the problems are investigated, visibly protect and reward the employees, and take them and their colleagues to lunch (Behn, 2017).

Several more types of institutionalization warrant attention. First, the Office of Inspector General is an oversight unit of a federal or state agency aimed at detecting and preventing fraud, waste, and abuse (Newcomer & Johnson, 2020). Some federal IGs are appointed by the president; others are designated by agency secretaries. While the IG Act of 1978 requires that these officials be selected based upon merit, presidential candidates, none the less, are considered political appointees because of their political and partisan relationships. Presidentially appointed IGs can only be removed from their positions by the president, whereas agency IGs can be terminated by the department head.

In 2020, the president replaced five IGs in less than two months. Legislators criticized the actions as politically motivated retribution and part of a pattern to neutralize constitutional checks and balances. Democrats introduced a House of Representatives bill in 2020 that would provide seven-year terms for IGs and protect against retaliation by requiring that removals must only occur for a just cause (also consult, US Government Accountability Office, 2020).

Second, while most agencies do not have a dedicated avenue for dissent, the U.S. State Department has had a long-standing, effective Dissent Channel that permits officials to directly contest policy with senior executives. The Secretary of State and his staff reply to messages within 60 days, and employees are shielded from retaliation. In recent years, however, the procedure has been criticized: "it is common for dissenters to receive a response that does not engage the merits of the dissent" (Foreign Service Officer quoted in Davidson, 2020; for a broader look at agency dissent channels, consult Van Schooten & Schwellenbach, 2020).

Various forms of institutionalization, then, hold the potential to enhance organizational life. An example from history is the 20th-century adoption of the merit system in federal government. Yet that transformation can be a slow, frustrating process (e.g., torture of alleged terrorists, and who is and who is not honored for their roles, as shown in Exhibit 8.4; also, consult Bowman et al., 2010, Ch. 5; also refer to Hajjar, 2021, February 17).

All of these initiatives can help employees translate values into honorable behavior. Training, in particular, can focus on making all personnel aware of their responsibilities by understanding ethical principles, behavioral standards, and legal requirements—not merely as just another organizational routine, but rather as integral to the core of the organization. To be effective, the program should engender recognition of critical values and how they may be interpreted in different contexts (also consult True Office Learning, 2021, on operationalizing code of conduct training). One creative FBI educational program, designed to ensure that trainees keep morality in mind, includes a visit to the Washington, DC, Holocaust Museum. Trainees must learn not only how to follow policies but also how to make decisions that speak to their spirit in situations not addressed by value statements, oaths, and codes. In addition to training, outreach activities—having personnel at all levels meet those who they serve, staff call-in public information and help lines, monitor social media, conduct web chats—will bring employees into contact with those affected by agency decisions (Newell, 2015, 161–162).

Exhibit 8.4	**Honoring Those Who Said No to Torture**

Thus far, only those public officials who approved torture, not those who vigorously protested against it as an abandonment of the rule of law and morality, have been honored. In 2004, President George W. Bush awarded the nation's highest civilian award, the Presidential Medal of Freedom, to the former Central Intelligence Agency director who had authorized "enhanced" interrogation. The Army general responsible for prisoners at Guantánamo was given the Distinguished Service Medal. One of the lawyers responsible for the Bush administration's "torture memos" received awards from the Justice Department, the Defense Department, and the National Security Agency (NSA).

President Barack Obama (a) prohibited cruelty as official American policy, (b) retained illegal rendition and detention practices in modified form, (c) opposed an official inquiry into the efficacy and legality interrogation methods, and (d) resisted investigation and prosecution of those responsible. Maintaining that the country should look forward, not back, the president appeared to consider torture to be an unfortunate policy choice instead of war crimes in violation of U.S. laws and international treaties.

While it may be impossible to prove that degrading and inhumane treatment never works, there is a great deal of evidence suggesting that it is an ineffective way to gather reliable intelligence. For example, the Defense Department's Intelligence Science Board found that there is no scientific evidence to demonstrate that cruelty produces valid information (see Case Study 11.1). But framing the controversy in terms of the efficiency of cruelty misses the point: "This is," as Senator John McCain (2011) indicates, "a moral debate. It is about who we are." The only way to resolve such a dispute is on the basis of principle. It is noteworthy that most of those who were willing to accept painfully excruciating methods are unwilling, on the grounds of national security, to document cases that they argue justified extreme techniques; they were also not prepared to state that, as a matter of principle, they favor torture (Neier, 2011):

> A refusal to torture, like a refusal to use terrorism, is a basic dividing line between civilized and uncivilized peoples. . . . The American republic rests upon the centrality of human liberty and dignity. . . . We must secure our principles as we secure our nation.
>
> (Bandow, 2011)

One way to do that is to recognize that those civil and military public servants who stayed true to American values, and stood up against cruelty, are worthy of a wide range of civilian and military commendations. Recognizing them is a way of encouraging the best in our public servants, now and in the future. It is a way of honoring the best in ourselves, a nation and people worthy of Jefferson, Washington, and Madison.

Note: In 2011, George W. Bush canceled a trip to Switzerland, where alleged victims of torture intended to file a criminal complaint against him.

Sources: Adapted from Bandow (2011), Jaffer and Siems (2011), McCain (2011), and Neier (2011).

Overall, a self-governance approach to ethical competency is needed. Beyond understanding policies and statutes, de las Fuentes, Willmuth, and Yarrow (2005) recommend that the workforce should learn to (a) develop moral reasoning skills, (b) appreciate the cultural contexts from which beliefs derive, and (c) comprehend the values on which codes are built. Rest's (1983) model is a useful guide for honing reasoning abilities, recognizing a dilemma, employing a cognitive understanding of the issues involved, deciding on a course of action, and implementing an appropriate response.

Recognizing the principles on which codes are written—duty, justice, equity, utility, public interest—can provide the basis for critically evaluating or justifying actions, when simply referring to a code is not sufficient. Assessments of ethical skill can be conducted using "360-degree" evaluations, whereby all of those in the learning environment provide feedback to the trainee. Critical incident methodology can also be useful in noting whether, or in what ways, the individual has recognized a dilemma and responded in an ethical manner using appropriate (or inappropriate) sensitivity. Finally, case studies, role plays, and vignettes based on ethics codes allow trainees to demonstrate logic and decision-making, and help reveal the thought processes used in code interpretation (West & Berman, 2013).

Another ethical infrastructure dimension is the cultivation of cultural awareness. Organizational values are not always understood by employees, even when managers attempt to communicate them in a variety of ways (Paarlberg & Perry, 2007). Further, organizational values, as determined by leaders and managers, are most effectively operationalized when they correspond to employees' existing values. This receptivity requires skillful values management within a changing public service. The intent is to develop cultural sensitivity among organizational members given the multiple identities of the workforce, including race, culture, ethnicity, gender, age, religion, disability, and sexual orientation. Additional differences in communication style, education, work style, organizational role, sectorial location, economic status, national/geographic origin, and conceptions of work (as a job, a career, or a calling) further complicate implementation of values management initiatives. What are some of the strategies and issues involved in cultivating shared organizational values in a diverse workforce and linking those with employees' existing values? How can ethical and cultural competency be promoted given system reforms and increased workforce heterogeneity?

A model based on the work of Arredondo et al. (1996, 11–27) is helpful in understanding how cultural competency contributes to ethical competency. Multicultural abilities encompass an acknowledgment of one's personal assumptions, values, and biases; an understanding of the different orientations of diverse colleagues; and the skill to think creatively. Arredondo and colleagues identify characteristics of culturally skilled personnel: (a) recognition of how personal cultural background and experiences shape attitudes, values, and biases; (b) knowledge about personal racial and cultural heritage and how these affect perspectives and behavior; and (c) skills acquired through educational, consultative, and training experiences to improve working with culturally diverse populations.

To comprehend the worldview of diverse coworkers, Arrendondo et al. (1996) point out that culturally skilled staff must be aware of prevailing stereotypes; discern how race, culture, ethnicity, and religion may influence attitudes and behaviors; and become involved with minority individuals outside the workplace. Their objective is to respect coworkers' values, recognize how convictions may affect work habits, be alert that the beliefs of cultural groups may clash, and be capable of promoting accurate and appropriate verbal and nonverbal communication among various groups.

Cultural competency alone is not sufficient in establishing norms that form the basis for individual and organizational ethical behavior. Recognition of cultural differences must be matched by an attempt to reach consensus on a set of universal values that transcend particular belief systems, create value links among different groups, and thus lead to a higher form of value formation (Barrett, 2006). Cultural sensitivity and value formation must take place within the context of the overall mission, for organizations cannot simply reflect the sum total of the beliefs of their employees. Without a clear mission based on a cohesive set of values, there is the danger that organizational fragmentation and empire-building lead to self-interest prevailing over the common good (116).

Diversity management plays a critical role in combining cultural competency with the integration of organizational values necessary to enhance performance. It is the process by which employee diversity is turned into a creative force by producing a synergy of values through workshops and activities that challenge "the way things are usually done." Diversity by itself may not be productive; in fact, without the proper management, it may result in poor morale, personnel problems, and decreased work-unit effectiveness (Choi, 2009; Dobbin, Kalev, & Kelly, 2007; Pitts & Jarry, 2007). Unmanaged diversity on company boards, for instance, has proved to be divisive and unproductive (Manzoni, Strebel, & Barsoux, 2010). Only through concerted management techniques can the creative potential of a multicultural workforce be fulfilled to contribute to the organizational mission (Collins, 2010, 107). Possible methods include sensitivity training, team-building, mentoring programs, and discussion of communication styles.

Managing ethics in institutions is not just about implementing specific initiatives. Rather, the ethical context or climate of the organization is at least as important. That context includes such elements as admirable leadership, reward systems, perceived "fairness" of the organization, and ethics as a topic of daily conversation (Weaver, Treviño, & Cochran, 1999). Ethics programs can help maintain a moral course in organizations and support employee growth. While they have many benefits, they should be established not simply for instrumental reasons but because it is the right thing to do (McNamara, 1998). A viable infrastructure includes exemplary officials, meaningful oaths and codes, a legal framework, accountability mechanisms, effective human resource systems, and a supportive citizenry. In many ways, as Exhibit 8.5 demonstrates, training opportunities serve as a centerpiece of an ethics program. Yet to the extent that such initiatives rely on untested assumptions and models about rationality—at the expense of understanding why people behave unethically—they have very real limitations in affecting change (see Chapter 7 for a discussion of behavioral ethics).

EXHIBIT 8.5	**Ethics Training**

Ethics instruction is a central component of any meaningful strategy for promoting an organizational environment. While both the tangible controls and the intangible nudges that constitute an organization's ethical infrastructure are essential, training is the key complement to both. It can provide realistic simulations of "the ways things are done around here," thereby increasing the probability of compliance. The resultant sharpening of ethical awareness and problem-solving can bolster proper behavior. Yet not all instructional programs are created equal.

West and Berman (2004) found that although ethics training initiatives are widespread in city governments, they vary widely in both purpose and form. Following Paine's (1994) high-road/low-road distinction, training can either take the low road, serving "defensive" purposes such as avoiding embarrassment or adverse legal action, or it can take the high road, furthering "aspirational purposes" like contributing to a positive organizational culture or developing employees' critical thinking skills.

These differing approaches are far from merely symbolic—their divergent emphases influence the content of instruction. Organizations that "take the high road" are more likely to delve into topics such as transparency and the importance of ethics, whereas those that opt for the low road focus on technical understandings of issues such as conflict of interest. The form that programs take is also important. Live instruction that is "reality based" and "practical"—exercises that include hypothetical scenarios and case studies and provide opportunities to practice decision-making skills—is the most effective pedagogical approach (West & Berman, 2004, 195–197).

Through the use of statistical models that suggest causality, it was found that "training is associated with fostering organizational cultures of openness, accountability, and performance that, in turn, are associated with increased employee productivity" (West & Berman, 2004, 202). This is not an all-too-surprising conclusion; a recurring theme of this book is that acting ethically and acting effectively often go hand in hand. The finding is nevertheless worthy of careful attention, as approximately 85 percent of city governments use training for at least some defensive purposes (195). They frequently pass up opportunities to enhance their strategies by employing such techniques as incorporating ethics training into new-employee orientation (197; for an account of similar shortcomings in state government, see Menzel, 2012, 82–86). Carefully crafting an instructional program should therefore be a primary concern of any manager seeking to grow an ethically oriented organization.

No strategy will be without criticism, but if all proposals are rejected until perfection is guaranteed, then improvement is unlikely. In the meantime, agencies should plant and cultivate standards by which an individual can measure his or her activities, encourage the correction of deficiencies, and aid in the identification and minimization of those institutional conditions that lead to unethical actions. This effort should establish a culture that encourages the asking of right questions to facilitate discussion. Most problems, including ethical ones, are more easily prevented than they are corrected. Effective prevention is an initiative that includes instruction, celebrates exemplary employees, holds wrongdoers accountable, and integrates ethics into the routines of the department. The issue is not whether norms of conduct will be communicated but rather what they are, how they are disseminated, and whether all personnel are fully conscious of the ethical dimensions of work. Such a program can provide a point of departure (like the top of a jigsaw puzzle box), offer guidance to know what to do in the absence of a specific rule, and serve as an empowering device to strive for high ideals. Not failure but low aim is a tragedy.

CONCLUSION

Ethics provides coherence to organizational policies and individual behavior. Without consistent behavior, there would be no working together. It is imperative to develop a widely shared vocabulary of ethics in institutions. Men and women in workplaces that value and nurture a reputation for integrity are the surest safeguard against corruption. If ethics, the cornerstone of organizational practice, is not explicit to each person, then the prospects of making praiseworthy decisions and accepting responsibility are diminished.

The steps detailed in this chapter will not by themselves build a moral community. The system cannot operate without leaders with formal authority, but what really makes it work is moral authority (Freidman, 2017, June 21). Ethics programs can only reinforce a moral climate, but they cannot create it—that remains the function of leadership. Ethics initiatives are difficult to establish and maintain (Gilman, 2005). Those involved must embed moral imperatives into the work of the agency. Underlying formal systems are influential informal norms that teach employees behaviors that are really expected at work. It is the task of leadership to align formal obligations with informal practices. In the absence of such an approach, expediency is likely to dominate. If organizations do not take action to prevent unethical conduct, it is an abdication of responsibility and they should be held responsible for the misconduct that occurs within them.

***

Mostly, we are good when it makes sense. A good society is one that makes sense of being good.

—Ian McEwan

DISCUSSION

1. Describe differences between immoral, amoral, and moral management. Identify examples of organizations that appear to be representative of each type, including those of which you are or have been a member (e.g., clubs; colleges; or business, nonprofit, or governmental organizations).

2. While an organizational ethics infrastructure can enhance individual judgment, it is not a substitute for it. Examine this claim.

3. The nonprofit sector is sometimes referred to as "America's conscience." Indeed, the sector historically has escaped the kind of scrutiny directed at government and business. Ironically, however, not-for-profit agencies have not generally developed ethical infrastructures common in the other sectors. This is especially surprising because their work often involves society's most vulnerable members. Discuss.

4. Discuss some ways that the informal ethics behaviors (e.g., hallway conversations, peer reporting, social rewards, or punishment based on work-group approval) may reinforce or be in conflict with formal ethics structures (e.g., codes of conduct, core value statements, ethics training).

5. One study found that ethics books were far more likely to be missing from libraries than other areas of philosophy. Consult a classmate to speculate why this is the case. (Hint: Are any behavioral science findings germane?)

EXERCISES

1. Complete:

    *   Analyze the code of ethics used by your university or place of employment using the ethics trinity (Chapter 7). Is the code largely based on results, rules, or rectitude? How could it be enhanced?
    *   Visit www.aspanet.org/public/, go to the "Resources" tab, and then click "Code of Ethics" to view the American Society for Public Administration's ethics code. Critique it.
    *   Provide brief general background information on the organizational size, sector, and geographic location of an organization familiar to you. Compare and contrast the ethical infrastructure of the organization with the material in this chapter.

2. You have a friend from a foreign country who is returning home to attend medical school. Unfortunately, admissions officials expect bribes. Your friend has asked for your help. What do you say and why? (This scenario is based on Randy Cohen's 2004 column in the *New York Times*.) Your response could employ materials in this chapter, the ethics triad and behavioral ethics (Chapter 7), or Kohlberg's moral development theory (Chapter 4).

3. Vienna subways, inexpensive and efficient, work on the honor system. There are no ticket turnstiles at stations and no routine ticket checks. However, purchasing a ticket is a good idea, as undercover agents randomly ask to see tickets. Riders with no tickets are fined $100. Comment on this system in light of compliance-based and integrity-based organizational ethics systems. Consider these points:

    *   You can have an ethical organization but not a quality organization; you cannot have a quality organization without being ethical.
    *   Does removing turnstiles encourage passenger integrity, or does it do more harm than good?
    *   Does random checking without warning constitute integrity-based practice?

4. Respond to these claims:

    *   "If you think you can get away with it, don't do it."—Texas senator Carl Parker
    *   "To be the best, you must be able to handle the worst."—Wilson Kanadi

5. In support of an independent, nonpartisan career service, #UpholdTheOath describes itself as "a digital project that celebrates America's federal civil servants and encourages them to publicly reaffirm their commitment to the ideals list in the oath of office." It requests that they record and submit a video of themselves retaking the pledge. It is planned that these videos will be released as a public service announcement to demonstrate commitment to the constitution. Visit #UpholdTheOath and report to the class what you found and the impact it may have had on you.

6. Summarize your notes and establish links between chapter and course objectives. Continue to do this as self-study exercise. While doing this, create sentence stems (see Chapter 1) for use in discussion.

7. Access and view "The Ghosts of Abu Ghraib" on YouTube. The Hajjar (2021) reference below may be helpful in thinking about the video.

REFERENCES

Anechiarico, F., & Jacobs, J. (1996). *The pursuit of absolute integrity: How corruption control makes government ineffective*. Chicago: University of Chicago Press.

Arredondo, P., Toporek, R., Brown, S., Jones, J., Lock, D., Sanchez, J. et al. (1996). *Operationalization of the multicultural counseling competencies*. Alexandria, VA: American Counseling Association.

Bandow, D. (2011, June 13). Getting Osama Bin Laden: The case against torture. *Huffington Post*. Retrieved from http://huffingtonpost.com/doug-bandow/getting-osama-bin-laden-t_b_861451.html

Barrett, R. (2006). *Building a values-driven organization: A whole system approach to cultural transformation*. Burlington, MA: Butterworth—Heinemann.

Bauer, C. (2016). *An ethics thought—Six values statement essentials*. Nashville, TN: The Author.

Behn, B. (2017). Take a whistleblower to lunch. *Performance Leadership Report*. Retrieved from https://thebehnreport.hks.harvard.edu/files/thebehnreport/files/behnreport_2017-8_aug.pdf

Berman, E., & West, J. (1994). Values management in local government. *Review of Public Personnel Administration*, *14*, 6–23.

Berman, E., & West, J. (2003). Psychological contracts in local government: A preliminary survey. *Review of Public Personnel Administration*, *23*, 267–285.

Berman, E., & West, J. (2012). Public values in special districts: A survey of managerial commitment. *Public Administration Review*, *72*, 43–54.

Bowman, J. (1983). Ethical issues for the public manager. In W. Eddy (Ed.), *Handbook of organizational management* (pp. 69–89). New York: Marcel Dekker.

Bowman, J., & West, J. (2020). Pointless or powerful: The case for oaths of office. *Administration and Society*, *52*(8), 1147–1169.

Bowman, J., West, J., & Beck, M. (2010). *The professional edge: Competencies in public service* (2nd ed.). Armonk, NY: M. E. Sharpe.

Brooks, R. (2019). *Bean counters: The triumph of the accountants and how they broke capitalism*. Halifax, NS: Atlantic Books.

Bruce, W. (1996). Codes of ethics and codes of conduct. In J. Bowman (Ed.), *Public integrity annual* (pp. 23–30). Lexington, KY: Council of State Governments.

Bruce, W. (2000). Breaking the psychological contract: An act of anti-ethics. *Global Virtue Ethics Review*, *2*(2), 134–174.

Carroll, A. (1987). In search of the moral manager. *Business Horizons*, *30*, 7–15.

Choi, S. (2009). Diversity in the US federal government: Diversity management and employee turnover in federal agencies. *Journal of Public Administration Research and Theory*, *19*, 603–630.

Clark, T. (2020, October 13). To foster innovation, cultivate a culture of intellectual bravery. *Harvard Business Review*. Retrieved from https://hbr.org/2020/10/to-foster-innovation-cultivate-a-culture-of-intellectual-bravery

Cohen, R. (2004, October 10). Acceptable bribe. *New York Times*. Retrieved from www.nytimes.com/2004/10/10/magazine/10ETHICIST.html?n=Top%2fFeatures%2fMagazine%2fColumns%2fThe%20Ethicist&_r=0

Collins, D. (2010). Designing ethical organizations for spiritual growth and superior performance: An organization systems approach. *Journal of Management, Spirituality, and Religion*, *7*, 95–117.

Davidson, J. (2020, July 31). Some federal agencies have dissent channels. A report says they aren't working. *Washington Post*. Retrieved from www.washingtonpost.com/politics/some-federal-agencies-have-dissent-channels-a-report-says-they-arent-working/2020/07/30/d242a114-d29e-11ea-af07-1d058ca137ae_story.html

de las Fuentes, C., Willmuth, M., & Yarrow, C. (2005). Competency training in ethics education and practice. *Professional Psychology: Research and Practice*, *36*, 362–366.

Dobbin, F., Kalev, A., & Kelly, E. (2007). Diversity management in corporate America. *Contexts*, *6(4)*, 21–28. Retrieved from https://scholar.harvard.edu/dobbin/files/2007_contexts_dobbin_kalev_kelly.pdf

Eblin, S. (2010, May 24). Why we need an MBA oath. *Government Executive*. Retrieved from www.govexec.com/excellence/executive-coach/2010/05/why-we-need-an-mba-oath/39874/

Freidman, T. (2017, June 21). Where did we the people go? *New York Times*. Retrieved from www.nytimes.com/2017/06/21/opinion/where-did-we-the-people-go.html

Gilman, S. (2005, Winter). Ethics codes and codes of conduct as tools for promoting ethical and professional public service: Comparative successes and lessons. *PREM Paper*. Washington, DC: World Bank.

Guest, D. (2000). *The psychological contract in the public sector*. London: Chartered Institute of Personnel Development.

Hajjar, L. (2021, February 17). *'The Mauritanian' rekindles devate over Gitmo deainees' torture— with 40 still held there*. Retrieved from 'The Mauritanian' rekindles debate over Gitmo detainees' torture – with 40 still held there (theconversation.com)

Heclo, H. (2008). *On thinking institutionally*. St. Paul, MN: Paradigm.

Hoekstra, A., Belling, A., & van der Heide, E. (2008). A paradigmatic shift in ethics and integrity management within the Dutch public sector? Beyond compliance—A practitioners' view. In L. Huberts, J. Maesschalck, & C. Jurkiewicz (Eds.), *Ethics and integrity of governance: Perspectives across frontiers* (pp. 143–158). Cheltenham: Edward Elgar.

House Ethics Manual: Code of Ethics for Government Service. (n.d.). Retrieved from www.house.gov/ethicsreform/Appendix_Code_of_Ethics.html

Jacobs, R. (2017, July 28). Building a 'core' culture: The public administrator as ethical leader and chief learning officer. *PA Times*. Retrieved from http://patimes.org/building-core-culture-public-administrator-ethical-leader-chief-learning-officer/

Jaffer, J., & Siems, L. (2011, April 17). Honoring those who said no. *New York Times*. Retrieved from www.nytimes.com/2011/04/28/opinion/28jaffer.html

Kernaghan, K. (2003). Integrating values into public service: The values statement as centerpiece. *Public Administration Review*, *63*, 711–718.

Lewis, C., & Gilman, S. (2012). *The ethics challenge in public service* (3rd ed.). San Francisco: Jossey-Bass.

Lowenstein, G. (1996). Behavioral decision theory and business ethics: Skewed trade-offs between self and other. In D. Messick & A. Tensbrunsel (Eds.), *Codes of conduct: Behavioral research into business ethics* (pp. 214–229). New York: Russell Sage Foundation.

Mabry, S. (2017, September 6). Why you should be asking for trouble. *Soul2Work*. Retrieved from https://soul2work.com/2017/09/why-you-should-be-asking-for-trouble/

Manzoni, J., Strebel, P., & Barsoux, J. (2010, January 25). Why diversity can backfire on company boards. *Wall Street Journal*, p. R3.

McCain, J. (2011, May 11). Bin Laden's death and the debate over torture. *Washington Post*. Retrieved from www.washintonpost.com/opinions/bin-ladens-death-and-the-debate-over-torture/2011/05/11

McNamara, C. (1998). *Complete guide to ethics management: An ethics toolkit for managers.* Retrieved from www.managementhelp.org/ethics/ethxgde.htm

Menzel, D. C. (2012). *Ethics management for public administrators: Leading and building organizations of integrity* (2nd ed.). Armonk, NY: M. E. Sharpe.

Miller, C. (2020, November 13). Just how dishonest are students? *New York Times*. Retrieved from www.nytimes.com/2020/11/13/opinion/sunday/online-learning-cheating.html

Neier, A. (2011, May 14). "Enhanced" to the point of torture. *Washington Post*. Retrieved from www.washintonpost.com/opinions/enhanced-to-the-pointof-torture/2011/05/013/AFQhDz2G

Newcomer, K., & Johnson, C. (2020). *U.S. inspectors general: Truth tellers in turbulent times*. Washington, DC: Brookings.

Newell, T. (2015). *To serve with honor: Doing the right thing in government.* Crozet, VA: Loftlands Press.

Newell, T. (2016, December 13). Beyond ethics: Honor and public service. *PA Times*. Retrieved from http://patimes.org/ethics-honor-public-service/

Organisation for Economic Cooperation and Development (OECD). (1996). *Ethics in the public service: Current issues and practice.* Public Management Occasional Papers No. 14.

Paarlberg, L., & Perry, J. (2007). Values management: Aligning employee values and organizational goals. *American Review of Public Administration*, *37*, 387–408.

Paine, L. (1994). Managing for organizational integrity. *Harvard Business Review*, *72*, 106–117.

Pitts, D., & Jarry, E. (2007). Ethnic diversity and organizational performance: Assessing diversity effects at the managerial and street levels. *International Public Management Journal*, *10*, 233–254.

Rest, J. R. (1983). Morality. In J. H. Flavell & E. M. Markman (Eds.), *Handbook of child psychology: Vol. 3: Cognitive Development* (pp. 556–629, 4th ed.). New York: John Wiley & Sons.

Rohr, J. (1986). *To run a constitution: Legitimacy of the administrative state*. Lawrence: University of Kansas Press.

Rohr, J. (1988). *Ethics for bureaucrats* (2nd ed.). New York: Marcel Dekker.

Schwartz, M. (2011). How to minimize corruption in business organizations: Developing and sustaining an ethical corporate culture. In R. Burke, E. Tomlinson, & C. Cooper (Eds.), *Crime and corruption in organizations: Why it occurs and what to do about it* (pp. 273–296). Farnham: Gower.

Selden, S. (2009). *Human capital: Tools and strategy for the public sector*. Washington, DC: CQ Press.

Sharp, B., Aguirre, G., & Kickham, K. (2010). *Managing in the public sector: A casebook in ethics and leadership*. New York: Pearson.

Thompson, D. (2009). Obama's ethics agenda: The challenge of coordinated change. *The Forum*, *7*, Article 8.

True Office Learning (2021). 6 steps to revitalize the last mile of code of conduct training. https://www.trueofficelearning.com/revitalize-code-of-conduct-training-in-6-steps-0

United Nations. (1996). *General Assembly Resolution 51/59: Action against corruption*. Retrieved from www.un.org/documents/ga/res/51/a51r059.htm

US Government Accountability Office. (2020, June 8). *Inspectors general: Independence principles and considerations for reform*. Washington, DC: Author.

Van Schooten, D., & Schwellenbach, N. (2020). *Stifling Dissent*. Retrieved from www.pogo.org/report/2020/07/stifling-dissent/ *Ss dissent how the federal*

Weaver, G. R., Treviño, L. K., & Cochran, P. L. (1999). Integrated and decoupled corporate social performance: Management commitments, external pressures, and corporate ethics practices. *Academy of Management Journal, 42*, 539–552.

West, J. (2016). Ethics and HRM. In R. Kearney & J. Coggburn (Eds.), *Public human resource management: Problems and prospects* (6th ed., pp. 297–311). Washington, DC: CQ Press.

West, J., & Berman, E. (2004). Ethics training in U.S. cities: Content, pedagogy, and impact. *Public Integrity, 6*, 189–206

West, J., & Berman, E. (2013). Ethics management and training. In N. M. Riccucci (Ed.), *Public personnel management: current concerns, future challenges* (3rd ed.). New York: Longman.

9 Corruption Control

A people that values its privileges above its principles soon loses both.

—Dwight Eisenhower

One indication of failure to develop a robust ethics infrastructure in institutions is the presence of corruption. Because most of it is clandestine, no one really knows the magnitude of corruption—it is only possible to discuss the actual exposure of foul play. This secrecy makes it difficult to accurately gauge overall severity and trends; dishonorable conduct may not be known to exist and, if discovered, may not be reported. Still, media coverage is more intensive (the sheer quantity of information) and extensive (the geographic spread of information) today than ever before, as pervasive malfeasance seems to be a common reality in the life of institutions. The previous chapter was an affirmative attempt to construct an ethical infrastructure in organizations; this one targets the absence of ethics by examining corruption and ways to deal with it. The chapter objectives include an understanding of

- the scope and definition of corruption,
- root causes of corruption in human nature and American history,
- individual and organizational ethical failure,
- moral hazards and gift giving,
- the role of scandals in civic life,
- reform efforts, and
- invalid reasons for not dealing with fraud, waste, and abuse.

An administrator can be lulled into a false sense of security if he or she assumes that organizational "right-doing" programs discussed in the last chapter will prevent wrongdoing. Given human frailty and institutional dysfunctions, there will always be the potential for duplicity. That does not, however, relieve individuals and institutions of the obligation to mitigate it.

SCOPE AND MAGNITUDE OF CORRUPTION TODAY

The greatest evil is not now done in those sordid dens of crime that Dickens loved to paint . . . but is conceived and ordered . . . in clear, carpeted, warmed, well-lighted offices, by quiet men with white collars and cut fingernails and smooth-shaven cheeks who do not need to raise their voices.

—C. S. Lewis

DOI: 10.4324/9781003203148-12

Public and private organizations in the world lose at least 5 percent of annual revenue (over $5 trillion) to corruption, according to the Association of Certified Fraud Examiners (2020b). Fraud occurs in all economic sectors, in all sizes of organizations, and originates not only from internal perpetrators anywhere in the institutions but also from external perpetrators. Organizations report that the overall level of fraud has increased with the onset of the COVID-19 pandemic, resulting in more cyber, unemployment, payment, and vendor frauds (Association of Certified Fraud Examiners, 2020a)

Although economic crime in the United States is at a record high, many organizations do not have formal corruption-risk programs despite the fact that most experts believe the worst fraud could be prevented through adequate controls (PriceWaterhouseCoopers, 2020). Further, much of the public believes that government wastes nearly half of its tax dollars; dispassionate estimates of spending lost to waste, fraud, or abuse range from 2 to 7 percent (Cooper, 2009; Nye, Zelikow, & King, 1997). Yet outliers are not uncommon as an internal Pentagon study revealed that nearly one-fourth of its $580 billion budget was spent on administrative waste (Whitlock & Woodward, 2016, December 5). In any case, the conventional wisdom about fraud is wrong: "entitlement programs, from food stamps to Medicare, don't see unusually high cheating rates—and the culprits are usually managers and executives, not 'welfare queens'" (Schnurer, 2013, August 15).

Simple dollar losses in direct expenditures are an inadequate measure of total costs of injustice. For example, related expenses include legal fees, internal investigations and remedial actions, lost time and productivity, training, recruitment, and opportunities forgone due to damaged brand credibility. Burke, Tomlinson, and Cooper (2011, 16) argue that the price of corruption is "huge and includes less organizational and country growth, lower levels of public spending on education and health care, less revenue from taxes, greater political instability, and lower levels of direct foreign investment."

For the fifth year in a row the top fear of Americans is "corrupt governmental officials," far exceeding disasters, crime, military threats, environmental degradation, and scores of other phenomena (Sheth, 2019). Improbity exists throughout society—"the extraordinary concentration of wealth in this new Gilded Age . . . is itself evidence of corruption" (Schmitt, 2019)—yet by international standards the United States has consistently been in the top 20 least corrupt countries.

Globally, corruption is key to understanding many problems (Jurkiewicz, 2019). Refugees drowning in the Mediterranean are fleeing corrupt states. International efforts to address to poverty are frequently undermined by corrupt governments. Corruption damages the global economy; the World Economic Forum estimates that it adds 10 percent to business costs, while the World Bank believes some $1 trillion is paid in bribes every year. Malevolence threatens not only prosperity; it also threatens security. For instance, kidnapping of children and tourists for ransom as well as recruitment of fighters by extremist groups is facilitated by governmental oppression and corruption (Cameron, 2015, June 6).

The levy paid by society is not evenly distributed, as wrongdoing (a) harms the poor severely (by diverting services from those who need them the most), (b) strangles commercial growth (by driving legitimate companies out of business), and (c) saps support for public initiatives (by creating the perception that all programs are corrupt). "By degrading social norms and civic virtues, not to mention rule of law upon which investment depends, corruption rots the foundations of a healthy economy" (Larmer, 2018, June 6). The old debate about whether corruption acts as a "grease" (lubricating economic transactions) or as "sand" (obstructing the system with illegitimate costs) is settled. When competent government and business—which provide the basis for economic development—are eroded, the only winners are the corrupt; the gains from villainy are specific and immediate, while the harms are diffuse and long-lasting.

While overall crime rates in the United States have flattened in recent years, there has been a marked increase in white-collar crime according to federal and state officials.[1] Despite the fact that corporate crime costs easily dwarf those of ordinary street crime, the federal government does not track the incidence and magnitude of the damage corporate crime causes—there is no national database for these crimes and their disposition. Even when enforcement of relevant laws occurs, the penalties are often so low that they are easily absorbed as a cost of doing business.[2,3] Not surprisingly, there is no shortage of problems, as news reports revealed "breathtaking" corruption in the wake of Hurricane Katrina in 2006, the epidemic of foul play during the attempted reconstruction of Iraq (Rich, 2007), and numerous coronavirus scams and the lucrative governmental contracts in the "New Age of Fraud" ("COVID Feature," 2020, July 27). An earlier study (Ashforth & Anand, 2003), in fact, examined how easily turpitude becomes institutionalized—and normalized—in organizations to the point that it not only can neutralize the stigma of deviant conduct but also can rationalize malfeasance in socially desirable terms.

Other indicators of ignoble behavior in public and private sectors include the following:

- Every year Corporate Accountability International www.corporateaccountability.org/) publishes its "Ten Worst Corporations of the Year," complete with a detailed analysis. Recent listings included Amazon.
- AOL-Time Warner, Bank of America, Bayer- Monsanto, Coca-Cola, Dow, General Electric, JPMorgan Chase, Koch Industries, McDonald's, Nestle, News Corporation (owner of Fox News), Wal-Mart, and numerous others that engaged in civil and criminal wrongdoing (many enterprises are repeat offenders).
- A study of the *Fortune* 100 found that 40 of the firms engaged in unethical behavior, suggesting that "the level of misconduct . . . is the highest in American history" (Clement, 2006, 317). To update that finding, consult the extensive listings at "Fraud of the Day" (www.fraudoftheday.com/).
- The Governmental Accountability Project (www.whistleblower.org) publishes an annual "Hall of Fame" and a "Hall of Shame," consisting of business and governmental organizations.
- Citizens for Responsibility and Ethics monitors government ethics, bringing egregious conduct to light and holding officials accountable for their misconduct (www.citizens-forethics.org/); it also maintains an annual list of the top ten scandals.
- Transparency International (www.transparency.org) compiles a yearly "Global Corruption Barometer" and the "Corruption Perception Index."
- Global Integrity (www.globalintegrity.org) publishes an annual report and index that tracks governance and corruption trends.
- The Association of Certified Fraud Examiners sponsors an annual International Fraud Awareness Week.

The need for watchdog programs was dramatically illustrated by a 2010 U.S. Inspector General for Iraq Reconstruction report. It found not only that 96 percent of the $9 billion reconstruction monies were unaccounted for by the Defense Department, but also that the expenditures resulted in few successful reconstruction projects (Spoth, 2010). At the state level of government, one study measured the risks of corruption, as reflected in the strength of laws and policies designed to ensure transparency and accountability in government. It revealed that most states avoid public scrutiny; do not enact or enforce ethics laws; cut, consolidate, or eliminate auditing agencies; and allow corporate interests to dominate policy (Center for Public Integrity, Global Integrity, & Public Radio International, 2012). A state-by-state assessment of their vulnerability to wrongdoing is shown in Figure 9.1.

State Vulnerability to Corruption

FIGURE 9.1

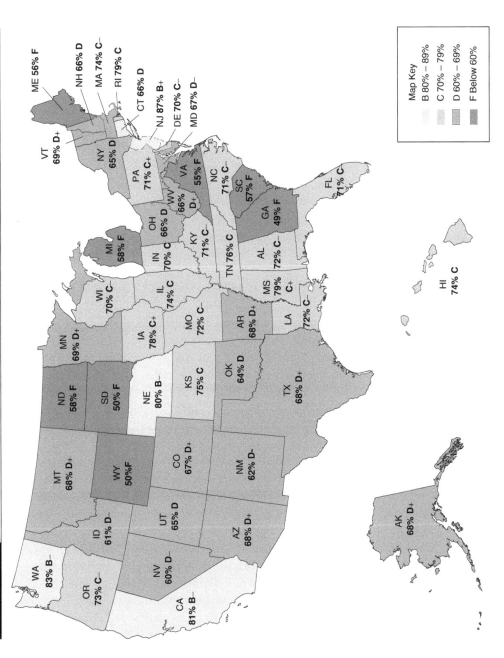

Map Key
B 80% – 89%
C 70% – 79%
D 60% – 69%
F Below 60%

ME 56% F
NH 66% D
MA 74% C–
RI 79% C
CT 66% D
NJ 87% B+
DE 70% C–
MD 67% D–

VT 69% D+
NY 65% D
PA 71% C+
VA 55% F
NC 71% C–
SC 57% F
FL 71% C
GA 49% F
WV 66% D+
OH 66% D
KY 71% C–
AL 72% C–
TN 76% C
IN 70% C–
MI 58% F
WI 70% C–
IL 74% C
MS 79% C+
LA 72% C–
IA 78% C+
MO 72% C–
AR 68% D+
MN 69% D+
ND 58% F
SD 50% F
NE 80% B–
KS 75% C
OK 64% D
TX 68% D+
MT 68% D+
WY 50%F
CO 67% D+
NM 62% D–
ID 61% D–
UT 65% D
AZ 68% D+
WA 83% B–
OR 73% C–
NV 60% D–
CA 81% B–
HI 74% C
AK 68% D+

Source: Center for Public Integrity, Global Integrity, & Public Radio International (2012).

Note: The numbers represent each state's integrity score. A high score (and letter grade) corresponds with a low vulnerability to corruption; a low score corresponds with a high vulnerability to corruption.

Such initiatives challenge the idea that impiety is someone else's problem and instead document the need for change. To that end, the discussion continues with a definition of corruption.

DEFINING CORRUPTION

Corruption is the abuse of position or power—a violation of public trust—often for personal gain by an individual or institution in the public or private sector. Government or business employees can be corrupt and organizations can be systemically corrupt. The term is derived from the Latin *corrumpere* for "distort." The word appeared in English medicine during the 14th century in reference to decomposition of the body and has subsequently referred to moral decay. Government is often an accessory to corporate misbehavior, and vice versa (Gitlow, 2005), as the public and private spheres are deeply intertwined and can collude for mutual benefit. Regulatory negligence, for instance, can enable corporate malfeasance, and the latter can reveal the former. Promises to "drain the swamp" did not mean attacking special interests and wealthy donors but rather public servants, as sources of independent expertise and analysis, who enforce laws, protect workers, help small business, and safeguard the environment (for more on the popular chant, see Dawsey, Helderman, & Fahrenthold, 2020, October 24).

There are many kinds of corruption such as bribery, nepotism, misappropriation of funds, kickbacks, extortion, spoils, smuggling, falsification of documents, abuse of office, breaches of democratic norms, and conflict of interest. Incidences differ in scale (small versus large) and duration (isolated versus repeated incidences). Thus, small-scale corruption could range from a single $50 bribe to routine payments of such amounts, whereas large-scale corruption could be either rare (a one-time $50,000 bribe) or repeated (systemic corruption). Reaction to each of these types—and their impact on business and government—can vary, from indifference to outrage (Thompson, 2000).

Corruption at the individual level can also be understood using role theory (Dobel, 1999). Thus, role distortion—the use of position for personal gain—may or may not involve massive greed. Whatever the form of wrongdoing, corruption violates public trust and generates unnecessary costs. Role failure occurs when an individual assumes office with laudatory goals but either loses sight of them or confuses them with his own views. Ethical violations may stem not only from failure but also from success (e.g., in the biblical "Bathsheba Syndrome," the highly regarded King David seduced Bathsheba with disastrous results including failed cover-ups, deaths, and dishonor with extreme personal misery). Senior executives feel invulnerable, control resources, and believe they are entitled to make up their own rules. ("The fish rots," the saying goes, "from the head.") But rank-and-file employees also engage in dubious behaviors to rationalize and compensate for low salaries. Both the powerful *and* the powerless can be corrupted (Bowman & West, 2007).

Finally, role rejection occurs when officials disdain public stewardship. Such people consider the workplace an extension of private life. They take advantage of the trust society places in institutions by exploiting opportunities for self-enrichment and rewarding friends. At the extremes of corruption, those with specific skills and access to valuable information become vulnerable to organized crime as it expands operations (Camilleri, 2011). Indeed, criminal networks overlap and cooperate with terrorists, an effective synergy because similar conditions give rise to both and because both depend on mutually beneficial relationships with well-known banks to launder their monies (Perri & Brody, 2011; Saviano, 2012).

There is no employee perpetrator profile, as wrongdoers may be very much like most people (Albrecht et al., 2011). Some analysts find the "20–60–20" rule to be useful. At the two ends of the spectrum, 20 percent of employees will always do the right thing and 20 percent will always be involved in wrongdoing when there is opportunity, high reward, and low risk. The remaining 60 percent may or may not be unethical depending on organizational culture (Brooks & Dunn, 2010) and on which 20 percent component is the more influential. Corruption incurs the loss of legitimacy and effectiveness, adds to taxpayer burden, and increases openings for organized crime. Exacerbated by an "epidemic of infallibility," powerful officials never admit making a mistake. "No error is ever admitted, there is nothing to apologize for: 9–11, the bungled occupation of Iraq, the botched response to hurricane Katrina" (Krugman, 2017, March 17), and the troubled approach to the pandemic. Given the implications, origins of corruption demand attention.

CAUSES OF CORRUPTION AND EVOLUTION OF ANTICORRUPTION STRATEGIES

Give a man a gun and he can rob a bank. Give a man a bank and he can rob the world.
—Anonymous

Root causes of corruption, according to Mahatma Gandhi, include wealth without work, pleasure without conscience, knowledge without character, commerce without morality, science without humanity, worship without sacrifice, rights without responsibilities, and politics without principles. Gandhi's causes often explain corruption in the worlds of government, business, and nonprofit organizations.

Government

In the public arena, the incubus of corruption provided much of the impetus for modern administration, which sought to address fraud, waste, and abuse by improving the quality of both personnel (via the merit system) and procedures (e.g., lowest bid, audits, council-manager government, and conflict of interest regulation). The evolution of corruption control can be depicted in stages with overlapping legacies, shown in Table 9.1. For each stage—the legacies of which remain today—the strategy, causes, prescriptions, and implications are outlined. For example, the strategy of the Progressive Movement at the turn of the 19th century was emphasis on professionalism to replace amateur, partisan administration. Important reforms included the creation of independent regulatory commissions and nonpartisan elections. Largely a response to scandal, however, the focus on corruption can come at the expense of effectiveness and efficiency when reforms become so burdensome as to defy common sense (Anechiarico & Jacobs, 1994). Thus, while the changes in each era were well meaning, they can lead to counterproductive actions in which the public good was not served. Regulations designed to prevent corruption, for instance, can be so annoying that they may actually encourage more illicit behavior.

The interplay between government and business is illustrated by the 2016 Morgan Stanley settlement with the Department of Justice. The Financial Crisis Inquiry Commission repeatedly documented that the bank was one of the largest criminal enterprises in the world. Yet, like in other settlements with Wall Street, the Department refused to prosecute the executives responsible, did not require that they return the monies they received from fraud, did not ask that they be terminated, or even require that they be named. It did not, in a word, apply the rule of law (Black, 2016, February 12). The Obama administration's concept of "systematically dangerous institutions" (SDIs), whose officials were "too big to jail," meant not only did bankers avoid prison time and collect bonuses but also dubious business practices of candidates for public office were normalized and no longer seemed to be an obstacle to election.

The upshot is despite the near collapse of the nation's financial system, efforts to reform the banking industry were limited to refining existing institutions responsible for the crisis. Rather than focusing on avoiding another crash, the emphasis was on precluding another bailout. Narrowly averting a depression, paradoxically, reduced the political pressure for restructuring the banks (Ferguson, 2019, March 29). In the years since then, the largest financial institutions have gotten bigger, which increases the likelihood that government will once again have to rescue them when their dangerous actions endanger the nation. "Banks fell right back into bad behaviour . . .—taking too many risks, hiding debt in complex instruments and off-balance-sheet entities, and generally exploit loopholes intended to rein in their greed" (Partnoy, 2020; also consult Vogel, 2020 on the dangers of another mortgage collapse, this one focusing on hotel and office properties).

The regulatory regime, in short, is proving once more that it is captive of Wall Street. Shelia Bair, the former chair of the Federal Deposit Insurance Corporation, believes that "it's naïve to think that our democracy could survive another financial crisis and another round of big bank bailouts. . . . If the financial sector is really that unstable, we should just break up the big banks now . . . or nationalize them" (2019). Instead, de-regulation in recent years has focused on bolstering the economy not policing the banking sector.

More broadly, during the Trump administration there was a comprehensive assault on the integrity, objectivity, independence, and quality of institutions that are the foundation of a functioning government. Seeking to improperly politicize, manipulate, and censor nonpartisan sources of expertise that bind the country together, there were consistent efforts to discredit: intelligence assessments, medical science, the election system, the military, consumer protection, weather predictions, the judiciary, the media, IGs, the census, the postal system, tax collection, environmental quality, and stock market regulation (see, e.g., Common Cause, 2020). Federal agencies responsible for such policy areas have seen their capacity deteriorate as cutbacks, vacancies, and defunding have put their missions at-risk.

Business

In the private sphere, revelations of slush funds and secret payments were regarded as a detriment to foreign policy, the image of American society, and citizen confidence in the integrity of markets, leading to the 1977 Foreign Corrupt Practices Act (FCPA). Intended to prevent bribery of foreign officials, the statute requires that firms maintain a responsible internal accounting control system. Criticized as a "horrible law," President Trump said it was "just so unfair that American companies aren't allowed to pay bribes to get business overseas" (Smialke, 2020). Although the administration wanted to change the law, there was little interest in Congress to do so. The Securities and Exchange Commission website shows a complete list of enforcement cases since 1978. Settlements frequently involve multimillion dollar penalties; 2019 broke records totaling $2.5 billion (Congressional Research Service, 2020).

Corruption also led to the following U.S. Federal Sentencing Guidelines:

1. The firm's standards must be tailored to its business operations.

2. Top leadership must be personally involved in the program.

3. Corporations must not delegate significant discretion to those who have shown themselves inclined to deviant conduct.

4. The policy must be effectively communicated throughout the company.

5. Businesses must have compliance standards and reporting systems.

6. There must be disciplinary procedures in place to address problems.

7. Companies must respond to offenses, report them to the government, and seek to deter future issues.

The statute mandates that firms develop programs that can then be used both as a deterrent to wrongdoing and as a means to limit corporate liability. Organizations are expected to create an ethical climate, develop an active oversight program, identify risk factors and offer training, and reduce the opportunities for, and increase the risks of, malfeasance. Often, the provision of a proper climate includes the creation of codes of ethics, ethics audits, ethics officers, and other components of an infrastructure discussed in the previous chapter. One reason why corporations might encourage whistleblowers (Chapter 10) to report problems internally may be so that they can turn themselves in and qualify for leniency.

TABLE 9.1 Visions of Corruption Control: Strategies, Causes, Prescriptions, and Implications

Corruption Control Vision	Anti-patronage (1870–1900)	Progressive (1900–1933)	Scientific Management (1933–1970)	Panoptic (1970–1990s)	Revisionist (1990s–Present)
Strategy	Credential and competence testing	Professionalism	External control	Law enforcement	Public entrepreneurship
c	Partisan control of personnel	Partisan, unprofessional administration	Inadequate organizational controls	Inadequate monitoring	Bureaucratic pathology
Key policy prescription	Merit system	Electoral reform, independent regulatory commissions, administrative expertise, apolitical administration	Government reorganization and centralization	Surveillance, investigation, fiscal controls	Market privatization
Implications for public administration	Peer enforcement of norms, personal controls	Enforced standards of efficiency	Oversight of agencies and appropriate span of control	Strong investigative and auditing agencies	Decentralized debureaucratized structures, deemphasize corruption control

Source: Anechiarico and Jacobs (1994, 466).

Another technique is the use of "honest services" fraud and conflict-of-interest legislation (18 U.S.C. & 1346). It requires that public and corporate officials act in the best interests of their constituents or employers by criminalizing schemes to defraud victims of "the intangible right of honest services," including the right to good government (Schwartz, 2009). Thus, a decision maker can be charged with depriving others of that right, if he or she puts his or her own interest or those of another person above the interests of citizens or shareholders.

David Brooks (2010) noted that after the controversial Vietnam War and the Watergate scandal, an "ethos of exposure" swept American culture. According to this view, the political and corporate elite, while appearing to be upstanding, are actually corrupt. The private lives of officials, once considered inconsequential, became at least as prominent as their performance. In many cases, the exposure ethos elevated the trivial above the significant while simultaneously corroding faith in the nation. Transparency has been dramatically magnified in the last generation by the development of the Internet and the proliferation of media outlets. As web-based public information sharing portals become more common (Chapter 11), scandals once revealed by employees may be teased out from aggregate data by citizens.

The historically low rate of waste in the 2009 federal stimulus package, for example, has been credited to Recovery.Gov: Track the Money (www.recovery.gov), an official website that provided public access to Recovery Act spending and allowed for reporting of potential corruption. Michael Grunwald (2012) argued that the "$800 billion package of spending and tax cuts" was fraud free and exceptionally well managed. Yet "more Americans think Elvis Presley is still alive than think that the stimulus was a success"—even Obama seldom mentioned it (Clark, 2012). More recently, the Coronavirus Aid, Relief, and Economic Security Act established oversight bodies to ensure transparency and accountability (Exhibit 9.1).

EXHIBIT 9.1   **Corruption: The Other COVID Crisis**

The Coronavirus Aid, Relief, and Economic Security (CARES) Act was passed in response to the COVID-19 contagion and established three oversight bodies concerned with coronavirus spending. The Act established three: the Congressional Oversight Commission (COC), Pandemic Response Accountability Committee (PRAC), and the Special Inspector General for Pandemic Recovery (SIGPR). Additionally, the U.S. House of Representatives established a Select Subcommittee on the Coronavirus Crisis, meant to provide its own oversight.

The four entities have separate but overlapping responsibilities during a time when the executive branch evinces hostility to checks and balances. Indeed, President Trump stated that he personally would "be the oversight." In a signing statement authorizing the Act, he also indicated that he would not consider the inspector general reporting requirements to be mandatory.

The need for review of coronavirus spending was evident: According to Accountable US *Coronavirus Corruption Newsletter* (2020, September 9), major relief programs were rife with mismanagement and lack of oversight. They were overrun with fraud and abuse due to poor design and implementation. The Act allowed well-to-do companies to cash in—sometimes double- and even triple-dipping into its funds. Private jet companies were given access to the programs, receiving up to $65.75 million at a time when demand for private jets were soaring and while hundreds of needy small businesses were shut out.

In addition, 27 clients of Trump-connected lobbyists received up to $10.5 billion, beneficiaries have included multiple entities linked to the family of Jared Kushner and other Trump associates, $273 million was awarded to more than 100 companies owned or operated by major donors to the president's election efforts, ethics waivers were applied to apparent conflicts of interest, and many other transactions meriting further investigation occurred.

Given concerns about personnel vacancies in COC (affecting its mission to assess the impact of CARES on the economy), the vulnerability of PRAC to presidential intervention, as well as the leadership of SIGPR, to do rigorous audits, the three units must achieve full functionality and the House Select Committee must play a robust role. They should derive lessons from the genuine success of the 2008 Recovery Act in the management of fraud that injected some $800 billion in stimulus funds during the Great Recession. The nonpartisan U.S. Government Accountability Office (2020) has identified issues needing attention: improvement of the medical supply chain function, collection of reliable data, development of accountability and transparency procedures, and protection against cyberthreats.

With trillions of dollars appropriated to deal with the disaster, emergency federal programs can benefit from and require extraordinary oversight. Since the CARES Act failed to provide adequate transparency measures, the COVID Bailout Tracker (https://covidbailouttracker.com/) was developed by Accountable US, a nonprofit watchdog group.

Source: Adapted from Mellman and Eisen (2020) and Accountable US *Coronavirus Corruption Newsletter*, Edition No. 22 (2020, September 9). Also see Miller and Shea (2020).

Nonprofit Organizations

The nonprofit sector is not immune from issues of corruption, asset manipulation, and fraudulent accounting (see, e.g., the end-of-the-chapter Exercise 5, the "Bad Boss"). Headline stories have exposed conflicts of interest, bribery, unlawful gratuities, economic extortion, as well as illegal financial and nonfinancial statements with growing frequency. Given the size and scope of the sector, with trillions in revenues and 10 million employees (NCCS Project Team, 2020), it is a ripe target for wrongdoers. Using data from the Association of Certified Fraud Examiners (2016), fraud losses in the nonprofit arena amount to about $40 billion annually.

The United Way, Boy Scouts of America, and other high-profile organizations have been embarrassed by disclosures of corruption in recent years (see, e.g., Baker, 2020). The Red Cross comes under repeated criticism for poor performance ("How to help the neediest Harvey victims," 2017). Congressionally charted, the charity is a monopoly provider of national first responder services; no other organization has a similar stature or scope. Its failures included operations during 9/11, Katrina, the 2010 Haiti earthquake, Super Storm Sandy and Hurricane Isaac (both in 2012), and the 2015 response to California fires. In 2017, a Red Cross executive was asked what percentage of funds donated in the wake of Hurricane Harvey would be devoted to relief; he did not know.

Additional examples of nonprofit problems abound both here and abroad:

- Potential donors seeking to provide assistance to Hurricane Katrina victims were likely deceived by more than 2,000 fraudulent Internet sites soliciting contributions (Aviv, 2005).

- The former CEO of the National Kidney Foundation Singapore was charged with corruption and jailed for questionable business practices, ranging from conflicts of interest to misrepresentations of organizational performance and wasteful spending (see Rowe & Dato-on, 2013, 94–107).
- The Association of Community Organizations for Reform Now (ACORN) was busted for voter registration fraud and for employees caught on videotape facilitating tax fraud and covering up a child sex slavery ring (McRay, 2009).
- The bankruptcy filing of the Miami-area James E. Scott Community Association listed $3.4 million in liabilities and only $1.7 million in assets after it lost government contracts over fears about its financial management. The charity had been administering programs for infants, teenagers, and the elderly in the city's poorest neighborhoods (Grimm, 2010; "Miami-Area Social-Service Charity," 2009).

How can nonprofits curb corruption and preserve both their reputations and funding base? Greenlee and her colleagues (2007, 688–691) provide numerous strategies: (a) establish clear lines of authority, (b) create proper procedures for authorizing transactions, (c) audit monthly financial transactions in addition to an annual audit, (d) train volunteers about theft risks, (e) recruit quality, independent board members, (f) authorize an audit committee to detect or deter financial mismanagement, (g) complete background checks on employees with access to cash or assets, and (h) provide whistleblower protection. Beyond root causes of corruption, as manifested in government, business, and nonprofit organizations, how else can individual and collective moral failure be explained?

INDIVIDUAL AND INSTITUTIONAL MORAL FAILURE

There is no right way to do a wrong thing.

—Howard S. Kushner

Individuals

Personal moral lapses can stem from the human genius for self-serving rationalization. Because there is often a grain of truth in rationalizations, it is easy to understand, and hard to deny, their seductive nature. Anand, Ashford, and Joshi (2004) highlight seven rationalization techniques and provide examples of each (Table 9.2). Most of these psychological defense mechanisms—used to mask the true reasons for behavior—cannot withstand the "front-page test" ("Would you be willing to see your actions in the newspaper?"), but two additional common excuses not included in the table warrant comment: contingent necessity ("If I don't do it, someone else will") and ignorance ("I didn't know").

First, conduct must be judged on its merit, not on a vague possibility of what a nameless "someone else" may or may not do. That is, ethics is about personal responsibility. One individual may not be able to do everything that needs to be done, but he or she can improve conditions around him or her by avoiding unethical behavior, setting an honorable example, and strengthening her character (Chapter 6). Second, what executives do not know may not be their fault, but it is their responsibility—they are accountable for organizational climate and due diligence. The official's obligation is not fulfilled unless everything possible is done to ensure proper standards of practice.

Looking at sexual harassment as a case study of rationalization, Bauer (2017, June 19) points out common, but toxic, claims by managers, colleagues, and victims:

- "The individual is being too sensitive" (blaming the victim is never an appropriate response).
- "The perpetrator is such a good person that this allegation is difficult to believe" (many caring people do untoward things).
- "If I endure this, others won't need to" (this self-destructive response ignores other past, current, and future victims).
- "This too will pass" (this condones the offensive conduct).
- "Complaining will only lead to retaliation" (while this may be true, it "kicks the problem down the road").

TABLE 9.2		Rationalization Techniques: Description and Summary	
Category	Rationalization Technique	Description	Examples
Justification	Appeal to higher loyalties Denial of injury	The actors argue that their violation of norms is due to their attempt to realize a higher-order value The actors believe that no one is harmed by their actions; so the actions aren't corrupt	"We answered to a more important cause" "I wouldn't report it due to loyalty" "No one was really harmed" "It could have been worse"
Social Excuses	Denial of victim Social weighting	The actors counter blame for their actions by arguing that the violated party deserved it The actors assume a practice that moderates the salience of corrupt behavior: condemn or compare	"They deserved it" "They chose to participate" "You have no right to criticize us" "Others are worse than we are"
Contextual Excuses	Denial of responsibility Denial of illegality Metaphor of the ledger	The actors engaged in corrupt behavior perceive that they have no choice but to participate Actors excuse corrupt practices on the basis that their actions are not illegal The actors rationalize that they're entitled to indulge in deviant behavior because of their accrued credits	"What can I do?" "It is none of my business what the corporation does overseas" "There's no law against it" "We've earned the right"

Source: Adapted from Anand et al. (2004, 11).

Establishment of an ethical infrastructure (Chapter 8), ethical audits, consultations with legal and human resource professionals, and "management by walking around"—and listening—can help protect against corruption. Not only do ordinary people populate the ranks of the corrupt, but many organizations are also prone to criminality (Ashforth & Anand, 2003). Recent incidents—the Flint, Michigan water disaster and the Wells Fargo scandal—implicating individuals as well as institutions are examined later.

Flint, Michigan Water Crisis. Water supplies, roads, bridges, airports, and dams are in a precarious state. The significance of maintenance and upkeep is not only unappreciated but also taken for granted by the general public. The result is the failure of physical and human infrastructure (Veruil, 2017). The American Society of Civil Engineers grades the nation's water system as a "D," requiring at least $400 billion to modernize (Leber, 2017, July 19; Russell & Vinsel, 2017, July 3). Taxpayers also fail to support blue- and white-collar maintenance workers with recognition and competitive salaries.

To save money and "run government like a business," in 2014 a state-appointed emergency manager switched Flint's water supply from a lake to the Flint River, and unqualified technical personnel were hired to oversee the change. For over a year, local and state managers denied the resulting contamination problems—even though General Motors and a Flint hospital stopped using the water because it was damaging metal automobile parts and medical instruments.

In 2017, the Michigan Attorney General charged 15 officials with neglect of duty, including the state's health department's secretary (involuntary manslaughter) as well as chief medical officer (obstruction of justice). His report found that the solution to the problem could have been handled easily at the outset by the use of common anti-corrosion chemicals (Atkins & Davey, 2017, June 14). Later that year, reduced fertility rates, increased miscarriages, and more fetal deaths were linked to the crisis (Delaney, 2017, September 21).

People may assume that by now the problem is fixed, but residents point out that thousands of lead pipes need to be replaced (a process that will take years), citizens may lose their homes if they do not pay dramatically escalating water bills, and they fear tap water will continue to make them sick. Flint, a town of nearly 100,000, is a majority Black community with 40 percent of residents living below the poverty line; it is doubtful that this crisis would have emerged in a white, wealthy community. The Environmental Protection Agency, at this writing, is posed to repeal the federal clean water rule which protects waterways that provide drinking water. The Flint physical infrastructure tragedy demonstrates the need for human infrastructure—technically and ethically competent professionals as well as responsible elected officials—to provide basic services to the citizenry.

As one of the largest public health disasters in history, it returned to the headlines in recent years. First, in 2019 criminal charges were dropped against officials and others took plea deals for misdemeanors, although they are being sued in civil court. In addition, families suffering from lead poisoning confronted the COVID-19 contagion, which also disproportionally affects communities of color. Third, in mid-2020 the state of Michigan settled class action claims for $600 million. After legal fees, this amounts to $12,000 per person, which observers characterized as "paltry" (Schofield, 2020). Once the settlement is approved by the court, the money would be appropriated through the state legislature, which is facing a pandemic-induced budget issues. Finally, in early 2021 the Michigan attorney general announced plans to indict up to ten individuals in the former governor's executive office, including the ex-governor, as well other state and local officials, on criminal charges.

The Flint case may be a preview of the future, as the water supply in selected major cities is contaminated with "forever chemicals" (Gardner, 2020; also, consult Clark, 2020 and Brockovich, 2020 plus the well-documented work by Hightower, 2021). Further, there were more than 12,000 health violations in 5,000 community water systems, as 19 million Americans are stricken each year after drinking contaminated water (Baptiste, 2017). Desperate to raise money to address the issue, communities across the country have gotten entangled in risky Wall Street transactions that endanger the local economy in pursuit of corporate gain at the expense of the public.

Known as "disaster capitalism" (Klein, 2007; see also Olaniran, 2018 on corporations taking advantage of weak state water laws), government and industries exploit crises to impose pro-corporate policies, as banks use their political power to persuade elected officials to cut local taxes resulting in reductions of revenue necessary to maintain infrastructure. City officials then seek ways to fund projects and are readily exploited by too-big-to-fail banks offering opaque, high-risk Wall Street financial deals. "When the deals fail and those responsible have collected their payday, there's always another profiteering company ready with more promises of 'cost savings' and 'efficiencies'" (Sloan, 2016, March 14).

Wells Fargo Scandal. In 2016, Wells Fargo, one of the nation's oldest, largest, and successful banks, announced that it would pay $185 million in fines to regulators; the action settled allegations that its employees created 2.1 million fraudulent credit card and checking accounts since 2002 without their customers' knowledge or permission. Hoping to put the issue behind them, the bank's decision sparked a firestorm instead. The predatory fraud was something people could easily understand and was done in the context of dozens of fines for other abusive practices costing the bank $15 billion.

A management-created sales pressure scheme with unrealistic quotas drove employees to falsify documents and game the system to meet sales goals. Failure to do so met with disciplinary action. This large-scale, brazen, systematic institutionalized program led a Republican congressman to charge that the bank was running a criminal enterprise and a Democratic legislator to call it a "school for scoundrels" (Merle, 2016, September 29).

Wells Fargo admitted no wrongdoing in the settlement and no high-level officials were singled out for prosecution. The fines are a "rounding error" compared to the company's multiple billion-dollar profits and assets of at least one trillion dollars. In connection with the scandal, 5,300 personnel were discharged over a period of five years (apparently including those who reported misconduct) with one exception: the executives in charge.

But is it reasonable to blame them for the actions of a relatively small number of employees in a huge institution with branches throughout the nation? The illicit behavior involving thousands of staff and millions of phony accounts cannot be dismissed as the work of a few bad apples. Systemic problems like this is *exactly* the responsibility of top executives (Ochs, 2016, September 15). A profit-over-people organizational culture led to gross mismanagement, according to the chair of the U.S. House of Representatives Financial Services Committee.

For a supposedly well-run bank—Wells Fargo's John Stump was named "CEO of the Year" in 2015—it is inconceivable that senior management could miss the creation of millions of bogus accounts. Executives were either complicit or should have been terminated for gross incompetence. Indeed, they repeatedly certified the accuracy of financial reports and the adequacy of quality controls. Stump, who enabled the massive scandal, got rich from it, and helped cover it up, resigned with a $130 million payout,

A year later more than 1.4 million additional fake accounts were identified (Cowley, 2017, August 31). As if to demonstrate that white-collar crime defendants do not limit their dishonest activity to just one crime (legendary investor Warren Buffett observed, "There's never just one cockroach in the kitchen"), a broader bank review revealed that hundreds of thousands of customers were affected by (a) unauthorized enrollments in the bank's online bill payment service, (b) unrequested auto insurance, (c) secret changes to mortgage repayments, (d) fictitious life insurance premium charges, and (e) improper withholding of refunds to automobile loan customers and repossessions of their cars.

The abusive practices were so widespread that the public interest group Americans for Financial Reform created an extensive Wells Fargo Scandal Tracker just to keep up with the bank's wrongdoing. Although financial regulators are pursuing far fewer cases as the nation enters the new decade, the Department of Justice and the Securities and Exchange Commission reached a $3 billion dollar settlement with the bank in 2020 to address criminal and civil violations. At the same time, the powers of the Consumer Financial Protection Bureau were under attack and its political appointees stopped: payments to victimized customers, career service hiring, new rule making, and ongoing investigations.

It is evident that years of tighter rules from legislators have done nothing to fix the "me-first" cultures that afflict large financial firms: Wells Fargo account scandal is hardly unique. Other well-known banks have a long list of fines and settlements, including bribery of foreign governments, violating American economic sanctions against rogue regimes, being involved in the Bernie Madoff Ponzi scheme, rigging interest rates, manipulating energy markets, and engaging in whistleblower reprisals (Carter, 2018, February 6). Bankers clearly are not willing to institute a system of self-regulation and personal liability. Despite the Wells Fargo scandal, the bank remains as a large institution, one that financed the caging of children during the 2019 immigration crisis, paid a multimillion dollar settlement in race and sex discrimination cases in 2020, and continues to underwrite fossil fuels.

In short, customers are vulnerable to fraud due to the complexity of many financial products, the opacity of fine print, and the lack of genuine recourse. Likewise, it is considerably easier for government to deal with common criminals than to pursue wrongdoers at Wells Fargo and other SDIs with their teams of corporate attorneys. Without real reform, citizens and governments will continue to be victimized (Ramirez & Ramirez, 2017). Among the ironies are that mega banks tend to underperform, inclining them to criminality that, in turn, undermines capitalism.

Institutions

As the aforementioned cases suggest, failure on the part of an organization to avoid corruption may originate from the nature of work itself, groupthink, management-induced fear, or retaliation. Awareness of individual and institutional pressures is the initial step toward addressing them. Consider two cases, one focusing on the private sector and one on the public: moral hazard and gift giving.

Moral Hazard refers to undue risks that organizations and people are likely to take if they are not responsible for the consequences (as when financial firms make high-risk investments with federally insured taxpayer money and are subsequently bailed out). Shirking fiduciary responsibilities, and saved from failure by government, such conditions increase moral hazard, inhibit trust in institutions, and permit failed capitalists to become corporate socialists.[4] A defense against moral hazard constitutes a system of controls that prevents firms from taking risks with other people's money—and at their expense—in the first place. The New Deal stock market regulations were an iconic anti-corruption system. Yet those provisions were repealed in the late 1990s. In their place, Congress deregulated the financial sector and allowed Wall Street to self-regulate, abandoning the idea that markets need oversight: The result was one of the biggest crime waves the country has ever experienced.

Turning to Gift Giving in public service, the practice is often regulated—unlike business norms wherein such goodwill courtesies are common. These prohibitions, however, are frequently criticized as ineffective, on the grounds that most individuals do not sacrifice their honor for gifts since most people believe that they are basically good.[5] The premise of this contention—predicated on valorizing self-interest and invalidating moral concern— may be correct: Many officials are not "for sale." As legendary California Assembly Speaker Jesse Unruh used to say of lobbyists, "If you can't eat their food, drink their booze and [expletive deleted] their women, and then vote against them, you have no business being up here."[6]

Yet as discussed in Chapter 7, the conclusion of this reframing—that inducements are acceptable—must be rejected as pernicious for three reasons. First, it is difficult to discern a defensible reason (as opposed to an expedient or self-serving reason) why an official should expect gratuities. Next, corruption requires nothing so crass as a quid pro quo, because such offerings introduce the possibility of favoritism. Bribing is generally not the issue; rather, it is access and the attendant appearance of impropriety, conflict of interest, entitlement, influence peddling, and self-dealing. The challenge for administrators to avoid corruption intensifies when the ethics of an action is unclear, as in the case of transition from public to private employment (Case Study 9.1).

Individual gifts, third, can help create organizational corruption—the creation of a system that encourages decisions based not on the substance of issues but rather on friendships and cronyism among the political and financial officialdom. Immersed in a culture of the comfortable:

> [T]he process of influence doesn't have to involve raw corruption (although that happens too). All that it requires is the tendency to assume that what's good for the people (those who you associate with the most), must be good for the economy as a whole.
>
> (Krugman, 2011)

As Dan Ariely (2012) points out, people are social creatures. Someone gives a person a present—even, or perhaps especially, a small one—and the recipient tends to feel a debt of gratitude. That sense of indebtedness, conscious or unconscious (Chapter 7), influences perceptions and behavior by the need to clear a perceived debt. Gifting, stated differently, is a technique of power exercised by one party over the other. Lobbyists spend a small part of their time with politicians on official business and most of the time "trying to implant a feeling of obligation and reciprocity in politicians who they hope will repay them by voting with their interest in mind" (78). Consider the case in Exhibit 9.2.

Exhibit 9.2	**Not-for-Profit Organization: Executive Director and Board Member Gift**

I work as the executive director of a nonprofit organization. Like so many, we are struggling through the pandemic with fewer resources. In the spring, I implemented belt-tightening with all staff, beginning with my salary and a short furlough.

Recently, a board member dropped by with a flower arrangement with an envelope containing several thousand dollars. This member does not have a conflict of interest or ulterior motive. She is well off and wanted to recognize my work. But my conscience is on high alert—a reward only for me when everyone here is working hard and is paid less than me? I am considering donating it to the organization. Yet I want to honor the intentions behind this kind gesture. Our organization does not have a gift policy, and the money would be a help my family. What should I do?

A gift can result in a changed relationship; it is now, in a personal way, a relationship between benefactor and beneficiary. A direct gift, one not mediated by the formal structures of the institution and the law, has a different meaning. It was doubtless intended to convey gratitude, but it is also, at least potentially, a way of turning you into a personal protégé.

Assuming you are okay with a changed relationship, you're still left with the issue you raise. Is it fair that this present goes to you and not to other staff who could use it even more? Because board members typically have relationships only with senior management, they are not likely to have that kind of bond with the staff.

Philanthropic gifts generally are not based on need; there is almost always a more deserving recipient. For example, the money you give to a museum is funding that could vaccinate children and save lives in a poor country. Whatever the case is for giving money to the museum, it is not that it has the greater need. That philanthropy is not guided by a pure calculus of utility is one reason for having a public system to address the basic needs of all citizens.

Still, a gift is a gift, and you are free to do with it what you will. Your scruples suggest that spending the money on your family may not reflect your moral priorities. Knowing the challenges facing your employees, you could use the money to help the organization. Because your gift is tax-deductible, it is possible that some part of the money may, in fact, end up in your pocket.

Source: Adapted from Appiah, K. (2020, December, 6). *The New York Times Magazine*, p. 20.

The financial industry, for instance, creates conflicts of interest, nurtures them, and the banking and political elite benefits from a shared ideology—a belief system that the continued existence of Wall Street firms, and business as usual, is in the best interest of the economy. It is not necessary for the wealthy to buy a lawmaker's vote. Rather, they "buy his mind" (Reich, 2011, 110). The 2007–2009 financial debacle—the third in 20 years after the 1980s Savings and Loan disaster and the Enron Era at the start of this century—was, at heart, a political crisis. Financiers elicit cooperation from elected officials who depend on them in the form of gratuities, campaign donations, and future employment.

Gifts are, in short, one manifestation of a deep culture of corruption as suggested by one state employee:

If corruption is defined as the abuse of position or power, this could be anything. Using your position to receive gifts is an example. I work for the Department of Economic Opportunity. Our gift policy (www.ethics.state.fl.us/publications/gifts%20 info_2007_web.pdf) requires filling out forms when receiving gifts valued at over $100. It was created to deal with corruption or the appearance of corruption. The forms are public record.

The problem is that the policy relies on self-reporting: the individual must act ethically to determine if any wrongdoing has occurred. It is very difficult to catch someone accepting presents and not reporting it unless the giver reports the receiver. I think that the $100 amount is arbitrary; the amount is not all that relevant. Taking gifts gives the appearance of bias and corruption, regardless of how much they cost.

(Anonymous, personal communication, November 1, 2016)

A sound policy should clearly define a "gift" (including what is not considered to be one), the ethical principles governing gift-giving, and prohibited actions (with examples), and penalties for violations. Stated differently, most conflicts of interest cannot be credibly rationalized. To avoid the corruption they produce, gifts should be made anonymously or simply be banned.

Jurisdictions lacking workable regulations and tax-supported campaigns for office should consider them. The imperative of serving citizens before self ought to be enough for a public official. Why should presents, cash donations, and promises of impending jobs be routinely anticipated? Does anyone really think that they are offered in the name of "good government"? Perhaps Plato said it best, "The servants of the nation are to render their services without any presents. The disobedient shall, if convicted, die without ceremony." Admittedly, prohibiting inducements may not be the preeminent issue—as long as privately funded political campaigns continue, the biggest source of corruption is legal—but it is a good place to begin.

Individual and institutional moral failure stems from a variety of sources, many of which are manifested in moral hazards and gift giving. When corruption is revealed, the dishonor it produces may have serious and long-lasting effects. The next section examines such *contretemps* with particular attention to government and corporate roles in recent events.

SCANDALS: TYPES AND IMPACTS

Corruptio optimi pessimum (The corruption of the best is the worst).

—Latin proverb

Types of Scandal

Scandals reveal opportunities for the public to obtain information not otherwise available. As they occur in public service, these issues often have shared characteristics:

- There is no clear connection between the gravity of misdeed and the controversy.
- Their impact may depend on electoral cycle, partisan balance, presidential or gubernatorial approval ratings.

- Good journalism is bad business (expensive investigatory journalism), and bad journalism is good business (sensationalized coverage of sex peccadilloes).
- Republican scandals reinforce the conservative claim that government is corrupt, while Democratic scandals undercut the liberal view that government can be trusted to do good (Brooks, 2012).

Simplicity, moral transgressions, and hypocrisy are also common features. A scandal refers to actions or events involving offenses that become known and are perceived to be sufficiently serious to merit a public response (Basinger, 2018, March 1; Thompson, 2000).

Several types of revelation combust in spectacular ways and are based on the fatal attraction of sex, money, and/or power (Thompson, 2000, 122). Sex incidents may or may not involve criminal offenses but generally reflect actions that are regarded as sanctimonious or unseemly. Over the years, coercion and criminality have trumped consent and morality in the political assessment of these events (Fisher, 2018, May 13) (see Appendix 9.1: The Statutory Rape Case in USA Swimming). The more citizens have to rely on the character and discretion of officials, the more significance is given to personal weaknesses—especially if they affect broader issues of public concern.

Financial scandals, second, disclose improper linkages between economic and political powerbrokers, and often involve violations of law because there is a well-developed set of statutes that cover them (this does not mean that such cases are easily resolved; see Case 9.1). Yet the mere presence of legislation means little, if laws are ignored or if ongoing investigations confront statutes of limitations. As noted earlier, there was, for example, a stunning lack of accountability for the crimes that helped create the 2007–2009 economic crisis. In a mockery of the rule of law, there has not been a single prosecution of a major Wall Street bank or executive for what the FBI termed "an epidemic of fraud" that blew up the entire economy (Dwyer, 2013; Morgenson & Story, 2011; "No Fault Corporate Crime," 2012).

The same can be said for the 2001 terrorist attacks, the extraordinary rendition and torture of detainees during the Iraq War, the 2010 BP Deep Water Horizon oil spill, and life-and-death problems with COVID-19 policies. For the most part, no one was terminated, resigned, or took responsibility. There has been, in other words, a de facto decriminalization of unethical behavior by organizations that act as though they are above the law and beyond the discipline of the market. One of the world's largest banking groups, HSBC, to illustrate, admitted to laundering billions for drug cartels and violating critical laws, including the Bank Security Act and the Trading with the Enemy Act (Protess & Silver-Greenberg, 2012).

Abuses of power, third, often do not involve extraneous factors such as sex and money but the illicit use of power itself. As Teddy Roosevelt observed, "You cannot give an official power to do right, without at the same time giving him the power to do wrong." Scandals reveal activities that transgress the rules of governance in the acquisition and exercise of power. The preemptive war against Iraq as a response to the 9/11 terrorist attacks, for instance, was described by the chief official in the White House situation room on 9/11 as making as much sense as "invading Mexico after the Japanese attacked us at Pearl Harbor" (Clarke, 2004, 30–31).

Finally, the miasma of scandals can stem from power but entangle money and sex—or just plain waste. An imbroglio involving sex, money, and power occurred in the Department of Interior's Minerals Management Service, a unit responsible for collecting $10 billion in royalties (one of the federal government's largest sources of nontax revenues). Regulators accepted bribes, negotiated for industry jobs, engaged in illicit drug use and sex with oil company employees, falsified reports, and waived regulatory requirements. In the wake of the 2010 Deep Water Horizon blowout, the agency was renamed and reorganized.

An instance of simple waste, in a time of fiscal austerity, was revealed by the General Services Administration (GSA) Inspector General—a lavish Las Vegas conference at a cost of $823,000. The convention featured mind readers, magicians, clowns, souvenirs, and expensive dinners. Some of those involved received bonuses. The agency head resigned, all travel expenditures and conferences were suspended, and a thorough review of personnel and planning practices was undertaken. Ironically, the U.S. Office of Government Ethics evaluated the GSA during the time it was planning the convention and praised it for using exemplary practices, while failing to address known risk factors that could have prevented the problem (Epstein, 2012).

Due to their unprecedented scale, more recent money, sex, and power outrages since 2017 had the paradoxical effect of obscuring their impact on democratic governance. Shamelessness seemed to actually be empowering as no one would be held to account, melodrama militated against genuine understanding, and failures could mendaciously be framed as successes. Troubling incidents would go through the daily news cycle only to be distracted and superseded by yet another scandal the next day (Alterman, 2020; vanden Heuvel, 2019, May 8). The idea, according to administration White House advisor Steve Bannon, was "to flood the zone with sh-t" so that there was so much disinformation that it was difficult to distinguish fact from fiction (Will, 2020, October 10).

Impacts on

If our civilization is destroyed, disaster will not be by . . . barbarians from below. Our barbarians come from the top.

—Henry Lloyd, Wealth Against Commonwealth

Government Service. Sex, financial, and power scandals belie the idea of public service: These abuses are problematic for democracies as they subvert governmental legitimacy and obstruct the rule of law.[7] It should be noted that such events have a Janus-faced nature about them (Garment, 1991). On the bright side, they can be seen as actually stabilizing the political system. The contention is that it needs pathologies for purification purposes, as exposures take the abstract values of democracy (such as due process and equal protection) and make them tangible. As a result, it is said that "the process works," and the system deserves support. What began as abuse of self-government culminates in a celebration of its values. Scandals also satisfy the need for the citizenry to participate, albeit vicariously, in public affairs.

On the dark side of the Janus face, revelations may not have the claimed beneficial effects. The lesson of the Watergate affair in the Nixon administration was not so much that the rule of law was effective but that few citizens since then wanted to experience a failed presidency again (Pierce, 2012).[8] Worse, scandals can become an alternative to dealing with important societal issues: The politics of scandal replaces the politics of democracy. Perversely, public attention can be diverted away from debate and discourse to fake scandals, which, in turn, spawn faux outrage obscuring actual, less easily reported problems. Such non-incidents (e.g., Barack Obama's birthplace; vote-by-mail fraud) create a culture of mistrust and undermine the polity.

In recent years, a playbook has been used when scandals emerge: Deny whatever has been revealed, wait for the outrage to burn itself out, and if necessary claim that whatever happened was proof of virtue because it happened in plain sight with no embarrassment or concealment (even if there was). In any case, the incident will be buried soon enough by the next one. "Never apologize, always play offense, attack the 'fake news,' and dismiss the issue as a partisan attack without merit" (Blow, 2019, October 20; Hemmer, 2020, January 24; Lerer, 2018, December 4). Eventually, when everything is a scandal, then nothing is a scandal, which raises the question, "does anything matter?"

The result of actual and specious scandals is that it is more difficult to govern. Ethics can even be used as a weapon to discredit reformers—all that may be necessary is a well-financed misinformation campaign aimed at their personal and professional lives to frustrate reform. Instead of stabilizing the system, Garment (1991) argues, scandals destabilize it as they are morally repugnant, economically distorting, and politically de-legitimating. Each round of revelations and allegations weakens democracy and diminishes public trust. As a consequence, citizens feel "perpetually dirty," have contempt for all officials, and believe government is dishonorable. If the whole system is rigged, and every politician corrupt, then issues are decided as raw power trumps principle. Instead of eliminating corruption, even those incidents that are "successfully" resolved damage faith in the republic.

Business. In every era marked by rapid technological change, entrepreneurial zeal is apt to be attracted to the lure of quick riches. The cavalcade of corporate scandals since the turn of the 21st century should not be surprising. Yet merely pointing out that dishonesty is not the norm in business is insufficient. For all the attention to the Wall Street crime wave, significant audit and accounting issues persist. The typical federal government's response to the crisis—to reestablish the status quo as soon as possible—is also not unexpected, given that those responsible for financial law enforcement are the same people who played important roles on Wall Street when it imploded. "There is an awful lot to do in the world of corporate fraud," according to the FBI (Johnson, 2006).

Further, there are ongoing lobbying efforts to thwart the landmark 2002 Sarbanes–Oxley Act (intended to curb accounting abuses) and the 2010 Dodd–Frank legislation (designed to avert another 2008-style meltdown of the financial system) (Chapter 10). As irresponsible stewards of the power surrendered to them through deregulation, investment firm CEOs wrecked the economy, received bailouts from the federal government, and are richer than ever (Dionne, 2010). "The dogma of 'free markets,'" Bill Black (2012) points out, "turned into an anti-regulatory creed that produces an environment so criminogenic that it drives our recurrent, intensifying financial crises." Ironically "the spectacular failure of financial markets," writes Michael Sandel (2012, 12), "did little to dampen the faith in markets generally," as public opinion polls showed that Americans blamed the government more than Wall Street for the economic collapse.

It is doubtful, in any case, that reforms have been institutionalized as the nation has yet to grasp the depth of the problem. There is a big difference between being accountable and being held to account. Examples of "failing upward" include:

- State and federal changes made in the early part of this century did little to prevent the 2007–2010 credit crisis (Chapter 1). In fact, investigations into banking practices—including widespread fraudulent documentation of mortgage loans run up against statutes of limitations (Note: Mortgage-backed securities are the biggest asset class in the world).

- In contrast to the Savings and Loan scandal and the Enron Era, there were very few investigations and many fewer prosecutions during the Great Recession, as miscreant financiers avoided jail, made sweetheart deals, paid modest fines (often covered by corporate insurance policies), and collected millions in bonuses (evaluation of executive performance typically excludes legal settlement costs) while many citizens lost much of their life savings, their jobs, and their homes.
- White-collar crime federal sentencing guidelines (www.ussc.gov/orgguide.htm) discussed earlier, which place responsibility for establishing an ethical organizational culture on top executives, were recently changed from mandatory to advisory in nature (see also Chapter 10).
- The epic corruption by military contractors reached twice the amount of money (adjusted for inflation) expended to rebuild Iraq as it did to rebuild Japan—"an industrialized nation three times the size, two of whose cities had been incinerated by atomic bombs" (Rich, 2007).
- The long-standing practice of permitting an organization or individual to neither admit nor deny wrongdoing ("no-fault" corruption) might not only encourage compliance but also enable widespread recidivism; it overlooks, in addition, that guilty pleas make it easier for victims to recover damages and take advantage of law that treats past offenders differently than one-time perpetrators.
- An emblematic case of these problems is the Federal Deposit Insurance Corporation that allowed the most notorious executives to walk away wealthy, proving itself to be lacking in integrity and courage and unfit to represent the nation (Black, 2013, March 12).
- Major investment banks were "dismissive, even defiant" when criticized for "business as usual" investment and compensation practices supported by bailout money (Anderson, 2009); "they were embarrassed for about 15 minutes," grew bigger than ever, and worked to block or repeal reforms (Clark, 2013, April 4). Going into 2020, it was clear that Wall Street need have no concern about any remaining reforms as they were diluted or ignored ("Why the return of bigger banks means more risks for everyone else," 2017, September 8).

At issue is not merely honest bookkeeping but the fact that governance of corporations and capitalism as a whole becomes increasingly predatory (Ferguson, 2012). Free markets are supposed to allocate capital efficiently to the benefit of everyone, but only if subject to meaningful oversight. Many major companies no longer exist to produce goods; rather, they are owned by global speculators and institutional investors who demand short-term profits, often achieved by eliminating jobs and slashing wages. Instead of building industrial capacity and public works infrastructure, investment banking created financial innovations for the sake of profit at the expense of social value. Indeed, much of the problem is what is legal when firms are rewarded for lobbying clout rather than contributing to the economic health of the nation. As Senator Richard Durbin (D-Ill.) said in 2009, despite having caused the financial crisis, the same firms "are still the most powerful lobby on Capitol Hill. And they, frankly, own the place" (quoted in Friedman, 2011).

A compelling illustration of this is the "shadow banking system"—unregulated, dangerous, speculative credit derivative markets that changed the way Wall Street made money—that played a key role in creating the 2007–2009 recession and its aftereffects. Shadow banking accounts for more assets than those held by the traditional banking system (Cowen,

2013). A particularly destructive form of capitalism, these opaque markets offer little or no social or economic purpose, while tying up billions of dollars that could otherwise be used to finance businesses to create jobs and produce goods and services. Much more of the system's assets are devoted to trading corporate securities than to supporting long-term investment in productive assets. Derivatives—what Warren Buffet called "weapons of mass financial destruction"—were devised to distribute risk broadly so that they made the system safe. But "they interlocked risk so completely that they brought the system down" (Meyerson, 2011) to the point that Wall Street banks stopped lending even to one another.

This is an example of the financial industry detached from the real economy it is supposed to serve (Brady, 2011; Pearlstein, 2012). Perhaps in recognition of the problem and as noted in Chapter 7, the influential Business Roundtable released an open letter in 2019, signed by 183 chief executives of the largest corporations in the world, redefining the role of companies in society. It proclaimed that they would pledge to protect the not only of shareholder interests, but also the long-term interests of all stakeholders impacted by their operations. Even business-friendly *Forbes* magazine panned it as a public relations ploy that contains no accountability mechanisms to ensure implementation (Eccles, 2020, August 19). In the meantime, corporate spending demonstrates how companies support a wide range of political issues antithetical to their public positions (Sorkin, 2020, July 21; Goodman, 2020, September 22). Profits continue to come at the expense of society. Signatories of the letter were more likely than other big companies to lay off employees during the pandemic while paying out dividends to shareholders. Wells Fargo fought back a shareholder proposal to implement the Roundtable pledge.

Until reforms address "a financial system that really serves society, rather than just trying to stay ahead of misdeeds of the one that doesn't, we'll struggle in vain to bridge the gaps between Wall Street and Main Street" (Foroohar, 2017, September 27). Corporations cannot be depended upon to reform themselves; stakeholders need to protect their own interests with voice and representation in board rooms (Meagher, 2019, September 26). In short, the impact of scandals makes it difficult to govern, to hold public and business officials accountable, and to chart reform.

Nonprofits. Not-for-profit organizations are also adversely impacted by scandals. Stories of the misdeeds tarnish the reputation not only of those smeared with the taint of corruption but also of legitimate programs that might lose favor with the public. Damaged reputation can sour potential donors who may withhold cash because of real or actual misdoings. Not-for-profits are especially susceptible to fraudsters because of their characteristics such as a trusting atmosphere, revenue streams that are hard to verify, insufficient knowledge and experience in business and financial matters, and unpaid volunteer boards of directors (Douglas & Mills, 2000). Add to this the legal system's inconsistent approach to the pursuit of white-collar criminals in the nonprofit setting (Croall, 2003), problems may escape detection and be allowed to fester. Because of these vulnerabilities it is important for nonprofits to defend themselves by fortifying their ethical infrastructure (Chapter 8) and by standing up for integrity.

Overall, then, focusing on scandals in government, business, and non-profits is important but should not divert attention from less spectacular corruption. Headline scandals, in fact, are often trivial when compared to the underlying failure of the system to come to terms with critical issues such as health care, environmental protection, financial regulation, social justice, immigration reform, and more. Yet while crises have a way of bringing out the worst of human vices, they also bring out the best of human virtues as illustrated by calls for reform.

AVENUES FOR REFORM

Power concedes nothing without a demand.

—Frederick Douglass

To prevent, deter, and expose corruption at least four elements are needed: an informed electorate, a vibrant media, transparency, and skilled investigators and prosecutors (Reilly, 2016, 149). Thus, a more successful, less crisis-prone system would include initiatives such as

- establishing a national commission on corporate crime, restricting the use off-shore tax havens, strengthening conflict of interest rules, limiting stock options,
- using the authority federal and state law enforcement agencies already have,
- acknowledging that fines and court settlements, "which don't even rise to the level of a minor inconvenience" (Gongloff, 2012), are meaningless unless coupled with executive exposure to criminal and civil liability,
- conducting periodic bank "stress tests" to determine financial soundness
- improving business accountability to not only company stockholders but also societal stakeholders by enacting legislation that prohibits making a profit at the expense of the environment, human rights, public safety, the welfare of the community in which the corporation operates, or the dignity of employees (several large cities have passed a Code for Corporate Citizenship or "responsible banking" ordinances that require banks to reveal their impact on the community and/or require city officials to only do business with banks that are responsive to local needs),
- forbidding corporate law breakers the right to bid on governmental contracts that are a significant source of business for most major companies,
- establishing a reparations fund—like the BP fund to reimburse 2010 Gulf oil spill victims—for Main Street victims of Wall Street avarice—the source of revenues would be a "Robin Hood" tax (Exhibit 9.3), and
- enacting a corporate "death penalty" by revoking the firm's charter after three criminal convictions (Exhibit 9.4).[9]

EXHIBIT 9.3   Robin Hood Tax

The "Robin Hood" tax would offset the cost of the financial sector-caused recession, suppress high-risk and high-speed trading that caused the crash, and limit the casino culture of Wall Street. The United States not only had this tax in the past (1914–1966) but also doubled it during the Great Depression to help pay for recovery. Revenues would be collected on financial transactions detailed in the proposed Wall Street Trading and Speculator Tax Act. The tiny levy, 0.03 percent of each transaction, is able to generate significant funds due to high frequency of billion-dollar trades (Gerard, 2012; van Gelder, 2002). The nation charges sales taxes on many consumer goods, but nothing on the sale of stocks, bonds, and derivatives—at a time when many other nations use the Robin Hood tax. Added impetus for this reform was provided by the May 2012 $5 billion loss sustained by JPMorgan and the credit downgrades of 15 major banks the next month. This was followed by the global Libor interest rate exposé. Even after being bailed out by the taxpayer in 2008, it was evident that banks continued to speculate and failed to protect themselves from future crashes. Critics maintain that these institutions need adult supervision.

EXHIBIT 9.4	**Corporate Charters**

I believe . . . that banking institutions are more dangerous than standing armies.

—Thomas Jefferson

A potential reform strategy is to reinvigorate corporate charters, the legal instruments by which state governments incorporate businesses (Kelly, 2001). Historically, corporations were creatures of, and subordinate to, state governments. The founders understood that "we the people" would be sovereign over not only the political but also the economic system. Since corporations were seen as a threat to democracy—the American Revolution was a reaction to British trading companies—citizens determined whether corporations had the right to exist.

Pointedly, Thomas Jefferson wanted an Eleventh Amendment to prevent companies from dominating entire industries or having power to influence government. He saw this as necessary because the Bill of Rights does not protect people against private institutions (employees, for instance, have no powers of free speech). The main reason it was not incorporated into the Constitution was that it was deemed unnecessary given the state-chartering process.

Corporations possessed no authority, as legislatures set the terms of their existence—public corporations were not private enterprises and not run to maximize shareholder value. It was a privilege to serve the commonweal. The public governed corporations by detailing rules and defining operating conditions in charters (few were granted, and then only after legislative debate). In short,

- corporations had to serve a public purpose,
- they were limited to what business they could pursue (they could not buy other businesses) and could amass only certain amounts of wealth,
- there was a 15- to 20-year limit to the charter, subject to renewal,
- corporations were prohibited from lobbying,
- the penalty for abuse was not a fine or plea bargain, but charter revocation, and
- stakeholders were to be treated responsibly by corporations (Hightower, 2003).

In 1886, however, a Supreme Court ruling—*Santa Clara v. Southern Pacific Railroad Co.*—was widely misinterpreted to mean that corporations were "persons" with the same inherent, inalienable rights, freedom, and mobility as human beings (Hartmann, 2010). In subsequent years, courts established new doctrines (freedom of contract, managerial prerogative) to weaken state laws and citizen sovereignty over corporations, as they bestowed on corporations authority over investment, production, and organization of work (Grossman, 2001). The result: Shareholder primacy over public interest was established and the role of government changed from defining corporations to attempting to regulate them. Corporations, accordingly, have claimed such rights as the Fourteenth Amendment right to stop cities from favoring local businesses over chain stores, the Fourth Amendment right against search and seizure to prevent surprise inspections of companies, and the First Amendment right to free exercise to spend unlimited monies in political campaigns. Many states, nonetheless, still retain formal charter revocation authority, and some businesses—notably those that are small with little political power—may lose their charters.

In 1976, a Supreme Court decision equated free speech with spending, resulting in corporations having the biggest, wealthiest, and most undemocratic voice in electoral process. This was dramatically reinforced by the Court's 2010 *Citizens United v. Federal Election Commission* decision, which removed limits on corporate contributions to political campaigns. Businesses are now able to tell employees which politicians they support, in effect, campaigning and collecting donations in the workplace. The implication is that "the rich and powerful transform free speech—our most important tool of bottom-up self-government—into a means of allowing top-down control" (Epps, 2012). Revisiting the origins of corporate charters, in brief, may hold promise as a reform strategy, one that might merit national standards for large corporations—the issuance of federal charters.

Senator Sheldon Whitehouse believes that the America "has been though a colossal test case in how (to) corrupt and incapacitate a great democracy. And failing to learn those lessons is a disservice to that democracy" (Goldberg, 2020, August 13). One place to begin is for every federal agency to conduct an internal review of its operations to identify areas that were corrupted during the past administration and take steps to address them.

Reforms specifically targeting banks include capital requirements, standardized and transparent derivatives, and independent auditing. Absent regulation, "capitalism's most dangerous enemies are capitalists" (Samuelson, 2008), not unlike the communists who destroyed communism. A "criminogenic" environment is created by speculation, chicanery, and outright fraudulent behavior. Analogous to Gresham's Law (counterfeit money drives legal currency out of circulation), regulatory negligence and corporate excess permit bad behavior, allowing honesty to wither.

Indeed, banks, according to U.S. Representative Maxine Waters (D-Calif.) (2012), "will fight against regulation even when it is in their own best interest." Thus, the head of JPMorgan acknowledged before Congress that reckless trading fueled by "greed, arrogance, hubris, and lack of attention to detail" continues, even as the industry resists rules to curb its toxic practices ("Mr. Dimon," 2012). Leading financial firms have been caught committing fraud, financing terrorists, and laundering money. For example, transgressions include the 2012 LIBOR (London Interbank Offered Rate) interest-rate rigging scandal (which affects the cost of borrowing for corporations and consumers), JPMorgan Chase's 2013 $6.2 billion trading fiasco (Morgenson, 2013), and the Wells Fargo fake customer accounts discussed earlier. There is, in brief, no shortage of ideas to reform the system; what is missing is political will. Failing to confront lawlessness contributes to citizen feelings of alienation and powerlessness that feeds corruption.[10]

An indicator of the validity of reform is the failure of opponents to make an honest case against them. The implacable, tenacious power of existing stakeholders cannot be underestimated. An important consideration in enacting change is what may happen when and if they are implemented. Many white-collar crimes are extraordinarily complex, and public service frequently does not have the necessary expertise and funding to pursue them in court. In addition, resource-poor government prosecutors typically face well-financed corporate defense teams (e.g., Enron's Kenneth Lay and Jeffery Skilling's legal defense cost at least $70 million). Business corruption is not just a corporate failure but also a failure of governmental oversight eviscerated by deregulation—the sheer volume of cases simply overwhelms prosecutors (Ramirez & Ramirez, 2017).

The inability or unwillingness to employ anti-corruption approaches amounts to the institutionalization of corruption that not only degrades democracy and the rule of law but also imperils the future of the nation. Corruption is a severe problem and although reform initiatives exist, when improper behavior is the norm the co-dependency of officials can make anti-corruption programs an instrument of cronyism and can exacerbate corruption (Liu, Moldogaziev, & Mikesell, 2017). Even the most egregious failures do not seem to be consequential to policymakers or businesspeople. Evidence matters much less than a narrative that supports their interests. In a fact-free environment, unaffected by conventional understandings of facts, no one pays the price for disinformation. Reality-based governing is at risk. In many respects, America has become a society that cannot self-correct. Edward Wyatt says this about the Securities and Exchange Commission:

> Critics of the agency have raised concerns about its settlement practices over the last decade. According to the *New York Times* analysis of enforcement cases, nearly all of the biggest Wall Street firms have settled fraud cases by promising never to violate the law that they had already promised not to break, usually multiple times. In addition . . . those settlements also repeatedly granted exemptions to the biggest Wall Street firms from punishments intended by Congress and regulators to act as a deterrent to multiple fraud violations.
>
> (2012; see also Smith, 2018 and Temin, 2020)

The 2011 Financial Crisis Inquiry Commission faulted two administrations and regulators with permitting fraudulent lending practices, bundling of toxic loans for sale to investors, and risky bets on securities backed by the loans. One commentator explained the importance of this finding, saying, "The greatest tragedy would be to accept the refrain that no one could have seen this coming and thus nothing could have been done. If we accept this notion, it will happen again" (Chan, 2011).

CASE STUDY 9.1

Applying Philosophical and Behavioral Ethics Approaches: Public to Private Approaches to Employment for Similar Work

Craig Weatherford has worked for many years in Metropolitan County government. Trained as an engineer, his job is to conduct evaluations for the county zoning board regarding engineering features of filed petitions. Weatherford decides to retire. He then opens a consulting business and does similar work in the private sector. Given his prior experience in government, he is approached by a fellow engineer from a development firm who is petitioning the county zoning board for a variance. Weatherford agrees to represent the client and is slated to offer expert testimony before the board regarding the technical soundness of a large water system and the ecological consequences for surrounding jurisdictions. Previously, while employed by the county, Weatherford had completed preliminary assessments of this petition. His status as an expert witness for the company was challenged by citizen groups who opposed approval of the zoning variance. They questioned Weatherford's involvement in this issue. Now, he is uncertain about whether to continue to testify and represent his client.

Results-Based Analysis. Like the case in the last chapter, this case study can be examined using both philosophical theory and behavioral ethics. Beginning with the former, a results-based analysis focuses on the greatest good for the greatest number. Thinking broadly about the case, it is hard to argue that allowing one side of a dispute to use insider knowledge not available to the other side serves the greater good, especially when it creates an unleveled and unfair playing field. More narrowly, Weatherford may be viewing results differently. He thinks his experience will likely enable him to be successful in persuading the board to approve the variance. Weatherford's clients would be pleased if he prevailed and his business would likely flourish as a result. He doubts that there would be any mistakes in his testimony because he has intimate knowledge not only about board policies and procedures but also regarding the nuances of the case based on his preliminary review. Nonetheless, the advocates opposing the variance will question the legitimacy of the process if the board relies on testimony from someone with the unfair advantage of inside information.

Weatherford is aware of his vulnerability to the charge of trading on insider knowledge, which undoubtedly will be emphasized by those opposing the variance. He is concerned that this allegation might be effective and undercut his credibility. Failure to win the variance for his client could damage his reputation for competence and lead people to question his integrity. He worries: Is he putting the end of achieving the variance ahead of the ethics of his profession regarding "avoiding the appearance of impropriety"? He realizes that there may be legitimate concerns regarding the ethical permissibility of his private employment following public service, but he is unwilling to withdraw.

Rule-Based Analysis. A rule- or principle-based analysis considers what is good for one is good for all. The privileged information is not available to all stakeholders. Weatherford does not seem willing to recognize that he may resent it if everyone was allowed to use the information in the way he intends to use it. Is giving an unfair advantage to one side of a dispute a practice he would want to universalize? Probably not, but he may feel that while the rules regarding conflict of interest and inside information are found in the relevant provisions of professional ethics codes, these provisions are vague and subject to interpretation. Further, he knows he is qualified professionally to evaluate the proposal objectively.

Weatherford recognizes he has an edge in this dispute because of his prior experience, but he also knows he will confront charges that he is violating standards. Despite fears that the citizen group would approach the media and publicly criticize his role, he is convinced that he can defend the variance on the merits and that the facts are on his side. The professional ethic requires him to represent his client to the best of his ability. Withdrawal from the case means failure.

Virtue-Based Analysis. A virtue ethics approach focuses on whether the decision makes him and his community better. Weatherford has promised to represent his client and to appear before the board; he is convinced that the variance will advance the community's interest and is loath to renege on this promise. Does he walk away from his client and give up midway through the case? Does he wither in the face of criticism? He thinks it is important to stand up and to be an effective advocate for those who are paying for his services. He owes them his best effort. He would not deny that his prior experience is an asset, but he would not apologize for using his skills acquired in civil service.

Yet does he have an unfair advantage over his opponents? Would the decision to continue pursuing the case reflect the actions of a person of good character? Can he look himself in the mirror and comfortably conclude he could live with himself if he continued to pursue the case? If not, he should withdraw. He wants to be prudent by carefully weighing the pros and contras of the case and consulting colleagues for advice before deciding definitively.

Behavioral Ethics-Based Analysis. Prior to a decision, however, it is important to consider insights from behavioral ethics that lead to consideration of other possible, sometimes unconscious, motivations and intuitions at play in Weatherford's actions. Recall that it is a universal human condition that people think that they are better than they really are. Self-serving bias, thus, can often influence decisions; Weatherford is likely making judgments based on what would advance his self-interest. The "want" and "should" selves might have been at odds with each other: He may have failed to distinguish between his emotional and impulsive "want" choice to take the case and the more thoughtful and deliberative "should" choice. This bounded ethical awareness could help account for the acceptance of the case and agreement to testify without giving sufficient attention to the possible appearance of impropriety. He may have framed the situation as one that he could win rather than considering the ethical implications, rationalizing that the rules on conflict of interest were vague and inapplicable. Upton Sinclair's famous line, "It is difficult to get a man to understand something, when his salary depends on his not understanding it," comes to mind.

Source: Online Ethics Center for Engineering (2006).

Indeed, years after the Wall Street debacle, several self-serving rationalizations—that no one saw it coming and bailing out the banks was the only responsible choice—attempted to provide exoneration of those responsible (Prasch, 2013). To the contrary, it was predicted by many analysts and economists (none of whom was later elevated to responsible positions in government or business). An alternative choice to subsidizing bankrupt investment firms would have been to follow the 1984 Continental Illinois bank collapse (one of the nation's largest banks), which was taken over by the Federal Deposit Insurance Corporation, the agency with extensive experience with resolving failed financial institutions.

Except for these widely overlooked studies, there have been no other authoritative examinations of the role that financial institutions played in the worst recession since the 1930s, no financial settlements proportionate to the crisis, and no criminal indictments of megabank executives. Stanford University economist Anat Admati (2013) wrote that huge banks "take enormous risks that endanger the economy. . . . We will never have a safe and healthy global financial system until banks are forced to rely much more on money from their owners and shareholders to finance their loans and investments."

Wall Street firms, whose resources easily surpass those of state and federal governments, may not only be too big to fail but also too big to investigate, prosecute, and jail (Eisinger, 2017).[11] Operating with impunity, the banking industry continues to imperil American society as crime without punishment prevails. Prosecutorial passivity in the face of overwhelming evidence remains, but there are several isolated exceptions. Federal criminal charges were leveled against the major hedge firm SAC Capital Advisors, and the nation's largest bank, JPMorgan, confronted multiple investigations by the U.S. Justice Department, the Securities and Exchange Commission, and the Commodity Futures Trading Commission (Douglas, 2013; Lattman & Protess, 2013). SAC pled guilty to insider trading and paid a $1.23 billion fine, and JPMorgan settled for $13 billion, the largest fine ever levied by the government (it represents one-half of the bank's 2012 profits). No individuals at either institution were held accountable ("JP Morgan Pays," 2013).

Overall, then, the past 50 years has ushered in an era of rank indifference to the perils of corruption (Foer, 2019, March 13), The lack of accountability that citizens felt about the Iraq War, the use of torture, and the dangerous response to the pandemic did not go away; it metastasized. Nearly every institution in American life has been affected. Beyond the Flint, Michigan and Wells Fargo cases—from bloated bonuses on Wall Street to sex predator Jeffrey Epstein to the college admissions scandal—there is no shortage of white-collar turpitude. Additionally, political scandals since 2016 that would have defined any other presidency occurred with little accountability on a regular basis.

While there are a few exceptions, the criminal justice system has given up the pretense that the crimes of the wealthy are worth taking seriously (Hobbes, 2020, February 10). Criminal penalties levied by the Department of Justice dropped from $3.6 billion to $100 million, illicit profits seized by the Securities and Exchange Commission have fallen by more than half, and white-collar prosecutions are at their lowest level in years. As one expert said, "there is no reason to fear prosecution from committing serious corporate crimes" (cited in Protess, Gebeloff, & Ivory, 2018, November 3). The administration's emphasis was on fortifying the economy, not policing Wall Street. The tragedy is that the expectation of integrity gave way to the cynical acceptance of deceit (Lozada, 2017). The country is simply not very good at being honest with itself or at holding elites responsible, a genuine concern for the rule of law as wrongdoing multiplies during the ongoing pandemic (recall, for example, Exhibit 9.1).

CONCLUSION

Only they deserve power who justify its use daily.

—Dag Hammarskjold

No organization is corruption proof. Dishonorable behavior is often easy, it pays, and getting caught is improbable. However, ignoble conduct cannot be minimized, as the costs of corruption are intolerably high in a democracy. Paradoxically, Daniel Kaufmann (2005) argues, "You don't fight corruption by fighting corruption." Most jurisdictions do not need more politically expedient studies, anti-corruption campaigns, laws, and agencies to serve as a scapegoat for lack of progress or a wall behind which to shield unethical conduct. What is needed is to (a) use the authority already present to pursue fundamental, systemic reforms; (b) end the deliberate underfunding of law enforcement and the judicial system; and (c) fortify a merit-based public service to deter and detect corruption. As Ariely and Garcia-Rada (2019) observe. "The mere exposure to corruption can be corrupting. Unless preventive measures are taken, dishonesty can spread stealthily and uninvited . . . eroding social norms and ethics—and once a culture of cheating and lying becomes entrenched, it can be difficult to dislodge."

For example, while the Securities and Exchange Commission charged 100 firms and 545 executive officers in connection to the 2008 economic collapse, the commission's budget is a fraction of those found in Wall Street firms. Further, federal regulations restrict the size of fines—most of which, in any case, are covered by corporate insurance policies. Investigations of institutions at the center of the Great Recession—Goldman Sachs, Lehman Brothers, Countrywide Financial, American International Group—were dropped. Stated differently, the financial debacle was exacerbated by a violation of the fundamental principles that make democracy and capitalism work: accountability and equal justice (Auerbach, 2018, August 28; Judson, 2011). Whether capitalism can be saved from itself in the pandemic, social justice, and economic crisis remains to be seen.[12]

In the meantime, it is useful to respond to common reasons for not dealing with corruption:

1. "Corruption is everywhere." The statement not only is self-defeating but also makes an assumption that is contestable. Poor health is worldwide, but no one concludes that treating it is a bad idea.

2. "Corruption is culturally determined." While cultural diversity is a fact, there are some practices condoned by none. No culture, for example, condones outright bribery. Exaggerating the importance of culture is often a facade for practices grounded in self-interest. When this happens, it may preempt policies to change culture and save it from itself (Chapter 3).

3. "Cleansing society of corruption requires vast change taking many years." While evil has been present for centuries, so has honor. There is no time like the present to close loopholes, create incentives and deterrents, and augment accountability. The objective is to change the perception of the problem from a low-risk, high-profit enterprise to one that is a high-risk, low-profit peril.

4. "Worrying about corruption is pointless; with free markets, corruption will disappear." Corruption can easily inflict serious harm on free markets, as today's Wall Street scandals, like the Enron Era and Savings and Loan disasters before them clearly demonstrate. Widespread misdoings have been exposed, annihilating the myth of self-regulating markets. Yet that does not stop many decision makers from fighting for the continuation of the same failed policies that caused the disaster. Markets, as imperfect human-created constructions of reality, eventually may be self-correcting, but not without considerable damage to society.

(Adapted from Klitgaard, MacLean-Abaroa, & Parris, 2000)

In brief, the beginning and end of wrongdoing starts with each person. It is important to be aware of the types of circumstances likely to disorient one's moral compass and the rationalizations used to excuse dubious behavior. If corruption problems are ignored, we will not be able to deal with them—they will deal with us.

To combat corruption, a strong civil society (legitimacy of open debate, reform movements, institutions designed to serve the commonweal), clear vision for reform, vigorous political leadership, and rigorous monitoring of progress are necessary. Unfortunately, these critical elements seldom emerge simply because they are needed. The combination of circumstances necessary to attract national attention occurs so rarely that once reforms pass, it is unlikely that such issues will gain widespread scrutiny for some time to come. It has been years since the near collapse of the economy in 2008, and the problems it caused remain only to be exacerbated by the current financial crisis.

The spreading scourge of corruption and the resulting systemic failures on Wall Street should mandate active, disinterested governmental regulation rooted in a "sober, conservative assessment of the human capacity of mistake and self-delusion, not to mention avarice and chicanery" (Meyerson, 2011). The economy should be a servant, not a master, of human needs. As James Madison famously said, "if men were angels, no government would be necessary." But the greed of an unchecked market system calls for regulation of corporate conduct that denigrates human worth and stifles social justice. Government is not a necessary evil but a necessary good. Yet, until genuine reform is achieved, major scandals can be expected in the years ahead. The indelible lesson to date is that perpetrators can act with impunity. If there are limits to corruption, perpetrators are still trying to find them. Discredited financial firms are transforming themselves into a larger, more centralized, and more virulent form, as they continue to corrupt the political system through campaign donations. At some point, a choice will have to be made: rescue investment banks or civil society.

***

The disposition to admire and almost worship the rich and the powerful is the great and most universal cause of the corruption of moral sentiments.

—Adam Smith

NOTES

1. Actual data are difficult to obtain for the reasons already noted and because statistics are ambiguous due to definitional issues. At the same time, Kaufmann, Kraay, and Mastruzzi (2006, 3–4) argue that imperfect proxies—informed stakeholder perceptions, institutional practices, project audits—furnish useful measures of corruption. In fact, "there should be no presumption that objective data is necessarily more informative than data that relies on survey responses from firms and citizens about the reality (of corruption) on the ground."

2. For a running commentary on these matters, see www.corporatecrimereporter.com. An interesting group of articles on white-collar crime can be found in the June 6, 2004, *New York Times Magazine*.

3. Mark Warren (2006) argues that the focus on corruption should be on how it undermines the processes of democracy. It does so by limiting the capability of governments to be responsive to the people when it excludes citizens from decisions that affect them.

4. Moral hazard is most often applied to individual consumers rather than too-big-to-fail institutions. "A lot of energy has gone into arguing that higher workers' comp payments, for example, make workers careless," writes Shaila Dewan (2012). "Far less is said about how lower workers' comp invites moral hazard for employers, making them less attentive to workplace safety."

5. See gift giving "point-counterpoint" feature in Public Integrity, 4(1) (Winter 2002); also examine Schultz (2010).

6. As noted in Lou Cannon, *Governor Reagan: His Rise to Power* (New York: Public Affairs, 2003).

7. The citizenry may have a pragmatic view toward many transgressions, overlooked so long as the elected official does not lie about them and can still be effective by providing for constituency needs. As one politico said, "[P]eople love a titillating story, but they care much more about who can deliver for them"—a fall from grace, followed by redemption, is the classic religious model of salvation. After reviewing the numerous sex scandals and the growing tolerance of some behavior, columnist Lenore Skenazy (2008) observed, "We

are officially adults now, just like the French people but without the delicious pastries and nude first lady."

8. Charles Pierce (2012) writes that "if the lessons of Watergate really were that 'the system' worked and that 'the people' triumphed," then Ronald Reagan would have been impeached for the Iran-Contra affair, George W. Bush would not have gotten away with what his 2000 campaign did in Florida (to say nothing of what was done once in office), and Barack Obama would have been under much more pressure than he was for continuing many of the Bush-Cheney civil liberties policies. "The lasting lesson of Watergate," Pierce writes, "is that self-government was too dangerous."

9. For additional ideas dealing with corporate disclosure, citizen rights, employee participation, and related issues, see Kelly (2001) as well as http://multinationalmonitor.org (click on archived issues, July/August 2002, Corporate Reform After Enron, especially the "Introduction"), www.citizensforethics.org, www.corporatecrimereporter.com, and www. corpwatch.org. Also refer to "USA: 12 Things to Do Now About Corporations" (van Gelder, 2002). On a lighter note, defense attorney Edward W. Hayes created several measurements for gauging the ups and downs of Wall Street: the HEGI and the HESI (the High End Girlfriend Index and the High End Stripper Index). When the financial sector's business is good, traders and bankers spend enormous sums of money on high-end girlfriends and in the VIP rooms of Manhattan's pricey strip clubs (Richberg, 2008).

10. Yet citizens do not have to wait for politicians to act; they can be imaginative when the need arises. In the classical Greek play Lysistrata, the women of Athens go on strike, refusing to have sex until war ended. Peace negotiations were quickly concluded (also see Miller, 2005).

    Likewise Liberia's women used the same strategy in 2003 to campaign for peace, as did women in Togo to demand the resignation of the country's president (Associated Press, 2012). In addition, as part of a 2012 Spanish national strike protesting austerity measures, the executive-class escorts refused bankers until they opened up credit lines to middle-class families and small businesses. Madrid's largest prostitute trade association (Moran, 2012) said, "We are the only ones with real ability to pressure [bankers]." Apparently, the idea for the strike came after one of its members pressured a bank employee to grant a loan to a struggling citizen by withholding her services.

11. Nonetheless, in 2007, the Justice Department decided to prosecute baseball star Roger Clemens for lying to Congress about steroid use (he was acquitted in 2012), while failing to prosecute government torturers and white-collar criminals.

12. After the 2008 economic crash, US bankers received huge bonuses, while reckless bankers in Iceland went to jail. An Icelandic study of the causes of the financial collapse concluded that bank officials were engaged in a "penis competition." Reformers replaced bank presidents with female executives in two of the country's three banks (Sandler, 2018, September 2).

DISCUSSION

1. To the extent that people tend to think of themselves as more ethical than others, they may overestimate the degree of improper conduct in organizations. They then might modify their own behavior accordingly, with the result that corrupt activity expands. Critique.

2. Comment:
   - "Behind every fortune lies a crime."—Balzac
   - "Behind the ostensible government sits enthroned an invisible government owing no allegiance and acknowledging no responsibility to the people. To destroy this invisible government, to befoul the unholy alliance between corrupt business and corrupt politics is the first task of the statesmanship of the day."—Theodore Roosevelt
   - "One of the most important duties of government is to put rings in the noses of hogs."—William Jennings Bryan

- "It is easy to get into trouble and hard to get out."—Anonymous
- "You can count on Americans to do the right thing—after they have tried everything else."—Winston Churchill
- "Always forgive your enemies—nothing annoys them so much."—Oscar Wilde

3. Choose at least one of the following topics for examination.

- The nation's nonprofit groups were held in high esteem immediately after September 11, 2001. In the months that followed, however, questions about the practices of the United Way, the American Red Cross, and others caused public confidence in not-for-profits to plummet. A survey conducted several years later by Paul Light (Brookings Institution) found public trust in nonprofit organizations had not been regained. Assuming that attitudes are slow to change, how can high esteem and confidence be restored?
- It is said the major banking institutions are "too big to fail." How does this explain (if it does) the failure to indict individual bank executives—an action that would not endanger the economy?
- Legal settlements with corporations accused of lawbreaking routinely and repeatedly.
- Allow the firms to buy their way out of the crimes they committed, deny wrongdoing, and protect executives who created the frauds.
- Corruption tends to prevail when the state is captured by elites who use it for their own purposes. Comment on this claim in the context of such concerns as campaign finance, low voter turnout, millionaires winning office, lack of competition for many congressional seats, absence of political attention to major issues affecting the average voter, and so forth.
- "In government, there is no comparison private sector; there is no escape route—you can't declare bankruptcy."
- The military dictator of the Democratic Republic of Congo built a palace in his native village. The air conditioning had to run continuously so the jungle heat would not tarnish the gold leaf on the chandeliers (Kingsolver, 2008, 547).

4. React to the following statements:

- "We have a formidable ethics program—we always catch and punish violators."
- "We have a very effective ethics program—we have 100 percent compliance; no one has ever been caught doing something wrong."
- "Without effective societal institutions—government and business transparency, checks and balances, a free press, independent judiciary—corruption control will be significantly hampered."

5. If there is a gap between how ethical people believe they are and how ethical they actually are, then gift-giving can be problematic. Should gift-giver and recipients nonetheless favor gifting, then there should be a policy making the donor anonymous (if the situation makes the giver is obvious, then gifts would be prohibited). What would be the effect of such a policy?

6. Role distortion, failure, and rejection are components of role theory. Select a well-known public figure and interpret his or her actions using role theory.

7. During the pandemic, some federal agencies were offered large-scale donations of

masks and related personal protective equipment. You are the department's human resource manager. What would you recommend the agency secretary do? Why?

8. Populist Jim Hightower (2013, 2) writes, "Wall Street's super-rich speculators are now making millions of super-fast, robotic financial transactions per second, generating trillions of dollars a year from them—but producing nothing of real value for us, which is distorting and endangering markets." Discuss.

EXERCISES

1. Check with the secretary of state in your state or a local corporation; ask for a copy of a corporation's state charter. Examine its content and critique.

2. Consult these websites for updates on corruption: www.corpwatch.org, www.corporate.policy.org, and www.citizensworks.org (which contains 12 reforms to crack down on white-collar crime).

3. Ralph Nader (2013) suggests that corporate CEOs should recite the Pledge of Allegiance at shareholder meetings because:

   [I]t is our country that chartered (their corporations) into existence and helped insure their success. . . . And these corporations now wield immense power in our elections, in our economy, over our military and foreign policies, and even in how we spend time with our friends and families. [This] is an ideal time to call out these runaway corporate giants who exploit the patriotic sensibilities of Americans for profit and, in wars, for profiteering, but decline to be held to any patriotic expectations or standards of their own.

   Contact businesspeople in your community for their views on this claim.

4. "The Wagon Wheel" (2020 Netflix Original, Jigsaw Production, 54 minutes) is a damning documentary of the ongoing fraud at Wells Fargo. View the film and report your findings to the class.

5. Examine the detailed investigation of corruption in nonprofit organizations by the *Washington Post* www.washingtonpost.com/investigations/inside-the-hidden-world-of-thefts-scams-and-phantom-purchases-at-the-nations-nonprofits/2013/10/26/825a82ca-0c26–11e3–9941–6711ed662e71_story.html?utm_term=.45c546ebec16.

6. *Bad Actor Tabletop Exercise 3:* The Bad Boss. Instructions (see Chapter 3, Exercise 6). Mark Sandsburg is the Director of Finance for Be a Friend, a local nonprofit organization that serves at-risk youth in the community. Most of his experience has been with for-profit organizations, and he has only recently become involved with the charity. He has a reputation of being good with numbers, but his methods are not completely sound. Mark has been shuffling funds between accounts to balance the budget and reporting some individual donations as unrestricted when they were collected for a specific cause. His methods, while shady, have lightened the financial burden the organization had been facing for the past year, but there is a chance that, if audited, his underhanded practices could come to light. The organization has recently canceled its annual voluntary audit.

Role 1: Executive Director

You are the Executive Director of Be a Friend. With no expertise in finance, Mark's practices have evaded you until recently. You have temporarily canceled your annual audit until you can resolve this issue. Mark assures you that no audit would uncover his practices and that you should continue business as usual. You can't be sure that's the right thing to do, but you do know Mark has improved the financial situation. There is a board meeting next week, and they expect an explanation as to why the audit was canceled. What do you do? Consider your obligations, ethical and otherwise. To whom are you accountable as the Executive Director of a nonprofit? What factors impact your decision?

Role 2: Chairman of the Board

You are the Chairman of the Board of Directors for Be a Friend. After finding out that the audit has been canceled, you decide to review this year's financial documents before the next meeting. In reviewing the documents, you find that Mark has been finagling the balance sheet. Despite the impropriety of these tactics, he has been able to free up funds for use on new initiatives. Do you bring this issue to the board for punitive action against Mark? Why or why not? Consider your obligations, ethical and otherwise. To whom are you accountable as a board member? What factors impact your decision?

Role 3: Donor

You are a representative for a private trust that funds Be a Friend. You know that it typically releases its annual audit in June, and it is nearly August. You have not been able to get a straight answer from anyone regarding the holdup. You become suspicious knowing that it recently replaced its Director of Finance and started several new initiatives. It is within your power to impose an independent audit to ensure your funds are being used as stipulated, but this organization is well connected within the community, and its events provide opportunities for your business to grow. What do you do? Consider your obligations, ethical and otherwise. To whom are you accountable as an investor? What factors impact your decision?

Role 4: Independent Auditor

You are an independent auditor. Be a Friend has hired your company to complete an audit. While reviewing their finances, you notice that funds have been changed around rather frequently, and are unsure whether you should investigate further. With the knowledge you have now, there appears to be no definitive wrongdoing, but if you continue your investigation, that may become an issue. Do you investigate the issue further, or clear the audit? Consider your obligations, ethical and otherwise. To whom are you accountable as an auditor? What factors impact your decision?

REFERENCES

Accountable US. (2020, September 9). *Coronavirus Corruption Newsletter*.

Admati, A. (2013, August 25). We're all still hostages to the big banks. *New York Times*. Retrieved from www.nytimes.com/2013/08/25/

Albrecht, C., Sanders, M., Holland, D., & Albrecht, C. A. (2011). The debilitating effects of fraud in organizations. In R. Burke, E. Tomlinson, & C. Cooper (Eds.), *Crime and corruption in organizations: Why it occurs and what to do about it* (pp. 163–185). Guildford: Gower.

Alterman, E. (2020). Lying in state: *Why presidents lie—and why Trump is the worst*. New York: Basic Books.

Anand, V., Ashford, B., & Joshi, M. (2004). Business as usual: Acceptance and perpetuation of corruption in organizations. *Academy of Management Executive, 19*, 9–23.

Anderson, J. (2009, August 6). Despite bailouts, business as usual at Goldman. *New York Times*. Retrieved from www.nytimes.com/2009/08/06/business/06goldman.html? pagewanted= all&gwh=7C3735518D2FCA44B002654FF16B628F

Anechiarico, F., & Jacobs, J. (1994). Visions of corruption control and the evolution of American public administration. *Public Administration Review, 54*, 465–773.

Ariely, D. (2012). *The (honest) truth about dishonesty: How we lie to everyone—especially to ourselves*. New York: Harper.

Ariely, D., & Garcia-Rada, X. (2019). Contagious dishonesty. *Scientific American, 321*(3), 62–66.

Ashforth, B., & Anand, V. (2003). The normalization of corruption in organizations. *Research in Organizational Behavior, 25*, 1–52.

Associated Press. (2012, August 27). Togo sex strike: Women's group plans to withhold sex in effort to unseat president Faure Gnassingbe. *Huffington Post*. Retrieved from www.huffington post.com/2012/08/27/togo-sex-strike-against-president-faure-gnassingbe_n_1832575.html

Association of Certified Fraud Examiners. (2016). *2016 report to the nation on occupational fraud and abuse*. Austin, TX: Author. Retrieved from www.acfe.com/fraud/report.asp

Association of Certified Fraud Examiners. (2020a). *Fraud in the wake of COVID-19: Benchmarking report*. Austin, TX: Author. Retrieved from www.acfe.com/uploadedFiles/ACFE_Website/Content/resources/Covid-19%20Benchmarking%20Report%20September%20Edition.pdf

Association of Certified Fraud Examiners. (2020b). *Report to the nations: 2020 global study on occupational fraud and abuse*. Austin, TX: Author. Retrieved from www.acfe.com/fraud/report.asp

Atkins, S., & Davey, M. (2017, June 14). 5 charged with involuntary manslaughter in Flint water crisis. *New York Times*. Retrieved from www.nytimes.com/2017/06.14/us/flint-water-crisis-manslaughter

Auerbach, M. (2018, August 28). White-collar criminals got off scot-free after the 2008 financial crisis—and helped fuel president Trump's rise. *Naked Capitalism*. Retrieved from www. nakedcapitalism.com/2018/08/white-collar-criminals-got-off-scot-free-2008-financial-crisis-helped-fuel-president-trumps-rise.html

Aviv, D. (2005, September 28). *Testimony to the U.S. Senate Finance Committee, hearing on Hurricane Katrina: Community rebuilding needs and effectiveness of past proposals*. Retrieved from www.senate.gov/~finance/hearings/testimony/2005test/092805datest.pdf

Bair, S. (2019, May 23). Bank bailouts propped up the financial system. But we should never repeat them. *Washington Post*. Retrieved from www.washingtonpost.com/outlook/bank-bailouts-propped-up-the-financial-system-but-we-should-never-repeat-them/2019/05/23/f50e001a-7bee-11e9-8ede-f4abf521ef17_story.html

Baker, M. (2020, November 15). Sex-abuse claim against Boy Scouts new surpass 82,000. *New York Times*. Retrieved from www.nytimes.com/2020/11/15/us/boy-scouts-abuse-claims-bankruptcy.html

Baptiste, N. (2017, May 8). Millions of Americans are drinking contaminated water—and don't even know it. *Mother Jones*. Retrieved from www.motherjones.com/environment/2017/05/millions-drinking-contaminated-water/

Basinger, S. (2018, March 1). There are far more major scandals brewing. So why is a $30,000 dining set in the news? *Washington Post*. Retrieved from www.washingtonpost.com/news/

posteverything/wp/2018/03/01/there-are-far-more-major-scandals-brewing-so-why-is-a-31000-dining-set-in-the-news/

Bauer, C. (2017, June 19). *The five most toxic reasons for not confronting harassment*. Retrieved from Christopher Bauer: chris=bauerethicsseminars.com@send.aweber.com; on behalf of Christopher Bauer chris@bauerethicsseminars.com

Black, B. (2012, August 9). Eduardo Porter's "folly"—Why we must end the "race to the bottom". *New Economic Perspectives*. Retrieved from http://neweconomicperspectives.org/2012/08/eduardo-porters-folly-why-we-must-end-the-race-to-the-bottom.html

Black, B. (2016, February 12). *The inaugural financial fraud lemons of the week award goes to DOJ*. Retrieved from www.nakedcapitalism.com/2016/02/bill-black-the-inaugural-financial-fraud-lemons-of-the-week-award-goes-to-doj.html

Black, W. (2013, March 12). Which aspect of the FDIC's litigation failure is the most embarrassing and damaging? *Naked Capitalism*. Retrieved from www.nakedcapitalism.com/2013/03/bill-black-which-aspect-of-the-fdics-litigation

Blow, C. (2019, October 20). No, we won't just 'get over it'. *New York Times*. Retrieved from www.nytimes.com/2019/10/20/opinion/trump-impeachment-united-states.html

Bowman, J., & West, J. (2007). Lord Acton and employment doctrines: Absolute power and the spread of at-will employment. *Journal of Business Ethics*, *74*, 119–130.

Brady, N. (2011, October 28). What, if anything, to do about Wall Street's wealth. *Washington Post*. Retrieved from www.washingtonpost.com/opinions/what-if-anything-to-do-about-wall-streets-wealth/2011/10/26/gIQASfYNNM_story.html

Brockovich, E. (2020). *Superman is not coming: Our national water crisis and what we the people can do about it*. New York: Pantheon.

Brooks, D. (2010, June 24). The culture of exposure. *New York Times*. Retrieved from www.nytimes.com/2010/06/25/opinion/25brooks.html

Brooks, D. (2012, January 9). Where are the liberals? *New York Times*. Retrieved from www.nytimes.com/2012/01/10/opinion/brooks-where-are-the-liberals.html

Brooks, L., & Dunn, P. (2010). *Business and professional ethics* (5th ed.). Mason, OH: South Western Cengage Learning.

Burke, R., Tomlinson, E., & Cooper, C. (Eds.). (2011). *Crime and corruption in organizations: Why it occurs and what to do about it*. Farnham: Gower.

Cameron, D. (2015, June 6). Corruption is the cancer at the heart of so many of the problems we face around the world. *Huffington Post*. Retrieved from www.huffingtonpost.co.uk/david-cameron/david-cameron-fifa-corruption_b_7524550.html

Camilleri, J. (Ed.). (2011). *Organized crime: Challenges, trends, and reduction strategies*. New York: Nova Science.

Carter, Z. (2018, February 6). The Fed took on Wells Fargo. What about everyone else? *Huffington Post*. Retrieved from www.huffpost.com/entry/janet-yellen-banks-trust_n_5a78c467e4b00f94fe9408a1

Center for Public Integrity, Global Integrity, & Public Radio International. (2012). *State integrity investigation: Keeping government honest*. Washington, DC: Authors.

Chan, S. (2011, January 25). Financial crisis was avoidable, inquiry finds. *New York Times*. Retrieved from www.nytimes.com/2011/01/26/business/economy/26inquiry.html

Clark, A. (2020). *The poisoned city: Flint's water and the American urban tragedy*. New York: Metropolitan Books.

Clark, C. (2012, August 16). Agency handling of Recovery Act praised in new book. *Government Executive*. Retrieved from www.govexec.com/technology/2012/08/agency-handling-recovery-act-praised-new-book/57481/

Clark, C. (2013, April 4). "Cassandras" of financial crisis blast Justice, Treasury departments. *Government Executive*. Retrieved from www.govexec.com/management/2013/04/cassandras-financial-crisis-blast-justice-treasury-departments/62298/

Clarke, R. (2004). *Against all enemies: Inside America's war on terror*. New York: Free Press.

Clement, R. (2006). Just how unethical is American business? *Business Horizons*, *49*, 313–327.

Common Cause. (2020). *Intentional disregard: Trump's authoritarianism during the COVID-19 pandemic*. Washington, DC: Author.

Congressional Research Service. (2020). *The Foreign corrupt practices act: An overview*. Washington, DC: CRS.

Cooper, M. (2009, September 18). On the lookout for stimulus fraud. *New York Times*. Retrieved from www.nytimes.com/2009/09/18/us/18fraud.html

"COVID Feature" (2020, July 27). *Fraud of the Day*. Retrieved from www.fraudoftheday.com/covid-19-fraud/covid-feature-new-age-of-fraud/

Cowen, T. (2013, September 5). The age of the shadow bank run. *New York Times*. Retrieved from www.nytimes.com/2012/03/25/business/the-ban-run-updated.html

Cowley, S. (2017, August 31). Wells Fargo review finds 1.4 million more suspect accounts. *New York Times*. Retrieved from www.nytimes.com/2017/08/31/business/dealbook/wells-fargo-accounts.html

Croall, H. (2003). Combating financial crime: Regulatory versus crime-control approaches. *Journal of Financial Crime*, *11*(*1*), 45–55.

Dawsey, J., Helderman, R., & Fahrenthold, D. (2020, October 24). How Trump abandoned his pledge to 'drain the swamp'. *Washington Post*. Retrieved from www.washingtonpost.com/politics/trump-drain-the-swamp/2020/10/24/52c7682c-0a5a-11eb-9be6-cf25fb429f1a_story.html

Delaney, A. (2017, September 21) Flint water crisis likely increased fetal deaths, Study shows another hint that the U.S. ought to quit using lead pipes for water. *Huffington Post*. Retrieved from www.huffingtonpost.com/entry/flint-water-fetal-deaths_us_59c2ae5ee4b06f93538bf1ce

Dewan, S. (2012, February 26). Moral hazard: A tempest-tossed idea. *New York Times*, pp. 1B, 7B.

Dionne, E. (2010, December 19). Even progressives need CEOs. *Washington Post*. Retrieved from www.washingtonpost.com/wpdyn/content/article/2010/12/19AR2010121903017.html

Dobel, P. (1999). *Integrity*. Baltimore, MD: Johns Hopkins University Press.

Douglas, D. (2013, August 20). Legal troubles mount at JP Morgan. *Washington Post*. Retrieved from http://articles.washingtonpost.com/2013-08-20/business/41429476_1_jpmorgan-chase-biggest-bank-jamie-dimon

Douglas, S., & Mills, K. (2000, August 16). Nonprofit fraud: What are the key indicators? *Canadian Fundraiser*. Retrieved from www.charityvillage.com/cv/research/rlega116.html

Dwyer, P. (2013, November 17). Why no bankers go to jail. *Bloomberg*. Retrieved November 17, 2013 from www.bloomberg.com/news/2013-11-17/why-no-bankers-go-to-jail.html

Eccles, B. (2020, August 19). An open letter to the Business Roundtable. *Forbes*. Retrieved from www.forbes.com/sites/bobeccles/2020/08/19/an-open-letter-to-the-business-roundtable-181/#62f651b14001

Eisinger, J. (2017). *The chickenshit club: Why the justice department fails to prosecute executives*. New York: Simon & Schuster.

Epps, G. (2012, April 16). Don't blame corporate "personhood". *American Prospect*. Retrieved from http://prospect.org/article/dont-blame-corporate-personhood

Epstein, D. (2012, August 13). Ethics office audit of GSA fell far short. *Federal Times*. Retrieved from www.federaltimes.com/article/20120812/ADOP06/308120001/Ethics-office-audit-GSA-fell-far-short

Ferguson, C. (2012). *The predator nation: Corporate criminals, political corruption, and the hijacking of America*. New York: Crown.

Ferguson, T. (2019, March 29). Bank regulation can't be heads banks win, tails taxpayers lose. *Naked Capitalism*. Retrieved from www.nakedcapitalism.com/2019/03/bank-regulation-cant-be-heads-banks-win-tails-taxpayers-lose.html

Fisher, M. (2018, May 13). Trump, Schneiderman, Greitens and the changing shape of sex scandals. *Washington Post*. Retrieved from www.washingtonpost.com/politics/trump-schneiderman-greitens-and-the-changing-shape-of-sex-scandals/2018/05/12/de8ba12e-52d9–11e8–9c91–7dab596e8252_story.html

Foer, F. (2019, March 13). We're losing the war on corruption. *The Atlantic*. Retrieved from www.theatlantic.com/ideas/archive/2019/03/manafort-and-huffman-show-elite-act-impunity/584860/

Foroohar, R. (2017, September 27). How big banks became our masters. *New York Times*. Retrieved from www.nytimes.com/2017/09/27/opinion/how-big-banks-became-our-masters.html

Friedman, T. (2011). Did you hear the one about the bankers? *New York Times*. Retrieved from www.nytimes.com/2011/10/30/opinion/sunday/friedman-did-you-hear-the-one-about-the-bankers.html

Gardner, T. (2020, January 22). US drinking water widely contaminated with 'forever chemicals,' watchdog says. *US News*. Retrieved from www.usnews.com/news/top-news/articles/2020-01-22/us-drinking-water-widely-contaminated-with-forever-chemicals-report

Garment, S. (1991). *Scandal*. New York: Crown.

Gerard, L. W. (2012, June 25). Robin Hood tax: Economic justice. *Huffington Post*. Retrieved from www.huffingtonpost.com/leo-w-gerard/robin-hood-tax_b_1622176.html

Gitlow, A. (2005). *Corruption in corporate America*. Lanham, MD: University Press of America.

Goldberg, M. (2020, August 13). After Trump, America needs accountability for his corruption. *New York Times*. Retrieved from www.nytimes.com/2020/08/13/opinion/trump-corruption.html

Gongloff, M. (2012, September 6). Risky business pays off for Wall Street: Financial crisis penalties pale compared to profits. *Huffington Post*. Retrieved from www.huffingtonpost.com/2012/09/06/wall-street-financial-crisis-penalties_n_1858738.html

Goodman, P. (2020, September 22). Stakeholder capitalism gets a report card. It's not good. *New York Times*. Retrieved from www.nytimes.com/2020/09/22/business/business-roudtable-stakeholder-capitalism.html

Greenlee, J., Jordan, T., & Keating, E. (2007). An investigation of fraud in nonprofit organizations: occurrrences and deterrent. *Nonprofit and Voluntary Sector Quarterly*, *36*(4), 676–694.

Grimm, F. (2010, July). A conspiracy of silence killed JESCA. *Miami Herald*. Retrieved from http://miamiherald.typepad.com/grimm_truth/2010/07/a-conspiracy-of-silence-killed-jesca.html

Grossman, R. (2001). Taking care of business: citizenship and the charter of incorporation. In D. Ritz (Ed.), *Defying corporations, defining democracy: A book of history and strategies* (pp. 59–72). Lanham, MD: Apex Press.

Grunwald, M. (2012). *The new new deal: The hidden story of change in the Obama era*. New York: Simon & Schuster.

Hartmann, T. (2010). *Unequal protection: How corporations became "people" and how to fight back* (2nd ed.). San Francisco: Barrett-Koehler.

Hemmer, N. (2020, January 24). Scandalize! Minimize! Repeat as necessary. *New York Times*. Retrieved from www.nytimes.com/2020/01/24/opinion/sunday/impeachment-fox-news.html

Hightower, J. (2003). How a clerical error made corporations "people." *Hightower LowDown*, 5(4). Retrieved from www.hightowerlowdown.org/node/664/

Hightower, J. (2021, May). Incompetents, idealogues, and Wall Street. *Hightower LowDown*, entire.

Hightower, J. (2013, Autumn). A modest proposal on student debt. *Hightower LowDown*, p. 2.

Hobbes, M. (2020, February 10). The golden age of white collar crime. *Huffington Post*. Retrieved from www.huffpost.com/highline/article/white-collar-crime/

Hobson, W. (2018, January 26). Sports: Twenty years of failure: Many groups missed chances to stop Larry Nassar. *Washington Post*. Retrieved from www.washingtonpost.com/sports/twenty-years-of-failure-many-groups-missed-chances-to-stop-larry-nassar/2018/01/26/f3f51c84–029d-11e8–9d31-d72cf78dbeee_story.html?utm_term=.b82c142aea86

"How to help the neediest Harvey victims" (2017, August 31). *Naked Capitalism*. Retrieved from www.nakedcapitalism.com/2017/08/help-neediest-harvey

Johnson, C. (2006, October 25). End of Enron's saga brings era to a close. *Washington Post*. Retrieved from www.washingtonpost.com/wp-dyn/content/article/2006/10/24/AR2006102401246.html

JP Morgan Pays. (20 November, 2013). *New York Times*. Retrieved November 20, 2013 from www.nytimes.com/2013/11/21/opinion/jpmorgan-pays.html?_r=0

Judson, B. (2011, December 2). Restoring capitalism: Occupy our homes shines a light on our great failure. *Huffington Post*. Retrieved from www.huffingtonpost.com/bruce-judson/restoring-capitalism-occu_b_1124841.html

Jurkiewicz, C. (Ed.) (2019). *Global corruption and ethics management: Translating theory into action* (3rd ed.). Lanham, MD: Rowman and Littlefield.

Kaufmann, D. (2005). Back to basics: 10 myths about governance and corruption. *Finance and Development*, 42(3). Retrieved from www.imf.org/external/pubs/ft/fandd/2005/09/basics.htm

Kaufmann, D., Kraay, A., & Mastruzzi, M. (2006). *Measuring corruption: Myths and realities*. Working paper. Retrieved from http://www1.worldbank.org/publicsector/anticorrupt/corecourse2007/Myths.pdf

Kelly, M. (2001). *Divine right of capital*. San Francisco: Barrett—Koehler.

Kingsolver, B. (2008). *The poisonwood bible*. New York: Harper Perennial.

Klein, N. (2007). *The shock doctrine: The rise of disaster capitalism*. New York: Picador.

Klitgaard, R., MacLean-Abaroa, R., & Parris, H. L. (2000). *Corrupt cities: A practical guide to cure and prevention*. Washington, DC: World Bank.

Krugman, P. (2011, June 11). Rule by rentiers. *New York Times*. Retrieved from www.nytimes.com/2011/06/10/opinion/10krugman.html/

Krugman, P. (2017, March 20). America's epidemic of infallibility. *New York Times*. Retrieved from www.nytimes.com/2017/03/20/opinion/americas-epidemic-of-infallibility.html

Larmer, B. (2108, June 6). Corruption scandals are taking down leaders around the world. *New York Times Sunday Magazine*. Retrieved from www.nytimes.com/2018/05/02/magazine/busted-leaders-boosted-economies.html

Lattman, P., & Protess, B. (2013, July 25). SAC Capital is indicated and called a magnet for cheating. *New York Times*. Retrieved from www.nytimes.com/2013/07/25sac-capital-is-indicted?pagewanted=print

Leber, R. (2017, July 19). Trump's big plan for EPA is already dead. *Mother Jones*. Retrieved from www.motherjones.com/environment/2017/07/trumps-big-plan-for-a-tiny-epa-is-already-dead/

Lerer, L. (2018, December 4). In the age of Trump, Can scandal still sink a politician? *New York Times*. Retrieved from www.nytimes.com/2018/12/04/us/politics/politics-scandal-2020-presidential-campaign.html

Liu, C., Moldogaziev, T., & Mikesell, J. (2017). Corruption in state and local debt expansion. *Public Administration Review*, *77*(September/October): 681–690.

Lloyd, H. (2009). *Wealth against the commonwealth*. Ithaca, NY: Cornell University Library Press. [Original work published 1894]

Lozada, C. (2017, December 21). The presidency survived Watergate, Iran-contra and Clinton scandals. *Washington Post*. Retrieved from www.washingtonpost.com/news/book-party/wp/2017/12/21/the-presidency-survived-the-watergate-iran-contra-and-clinton-scandals-trump-will-exact-a-higher-toll/

McRay, G. (2009, September 16). Bad seeds—Why the ACORN scandal matters to other nonprofits. *Foundation Group*. Retrieved from www.501c3.0rg/blog/acorn-scandal-matters-to-nonprofits

Meagher, M. (2019, September 26). We can't rely on corporations to reform themselves—we must challenge their power. *Open Democracy*. Retrieved from www.opendemocracy.net/en/our economy/we-cant-rely-on-corporations-to-reform-themselves-we-must-challenge-their-power/

Mellman, A., & Eisen, N. (2020, July 22). Addressing the other COVID crisis: Corruption. *Brookings Institution Report*. Retrieved from www.brookings.edu/research/addressing-the-other-covid-crisis-corruption/

Merle, R. (2016, September 29). Lawmakers to Wells Fargo CEO: "Why shouldn't you be in jail?" *Washington Post*. Retrieved from www.washingtonpost.com/news/wonk/wp/2016/09/29/wells-fargo . . .

Meyerson, H. (2011, March 15). From Japan's devastation, our Lisbon moment? *Washington Post*. Retrieved from www.washingtonpost.com/opinions/from-japans-devastation-our-lisbon-moment/2011/03/15/ABPH0yZ_story.html

Miami-area social-service charity files for bankruptcy. (2009). *Philanthropy Today*. Retrieved from http://philanthropy.com/blogPost/Miami-Area-Social-Service-c/18013

Miller, L., & Shea, R. (2020, March 24). COVID-19 Stimulus must include oversight to block fraud. *Government Executive*. Retrieved from www.govexec.com/oversight/2020/03/covid-19-stimulus-must-include-oversight-block-fraud/164051/

Miller, M. (2005, May 25). Listen to my wife. *New York Times*. Retrieved from www.nytimes.com/2005/05/25/opinion/25miller.html

Moran, L. (2012, March 27). A national sex strike! *Daily Mail Online*. Retrieved from www.dailymail.co.uk/news/article-2120984/Spains-high-class-hookers-ban-sex-bankers-provide-credit-cash-strapped-economy.html

Morgenson, G. (2013, March 17). JP Morgan's follies for all to see. *New York Times*, BU, p. 1.

Morgenson, G., & Story, L. (2011, April 14). In financial crisis, no prosecutions of top figures. *New York Times*. Retrieved from www.nytimes.com/2011/04/14/business/14prosecute.html?pagewanted=all

Mr. Dimon on the hill. (2012, June 13). *New York Times*. Retrieved from www.nytimes.com/2012/06/14/opinion/jamie-dimon-on-the-hill.html

Nader, R. (2013, July 3). To big US corporations: What about some patriotism for America? *Huffington Post*. Retrieved from www.huffingtonpost.com/ralph-nader/corporate-patriotism

NCCS Project Team. (2020). The Nonprofit Sector in Brief 2019. *Urban Institute*. Retrieved from https://nccs.urban.org/publication/nonprofit-sector-brief-2019#the-nonprofit-sector-in-brief-2019

No fault corporate crime. (2012, April 3). *Corporate Crime Reporter*. Retrieved from www.corporatecrimereporter.com/news/200/no-fault-corporate-crime/

Nye, J., Zelikow, P., & King, D. (1997). *Why people don't trust government*. Cambridge, MA: Harvard University Press.

Ochs, M. (2016, September 15). In Wells Fargo scandal, the buck stopped well short. *New York Times*. Retrieved from www.nytimes.com/2016/09/15/opinion/in-wells-fargo-scandal-the-buck-stopped-well-short.html

Olaniran, T. (2018, April 15). I am a Flint resident. I am done paying for water that is not safe. *Washington Post*. Retrieved from www.washingtonpost.com/news/posteverything/wp/2018/04/16/im-a-flint-resident-im-done-paying-for-water-that-isnt-safe/

Online Ethics Center for Engineering. (2006, June 10). *Related work done by a private party following public employment (adapted from NSPE Case No. 78–10)*. Retrieved from www.onlineethics.org/Resources/Cases/ec78-10.aspx

Partnoy, F. (2020). The looming bank collapse. *The Atlantic*. Retrieved from www.theatlantic.com/magazine/archive/2020/07/coronavirus-banks-collapse/612247/

Pearlstein, S. (2012, May 20). JP Morgan's soap opera makes clear that Wall Street is detached from reality. *Washington Post*. Retrieved from www.washingtonpost.com/jpmorgans-soap-opera-makes-clear-that-wall-street-is-detached-from-reality/2012/05/18/gIQAIJwvbU_story.html

Perri, F., & Brody, R. (2011). The dark triad: Organized crime, terror, and fraud. *Journal of Money Laundering Control, 14*, 44–59.

Pickel, J. (2019, May 15). Penn State Child sex abuse scandal timeline: Sandusky's crimes continue to cast shadows. *PennLive*. Retrieved from www.pennlive.com/news/2016/05/jerry_sandusky_timeline.html

Pierce, C. P. (2012). The lessons of Watergate do not belong to us. *Esquire*. Retrieved from www.esquire.com/print-this/watergate-40-years-later-9747335?page=all

Porter, J. (1768). *Observations on the religion, law, government and manners of the Turks*. London: Nourse.

Prasch, R. (2013, September 22). The "lessons" that Wall Street, Treasury, and the White House need you to believe about the Lehman Collapse. *Huffington Post*. Retrieved from www.huffingtonpost.com/robert-e-prasch/the-lessons-that-wall-str_b_3953321.html?view=print&comm_ref=false

PriceWaterhouseCoopers. (2020). Fraud and economic crime: A seemingly never-ending battle. US edition. *PwC*. New York: Author. Retrieved from www.pwc.com/us/en/services/forensics/library/global-economic-fraud-survey-2020.html

Protess, B., Gebeloff, R., & Ivory, D. (2018, November 3). Trump administration spares corporate wrongdoers billions in penalties. *New York Times*. Retrieved from www.nytimes.com/2018/11/03/us/trump-sec-doj-corporate-penalties.html#:~:text=Trump%20Administration%20Spares%20Corporate%20Wrongdoers%20Billions%20in%20Penalties,as%20the%20Obama%20era%20came%20to%20a%20close.

Protess, B., & Silver-Greenberg, J. (2012, December 10). HSBC to pay $1.92 billion to settle charges of money laundering. *New York Times*. Retrieved from http://dealbook.nytimes.com/2012/12/10/hsbc-said-to-near-1-9-billion-settlement-over-money-laundering/?_r=0

Ramirez, M., & Ramirez, S. (2017). *The case for the corporate death penalty: Restoring law and order on Wall Street*. New York: New York University Press.

Reich, R. (2011). *Aftershock*. New York: Knopf.

Reid, S. (2018, February 16). Sports—100s of USA swimmers were sexually abused for decades and the people in charge knew and ignored it, investigation finds. *Register*. Retrieved from www.ocregister.com/2018/02/16/investigation-usa-swimming-ignored-sexual-abuse-for-decades/

Reilly, T. (2016). *The failure of governance in Bell, California*. Lexington, MA: Lexington Books.

Rich, F. (2007, October 21). Suicide is not painless. *New York Times*. Retrieved from www.nytimes.com/2007/10/21/opinion/21rich.html

Richberg, K. (2008, September 28). Power shifts from N.Y. to D.C. *Washington Post*. Retrieved from www.washingtonpost.com/wp-dyn/content/article/2008/09/27/ArR200909027021.html

Rowe, W., & Dato-on, M. C. (Eds.). (2013). *Introduction to nonprofit management*. Thousand Oaks, CA: Sage.

Russell, A., & Vinsel, L. (2017, July 3). Let's get excited about maintenance. *New York Times*, SR 3.

Samuelson, R. J. (2008, January 23). Capitalism's enemies within. *Washington Post*. Retrieved from www.washingtonpost.com/wp-dyn/content/article/2008/01/22/AR2008012202615.html

Sandel, M. (2012). *What money can't buy: The moral limits of markets*. New York: Farrar, Straus, & Giroux.

Sandler, L. (2018, September 2). To solve America's sexism, make workplaces more like Iceland's. *Huffington Post*. Retrieved from www.huffpost.com/entry/opinion-iceland-gender-equality-workplace-sexism_n_5b8ab6e1e4b0162f4723fb2e

Saviano, R. (2012, August 25). Where the mob keeps its money. *New York Times*. Retrieved from www.nytimes.com/2012/08/26/opinion/sunday/where-the-mob-keeps-its-money.html

Schmitt, M. (2019, September 2). Why has Trump's exceptional corruption gone unchecked? *New York Times*. Retrieved from www.nytimes.com/2019/09/02/opinion/trump-corruption-drain-the-swamp.html

Schnurer, E. (2013, August 15). Just how wrong is conventional wisdom about government fraud? *The Atlantic*. Retrieved from www.theatlantic.com/politics/archive/2013/08/just-how-wrong-is-conventional-wisdom-about-government-fraud/278690/

Schofield. (2020, August 23). Paltry toxic water settlement. *Naked Capitalism*. Retrieved from www.nakedcapitalism.com/2020/08/paltry-flint-toxic-water-settlement-lets-not-kill-all-the-lawyers-at-least-not-some-of-them.html

Schultz, D. (2010). Ethics regulations across the professions: The problem of gifting. *Public Integrity*, *12*, 161–172.

Schwartz, J. (2009, December 7). Justices to weigh honest-services law. *New York Times*. Retrieved from www.nytimes.com/2009/12/07/us/07honest.html

Sheth, S. (2019). America's top ten fears. *Chapman University*. Retrieved from www.chapman.edu/wilkinson/research-centers/babbie-center/_files/americas-top-fears-2019.pdf

Skenazy, L. (2008, August 12). A mistress, a baby, a men's room. *New York Sun*. Retrieved from www.nysun.com/opinion/a-mistress-a-baby-a-mens-room/83674/

Sloan, C. (2016, March 14). Wall Street is causing the water crises in American cities. *Whistleblow Wall Street*. Retrieved from https://whistleblowwallstreet.com/wall-street-is-causing-the-water-crises-in-american-cities/

Smialke, J. (2020), January, 16). Trump Tried to Scrap Anti-Bribery Law, New Book Says. *New York Times*, p. B3.

Smith, R. (2018, March 20). Once an SEC regulator, now thriving as a lawyer for whistle-blowers. *New York Times*. Retrieved from www.nytimes.com/2018/03/20/business/jordan-thomas-sec-whistleblower-settlement.html

Sorkin, A. (2020, July 21). A company backs a cause. It funds a politician who doesn't. What gives? *New York Times*. Retrieved from www.nytimes.com/2020/07/21/business/dealbook/corporate-political-donations.html

Spoth, T. (2010, July 27). IG: DoD can't account for almost 9 billion in Iraq funds. *Federal Times*. Retrieved from www.federaltimes.com/article/20100727/DEPARTMENTS01/7270304/IG-DoD-can-t-account-almost-9-billion-Iraq-funds

Temin, T. (2020, November 2). Is the SEC short changing corporate whistleblowers? *Federal News Network*. Retrieved from https://federalnewsnetwork.com/agency-oversight/ . . .

Thompson, J. (2000). *Political scandal*. London: Blackwell.

USA Swimming number of members from 2000 to 2017. (2019, May 15). Retrieved from Statista: www.statista.com/statistics/513081/usa-swimming-membership/

U.S. Government Accountability Office. (2020). *COVID-19: Federal efforts could be strengthen by timely and concerned actions*. GAO_20–701; September 21. Washington, DC: Author.

Vagianos, A. (2018, February 19). Sports-explosive report says USA swimming covered up hundreds of sexual abuse cases. *HuffPost*. Retrieved from www.huffpost.com/entry/usa-swimming-sexual abuse_n_5a8ad81fe4b004fc3194c4b2?guccounter=1&guce_referrer=aHR0cHM6Ly9zZWFyY2gueWFob28uY29tLw&guce_referrer_sig=AQAAAK73mTIdRAJteELt6rlvCeSL5dEnFoEpQ7QQPVdttwSZ_5VMBc-ln4jH

vanden Heuvel, K. (2019, May 8). Trump's tweets distract us from the biggest scandal of all. *Washington Post*. Retrieved from www.washingtonpost.com/opinions/trumps-tweets-distract-us-from-the-biggest-scandal-of-all/2018/05/08/0212817e-520a-11e8–9c91–7dab596e8252_story.htm

van Gelder, S. (2002, September 30). 12 things to do now about corporations. *Yes! Magazine*. Retrieved from www.yesmagazine.org/issues/living-economies/12-things-to-do-now-about-corporations

Vazquez, M. (2020, March 14). *How Dr. Anthony Fauci became Trump's coronavirus truth teller*. Retrieved from https://www.cnn.com/2020/03/14/politics/anthony-fauci-trump-coronavirus/index.html

Veruil, P. (2017). *Valuing bureaucracy: The case for progressive government*. New York: Cambridge University Press.

Vogel, H. (2020, May 15). Whistleblower: Wall Street has engaged in widespread manipulation of mortgage funds. *ProPublica*. Retrieved from www.propublica.org/article/whistleblower-wall-street-has-engaged-in-widespread-manipulation-of-mortgage-funds

Warren, M. (2006). Political corruption as duplicitous exclusion. *PS: Political Science and Politics*, *37*, 803–807.

Waters, M. (2012, May 22). Wall Street should stop trying to gut financial reform. *The Hill*. Retrieved from http://thehill.com/blogs/congress-blog/economy-a-budget/228597-wall-street-should-stop-trying-to-gut-financial-reform

Whitlock, C., & Woodward, B. (2016, December 5). Pentagon buries evidence of $125 billion in bureaucratic waste. *Washington Post*. Retrieved from www.washingtonpost.com/investigations/pentagon-buries-evidence-of-125-billion-in-bureaucratic-waste/2016/12/05/e0668c76-9af6-11e6-a0ed-ab0774c1eaa5_story.html?utm_term=.1ebf7b981e71

Why the return of bigger banks means bigger risks for everyone else. (2017, September 8) *New York Times*. Retrieved from www.nytimes.com/2017/09/08/opinion/why-the-return-of-bigger-banks-means-bigger-risks-for-everyone-else.html

Will, G. (2020, October 10). Trump's presidency is one giant act of trolling. *Washington Post*. Retrieved from www.washingtonpost.com/opinions/trumps-presidency-is-one-giant-act-of-trolling/2018/10/10/d6aa4632-cbe6-11e8-920f-dd52e1ae4570_story.html

Wyatt, E. (2012, February 22). Responding to critics: S.E.C. defends "no wrongdoing" settlements. *New York Times*. Retrieved from http://dealbook.nytimes.com/2012/02/22/s-e-c-chairwoman-defends-settlement-practices/

Appendix 9.1
The Statutory Rape Case in USA Swimming

Scandals involving Jerry Sandusky, an assistant football coach at Penn State (see Chapter 2) and Larry Nassar, a USA Gymnastics team doctor, have grabbed headlines across the United States beginning with Sandusky's story breaking in 2011. As noted in Chapter 2, Sandusky was charged with 48 counts of child molestation and ultimately convicted on 45 counts. He was sentenced in 2012 to 30–60 years in state prison (Pickel, 2019). Nassar was accused of molesting more than 350 victims across the nation and was sentenced to 40–175 years in prison in February of 2018 (Hobson, 2018). While these cases offer a restitution to some victims, and provide society with some measure of comfort in that these pedophiles are no longer a threat to society or our children, there is another scandal that has failed to garner attention, and it dwarfs both Sandusky and Nassar's crimes in the scale and scope of devastation.

USA Swimming, the umbrella organization for the Olympic Swim Team, and the proud tradition of excellence that produced such world-class swimmers as Michael Phelps and Jenny Thompson, has a systemic problem with sexual misconduct dating back to 1997 and affects at least 590 victims. At least 252 coaches and officials were arrested, charged or disciplined by USA Swimming for sexual assault or sexual misconduct against minors (Vagianos, 2018, np). Furthermore, some 20 other swim coaches have been arrested, charged, or convicted for sex crimes in four of the previous six years (Vagianos, 2018). The USA Swimming organization represented more than 350,000 as of 2019, (USA Swimming number of members from 2000 to 2017, (2019))

Historically, USA Swimming has been portrayed as being responsive to many sexual abuse cases. Instead, this approach has been used to mitigate the damage to its reputation by settling cases before they are filed in court, silencing victims and allowing predators to continue their abuse.

An Orange County Register investigation (Reid, 2018) found that in 2005, then-USA Swimming President, Ron Van Pool, pushed for a more aggressive approach to taking on sexual abuse in his annual State of Swimming address; however, no changes occurred and the abuse continued. The USA Swimming executive director, Chuck Wielgus, failed to take any action, even after he was deposed five years later, as part of a sexual abuse case.

Some of the Register's findings included:

- USA Swimming executives, board members, top officials and coaches were aware of sexually predatory coaches for years and in some cases even decades but did little in response. The very person responsible for administering the organization's "Safe Sport" initiative, Susan Woessner, decided to not pursue legal action against abusers.
- One coach, despite abusing a 12-year-old female swimmer, was allowed to continue coaching for an additional 25 years, and received more than $40,000 in grants from USA Swimming.
- Since 1997, at least 252 swim coaches and officials have been arrested, charged by prosecutors, or disciplined by USA Swimming for sexual abuse or misconduct against individuals under 18.
- USA Swim board members and coaches acknowledged they were aware of statutory rape cases that occurred during team trips to international competitions.
- The USA Swim organization maintains a list of more than 30 coaches and officials who have been arrested or accused by law enforcement of sex crimes including rape and child pornography. None of these individuals have been disciplined nor banned despite being convicted of felonies. The list is unavailable to the public.
- The organization spent more than $77,000 to lobby against legislation in California that would have made it easier for sexual abuse victims to sue their abusers and the organizations for which they worked.

The Register found that the coach-centric power base of USA Swimming and its obsession with protecting its brand were critical contributing factors that supported the environment of abuse for so many years (Reid, 2018). There are several factors that contributed to the ongoing mistreatment. One insider indicated that it's "the old boy—the good old boy mentality that USA Swimming still has because of those good old boys that still run that organization. . . . (Sexual relationships are) acceptable. That's not acceptable. That's not protecting children" (cited in Reid, 2018).

That's not acceptable. That's not protecting children" (Reid, 2018). And yet, this voice of reason was ignored. Sir James Porter (1768) may have established a most adept description for this situation when he noted in 1768 that "the fish rots from head down." The Hall of Fame coach of Olympic medalists and world record holders, Richard Shoulberg, wrote in an email to members of a USA Swimming task force that "I would hate to see our organizations ever in the predicament of the current Roman Catholic Church—protecting child molesters!" (Reid, 2018) It was all for naught. The crimes continued, and USA Swimming sought not to protect the swimmers but rather the organization, itself.

Finally, in 2013 the U.S. Olympic Committee (USOC) upon learning about the problem threatened to cut off funding for USA Swimming. It was only then that the rule prohibiting any romantic or sexual relationships between coaches and athletes became part of USA Swimming's Code of Conduct (Reid, 2018). While this show of force by the USOC produced results, even coaches convicted of violent sex crimes were not immediately banned from USA Swimming. Erick Lans, a Massachusetts coach arrested in January 1999 for rape and sex abuse charges, was not banned until March 2013, fully 12 years after he was convicted of intent to commit rape and other charges. He had raped a 12-year-old girl and forced a 10-year-old girl to perform oral sex on him at the facility where he coached (Reid, 2018).

The corporate sponsors of USA Swimming included organizations like Omega, swim gear providers Speedo and TYR, Marriott, NBC Universal and BMW. It is difficult to imagine that these companies willingly associate with an organization that protects sexual predators, but they did, and yet, USA Swimming reported $7.27 million in annual sponsorship revenue in 2016 (Reid, 2018)

A 2014 investigation by a U.S. House of Representatives Committee found that detailed actionable information about sexually abusive coaches "has been well known to USA Swimming leadership, yet because of inaction, these predators were allowed to prey with impunity" (Reid, 2018), and the abuse persisted.

It took the USA Gymnastics Larry Nassar case to compel national legislators to take action. On February 14, 2018, Public Law 115–126, titled "Protecting Young Victims from Sexual Abuse and Safe Sport Authorization Act of 2017" was passed. It requires the reporting of child and sexual abuse and makes accommodations for civil remedies for personal injuries and punitive damages. While this legislation seeks to protect young athletes going forward, there is a generation of swimmers who may have suffered unthinkable harm, and their stories may never be heard.

Adapted with permission from a paper by Karen Cinkus

10 Whistleblowing in Organizations

The ultimate measure of a man or woman is not where he stands in moments of comfort and convenience, but where he stands at times of challenge and controversy.

—Martin Luther King

The last chapter demonstrated that corruption is a significant problem in society. Indeed, many scandals are revealed by "whistleblowers," those who disclose organizational misconduct. Whistleblowing is a manifestation of serious issues; as long as fraud, waste, and abuse exist, so will the need to expose them. Consistent with legal usage, blowing the whistle is a process, as external reports of wrongdoing typically start with internal reports. Although dissent on the job is at least as old as the republic—the 1778 Continental Congress voted unanimously for the first U.S. whistleblower legislation—it crystallized into a social movement in the 1970s as public interest groups formed, professional associations sponsored symposia, universities encouraged research, unions protected members, national conferences convened, and legislatures held hearings and passed laws. As Stanger (2019) and Gold (2019, April 5) observe, whistleblowing has a long and storied saga in contemporary times, including involvement in Vietnam, the Watergate coverup, Enron's financial fraud, the NSA's mass surveillance program, and more recent wrongdoings from Big Pharma to Wall Street to Washington as noted here.

The importance of the whistleblower in responsible administration—an individual who reveals information about illegal, immoral, or inefficient organizational action that endangers the health, safety, or freedom of the public—is undeniable.[1] The U.S. Senate, in fact, unanimously passed the National Whistleblower Appreciation Day resolution on July 14, 2014, celebrating the 236th anniversary of the initial whistleblower law. There is a long-standing tradition of bipartisan support for whistleblowing legislation as most of it is passed without opposition. To help those who blow the whistle during the pandemic, the COVID-19 Whistleblower Protection Act has been introduced in the Senate and remains in committee early in 2021.

Among the many contemporary examples are the following:

- University of Massachusetts student J. Stone Laraway, in the face of a national cheating epidemic, blew the whistle on "crime in the classroom," saying that "this is my school, and I will not tolerate it."
- A Georgia high school principal suspended a student who used social media to publicize pictures of crowded hallways with mask-less students (she was reinstated).

DOI: 10.4324/9781003203148-13

- The manager of the Pentagon's largest contract in Iraq was discharged when he refused to pay $1 billion in questionable charges to a contracting firm (the bill was later paid and the company was awarded performance bonuses, plus a new $150 billion contract).
- An NSA official—who blew the whistle on massive fraud, waste, and abuse—was indicted on espionage charges for allegedly making unauthorized contact with a newspaper (the court proceedings collapsed when the judge ruled that the government had no case).
- Whistleblowers revealed that BP and the federal government made long-term public health and environmental effects of the Gulf oil spill worse by using a chemical to disperse oil that was more toxic than the crude oil alone.
- The U.S. Department of State paid an informer $25 million it had offered for the capture of Osama bin Laden.
- A Veterans Administration (VA) employee blew the whistle on poor care for mental-health patients at the Phoenix VA hospital—the same facility involved in the agency's wait-time scandal (see Chapter 12); he faced retaliation, but was assigned to the new VA Office of Accountability and Whistleblower Protection.
- A U.S. Environmental Protection Agency and Justice Department employee team won a Service to America medal for exposing a scheme by Volkswagen to rig over half a million vehicles to circumvent auto emission standards.
- A company official revealed Boeing Co. and the Federal Aviation Administration for flouting regulations and ignoring safety concerns for the 737 Max jetliner, whose crashes killed 346 people.
- A current and former Department of Homeland Security received whistleblower award for exposing the practice (since repealed) allowing separation of children from their families that crossed the border with Mexico.
- A top scientist at the Department of Health and Human Services lost his job when he revealed pandemic personal protective equipment supply chain problem and political pressures to support distribution of unproven drugs.
- An unnamed Central Intelligence Agency official filed a complaint concerning a promise the president made to a foreign leader leading to his impeachment.
- Reflecting a cultural shift, the #MeToo sexual harassment movement—by publically exposing employer wrongdoing—is the first mass whistleblowing phenomenon (for an extensive list of whistleblowers since 1773, see www.whistleblower.org/time-line-us-whistleblowers and https://en.wikipedia.org/wiki/List_of_whistleblowers; see also Stanger, 2019).

There are numerous cases in the business and nonprofit sectors as well: for example, employees successfully pressured Google to drop its bid for a controversial military artificial intelligence project, "liar loans" and "robo signings" in home mortgage approvals, the use of beef trimmings known as "pink slime" in the meat-packing industry, widely reported misdoings in pharmaceutical firms and tobacco corporations, and scandals at the Red Cross, United Way, and Boy and Girl Scouts. While not all disclosures become headline news, these "moral sentinels," "bravehearts," "truth tellers," or "insider threats" have been responsible for revealing problems in such areas as regulatory corruption, merit system abuses, dangers to public health, and conflict of interest irregularities. It should be evident that whistleblowing is a symptom of a society in stress.

Common to all incidents is the realization that organizations can be held to account by those willing to put principles into practice by "speaking truth to power." Yet the majority of ethical rebels exist in obscurity and never receive vindication as lionized persons of conscience. Those who are vindicated "are the rare exception, and even most of them pay a horrible price with lifelong scars" (Devine & Maassarani, 2011, 18; for a more optimistic, albeit cautious, assessment, see Hesch, 2008).

In light of such events, the chapter objectives are to

- understand the importance of conscientious employees in contemporary affairs,
- describe relevant statutes,
- analyze cases,
- comprehend the pervasiveness of organizational power, and
- evaluate current trends in whistleblowing.

The overall challenge is not only to achieve new civil rights for those who speak out but also to reduce the need to blow the whistle.

SIGNIFICANCE OF WHISTLEBLOWING

Whistleblowing occurs when micro-level personal ethics compel a person to bring meso-level organizational wrongdoing to light, sometimes for macro-level reform. Employee efforts to detect and correct fraud or waste committed by an employer demonstrate the permeable nature of the boundaries between the three levels of ethics.

As insiders, employees are well positioned to uncover—and help control—waste and fraud in the workplace. Given the low public visibility and high technical complexity of organizational activities, detection of abuse rests in large part with the workforce. In fact, it is amply documented that public and private sector whistleblowers are the single most important source for detecting and preventing crime—more than government regulators, law enforcement personnel, and professional auditors combined (Association of Certified Fraud Examiners, 2016; U.S. Department of Justice, 2010). The federal government, for instance, recovers $7 for every $1 spent fighting fraud, much of which comes from such insider information (Kennedy, 2012).

Rothschild and Miethe (1999) estimate that while one-third of employees have seen unethical conduct, over half of them remain silent probably from either a fear of consequences or a sense of futility ("Why bother?"). Revelations in 2011, for instance, revealed that Pennsylvania State University administrators and football coaches knew of criminal sexual conduct for years but failed to report it to police (see Case Study 2.1). Silence, while understandable, is ethically problematic from results, rules, and rectitude perspectives (Chapter 7). Nondisclosure does not represent the greatest good for the greatest number; it is a form of deceit that causes harm and compromises personal integrity. Rates of disclosure are the highest in public service when compared to business and nonprofit sectors (Brewer & Selden, 1998).

There are a variety of reasons for this; one is the oath of office that obligates civil servants to uphold the constitution, not necessarily one's supervisors. Corporate America, in contrast, often requires employees to sign a non-disparagement, nondisclosure, or mandatory company-dominated arbitration agreement in case of disputes, all of which discourage people from speaking out. Donald Trump planned to require all those who worked in his administration to sign nondisclosure agreements; it is unclear how many signed these agreements, but he was advised that they were not viable in government, which already had restrictions on release of classified information.

In any case, "[t]he wave of corruption," one observer noted, "has been the catalyst for a public mandate to protect whistleblowers. There's been more raw material . . . than at any time since Watergate" (Beutler, 2007), a statement that continues to be true, as noted here. An audit by the U.S. Department of Treasury found that in just one year tipsters reported $65 billion in unpaid taxes (Kocieniewski, 2010). In 2011, the federal government broke all records, bringing nearly $2.3 billion in whistleblower settlements and judgments. Yet complaints that contractors have defrauded taxpayers out of billions of dollars languish at the U.S. Department of Justice because of case backlog—by 2012, over 3,500 fraud cases had not been investigated due to lack of resources (Kennedy, 2012), a problem yet to be fully rectified. By 2016, however, over $37 billion had been collected since 1986 as a direct result of whistleblower information (Kohn, 2017, 12).

Although comparable data are not readily available, the trend continues due to new laws to protect informants, the Internet, and social media to collect and spread information; decline of watchdog functions in the nation's press and government; the normalization of fraud (e.g., "creative accounting"); privatization of public work (e.g., producing conflicts of interest); and events during the Trump administration (Berman, 2019, April 4; Mueller, 2019, 192ff. and 530ff.). Indeed, the number of whistleblowers during that time was higher than in previous administrations.

The larger, more systemic, and more institutional nature of the problem, the greater the managerial effort is to punish the truth teller. It is unusual for employees to be victims of adverse personnel actions when they report the behavior of subordinates. It is when superiors are implicated that retaliation occurs. Workers are also more likely to blow the whistle when wrongdoing is serious, frequent, or widespread—but under these conditions, they are also less likely to persuade the management to correct the problem and more apt to suffer reprisal (Near & Miceli, 2008, 277).

Organizations create a self-contained, self-serving worldview wherein dissent is seen as a challenge to the legitimacy of the leadership. Blowing the whistle is a perilous activity in any jurisdiction, but it is particularly treacherous for international civil servants who staff some 800 transnational governmental institutions. These organizations in the global governance system—unlike sovereign-level checks and balances in democratic countries—lack autonomous executive, legislative, and judicial branches as well as enforcement mechanisms—upon which the ethical resister might rely. Accordingly, tipsters are unusually vulnerable to issues of loyalty, immunity, procedural justice, and visas and employment contracts (Moloney, Bowman, & West, 2019). This international whistleblower vulnerability is vividly depicted in the movie *The Whistleblower* (see Appendix 10.1 for film summary).

Ironically, ethical resisters are often competent professionals who possess the attributes that employers claim they desire—in reporting one's superior, the ultimate act of loyalty becomes an act of betrayal (Matt & Shahinpoor, 2011). Conscientious employees usually believe their organizations will be gratified that they reported misconduct, instead of recognizing that their unwelcome allegations can make their superiors' life—and their own—far more difficult. Nonetheless, as shown in Case Study 10.1, blowing the whistle may be protected by law, but only when certain conditions are fulfilled.

The act of whistleblowing can be justified when

- it is done with an appropriate moral motive,
- internal channels of dissent have been judiciously considered,
- it is based on evidence that would persuade a reasonable person,
- analysis has been made of the seriousness, immediacy, and specificity of the problem,
- possible solutions to the issue are offered,
- it is commensurate with the employee's responsibility,
- it has some chance of success, and
- the employee is ready to accept the personal and professional consequences that accompany the decision.

(Adapted from Bowman, 1983, 91; see also Bauer, 2015,
August 24 and Feinstein & Devine, 2021)

It is common for personnel to work within the system. But when superiors do not do anything about illegal conduct or when individuals experience retaliation, the employee may feel the only ethical choice is to go public. Stated differently, can information be turned into power? Can disclosure make a difference? Did intelligence analyst Edward Snowden fulfill the elements of justified whistleblowing (Exhibit 10.1)?

A valid concern is no defense from organizational revenge. Thus, while one survey of civil servants reports that employees claiming direct knowledge of waste and fraud decreased during the last two decades, a significant number of those who reported problems experienced either threats of reprisal or reprisal (U.S. Merit Systems Protection Board, 2011). Retaliation can be subtle and occur without witnesses or happen for otherwise routine administrative reasons (changed duties, job transfers, performance evaluations, and otherwise marginalized). In many other instances, employees also often lose their jobs, their family, their careers, their retirements and their savings, as employers find it more expedient to "shoot the messenger."[2] Being right is no protection from revenge, as organizations transform whistleblower issues into employee subordination. The truth teller has the burden of proof to show that he was a victim of retaliation.

CASE STUDY 10.1

Problem-Solver or Troublemaker?

Vera English worked in a laboratory at the General Electric (GE) plant in Wilmington, North Carolina, as a quality control specialist responsible for the handling of radioactive materials. Dangerous practices and resulting hazards—contamination, defective equipment, leaks, and employee exposure—were common to everyday work conflicting with Vera's personal, micro ethic of employee safety at work. Her complaints led to work stoppages and caused the Nuclear Regulatory Commission to cite GE for safety violations.

The company, espousing a starkly different meso-level ethic of allowing lax safety standards, barred her from the lab and gave her 90 days to find another position at the facility; when that failed, she was terminated. Under the federal law at the time, she filed a wrongful discharge claim within 30 days of her firing. In court, GE was found guilty of illegal retaliation. English was reinstated and awarded damages.

The company, however, "was not finished. . . . [It] fought English's case every step of the way. . . . Numerous legal technicalities were raised, and they finally found one that would stick: failure to file a timely complaint. . . . GE argued that because she was told that she had 90 days to find a new position within the company, her 30-day filing period commenced to run even before her last day of work. The courts agreed, and her case was thrown out."

Questions to Consider

1. What, if anything, should English have done differently?
2. What lessons can be drawn from this case?

Source: Adapted from Kohn (2017, 68–69, 258–260).

EXHIBIT 10.1   **Is Edward Snowden a Whistleblower? Turncoat or Patriot?**

Revelations by NSA contract employee Edward Snowden sparked a global firestorm of controversy over surveillance and privacy. What are people entitled to know about their government, and what is government entitled to know about its people (Clark, 2013)? A free society requires an informed citizenry to protect both national security and personal privacy. Appropriate measures of transparency and accountability are essential components of that goal.

In June 2013, intelligence analyst Snowden revealed to the *Washington Post* and *The Guardian* (UK) illegal NSA surveillance, done under the mantle of national security, of hundreds of millions of Americans and foreigners through a secret data-mining program. The disclosure of thousands of secret, heavily encrypted documents in the release confirmed what advocacy organizations have known or suspected.

Is Snowden a traitor or a profile in courage? A naïf or a hero? A spy or a whistle-blower? Some officials, including the Speaker of the U.S. House of Representatives, found him guilty of espionage for taking top-secret records out of the country to China and Russia (Thiessen, 2013). Others pointed out that leaking classified information, and ignoring internal procedures to address problems, is against the law; in contrast, bravehearts often engage in lawful disclosures and use approved channels for raising concerns (Hicks, 2013). Perhaps, Snowden is more of a conscientious objector than a whistleblower, according to R. Scott Osward of the Employment Law Group (as cited in McElhatton, 2013), although some practitioners of civil disobedience believe that they should accept punishment for violating the law. Still others see Snowden as a "classic" whistleblower because he disclosed information about a rogue program and was then subjected to derogatory characterizations by the government in an effort to shift attention from the message to the messenger (Jesslyn Radack, as quoted in Wemple, 2013).

While Snowden is criticized for releasing classified information:

[P]ervasive surveillance does not meet the standard for classified information. Documents are properly classified only if they reveal sources or methods of intelligence gathering used to protect the US from its enemies. Information on domestic surveillance cannot be classified unless the US government deems its own population as an enemy.

("GAP stands with Snowden," 2013)

The public has a constitutional right to know how and why the government is conducting domestic surveillance. Like Wall Street (Chapter 9), the intelligence community exercises vast powers and lacks genuine accountability. Tellingly, the Obama administration did not label Snowden a spy. Even though he was indicted under the Espionage Act, the charges were theft of government property and unauthorized communication of national defense data.

Danah Boyd (2013) argues that what it means to protest may be changing in today's information age. Traditional forms of dissent and civil disobedience no longer create iconic narratives, and increasing secrecy since the 2001 terrorist attacks has made the rule of law ineffective as a check on power. Instead, Snowden created a new model of how to expose information (Rosen, 2013), at least so long as the Snowden "effect" (public attention to secret surveillance) outlasts the Snowden "saga" (his personal story in seeking asylum). While claiming a moral motive for his actions, Snowden left the country because, in the words of Project on Government Oversight executive director Danielle Brian, "there are very weak protections for intelligence whistleblowers and none at all for intelligence contractors" (quoted in Davidson, 2013).

When *The Guardian* asked if there was evidence that Snowden had cooperated with any intelligence service or American adversary, the administration and Congress declined to provide any (Ackerman, 2013). Snowden's remaining stockpile of stolen documents is designed to automatically become public knowledge should something happen to him (Publius, 2013). Instead of just divulging information and being forgotten, his approach may be a more effective form of opposition because it threatens the authority of the state and invites "the American people to consider . . . less militaristic and more democratic approaches to national security" (Bacevich, 2013). In the meantime, a government that employs massive secrecy, paradoxically, makes it harder to keep genuine secrets. "When far too much information gets classified, nothing is really classified" (Sanger, 2013) as much of what is secret is misclassified and publicly available. Gellman (2020), in a detailed and balanced treatment of the case, argued that Snowden did more good than harm. Prior to assuming the presidency, Donald Trump called Snowden a "traitor . . . who should be executed" but indicated in mid-2020 that he would consider pardoning Snowden.

Sources: Ackerman (2013), Bacevich (2013), Boyd (2013), Clark (2013), Davidson (2013), "GAP stands with Snowden" (2013), Hicks (2013), McElhatton (2013), Publius (2013), Rosen (2013), Sanger (2013), Thiessen (2013), Touchton et al. (2020), Wemple (2013).

In light of the economic, emotional, and psychological risks, the existence of whistleblowing in organizations is remarkable. The pressure to hide bad news is often intense—efforts to discredit and remove the employee are equally intense. The irony is that the bias against dissenters is counterproductive: Silencing complaints does not solve the problem, and when the cover-up is revealed, the institution is discredited. According to a landmark empirical study, organizations that react in a responsible manner to whistleblowing benefit themselves and society as a whole by reducing corruption (Micheli, Near, & Dworkin, 2008). Further, Wilde (2017) finds that whistleblowing has an important deterrent effect on firm financial misreporting: Using a large sample of cases, companies subject to whistleblowing allegations are substantially less likely to engage in dubious conduct for at least two years. Moreover, he and his colleagues (Call et al., 2017) reveal that whistleblower involvement is a key source of information for officials who investigate and prosecute wrongdoing that results in higher penalties for companies and potentially for executives.

WHISTLEBLOWER LAWS: THE LEGAL LABYRINTH

Unlike other areas of employment law (such as antidiscrimination policy), there is no uniform national whistleblowing law. Instead, there are over 50 separate federal statutes and literally hundreds of state statutory or common-law protections. This body of law consists foremost of legislation in specific policy areas (which includes reprisal protection measures) and, second, statutes designed to encourage whistleblowing. Under law, the dissenter does not have to be right to receive protection but must reasonably believe that a violation occurred. Legal safeguards, however, are denied for bad-faith whistleblowing.

The complex patchwork of legislation may safeguard the jobs of staff, forbid adverse personnel actions, allow employees to sue for back pay and legal fees, or award the critic a percentage of the money recovered in fraud cases—but only under specific circumstances and depending on the jurisdiction, the industry, and the issue in question. Although the numerous statutes are too diverse to summarize here (cf. Kohn, 2017, Chapter 4), some of the most important are described here.

The landmark 2002 Sarbanes–Oxley Public Corporation Accounting Reform and Investor Protection Act (SOX) was enacted in response to Enron Era scandals at the beginning of the century. It broadened whistleblower protections, for the first time, to include employees of publicly traded private companies and their contractors. SOX also mandates that companies establish processes to handle employee claims. Further, legislation later in the decade—the economic stimulus bill, health-care reform, as well as financial reform—contain informant safeguards. Those improvements, the Dodd–Frank 2010 Wall Street Reform, and the Consumer Protection Act defend workers against retaliation, while also providing considerable financial inducements to blow the whistle on securities fraud. Under Dodd–Frank, the Securities and Exchange Commission's whistleblower program has paid out more than $160 million over seven years to informants, a low and declining amount according to critics (Scofield, 2017, November 20; cf., Kohn, 2017, 114).

The historic example of laws that support dissent through the use of incentives, the False Claims Act (FCA) of 1863 covers fraud in federal procurement and contracting. Originally used against war profiteers during the Civil War, it authorizes citizens, acting as "private attorney generals," to file charges on behalf of the taxpayer and receive a percentage of the financial penalties collected by government. In 1986, the law was amended in response to the failed whistleblower effort to stop the launch of the space shuttle *Challenger*, as well as contracting scandals over $435 hammers and $600 toilet seats.

Since then, these *qui tam* suits have enabled the federal government to recover $62 billion, and an estimated $1 trillion in deterrence of further fraud, as the FCA has become the premier whistleblowing tool (Lipton, 2012; Mueller, 2019, October 18). The Department of Justice (DOJ) program under the statute has been so successful that many states have similar programs (see www.whistleblowerlaws.com/ on the content of state FCA laws). Rather than publicly calling attention to wrongdoing, the act encourages citizens to quietly inform the government so that investigations may take place before culprits hide their misdeeds (Kohn, 2017, 21ff.; also see Pugh & Rowan, 2021, June 8). Tipsters benefit only if their charges result in a fine of at least $1 million (thereby minimizing baseless complaints); some payouts are substantial, but they are a faction of the total amount of money that government recovers. Yet DOJ can be antagonistic to whistleblowers as *qui tam* suits can interrupt its daily business, imply that the department is not doing its job, and suggest that some corporations, in the end, are "too big and fraudulent to fail" (Mueller, 2019, 158). Indeed, in recent years DOJ has been hostile toward the FCA, which could lead to a court decision on its constitutionality.

The Internal Revenue Code (Section 406) was enacted in 2006 to resolve the difficulty of detecting large-scale tax fraud and underpayment in offshore accounts when there were few incentives—and many disincentives—for bankers and accountants to expose illegality. The IRS has long received tips from informants, but now with the payouts in its Whistleblower Reward Program, the number of cases and payments has dramatically increased; since 2007, the Whistleblower Office has collected over $5.7 billion and made awards in the amount of $931.7 million (Clark, 2018, November 1; U.S. Governmental Accountability Office, 2015; Internal Revenue Service, 2020). Corporate Sentencing Guidelines (Chapter 9) also use incentives to benefit employers, encouraging them to have an ethics code and to establish reporting channels for protesters. Doing so reduces fines and penalties if the organization is convicted of crimes.

For reasons to be discussed, much of this legislative activity functions as little more than a "mirage of protection" for dissenters, because much of it lacks due process and adequate remedies. The laws are not only confusing and riddled with loopholes but also not comprehensive or consistently enforced by government agencies and the courts. For example, according to Devine and Maassarani (2011, 197), "SOX is a pioneering reform because it systemically extends corporate freedom of speech in principle, solidifies modern legal burdens of proof, and creates the right to seek justice from a jury." However, "it has helped few actually achieve justice," as just 1.4 percent of over 2,000 claims resulted in truth teller victories (166). Explanations for the state of affairs include procedural complexity in bringing a claim, short statutes of limitations, inadequate agency staffing, and narrow or incorrect interpretations of the law (Micheli et al., 2008, 169–170).

A best practice standard, based on national laws and international organization policies, contains 20 specific criteria organized by

- the definition scope of whistleblowing coverage (the presences or absence of loopholes),
- the forum for whistleblower cases (adjudication bodies that provide fair process),
- rules needed to prevail (realistic burdens of proof and statutes of limitations),
- scope of relief (victim obtains benefit and wrongdoer is held accountable), and
- making a difference (positive results for not only the employee but also society) (Devine & Maassarani, 2011, 256ff).

The Whistleblower Protection Enhancement Act of 2012 (S743), reflective of many of these standards, was over 12 years in the making. Among the provisions are an increased protection of disclosures and retaliatory actions taken against them (both generally and for defense contractors), inclusion of Transportation Security Administration baggage handlers, expanded appeal rights in federal courts, provision of economic reparations for ethical insiders, and creation of an ombudsman office to train employees on their rights. The law does not provide jury trial rights for federal employees, cover national security persons of conscience who disclose information within their agencies, or cover nondefense contractors. Recommendations to improve the law include whistleblower jury trials, fortified protection against reprisals, financial relief during long cases (which often go on for five years and leave employees without income), each Inspector General to have a whistleblower ombudsman, and formal disciplinary system for superiors who harass dissenters (Burleigh, 2017, July 27).

As noted, many states have whistleblower laws (for a summary, see West & Bowman, 2020; also Kohn, 2017, chapter 5), which vary considerably. Like federal legislation, these state laws often protect a narrow range of speech, impose burdensome procedures on employees, and provide weak remedies. The most robust laws are found in California, Florida, Michigan, New Jersey, and the District of Columbia, but it is difficult to receive protection under most state statutes. Patrick (2010) examined a random sample of statewide cases between 1994 and 2009 and found that 74 percent of bravehearts were terminated, 6 percent suspended, 5 percent transferred, and 15 percent given poor evaluations.

Since 2013, over half of the states have introduced legislation that seeks to ban videotaping of animal, environmental, and food safety abuses—a critical form of evidence to substantiate claims by moral sentinels. These "ag-gag" bills would criminalize agricultural whistleblowers, instead of holding those responsible for wrongdoing accountable. Many of these bills were thwarted, and those that became law either have been overturned by courts as violations of the First Amendment or have lawsuit pending. Arkansas passed a bill that also makes it a crime to report patient abuse, elder abuse, and puppy mills

Overall, federal and state legislative initiatives imply it is prudent for organizations to have meaningful internal compliance programs (see Chapter 8). In the wake of the U.S. GSA Las Vegas conference scandal (Chapter 9), the public interest group Cause of Action Institute requested that the U.S. Office of Management and Budget conduct a government-wide audit to verify whether agencies are following whistleblower protection laws (no such audit was conducted). It also asked that the Office of Government Ethics disclose information on GSA's compliance with the 1989 Standards for Ethical Conduct for Employees of the Executive Branch (the Office of Government Ethics found GSA to be in compliance but did not audit the agency).

Blowing the whistle on whistleblowing protections, five reports have documented widespread problems. Historically, the U.S. Office of Special Counsel, the small bureau created to protect dissenters, had a poor reputation: Just 5 percent of its clients were satisfied with the treatment their cases received (Sandler, 2007). In response to a surge of disclosures, however, the agency reported favorable outcomes in 75 percent of retaliation cases (Tully, 2013). The U.S. Government Accountability Office (2010), second, examined the Labor Department's Occupational Health and Safety Administration (OSHA), the department which investigates retaliation against employees under more than 20 federal laws. It criticized OSHA for ineffective whistleblower protections that have persisted for 20 years after the accountability office first reported weaknesses (for more information, consult http://oshlaw.org and Devine & Maassarani, 2011, 166). Next, the agency's Inspector General established that it failed 80 percent of the time to meet all elements essential to the investigative process (U.S. Department of Labor, 2010). The report further revealed that the Administration dismissed 1,066 claims of business fraud and upheld only 25 claims under SOX.

The U.S. Merit Systems Protection Board, an appeals panel for federal civil servants, rules against whistleblowers in 95 percent of cases (Davidson, 2010). The research arm of the same agency, however, documented how the treatment of dissenters has deteriorated since 1992. Ethical resisters are substantially more likely to be terminated, suspended, demoted, reassigned, or denied a promotion (U.S. Merit Systems Protection Board, 2011). Finally, the 1994–2012 record of the Federal Circuit Court of Appeals (the only review body for all 1989 Whistleblower Protection Act cases) was 3–220 against employees (Devine & Clark, 2012, 21). There are many factors to explain the results reported here—poor management, meager funding, inconsistent interpretation of laws, lengthy processing time, lack of training, and insufficient staff are among them (for a discussion of OSHA's problems, see Kohn, 2017, 57–60).

To be covered by the relevant statutes, the concerned employee must act in good faith—the disclosures are to be objectively reasonable, specifying what misconduct is unlawful. A general claim is not sufficient. The majority of whistleblowers—at least once those making frivolous claims are excluded—are not malcontents, misfits, neurotics, crusaders, crackpots, or radicals. Typically, they are middle managers or professional staff persons, knowledgeable individuals able to observe problems, but may not have a vested interest in ensuring they are never made public. Most resisters are normal people with no record of animosity toward the organization. They are "just doing their job," not considering themselves to be protesters, and expecting problems to be addressed when brought to the attention of those in authority (see Case Study 10.2). When problems are not rectified, and corruption goes unchallenged, conscientious employees expose the issue. Nonetheless, it is important not to romanticize such individuals—they may speak out for selfish as well as altruistic motives.[3] While some dissenters may have mixed motives, this does not mean that they are wrong. The ideal case—where the cause is just, where all administrative appeals have been tried, where responsibility is openly accepted, and where the employee is above reproach—may not always emerge.

Heumann et al. (2013–2014), contrary to most literature, claim that there is insufficient evidence to demonstrate whether protection laws are "failing spectacularly" to care for employees ("the whistleblower-as-hero") or are working well to screen out malcontents ("the dissenter-as-false accuser"). There is little systematic research on the proportion of whistleblower complaints judged to have merit. Governmental watchdog agencies typically report that most cases fail, while anonymous employee surveys suggest that wrongdoing is widespread. Micheli et al. (2008, 21–22) believe that employee perceptions may sometimes be erroneous but point out that most have no incentive to distort their perceptions on confidential questionnaires. Such data imply that the validity of estimates offered by official compliant recipients are too low.

CASE STUDY 10.2

Applying Rational and Behavioral Ethics Approaches: Cooking the Books

Grant monies for Program X in nonprofit agency MNO are insufficient to cover client needs. The chief executive officer authorized expenditures for the program from grant monies awarded to unrelated Program Y. She would change line items in the budget and modify supporting documentation (e.g., purchase orders, travel expenses, supplies) to make it appear that Program Y made purchases which in reality applied to Program X. These expenditures sometimes amounted to thousands of dollars, occasionally for questionable items. Sophia Rasmussen, a senior staffer, was disturbed by this practice. When she mentioned this to her superiors, she was told, "This is the way things are done around here." Sophia's dilemma is whether to press the issue further.

Following the approach described in Chapter 7 and used in case studies in the previous two chapters, this dilemma can be explored from the perspective of rational decision-making theory as well as the behavioral ethics approach.

Results-Based Analysis. Starting with philosophical theory, consider the issue by centering on results—the greatest good for the greatest number— Sophia can see that Program Y's resources are being depleted to augment funds in Program X. She knows that both programs provide valuable services that together benefit the entire community, but denial of services to Program Y recipients narrows the impact by depriving deserving service recipients. She could report this to the external auditors or, if the government agency is the funding source, to appropriate authorities. Doing so would potentially satisfy those benefiting from Program Y's services and possibly advance the greater good.

The result for Sophia may not be positive. While she will feel better about herself for acting on her convictions, she will undoubtedly anger the CEO and those assisted by Program X. She may also find that blowing the whistle may not solve the problem. If the lax attitude reflected by her superiors is one permeating the organization, her objection falls on deaf ears. If she goes outside the organization, the external entity she contacts may not be empowered to correct the situation. It is unlikely that an aroused public would apply sufficient pressure to force a change to this practice, unless some dramatic event (e.g., media coverage) prompted the need for drastic action.

Rule-Based Analysis. Second, focusing on rules and principles, Sophia is aware that federal law mandates that nonprofits have reporting channels for whistleblowers and protects them from retaliation. As an astute observer of organizational behavior, she also knows that her organization is often noncompliant and lax in enforcing legal strictures. If funds are being misallocated, this could lead to criminal charges against the CEO. If the funds are coming from a person whose intent for the use of the monies was made explicit, then the use of Program Y funds to cover Program X's expenses is a clear contravention of donor intent. The criterion "what is good for one is good for all" is being violated; one also would not want to universalize the deceptive modification of documents and disregard of donors' intentions.

Sophia sees the misallocation of funds as a form of lying and wonders if she can live with herself knowing that she has not pursued every avenue to correct this wrongdoing. She prides herself on her honesty; one of the reasons she decided on a career in nonprofit organizations is her commitment to public service, which she sees as being subverted and harming innocent clients of Program Y. She thinks those higher up need to be held accountable for their behavior and pay the penalty for their actions.

Virtue-Based Analysis. Third, from a virtue ethics perspective, excellence in individual and community character is not promoted by the CEO's actions. Sophia believes that moral courage is required to stand up for ethical principles. She does not like to back down from a fight when a principle is at stake. She feels her views were discounted and disregarded but is convinced that she is right. Her individual responsibility requires her to act to correct what she knows to be improper behavior, but prudence requires her to carefully weigh the costs and benefits of ways to resolve the issue.

She is also concerned about the damage to her self-esteem and character if she remains silent on this issue, and she wonders whether she has the moral courage to pursue this matter outside the organization. She has a well-deserved reputation as a principled, cooperative, and competent member of the senior staff team. By going outside, she risks alienating not only her superiors but also her coworkers, whose friendship and support she values. Her reputation is important to her, as is her character; she is torn between wanting to do the right thing and hoping to avoid being branded as a troublemaker.

Behavioral Ethics-Based Analysis. Behavioral ethics concepts can be used to help explain actions of the CEO and Sophia in this case; recall that many of the behavioral phenomena occur at the unconscious level—that is, decision makers may well believe that they are rationally addressing the issue at hand. Yet feelings and perceptions are at least as important in understanding why people do what they do. The CEO is likely confident that he has the discretion to move funds from one program to another and could be annoyed by the suggestion that his behavior was inappropriate. His moral blindness is most evident in his modification of documents, which his "want" self might think is OK but his "should" self may later regret. Ethical fading happens when one is so focused on a specific matter to the exclusion of other matters that may occur at the same time. His single-mindedness in pursuing Program X may have led him to discount the importance of Program Y and to believe that no one would care about the diversion. Sophia cares, but she needs to be mindful of the tendency she may have to be overly optimistic and overconfident that her whistle-blowing will result in the successful resolution of the problem and the elimination of wrongdoing.

As in other cases (e.g., Case Study 8.1), decision makers would do well to take steps to ensure that easily overlooked behavioral ethics phenomena receive attention (Chapter 7). Believing in something is not the same as knowing the correct judgment to make; the basis of a decision may stem not from moral reasoning but rather from an after-the-fact rationalization for a dubious decision already made. Referring to Chapter 7, specify other behavioral ethics tenets that are likely to be present in this scenario.

DISSENT IN ORGANIZATIONS

A milestone book by C. Fred Alford (2000) presents a dark, chilling, sobering account of institutional power and employee character. The grim contention of the rich, complex analysis is that the organization is a feudal institution dedicated to the neutralization of its members' moral individuality—the ability to think seriously about what one is doing (recall the Milgram experiment in Chapter 4). Public, nonprofit, and private bureaucracies resemble authoritarian states that do not permit legitimate opposition. The same organizational DNA appears everywhere as whistleblowers are seen as a threat to be exterminated (Taibbi, 2012, May 10). If dissenters tend to be rule- or virtue-based ethicists whose morality consists of clear norms or defined character, managers are apt to be results-based decision makers seeking the greatest good for the greater number—narrowly defined as the institution. Anyone questioning the organization is seen as a disloyal defector to be dealt with severely. The institution's greatest fear is not corruption but rather that its most competent people will blow the whistle on misdoings. Echoing Jackall (1988), what matters most to the organization is that the person be subservient.

The employee need not go outside the workplace to get in trouble—as a whistleblower, he or she is one who remembers that there *is* a world outside the organization. Alford (2000) argues that when a person comes forward to protest malfeasance, the institution is inherently unable to properly deal with the challenge because of its imperative for survival. When six experts on a National Space and Aeronautics Administration safety panel, for example, issued warnings prior to the 2003 *Columbia* space shuttle explosion, they were discharged. In contemporary times, it seems that admiring moral bravery is far less common than is admiring physical bravery; in fact, there is often suspicion toward those who expose problems (for a commentary on this worldwide problem, see Rushdie, 2013).

Public reaction to whistleblowing depends in part on how the issues are framed (see Chapter 7). For example, the high-profile criminal cases of Julian Assange, Chelsea Manning, and Edward Snowden involving the release of classified documents through outlets like WikiLeaks can be framed in ways that influence opinions. This is confirmed by a recent study based on national survey data (Touchton et al., 2020). Researchers used embedded experiments to test the effects of two forms of framing on favorability ratings toward the three leakers. The first frame addressed partisanship (i.e., which political party is harmed by the information release), and the second addressed how the action is framed (i.e., did the question refer to the person as "leaking" or "blowing the whistle"). The findings show that both the party and leaking/whistleblowing frames significantly affect public favorability in expected ways. The release of classified materials comes with both costs and benefits, but public opinion appears to be more sensitive to its implications for partisan competition.

Regardless of the way the issue is framed, the likelihood of success in a whistleblower case can be characterized, according to one dissenter, as, "If you have God, the law, the press, and the facts on your side, you have a 50–50 chance of victory." In Alford's view, the organization simply cannot—and will not—tolerate individuality. Eventually, insiders with outsider values are branded as "nuts or sluts"—or both. When the subordinate confronts the employer he must make a "choice less choice," risking career and family in order to stay true to self. The biggest shock comes when he realizes that nothing he believed is true, including that

- the individual matters,
- law and justice can be relied on,
- government is of laws, not people,
- one's friends will remain loyal even if one's colleagues do not,
- the organization is fundamentally moral,
- it makes sense to stand up and do the right thing,
- someone, somewhere who is in charge knows, cares, and will do what is right, and
- the truth matters, and someone will want to know it.

(Alford, 2000, 49)

As Martin Luther King said, "Our lives begin to end the day that we become silent about things that matter." The protester blows the whistle because the dread of living with a corrupted self outweighs the risk of recrimination. These persons do not take the easy way out. They are not good at "doubling," living morally compartmentalized lives, one at work and one at home. However, most employees, as suggested later, can do so. Particularly insidious, Alford believes, is the way the organization uses someone's personal responsibility to her family to justify behavior at work upto and including doing nearly anything for her superiors.

This may explain failures to speak out. For instance, scores of personnel at Enron and Arthur Andersen, as well as Ford and Firestone at the beginning of the century, knew about dubious accounting practices and tire safety concerns for years and said nothing. The same phenomenon was true of Tyco, WorldCom, General Electric, Halliburton, and hundreds of other organizations, private, nonprofit, or public, as well as leading banks that facilitated duplicitous transitions during the Enron Era (Bowman, West, & Beck, 2010, 150). Further, there were numerous people in the nation's vast civilian and military intelligence bureaucracy who knew that pre–Iraq War intelligence was being misused but did little. It is likely also that conscientious employees could have helped avert the 2008 financial crisis. Case Study 10.3 portrays a case when the whistle was silent, and Case Study 10.4 reports an incident when sounding the alarm was successfully accomplished.

If a person knows what his values are (Chapter 3), difficult decisions to speak out become easier to make. In the face of institutional power and pressure, it is critical to understand where the organization ends and the individual begins. It is ethically suspect to remain silent because harm could occur. Silence is a type of deceit; failure to protest likely is self-compromising. Consequences of inaction, duty, and virtue should be part of decision-making in organizations that strive for integrity (Chapter 7; Verhezen, 2010).

As 18th-century philosopher and statesman Edmund Burke observed, "All that is necessary for the triumph of evil is for good men to do nothing." Passive complicity is a far bigger, more telling concern than whatever catalyst finally brought scandals to light. Too often, when the dissenter makes a commitment and is seemingly alone, there are others who want to make a like commitment but will not (see also Reed, 2015). It is advisable, in any event, to have professional liability insurance that provides legal defense protection when contending with agency investigations and/or disciplinary proceedings.

CASE STUDY 10.3

The Silent Whistle

In 2008, sickness and death were caused by contaminated peanut butter sold by the Peanut Corporation of America in Blakely, Georgia. Eight people died, and an estimated 19,000 people were sickened in 43 states. No employees had attempted to blow the whistle to the public or government agency in an effort to stop shipments of the product. They not only knew of conditions that contributed to contamination (water leaks, rats and roaches, failure to clean the facility), but they also knew that the peanut butter tested positive for salmonella. Some expressed concern within the company, but most remained silent. Knowing the delay caused by stopping shipments cost money, managers and owners did nothing.

If a worker had spoken to an attorney, would he have been protected under state or federal law from retaliation? No, he would have been on his own. Because there was no food safety whistleblower law in Georgia, the employer could terminate the employee. There are many federal whistleblowing protection laws, but none covers food safety. The most germane law was the 2002 Sarbanes–Oxley Act. However, that statute covers fraud in publicly traded companies, and the peanut firm was a family-owned business. Had the lawyer asked if any public organization purchased the peanut butter, he would have learned that federal agencies and the state of California, as well as their contractors, did. The worker, accordingly, would be protected by national and California laws aimed at preventing fraud in government procurement and contracting. The key in this case, then, was not merely the sale of poisoned product but also that taxpayer-supported agencies had paid for it.

Questions to Consider

1. Review the behavioral ethics discussion in Chapter 7 to help explain why employees did not speak out (one starting point: bounded ethicality).

2. Use the ethics triad in the same chapter to determine what you might have done. What might have stopped you from taking action?

Source: Adapted from Kohn (2017, 51–52).

While some organizations say they welcome criticism, common techniques—such as suggestion boxes, hotlines, and "open door" policies—not only lack the power to compel officials to examine criticisms they are reluctant to deal with but also could turn out to be a trap for the employee. Since he is objecting to policy, it is not reasonable to expect an unbiased review of the compliant—or the person. For example, internal hotline programs have no responsibility to assist callers or inform them of their legal rights; they exist for the benefit of the organization, not the individual. In one case, a major corporation assumed that callers were a potential litigation risk and forwarded concerns to in-house attorneys. "While the worker was manipulated into thinking he or she was doing a good job, the company . . . started to build a case that could justify disciplinary action" (Kohn, 2011, 18; also consult Mueller, 2019, 168). While conceding that many organizations ignore or misuse hotlines, Stubben and Welch (2018, February 14) offer some evidence that the use of hotlines may be a sign of a healthy organizational culture.

More systematic procedures, both internal and external to the institution, may not entirely deal with these problems, but they can have a deterrent effect if employers know that their actions are subject to review. Indeed, how agencies handle ethical resisters can be seen as an indicator of its level of moral development (Chapter 8). Organizations could, for instance, provide their staff with independent disclosure systems that genuinely aim to uncover and correct problems. Bok (1980, 292) suggests that the organization develop and specify conditions, perhaps in a code of ethics, under which the whistle *must* be blown. The absence of such provisions virtually guarantees that the issue will develop into a confrontation between management and the subordinate. In light of the significance of whistleblowing, and the development of current law, and the nature of large bureaucracies, what does the future hold?

CASE STUDY 10.4

Successful Whistleblowing

The contract in this case was a sole-source bid and no one really knew how much it would cost to build something that had not been done before. The military asked FlyX to come up with its best estimate of costs. Based on the estimation, the military would negotiate a fair contract price. The concerned employee possessed evidence revealing the "financial program plan" cost compared to the "contract value" cost given to the government. At the bottom of a key document was a line labeled "risk/reserve," a $700,000 difference between the financial plan and contract value. This figure was the extra amount the company built into the contract price. The practice was not limited to one contract; the risk/reserve was part of all their sole-source contracts, meaning that they cheated by some $100 million. The U.S. Department of Justice and the FBI agreed to pursue the case, creating an investigative strategy that included hiring more auditors and attorneys. After the preliminary investigation was completed in four months' time, agents went to the homes of six FlyX employees to gather additional information for corroboration.

Several months later, subpoenas were served at the corporation seeking documents. It took five months for the company to produce the materials, at which time the case became public information. The employee was no longer invited to business meetings, lost his administrative assistant in a reorganization, and was assigned complex tasks that could not be completed by nonnegotiable, unrealistic deadlines. When the company produced the requested information, it provided 40 boxes of papers. This was viewed as an attempt to bury the government in paper. Months passed, but it became increasingly evident that FlyX could not escape the fact that it failed to report its true best estimates in violation of the Truth in Negotiation Act. Still, it refused to repay any funds.

Instead, it counterattacked through fierce litigation, filing numerous motions to dismiss the suit and attempting to disqualify the whistleblower from receiving any payments from the government's reward program should the case go forward. In the meantime, the employee received poor performance evaluations for the first time in his career, was demoted, and was moved to a small storage area in the building basement with a desk, but with no telephone or computer. After a year of active ligation, the judge denied the corporation's motions. Under the FCA, FlyX would have to pay triple the amount of loss, a liability of $210 million. It filed for bankruptcy.

It was uncertain whether this action was part of a strategy aimed at reducing the amount it would pay in a settlement or if the expenses incurred from hiring outside law firms to defend itself was weighing heavily on the company. It was clear that it would not be able to pay the full amount of the judgment. The question became, "What could the company afford and still keep its doors open?" After weeks of negotiation, the parties settled for $70 million. FlyX changed its bidding practices and continued providing much needed equipment to the military. The government, which earned millions for taxpayers in this case, would not have known about it had the person not blown the whistle. The employee was awarded $13 million three and a half years after he first alerted the government of his suspicions.

Questions to Consider

1. Make a case that all parties to the settlement were "winners."
2. Make an argument that, in some sense, all parties were "losers."

Source: Based on and adapted from Hesch (2008, 23–29).

TRENDS IN BLOWING THE WHISTLE

Since the September 11, 2001, terrorist attacks, conditions may have become worse for dissenters. Growing corporate power and congressional and judicial deference to the executive branch (regarding suppression of information or punishment of nonconforming employees) illuminate three trends: the fate of recent reforms, whistleblowing case disposition data, and treatment of dissenters during the Obama and Trump administrations.

As noted earlier, the 2002 Sarbanes–Oxley Act (passed to reform corporate practices and protect those who report wrongdoing) has been criticized as costly, overreaching, and unnecessary. Some say the "swagger" of American business is back, suggesting the changes, rather than being embedded into corporate practices, have simply been undermined and unenforced (Moberly, 2008). Similar concerns exist for the 2010 Dodd–Frank Act enacted to restore selected Depression Era banking regulations, regulate new financial instruments that contributed to the 2008 crash, safeguard consumers, and avoid future bailouts. The act is being systematically exploited for loopholes, litigated against, and delayed or disregarded (Taibbi, 2012). As a result, employees may simply quit. The abuse of both laws clearly demonstrates that a legislative victory is just the start, not the end, of a policy battle.

Second, data from the U.S. Office of Special Counsel, the department charged with whistleblower protection, reported that in 2003 it received 535 cases. It determined that 11 merited investigation and sent them back to the agency where the problem originated. While the Office became much more effective during the Obama years, it remained under-resourced, operated "at a molasses pace," and hesitated to take legal action against agencies that violated whistleblower rights (Davidson, 2017, June 7); the pattern continued during the next administration. Similar findings occurred at the IRS, and although there were improvements during the Obama years (discussed earlier), Congress continued its multiyear defunding of the IRS, notably the enforcement division. Likewise, as indicated earlier, the U.S. Government Accountability Office (2010) audited the Occupational Safety and Health Administration with comparable results. Also consider the experience of Eileen Foster (Exhibit 10.2), who blew the whistle but no one heard it. The evidence here is hardly surprising in light of Alford's thesis.

The final trend concerns an apparent change on the part of Barack Obama as well as Donald Trump when they were president. As a private attorney, Obama defended a moral sentinel and, later as a Senator, voted for the then-pending Whistleblower Protection Enhancement Act of 2012. On assuming office, the president ordered departments to be responsive to freedom-of-information requests, banned them from altering scientific findings for political purposes, and appointed employee advocates to key positions. And in 2012, he issued a presidential directive that prohibited retribution against intelligence community employees who reveal abuse when it became evident that they would not be included in the new reform law.

Yet during the Obama administration, there was a historic increase in the "criminalization" of whistleblowers, as officials attacked the news media and initiated prosecutions against WikiLeaks, Army private Bradley Manning, and Edward Snowden. As stated earlier, it also indicted a national security agent under the 1917 Espionage Act, a law intended for prosecution of spies, not whistleblowers. The agent was the sixth official so indicted by the administration, more than all other presidencies combined. While the Whistleblower Protection Enhancement Act made it more difficult to terminate employees, it did not protect against retaliatory and harassing investigations: Investigations are easier for the government than time-consuming lawsuits as they present the truth teller the choice of resigning or risking indictment.

Finally, the administration supported a reform act provision that permits agencies to bypass due process and whistleblower rights in the name of national security. In a related development, the U.S. Court of Appeals issued a ruling—a "sensitive jobs loophole"—that "openly backed a proposed administration rule to declare virtually any job as national-security sensitive." Critics point out that this would mean agencies could retaliate against dissenters (Hicks, 2013). Some commentators claimed that the president's transparency legacy would be known as a "war on whistleblowers."

The next administration reflected its predecessor's equivocal position in at least two ways. During the 2016 campaign, Mr. Trump enthusiastically supported WikiLeaks, but once in office he has regularly denounced leaks, creating a chilling effect among employees. And like Mr. Obama, he made well-regarded appointments to oversight offices. Some pundits even saw him as his own unwitting whistleblower given his tendency to justify his actions that frequently backfired and resulted in self-incrimination (Burleigh, 2017, July 27; Sargent, 2020, July 29).

EXHIBIT 10.2	**Sounding the Alarm, No One Is Listening**

Whistleblower Eileen Foster asks, "Why, four years after large banks brought our economy to the brink of disaster, are we still reading about fraud, deceit, and reckless gambling by leading banks?" An important part of the answer is that the U.S. Department of Justice (DoJ) has failed to use evidence provided to them by whistleblowers.

Foster supervised Countrywide Home Loans internal fraud investigators and reported to federal regulators and the company's board of directors. The investigations showed that commission-hungry loan officers routinely forged borrowers' signatures and falsified income statements. With detailed evidence of fraud, she reported the findings to her superiors. "At that point I became a target. Countrywide managers went after my job and reputation, intimidating witnesses and altering statements to produce derogatory—and entirely phony—'findings,' which they passed on to Bank of America (BofA)," then in the process of buying out Countrywide. Both Countrywide and BofA worked "to silence employees, using weapons like blacklisting, hush money and confidentiality agreements. The upper echelons at BofA attempted to buy my silence with more than $200,000," which she rejected.

Three years later, she offered evidence of systemic fraud to the Financial Crisis Inquiry Commission. The commission's final report found widespread fraudulent actions in financial institutions and referred their findings to DOJ. Yet no successful criminal prosecutions have resulted. DOJ says it cannot indict and convict company officials just because they behaved badly; greed, they point out, is not a crime. "Together with other Commission witnesses," Foster writes, "I alleged *fraud*, not greed, and that *is* a crime."

Foster concludes:

Today, millions of Americans are paying more on their mortgages than their homes are worth, and millions more are facing foreclosure. Meanwhile, those who cashed in while ordinary Americans lost their homes and their jobs remain at large. . . . Whistleblowers like me know who they are. . . . Why won't the government listen?

Source: Adapted from Foster (2012).

Donald Trump signed a 2017 Veterans Administration law containing important whistleblower reforms, notably agency employees now have unique anti-retaliation rights. Yet unprecedented challenges regarding censorship of information and employees, as well as violation of ethical norms and rules, suggest increasing reports of misconduct to counterbalance understaffed oversight functions. In fact, whistleblowers documented improper granting of security clearances, a plan to secretly provide nuclear technology to selected Middle Eastern countries, removal of climate and pandemic scientists, and scandals at immigration centers. Contemporary times are ripe for persons of conscience to step forward as today's workforce is said to be more willing to buck the system and voice discontent than may have been the case in the past (Conway-Hatcher & Bourelly, 2017, January 30). Consistent with this tendency, President Biden has promised stronger protection for dissenters.

Overall, the uncertain destiny of corporate reform, troublesome handling of cases, and government proceedings against its employees suggest the tensions between individual democratic rights and organizational authoritarianism in American life are likely to continue.

Nonetheless, it is also true that there has been a "revolution" in whistleblower rights (Kohn, 2017), suggesting that a new era (Hertsgaard, 2016) may be emerging in the attitudes about, and the actions by, whistleblowers. Louis Clark, president of the potent Government Accountability Project (GAP), says that "today, more than any other time in history, whistleblowers are refusing to remain silent" (2019) as GAP is "experiencing a groundswell of new clients" (2020). Not only do large majorities of the public support them, but they favor increased protections for conscientious employees because they can get results (National Whistleblowers Center, 2007). In law, a complex framework has been developed in recent decades to facilitate blowing the whistle and to protect those who do. Indeed, there as been an impressive series of recent Congressional victories enacting new laws and strengthening existing legislation (Government Accountability Project, 2021).

Employees and employers, however, may not be generally aware of their rights and obligations—those that speak out continue to assume the best outcome only to be victimized in the end. Although whistleblower law has arguably matured, it nonetheless confronts deep-seated cultural biases in organizations. They seldom acknowledge that disclosures are in their long-run best interest. While truth tellers have better legal protection than ever, they still face intimidating social, professional, and legal challenges (Clark, 2019; also consult Bellman, 2020). The legal framework for changing administrative cultures exists, but the risks confronting dissenting employees remain—even advocates agree that strong, well-documented whistleblower cases are hard to win (e.g., Devine & Maassarani, 2011; Hesch, 2008; Kohn, 2017).

CONCLUSION

Whistleblowing is a compelling and problematic aspect of organizational life. On the front-lines in the fight against corruption, responsible personnel confront a bleak choice between becoming self-compromised by not acting ethically or being vilified for acting ethically. It is evident that judicious leaders—as ethical agents—can act strategically to protect organizational reputations, deter wrongdoing, avoid lawsuits, retain thoughtful employees, and reduce regulatory intervention. This can be accomplished by creating an ethical infrastructure (Chapter 8) to heighten transparency and encourage sound decision-making. The real issue about blowing the whistle is not who does it but why the government, business, and nonprofit organizations respond as they do (Alford, 2016).

Despite promising signs of change, little can be expected from whistleblower programs and offices plagued by lack of resources and case backlogs. If internal checks (such as reporting procedures) are treated as little more than window dressing and external checks (like statutes) are ignored or turned into management tools, dealing with corruption will remain difficult. But without attempts to encourage and protect moral sentinels, society risks one scandal after another. Whistleblowing can and does make a difference. The United States must not be a nation where standing up to authority is a hazardous act, when responsible men and women cannot speak truth to power, and when character and conviction do not matter. Reforms must become ingrained in a process that deals with the substance of dissent. The act of whistleblowing should be routinized and recognized as essential to ethical governing. If the daily interactions among employees and employers do not provide for the exercise of integrity, whistleblowing will remain a dangerous, if essential, task.

***

To see what is right and not do it is cowardice.

—Confucius

NOTES

1. Small parts of this chapter are adapted from Bowman (1980).
2. One study of 27,000 whistleblowers from 1994 to 2008 who filed retaliation complaints with the Occupational Safety and Health Administration found that 78 percent struggled financially for the first five years after blowing the whistle, 83 percent found it "extremely difficult to impossible" to find a new job in their field, 66 percent found it "extremely difficult to impossible" to find a new job after changing professions, and 54 percent could not find work until they changed profession (cited in Devine & Maassarani, 2011, 31).

   According to Micheli, Near, and Dworkin (2008, 25–26), there exists substantial variation among organizations regarding the incidence of whistleblowing, the frequency of retribution, and the impact of dissent. Such differences result from not only operational differences from organization to organization but also difficult, perhaps inherent, methodological problems in data collection.
3. Heumann et al. (2013–2014) developed a tentative typology of whistleblowers: the Altruist who acts as the conscience of the organization by fighting for justice in the public interest; the Organization Man who interprets the organization's action from his perspective and issues a warning to superiors. If ignored, the public will never hear from him; if the problem becomes known, he exposes management's cover-up; the Avenger who, for selfish and dishonorable reasons, seeks retribution against the organization; the Alarmist who repeatedly, and wrongly, predicts dire consequences of a policy; the Bounty Hunter who demands financial gain by suing the organization (the odds for which are akin to winning the lottery, according to Devine & Maassarani, 2011, 43).

DISCUSSION

1. Critically evaluate these statements and questions:

   - Whistleblowers reveal a loss of innocence: the gap between American ideals and the reality of governing.
   - Organizations create whistleblowers.
   - The biggest shock to dissenting employees: Nothing they believed in is true.
   - The term "whistleblower" may have the effect of focusing on the messenger while distracting from the message of fraud, waste, and abuse.
   - Is whistleblowing on the increase or decrease? Why?
   - How well an organization treats truth tellers is an indication of how ethical it is.
   - "Here I stand. I can do no other."—Max Weber
   - Whistleblowing, paradoxically, tends to bring out both the best and the worst in American institutions.
   - What lessons, if any, have been learned by government and business as a result of recent scandals?

2. U.S. Army private Bradley (now Chelsea) Manning released hundreds of thousands of classified documents and was found guilty in largely secret military court proceedings. Over 80,000 people signed a petition nominating him for the Nobel Peace Prize. Discuss.

3. Less sensational cases of ethical incidents are useful to understanding whistleblowing. To take a classroom dishonesty example, have you or anyone you know had an opportunity to blow the whistle on cheating (an obligation common in university honor codes)? Was it blown or not? Why? What, if anything, happened as a result?

4. Discuss a relevant incident in the news or from your own organization or experience.

5. Analyze the implications of these queries:

   - Alford's work calls into question ethics laws and organizational ethics programs. What good, if any, do they do? What limitations do they have?
   - What does it mean to be a professional? Who is the "traitor"—the dissenter or the non-dissenter? What is the lesson(s) that might be drawn from Alford's views?
   - Doing the right thing does not mean right things will happen to you.
   - Whistleblowers remind the rest of us that we are children of Milgram (Chapter 4).
   - The whistleblowing paradox: Society commends truth tellers but acquiesces to their persecution.

6. America does not have a tradition of "resignation in protest," an honorable practice in England—that is, when a high appointee cannot support a policy, she resigns and clearly states why, which might have an effect on policy. In the United States, rather than regarding speaking out as a public duty, whistleblowers are often seen as "troublemakers" or "squealers" and endure the consequences. Accordingly, most officials tend to remain "loyal" by staying in office, then resigning quietly, and waiting for their book to be published before telling the citizenry about their concerns.

   Discuss whether or not an official should leave her agency or stay to help ensure that she is not replaced by someone not qualified as well as to be part of a core of employees who say "never again" will the agency be victimized by political interference. Note: While there were some resignations in protest during the controversial tenure of the 45th president, what is remarkable is that there were so few (see, e.g., Rubin, 2020, September 27 and Diamond, 2021, March 30).

7. Technology is a double-edged sword for concerned employees: It is easier both to leak information and to trace the source of the leak (see, e.g., Touchton et al., 2020).

8. Many employees who see fraud, waste, and abuse may initially believe that *res ipas loquitur* ("the thing speaks for itself"). Explain why this may be the case and why the moral sentinel may find it is simply not true.

9. As this chapter pointed out, whistleblowing cases often take years to resolve while whistleblowers may be without an income due to retaliatory termination. Discuss whether or not future legislation should include a fund similar to federal and state crime victims funds (these funds compensate victims for expenses related to the crime).

EXERCISES

1. Explore these websites:

   - The Project on Governmental Oversight (www.pogo.org) and the Government Accountability Project (www.whistleblower.org) are independent watchdogs that investigate fraud, waste, and abuse and assist dissenters. They publish newsletters, blogs, or reports, and their activities can be followed on Facebook and Twitter.
   - The National Whistleblowers Center (www.whistleblowers.org) is a nonprofit advocacy organization that deals with corporate issues, cases, historical information, and legislation. The National Whistleblower Legal Defense and Education Fund independently manages the legal programs supported by the Center.

- The mission of the Office of Special Counsel (www.osc.gov) is to assist federal personnel who report fraud, waste, and abuse.
- The law firm Labaton Sucharow (www.labaton.com/) sponsors a whistleblower program and a corporate ethics clearinghouse; it is a comprehensive resource to assist individuals and organizations in building cultures of integrity.
- The Securities and Exchange Commission maintains a comprehensive website (www. secwhistlebloweradvocate.com) that includes an insider's guide, a whistleblower handbook, a legal primer, videos, webinars, and podcasts.
- Whistleblow Wall Street (htttps: www.whistleblowwallstreet.com) provides a secure platform and attorneys to help employees to anonymously expose the worst practices of the financial industry.
- ExposeFacts.org encourages secure, anonymous disclosure of information that examines the material and, if appropriate, arranges for the release of information to the media.
- Whistleblower Aid (https://whistlebloweraid.org) offers a legal alternative to illicit leaking without exposure to criminal liability by helping federal investigators gather evidence, file complaints, and meet with officials.

2. For a compelling documentary on the plight of conscientious federal employees, view "War on Whistleblowers: Free Press and the National Security State" (Brave New Foundation, 2013, 66 minutes), available for purchase or rental from Amazon, iTunes, Netflix, or Hulu.

3. In addition to dramatic incidents that make the front page of the newspaper, there are many less publicized instances of fraud, waste, and abuse that occur in everyday management, such as the following one (adapted from Cohen, 2009):

I am an employee of a large contractor working on a small government office restoration project with a $800,000 construction budget. Because of poor work by a subcontractor (an old friend of my boss's), the paint was not properly applied and will fade and peel in the near future. The project is almost finished. The boss will not inform the government and we were clearly told to say nothing. What should I do?

Randy Cohen, the *New York Times* "ethicist," replies:

Your boss's actions are, of course, also unethical. Declining to report others' misdeeds is one thing; committing your own is quite another (e.g., if you act to disguise the bungled paint job).

My guideline for duty-to-report questions is this: You must come forward when doing so will prevent imminent harm; that is not the case here, and ethics does not require you to sacrifice your job. Yet, informing the government is desirable. How much jeopardy should you shoulder? That depends on your tolerance for risk (and the advice of an attorney), the quality of the evidence you have in hand to prove the case, the likelihood that the problem will be corrected, and other factors.

Apply the ethical schools of thought found in the three-pronged decision-making approach (Chapter 7) to the problem to achieve a more fully considered judgment about what to do. Using the prompts representing each approach—the greatest good for the greatest number, what is good for one is good for all, excellence in individual and community character—will help ensure that all dimensions of the issue are explored, especially when tempered by the insights from behavioral ethics. Consider also the micro, meso, macro levels of ethics (Chapter 2) interacting in the dilemma on the part of participants (the individual, the manager, the subcontractor) and how they affect the decision.

4. Choose an episode of *Whistleblower* (www.cs.com/shows/whistleblower/), summarize it in one paragraph, and analyze the case with using selected concepts from this chapter.

REFERENCES

Ackerman, S. (2013, July 5). Edward Snowden is a whistleblower, not a spy—But do our leaders care? *The Guardian*. Retrieved from www.guardian.co.uk/world/2013/jul/05/edward-snowden-nsa-whistleblower-spy

Alford, C. (2000). *Whistleblowers: Broken lives and organizational power*. Ithaca, NY: Cornell.

Alford, C. (2016). What makes whistleblowers so threatening? *International Journal of Health Policy and Management*, 5(1), 71–73.

Association of Certified Fraud Examiners. (2016). *Report to the nations on occupational fraud and abuse: 2016 global fraud study*. Retrieved from www.acfe.com/rttn2016.aspx

Bacevich, A. (2013, August 6). Are Manning and Snowden patriots? That depends on what we do next. *Washington Post*. Retrieved from www.washingtonpost.com/opinions/are-manning-and-snowden-patriots-thatdepends

Bauer, C. (2015, August 24). *An ethics thought before you get to "enough is enough"*. Retrieved from www.aahamwesternregion.org/docs/ethicsthought-enough2.pdf

Bellman, B. (2020). *Dark mirror: Edward Snowden and the American surveillance state*. New York: Penguin.

Berman, R. (2019, April 4). 'Dozens' of whistleblowers are secretly cooperating with House Democrats. *The Atlantic*. Retrieved from www.theatlantic.com/politics/archive/2019/04/trump-administration-whistleblowers-democrats-congress/586459/

Beutler, B. (2007, October 12). Short arm of the law. *American Prospect*. Retrieved from http://prospect.org/article/short-arm-law

Bok, S. (1980). Whistleblowing and professional responsibility. In D. Callahan & S. Bok (Eds.), *Teaching ethics in higher education* (pp. 277–295). New York: Plenum.

Bolkovac, K. (2011). *The whistle blower: Sex, trafficking, military contracters, and one woman's fight for justice*. New York: St Martin's Griffin.

Bolkovac, K. (2018). *The Whistleblower*. Retrieved May 18, 2019, from https://video.search.yahoo.com/search/video?fr=mcsaoffblock&p=bolkovac+kathryn#id=2&vid=ab34bca62167b5b9937a4f12d37eba35&action=view

Bowman, J. (1980). Whistle-blowing in the public service: An overview of the issues. *Review of Public Personnel Administration*, 1, 15–27.

Bowman, J. (1983). Ethical issues for the public manager. In W. Eddy (Ed.), *Handbook of organization management* (pp. 69–103). New York: Dekker.

Bowman, J., West, J., & Beck, M. (2010). *Achieving competencies in public service: The professional edge* (2nd ed.). Armonk, NY: M. E. Sharpe.

Boyd, D. (2013, September 2). *Whistleblowing is the new civil disobedience: Why Edward Snowden matters* [Web log post]. Retrieved from www.zephoria.org/thoughts/archives/2013/07/19/edward-snowden-whistleblower.html

Brewer, G., & Selden, S. (1998). Whistle-blowers in federal civil service: New evidence of the public service ethic. *Journal of Public Administration and Theory, 8,* 413–439.

Burleigh, N. (2017, July 27). Trump hates leaks, but some federal whistleblowers love him. *Newsweek.* Retrieved from www.newsweek.com/trump-scaramucci-tsa-whistleblowers-leaks-642866

Burleigh, N. (2017). Trump hates leaks, but some federal whistleblowers love him. *Newsweek.*

Call, A., Martin, G., Sharp, N., & Wilde, J. (2017). *Whistleblowers and outcomes of financial mis-representation enforcement actions (April).* Available at https://ssrn.com/abstract=2506418 or http://doi.org/10.2139/ssrn.2506418

Clark, C. (2018, November 1). IRS may be unintentionally discouraging whistleblowers from report-ing tax cheats. *Government Executive.* Retrieved from www.govexec.com/oversight/2018/11/irs-may-be-unintentionally-discouraging-whistleblowers-reporting-tax-cheats/152515/

Clark, L. (2013, August 1). Whistleblowers and the national security state. *Government Accountability Project.* Retrieved from www.whistleblower.org/press/gap-op-eds/2941-washington-spectator-whistleblowers-and-the-national-security-state

Clark, L. (2019, Winter). No regrets. *Whistleblower,* p. 2.

Clark, L. (2020, Spring). This too shall pass? *Whistleblower,* p. 2.

Cohen, R. (2009, March 15). Painted into a corner. *New York Times Sunday Magazine.* Retrieved from www.nytimes.com/2009/03/15/magazine/15wwln-ethicist-t.html

Conway-Hatcher, A., & Bourelly, A. (2017, January 30). Today's whistleblower realities: Learning to expect and effectively respond to the unexpected. *Corporate Law & Accountability Report.* Retrieved from www.bna.com/todays-whistleblower-realities-n57982083035

Davidson, J. (2010, August 27). Nod to national security advances whistleblower protec-tion bill. *Washington Post.* Retrieved from www.washingtonpost.com/wp-dyn/content/article/2010/08/26/AR2010082606569.html

Davidson, J. (2013, June 25). How do whistleblower advocates deal with Edward Snowden's case? *Washington Post.* Retrieved from www.washingtonpost.com/politics/federal_government/how-do-whistleblower-advocates-deal-with-edward-snowdens-case/2013/06/24/180df296-dd03–11e2–9218-bc2ac7cd44e2_story.html

Davidson, J. (2017, June 7). Special counsel Lerner leaves office as Trump rejects highly praised whistleblower advocate. *Washington Post.* Retrieved from www.washingtonpost.com/news/powerpost/wp/2017/06/07/lerner-leaves-office-of-special-counsel-as-trumps-rejects-highly-praised-whistleblower-advocate/

Devine, T., & Clark, L. (2012, May 21). Now more than ever, stronger whistleblower protections essential. *Federal Times,* p. 21.

Devine, T., & Maassarani, T. (2011). *The corporate whistleblowers' survival guide: A handbook for committing the truth.* San Francisco: Barrett-Koehler.

Diamond, D. (2021, March 29). Feuds, fibs and finger-pointing. *Washington Post.* Retrieved from https://www.msn.com/en-us/news/politics/feuds-fibs-and-finger-pointing-trump-officials-say-coronavirus-response-was-worse-than-known/ar-BB1f4WJ2

Foster, E. (2012, August 9). Obama administration needs to tap, not stiff-arm Wall Street whistleblowers. *Rolling Stone.* Retrieved from www.rollingstone.com/politics/blogs/national-affairs/the-obama-administration-needs-to-tap-not-stiff-arm-wall-street-whistleblowers-20120809?print=true

Feinstein, S., & Devine, T. (2021). *Truth-telling in government: A guide to whistleblowign for federal employees, contactors, and grantees.* Washington, DC: Government Accountability Project.

GAP stands with Snowden. (2013, Autumn). *Bridging the Gap,* pp. 1, 3, 4, 6.

Gellman, G. (2020). *Dark mirror: Edward Snowden and the American surveillance state*. New York: Penguin.

Gold, D. (2019, April 5). Five myths about whistleblowers. *Washington Post*. Retrieved from www.washingtonpost.com/outlook/five-myths/five-myths-about-whistleblowers/2019/04/05/8a5de2ac-5624-11e9-814f-e2f46684196e_story.html

Hertsgaard, M. (2016). *Bravehearts: Whistleblowing in the age of Snowden*. New York: Hot Books.

Hesch, J. (2008). *Whistleblowing: A guide to government reward programs*. Lynchburg, VA: Goshen Press.

Heumann, M., Friedes, A., Cassak, L., Wright, W., & Joshi, E. (2013–2014). The world of whistle-blowing: From the Altruist to the avenger. *Public Integrity*, *16*, 25–52.

Hicks, J. (2013, September 6). Grassley calls on Obama to ensure protections for federal whistle-blowers. *Washington Post*. Retrieved from www.washingtonpost.com/blogs/federal-eye/wp/2013/09/06/grassley-calls-on-obama-to-ensure-protections-for-federal-whistleblowers/

Internal Revenue Service. (2020). *Whistleblower program fiscal year 2019: Annual report to Congress*. Washington, DC: IRS.

Jackall, J. (1988). *Moral mazes: The world of corporate managers*. New York: Oxford University Press.

Kennedy, K. (2012, February 23). Whistleblowers key in health care fraud fight. *USA Today*. Retrieved from www.usatoday.com/news/washington/story/2012-02-22/health-care-fraud-whistleblowers/53212468/1

Kocieniewski, D. (2010, May 19). Whistleblowers become investment option for hedge funds. *New York Times*. Retrieved from www.nytimes.com/2010/05/20/business/20whistleblower.html?pagewanted=all

Kohn, S. (2011). *The whistleblower handbook: A step-by-step guide to doing what's right and protecting yourself*. Guilford, CT: Lyons Press.

Kohn, S. (2017). *The new whistleblower handbook: A step-by-step guide to doing what's right and protecting yourself*. Guilford, CT: Lyons Press.

Kondracki, L. (Director). (2010). *The Whistleblower* [Motion Picture].

Legislative victories for *whistleblower* rights (2021, Spring). *Whistleblower*, p. 34.

Lipton, E. (2012, October 1). A legal circle reached deep to aid Obama. *New York Times*. Retrieved from www.nytimes.com/2012/10/02/us/politics/whistle-blower-lawyers-donate-to-obama-campaign.html

Long, M. (2019, May 18). *Basic stages of grooming for sexual exploitation*. Retrieved from End Slavery Now: https://www.endslaverynow.org/blog/articles/basic-stages-of-grooming-for-sexual-exploitation

Matt, B., & Shahinpoor, N. (2011). Speaking truth to power: The courageous organizational dissenter. In D. Comer & G. Vega (Eds.), *Moral courage in organizations: Doing the right thing at work* (pp. 157–171). Armonk, NY: M. E. Sharpe.

McElhatton, J. (2013, June 11). Snowden the whistleblower? Not exactly. *Federal Times*. Retrieved from http://blogs.federaltimes.com/federal-times-blog/2013/06/11/snowden-the-whistleblower-not-exactly/

Micheli, M., Near, J., & Dworkin, T. (2008). *Whistleblowing in organizations*. New York: Routledge.

Moberly, R. (2008). Protecting whistleblowers by contract. *University of Colorado Law Review*, *79*, 975–1042.

Moloney, K., Bowman, J., & West, J. P. (2019). Challenges confronting whistleblowing and the international civil servant. *Review of Public Personnel Administration*, *39*(4), 611–634.

Mueller, T. (2019). *Crisis of confidence: Whistleblowing in an age of fraud*. New York: Riverhead Books.

Mueller, T. (2019, October 18). The law doesn't care about whistleblowers' grudges. *Washington Post*. Retrieved from www.washingtonpost.com/outlook/the-law-doesnt-care-about-whistle blowers-grudges/2019/10/18/b6b29a10-f100-11e9-b648-76bcf86eb67e_story.html#:~: text=The%20law%20doesn%E2%80%99t%20care%20about%20whistleblowers% E2%80%99%20grudges%20Personal,of%20the%20top%20candidates%20to%20 be%20%22Deep%20Throat.%22

National Whistleblowers Center. (2007). Retrieved from www.whistleblowers.com

Near, J., & Miceli, M. (2008). Wrongdoing, whistle-blowing, and retaliation in the U.S. government: What have researchers learned from the Merit System Protection Board (MSPB) survey results? *Review of Public Personnel Administration, 28*, 263–281.

O'Leary, R. Jurkiewicz, C., & Giacalone, R. (2000). Using film to demonstrate ethical decision making. *Journal of Public Affairs Education, 6*(4), 257–265.

Patrick, P. (2010). Be prepared before you blow the whistle: Protection under state whistleblowing laws. *Fraud Magazine*. September/October. Retrieved from www.fraud-magazine.com/article. aspx?id=4294968656

Publius, G. (2013, August 16). *Whistleblowing is the new civil disobedience: Why Snowden matters* [Comment]. Retrieved from http://americablog.com/2013/08/whistleblowing-is-the-new-civil-disobedience-why-snowden-matters.html

Pugh, P., & Rowan, D. (2021, June). DOJ is getting more imaginative with False Claims Act enforcement and hitting a growing number of organizations. *Corporate Compliance Insights*. Retrieved from https://www.corporatecomplianceinsights.com/doj-expanding-false-claims-act-enforcement/

Reed, G. (2015). Expressing loyal dissent: Moral considerations from literature on followership. *Public Integrity, 17*(1), 5–18.

Rosen, J. (2013, July 5). *The Snowden effect: definition and examples* [Web log post]. Retrieved from http://pressthink.org/2013/07/the-snowden-effect-definition-and-examples/

Rothschild, J., & Miethe, T. (1999). Whistle-blower disclosures and management retaliation: The battle to control information about organization corruption. *Work and Occupations, 26*, 107–128.

Rubin, J. (2020, September 27). A message to Justice Department lawyers: It's up to you to protect democracy. *Washington Post*. Retrieved from www.washingtonpost.com/opinions/2020/09/27/an-open-letter-justice-department-lawyers/

Rushdie, S. (2013, April 28). Whither moral courage? *New York Times*, p. SR 5.

Sandler, J. (2007, November 1). The war on whistle-blowers. *Salon*. Retrieved from www.salon.com/2007/11/01/whistleblowers/

Sanger, D. (2013, August 3). A Washington riddle: What is "top secret"? *New York Times*. Retrieved from www.nytimes.com/2013/08/04/sunday-review/a-washington-riddle-what-is-top-secret.html?_r=0

Scofield, J. (2017, November 20). SEC continues to tout performance of underwhelming whistleblower program. *Naked Capitalism*. Retrieved from https://macro.economicblogs.org/naked-capitalism/2017/11/scofield-sec-continues-tout-performance-underwhelming-whistleblower/

Stanger, A. (2019). *Whistleblowers: Honesty in America from Washington to Trump*. New Haven, CT: Yale University Press.

Stubben, S., & Welch, K. (2018, February 14). Research: Whistleblowers are a sign of healthy companies. *Harvard Business Review*. Retrieved from https://hbr.org/2018/11/research-whistle blowers-are-a-sign-of-healthy-companies

Taibbi, M. (2012, May 10). How Wall Street killed financial reform. *Rolling Stone*. Retrieved from www.rollingstone.com/politics/news/how-wall-street-killed-financial-reform-20120510

Thiessen, M. (2013, July 1). The danger of what Edward Snowden has not revealed. *Washington Post*. Retrieved from www.washingtonpost.com/opinions

Touchton, M., Klofstad, C., West, J., & Uscinski, J. (2020). Whistleblowing or leaking? Public opinion toward Assange, Manning, and Snowden. *Research and Politics*, *7*(1), 1–9.

Tully, M. (2013, July 14). OSC: Whistleblower disclosures "skyrocketed." *Fedsmith*. Retrieved from www.fedsmith.com/2013/07/14/osc-whistleblower-disclosures-skyrocketed/

U.S. Department of Justice, Civil Division, Commercial Litigation Branch. (2010). *Fraud statistics— Overview: Oct. 1, 1987—Sept. 30, 2010*. Retrieved from www.taf.org/FCA-stats-2010.pdf

U.S. Department of Labor, Office of Inspector General. (2010, September 30). *Complaints did not always receive appropriate investigation under the Whistleblower Protection Program* (Report No: 02-10-202-10-105). Retrieved from www.oig.dol.gov/public/reports/oa/2010/02-10-202-10-105.pdf

U.S. Government Accountability Office. (2010). *Whistleblower protection: Sustained management attention needed to address long-standing program weaknesses (GAO-10–722)*. Retrieved from www.gao.gov/assets/310/308767.pdf

U.S. Governmental Accountability Office. (2015). *IRS whistleblower program: Billions collected, but timeliness and communication concerns may discourage whistleblowers*. Washington, DC: GAO-113–318, March.

U.S. Merit Systems Protection Board. (2011). *Blowing the whistle: Barriers to federal employees making disclosures*. Retrieved from www.mspb.gov/netsearch/viewdocs.aspx?docnumber=662503&version=664475&application=ACROBAT

Verhezen, P. (2010). Giving voice in a culture of silence: From a culture of compliance to a culture of integrity. *Journal of Business Ethics*, *96*, 187–206.

Wemple, E. (2013, June 10). Edward Snowden: "Leaker," "source," or "whistleblower"? *Washington Post*. Retrieved from www.washingtonpost.com/blogs/erik-wemple/wp/2013/06/10/edward-snowden-leaker-source-or-whistleblower/

West, J., & Bowman, J. (2020). Whistleblowing policies in American states: A nationwide analysis. *American Review of Public Administration*, *50*(2), 119–132.

Wilde, J. (2017). The deterrent effect of employee whistleblowing on firms' financial misreporting and tax aggressiveness. *The Accounting Review*, *92*(5), 247–280.

Appendix 10.1
The Whistleblower: UN Peacekeeper Sex-Trafficking Scandal

Film Title *The Whistleblower.*

SUMMARY

The film is based on the experiences of Kathryn Bolkovac, a police officer from Nebraska who served as a United Nations (UN) peacekeeper in postwar Bosnia. During Bolkovac's tour of duty, she discovered a sex-trafficking scandal that involved some of the UN peacekeepers with whom she served. Bolkovac finds resistance from the very leadership team that is supposed to protect and serve the victims, a clear case of role distortion. She was stripped of her credentials when she threatened to disclose the unethical and illegal practices of the peacekeepers (Kondracki, 2010).

THE SITUATION ON THE GROUND

While Bolkovac is initially assigned to a general peacekeeping role, she indicates to the leadership that she is interested in making a difference and is willing to take on a more challenging role. She is assigned to work with a prosecutor who has experienced difficulties representing female victims of sex crimes. When she begins to have an impact, she is sought out by a representative of the UN Office of the High Commissioner for Human Rights who noted that Bolkovac is able to "do in two months what we (the Commission has) have failed to do in four years" (Kondracki, 2010). In response to her outstanding accomplishments, Bolkovac is offered the opportunity to lead the International Police Task Force (IPTF) Gender Affairs office. While this is a substantial career opportunity, Bolkovac is conflicted between choosing her career and choosing parenthood. She decides to honor both options, just not simultaneously. The career move can allow her to be located closer to her child when she returns to the United States.

Bolkovac quickly finds that her work is going to be more intractable than she expected, as she faces sexism and cultural bias against women, especially those who are sex victims. She is called to a local bar and arrives as sexually exploited women are being escorted from the premises, ostensibly to be cared for in a women's shelter. Bolkovac enters the facility and finds photos of UN peacekeepers performing lewd and degrading sex acts on the trafficked women. She also learns that the women she was initially sent to retrieve have been diverted and, through a web of corruption, returned to their captors.

Bolkovac works through the internal reporting structure, presenting information to her superior, who advises her that these predators breach protocol but operate with diplomatic immunity. In addition, the stateless condition of the victims prevents the UN from providing repatriation services. Corruption within the local police organization, which operates in conjunction with the unethical peacekeepers, creates an environment that consistently works against Bolkovac. Further complicating her work is that the women who are trafficked are reluctant to testify against their captors, fearing retribution.

At many turns, Bolkovac was surrounded by a system that failed to support her in an effort to do her job to the best of her ability. From diplomatic immunity for the perpetrators of kidnapping and human trafficking, to the UN's reluctance to shut down the trafficking operations, citing the loss of public trust that comes with a publicized scandal, Bolkovac struggled to find a way to do the right thing and protect the women. Holding on to her sense of right and wrong, she never succumbed to "contingent necessity," the tendency to believe that when individuals fail to act, someone else will step up.

Further complicating the situation was the public/private partnership between the United States and the contractor responsible for staffing the mission in Bosnia. In the film, the "Democra" company, actually DynCorp, exhibited the common failures of organizations, as the nature of the workplace supported unethical behavior, there was groupthink, and there was retaliation and management-induced fear.

"Democra" used "Grooming," a recruitment process for training someone for a purpose (in this case, prostitution), including

- targeting,
- gaining trust (the trafficker is known to the victims),
- filling a need (trafficker told the victims that they would have access to lucrative jobs in a hotel, far from their war-ravaged area),
- isolating (removed the women from their social structure/family life),
- abusing, and then
- maintaining control.

Aligning the moral decision-making process against the grooming process, it is very difficult for victims to establish any leverage or control over their decision to participate. The process is incredibly successful by design (Long, 2019). Grooming violates virtue-based ethics, as it is exploitation; it violates rules-based ethics, as it creates and enslaves victims; and it violates results ethics, as it fails to deliver the most good to the most people.

ISSUE RESOLUTION

The issues were ambiguously addressed in the film. While Bolkovac ultimately found an advocate within the UN Internal Affairs who helped her to remove critical documents from the country and bring the situation to light, the process took far too long and was devastating to the victims. Bolkovac worked with Internal Affairs, requiring her to use deception in order to successfully complete the investigation. The inquiry identified military officers and multinational police officers who were trafficking the women, selling them among themselves and using UN vehicles to transport the women around the area.

ANALYSIS

One way to analyze the film is to use some components of Montgomery Van Wart's typology—individual values, organizational culture, and public sector principles—to compare and contrast the values the characters exhibited. Applying the typology to the main characters in the film provides an interesting assessment of human behavior (O'Leary, Jurkiewicz & Giacalone, 2000). The lead character had a strong sense of her individual values, which were aligned with public sector values, but was thwarted by an organizational culture that sought to ignore problems rather than correct them.

The officials who were involved in human trafficking and sexual exploitation lacked individual values, exploited the weaknesses of the organizational culture, and absolutely did not align with public sector principles. The actors portraying managers of the UN Mission failed to demonstrate individual values, supported an organizational culture that was inconsistent with the UN Mission, and defied the most basic public sector principles.

The character portraying an Internal Affairs investigator and the official responsible for Gender Affairs oversight exhibited strong individual and public sector values, and infused their work with an organizational culture that was consistent with the foundational moral and ethical beliefs of the UN. Although the movie suggested that the Internal Affairs Officer was in fact not espousing organizational values, he did so in an effort to facilitate the removal of key documents, which were used to alert the world to the horrors being committed within Bosnia.

As public/private partnerships become an increasingly significant share of public service delivery, the gap between accountability and prosecutorial immunity must be addressed. As noted by Vanessa Redgrave's movie character, it is "diplomatic immunity, not diplomatic impunity." The exploitative behavior that prevailed in Bosnia was antithetical to the moral foundation of the UN, and DynCorp ignored that foundation.

The moral judgments of the filmmakers included positions against human trafficking, diplomatic immunity, and state-sponsored exploitation of war-ravaged populations. The manner in which many of the survivors were referred to, such as "war whores" and Croates/Serbs, "demonstrated a lack of humanity toward the population being served by the peacekeepers." De-humanizing individuals is one of the first steps to breaking a person's spirit and controlling them. There was a lack of adherence to the ethics triangle, with a complete disregard for the results of action by those who were conducting illegal human trafficking while hiding behind their UN credentials. There was no concern for the greatest good as DynCorp's actions were illegal and immoral. There was a lack of adherence to pertinent rules; in fact, the behavior by the traffickers was the antithesis of rules-based behavior. Personal integrity and character were also completely absent.

RECOMMENDATIONS

In supplemental data published by Bolkovac (2011) after her case was made public, she speaks of concerns about orientation training prior to leaving for Bosnia. It is disturbing, indeed, to learn that she was stepping into a minefield and saw little opportunity to establish effective communications with those within her organization to facilitate an ethical resolution and appropriate action (Kathryn Bolkovac, 2018).

Since the problems with peacekeeping are by no means limited to Bosnia (Moloney, West, & Bowman, 2018), training is needed. To set the tone for a training exercise, a mandatory viewing of *The Whistleblower* and/or *Kathryn Bulkovac* (2018) could be assigned to establish a baseline learning exercise for all staff. Training should include

- ethical foundations of the United Nations mission, including a brief history of the UN and its role,
- detailed rules of engagement as UN representatives,
- role-playing exercises,
- protocols and best practices for reporting suspected unethical behavior,
- stated policy indicating that suspected traffickers will be reported to their home country and returned to local law enforcement along with all supporting documentation to facilitate the prosecution of the perpetrator, and
- provision of international phone numbers to report ethics abuses.

CONCLUSION

The Whistleblower is a compelling portrayal of a real-life dilemma experienced by a dedicated professional. While the wrongdoing of the peacekeepers was documented and publicized, none of the participants in the human-trafficking scheme were brought to justice, and Bolkovac was required to file a legal claim against DynCorp to recover lost wages and damages for the impact of her ethical behavior. The long-term loss to her reputation is significant. She has not been recruited to join any other security operations, effectively being black-listed. Her career is stalled, and she no longer works in a role where she can bring her public sector values to the betterment of society.

Adapted with permission from paper by Karen Cinkus.

PART IV
Issues in Public Service Ethics

11 Ethics and Elected Officials

Art, like morality, consists of drawing the line somewhere.

—G. K. Chesterton

This chapter represents the first of four chapters in Part IV of the book, "Issues in Public Service Ethics." Here, attention is turned from ethical issues confronting appointed public servants who implement programs to those faced by elected officials who seek to reach agreement with other policymakers to advance a particular agenda. Some may conclude that "political ethics" is an oxymoron, assuming a bright line distinguishing ethical from unethical behavior that is routinely crossed by politicians. The reality of politics is not that simple—the boundary between right and wrong is often indistinct and vague.

Chapter objectives are to

- understand the ethical obligations of elected officeholders and their appointees;
- examine the character of these public servants;
- analyze the influence of partisanship, publicity, and polarization on congressional ethics;
- consider questions of ethics in presidential decisions; and
- explore citizen and media ethics when dealing with officials.

The sources and types of ethical obligation of civil servants include broad duties to protect the constitution, law, nation or country, and even democracy. Narrower responsibilities include adherence to organizational norms and professional standards, as well as obligations to family, friends, self, and "mid-range collectivities" (e.g., party, socioeconomic class, ethnicity) (Waldo, 2009). More general responsibilities shared by both appointed career civil servants and elected officials or their political appointees serve as guides to action to promote the public interest.

However, contradictions or dilemmas arise because of conflicts between and among these duties. For example, a decision may pit an official's partisan concerns against the public good he or she has been elected or appointed to serve. Reconciling such conflicts is an ongoing challenge to conscientious government employees. Failure to adequately consider these duties can lead to misconduct. (See Exhibit 11.1 to contrast the perspectives of political appointees and career staff and how to bridge the gap.) Two ethical problems elected incumbents encounter, especially members of Congress, also confront civil servants: conflict of interest and insider trading. An ethical choice the U.S. president faces is between truth telling and deception when dealing with national security.

DOI: 10.4324/9781003203148-15

EXHIBIT 11.1	**Need for Bridge-Building Leaders**

How political appointees and career civil servants view each other?		What can be done to bridge the gap?	
Political Appointees	*Civil Servants*	*Political Appointees*	*Civil Servants*
The Commissar: In charge of enforcing fidelity to the cause of power	**The Troll**: The career staffer with the reflexive, "we're already doing that"	Leap No.1: **Seek out the mavens**: The true federal experts with deep knowledge and experience	Leap No.1: **Put your fixer forward**: Counsel the political team to articulate the desired outcomes while the fixers work with the career staff to make it happen
The Hack: Sole interest in their own advancement	**The Turtle**: Withdraws into his shell and waits for better times	Leap No.2: **Don't ignore the trolls**: This will reveal the legislative, regulatory, budget and policy constraints that could get in the way	Leap No.2: **Make the political calendar work for you**: The career staff needs to understand the best time to float new ideas. It's vital to understand the importance of quick wins in any long-term effort
The Closer: Possesses the juice to work the bureaucracy, and puts the agency's mission over personal advancement	**The Maven**: Subject matter experts Treasure trove of expertise and institutional knowledge	Leap No.3: **Play fair**: Fairness, integrity, competence, and predictability are the bedrock behaviors for promoting organizational trust	
The Wonk: Honest effort to advance the work of the department	**The Translator**: Provides both the context for the latest initiative as well as the winning turn of phrase that conveys the career staff's view in a language that can win over balky political appointees	Leap No.4: **Have the conversation**: Leaders on both sides need to figure out how to discuss issues where political leadership can clearly articulate their needs and expectations Career folks need to think how they might reframe old and new problems to release the talents and reduce bureaucratic restraints	
The Visionary: Seeks alignment of mission and talent, inspires passion	**The Fixer**: The seasoned federal manager requires technical knowledge and bureaucratic savvy to solve		

Source: Adapted from Levine (2017).

Elected officials in both the legislative and executive arenas are influenced by their obligations, their roles, their character, institutional constraints, partisanship, and circumstances. The chapter begins with two congressional cases highlighting issues of conflict of interest and insider trading. That discussion is followed by a broader consideration of ethics and legislative decision-making.

The first congressional incident presents a situation in which one person's perception of constituent service can be another's perception of conflict of interest or public corruption; the second case shows how privileged access to nonpublic knowledge can lead to charges of insider trading. Congresswoman Shelley Berkley (D-NV) has been walking a fine line between constituent service and public corruption for several years. Representing Nevada's first district in the House of Representatives, Berkley has fought hard against federal termination of Medicare programs that allow for kidney transplants in her state.

In recent years, Nevada's University Medical Center—the only medical center for kidney transplants in the state—experienced a decline in the effectiveness of its transplants. A large number of patients died or experienced transplant failure following their operations—a rate far above the norm. In its wake, the federal government began taking steps to shut down the center's kidney transplant programs, which are almost fully covered by Medicare, regardless of the patient's age or the severity of the chronic illness. Berkley took a stand against government intervention and kept the government from terminating the program.

While Berkley's actions surely benefited some of her constituents and patients, it also privileged another group of individuals—including Berkley's husband, Dr. Lawrence Lehrner, who is a well-known nephrologist. He owns 11 dialysis centers throughout the state and was instrumental in making a lucrative deal with the University Medical Center. Not only is his profession directly connected with the political issue at hand, but Lehrner himself is also the leader of a political action committee that he created on behalf of renal physicians, making him an unofficial lobbyist. He also co-owns his dialysis centers with DaVita, Inc., which contributes large sums to Berkley's campaigns, including her 2012 campaign for Nevada's vacant Senate seat.

The possibility of conflict of interest and corrupt activity was brought to the attention of the House Ethics Committee in March 2012. While the Committee chose to delay weighing in on the issue until after the fall election, Berkley's support for her husband's industry and agenda was a key point throughout the race between her and Senator Dean Heller. Heller's campaign, as well as members of the Republican Party, accused Shelley of directly profiting from her political actions at the expense of federal dollars.

According to legislative acts, as well as reports from the House of Representatives, a conflict of interest is generally defined as "a situation in which an official's private financial interests conflict or appear to conflict with the public interest." While it seems as though Berkley's actions are not in conflict with her constituents' interests, another rule obscures the fine line. According to House ethics policies, a conflict of interest "becomes corruption when an official uses his position of influence to enhance his personal financial interests," which is what many accused Berkley of doing. The problem before the Ethics Committee lies between these two rules. The ambiguity and leeway in between these statements is where corruption certainly lies, and it is up to the committee to decipher on which side of the line Shelley Berkley's actions fall. No decision had been rendered up to the time of the 2012 election. However, Berkley's fate was determined by her electoral defeat in a close contest that centered on the ethics charges she was facing (Lipton, 2011; U.S. House of Reprentives Committee of Ethics, n.d.,; 5 USC. app. 4 SS101–111).

Thus, the initial case contrasts the imperative legislators have to serve their constituents with the tendency to serve their own personal and financial interests at the expense of taxpayers. The subsequent scenario illustrates the privileged access to information available to members of Congress that can lead to congressional insider trading. The House Ethics Committee must decide at what point their colleagues depart from acceptable to unethical behavior, not always an easy task. Punishment has typically been slow in coming and weak in consequences, except for the most egregious violations. This mild response is also typical of Senate Ethics Committee action (see Appendix 11.1 for a brief history of congressional ethics committees). Reforms with clearer standards and stronger sanctions, together with greater public and media scrutiny, are a prerequisite to reduce wrongdoing and increase citizen confidence. This raises a broader question: What is the role of ethics in legislative decision-making?

While the supremacy clause of the U.S. Constitution subjects all elected officials to the laws of the nation, some officeholders question whether certain laws truly apply to them. For example, many Americans believe that members of Congress, the president, and other executive personnel partake in insider trading based on the unique knowledge their positions bestow on them. One of those accused of benefiting from nonpublic knowledge is Senator Richard Burr (R-NC), chair of the Intelligence Committee and a 25-year Capitol Hill veteran. He was included in closed-door confidential briefings in late January and early February 2020 on the threat of the emerging COVID-19 virus. Burr, together with his wife, sold shares on February 13 worth as much as $1.7 million, resulting in savings for them of $250,000 in losses based on the stocks worth on March 19.

Senator Burr denies wrongdoing, claiming his stock trades prior to the March 20 market crash were based on public information, such as CNBC's reports out of Asia. Following the FBI's seizure of potential evidence from his cell phone and his iCloud data, he agreed to temporarily step down as chair of the Intelligence Committee and requested an investigation by the Senate Ethics Committee in the interest of "full transparency." The Department of Justice investigation of Senator Burr is ongoing, but it is difficult to prove that such stock trades are specifically based on nonpublic information gained through one's official position. No one has been successfully prosecuted under the existing law.

To reduce conflicts of interest or the appearance of them, Georgia's Senate candidates in a 2021 runoff election agreed that owning and trading individual stock shares no longer makes sense. Some members of Congress have introduced bills that would restrict stock ownership. While such measures are unlikely to pass, there are some calling for new members of Congress to follow the lead of the Georgia Senate candidates to avoid the appearance of impropriety and take a no stock pledge (Lieber, 2020). Both of the senators lost the run-off race in January 2021.

Since over half of the members of Congress own stock, many with stock investments exceeding $100,000 (excluding mutual funds and other holdings), and given that a majority of lawmakers are millionaires, their legislative actions can be affected by such financial ties to businesses. They may be aware of nonpublic information regarding pending legislative proposals that could be helpful to companies where they have investments. This could influence the decisions of stockholding lawmaker actions on legislation, regulations, subsidies, taxes, or contract awards (Hill, Ridge, & Ingram, 2017).

Congress has taken to burnishing their public image regarding financial transactions. The Stop Trading on Congressional Knowledge (STOCK) Act passed in 2012 prohibits elected officials and senior government personnel from trading on confidential information they are privileged to by virtue of their positions. To promote honesty and improve public trust, the bill also mandates that these officials (about 28,000) disclose their stock trades, real estate transactions, bonds, and other securities within 45 days of the transaction occurring. Transparency is one of the truest safeguards of democracy. In a nearly unanimous vote, Congress took steps to ensure its place in government affairs. Unfortunately, a year later, Congress unanimously amended the STOCK Act, quietly repealing the plan for Internet financial disclosure, effectively taking the teeth out of the regulations.

They did so without a hearing or a recorded vote in either the House or Senate, thereby undermining the intent of the law that was to ensure that government officials did not profit from nonpublic information. It is still legally permissible for stockholding lawmakers to sponsor legislation that could benefit the firms family members have investments in (Abad-Santos, 2012).

Potential solutions to these issues exist: requiring members of Congress to put their investment holdings in blind trusts and to recuse themselves from votes where conflicts of interest are involved as well as improving the accuracy and timeliness of reporting on stock holdings of members of Congress and expanding the disclosure system to encompass congressional staff (Hill et al., 2017; Public Citizen, 2017, June 22).

Questions to Consider

1. Why do you think Congress repealed the plan for Internet financial disclosure?

2. Can insider trading by public officers be stopped? If not, why not? If so, how?

Sources: Abad-Santos (2012), Pear (2012), Margasak (2012), Lawder and Cowan (2013), Feldman (2013), Hill et al. (2017), Lieber (2020), Public Citizen (2017)

ETHICS AND LEGISLATIVE DECISION-MAKING

Ethics cases involving members of Congress have received considerable attention in recent years—sometimes corroborated with substantial evidence, other times politically motivated and without merit—and the push for ethics reform continues despite questions about the likelihood of success (Public Citizen, 2017). A brief review of past cases illustrates the increasing prominence of the problem of legislative corruption.

Some of the most visible incidents involving legislators and ethics since the 1950s have been detailed by Tolchin and Tolchin (2001). One case involves Senator Joe McCarthy, condemned for disgracing the institution of the Senate with his anticommunist vendetta. In another, Senator Herman Talmadge was denounced for financial carelessness. Still others detail Representative Adam Clayton Powell's censure for tax evasion, travel junkets, plus additional offenses, and Senator Bob Packwood's threatened expulsion for sexual misconduct, which led to his resignation. Sex, money, and power remain strong temptations for ethical misconduct. Two cases that garnered considerable attention are Abscam and the Keating Five.

Abscam (an abbreviation of Abdul, a cliché for an Arab name, and Scam) was the most complete investigation and prosecution of legislative corruption in U.S. history, bringing down more members of Congress than any other scandal. The operation began with an FBI sting operation in the late 1970s and early 1980s targeting traffickers in stolen securities and art objects that quickly morphed into a public corruption investigation. Agents posing as Middle Eastern sheikhs offered bribes to numerous congressmen and senators in exchange for promised assistance with business and immigration problems. Politicians were video recorded receiving tens of thousands of dollars in bribes for agreeing to offer requested services. The investigation led to the conviction of a U.S. senator, five members of the House of Representatives, and other federal, state, as well as local officials (for details, see Grossman, 2008; Marion, 2010; Tolchin & Tolchin, 2001).

The Keating Five exposé refers to a 1989 imbroglio involving Charles Keating, owner of California-based Lincoln Savings and Loan, and U.S. Senators Alan Cranston (D-CA), Dennis DeConcini (D-AZ), John Glenn (D-OH), John McCain (R-AZ), and Donald Riegle (D-MI). When Keating ran into financial problems, the federal government prepared to take over Lincoln Savings and Loan. Keating gave hefty donations to five senators, requesting that they assist him in avoiding regulation. The Senate Ethics Committee formally rebuked the senators for intervening on Keating's behalf with regulators after accepting large campaign contributions from him.

Although the Abscam scandal is a clear case of wrongdoing, the Keating Five case illustrates the vague boundaries between corruption and constituent service. The Keating revelation involved campaign donations or charitable contributions, not money for their own pockets. While as candidates for reelection they would benefit from the monies, the funds were for political rather than personal use. Nonetheless, the senators' interference with regulators was seen as unfair, disrupting the mythical "level playing field" implying fair treatment for all in the regulatory process. The case also illustrated how vague ethics rules make deliberations about wrongdoing difficult to judge. The ignominious Abscam law enforcement sting was not problematic in that regard—it involved legislators lining their own pockets for personal gain.

Among the factors that determine congressional action are partisanship and publicity. Partisanship explains the use of ethics charges—deserved or not—to attack political opponents and provide justifications for retaliation. Party politics comes into play when determining punishment for ethical transgressions—condemnation, denunciation, expulsion, censorship, reprimand, rebuke. There is a tendency for legislators to consider "there but for the Grace of God go I," suggesting that they, too, feel uneasy about the boundaries of appropriate behavior and are reluctant to be too harsh in judging colleagues. Legislators also defer to loyalty, evident in their hesitance to condemn their allies. Such forces can lead to the "ethical fading," discussed in Chapter 7, and act as a deterrent to the whistleblowing, considered in Chapter 10.

Publicity is one potentially effective way to nudge Congress to take action on ethical issues; while they may be reluctant to condemn, they do not want to be seen as condoning unethical behavior. Another strategy is to overcome loyalty—to the institution, the party, and fellow members of Congress. As Tolchin and Tolchin (2001, 47) opine, "[M]ost lawmakers have to be pushed hard before they will go after a colleague, however low those colleagues may have fallen," suggesting that loyalty has its limits and will give way when public pressure is intense.

Dennis Thompson (1981a) warns against the dangers of "excuses of roles," pointing out that officials need to retain a sense of moral responsibility above and beyond their political responsibility. This is reinforced by the three-pronged model of ethical obligation for government officials: process, general duty of beneficence (public interest), and colleagues/subordinates (Moore, 1981). With regard to process, Moore cites the obligation of officials to share authority with others and to subject governmental actions to the scrutiny of citizens. Beneficence implies the exercise of government authority to effectively, efficiently, and decently achieve public purposes. Treating colleagues and subordinates with respect implies engaging in honest and fair dealings with them on a daily basis. These potentially conflicting roles and obligations are evident in the case of Robert Torricelli.

CASE STUDY 11.1

Robert Torricelli and the CIA

In the early 1990s, two murders in the jungles of Guatemala caught the attention of the public. One victim was an American innkeeper, the other a Guatemalan rebel leader. The faraway murders burst onto the media scene when evidence of U.S. involvement began to surface. The widows of the victims tried desperately to obtain information from the White House, but their efforts were conducted in vain until Rep. Robert Torricelli (D-NJ) stepped into the fray. Torricelli, a member of the House Intelligence Committee, suddenly went public with some disturbing classified information—the Guatemalan military officials responsible for the deaths were linked to the Central Intelligence Agency (CIA) and the agency had withheld information about the murders from the president. While the public was outraged at these allegations of a CIA cover-up, Torricelli's colleagues were furious that he had disclosed information he had obtained as a member of the Intelligence Committee. Despite attacks from both Democrats and Republicans, Torricelli stood firmly by his decision, declaring, "No oath imposed by the leadership can ask a member of Congress to conceal criminal activity" (quoted in Tolchin & Tolchin, 2001, 105).

Torricelli felt the ends—peace for the widows—justified the means—exposing the CIA. He weighed his loyalty to Congress against his personal, micro-level commitment to a higher order—a moral obligation to shed light on appalling CIA meso-level ethics permissive of such practices. His position on the issue matched prevailing public opinion. Had he not taken on the problem—and relentlessly pursued answers—it is unlikely that the resultant reform of congressional oversight of the CIA would have occurred through normal committee hearings or inquiries. Torricelli was guided by his character and by his perception of his role as a policymaker at the micro level. The next section examines these two influences—character and roles—on elected officials.

Questions to Consider

1. Do you think Torricelli was justified in disclosing this confidential information? Why or why not?

2. Would Torricelli have been right to allow the CIA to conceal criminal activity? Why or why not?

THE INFLUENCE OF CHARACTER AND ROLES ON ELECTED OFFICIALS

What is the appropriate role of members of Congress: Are they primarily emissaries (delegates) or leaders (trustees) of the people? As emissaries, they represent their constituents, remaining aware of what their support base is likely to advocate or oppose, and voting accordingly. As Frank E. Smith, former congressman from Mississippi, volunteers, "All members of Congress have a primary interest in being reelected. Some members have no other interest" (quoted in Falvey, 1991, 323). The role of conviction or belief is less significant if the primary duty is seen as serving the will of the people and the primary objective is self-preservation: The people are the true masters.

The leader or trustee, meanwhile, has an agenda. He or she identifies the most important issues, proposes solutions, explains the advantages and disadvantages, and persuades the voters of his or her views. This is consistent with Edmund Burke's (1774) advice to voters in Bristol regarding a representative's role, "Your representative owes you, not his industry only, but his judgment; and he betrays instead of serving you if he sacrifices it to your opinion." The role requirements of the leader are more demanding, the consequences less certain, than those of the emissary. When addressing new issues, the trustee would rely on his or her conscience, even when confronting opposition, with the intent of responding both to the demands of constituents and personal convictions.

Modern-day presidents and legislators are more accurately characterized as emissaries than leaders. Typically, they keep a finger elevated to gauge prevailing winds when making decisions. Emissaries in Congress are usually reluctant to be closely identified with a president during campaigns, only publicly supporting him when he has high ratings in their district or state. Why are there so few leaders? In part, because politicians are risk averse. As former Senator William Saxbe said, "If you don't stick your neck out, you don't get it chopped off" (quoted in Mayhew, 2004, 11). Elected officials want to retain power, some sacrificing their ethical beliefs to do so. Also, partisanship requires a certain amount of conformity to party leader preferences, because politics is a team sport. There is a price to pay when legislators go against the party, evidenced by the late Speaker Sam Rayburn's advice to Congressional freshmen, "You have to go along to get along" (quoted in MacNeil, 1963).

Given the differences in roles of officeholders and the paucity of leadership, what criteria can be used to evaluate their behavior? What principles and values can be reasonably expected from politicians regardless of trustee/delegate style to exhibit so that she might be held accountable? Scholars have identified moral criteria (see Carter, 1996, 1998; Cooper & Wright, 1992; Dobel, 1999; Planas, 2012; Thompson, 1995), including several discussed in earlier chapters:

- *Integrity*—having incorruptible honesty, playing by the rules, not being unduly influenced by friendship and family in conducting affairs of government, leading by example.
- *Civility*—respecting one's coworkers, displaying sportsmanlike conduct.
- *Upholding principles*—drawing on one's religious or philosophical moral values, taking the high road, following one's convictions, avoiding judgment of one's opponents.
- *Sincerity*—being forthright, avoiding hypocrisy and cynicism, not having a hidden agenda.
- *Political sensitivity*—seeking the good of the nation as a whole, responding to the needs of all citizens, showing compassion to those in need, being concerned about issues and problems.

- *Honor*—acting to bring credit and worth to one's work, profession, and institution.
- *Conviction*—having strong and consistent beliefs and the courage to stand by one's values while being open to new information and change where warranted.

Michael Josephson (2006) has posited "The Six Pillars of Character," to include trustworthiness, respect, responsibility, fairness, caring, and citizenship. These core values, together with those summarized previously, provide a yardstick for evaluating the ethical behavior of elected as well as appointed officials. One form of recognition singles out public servants with core values and character. An example is the Profile in Courage Award given to selected appointed and elected officials. Winners displayed courage of conscience by putting their careers at risk by pursuing the public interest in opposition to popular opinion or political pressures. Prominent recipients include Gerald Ford and John Lewis. But in today's climate of polarized politics, the character of elected officials is sorely tested.

POLARIZATION OF POLITICS AND ETHICAL IMPLICATIONS

Every American has seen signs of the hyperpolarization that characterizes the contemporary political environment, from the bumper stickers either lauding or lambasting political figures, to the "talking heads" on radio and TV deflecting charges of bias right back at their competitors, to ubiquitous partisan commentary on social media, and to elected officials who, instead of reaching across party lines, choose to lob accusations across the aisle. Collective political discourse suggests partisan differences have surpassed mere bickering to enter a state of animosity. As Mike Lofgren, former long-term Republican staffer, observed, "[L]egislating has now become war minus the shooting" (quoted in Mann & Ornstein, 2012, 55). A wall separates acceptable and stable forms of politics that fall short of consensus from the slippery slope of incivility that fuels feuding and strife ultimately leading to violence (see Figure 11.1).

A line figure depicting polarization of politics on the left side is labeled consensus and as polarization increases the movement across the line goes from disagreement and dissension to animosity in the middle and then to conflict and violence on the right side. The movement from the center (animosity) to violence (on the left end) is shown by a downward bend in the line figure.

FIGURE 11.1	Polarization of Politics

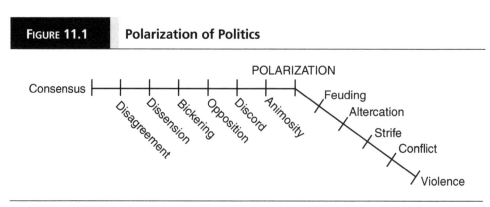

Source: Adapted from Planas (2012).

Despite incivility in political discourse, the historical nadir of partisanship was characterized by the doctrine of nullification (a doctrine devised by Jefferson and Madison to circumvent the acts of their political rival, President John Adams). Nevertheless, the state-led constitutional challenge to the 2010 Affordable Care Act, the fiercely partisan nomination hearings for Supreme Court justices, the 2020 protracted impeachment process, the contested 2020 election, and a second impeachment in 2021 suggest American government is heading in that direction (Nivola, 2010). Studies show that uncivil speech on the floors of both congressional chambers is on the rise (Kelman, 2018; Maisel, 2012) and that the accompanying party polarization has contributed to legislative gridlock (Farina, 2015). Mann and Ornstein (2012) call attention to the asymmetric partisan polarization attributing this in large measure to the growing ideological gap between the two political parties. The environment is so polarized that some politicians will vote against issues that they are for if they believe the other party will benefit as a result. If they block whatever their opponents support, it is thought that it will weaken their rivals.

While the political consequences of polarization are clear, the ethical implications are subtler. As observed earlier, whether as an emissary or a leader, an elected official bears a solemn responsibility to serve the interests of her constituents. However, when these politicians are preoccupied with partisan attacks and thereby foreclose the possibility of compromise, they generate a status quo bias that blocks the passage of policies necessary to promote the greater good (Gutmann & Thompson, 2010, 1129).

In fact, unwillingness or inability to compromise strikes at the very core of the American democratic political system. As Gutmann and Thompson (2010, 1130) observe:

> When parties enter into negotiations in bad faith, deliberately misrepresent their opponents' positions, and refuse to cooperate even on matters on which they could find common ground, they undermine relationships of respect that are necessary to sustain any morally justified democracy.

Problematically, the "uncompromising mindset" only serves to compound the effects of polarization, yet can be integral part of the democratic process. The uncompromising stance is a staple of successful political campaigns and a source of the type of principled argumentation that can nourish a democracy.

Yet, as Gutmann and Thompson (2010, 2012) demonstrate, there exists an urgent need to distinguish between the exigencies of campaigning and those of governing. To gain power in a democracy, elected officials must assume a firmly principled mindset. But to wield this power in accordance with their overriding ethical duties to their constituents, they must take on a more compromising posture. It is therefore a matter of duty for elected officials, regardless of the political climate, to keep politics off the dangerous slope to the acrid discourse that thwarts progress and corrodes mutual respect. It may not be clear exactly what this obligation implies. Does this mean that candidates must avoid negative campaigning? In the next section, the ethics of officials are put to the test in deciding whether to participate in that sort of activity.

NEGATIVE CAMPAIGNING

The strongest argument in favor of negative campaigning is that it works. Both the public and political candidates perceive it as an effective part of running for office (Geer, 2006). But is it ethical? Former Senate Majority Leader Tom Daschle has asserted that "negative advertising is the crack cocaine of politics" (Rich, 2012). It is widespread and addictive, especially in swing states and close elections. While most would agree that candidates should inform voters of any potential negative outcomes that would result from their opponents' policies or character, they would also likely contend that this should be done within the boundaries of civility and decorum. Deterioration of campaigns into the "ethics of the jungle"—name-calling, distortion, disinformation, false insinuations—where anything goes should be avoided.

Planas (2012, Chapter 13) makes the important distinction between "how things are and how they should be." "All's fair in love and politics" is an oft-used expression; indeed, it inspired the title of Matalin and Carville's classic 1994 campaign primer, but crossing the "fairness line" raises ethical concerns. While negative ads that are mean, rude, deceptive, insensitive, and vicious may be effective, applying the core values above would not lead to the conclusion that these "ought to be made the practice of politics" (382).

Nonpartisan organizations such as FactCheck.org and PolitiFact.com, along with organizations including Project Vote Smart and visual devices such as "Truth-O-Meters," have provided information to help voters sift through false claims generated by negative campaigning. These websites and organizations challenge duplicitous statements from both ends of the political spectrum. They can enable citizens to determine the truth behind campaign statements, news stories, and advertisements.

Yet the cost has been lowered for politicians as fact-checkers have become an unremarkable part of the process, and politicians seemingly pay little price for fabrications. Ideology trumps facts; slogans trump reality. Flatly, grossly, and shamefully untrue statements are often repeated as if they were true. No one is condemned for mendacity, to say nothing of its consequences for democratic governance. As one commentator observed, there is now a "liberty to lie"; truth has lost its honor and falsehoods have lost their stigma (Blow, 2012).

Lying is an emotional term that elicits a negative reaction, but it is so frequently part of government discourse that deception is often communicated more euphemistically. Terry Newell (2015, 133) has identified less brazen ways to deceive, some of which include parsing the meaning of words, pretending memory loss, staying silent, withholding information, evading the issue, using partial truths, silencing dissenting ideas, disregarding opposing arguments, leaking information, drawing false analogies, spinning the message, and assuring plausible deniability. More recently, blatant lying has become so ubiquitous that these more disguised forms of falsehoods have been less evident. But there is a risk and a cost to lying. As Joseph Nye (2020, 23–24) reminds us "the amount and type of lying makes a difference in terms of effects on credibility, trust and institutions." The more leaders or candidates rely on deception, the more they "erode trust, weaken institutions and create damaging precedents."

The issue for candidates is whether they are willing to be truthful, take charge of their campaigns and remove staffers who engage in questionable strategies. If elected, whether as a result of negative or positive campaign tactics, other ethical tests await them. Can it be expected that newly elected politicians will suddenly turn their backs on special interests that supported their campaigns financially? If so, how far can elected officials be obliged to go in their quest to be ethical? Should they do as Supreme Court justices are expected to do—recuse themselves from voting on matters related to special interest groups who may have contributed to their campaign? Should they refuse any financial support (e.g., meals, trips) paid for by special interest groups? Where is the line drawn on such matters if the law is unclear? Fuzzy limitations tempt unethical behavior, particularly when enforcement of campaign violations is slow and ineffective. Unfortunately, these questions are not being either asked or answered by policymakers in today's toxic political environment.

In sum, candidates and legislators must deal with a host of ethical dilemmas. The examples discussed here highlight a wide range of issues confronting members of Congress, including insider trading, conflict of interest, inappropriate constituent service, ideological vendettas, financial and sexual misconduct, bribe taking, uncivil speech, unfair treatment on behalf of campaign contributors, negative campaigning, and unauthorized disclosure of privileged information. While most of these concerns are illegal, government incumbents can also encounter the ethically troubling "dirty hands" problem, a subject discussed next.

THE PROBLEM OF DIRTY HANDS

The problem of "dirty hands" is traceable to Machiavelli, who advised that the Prince "must learn how not to be good." Political theorist Michael Walzer (1974) gave Machiavelli's principle the title of dirty hands, adapting the term from a play by Jean-Paul Sartre. The issue is thus: Sometimes the wrong thing is the right thing to do. But, Walzer qualifies, only in situations of dire or "supreme" emergency is the disutility of abiding by the prohibitions or rules great enough to override the utilitarian value of keeping to the rules (Coady, 2009). A classic controversial example: A political leader must decide whether to torture a terrorist to find the whereabouts of a bomb. Without this coercion, innocent people could die (Cunningham, 1992, 239; see also Case Study 11.1 and Chapter 4, Exercise 3).

Walzer argued that the dirty hands conundrum "is posed most dramatically in politics," where officials sometimes face violating their principles for the sake of achieving some morally weighty political end. This then is not just a problem, but a paradox. Dovi's (2005, 130) recommendation to citizens is to "accept the paradox and seek what solace is available by choosing political actors who are willing to get their hands dirty and will feel guilty doing so." The condition of guilt serves as an information mechanism of public accountability, given the assumption that guilty politicians will be disposed to confess their violations of moral principles or willingly subject their decisions to scrutiny.

Walzer (1974, 160) further claims the pervasiveness of dirty hands in politics as "a central feature of political life, one that arises not merely as an occasional crisis in the career of this or that unlucky official but systematically and frequently." The most common form of dirty hands is lying (e.g., falsehoods, evasion, duplicity). It may be permissible to deceive the public for its own good, so long as the official understands her overall obligation of truth telling embodied in the oath of office. Walzer divides political actors into two broad categories: consequentialists who ignore the obligations of morality and make decisions based solely on the considerations of expediency, and absolutists who act solely according to their moral principles. Like the contrasting styles of congressional representatives, both absolutists and consequentialists are needed for a morally healthy polity. Without the presence of some individuals refusing to compromise on their integrity, the polity would suffer.

Dovi cautions against the cumulative effects individual dirty-handed decisions can have. Continually compromising principles can result in officials—and the public witnessing the compromising—weakening their commitment to political ideals. A second cumulative effect is narrowing the scope of availability of policy options. Repeated exposure to dirty-handed decisions—even those made for morally important gains—can dull the intensity of certain commitments. If more and more decision makers accept torturing or bribing for preferable political ends, then the ordinariness and routine of these practices can numb moral repulsion. Politicians, soldiers, law enforcement agents, public defense attorneys, and resistance fighters are all people who often operate in dirty arenas and must constantly struggle against losing their moral sensitivity (Cunningham, 1992, 244).[1]

No precise decision procedure exists to inform people in advance when they can or must embrace evil to minimize it, or when they can forsake the battle against evil without becoming a partner in crime. The ethics triad and behavioral ethics, nonetheless, can aid in the decision procedure, illustrated in Case Study 11.2.

Presidents, too, cannot avoid ethical quagmires and must decide how to deal with them. Some of the same issues that confront Congress also challenge presidents (see, e.g., "The Bad President" Tabletop Exercise at the end of the chapter). However, one special concern singled out for attention here is adherence to truthfulness, the topic of the next section.

 CASE STUDY 11.2

Applying Philosophical and Behavioral Ethics Approaches: Interrogation Methods

You are Major Smith, the new counterintelligence operations officer for a battalion deployed last week to support Operation A. The infantry brigade is deployed throughout a major city, patrolling the streets. Things have not been going well in the last month. A number of soldiers have been killed by improvised explosive devices (IEDs) set by insurgents. As the senior officer, you get a call from your commander, who reports he just caught an insurgent leader. The commander says the leader is bragging that a car bomb has been set to go off in the next 30 minutes and said, "There's nothing you can do about it." The company commander is prepared to do some "serious persuasion" to find out where the bomb is, saying, "Your interrogators are too far away. I know the new directives say they have to do all interrogations by the book—but time is running out. I know how to make a man talk, so I can get the information. These attacks have to come to an end. Request guidance, sir." What should you do, Major?

A similar case occurred in the reality of war in Afghanistan (Operation Enduring Freedom), resulting in the deaths of two detainees in the Bagram Theater Internment Facility in December 2002. In February 2003, Lieutenant General Daniel K. McNeill, commander of American forces in Afghanistan in 2002 and 2003, said prisoners Mullah Habibullah and Dilawar had died of natural causes. He did not disclose that military pathologists had described both deaths as homicides caused by beatings.

Sergeant James P. Boland watched a subordinate beat prisoner Habibullah. Boland chained the hands of Dilawar above his shoulders and denied him medical care. Nearly two years later, the Army charged Sergeant Boland with criminal offenses in the Dilawar case, ranging from dereliction of duty to maiming and involuntary manslaughter. The findings of the military investigation support accounts by former Afghan prisoners that they were subject to abuse. The interrogation methods described were authorized in Guantanamo Bay, Cuba—not Bagram—including removal of clothing, isolation for long periods, stress positions, and sleep and light deprivation. Three men arrested with Dilawar said they were hooded with their arms raised and chained to the ceiling for hours and days at a time in Bagram. One of the three men said he was forced to lie on his stomach and a solider jumped on his back. Was the price of immorality of abuse worth paying? Did obtaining intelligence from the prisoners constitute a supreme emergency?

Results-Based Analysis. The two cases (based on Gall & Rohde, 2004; Kern, 2006) can be analyzed using the ethics triumvirate. Concentrating first on results—the greatest good for the greatest number—both the company commander in the first case and Sergeant Boland in the second thought they could obtain actionable intelligence by using "enhanced" interrogation techniques. In the best-case scenario the insurgent suffers but lives are saved if accurate information is divulged. The end of preventing the car bombing or obtaining information from detainees at Bagram justifies means of unauthorized interrogation methods. The major and the sergeant may believe that their action requires moral courage and that their decisions would lead to the greater good—fewer American casualties.

There is no certainty, however, that the fictional insurgent leader or the real-life detainees had the information necessary to prevent the bombing or advance the military mission in Afghanistan. Use of extreme methods may or may not have extracted useful intelligence. Subjecting others to harsh treatment undoubtedly takes a toll not only on the victim of the extreme tactics but also on those administering it, especially if the information gleaned fails to yield expected results. In the first case, authorizing unlawful methods could irreparably damage the major's reputation and media coverage could erode public support for the military.

Rule-Based Analysis. Assessing rules and principles, neither organizational rules nor the fundamental ethical rule "what is good for one is good for all" endorses the methods used to obtain information about enemy actions. The officers violated established procedures regarding the conduct of interrogations. Recall the Department of Justice memos used to authorize torture. In the first scenario, the major should not authorize the company commander to engage in actions that fall outside the rules and that violate moral principles. He might have done so because of giving higher priority to loyalty to his fellow soldiers and innocent civilians. The second case violated both the law and ethics with flagrant examples of detainee abuse. Following the Moral Minimum (avoid and correct social injury) and the Kew Gardens principles (they felt there was a compelling need, they were in proximity, possessed capability, and, at least in the first case, the major may have considered himself the last resort), they might argue that their choice was reasonable: The soldiers and the mission come first.

Under the extreme circumstances in the first case, wherein time was of the essence—delay could mean deaths—the major might have authorized unorthodox methods and subsequently defended his actions to his superiors claiming that he had to do a wrong thing to do the right (obtain information that would prevent harm and loss of life), the "dirty-hands" defense. While there is no assurance that the information would be accurate and achieve the desired result, the major is able to justify his decision and is willing to accept the consequences of his action if it comes to a court-martial. He may believe that anyone confronting this specific dilemma would be willing to endorse the universality of such action. Engaging in unauthorized interrogation caused harm and pain to the insurgents and involved techniques that, in the latter case, violated the law, resulting in criminal charges against Sergeant Boland.

Virtue-Based Analysis. From a virtue theory perspective, the action will be influenced by the ingrained dispositions of the decision maker. Moral courage will be required whichever choice is made. It takes courage to act when the stakes are so high, taking responsibility for the lives and well-being of others. In the first case, the major did not have time to think it over; there were two stark options with no middle course available. Prudence and thoughtful deliberation had to give way to decisiveness and valor. He had to act in the moment and make a snap decision. The major and the sergeant then must live with their decisions and the way their actions will be viewed by those they respect. Will their conduct survive the self-evaluation test posed when they look at themselves in the mirror and ask, "Is this someone who did what a moral exemplar would do?" Will it pass the after-event assessment by review boards, which will render a judgment on the action? Ultimately, both of them will have to decide whether they are comfortable with the rightness—or wrongness—of their decision: That is what makes it a moral choice.

Behavioral Ethics-Based Analysis. The first and second case can be further considered using some concepts from behavioral ethics. Ethical fading is a form of self-deception whereby people fail to recognize the moral dimension of an issue. This is most likely to occur when a visceral response occurs around a high-stress decision point. The major in this scenario, while he no doubt realizes his decision has moral implications, is forced to make a high-stakes decision with inadequate information. There is little time for System 2 thinking (slow-paced, cool and deliberative) given the circumstances, so it is not surprising that System 1 thinking (rapid, intuitive, gut reaction) is used even though System 2 might be preferred. Depending on the outcome, the major may regret that his "want" self prevailed over his "should" self in approaching the interrogation, a concern that may become more apparent after the event itself. Under the circumstances, the major was forced to decide quickly and later may be required to think more carefully when he is asked to justify his actions.

The overarching difficulty with concocted and—far rarer—actual "ticking bomb" cases is that they tend to obscure the need to think clearly not only about the limits of routine interrogations but also about what happens after the decision to torture is made. Impossible questions arise: How many people must be endangered? How certain must decision makers be of the danger? How convinced must they be that the victim will be susceptible to brutality? If necessary, are they prepared to engage in cruelty against his family to obtain accurate information? Stated differently, the argument for torture has no beginning and has no end (Fried & Fried, 2011; see also Chapter 4, Exercise 3, and Exhibit 8.4).

PRESIDENTS AND TRUTHFULNESS

For a moment the lie becomes the truth.

—Fyodor Dostoevsky

Consider Lyndon Johnson and the Vietnam War, Richard Nixon and Watergate, Jimmy Carter and Iranian hostages, Ronald Reagan and the Iran-Contra affair, George H. W. Bush and tax increases, Bill Clinton and the Monica Lewinsky affair, George W. Bush and the Iraq War, Barack Obama and Guantanamo, Donald Trump and campaign promise keeping. In each case, be it policy or politics, private or public behavior, the president had to decide whether to be truthful or deceptive. While a broken promise is not technically the same as a lie, "promise keeping" is an important principle and breaking a promise suggests one is untrustworthy (see Bad Actor Exercise 4: The Bad President at the end of this chapter). This requires qualification: If the promise is broken because of something you could not control, it is not a lie, but if it is betrayed for no good reason, it is a lie:

- Lyndon Johnson deliberately suppressed information about the Vietnam War, selectively revealing reports about the war's progress to put the best possible face on American success, thereby creating "an illusion of imminent victory" (Ekman, 2009, 307).

- Richard Nixon lied to cover up the fact that people working for the White House were caught at the Watergate complex while breaking in to the Democratic Party headquarters. Audiotapes of conversations in the Oval Office indicated that he was abusing the power of his office, concealing a crime to stay in power, and deceiving the people.

- Jimmy Carter misled the public when he said at a January 8, 1980, press conference that a military rescue of American hostages who had been seized by Iranian militants at the U.S. embassy in Tehran "would almost certainly end in failure and almost certainly end in the death of the hostages." He said this knowing that he had secretly authorized military training for just such a rescue operation.

- Ronald Reagan lied to the nation about the extent of American involvement in Iranian affairs. When an Iranian newspaper broke the story that the administration had secretly sold weapons to Iran through Israel in the hope of triggering the release of hostages, Reagan at first categorically denied the allegations. He then backpedaled and asserted that the arms sale was simply a minor one, and then days later went back to denying the sale altogether. When it was later discovered that the funds from the Iranian arms sale were diverted to fund rebels in Nicaragua, in contravention of a congressional prohibition of such funding, the administration quickly became entangled in the infamous Iran-Contra scandal (Alterman, 2004).

- George H. W. Bush in August 1988 accepted the Republican Party's nomination for president, saying in his acceptance speech, "The Congress will push me to raise taxes, and I'll say no. And they'll push, and I'll say no, and they'll press again. And all I can say to them is read my lips. No new taxes." In retrospect, this is reminiscent of the joke about lies told by politicians: "How can you tell when a politician is lying? When he moves his lips." He reneged on his unequivocal "no new taxes" pledge two years later when he signed the 1990 Omnibus Budget Reconciliation Act.

- Bill Clinton's infamous statement, "I did not have sexual relations with that woman, Miss Lewinsky," was a lie to the nation about his extramarital sex life. David Gergen, editor at large of *U.S. News and World Report*, who had experience working for Reagan, Nixon, and Clinton, took particular umbrage at Clinton's lie. "The deep and searing violation took place when he not only lied to the country, but co-opted his friends and lied to them" (quoted in Alterman, 2004, 11; see also Kinzer, 2007).

- George W. Bush was interviewed by NBC's Matt Lauer on November 8, 2010, and said, in reference to dealings with Iraq, "I gave diplomacy every chance to work." Yet insider accounts from inside Bush's national security team (e.g., Clarke, 2009) and others (e.g., Fromkin, 2010; Isikoff & Corn, 2006) indicate that a year prior to the invasion and immediately after 9/11, the administration had its sights set on military action against Iraq.

- Barack Obama made many promises to the American people during the campaign of 2008. According to PolitiFact.com's "Obamameter," composed of 533 of the president's promises, by the end of his eight years in office he had kept 48 percent of his promises and broken 24 percent of them, while another 28 percent were part of a compromise. One of the more prominent broken promises listed was Obama's pledge to close Guantanamo detention center, but the decision was not completely under his control (Congress refused to support closure of the prison).

- Donald Trump also made promises to the public during the 2016 campaign. PolitiFact. com's "Trump-O-Meter" identified 100 promises. By early September 2020 his report card showed he had kept 25 promises (24 percent), compromised on 21 promises (20 percent), broke 50 promises (49 percent), stalled on 6 promises (5 percent), and 0 promises are "in the works." PolitiFact also had a Truth-O-Meter making fact-checks on Trump's statements and those of other elected officials, classifying them as mostly true, half true, usually false, or "pants on fire."

Trump did not fare well on this "truth" criterion or standards used by other fact-checking sources. According to the Fact-Checkers database, he made 10,000 false or misleading statements in his first 827 days in office (average of 12 claims per day); and by July 9, 2020 (440 days later his average during the latter period was 23 claims a day), he had made 20,055 false or misleading claims in 1,267 days.

Trump's numerous false statements concerning the coronavirus, impeachment hearings, and taxes accounted for a few thousand of his falsehoods. He frequently repeated claims that stated today's U.S. economy is the best in history (360 times during his presidency), asserted the border wall is being built (261 times), believed he passed the largest tax cuts in history (210 times), deliberately lied about the lethal nature of COVID-19, and alleged without evidence widespread voter fraud (Kessler, Kelly, & Rizzo, 2020; see also Editorial board, 2020, December 26, and Kessler, 2020, December 18). His most controversial comments were often qualified by phrases such as "people think" or "some say" or "I was told that" (Blow, 2017, October 19).

Falsehoods continued after the 2020 election with the former president challenging the outcome (see Exhibit 11.2), despite the fact that the president's own election fraud commission and attorney general found no evidence of misdoings; the same proved to be true in recounts in selected states and in scores of court cases. It was not surprising, then, that election officials in all 50 states, the Electoral College, and Congress certified the election results (see Joint Statement from Elections Infrastructure, 2020).

EXHIBIT 11.2   Contesting the 2020 Presidential Election Outcome

The results of the election were deemed suspect due to alleged fraud, a charge that predates the election itself: There would be fraud, the president claimed—and then when he lost, he said that his prediction had come true. Yet no evidence of corruption was presented.

What Does *Not* Count as Systemic Fraud?

First, surges in vote totals benefited Biden. As polls closed, those ballots were added to the totals; since mail-in ballots tended to favor Biden, the results shifted.

Next, other suspicious-seeming things happened but are not fraud. Just because a suspicious van pulled up to a polling place does not mean anything other than a photographer unloading equipment.

Third, hundreds of people signed sworn statements about things they found suspicious. This does not mean they are proof of wrongdoing. A review of the affidavits made it clear that there were almost no actual allegations of wrongdoing but instead activity that seemed curious to those unfamiliar with vote counting procedures. A large number of accusations are not itself evidence.

Fourth, suspicious-seeming things that did not happen simply because claims were untrue. This includes more absentee ballots turned in than sent out, dead people voting, and a postal worker indicating that ballots were tampered with (a statement later recanted)

Fifth, foul play might have occurred, but did not, such as allegations that voting machines changed votes. There's no proof that this happened; even claims that it could technically have been done are not evidence that it was (further, the company leasing the equipment said that its machines cannot do it). It is also possible to throw out every Trump paper ballot before it can be counted. That does not mean that any were, particularly in the absence of verification. The claims were either false, obviously irrelevant, or both.

Last, "statistical analysis" suggests that vote totals were unexpected. Statistical analysis can illuminate possible problems, but does not by itself constitute proof of deception, and such analyses can often be misleading.

Things That *Do* Count as Evidence of Systemic Fraud

Demonstrated examples of impropriety affecting a large number of votes would qualify. This could be discovery and confirmation of votes cast on behalf of a large number of dead people or votes on behalf of hundreds of people who had no intention of voting.

What constitutes evidence? Something that strongly suggests misdoings occurred, withstands scrutiny, and cannot easily be debunked. Sworn affidavits from participants in schemes, or criminal investigations suggesting that the plots existed, could be counted as evidence. Nothing was offered that met this not-very-high standard. Instead, it was simply assumed that fraud occurred. The election aftermath was without precedent in American history. "Calling an election unfair," said one judge, "does not make it so" (Rucker et al., 2020, November 29). The head of the Cybersecurity and Infrastructure Security Agency, a life-long Republican appointed by the president, found no evidence of votes being compromised in any way, stating, "The 2020 election was the most secure in U.S. history" (Krebs, 2020, December 1).

The losing candidate's determined efforts to overturn the people's verdict—lawsuits, political agitation, pressure on state and local officials—were all unsuccessful. They did, however, endanger America's democracy, undermine national security and public health, and lead supporters to believe that the winner was elected illegitimately.

Source: Adapted from Bump (2020, November 28). Also see Krebs (2020, December 1) and Rucker et al. (2020, November 29).

Patrick Dobel (1999) has argued that prudence is a virtue of political leaders. "Diligence in obtaining information . . . and attentiveness to the fit and proportionality of means and ends" is required because of their "responsibility for the welfare of the polity" (57–75). Robert Dallek (2010) concludes that presidential deception is ethical in foreign policy if it is necessary for national security and produces substantially better outcomes. He maintains, however, that deception culminating in foreign policy debacles (e.g., George W. Bush and Iraq; Johnson and Vietnam) is unethical. One drawback of this view is that it explicitly links ethical judgments to outcomes. Dallek is right to focus on the pragmatic element of presidential deception, but there will always be factors outside the president's control for which he should not necessarily be held responsible.

What is the purpose behind the lie? Jimmy Carter lied about a rescue mission for the Iranian hostages. Ekman's (2009, 304–306) analysis of this deception concludes that he had to lie to "gain an advantage over the enemy." The attempt failed, but Carter was held responsible for only the failure and not the falsehood. When assessing an untrue statement by an official, it is crucial to determine the motivation for lying and to whom the lie is addressed. To evaluate the ethics of presidential deception, it is important to remember a now famous question asked by Howard Baker, then U.S. Senator and ranking minority member of the Senate committee investigating the Watergate scandal—"What did the president know and when did he know it?"

History repeated itself multiple times during the Trump administration, first in the context of former national security advisor Michael Flynn's resignation because of failing to disclose the details of his conversation with a Russian diplomat and his links to Russian President Vladimir Putin (Chapter 3). The question of what the president knew and when involved President Trump's alleged complicity in Flynn's questionable relations with Russia (Kristof, 2017). This occurred once more during the 2020 impeachment process and his dealings with Roger Stone (Nichols, 2019). It happened yet again based on his knowingly downplaying the threat of the coronavirus pandemic (Woodward, 2020).

In making judgments regarding truthfulness and character, Dennis Thompson (2010, 24) cautions that "ethical character is fragmented," and one needs to consider both private and public virtues. Presidents sometimes fail to display both private and public rectitude (e.g., Clinton's lies about the Lewinsky affair), but the question is whether they need to exhibit both. In his view, the qualities that constitute "Constitutional character" should take priority—"the disposition to act, and to motivate others to act, according to the principles that constitute the democratic process" (24). Actions in this regard may vary according to the respective responsibilities of different public offices, but they would include things like sensitivity to basic rights of citizenship, respect for due process, sense of responsibility, tolerance of opposition, willingness to justify decisions, and commitment to candor. Private virtues might make a president more capable or respectable, Thompson maintains, but constitutional virtues should be required as a condition for holding office.

Yet the behavior of politicians too often fails to reflect the core values and "Constitutional character" described here (e.g., see Exhibit 11.2). At the close of the Trump administration and beginning of the Biden presidency there was a push by legislators and pressure groups to tighten ethics rules. Trump's actions inciting attacks on the Capitol, directing tax dollars to advance family business interests, attempting to overturn the outcome of elections, failing to support enforcement of the Hatch Act (see chapter 14 for details on the Act), pardoning political appointees who supported him, and weakening enforcement powers of independent watchdog agencies prompted calls for reform.

Two proposals—Protecting Our Democracy Act and House of Representatives 1—would implement much tougher policies. Among these proposed reforms are requiring presidents to release their tax returns, increasing protection against retaliation for whistleblowers and IGs, tightening rules on accepting gifts (emoluments), limiting the pardon powers, bolstering the power of the Office of Government Ethics, and expanding the authority of the Office of Special Counsel to enforce the Hatch Act. Efforts to approve these safeguards will be contentious, but reformers see a window of opportunity to act by fortifying ethics rules (Williamson, 2021). New rules are not the only way to influence the decisions and actions of elected officials. In what ways do citizens' and media's dealings with officials affect their ethical behavior? This is the topic of the final section.

THE INFLUENCE OF CITIZENS AND THE MEDIA ON POLITICIANS

The populace and the media have subjected the private lives of officials to increased scrutiny with the advent of 24/7 "gotcha media" and the citizens' voracious appetite for tabloid-like stories. Back in the 1880s, when President Chester A. Arthur said, "I may be president, but my private life is nobody's damned business" (Hagopian Institute, 2008), he may have been able to make it stick. Now it is common to see headlines discussing the drinking habits, driving record, sexual conduct, and family life of presidents and other officials. This led Dennis Thompson (1981b, 2006) to examine when the private life of public servants should become an issue of public concern. Privacy laws provide limited clarity, and ethical principles sometimes conflict on this issue, making it difficult to identify precise rules regarding officials' rights to privacy.

Thompson (1981b) provides the following distinction between instrumental and intrinsic justification for the value of privacy: (a) Instrumental arguments maintain that privacy is linked to liberty by enabling a person to engage in certain activities unhampered by observation or intrusive interventions; (b) intrinsic arguments focus on the nature of intimate relations (love, friendship) and trust, which typically require privacy to develop. Clearly, officials must surrender some of their privacy rights, but how much and what kind? Here, Thompson considers the "principle of diminished privacy," which can be justified on utilitarian grounds—the interests of the many (citizens) trump the rights of the few (elected officials), with limitations on the privacy rights of officials, but not to an unlimited extent. In general, the more influential the position, the less privacy protection is afforded. The nature and type of the issues dealt with by the policymaker (intimate/personal versus policy/job related) and the effect of those issues (public/media perception; adverse impact on the job) are also important. Exhibit 11.3 highlights the problem of holding public officials accountable.

EXHIBIT 11.3   **Mendacity and American Democracy: An Editorial**

"The whole art of government consists in the art of being honest."

—Thomas Jefferson

Today's political environment presents unprecedented challenges to holding government accountable: a flagrant disregard of truth, censorship of public information, and disrespect for ethical norms. The nature of the dishonesty—its sheer volume and spontaneity as well as its repetition of easily disproved statements—distracts, confuses, and overwhelms the public and punditry alike. It leads to familiarity, and familiarity leads to acceptance, ultimately rendering those who would question government ineffectual. It is difficult to have meaningful dialogue with those who do not believe in facts but instead depend upon intimidation and denial to create doubt. Liars lie not only about their own policy positions but also about the views of their opponents. As Michael Ford (2021, March 22) observes, "the point of a lie is often not that the spreader believes it, but rather to demonstrate that truth does not matter...." A "liars dividend" may result: When it is unclear what is real and what is fake, liars can benefit, especially when debunking efforts backfire and reinforce the falsehoods.

Among the numerous widely spread false claims are disinformation about September 11 celebrations, Iraq War opposition, Iraq War spending, the birther conspiracy, inaugural crowd size, the Electoral College majority, voter fraud, the status of the Affordable Care Act, tax-cut beneficiaries, the United States having the highest taxes in the world, the North American Free Trade Agreement, the Iran nuclear deal, contributions to NATO, Mexican and Muslim immigrants, the unemployment rate, the murder rate, pandemic masks are infectious, and sexual harassment. The fact that such lies are not concealed—indeed, they are repeated—is seen as proof of their virtue.

Indifference to facts, and no penalty for being wrong, represents a societal breakdown in the ability to face objective reality, as well as to morally and intellectually compromise government. Post-truth politics undermines the very idea of facts; the issue becomes not what is right but what you can get away with. PolitiFact rates nearly 70 percent of presidential statements as mostly false, false, or "pants on fire" (this site keeps track of all assertions on a daily basis: www.washingtonpost.com/news/fact-checker/wp/2017/07/20/president-trumps-first-six-months-the-fact-check-tally/?utm_term=.d5d4af8b7a63). Easy falsehoods often sound more true than hard facts, as humans are often swayed more by fiction than reality. Mark Twain observed that it is easier to fool a person than to convince him that he has been fooled. Incriminating truth is seldom preferred over flattering fabrications that win applause. Incapable of acknowledging wrongdoing, it is not a deception if top officials believe it. Oblivious to the idea that ethics is relevant to decisions, a lie is not a lie; rather, it is just what they happen to think.

With no standard of propriety, the disdain for truth embodies contempt for democracy and a challenge to legitimacy of its institutions. In an apparent "us-against-them" attacks on the rule of law and constitution government, separation of powers (the courts, the Congress, executive agency secretaries, the intelligence community, the military), Gold Star families, political party allies, defense treaties, the free press, labor unions, as well as business advisory councils erode the sense of trust in society—and ourselves.

Democracies depend upon acceptance of shared facts such as the certification of elections as valid (including accurate counting of votes and the absence of illegally cast votes) as well as respect for the electoral process and one's opponents. The existence of facts, a conception of truth outside what government says is true, as well as the force of law are foundational to, and a test of, democracy. Duplicity distracts attention from other ethical concerns such as undermining the capacity for evidence-based governing and upholding laws policymakers are sworn to protect. Falsification, deceit, denial, habitual lying, imperviousness to correction, and political chicanery must be called out for what they are. Ethical competence is not to be confused with confidence; attitude is not the same as aptitude. Conservative columnist Max Boot wrote this about Donald Trump, "It's bad enough that the president lies so much; what's worse is that so many think he is telling the truth." "When you tell a lie," concludes Khaled Hosseini, "you steal someone's right to tell the truth."

Sources: Blake (2020, September 10), Boot (2020, October 13), Brooks (2017, July 14), Gold (2017), Hohmann (2017, August 2 Ford (2021, March 22), Jurecic (2017, January 27), Kessler, Lee, and Kelly (2017, July 20), Paul and Matthews (2016), Sargent (2017, March 6).

What is the benefit and cost of exposure of the private lives of public servants? On the upside, Thompson argues that it enables citizens to form judgments about an official's physical and moral competence, the likelihood that they would put the public interest ahead of private interests and support politically popular policies. Public exposure offers clues about officials' or candidates' moral sensitivity and provides a basis for holding them accountable. In the 2012 presidential campaign, Republican nominee Mitt Romney told a group of Florida donors that 47 percent of the citizenry would not vote for the GOP because they were, essentially, parasitic "takers" dependent on government largess. An enterprising bartender taped the "private" talk, and *Mother Jones* magazine broke the story. This reinforced a stereotype that Democrats had been pushing of Romney as an out-of-touch plutocrat, too aloof and arrogant to care about the needs of less privileged voters. Was this recording of the speech an invasion of privacy? While some may doubt it, others may see it as a public service, as Wasserman (2013) opined in an op-ed for the *Miami Herald*: "[W]hat it revealed and what might not have been heard otherwise," justified its reporting.

Another revealing quote comes from Democratic nominee Hillary Clinton's speech in 2016 at a New York City fund raiser during a heated campaign: "You know, to just be grossly generalistic, you could put half of Trump's supporters into what I call the basket of deplorables. Right?" She said: "The racist, sexist, homophobic, xenophobic, Islamaphobic—you name it. And unfortunately there are people like this. And he has lifted them up" (quoted in Reilly, 2016). The candidates opposing them quickly used Clinton's and Romney's quotes to portray them in a bad light, escalating the rhetoric and name-calling in the campaign.

An additional downside of negative campaigns: Exposure is a distraction from the more significant issues of the day. The amount of the media's time and space devoted to salacious stories and the viewer's/reader's attention to such matters means the decision maker's time and attention likely will be occupied by these concerns as well—diverting them from the more substantive policy matters for which they were elected to deliberate. Also, "the private lives of public officials deserve protection because the privacy of all citizens has value" (Thompson, 1981b, 240), and these rights have been progressively eroded for politicians as well as candidates.

For example, *Mother Jones* also published reports of Senate minority leader Mitch McConnell planning with campaign aides to release an unflattering secret video of film star Ashley Judd, a rumored challenger for McConnell's seat. It included comments about her history of mental instability and personal, private comments she had made that were likely to annoy Kentucky voters. (Judd opted not to run prior to publication of the article.) Clearly, the zone of candidate privacy, like that of elected incumbents, has diminished considerably. Some aspects of the private lives of public officials and those seeking office, such as sexual orientation and gender identity, have no bearing on their performance. Media exposure of such characteristics (especially when the person wishes them to remain confidential) is unethical when it causes undue professional or personal harm (Case Study 11.3).

Some balance must be struck between the public's right to be informed about the actions of their elected officials or candidates and the officials' and candidates' right to privacy.

CASE STUDY 11.3

Applying Philosophical and Behavioral Ethics Approaches: A Transgender City Manager

Susan Stanton, then known as Steve, had been working as city manager for the city of Largo, Florida, for more than 14 years and was a recent recipient of a sizable merit pay increase. In 2007, someone leaked to the local newspaper the fact that Stanton was in the midst of a gender transition. The *St. Petersburg Times* published the story and "outed" Stanton against her wishes. Stanton's wife was already aware of her circumstances, but her 13-year-old son was not. Stanton rushed home the afternoon before the story broke to share her struggle firsthand with her son, whom she feared would be harassed at school following the disclosure.

The news about Stanton's new identity came as a shock to the citizens of Largo, who had known Steve Stanton as an esteemed community member and as their city manager for years. Once the news was published, there was an immediate outcry from residents demanding that Stanton be fired. City Commission members were inundated with phone calls and emails denouncing Stanton as "disgusting." One religious official went so far as to publicly claim that Jesus would want Stanton fired. Prior to this, Stanton's job performance was never in question—indeed, Stanton had proved competent and effective at managing the city. Stanton wanted to continue in her position, a job that she enjoyed and at which she was successful (Escobedo, 2010). A minority cohort of community members rallied in support of Stanton, arguing that job retention should be based on merit and not on aspects of identity. There were, however, no legal protections in Largo that prohibited discrimination on the basis of gender identity or expression. What should the City Commission do?

The ethics triad can help provide a defensible evaluation to an ethical conflict derived from a comprehensive consideration of three elements: results, rules, and virtue. This framework allows for the interplay of the competing interests involved in decision-making. However, the tripartite analysis can be perverted as well. For it to work as intended the results must be based on the greatest good, not self-interest; the rules interests must pivot on a sense of justice and fairness, not organizational rules; and the value interests must be predicated on integrity, not conformity.

Results-Based Analysis. This case presents an example of instances when results interests may not lead to sound ethical decision-making. The greatest good is served if the city manager is discharged because that is what the community desires, and the community is an emblem of the greatest good. However, serving the greatest good by meeting public demands is unethical in this context because its motives are driven by prejudice and ignorance. Therefore, even though retaining the city manager will cause discontent, it is nevertheless the proper course of action.

Rule-Based Analysis. The council should look to its code of ethics, its oath to protect and serve the public interest, its employment contract with the city manager, as well as its state and federal employment laws when evaluating how to address the issue. The rules contained in each of these documents will help inform the council of the best course of action. Likely, such rules will support retaining the manager—as long as her personal transition does not interfere with her ability to fulfill her professional responsibilities. And even if the rules do not direct the council how to proceed ethically, the underlying notions of justice and fairness inherent in the rules interests should indeed inform the council that prejudice and ignorance serve no purpose in ethical decision-making. "What is good for one is good for all" is the key criterion in rule-based decision-making.

Virtue-Based Analysis. The virtue interests involved in this conflict will be determined by the values that the city council chooses to demonstrate through its actions. Robert Greenleaf's (2002) theory of Servant Leadership suggests that the council should be attentive to the concerns of constituents and empathize with them. This theory would justify heeding the call of citizens who wish to see the city manager fired. However, such a decision would undoubtedly violate several of the "Six Pillars of Character" (Josephson, 2002)—namely, respect, fairness, and caring. Therefore, a decision to terminate the manager would reflect poor character on the part of the city council members.

Actual Outcome. Within days of the initial newspaper article, Largo's City Commission held a highly emotional emergency hearing. At the conclusion, it voted to terminate Stanton's employment. Several commissioners cited as justification their belief that the public had "lost confidence" in the manager and, under those circumstances, Stanton could not be retained. In making this decision, the Commission stood with the majority of vocal residents and argued that their actions led to a "good" outcome for the maximum possible number of people ("Susan Stanton's Story," 2012). In October 2012, Stanton was hired as the city manager of Greenfield, California.

Lesson. This scenario should not present an ethical conflict. If the city manager were somehow unable to perform at the same caliber because of being transgendered, then the scenario could merit termination. But for the Commission to make such an evaluation based solely on citizen outcry—any credence to the employee's actual performance notwithstanding—is wholly improper and sends a signal to the community that it is acceptable to be biased and ill-informed.

Questions to Consider

1. Did the *St. Petersburg Times* dutifully fulfill a journalistic duty to publish the story that "outed" Stanton, despite being against her wishes?

2. Does one's gender identity affect his or her ability to fulfill professional responsibilities?

3. Was the Commission correct in hearing citizen comments regarding Stanton's transition in a public forum?

4. Should the public's opinion regarding a personal element of an official's life influence the official's employment standing?

5. Did Stanton have an obligation to make her transition known to the Commission prior to the article being published?

Behavioral Ethics-Based Analysis. The language of behavioral ethics can be used to further dissect this scenario. System 1 thinking based on rapid, intuitive, visceral reactions characterized the general reaction to Stanton's gender reassignment, precluding more reflective and deliberative System 2 consideration of the matter. By becoming the "political issue," Stanton misjudged the reaction of her colleagues and community, perceiving them to be more progressive in their attitudes than they were. Alternatively, she knew of the risks and decided to go public with her gender reassignment anyway. The bias and stereotypic thinking demonstrated by the press, the Commission, and the vocal portions of the community compromised Stanton's ability to continue in her managerial role. The absence of transgender support groups and an ethics code with teeth provided no counterweight to the overwhelming negative response to Stanton's transgender status.

CONCLUSION

The distinction between political ethics and administrative ethics is often overdrawn. Many of the same values and ethical principles—problems and dilemmas—are encountered by both appointed and elected public servants. Conflicts of interest, insider trading, competing roles and obligations, significance of personal character, temptations to compromise, the value of ethical tenets—these challenges are present regardless of whether one is elected or appointed. However, some issues are more pronounced for elected officials. Citizen and media scrutiny is often more intense, legal requirements are more ambiguous, and political polarization and partisanship make decision-making slower and more treacherous. Expectations for performance are higher for elected officials than for appointed officials, vulnerability to personal attack is greater, and privacy rights are less protected. Similarly, external pressures are more overt, job security is less certain, and accountability is regularly demanded.

Elected legislators and executives face particular challenges. They can be leaders or emissaries, truthful or deceptive. They can be guided by core values and public service obligations, or succumb to the pressures and temptations that lead to compromising ethical principles and violating their oath of office. The citizenry, unfortunately, is exposed to too many instances of the latter and too few of the former. Recall the epigram opening this chapter ("Art, like morality, consists of drawing the line somewhere"). Public officials—elected or appointed—have to make distinctions between what they "should" and "should not" do, realizing that some lines are drawn for them and some are drawn by them. Then they need the moral courage to do the right thing.

***

The whole art of government consists in the art of being honest.

—Thomas Jefferson

NOTE

1. For a compelling argument that virtue ethics (Chapter 6) is a way to deal with the struggle, see Tholen (2013); also consult Anderson (2014).

DISCUSSION

1. How would you assess the effectiveness of the House and Senate Ethics Committees? Read Appendix 11.1 before answering. What reforms would you propose for handling ethical wrongdoing by members of Congress? How likely is it that your suggestions would be feasible and effective?

2. Discuss the following statements and questions:

   - "We expect leaders to be truthful even though we suspect that they will not be."
   - Where is the line drawn between constituent service and conflict of interest? Current methods of campaign finance amount to informal bribery. How would you refute or support this assertion?
   - How can insider trading among public officials be stopped? Is new legislation needed? How likely is it that your suggestions would be feasible and effective?
   - "All members of Congress have a primary interest in being reelected. Some members have no other interest."
   - Why are there far more emissaries than leaders among today's politicians?
   - What criteria can and should be used to evaluate the performance of politicians? What role should ethics play in such assessments?

- What can be done to curb polarization of politics? How likely is it that your suggestions would be efficacious?
- Which of the examples of presidential deception listed is most egregious? Why?

3. In a polarized political climate, many legislators vote the "party line," seemingly irrespective of the merits of issues or what is for the greater good. Using the ethics triad and the tenets of behavioral ethics (Chapter 7), is such conduct ethical? Why or why not?

4. Comment on this observation:

- "God has a special providence for fools, drunks, and the United States of America."— Otto von Bismark

5. The Liar's Paradox—"I am lying"—provokes an odd sequence: If the assertion is true, then it is false; if it is false, it then seems true. Contemplate this statement and apply it to a current event or political figure.

6. The chapter ends by discussing how public servants often confront difficult choices and need political courage to act. Consider the advice that Eleanor Roosevelt ("Do what you feel in your heart to be right, for you'll be criticized anyway") and Ernest Hemingway ("I know only that what is moral is what you feel good after and what is immoral is what you feel bad after") offer as officials respond to compelling challenges.

EXERCISES

1. Identify any one of the 535 members of the current Congress who you believe meets the qualifications of a moral exemplar (consider criteria discussed in this chapter). Write a two-page essay justifying your selection of this person and the criteria used.

2. Visit PolitiFact.com's Truth-O-Meter and examine the facts provided on an issue or candidate. How useful is such a source in determining whether to support candidates for public office? Why?

3. **Bad Actor Tabletop Exercise 4:** "The Bad President." Instructions (see Chapter 3, Exercise 6)

   Senator John Ross III is currently running for office as the President of the United States of America. The public is wary of Senator Ross because of his position on a number of issues during his time on the Senate. Ross knows that his chances of being elected will be much higher if he changes his stance on critical issues during his campaign. He plans to release a campaign video making promises to push issues during his presidency that he did not support in the Senate. If elected, the Senator has no intention of keeping those promises.

   Role 1: Independent Journalist
   You are a journalist who hears from a credible source that Senator Ross plans on breaking his campaign promises. The source is willing to go on record. In light of this information, how do you react? Consider your obligations, ethical and otherwise. To whom are you accountable as an independent journalist? What factors impact your decision?

Role 2: Campaign Manager

You are Senator Ross' campaign manager. As you have firsthand knowledge of the Senator's platform, Ross comes to you to advise him regarding this new campaign video. Do you support his decision or try to persuade him to take a different approach? Consider your obligations, ethical and otherwise. To whom are you accountable as campaign manager? What factors impact your decision?

Role 3: Running Mate

Senator Ross has tapped you to run alongside him during his presidential campaign. You become aware of his intent to make false campaign promises. How do you react? Do you accept the Senator's offer or decline? Consider your obligations, ethical and otherwise. To whom are you accountable as the potential Vice President of the United States? What factors impact your decision?

Role 4: Industry Executive/Donor

You are a top executive in a leading industry. You have been negotiating with Senator Ross, who is seeking funding from you for his campaign. In return, you expect to have some influence on forthcoming policy that impacts your industry. You are informed of the Senator's intent to renege on the campaign promises. How does this knowledge impact your decision to fund his campaign? Consider your obligations, ethical and otherwise. To whom are you accountable as a professional? What factors impact your decision?

Role 5: Public Official/Supporter

You are a public official in the same state as Senator Ross. As such, you have decided to publicly support his campaign. Just before you have made your statement, you become aware that he has been making false campaign promises. Does this impact your decision to support the Senator? Do you feel obligated to inform the public of his intentions? Consider your obligations, ethical and otherwise. To whom are you accountable as an official? What factors impact your decision?

REFERENCES

Abad-Santos, A. (2012, October 8). Lucky for Congress, blatant conflict of interest is still perfectly legal. *The Atlantic*. Retrieved from www.theatlantic.com/.../lucky-congress-blatant-conflict-interest-still-perfectly-legal/322790/

Alterman, E. (2004). *When presidents lie: A history of official deception and its consequences*. New York: Penguin.

Anderson, J. (2014). An open letter to "dirty hands" theorists from a public manager. *Public Integrity*, *16*(3), 305–316.

Blake, A. (2020, September 10). The remarkable—and growing—onslaught of bad news for Trump. *Washington Post*. Retrieved from www.washingtonpost.com/politics/2020/09/10/remarkable-growing-onslaught-bad-news-trump/

Blow, C. (2012, November 1). Liberty to lie. *New York Times*. Retrieved from http://campaignstops.blogs.nytimes.com/2012/11/01/liberty-to-lie/

Blow, C. (2017, October 19). Trump isn't Hitler, but the lying . . . *New York Times*. Retrieved from https://nyti.ms/2zlXjPA

Boot, M. (2020, October 13). How can 42 percent of Americans still support the worst president in our history? *Washington Post*. Retrieved from www.washingtonpost.com/opinions/2020/10/13/how-can-42-percent-americans-still-support-worst-president-our-history/

Brooks, D. (2017, July 14). Moral vacuum in the house of Trump. *New York Times*. Retrieved from www.nytimes.com/2017/07/14/opinion/donald-trump-family-ethics.html

Bump, P. (2020, November, 28). If there is any real evidence of fraud, Mr. President, it's time to put up. *Washington Post*. Retrieved from www.washingtonpost.com/politics/2020/11/28/if-there-is-any-real-evidence-fraud-mr-president-its-time-put-up/

Burke, E. (1774). *Speech to the electors of Bristol*. Retrieved from http://press-pubs.uchicago.edu/founders/documents/v1ch13s7.html

Carter, S. (1996). *Integrity*. New York: Harper Perennial.

Carter, S. (1998). *Civility*. New York: Basic Books.

Clarke, R. (2009). *Against all enemies: Inside America's war on terror*. New York: Free Press.

Coady, C. (2009). The problem of dirty hands. In E. N. Zalta (Ed.), *The Stanford encyclopedia of philosophy* (summer 2011 ed.). Retrieved from http://plato.stanford.edu/archives/sum2011/entries/dirty-hands/

Cooper, T., & Wright, D. (1992). *Exemplary public administrators: Character and leadership in government*. San Francisco: Jossey-Bass.

Cunningham, A. (1992). The moral importance of dirty hands. *Journal of Value Inquiry, 26*(2), 239–250.

Dallek, R. (2010). Presidential fitness and presidential lies. *Presidential Studies Quarterly, 40*, 9–22.

Dobel, J. (1999). *Public integrity*. Baltimore, MD: Johns Hopkins University Press.

Dovi, S. (2005). Guilt and the problem of dirty hands. *Constellations, 12*(1), 128–146.

Editorial Board. (2020, December 26) The U.S. was supposed to be equipped to handle a pandemic. So what went wrong? *The Washington Post*. Retrieved from www.washingtonpost.com/opinions/the-us-was-supposed-to-be-equipped-to-handle-a-pandemic-s-what-went-wrong/2020/12/24/021ec42c-453f-11eb-97c-d17b8815a66d_story.html

Ekman, P. (2009). *Telling lies: Clues to deceit in the marketplace, politic and marriage*. New York: W. W. Norton.

Escobedo, T. (2010, March 12). *Journey from Steven to Susan captured in new documentary*. Retrieved from http://www//cnn.com/2010/LIVING/03/10/her.name.was.steven/index.html

Falvey, J. (1991). The congressional ethics dilemma: Constituent service or conflict of interest. *American Criminal Law Review, 28*, 323–382.

Farina, X. (2015). Congressional polarization: Terminal constitutional dysfunction. *Columbia Law Review* Retrieved from https://columbialawreview.org/content/congressional-polarization-terminal-constitutional-dysfunction-2/

Feldman, J. (2013, April 23). *John Stewart tears up Congress for quietly scaling back insider trading law: The "f*cker Act."* Retrieved from www.mediaite.com/tv/jon-stewart-tears-up-congress-for-quietly-scaling-back-insider-trading-law-the-fcker-act/

Ford, M. (2021, March 22). Much ado about masks. *PA Times*. Retrieved from https://patimes.org/much-ado-about-masks/

Fried, C., & Fried, G. (2011, May 5). Torture apologists stain triumph over bin Laden. *Washington Post*. Retrieved from http://articles.washingtonpost.com/2011-05-05/opinions/35232191_1_osama-bin-laden-abbottabad-torture

Fromkin, D. (2010). The two most essential, abhorrent, intolerable lies of George W. Bush's memoir. *Huffington Post*. Retrieved from www.huffingtonpost.com/2010/11/22/the-two-most-essential-a_n_786219.html

Gall, C., & Rohde, D. (2004, September 17). New charges raise questions on abuse at Afghan prisons. *New York Times*. Retrieved from www.nytimes.com/2004/09/17/international/asia/17afghan.html?_r=0

Geer, J. G. (2006). *In defense of negativity: Attack ads in presidential campaigns*. Chicago: University of Chicago Press.

Gold, D. (2017). The challenge: Making truth-telling the norm. *Whistleblower*, Spring, p. 3.

Greenleaf, R. K. (2002). *Servant leadership: A journey into the nature of legitimate power and greatness*. New York: Paulist.

Grossman, M. (2008). *Political corruption in America*. Amenia, NY: Grey House.

Gutmann, A., & Thompson, D. (2010). The mindsets of political compromise. *Perspectives on Politics, 8*, 1125–1143.

Gutmann, A., & Thompson, D. (2012). *The spirit of compromise: Why governing demands it and campaigning undermines it*. Princeton, NJ: Princeton University Press.

Hagopian Institute. (2008). *Quote junkie presidents edition: Hundreds of the greatest quotes from the greatest men ever to run our fine country*. CreateSpace Independent.

Hill, A., Ridge, J., & Ingram, A. (2017, February 24). The growing conflict-of-interest problem in the U.S. Congress. *Harvard Business Review*. Retrieved from https://hbr.org/2017/02/the-growing-conflict-of-interest-problem-in-the-u-s-congress

Hohmann, J. (2017, August 2). The Daily 202: Jeff Flake delivers the most courageous conservative rebuttal of Trump yet. *Washington Post*. Retrieved from www.washingtonpost.com/news/powerpost/paloma/daily-202/

Isikoff, M., & Corn, D. (2006). *Hubris: The inside story of spin, scandal, and the selling of the Iraq War*. New York: Crown.

Joint Statement from Elections Infrastructure Government Coordinating, Council and the Election Infrastructure Sector Coordinating Executive Committees (2020, November 12). Washington, DC: Cybersecurity and Infrastructure Security Agency.

Josephson, M. (2002). *Making ethical decisions*. Los Angeles: Josephson Institute of Ethics.

Josephson, M. (2006). The six pillars of character. In J. West & E. Berman (Eds.), *The ethics edge* (pp. 18–23). Washington, DC: International City/County Management Association.

Jurecic, Q. (2017, January 27). Can a president who disregards the truth uphold his oath of office? *Washington Post*. Retrieved from www.washingtonpost.com/posteverything/wp/2017/01/27/can-a.

Kelman, L. (2018). Rising trash talk in our politics: The latest uncivil debate. *AP News*. Retrieved from https://apnews.com/article/fdd079d501f7433c915f8b31d9f7ffdd

Kern, J. (2006). The use of the "ethical triangle" in military decision making. *Public Administration and Management, 11(1)*, 22–43.

Kessler, G. (2020, December 18). The biggest Pinocchios of 2020. *The Washington Post*. Retrieved from www.washingtonpost.com/politics2020/12/18/biggest-piocchios-2020/

Kessler, G., Kelly, M., & Rizzo, S. (2020, July 15). Analysis: President Trump has made more than 20,000 false or misleading claims. *The Washington Post*. Retrieved from www.washingtonpost.com/

Kinzer, S. (2007). *Blood of brothers: Life and war in Nicaragua*. Cambridge, MA: Harvard University Press.

Krebs, C. (2020, December 1). Trump fired me for saying this, but I'll say it again: The election was not rigged. *Washington Post*. Retrieved from www.washingtonpost.com/opinions/christopher-krebs-trump-election-wasnt-hacked/2020/12/01/88da94a0-340f-11eb-8d38-6aea1adb3839_story.html

Kristoff, N. (2017). What did the president know and when did he know it. *New York Times*. Retrieved from www.nytimes.com/2017/02/15/opinion/what-did-trump-know-and-when-did-he-know-it.html

Lawder, D., & Cowan, R. (2013, April 12). U.S. Congress quietly repeals plan for internet financial disclosures. Retrieved from www.reuters.com/assets/print/aid-USL.2N0C120130412

Levine, N. (2017, August 10). *Bridging the gap between political appointees and civil servants*. Retrieved from www.govexec.com/excellence/promising-practices/2-17/08/bridging-gap-between-political-appointees-and-civil-servants/140146/WY97?BocJrhM.email

Lieber, R. (2020, November 14). Time to take a pledge: No stocks if you are a member of Congress. *New York Times*. Retrieved from www.nytimes.com/2020/11/14/your-money/congress-stocks-divest.html

Lipton, E. (2011, September 5). A congresswoman's cause is often her husband's gain. *New York Times*. Retrieved from www.nytimes.com/2011/09/06/us/06berkley.htmPpagewanted=all

MacNeil, N. (1963). *Forge of democracy: The House of Representatives*. New York: D. McKay.

Maisel, L. (2012). The negative consequences of uncivil political discourse. *PS: Political Science & Politics*, *45*, 405–411.

Mann, T., & Ornstein, N. (2012). *It's even worse than it looks: How the American constitutional system collided with the new politics of extremism*. New York: Basic Books.

Margasak, L. (2012, February 28). Insider trading in Congress: New regulations to open window into transactions. *Huffington Post*. Retrieved from www.huffingtonpost.com/2012/02/28/insider-trading-congress-stock-act_n_1306301.html

Marion, N. (2010). *The politics of disgrace*. Durham, NC: Carolina Academic Press.

Mayhew, D. (2004). *Congress: The electoral connection*. New Haven, CT: Yale University Press.

McBride, A. (1990). Ethics in Congress: Agenda and action. *George Washington Law Review*, *58*, 451–487.

Moore, M. (1981). Realms of obligation and virtue. In J. Fleishman, L. Liebman, & M. Moore (Eds.), *Public duties: The moral obligations of government officials* (pp. 3–21). Cambridge, MA: Harvard University Press.

Newell, T. (2015). *To serve with honor: Doing the right thing in government*. Crozet, VA: Loftland Press.

Nichols, J. (2019, January 25). What did the president know and when did he know it? *The Nation*. Retrieved from www.thenation.com/article/archive/roger-stone-trump-impeachment-nixon/

Nivola, P. (2010). Partisanship in perspective. *National Affairs*, *5*, 91–104.

Nye, J. (2020). *Do morals matter? Presidents and foreign policy from FDR to Trump*. New York: Oxford University Press.

Paul, C., & Matthews, M. (2016). The Russian "firehose of falsehood" propaganda model: Why it might work and options to counter it. *RAND Corporation Perspective Series Paper*. Retrieved from www.rand.org/pubs/perspectives/PE198.html

Pear, R. (2012, March 22). Insider trading ban for lawmakers clears Congress. *New York Times*. Retrieved from www.nytimes.com/2012/03/23/us/politics/insider-trading-ban-for-lawmakers-clears-congress.html

Planas, R. (2012). I'm right, you're wrong no, you're wrong, I'm right. *Reason & Politics*. Retrieved from www.reasonandpolitics.com/home.html

Public Citizen. (2017). *Congressional ethics*. Retrieved from www.citizen.org/our-work/government-reform/government-ethics-and-lobbying-reform/congressional-ethics

Public Citizen. (2017, June 22). *The impact of the STOCK act on stock trading activity by U.S. senators, 2009–2015*. Retrieved from www.citizen.org/system/files/case_documents/2017_stock_act_report.pdf

Reilly, K. (2016, September 10). Read Hillary Clinton's 'basket of deplorables' remarks about Donald Trump's supporters. *Time*. Retrieved from https://time.com/4486502/hillary-clinton-basket-of-deplorables-transcript/

Rich, F. (2012, June 17). Frank Rich: Nuke 'em. *New York Times*. Retrieved from http://nymag.com/news/frank-rich/negative-campaigning-2012-6/

Rucker, P., Parker, A., Dawsey, J., & Gardner, A. (2020, November 29). 20 days of fantasy and failure: Inside Trump's quest to overturn the election. *Washington Post*. Retrieved from www.msn.com/en-us/news/politics/20-days-of-fantasy-and-failure-inside-trumps-quest-to-overturn-the-election/ar-BB1bs02h

Sargent, G. (2017, March 6). At the root of Trump's new fury: Total contempt for American democracy. *Washington Post*. Retrieved from www.washingtonpost.com/blogs/plum-line/wp/2017/03/06/at.

Straus, J. (2011a). *Enforcement of Congressional rules of conduct: An historical overview (Congressional Research Service Report)*. Retrieved from www.fas.org/sgp/crs/misc/RL30764.pdf

Straus, J. (2011b). *House Committee on Ethics: A brief history of its evolution and jurisdiction (Congressional Research Service Report)*. Retrieved from http://ethics.house.gov/sites/ethics.house.gov/files/HouseCommitteEthics3%202011%20Straus.pdf

Straus, J. (2011c). *House Office of Congressional Ethics: History, authority, and procedures (Congressional Research Service Report)*. Retrieved from http://waxman.house.gov/sites/waxman.house.gov/files/House%20Office%20of%20Congressional%20Ethics%20History%20Authority%20and%20Procedures.pdf

Straus, J. (2011d). *Senate Select Committee on Ethics: A brief history of its evolution and jurisdiction (Congressional Research Service Report)*. Retrieved from www.fas.org/sgp/crs/misc/RL30650.pdf

Susan Stanton's Story. (2012, January 19). Unitarian Universalist Association of Congregations. Retrieved from www.uua.org/re/tapestry/adults/ethics/workshop3/workshopplan/stories/191788.shtml

Tholen, B. (2013). Dirty hands or political virtue? Walzer's and MacIntyre's answers to Machiavelli's challenge. *Public Integrity*, *15*, 187–202.

Thompson, D. (1981a). Moral responsibility and the New York City financial crisis. In J. Fleishman, L. Liebman, & M. Moore (Eds.), *Public duties: The moral obligations of government officials* (pp. 266–289). Cambridge, MA: Harvard University Press.

Thompson, D. (1981b). The private lives of public officials. In J. Fleishman, L. Liebman, & M. Moore (Eds.), *Public duties: The moral obligations of government officials* (pp. 221–248). Cambridge, MA: Harvard University Press.

Thompson, D. (1995). *Ethics in Congress*. Washington, DC: Brookings Institution.

Thompson, D. (2006). Private life and public office. In J. West & E. Berman (Eds.), *The ethics edge* (pp. 156–166). Washington, DC: International City/County Management Association.

Thompson, D. (2010). Constitutional character: Virtues and vices in presidential leadership. *Presidential Studies Quarterly*, *40*, 23–37.

Tolchin, M., & Tolchin, S. (2001). *Glass houses*. Boulder, CO: Westview Press.

U.S. House of Representatives Committee on Ethics. (n.d.). *Policies underlying disclosure*. Retrieved from http://ethics.house.gov/financial-dislosure/policies-underlying-disclosure

Waldo, D. (2009). Public administration and ethics: A prologue to a preface. In R. Stillman (Ed.), *Public administration: Concepts and cases* (pp. 472–482). Boston, MA: Wadsworth.

Walzer, M. (1974). Political action: The problem of dirty hands. In M. Cohen, T. Nagel, & T. Scanlon (Eds.), *War and moral responsibility*. Princeton, NJ: Princeton University Press, 62–82.

Wasserman, E. (2013, April 22). Privacy invasion requires good reason. *Miami Herald*, p. 13A.

Williamson, E. (2021, January 12). Trump's conduct spurs push for ethics rules tougher than shame. *New York Times*. National Section, p. A10.

Woodward, B. (2020). *Rage*. New York: Simon & Schuster.

Appendix 11.1

Ethics Committees

Article I, Section 5, of the Constitution delegates to the House and Senate the exclusive authority to draft rules of conduct for their members, as well as the sole discretion to discipline and expel them. However, for much of the nation's history, Congress operated without a formalized code of ethics or standardized procedures for adjudicating allegations of improper conduct. It was not until the 1960s that Congress began to shift away from the regime of informal rules and ad hoc procedures that left punishment to be meted out mainly by public opinion and electoral outcomes. In 1964, in the wake of a bribery scandal involving the secretary to the Senate Majority Leader, the Senate created the Select Committee on Standards and Conduct (now the Select Committee on Ethics). The House followed suit in 1967, establishing the Committee on Standards of Official Conduct (now the Committee on Ethics). Both committees immediately went to work on drafting codes for their respective members, staff, and employees. When first drafted, they covered such topics as campaign finance and financial disclosure. They have since been amended to include rules governing gifts, outside earned income, conflicts of interest, foreign travel, franking, political advertising, and lobbying.

Both committees are unique in that their membership is constituted in a bipartisan fashion. They consist of equal numbers of members from each party (five from each party in the House and three from each party in the Senate). Such a balanced structure is intended to avoid the politicization of the ethics process. The work of each committee is divided between advising members and staff on rules of conduct and investigating and adjudicating cases of misconduct. Yet it is here that the similarities between the two committees end. While the structure and jurisdiction of the Senate committee has remained fairly static over the years, the House committee has a more colorful history, which has resulted in a more complex structure that has expanded to include an external review body. The three major periods of House ethics reform—1989, 1997, and 1998—serve to illustrate the structural and procedural differences between the two chambers' ethics committees.

While many minor procedural changes were adopted in the 1970s, substantive House ethics reform was not seriously considered until 1989, a high-profile year for ethical controversy in the House. That year the Savings and Loan crisis precipitated numerous investigations into the "constituent service" activities of members. These investigations did not stop at the Keating Five in the Senate. Speaker of the House Jim Wright was forced to resign after the Ethics Committee found evidence of upwards of 60 violations of House rules. He was followed out by the Majority Whip. The sights were set on the Minority Whip, who had begun the investigation, and then the chairmen of the Banking Committee and Defense Appropriations Subcommittee (Falvey, 1991; McBride, 1990).

Out of the chaos emerged the Ethics Reform Act of 1989, which stipulated, among other things, a meso-ethics strategy that the investigative and adjudicative functions of the committee be segregated. Thus, when allegations of ethics violations are brought to the committee, an ad hoc investigative subcommittee is convened. If this subcommittee discovers any violations and submits formal charges to the chair, a separate ad hoc adjudicative subcommittee consisting of the chair, ranking member, and the committee members who did not participate in the investigative subcommittee is formed. In contrast, the Senate committee does not require that the investigation and adjudication of ethics violations proceed separately. The full Senate committee also assumes the burden of advisory and educational (i.e., ethics training) responsibilities, which the 1989 Act delegated to a separate Office of Advice and Education in the House Committee on Ethics.

The legislation addressed the meso level of ethics by attempting to alter the organizational culture of the institution. The presence of impartial committees with genuine jurisdiction over ethical violations is a signal to members in the House and Senate that ethics is taken seriously. The 1997 House Ethics Reform Task Force analyzed some of the lingering concerns over the process. Most notably, the Task Force recommended a requirement that nonmembers be prohibited from filing an ethics complaint unless a member can certify that the complaint is submitted in good faith and warrants consideration. No such requirements exist in the Senate, where anybody inside or outside Congress can bring forth charges of ethical impropriety against a senator. Ten years later, in 2007, another task force, the Special Task Force on Ethics Enforcement in the House of Representatives, was established to consider whether establishing an outside enforcement entity would address growing concerns over the closed nature of the Committee on Ethics' proceedings. The following year the House voted to create the Office of Congressional Ethics composed of six members jointly appointed by House leaders, which can initiate independent investigations of allegations lodged by the general public. The Senate has not created a corresponding external entity. Its Select Committee on Ethics continues to collect and investigate internally all allegations of senatorial misconduct.

Sources: Unless otherwise noted, the narrative is drawn from Straus (2011a, 2011b, 2011c, 2011d).

12 Organizational Gaming and Performance Measurement

Integrity is one of several paths. It distinguishes itself from the others because it is the right path, and the only one upon which you will never get lost.

—M. H. Mckee

This chapter is limited in scope to efforts by organizations to take advantage of "loopholes in the rules and system" and, even more specifically, to "manipulate performance criteria" or "gaming" (Bohte & Meier, 2000, 175; Fisher & Downes, 2008, 248). While Chapter 9 presented an overview of both individual and organizational corruption, here the focus is exclusively on this narrower concept of organizational cheating. The chapter objectives include examining:

- what motivates organizational gaming,
- ways to ethically evaluate cheating,
- types of institutional manipulation,
- a program design to affect organizational "fudging,"
- the link between performance measurement and gaming behavior,
- the consequences of fraud, and
- strategies to prevent or minimize fakery.

The epigram alludes to integrity as the right path whereupon one will never be lost. Manipulation would be a wrong path that often—but not always—leads to bad outcomes. Stated differently, manipulation is an example of what Stephen Carter (1996, 13) refers to as "unintegrity". Repeated acts of this kind can result in getting away with things known to be wrong. The discussion begins by considering some of the pressures that contribute to cheating, and the nexus between performance measurement and manipulation. Specific cases of gaming the system in education are considered. Attention then turns to different types of organizational gaming, followed by a brief section on the role of politicians and public opinion. The last two topics, prior to the conclusion, consider ethical evaluation of fudging and ways to prevent or minimize it.

DOI: 10.4324/9781003203148-16

DUPLICITY PRESSURES

What stresses contribute to cheating? In a competitive economy, the need to perform, meet expectations, achieve standards, and avoid failure is intense in all sectors of the economy. As contracting and outsourcing have become more common, governments and nonprofit organizations have had to step up their game to retain their monopoly power or to have their service contracts renewed. The more competitive the environment, the greater temptations there are to deceive, especially when safeguards against wrongdoing are absent. There are often substantial rewards associated with fraud, at least in the short term. Indeed, as Callahan (2004, Chapter 6) has observed, a "trickle-down" effect occurs when people make up their own moral code because they think the system is not fair; they start cheating a little more, and then it accelerates into cheating a lot. The same effect can occur in organizations (Haines, 2003–2004). Such spillover occurs between the micro, meso, and macro levels of ethics. Individuals within an organization can alter the institution as a whole (micro–meso), and organizations can influence markets and civil society (meso–macro).

Coupled with external pressures are those internal to the organization. Sometimes there are counterintuitive influences—setting goals can actually incentivize unethical decision-making. For example, the overcharging of customers and hiding of financial losses conducted by Sears and Enron employees can be traced back to how goals were set for the corporations. Sears set difficult sales goals ($147/hour) and linked commissions to meeting these quotas. Enron established a "performance unit plan" whereby executives received large bonuses based on the company's financial success (Barsky, 2008, 63–64).

Similar goal setting and performance plans are created in government and nonprofit organizations, often mandated by law or required by contract (Berman, 2006; Cooper, 2000; DeHoog & Salamon, 2002; de Lancer Julnes & Gibson, 2015; James et al., 2020; Liff, 2014). For instance, the 1993 Government Performance and Results Act requires that every federal department submit a strategic plan to Congress, plans that typically include productivity measures. Such measurement gone awry can lead to gaming the system. To use some examples from local government, consider solid waste haulers who water down the garbage before weighing the truck (to gain rewards based on performance targets measured by the full truck weight), school enrollment specialists (who inflate the number of enrollees in order to get more state funds), or police officers who increase the number of tickets issued (to meet a standard and earn a reward).

Autocratic goal setting led to Air Force officers cheating on exams measuring ICBM launching ability because commanders insisted on a 100 percent test score and used the exam as the only promotion criterion (Cooper, 2014). The Department of Veteran Affairs faced with too many service demands from returning veterans and too few staff, imposed an unrealistic work standard that each patient be seen within 14 days of requesting an appointment, thereby incentivizing cheating as staff misreported the number of veterans asking for and waiting for care in order to meet the standard (Jaffe & Hicks, 2014). In other words, goals can have a downside when employees are too fixated on them (neglecting non-goal areas), when goals prompt risky behavior, when external motivators override intrinsic motivation, and when objectives nudge employees toward more unethical behaviors than they would engage in absent the goal (Ordonez et al., 2009).

The conceptual link between falsification and performance measurement is that democratic governance requires both a large technical bureaucracy as well as accountability.

Because it is difficult to gauge the often intangible ends of public service delivery, elected officials frequently fall back on shorthand indicators when judging agency action. The resultant problem? "Rather than measuring the final *outcomes* of bureaucratic activity, those who evaluate the performance of public bureaucracies often pay more attention to the *outputs* these agencies produce" (Bohte & Meier, 2000, 174). This can result in goal displacement, as "agencies focus on generating numbers that please political officials, rather than devoting their energies to achieving more meaningful policy outcomes" (174).

This myopia is a dangerous dynamic because continued political and financial support is predicated on a measurement scale that does not necessarily match up with the overarching mission of the organization. Thus, the dilemma:

> Engage in goal displacement and seek to meet the standard even if it affects performance in a detrimental manner, or continue to seek the larger goal and hope that success in the actual mission will also produce success on the performance standard. (179–180)

This can encourage gaming—reliance on loopholes and manipulation of evaluation criteria to meet expectations. Considerable vulnerability occurs when monitoring of service providers is limited and bureaucracies are decentralized, as is often the case in social welfare, health, and education programs. This is especially true in institutions wherein resources are scarce and expectations are overwhelming—a typical circumstance in many jurisdictions. "Outside observers demand results, regardless of how intractable an agency's task may be" (180).

As such, the nature of goal setting in organizations generates natural/internal incentives to cheat/game. However, these internal incentives can be compounded by tangible, external incentives, such as incentive-based structures embedded in program designs. Some structures abet manipulation to receive program benefits, like cities that dismissed employees, later hiring them back with federal monies available under the Comprehensive Employment and Training Act of 1973 or school districts that offer bonuses to teachers, contingent on student test scores. In more than a few cases, teachers or principals have been involved in erasing or correcting student answers on exams to boost performance ratings (see Case Studies 12.1 and 12.2, Exercise 3, the "Bad Teacher"; see also Chapter 7). Thus, the incentive structure is decisive in influencing the decision to game the system. The cases below illustrate the ways cheating occurs by gaming the system to gain advantage in the field of secondary and higher education.

CASE STUDY 12.1

Organizational Cheating in Education

During the last generation, cheating has permeated the education system. From elementary to university levels, and from student to administrative perpetrators, it has become a grave issue in American education. In light of reforms such as No Child Left Behind and Race to the Top initiatives—as well as growing pressures placed both on students and on teachers to increase performance—the country has become a petri dish for cheating experimentation. Students have been compelled to achieve certain numerical scores on standardized tests and school examinations to succeed through the increasingly competitive university application and selection process. Similarly, public schools have felt great pressure under the implementation of teacher performance measures tied directly to student achievement, federal grants linked to standardized test scores, and cash bonuses for improved test results.

The Atlanta Public School System, like many others across the country, revolves around a standardized test to measure student success, teacher ability, and, most significantly, state and federal funding. The state of Georgia has received recognitions for its improvement in elementary education. These acknowledgments are attached to monetary aid and depend directly on the results of the state's Criterion Reference Competency Test (CRCT). Bonuses were given to every employee of the schools with high passing rates. Georgia's superintendent at the time, Beverly Hall, focused solely on the exam scores to begin measuring teacher achievement rather than student aptitude (Aviv, 2014; Frysh, 2011). Over 178 teachers and principals were investigated in 44 schools and charged with cheating on the statewide examination; later, nearly three dozen would be indicted on racketeering, false statements, and theft (Brumback, 2013; Strauss, 2011). Using several different methods, these professionals directly and indirectly altered exam results to keep their jobs, receive bonuses, and ensure federal and state funding. The national attention the case received spurred investigations in Denver, Washington, DC, and elsewhere.

State auditors in Denver found that school administrators had been allegedly erasing student responses on state standardized exams and filling in the correct answer, much like their colleagues in Georgia. In Denver, two teachers "met with the School's [Beach Court Elementary] Administration to discuss the fact that their students' Colorado Student Assessment Program scores were not reflective of the students' classroom performance" (Auge, 2012). In Washington, DC, 103 schools "had test erasure rates that indicated possible cheating from 2008 to 2010" (Whitesell, 2012). In DC, however, it was the teachers, who feel great stress over job stability and the need for federal aid, who had been allegedly participating in the scandal.

While they were not changing answers on exams, other school districts resorted to misusing and misreporting data to receive funding. For example, in Ohio, several districts were found to have been tampering with attendance records to improve school and district report cards. Over 2 million absences were wiped from the system in a practice known as "scrubbing": dropping students from the roster and adding them later in the year, because scores for students who are not enrolled from beginning to end do not affect the school's report card (Zhao, 2012). In essence, administrators were cherry picking pupils who perform well as the only determinants of the school report card, omitting the scores of underperforming students resulting in misreported and false data.

Claremont McKenna College, along with many other universities, is not exempt from the gaming phenomenon. With the heightened weight given to college rankings, higher education has also fallen into cheating through the misreporting of data to climb the ranks. For the last 25 years, the small university had fallen outside the rankings' top ten liberal arts colleges. That all changed in the years following 2005. Since then, Claremont McKenna has boasted the ninth and tenth spots on the popular ranking in *U.S. News & World Report*. However, in 2012, the president of Claremont McKenna, Pamela Gann, revealed that a manager of the admissions office had been inflating student SAT scores by 10–20 points to remain competitive in nationwide rankings (Strauss, 2012). Colleges such as Baylor University, Villanova University, and Iona College have all been found guilty of similar fraudulent and deceptive actions resulting in higher application rates and improved rankings (Perez-Pena & Slotnik, 2012).

A college rankings scandal at the Temple University's Fox School of Business resulted in a $700,000 fine to be paid to the U.S. Department of Education. A settlement was reached in 2020 with the Department to address complaints that the Fox School lied to *U.S. News & World Report* for years (2015–2018) about student scores on the Graduate Management Admission Test (GMAT) in order to achieve a number one ranking for its online MBA program and to bolster enrollments. The scandal erupted in 2018 when *U.S. News* deleted Temple's online MBA program its list of Best Online Programs.

Misinformation was provided regarding the number of student admits reporting GMAT scores when applying, mean grade point averages (GPAs) of admitted students, the number of admissions offered those applying, debt levels of students who borrow, the number of students taking standardized admission tests, and other measures. False information inflated the grade point averages of undergraduate students in some Fox business programs. Education Secretary Betsy DeVos said in a statement about the case, "We know many students rely on rankings to make decisions, and in this case students were presented deliberately falsified information by Temple's Fox School" (Inside Higher Education, 2020).

In light of rampant cheating throughout the country, there have been calls to reform the system and help diminish the need and ability to cheat. The U.S. Department of Education requested that educators and administrators provide ideas on the causes and issues surrounding cheating, including how to restore credibility to a school or district following a scandal (Whitesell, 2012). However, many critics and scholars believe that cheating is inherent in the system that has developed. For example, Leonie Haimson (2012), writing for the *New York Times*, states that "Campbell's Law predicts that any time huge stakes are attached to quantitative data, the data itself will become inherently unreliable and distorted through cheating and gaming the system."

As long as standardized tests and rankings dominate the system, cheating is unlikely to stop. To change the climate in school districts, there needs to be a shift in focus from quantitative data to a holistic approach in which student and teacher assessments go beyond the scores of a single exam. Until such time, there is a small but growing national movement to "opt out" of standardized testing on the grounds that it encourages how to answer multiple-choice questions at the expense of reasoning and critical thinking. Some school administrators have called for a testing moratorium (Layton, 2013). However, the problem continues as shown in Case Study 12.2.

Questions to Consider

1. What are the pros and cons of quantitative performance measurement systems?

2. How can actions gaming the system be reduced?

CASE STUDY 12.2

Gaming the System—College Cheating Scandal

More than 50 people—33 wealthy parents and more than a dozen in colleges who aided and abetted them—were charged in the college admission scam (Eaton, 2019; Richer, 2020). The lure of gaining admission to an elite institution like Stanford, Yale, University of Southern California, and others led privileged parents to game the system by sneaking into the "side door" of college admissions. Some privileged parents may do so feeling they are above the rules of a game that is already unfair. Others may resort to bribing and cheating to get their kids in top schools because they have the resources to do so, something less privileged parents cannot afford (Colarco, 2019). According to the FBI (*New York Times*, 2019), tactics of those involved with the scam were multiple and varied, including

- claiming falsely that their children had learning disabilities to get extra time on admission tests,
- paying stand-ins to cheat on standardized exams,
- paying kickbacks to college coaches and administrators to gain admission,
- photoshopping students' faces onto the bodies of athletes,
- doctoring athletic profiles with fake accomplishments,
- disguising payments as charitable donations.

Payments to secure admission ranged from $15,000 to $75,000 to rig an ACT or SAT test to reports of an anonymous person paying $6.7 million to get his/her children into top schools (Winton, 2019). A fixer with more than 700 clients, William "Rick" Singer, founder of The Edge College and Career Network, was a major player in the scam as a paid intermediary between parents and college personnel to arrange the admissions. Among the charges to those involved in "Operation Varsity Blues" were conspiracy to commit mail and wire fraud, honest service mail and wire fraud, and money laundering. Those who pled guilty and agreed to a plea deal either faced no prison time or a "low end" prison term (four to ten months and a fine around $20,000), and at the "high end" (a prison term of 20 years and a fine of $250,000 to $500,000). Those who pled not guilty and rejected the plea deal would have spent 18–24 months in jail (Kaplan, 2019; Palus, 2019; Surlgua, 2019).

A year following the arrests, the scandal update showed eight parents awaiting trial (including "Full House" star Lori Loughlin and her husband, Mossimo Giannulli); four coaches continuing to contest allegations; 21 parents acknowledging paying bribes or fraudulently subverting the admissions system (including "Desperate Housewives" actress Felicity Huffman); five coaches pleading guilty; and two coaches sentenced with penalties ranging from no prison time to six months in prison (Richer, 2020). Singer pleaded guilty to racketeering, conspiracy, money laundering and obstruction of justice (Surlgua, 2019)

Laughlin and Mr. Giannulli fought the charges for more than a year, but finally pleaded guilty to paying $50,000 as part of the scheme. Ms. Loughlin ultimately completed a two-month prison sentence in December 2020, and Mr. Giannulli was sentenced to five months with scheduled release in April 2021. Ms. Huffman pleaded guilty to paying $15,000 to inflate her daughter's SAT score and expressed contrition. She served 11 days in prison (Taylor, 2020, December 29).

Questions to Consider

1. Should students caught up in the university cheating scandal be punished?

2. How should colleges reform their admission policies?

3. What are the macro, meso, and micro dimensions (Chapter 2) of the scandal?

4. Use the ethics triad to evaluate the sentences and penalties given to those involved in the scam?

5. What behavioral ethics biases (Chapter 7) are useful in understanding this case?

TYPES OF GAMING

When the focus is narrowed to organizational cheating, gaming can take a variety of additional forms: ratchet effects, output distortion, output tunnel vision, cherry picking, favorable focus, and cutting corners (Hendrick & Yazici, 2011).

Ratchet Effects

This phenomenon involves a deliberate attempt by managers to freeze existing performance levels to avoid having expectations ratcheted up in the future. Navy recruiters, for example, are required to be part of a program that rewards high performance. Asch (1990) found that recruiters would calibrate and time their effort to win rewards. In some cases, recruiters stalled their efforts until the deadline for the award was near, or they ramped up their effort by amassing an inventory of potential recruits but deliberately failed to enlist them until their eligibility for an award was established. Once an award is earned, productivity drops, in part because intense effort to gain the reward requires recruiters to scale back and rest, but also because "in order to win a reward they pursued enlistments that they otherwise would have garnered in future months" (104).

Output Distortion

This strategy is among the most common gaming practices. It involves intentional manipulation of results by modifying information and misrepresenting performance as in the Claremont McKenna College and Temple business school cases. In some instances, it includes outright falsification of data (Bohte & Meier, 2000, 175). This makes it difficult for policymakers and stakeholders to know what is going on. Congressional oversight committees and watchdogs are at an "information disadvantage" relative to the agencies they oversee because they cannot keep track of all their activities. Output distortion gives the advantage to managers capitalizing on these "information asymmetries" by divulging to policymakers and citizens distorted data that convey a rosy picture while downplaying less favorable information. Figure 12.1 reports the levels of deceit, from less honest to more honest, in communication manipulation, of both quantitative and qualitative data.

The Environmental Protection Agency's Superfund toxic waste cleanup program under the leadership of Rita Lavelle is one example (Meier, 1985, 64–65). She deliberately misrepresented her record of inspecting toxic waste sites, claiming that objective criteria were used, when it was really political criteria that guided enforcement. Bohte and Meier (2000, 175) caution that "lying essentially violates the trust between bureaucrats and politicians that is necessary for effective governance"; therefore, it is "an extremely high-risk method of cheating." Other high-profile examples of such misleading claims include exaggerated body counts in Vietnam or undercounting "collateral damage," including civilian deaths in Afghanistan.

Exposure of blatant cheating can be a costly deterrent, but cheating is harder to prevent when it is interwoven into the organizational rules and processes. This interweaving, Meier (2008, 4) asserts, is especially evident in educational organizations, given their tendency to

FIGURE 12.1	Levels of Deceit in Data and Information Manipulation

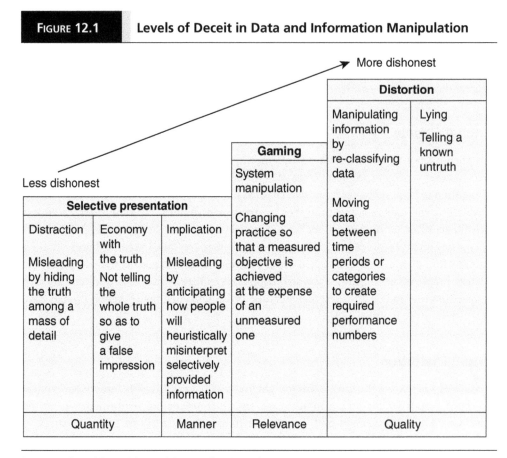

Quantity			Manner	Relevance	Quality	

More dishonest

Distortion

Manipulating information by re-classifying data	Lying Telling a known untruth

Gaming

System manipulation

| Changing practice so that a measured objective is achieved at the expense of an unmeasured one | Moving data between time periods or categories to create required performance numbers |

Less dishonest

Selective presentation

Distraction	Economy with the truth	Implication
Misleading by hiding the truth among a mass of detail	Not telling the whole truth so as to give a false impression	Misleading by anticipating how people will heuristically misinterpret selectively provided information

Quantity	Manner	Relevance	Quality

Source: Adapted from Fisher and Downes (2008, 247).

sort and classify students. Bohte and Meier (2000) found a "moderate amount of cheating" in Texas school districts, with some schools illegitimately exempting low-scoring students from the Texas Assessment of Academic Skills exam under the guise of being special education students or limited English proficiency pupils. This was especially the case in low-income school districts. Similarly, Figlio and Getzler (2002) discovered that Florida schools reclassified low-income and previously low-performing students as disabled—and therefore ineligible to contribute to the school's aggregate Florida Comprehensive Assessment Test score.

Figlio's (2005, 5) subsequent study found that schools "act on the incentive to re-shape the testing pool through selective discipline in response to accountability pressures," a "high-stakes testing regime" implemented in accordance with the No Child Left Behind Act of 2001. Some Florida schools went so far as to allocate longer suspensions to potentially low-performing students than to their high-performing counterparts to ensure that the high performers would be present at test time and low performers would not. Figlio and Winicki (2005) further revealed that schools experiencing accountability pressures upped the caloric content of school lunches in an apparent attempt to improve short-term student cognitive performance on test days.

TABLE 12.1	Types of Gaming	
Type of Gaming	**Behavior Involved**	**Examples**
Ratchet Effects	Deliberately restraining current performance to avoid having to achieve higher levels in the future	Navy incentive program to reward high performance—recruiters calibrated effort to reward
Output Distortion	Deliberately manipulating data and results by various forms of cheating, including altering performance data or misreporting performance	Faked improvements in U.K. A&E hospital wait times to improve rating
Output Tunnel Vision	Improving performance only for qualities that can be measured at the expense of qualities that cannot be or are not measured	Effort substitution to reduce A&E wait times at expense of quality care
Cherry Picking	Reporting on or servicing only cases where high performance can be achieved more easily while neglecting or not reporting hard cases that are costly to handle	Self-selection by police of easy-to-clear crimes versus more difficult cases
Favorable Focus	Supplying, developing, or promoting performance measures that are easy to obtain and favorable of abandoning those that are hard to obtain or unfavorable	Elected officials selecting easy performance targets to reap electoral benefits
Cutting Corners	Doing sloppy work or quick-and-dirty delivery of services in order to boost performance measures	Quick-and-dirty regulatory inspections to look tough on regulation

Source: Adapted from Hendrick and Yazici (2011, 7).

Output distortion is also documented in the airline industry, federal job training programs, and health care (Table 12.1). Gormley and Weimer (1999, 149) reported that "an airline may improve its 'on-time' punctuality performance by 'increasing the predicted length of a flight,'" thus improving "their official statistics without actually improving their performance." Courty and Marschke (2003) examined gaming in federal job training by observing student dismissal patterns in the training system. Training centers were directed to set up programs targeting the economically disadvantaged, and those encountering serious employment barriers, so they could gain needed job skills, achieve better income, and reduce reliance on welfare.

The researchers found that discretion given to centers to terminate enrollees produced sub-optimal results. To cover up poor findings, "centers could postpone terminating enrollees who were unemployed, or if employed, had low wages" because the termination date corresponded to the measurement date of a particular center's employment and wage rates (Courty & Marschke, 2003, 908). In response, the U.S. Department of Labor implemented a 90-day rule that required training agencies not only to measure performance on the termination date but also to discharge any participant who had not received any services for 90 days. The response triggered more cheating.[1]

Police have long recognized the value of gaming the system by relying on number manipulation. Don Winslow in his 2017 novel, *The Force*, illustrates this by showing how administrators, "suits," use numbers as "moneyball" tactics to demonstrate crime reduction:

> The suits love their numbers. . . . This new 'management' breed of cops are like the sabermetrics baseball people—they believe the numbers say it all. And when the numbers don't say what they want them to, they massage them . . . until they get a happy ending. (p. 37)

Winslow shows how this is done:

> The . . . way to manipulate the numbers is to let officers know they should downgrade charges from felonies to misdemeanors. So you call a straight up robbery a "petit larceny," a burglary becomes "lost property," a rape a "sexual assault." Boom—crime is down. Moneyball. (p. 38)

A similar practice is found in programs addressing work and poverty as noted by Soss, Fording, and Schram (2011, 209):

> [S]erious reforms designed to deal with problems of poverty and work are (not surprisingly) often viewed as difficult to achieve, and their performance effects are usually seen as distant and uncertain. It is far easier to change how one classifies existing activities and count measured behaviors. As a result, as one local official told us forthrightly, "people game the numbers all the time."

The final example of output distortion is based on research in U.K. hospital emergency rooms. In 2003, the Department of Health, which oversees the National Health Service (NHS), announced a new initiative regarding wait times in "accident and emergency" (A&E) (equivalent to the American ER) departments. Wait times would be included in the "star rating" system used to rank hospitals. The following year, it was announced that £100,000 would be given to hospitals that showed an increase in the percentage of patients treated within four hours. The Department announced that the A&E performance measurements would be conducted in the final week of March. *The Guardian* reported on the efficacy of the reform: "Two-thirds of NHS A&E departments faked improvements in their wait times during the week chosen by ministers to measure their performance" (Carvel, 2003, 12).

Output Tunnel Vision

This technique seeks to improve achievement, but only for measurable quantities at the expense of qualities incapable of measurement. As Kelman and Friedman (2009, 922–923) point out, "the focusing function of performance measures—'what gets measured gets *noticed*'—can have a dark side—'what gets *measured* gets noticed.'" Examples of "effort substitution" or output tunnel vision include reduced wait time at the expense of quality care, resource transfers (e.g., doctors and nurses) from nonemergency activities to A&E to achieve wait-time goals, and redistribution of wait times so patients who would normally experience short wait times are left waiting for nearly four hours to focus attention on patients who would normally exceed the four-hour threshold.

Cherry Picking

This next form of trickery involves focusing exclusively on cases where high performance is achievable, while costly and difficult cases are neglected or disappear from reports. Cherry picking (sampling bias) occurs in law enforcement agencies as they classify crimes. When officers are evaluated based on clearance rates rather than public safety, there is an incentive to focus on solving crimes. The more difficult cases to solve (break-ins and burglaries) may be classified as "unfounded" in reports, instead of classifying them as real crimes. When assessing probabilities, personnel may conclude that the probability of catching some law breakers (prostitutes, drug dealers) is higher than that of catching a burglar. To achieve high clearance rates, police tend to focus on the easier crimes with less attention to the more difficult cases (Bohte & Meier, 2000, 174; Stone, 1988, 141). This tendency is not restricted to local police; self-selection of easy-to-clear crimes was also a tactic of the FBI under J. Edgar Hoover (Bohte & Meier, 2000, 181). Managers may also focus on highly visible cases, neglecting or excluding those less visible.

Another kind of cherry picking is "cream skimming." This happens when it is clear that a program fails to contribute to a jobseeker's employment prospects, and administrators claim credit for success that would have occurred without the program (Kelman & Friedman, 2009, 925). Further, this effort that added no value (assisting someone who was easy to place) might have been devoted to aiding the prospects of the hard-to-place person.

Favorable Focus

This fifth type of cheating occurs when selecting performance measures that are readily available, easy to get, and favorable, while abandoning measures that are harder to obtain and unfavorable. Arguably, this occurred at the executive level in the British hospital case when the Department of Health chose wait times as the key measure. Hood, Dixon, and Beeston (2008) theorized that elected officials are confronted with political incentives to formulate "ambitious performance target systems" to reap electoral or symbolic benefits. They are likely to choose those targets that will be most likely to bring the desired benefits, and not accurate assessment parameters.

Cutting Corners

This final form of fraud occurs when performance measures are selected with an eye to conserving resources. This might be viewed as a "quick fix" by those choosing the metric that enables them to claim they are enhancing achievement. If the measure is based on a "more is better" mentality, it conveys the message to service recipients that the emphasis is on quantity of output rather than quality. This can be seen when regulatory agencies or financial auditors resort to "quick-and-dirty" inspections or audits to increase the overall number they conduct as a means of appearing tough on those regulated. During the 1960s, Federal Housing Administration housing inspectors were found "guilty of conducting inspections from their cars" (Bohte & Meier, 2000, 175). In the UK study, patients coming into the A&E with serious injuries that could not be treated within four hours were admitted to inpatient wards, taking up valuable space and resources. If an A&E were too crowded, ambulances would stay outside with the patient still inside to delay the four-hour countdown from starting until the hospital was ready (Kelman & Friedman, 2009).

In sum, there are many types of organizational falsification, cheating or gaming, but the results of all types of deception present adverse effects on citizens. Metric manipulation misleads the public and makes it difficult to accurately assess service efficacy. Service users are forced to be skeptical of claims by providers, reinforcing public cynicism. The next section moves from the six-item gaming typology to briefly explore issues involving cheating, politicians, and public opinion.

CHEATING, POLITICIANS, AND PUBLIC OPINION

Elected officials are notorious for claiming credit whenever positive outcomes occur and for "blaming the bureaucrats" when negative outcomes result. In bureaucracies, executives make the good-news announcements but distance themselves and blame subordinates for bad news. Likewise, administrators face incentives to "[take] credit when times are good but [find] ways to pass blame back to politicians (by claiming inadequate resources, lack of authority, backdoor interference) when adverse events occur" (Hood, 2002, 326). The pessimistic takeaway from these "blame-game" cheating tendencies is that:

> [I]n the rare cases where politicians and other actors do not cheat by heavily encroach-ing on public managers' decision space, the latter will find it harder to escape blame and may therefore be led to play a highly defensive type of blame game . . . a managerial approach geared toward limitation of liability and tight control of potentially damag-ing information rather than bold and open initiatives—exactly the opposite of what managerial regimes were ostensibly designed to achieve. (329)

Hood also notes the inclinations of managers to fail to comply or engage in "creative compli-ance" when confronted with freedom of information requests or other transparency require-ments (328; see also Chapter 11).

Cheating can affect public opinion: Elected officials might construe citizen opinion as a form of performance system, which then raises the question of cheating. For example, presi-dents routinely try to stoke public opinion in support of an agenda. (Meier (2007, 6) asks, "If enough administration spokespersons contend that weapons of mass destruction were found in Iraq, will the public believe it?" Analogously, this is equivalent to school districts changing answers on tests to generate better scores.

A subtler form of gaming occurs by omission. This occurs when managers fail to exercise due diligence by being too willing to believe information they are given. Hood (2006, 519) detects "an eagerness by the central managers of the system to accept 'good news' perfor-mance data at face value without putting substantial resources into probing those numbers." Having considered the forces prompting duplicity, the motivations behind gaming, and the forms of cheating, the discussion now shifts to ethical evaluation and strategies to reduce this form of wrongdoing.

ETHICALLY EVALUATING AND MINIMIZING CHEATING

Integrity is like the weather: everybody talks about it but nobody knows what to do about it.
—Stephen Carter

How can cheating be ethically evaluated? Selected decision frameworks, such as the ethics triad, were presented in Chapter 7. They could be applied to any one of the six types of cheating discussed here to aid in determining the appropriateness of implementation in the organization.

Doing so, all three components of the trilogy—results, rules, virtue—suggest that cheating is unethical. It does not represent the greatest good, causes harm, and reflects poorly on personal integrity. But sometimes the consequences of cheating may be good, coloring judgments about character. For example, doctors deceiving insurance companies to help patients (Callahan, 2004, 61) or law enforcement tricking suspected criminals in sting operations (see discussion of Abscam in Chapter 11). But virtue ethics is a double-edged sword—it can restrain people while at the same time giving them latitude to stray from the ethical within those restraints (see, e.g., Ariely, 2012; see also Exhibit 12.1).

Yet since cheating is considered unethical, how can it be minimized? Sometimes management's desire to detect and correct unproductive or unethical work behavior can lead to decisions with unanticipated adverse consequences. Case Study 12.3 on electronic surveillance shows that using monitoring software and videotaping to address "cyberlollygagging" and low productivity can yield both positive and negative results.

Exhibit 12.1 **The Fudge Factor: The Dishonesty of Honest People**

From an adult filling out tax returns to a student taking an exam, scholars argue that everyone may be unethical to a certain degree at one time or another. As fallible human beings, people tend to cheat a little here and a little there every day. But it is blatant and extensive dishonesty that most find disturbing. Rather than weigh every decision in light of traditional economic cost-benefit analysis, new studies show that there is more that comes into play when considering a decision. Individuals try to maintain a balance between cheating and still view themselves as dignified, honest people. Dan Ariely (2012), professor of behavioral economics and psychology at Duke University, calls this phenomenon the *fudge factor*.

After conducting experiments both in academic, controlled settings and out in the real world, Ariely discovered that the further away an individual is from the unethical act—the more steps between a person and the dishonest action he is engaging in—the more likely the individual is to carry it out. As the nation moves to a cashless society, Ariely wonders whether our moral compass is more likely to slip. Is stealing a credit card number easier from a moral standpoint than taking cash from someone's purse? Using the game of golf, where lies and cheating are not unknown, he observes that players are more likely to move the ball with their shoe or their club than with their own hand. Since people want to be able to think of themselves as morally just individuals, the degree and the manner in which they cheat is downplayed and fudges moral boundaries.

Source: Adapted from Ariely (2012, Ch. 2B).

CASE STUDY 12.3

Applying Philosophical and Behavioral Ethics Approaches: Electronic Surveillance in the Workplace

Marisol Sanchez is the newly appointed director of the productivity improvement unit in the metropolitan county government of a Southwestern state. After surveying the performance of the major departments during her first year on the job and benchmarking productivity indicators against those from comparable jurisdictions elsewhere, she is convinced that changes are needed. She is considering installing new monitoring software on all office computers because of concerns about "cyberlollygagging" (wasting time on non-work-related websites). This will allow her to examine employee browsing patterns and determine whether they are visiting websites that the software categorizes as "productive," "unproductive," or "neutral." The software makes it possible to grade employees according to their browsing habits, singling out the most frequent users and the most commonly visited websites. She could also use the software to search emails and close access to objectionable websites. While she has been assured by general counsel that this strategy is legally acceptable, she has some ethical reservations about proceeding.

Consider Marisol's dilemma using the philosophical approach to decision-making followed by behavioral ethics.

Results-Based Analysis. From a results perspective, Marisol believes this program will improve productivity, reduce wasted time, and keep employees honest. She thinks it will help employees as well as employers—workers are aided in reaching their career goals free of distractions, and employers can reward high-performing employees. It also helps to foster a positive, task-focused organizational culture and professional work environment. It will likely be cost effective and advance government's core purpose. It can also result in improved citizen service and reinforce the idea that time at work should be spent working.

The downside may be that employees resent the intrusion by the employer and feel the psychological contract—shared perceptions of expectations and obligations—has been broken. They may respond with anger and consider the monitoring to be an invasion of privacy. Surveillance may increase competition and stress while simultaneously lowering morale and eroding trust. Employees may object to the initiative, especially if the employer's motives are suspect or if they think the severity of the problem is insufficient to warrant management's overreaching with the monitoring approach.

Rule-Based Analysis. When rules or principles become the focus, it is the agency's prerogative to make and implement workplace policies. Legal counsel has assured Marisol that the policy has been tailored in a way that complies with existing statutes. It is Marisol's duty to work responsibly to improve employee performance and public service. Monitoring helps managers to manage. By implementing monitoring in all departments, it is applied fairly. As stewards of government resources, officials can be confident that government property (computers) is being used for government work. "What is good for one, is good for all."

Among the disadvantages of overreliance on surveillance is that employees may believe their privacy rights are violated. They may resent not being included in the formulation of the policy and object to the secrecy of its implementation. They may feel their trust has been violated, reinforcing feelings of alienation from management. They may question whether due diligence will be observed regarding the access and use of the gathered information. It may be that highly productive employees are able to finish a task and be refreshed by a brief diversion browsing the Internet. The means (privacy invasion) do not justify the ends (productivity).

Virtue-Based Analysis. Virtue ethics provides a third lens in assessing this program. Aristotle argued for balance and the need to avoid both excesses and deficiencies. Marisol may feel that the surveillance is balanced, respecting both the county's interests and the employee's rights. She believes this action is necessary and that data will not be misused. It is a way to hold employees accountable. Abusers deserve to be caught. Those who are not violating policy should not mind. Protecting government property from misuse is an obligation of management. Surveillance indicates the caring of government in promoting government's public service function. Marisol thinks that the program will make her a better manager and likewise will improve metropolitan government.

Employees may feel that their rights are being compromised by overly aggressive, intrusive management monitoring. They could believe that surveillance disrupts the power balance between employer and employee and fear the misuse of data collected. Workers may think that the program is unfair, likely to result in fewer rewards or undeserved punishment. The monitoring might be seen as a violation of civil liberties. Some will likely try to "work around" the policy (use their own iPad or cell phone) and point to the "chilling effect" surveillance has on the work environment. Performance could suffer if the worry, concern, and dislike of employees negatively alter the organizational climate. In the interest of integrity, employers should respect and protect employee privacy.

Outcome. After weighing the electronic surveillance issue, Marisol decides to buy and install the new monitoring software. Indeed, she goes so far as secretly installing videotaping equipment in all offices to further monitor employee work. It does not take long for Marisol to begin getting employee feedback about these initiatives. Two cases cause her to second-guess her decisions: (i) Bonnie Albright was surprised and distressed to find out that her employer, Metropolitan County Government, had secretly videotaped her office 24/7 for several months because of concern about subpar performance in her department. Bonnie often changed clothes in her office before leaving for the day, having no knowledge that this was caught on videotape. She was mortified that she had not been told of this practice, especially when she discovered that the employer had viewed the tapes. (ii) Burton Christianson complained when he saw his supervisor printing out emails sent among his fellow employees.

Questions to Consider

1. How do you assess Marisol's strategy for improving county performance?

2. Is there anything that could or should have been done prior to implementation?

3. Are there any design flaws in these two productivity improvement initiatives?

4. What ethical problems can you identify?

5. What advice would you give to Marisol regarding her efforts to monitor employees?

Behavioral Ethics-Based Analysis. Recall that the approach used here is considered incomplete because it ignores the importance of emotions and tacit understandings in behavior. Behavioral ethics, thus, introduces considerations like ethical fading, focalism, and motivated blindness that provide insights into the case. Marisol's mono-focus on curbing employee "cyberlollygagging" and improving productivity has led her to downplay privacy concerns. This form of ethical fading can lead to motivated blindness that unintentionally minimized legitimate moral concerns. It may be that the initial introduction of monitoring software was implemented with few objections and resulted in limited legal exposure, but the subsequent intrusive videotaping led to escalating legal and ethical concerns. Failure to involve employees in designing the policy and to inform them of the videotaping was—surprisingly—an unanticipated error. Supervisors circulating employee emails to coworkers shows bad judgment and suggests the absence of guidelines on appropriate use of information technology and protection of employee privacy rights. Identify other behavioral ethics phenomena that shed light on what happened. (See other cases for analysis in the Exercises section at the end of this chapter.)

Bohte and Meier (2000, 180) argue, "The most likely proposed solution, and perhaps the least likely to work, is to simply add rules to circumscribe the behavior." However, adding rules may lead to a vicious cycle in which stricter rules prompt more efforts to "circumvent control," which, in turn, produces even stricter policies, decreasing productivity and morale, because increasing rules implies distrust of employees. An extreme case of strict enforcement of rules that occurred in the JC Penney Company ended in mass firings.

In 2012, the 4,800 employees of Penney's headquarters watched a combined 5 million YouTube videos while working, using over 30 percent of the headquarters' bandwidth. CEO Ron Johnson brought in Michael Kramer, chief operating officer, to transform the company's culture. Kramer's "transformation" reduced the number of employees at headquarters by 1,600 people. Despite research such as the 2009 University of Melbourne study that found Internet browsing at work boosts productivity, companies like JC Penney take a hardline position on "cyber loafing"—lay off the YouTube videos or be laid off ("JC Penney Exec," 2013).

Professional or organizational norms to control cheating are a more likely effective corrective, according to Bohte and Meier (2000), because they involve a broader understanding of organizational goals and the possible inconsistencies between these goals and the narrower incentive system in place. Such norms are also likely to take into account the difficult tasks assigned to employees. They need to be buttressed by procedures and structures, including policies that look beyond short-term gains. It is also important to pay attention to the incentive structure (the basis for rewards and sanctions) and the kind of behavior it encourages.

Before attempting to prevent or minimize fakery, managers need to understand why it is occurring. A common form of cheating is metric manipulation. Prevention efforts can be aided by increased awareness of the motivation behind cheating via measurement manipulation and the organizational contexts that give rise to it. Fisher and Downes (2008, 249–250) identified seven reasons that help explain why people and organizations manipulate target and performance measures: (1) to avoid the hassle and scrutiny of managers, (2) because current metrics are inappropriate or unfair, (3) because there is the perception that the data are misleading or untrue, (4) the desire to achieve a target that yields a big bonus, (5) the desire to achieve a target that yields a small bonus, (6) to make performance appear worse that it really is as a way to argue for more resources, and (7) to make productivity appear better than it is in cases where income is tied to organization targets. Governance can be improved with performance measurement by removing inducements that trigger manipulative actions and providing inducements that encourage good practice.

Subtle reminders that others within the organization are observing behavior are sometimes sufficient to quell cheating. For years, an office kitchen operated in a manner that relied on employee honesty. Tea and coffee were available, along with a suggested price list and an "honors system" box into which people were expected to contribute. A poster was placed above the box that alternated between an image of a flower and an image of eyes. When it showed eyes staring at the employee, there was a spike in the money put in the box. The experiment illustrates that even simple symbolic reminders can deter cheating (Kahneman, 2011, 57–58). In organizations in which performance is scrutinized, there is less likely to be flagrant dishonesty.

Schweitzer, Ordonez, and Douma (2004, 422) found that "in addition to motivating constructive effort, goal setting motivates *unethical* behavior when people fall short of their goals." Thus, "when employees are close to a goal or a deadline, managers should be particularly vigilant," because under conditions of low transparency and asymmetric information, vulnerability to cheating is high (430). Recall the Sears case mentioned earlier—when difficult goals for automotive service advisors were set, repairs were unnecessary 90 percent of the time. Managers need to employ risk-assessment strategies and consider an ethics audit to determine their vulnerability to cheating behaviors.

Unlike incentive-based systems, performance measurement—the collection and analysis of information on program outputs and impacts—can be harnessed for ethical governance. Honest measurement promotes efficiency and effectiveness because it encourages dialogue between stakeholders and contributes to transparency. However, performance measurement is effective only when it is not "simply viewed as a system for accountability" (de Lancer Julnes, 2009, 1–2). Instead, the development and use of performance systems should include training that emphasizes ethical considerations. For example, systems can be designed and used to evaluate individual achievement in an ethically responsible way, according to Drongelen and Fisscher (2003, 55–57). Their suggestions are valuable for individual evaluation as well as for program assessment:

1. Be upfront and candid about the intended use of performance information. Avoid changing intended uses without proper consultation with relevant stakeholders.

2. Choose a variety of well-balanced measures.

3. Select measures that are closely aligned with program goals and realities.

4. Ensure that data collection methods are an appropriate fit for the task.

5. Offer feedback so that necessary changes can be made to achieve program goals.

6. Use accessible information to clearly explain the selected indicators.

7. Involve citizens in the overall process.

It is critical to recognize that accountability provided by productivity measures can both encourage and hinder the use of information (de Lancer Julnes, 2006, 2009). Thoughtful evaluation of a performance measurement after its implementation aids in weighing the costs and benefits of permanent adoption.

Thus, while performance measurement can support the value of accountability, it can also support other values (efficiency, effectiveness, responsiveness, equity) essential to advance public welfare. Managers need to consider some of the strategies discussed here to minimize fabrication. Formulating rules, establishing organizational norms, increasing awareness of the reasons for cheating, providing periodic reminders, routinely monitoring operations, and carefully designing program assessments are potentially useful strategies.

CONCLUSION

Cheating or gaming the system occurs in government as a result of both external (economic, political, and social) forces and internal pressures (high-performance goals). Goal setting and performance measurement are worthwhile activities that can enhance productivity and improve perceptions of public service. Citizens are likely to be concerned about the quality of services and their relative standing vis-à-vis other jurisdictions, departments, or vendors. Agencies are ranked and rated, the equivalent of organizational report cards, on a variety of measures at federal, state, and local levels, just as businesses and nonprofit organizations are evaluated.

Unfortunately, a by-product of relying heavily on targets and metrics is that it can be dysfunctional, as this chapter illustrates. Pressures to do well on rankings have resulted in fudging the numbers or manipulating the metrics, especially when substantial rewards or sanctions are linked to performance, deadlines are looming, and scrutiny is lacking. Cheating can be ethically evaluated by focusing on results, rules or virtues and gaming behavior often comes up short on one or more of them.

While not all gaming harms citizens, it nevertheless misleads them and erodes trust in business practices, government statistics, or nonprofit data. Falsified data mask the effort that went into performance when metrics are deceitfully raised or lowered, making legitimate comparisons among units impossible. When these actions come to light—and they often do—it can harm careers, tarnish reputations, and embarrass individuals and institutions that skirt the rules or manipulate evaluation criteria.

Organizational cheating will never be eradicated completely, but strategies exist that can be used to minimize it: risk assessments, new rules, organizational and professional norms, ethics training, managerial attentiveness, stakeholder participation, and honest reporting. As Stephen Carter (1996) said, "repeated acts of unintegrity often result in getting away with things that are known to be wrong." Integrity, in contrast, "is the right path . . . upon which you will never get lost," according to M. H. McKee. Public administrators need to use prudent leadership to keep public service on the right path.

***

What lies behind us and what lies before us are tiny matters compared to what lies within us.
—Ralph Waldo Emerson

NOTE

1. Enrollees who had jobs at the end of the training were usually terminated at that time. Those who were unemployed on the last day of training, but obtained jobs within 90 days, were discharged when employment started. Enrollees who did not gain jobs were usually released on the final day of the 90-day period.

   The terminations served to maximize performance scores of the training centers because the centers would have achieved an employment rate outcome substantially lower if they had been required to terminate enrollees (and record their performance results) on the day trainees completed training. However, the researchers concluded "the kind of monitoring of the caseload necessary to optimally time termination diverts resources from training activities" (Courty & Marschke, 2003, 908–909), resulting in lower quality training, thereby undermining the overarching goal of the program.

Courty and Marschke's broader discovery delineates a "trial-and-error" dynamic, "characterized by a feedback loop" (904), whereby the federal agency implements measures, local managers game them, the feds discover the gaming and revise the metrics thereby promoting possible new gaming, and so on. This dynamic highlights a lesson for those implementing a performance management system—accurate assessment is a challenge that requires careful monitoring and continuous improvement.

DISCUSSION

1. It is claimed that cheating in the classroom pervades American schools. Have you witnessed this behavior? What was the cause(s)? If it was discovered, what, if anything, was done about it by students, instructors, or administrators? Are there exemplary models (e.g., institutions with effective honor codes) where dishonesty is rare or absent?

2. In a climate where cheating becomes so pervasive that people use the excuse "everybody does it" (see Tuckness, 2010, for a commentary on this rationalization in the workplace) employees may be inclined to discount ethics because they do not want to put themselves at a competitive disadvantage when they conform to the official policies rather than the *real* policies. Discuss examples of when this might occur in public service settings and what managers can do to avoid or correct it.

3. Some organizations are too relaxed and others are too stressed. When the work environment is being revitalized, it can create excessive pressure to perform, causing uncertainty, anxiety, stress, and sometimes impaired ethical judgment. Discuss (a) examples of how wrongdoing can occur under such circumstances and (b) ways that institutions might achieve the golden mean between too much comfort and too much pressure.

EXERCISES

1. This chapter presented six different types of gaming, and ways in which to distinguish one from the other. Using this information and your own experience, provide two examples for each of the types (other than those provided in the chapter). How can selected types of gaming be avoided?

	Example 1	Example 2
Ratchet Effects		
Output Distortion		
Output Tunnel Vision		
Cherry Picking		
Favorable Focus		
Cutting Corners		

2. Ethically evaluating cheating is an important part of this chapter. Using the ethics triumvirate, evaluate the situations presented here from a rules, results, and virtue perspective:

Scenario 1
You are a fifth-grade teacher in a low-performing school working with underprivileged students. You have just been informed that the new principal has made it clear that if scores do not dramatically increase, the teachers with low-scoring classrooms will lose their jobs. The state standardized exam begins next week, and you know your students are not prepared. In a desperate effort to keep your job, you decide to walk around the room and "help" students on questions.

    Results:
    Rules:
    Virtue:

Scenario 2
You have just finished your master's in business administration and are now working for a prestigious lending company. After your first week successfully assisting people in setting up their loans, and providing them with the information they need and telling them of their best options, you are confused when your boss calls you in to discuss your performance. After the meeting, you now know that your boss encourages subprime loans for all clients rather than the safer options that you know are the proper thing to offer. However, you begin offering clients risky subprime loans, assuring them that there is low risk and that their money is safe.

    Results:
    Rules:
    Virtue:

Recalling the research results on behavioral ethics from Chapter 7, what are the possible explanations for and implications of the actions taken in this case?

Scenario 3
Samantha works for the administrative offices of Memorial Hospitals in a large metropolitan area. Her office is the managing body that oversees a chain of hospitals in the region. Samantha's recent task is to interpret performance measurement data that has been submitted in light of recent changes to hospital protocol. In an effort to improve efficiency and reputation, management had implemented a series of targets that the hospitals meet with regard to readmission rates and emergency room wait time.

    A few months after implementation, it is Samantha's duty to analyze the reports from the hospitals and provide her supervisor with feedback concerning performance in relation to the new targets. Samantha realized that one of the hospitals provided reports in which the hospital met every target, yet Samantha's own observations indicated it was falling short of each objective. When Samantha informed her supervisor of the inconsistencies between her report and the hospital's, her supervisor was not alarmed or surprised, and advised her to analyze the reports "as is." After that encounter, Samantha got the impression that her supervisor was more concerned with publishing reports that look good even if the information they represent is incorrect.

Results:
Rules:
Virtue:

Based on behavioral ethics findings, how might the conduct here be understood? What explains the dishonesty of honest people? T. S. Eliot thought, "Half of the harm that is done in this world is due to people who want to feel important . . . they do not mean to do harm . . . they are absorbed in their endless struggle to think well of themselves." What do you think?

3. **Bad Actor Tabletop Exercise:** The Bad Teacher. Instructions (see Chapter 3, Exercise 6) Miss English is a history teacher at Breakwood High School. She teaches 9th through 12th grade American and world history. In order to encourage teachers to perform according to standards, the school awards bonuses based on student performances on state exams. Knowing this, Miss English purposefully neglects any information that is not included in the scope of state exams. Although her students do well in the exams, the course does not cover the majority of the material outlined in her approved curriculum. Instead, students are pressured to study on their own right before test time and spend most of the year watching videos and completing marginally relevant assignments.

Role 1: Principal
You are the principal, and it has come to your attention that Miss English has been deviating from her approved curriculum and "teaching to the test." You know that this is frowned upon, but English's students are among the highest performing in state exams, which reflects well on the school. Do you feel compelled to address this issue with English? Why or why not? Consider your obligations, ethical and otherwise. To whom are you accountable as a school principal? What factors impact your decision?

Role 2: Coworker
You are also a history teacher at the school. You go to Miss English for advice on improving your students' performances on state exams, and she informs you of her teaching methods. You know that teaching to the test is wrong, but it seems to be working for her. What do you do? Do you report English's behavior? Why or why not? Consider your obligations, ethical and otherwise. To whom are you accountable as an educator? What factors impact your decision?

Role 3: Student
You are a student in English's 12th-grade world history course. You have always been interested in history and want to major in that field in college. After having swapped English for American history, you know that you will not be challenged academically, and will need a strong foundation to go into your major next year. What do you do? Do you complain to the principal and seek a transfer? Consider your obligations, ethical and otherwise. To whom are you accountable as a student? What factors impact your decision?

Role 4: PTA President

You are the president of the parent teacher association at Breakwood High. You have heard of Miss English's teaching practices and are aware that some parents and students are concerned about the quality of their education. You also know that English's students test well at the state level. How do you manage this situation? Consider your obligations, ethical and otherwise. To whom are you accountable as the PTA president? What factors impact your decision?

Role 5: Member of the Board of Education

You are on the Board of Education which is meeting to discuss taking punitive action against Miss English. Knowing the details of her teaching methods and her students' results on exams, do you vote in favor or against taking action? Why? Consider your obligations, ethical and otherwise. To whom are you accountable as a board member? What factors impact your decision?

4. Case: Julie Gaming the System

Case

Mary works for a fast-growing nonprofit organization. She recently referred a friend of hers, Julie, to an open position and Julie was offered the job. Following the acceptance of the offer, Julie tells Mary that she intends to keep her current job while simultaneously working for the nonprofit. She feels justified in doing this because both employers permit remote work and she is confident she can divide her time equally between both jobs. The nonprofit has an explicit policy dealing with this issue of dual employment and requires disclosure and approval of any offsite work. When Mary learns of Julie's intent to do both fulltime jobs without disclosure or approval, she advised Julie not to take this course of action, but Julie remained adamant about her decision. Mary was concerned about the potential consequences of her friend's decision, but also the potential tarnishing of her own professional reputation were the deception to be discovered. Mary is debating whether to warn her employer.

Analysis:

Julie is violating the terms and conditions of her employment and taking advantage of trust from her employer that provides a telework option for employees to work unsupervised at home, and she is doing so in ways that are unfair to other employees who are working remotely and complying with the organization's policies. She is not receptive to advice from Mary, a friend who referred her expecting that Julie would give full attention to her fulltime position. Her action is not what one would expect from a friend. Julie's deception could be divulged in a variety of ways, such as, office talk among employees or posting of an online organization directory.

If the details were less clear, the discussion could explore the obligations Mary has to her employer and those she has to her friend. But the case makes it clear that Julie has recklessly broken the bond of trust with a friend, so Mary would be within her rights to disclose the situation to her employer. Since the impact of Mary's disclosure could be serious, she should give Julie the choice of volunteering to stop the dual employment or Mary would disclose her deceit to the employer.

Source: Adapted from Appiah (2020)

QUESTIONS FOR CONSIDERATION:

1. Do you agree with the advice provided to Mary? Why or why not?

2. Analyze this case using one or more of these ethical analytical frameworks:

   (a) the ethics triad (Chapter 7), (b) macro-meso-micro perspectives (Chapter 2), ethical principles approach (Chapter 5), (d) behavioral ethics (Chapter 7), or the 5-step approach (Chapter 5).

QUESTIONS TO CONSIDER:

1. What meso-level reforms would make gaming the system less attractive to fraudsters?

2. Why weren't such reforms part of the initial design of the Paycheck Protection Program?

3. How can the methods used by fraudsters be effectively addressed by anti-corruption units? Why will this be difficult?

4. Case: Fraudsters Gaming the System

   The federal government's $523 billion Paycheck Protection Program offering coronavirus relief for small businesses has resulted in scammers trying to game the system. As of late 2020 criminal charges have been filed accusing more than 80 people for stealing up to $127 million from relief funds; however, the House Select Committee on the Coronavirus Crisis estimates improper loans could amount to more than $4 billion.

   A combination of substantial government funds available in a short time period, low application standards, absence of requirements that borrowers document specific injury from the virus, frequently revised rules, swift loan application approvals, self-certification eligibility procedures, and the lack of adequate oversight has attracted those who are willing to break the law to get access to the funds.

   Among the methods used by fraudsters are doctoring payroll lists, faking business tax returns, forging documents, and modifying bank statements. Investigations of such actions are underway by more than a dozen government agencies. The chief executive of Fountainhead Commercial Capital commenting on the fraud said, "We couldn't believe how many people were trying to take advantage and game the system" (Cowley, 2020).

REFERENCES

Appiah, K. (2020, July 10). The ethicist. *New York Times Magazine*, p. 20.

Ariely, D. (2012). *The (honest) truth about dishonesty*. New York: HarperCollins.

Asch, B. J. (1990). Do incentives matter? The case of Navy recruiters. *Industrial and Labor Relations Review*, *43*, 89S–106S.

Auge, K. (2012, June 7). "Principal-level" cheating on CSAP at Denver school, probe finds. *Denver Post*. Retrieved from www.denverpost.com/breakingnews/ci_20800253/principal-level-cheating-csap-at-denver-school

Aviv, R. (2014, July 21). Wrong answer. *The New Yorker*. Retrieved from www.newyorker.com/magazine/2014/07/21/wrong-answer

Barsky, A. (2008). Understanding the ethical cost of organizational goal-setting: A review and theory development. *Journal of Business Ethics, 81(1)*, 63–81.

Berman, E. (2006). *Performance and productivity in public and nonprofit organizations* (2nd ed.). Armonk, NY: M. E. Sharpe.

Bohte, J., & Meier, K. J. (2000). Goal displacement: Assessing the motivation for organizational cheating. *Public Administration Review, 60*, 173–182.

Brumback, K. (2013, March 29). 3 dozen indicted in Atlanta cheating scandal. *Washington Post*. Retrieved from www.washingtonpost.com/politics/3-dozen-indicted-in-atlanta-cheating-scandal/2013/03/29/86711356-98c2-11e2-97cd-3d8c1afe4f0f_allComments.html

Callahan, D. (2004). *The cheating culture*. New York: Mariner Books.

Carter, S. (1996). *Integrity*. New York: Harper Perennial.

Carvel, J. (2003, May 13). Hospitals "faked" wait times test. *The Guardian*. Retrieved from www.guardian.co.uk/society/2003/may/13/hospitals.nhs

Colarco, J. (2019, March 22). Cheating in college admissions plays out on several different levels (opinion). *Inside higher ed*. Retrieved from www.insidehighered.com/advice/2019/03/22/cheating-college-admissions-plays-out-several-different-levels-opinion

Cooper, H. (2014, February 14). For a new air force secretary, a baptism by fire. *New York Times*. Retrieved from www.nytimes.com/2014/02/14/us/for-new-air-force-secretary-a-baptism-by-fire.html

Cooper, P. (2000). *Public law and public administration*. Itasca, IL: F. E. Peacock.

Courty, P., & Marschke, G. (2003). Making government accountable: Lessons from a federal job training program. *Public Administration Review, 67*, 904–916.

Cowley, S. (2020, December 9). How bad was virus aid fraud? One banker was "frustrated with humanity". *New York Times*. Retrieved from www.nytimes.com/2020/12/09/business/ppp-fraud-paycheck-protection-program.html

DeHoog, R., & Salamon, L. (2002). Purchase of service contracting. In L. Salamon (Ed.), *The tools of government: A guide to the new governance* (pp. 319–339). New York: Oxford University Press.

de Lancer Julnes, P. (2006). Performance measurement: An effective tool for government accountability? The debate goes on. *Evaluation, 12(2)*, 219–235.

de Lancer Julnes, P. (2009, October). *The role of performance measurement in ethical and effective government*. Paper presented at the Fourteenth International Congress of CLAD (Latin-American Center of Administration for Development) on Reform of the State and Public Administration, Salvador de Bahia, Brazil.

de Lancer Julnes, P., & Gibson, E. (eds.) (2015). *Innovation in public and nonprofit organizations: A public solutions handbook*. New York: Taylor & Francis/Routledge.

Drongelen, I., & Fisscher, O. (2003). Ethical dilemmas in performance measurement. *Journal of Business Ethics, 45*, 51–63.

Eaton, C. (2019, March 19). Wealthy wall street donors have legal admissions advantages that should be curtailed (opinion). *Inside higher ed*. Retrieved from www.insidehighered.com/views/2019/03/19/wealthy-wall-street-donors-have-legal-admissions-advantages-should-be-curtailed

Figlio, D. (2005). *Testing, crime and punishment* (Working Paper 11194). Cambridge, MA: National Bureau of Economic Research. Retrieved from www.nber.org/papers/w11194

Figlio, D., & Getzler, L. (2002). *Accountability, ability and disability: Gaming the system* (Working Paper 9307). Cambridge, MA: National Bureau of Economic Research. Retrieved from www.nber.org/papers/w9307

Figlio, D., & Winicki, J. (2005). Food for thought: The effects of school accountability plans on school nutrition. *Journal of Public Economics, 89*, 381–394.

Fisher, C., & Downes, B. (2008). Performance measurement and metric manipulation in the public sector. *Business Ethics: A European Review*, *17*, 245–258.

Frysh, P. (2011, August 8). Cheating report confirms teacher's suspicions. *CNN*. Retrieved from www.cnn.com/2011/US/08/05/atlanta.public.schools.scandal/index.html

Gormley, W. T., & Weimer, D. L. (1999). *Organizational report cards*. Cambridge, MA: Harvard University Press.

Haimson, L. (2012, July 29). Tests don't assess what really matters. *New York Times*. Retrieved from www.nytimes.com/roomfordebate/2012/07/29/can-school-performance-be-measured

Haines, D. (2003–2004). Fatal choices: The routinization of deceit, incompetence, and corruption. *Public Integrity*, *6*, 5–24.

Hendrick, R., & Yazici, N. (2011, June). *Strategic behavior and performance measurement in government*. Paper presented at the Seventh Transatlantic Dialogue on Strategic Management of Public Organizations, Rutgers School of Public Affairs and Administration, Newark, NJ.

Hood, C. (2002). Control, bargains, and cheating: The politics of public-service reform. *Journal of Public Administration Research and Theory*, *12*, 309–332.

Hood, C. (2006). Gaming in targetworld: The targets approach to managing British public services. *Public Administration Review*, *66*, 515–521.

Hood, C., Dixon, R., & Beeston, C. (2008). Rating the rankings: Assessing international rankings of public service performance. *International Public Management Journal*, *11*, 298–328.

Inside Higher Education. (2020, December 4). *Education department fines temple $700,000 in rankings scandal*. Retrieved from www.insidehighered.com/admissions/article/2020/12/07/education-department-fines-temple-700000-rankings scandal?utm_source=Inside+Higher+Ed&utm_campaign=a3dd98e9f4-DNU_2020_COPY_02&utm_medium=email&utm_term=0_1fcbc04421-a3dd98e9f4–199906201&mc_cid=a3d

Jaffe, G., & Hicks, J. (2014, June 9). VA audit: 57,000 veterans waiting more than 90 days for appointment at medical facilities. *Washington Post*. Retrieved at www.washington-post.com/politics/va-audit-57000-veterans-waiting-more-than-90-days-for-appointment-at-medical-facilities/2014/06/09/599d26ee-f014–11e3–9ebc-2ee6f81ed217_story.html?utm_term=.00fc6e4b7b5f

James, O., Olsen, A., Moynihan, D., & Van Ryzin, G. (2020). *Behavioral public performance: How people make sense of government metrics*. New York: Cambridge University Press.

JC Penney exec admits its employees harbored enormous YouTube addiction. (2013, February 25). *Wall Street Journal*, p. A12.

Kahneman, D. (2011). *Thinking, fast and slow*. New York: Farrar, Straus, & Giroux.

Kaplan, E. (2019, June 3). Parents in college cheating scandal say money was for charity not a bribe. *NBC News*. Retrieved from www.nbcnews.com/news/us-news/parents-college-cheating-scandal-say-money-was-charity-not-bribe-n1013391

Kelman, S., & Friedman, J. N. (2009). Performance improvement and performance dysfunction: An empirical examination of distortionary impacts of the emergency room wait-time target in the English National Health Service. *Journal of Public Administration Research and Theory*, *19*, 917–946.

Layton, N. (2013, April 14). Bush, Obama focus on standardized testing leads to "opt-out" parents' movement. *Washington Post*. Retrieved from http://articles.washingtonpost.com/2013-04-14/local/38537469_1_no-child-students-such-testing

Liff, S. (2014). *98 opportunities to improve management in government*. Tysons Corner, VA: Management Concepts Press.

Meier, K. J. (1985). *Regulation: Politics, economics and bureaucracy*. New York: St. Martin's Press.

Meier, K. J. (2007). The public administration of politics, or what political science could learn from public administration. *PS: Political Science and Politics*, *40*, 3–9.

Meier, K. J. (2008). The scientific study of public administration: A short essay on the state of the field. *International Review of Public Administration*, *13*, 1–10.

New York Times. (2019, March 12). Here's how the F.B.I. says parents cheated to get their kids into elite colleges. *New York Times*. Retrieved from www.nytimes.com/2019/03/12/us/admissions-scandal.html

Ordonez, L., Schweitzer, M., Galinsky, A., Bazerman, M. (2009). On good scholarship, goal setting, and scholars gone wild. *Academy of Management Perspectives*, *23*(3), 82–87.

Pauls, S. (2019, March 12). The college admissions scam shows how parents duped their kids, too. *Slate*. Retrieved from https://slate.com/human-interest/2019/03/college-admissions-scam-imagine-finding-out-your-parents-bought-your-way-in.html

Perez-Pena, R., & Slotnik, D. E. (2012, January 31). Gaming the college rankings. *New York Times*. Retrieved from www.nytimes.com/2012/02/01/education/gaming-the-college-rankings.html?_r=1&pagewanted=print

Richer, A. (2020, March 11). A look at the college admissions cheating case 1 year later. *U.S. News*. Retrieved from www.usnews.com/news/us/articles/2020-03-11/a-look-at-the-college-admissions-cheating-case-1-year-later

Schweitzer, M. E., Ordonez, L., & Douma, B. (2004). Goal setting as a motivator of unethical behavior. *Academy of Management Journal*, *47*, 422–432.

Soss, J., Fording, R., & Schram, S. F. (2011). The organization of discipline: From Performance Management to perversity and punishment. *Journal of Public Administration Research and Theory*, *21*(supp 2), i203–i232.

Stone, D. (1988). *Policy paradox and political reason*. New York: HarperCollins.

Strauss, V. (2011, July 5). Probe: Widespread cheating on tests detailed in Atlanta. *Washington Post*. Retrieved from www.washingtonpost.com/blogs/answer-sheet/post/probe-wide-spread-cheating-on-tests-detailed-in-atlanta/2011/07/05/gHQAURaczH_blog.html

Strauss, V. (2012, January 31). College admits inflating SAT scores to boost ranking. *Washington Post*. Retrieved from www.washingtonpost.com/blogs/answer-sheet/post/college-admits-inflating-sat-scores-to-boost-ranking/2012/01/31/gIQA00H1fQ_blog.html

Surlgua, S. (2019, April 19). Lori Loughlin and 15 other parents face additional charges in college admissions scandal. *The Washington Post*. Retrieved from www.washingtonpost.com/education/2019/04/09/lori-loughlin-other-parents-face-additional-charges-college-admissions-scandal/

Taylor, K. (2020, December 29). Loughlin completes sentence in college admissions fraud. *New York Times*. Retrieved from www.nytimes.com/2020/12/28/us/lori-loughlin-released-prison.html?searchResultPosition=1

Tuckness, A. (2010). "Everybody does it": An analysis of a common excuse. *Public Integrity*, *12*, 261–272.

Whitesell, G. (2012, January 20). Government seeks help to stop teacher-led cheating. *USA Today*. Retrieved from www.usatoday.com/news/education/story/2012-01-19/teacher-testing-cheating/52683838/1

Winslow, D. (2017). *The force*. New York: William Morrow.

Winton, R. (2019, March 24). Mystery parent paid $6.5 million to get kids into top universities as part of admissions scandal. *Los Angeles Times*. Retrieved from www.latimes.com/local/lanow/la-me-college-admissions-bribe-fixer-20190324-story.html

Zhao, E. (2012, July 27). Ohio state auditor will launch investigation into school cheating, attendance record tampering. *Huffington Post*. Retrieved from www.huffingtonpost.com/2012/07/27/ohio-state-auditor-will-1_n_1711448.html

13 At-Will Employment

Those who are fear'd, are hated.

—Benjamin Franklin

The nature of the employer–employee relationship has undergone change during the last two generations from a long-term career system to a short-term employment system (Bowman & West, 2006b). The risks of management decisions and market fluctuations, previously borne by institutions, have increasingly been shifted to individuals. As a result, the traditional social contract at work—job security in exchange for organization loyalty—has been eroded (Stone, 2004; West, 2013). One of the most sweeping measures is the at-will employment doctrine. It has been used to eliminate existing employee protections not only in private companies but also in government service (Hays & Sowa, 2006).

This chapter analyzes the at-will doctrine by emphasizing the complementarity and interdependence of results-based utilitarian ethics, rule-based duty ethics, and virtue-based character ethics. The chapter objectives include examining

- the importance of the problem,
- its evolution and current status,
- evaluation of the employment at-will doctrine, and
- implications of the findings.

In so doing, Lord Acton's (1834–1902) adage—"Power tends to corrupt and absolute power corrupts absolutely"—provides a useful perspective on contemporary trends in employment relations.

THE EMPLOYMENT AT-WILL DOCTRINE

Historical Development

Early American labor-management law was based on British master–servant law, which assumed employment would last one year.[1] However, consistent with the laissez-faire capitalism of the Industrial Revolution, the approach was abandoned for the American Rule near the end of the 19th century. Under this rule, employees work for an unspecified period of time at the will of the employer (Hugh, 2001; see also Holger, 2004; Werhane, Radin, & Bowie, 2004). The relationship would be defined by the freedom to contract

DOI: 10.4324/9781003203148-17

where neither party was compelled to create the affiliation and either party could terminate it at will. The discipline of the free market would ensure the societal efficiency of these voluntary agreements as both parties would have incentives to recover their investments made in each other (Epstein & Rosen, 1984). With the exception of unionized industries and most civil servants, the majority of the U.S. workforce today works at will.

In concept, the absolute right of the employer to discharge a worker coincides with the sovereignty doctrine in the public sector. Because employment is a privilege, not a right, it was subject to terms specified by government. Government is sovereign; it is inappropriate to dilute its management rights (e.g., no person has a right to a public job). Indeed for much of the 1800s—the last time that at-will employment was used in public service—the spoils system dominated personnel policy. Citizens sought a position not on the basis of character or competence but on political connections, and they could be terminated on the same basis. Public office was perverted into a private fiefdom as arrogance, greed, and opportunism prevailed over honor, openness, and prudence.

Favoritism, cronyism, intimidation, corruption, and rampant dismissals were widespread in that squalid era. Rather than emphasizing good government and policy, the system encouraged mediocre governance—its highest priority was to reward its friends, to grant favors for favors given. To protect the legitimacy of the state from private interests and to cleanse public service of partisan interference, English merit principles (including entrance examinations, job tenure, career service, political neutrality) were adopted in the 1883 Pendleton Act (and state "mini-Pendleton" laws) as well as the 1912 Lloyd–LaFollette Act. As the spoils system gradually eroded (only 10 percent of employees were initially covered by the Pendleton Act), the merit system, as well as the federal courts, progressively strengthened employee rights under the Constitution.

A merit-based civil service—as a moral guardian of democracy—would shield employees from politically inspired employment actions. Public servants would be loyal to the system of government, not to a particular political party. They would only give free and candid advice if their positions were safeguarded. Clean government would mean effective government as job security facilitated government responsiveness and ensured efficient service delivery. Competence would be the foundation of ethical public management; government would be run like a business when organized by administrative principles, led by an executive, and staffed by nonpartisan employees shielded from unscrupulous politicians.

Although the merit system was created to "clean up government" by eradicating spoils, it is not surprising that with the passage of time the past would be forgotten. Toward the end of the 20th century, a simpler, private sector–inspired employment model gained favor. Based on a liberal market ethos, it stresses a laissez-faire employment relationship that celebrates self-interested behaviors and economic incentives. The NPM/Reinventing Government movement emphasized "letting managers manage" by increasing their discretion and using corporate management styles to ensure improved performance and results (Ferlie, Ashburner, & Pettigrew, 1996; Gore, 1993; Pollitt, 1990; Salamon & Elliott, 2002). Relaxing job protections for civil servants has been seen as a key method to accomplish these objectives. Policy advocates favor substituting tenured employees for contract workers who are obliged to provide specific outputs with few job guarantees (Pollitt & Bouckaert, 2004; Sulieman, 2003). At-will employment, in short, is now seen as solving, instead of causing, public management problems.

Contemporary Reform

Fueled by entrepreneurial strategies, budget cutbacks, and devolution, the reform movement (Condrey & Maranto, 2001) has gained exceptions from merit systems across the nation by expanding management prerogatives and restricting employee rights (Kellough & Nigro, 2006). In recent years, a variety of federal departments received full or partial waivers from Title 5 of the U.S. Code, which covers the merit system. Further, in the wake of the September 11, 2001, attacks, the Transportation Security Agency established at-will employment for its personnel. Subsequently, the Departments of Homeland Security and Defense were authorized in the name of the "war on terror" to create new human resource management systems that strengthen administrative discretion and diminish employee protections. Reformers sought to use these approaches as templates for government-wide change.

At the state level, major reform examples also exist: Texas nullified its merit system in 1985, making all state employees at will; a 1996 Georgia law mandated that all new civil servants be hired on an at-will basis; and in 2001, Florida eliminated job tenure for most incumbent middle managers (Walters, 2002). South Carolina and Arkansas abolished their merit systems; less dramatically, many states including Indiana, Delaware, and Kansas have reclassified career service positions to unclassified ones as a consequence of reorganizations, reductions-in-force, or attrition. Such strategies are often mutually reinforcing in a manner that promotes the ongoing decline of career public service.

The effect is that the status and role of the public employee today is increasingly not too different than that found in business (Hays & Sowa, 2006). Changes reducing or abolishing job security (and otherwise altering basic merit system tenets), then, have occurred throughout the country, despite International Labor Organization standards that forbid unjust dismissal.

The most recent development was a 2020 presidential Executive Order that has been called "the most direct assault on the career civil service since the passage of the Pendleton Act in 1883" (Neal, 2020, October 23) which outlawed the spoils system (Chapter 1). Drafted in secrecy and unprecedented in scope, it created a new "Schedule F" category of exempt positions for political appointees. Agencies were are to identify personnel in policy-related positions "to be involuntarily reclassified from jobs with constitutional and legislative due process safeguards to hiring and firing at-will employees." It is important to keep in mind that "these protections do not exist for the sake of civil servants themselves, but rather to ensure that government delivers services insulted from undue political influence" (Wagner, 2020, November 23).

The order could have affected tens of thousands, perhaps hundreds of thousands, of workers and undermine the professional, nonpartisan merit system, a repository of knowledge that distinguishes the national government and a key foundation of American democracy. It would have changed more than a century of employment laws, including the Hatch Act (see Chapter 14), legislated to assure an impartial, merit-based workforce. By putting institutional knowledge at-risk, converting the workforce to at-will status makes it more likely that employees would implement policies that were dangerous, illegal, and unethical. The order, in short, sought to redefine the competitive service into a politically loyal component of the presidency instead of fealty to the constitution (Wagner, 2020, October 27). While civil service reform is needed (Berman et al., 2022), this directive would have further marginalized the career service (Kettl, 2020, October 29). President Biden, who regards the career service as "the heart and soul of government," rescinded the order shortly after taking office. However, at least one advocacy group, based on initiatives in state and local government (which could affect the federal civil service), believes that interest in at-will reforms will continue especially if parties controlling the presidency and Congress change in future elections (Sherk, 2021).

APPLYING THE ETHICS TRIAD TO AT-WILL EMPLOYMENT

The spread of at-will employment has led to concerns about whether the doctrine is ethical. As discussed in Chapter 7, various ethical models may be helpful, but one is particularly useful because its comprehensive nature reduces the chances of an incomplete, flawed judgment. The decision-making tool acknowledges the imperatives in three approaches based on (1) expected results of an action (consequentialism or teleology), (2) application of pertinent rules (duty ethics or deontology), and (3) personal rectitude or character (virtue ethics).[2] Although the synthesis developed from triangulation does not provide definitive solutions, it does offer guidance by identifying the underlying logic by which decisions are justified (for further discussion, see Bowman, West, & Beck, 2010, Chapter 3). The goal is to strive for balance; governance is not geometry but the art of the possible. Ethical theories may lead to different evaluations of at-will employment, but Acton's epic-warning challenges decision makers to confront these differences, not suppress them. Management ethics need not be an oxymoron. The at-will doctrine will be analyzed here using the three perspectives.

Results-Based Analysis

In consequentialism, the best policy results in "the greatest good for the greatest number." What is right is that which creates the largest amount of human happiness with the least harm. This school of thought is associated with John Stuart Mill's ideas that "[d]ecisions are judged by their consequences depending on the results to be maximized" (Frederickson, 1997, 167–168). A similar emphasis is found in G. W. F. Hegel's (1821/1996, 113) writings where he articulates the principle, "[J]udge an act by its consequences, and make them the standard of what is right and good." This approach is useful for administrators seeking the common good for the public. Accordingly, consideration of an employment at-will policy examines affirmative and negative arguments on (a) productivity, (b) flexibility, (c) responsiveness, (d) merit, and (e) loyalty grounds.

In Support of At-Will Employment. Reformers maintain that use of a corporate-style "bottom-line" standard results in exemplary performance. Overprotective employment requirements entitle civil servants to their jobs regardless of results achieved (Howard, 2001). Moving from "protection to performance" means employees are not shielded by procedural requirements if they fail to produce (Florida Council of One Hundred, 2000). The threat of job loss is needed to keep employees motivated; they will have incentive to perform because they can be replaced at any time by others willing to work harder (Bardwick, 1995).

Among the benefits are gains in *productivity* (Epstein & Rosen, 1984). Charged with the responsibility to serve the public interest, political leaders have considerable leverage over at-will employees. When serving "at the pleasure of" the appointing official, efficiency is maximized and waste minimized. Time and resources expended dealing with burdensome due process rights and "just cause" dismissal rules are thereby saved for regular business that increases effectiveness. This assurance is grounded in employee confidence that government officials make decisions based on their merits. Prime beneficiaries of increased productivity are citizens who pay for and receive public services.

Running government like a business produces not only cost savings and enhanced efficiency but also greater *flexibility* in implementing the will of the voters. Elected officials are responsible to the people and, in turn, civil servants must be held accountable. Absent the protection of job security, elected officials can pinpoint responsibility and ensure accountability from civil servants. At-will status, for example, can disempower "bureaucratic guerillas" who directly or indirectly subvert plans of their organizational superiors (O'Leary, 2006). Political appointees, in short, can expect that civil servants will be more *responsive* when their job is at risk. With emphasis on performance, it follows that *merit* can be readily rewarded, using programs such as pay for performance. The overall result is that employee *loyalty* is assured (Epstein & Rosen, 1984; Maitland, 1989).

In the 21st century, then, absolute power does not corrupt (as it might have done in Lord Acton's time) because it is limited by legal safeguards such as antidiscrimination statutes. Running government like a business by encouraging productivity, flexibility, and responsiveness enables the will of the people to be fulfilled. The payoff is greater workforce merit and loyalty, as well as enhanced public trust. Because the marketplace does not naturally produce job security contracts, this demonstrates that they are inefficient. For all these reasons, it is evident that removing job tenure and instituting at-will employment serves the greatest good for the greatest number.

In Opposition to At-Will Employment. Skeptics argue that reformers base their views on "common sense" or anecdotes that are suspect justifications for abandoning constraints on power that so concerned Lord Acton. There is a lack of empirical evidence of improved *productivity* when workers lose job security (e.g., McCall, 2003). Indeed, tenure, together with other workplace initiatives (e.g., employee participation, empowerment, incentive programs), is associated with higher productivity (see literature review in Levine & Tyson, 1990; also review Freeman & Medoff, 1984; Ichniowski, 1992; Pfeffer, 1998). Substantial cost saving can be incurred with a stable and loyal workforce (Reichheld, 1996).

Job tenure, in addition, does not require employers to retain unproductive workers or require them to keep employees if economic conditions mandate reductions in force. The real problem is not employment security provisions but rather that administrators "do not want to go through the aggravation of giving marginal employees an unsatisfactory rating. If that is so, wouldn't managers under the new system also be reluctant to do so?" (Underhill & Oman, 2006). Finally, critics hold that fear of job loss is a poor motivator, because "KITA" (Kick in the Ass) is counterproductive (Herzberg, 1987). Indeed, they see "Theory X" managerial control policies, and its assumptions about human nature that guide reform (McGregor, 1960), as unfortunate throwbacks to an earlier era. Expectations of enhanced productivity are likely to be dashed, with heightened cynicism and low morale preventing even plausible outcomes as employees spend more time concerned "about antagonizing the current political party" than providing citizen services (Bowman & West, 2006a, 150). There is a paucity of evidence, in brief, that job security is related to productivity losses.

Defenders of "just cause" standards also point out that existing public personnel systems provide for ample *flexibility* when officials understand procedures, take advantage of opportunities to provide feedback, and use progressive discipline. This can lead to increased *responsiveness* since the public service ethos, by definition, encourages service to the citizenry. The absence of assurance of a job in the future may lead to high turnover, and less capacity for responsiveness, as employees use their positions as stepping stones to higher paying openings elsewhere. Upholding the principles of *merit* has been the important distinguishing feature of modern personnel systems for many generations. Indeed, historically government has been a "model employer," as recruiting, rewarding and retaining employees based on merit characterized best practices in public management (Berman et al., 2022).

In contrast, at-will employment exemplifies "hard" human resource management derived from Taylorism and scientific management (Greenwood, 2001; Guest, 1987, 1998; Truss & Gratton, 1997). Its instrumental emphasis focuses on organizational ends, with employees seen simply as means in achieving these ends. The doctrine allows "inconsistent, even irrational, management behavior by permitting arbitrary, non-work-related, treatment of employees—behavior that is not considered a good management practice" (Werhane et al., 2004, 197). "Soft" human resource management, however, grew out of the human relations movement, and values people as assets to be developed more than costs to be reduced. Organizations, in fact, have a moral obligation to treat individuals with dignity by pursuing exemplary practices such as staff empowerment, participation, training, and skill-building (Greenwood, 2002, 269).

One way to meet this obligation is to invest in employee skills and abilities and to use them effectively over the long term. This is more apt to occur where people are valued and protected from wrongful discharge (Burke & Little, 2002–2003). It is also likely that jurisdictions will experience a return on this investment in the form of greater employee *loyalty*, satisfaction, job commitment, and cooperation (Ashford, Lee, & Bobko, 1989; Green et al., 2006; Guest, 1998; Lim, 1996; Niehoff & Paul, 2001; West & Bowman, 2004).

Absent security, people may well ask, "If the employer is not loyal to me, why should I be loyal in return?" If government employment is just a job and not a calling, and if the traditionally below-market pay is not compensated for by tenure, then key staff are likely to leave. Indeed, at-will employment and privatization often has meant public employees lose their positions and do the same work done previously, but now as contract "shadow workers," with no security or benefits. Those who remain in the more politicized workplace may displace their loyalties from serving the public to obeying political masters. Manipulating public servants as disposable commodities or interchangeable parts is demeaning and misguided. In brief, the greatest good for the greatest number is achieved not by Theory X but rather by Theory Y management policies.

To summarize this section, in result-based ethics, only consequences matter. At-will advocates seek the greatest good by emphasizing expected results from corporate, bottomline approaches said to enhance productivity, flexibility, responsiveness, merit, and loyalty. To do otherwise, by authorizing job tenure, risks employee self-serving, expedient behavior. On these same grounds, however, skeptics argue that abandoning the keystone of the merit system hardly serves the citizenry. Instead, it encourages not only managerial opportunistic behaviors but also expedient and, ultimately, counterproductive actions. Further, little theoretical or empirical evidence exists to suggest that the at-will doctrine has the results supporters claim. Because an overemphasis on any one point of the ethics triad may put a proposed policy at risk, attention now turns to another approach.

Rule-Based Analysis

Rule-based decision-making provides a different lens for evaluating at-will employment. Certain actions are inherently right (e.g., promise keeping) or wrong (e.g., inflicting harm), irrespective of predicted consequences. This approach is useful for administrators who are

obligated to follow the morality found in the Constitution, court cases, and laws and regulations (Rohr, 1988). Principle- or rule-based ethics is closely identified with Immanuel Kant's
categorical imperative and Thomas Hobbes's social contract theory. Kant's (1785/1959, 17)
imperative is to "act as if the maxim of your action was to become a universal law of nature,"
which, in turn, is rooted in the belief that humans are capable of rational thought and
self-governance. Hobbes refers to "natural law" wherein human nature is a combination of
all one's experiences and competencies, the consequence of which is a common understanding of right and wrong (Kem, 2006).

In a rule-based analysis, what is right is what conforms to moral rules; one must see one's
duty and do it. In deciding what rule to apply, the person asks, "Would I want everyone else
to make the decision I did?" Here the emphasis is on ethical principles such as autonomy,
fairness/justice, and mutual respect in examining the affirmative and negative positions on
civil service reform.

In Support of At-Will Employment. Proponents stress the importance of managerial
proprietary rights and prerogatives, and their need for *autonomy* to run their agency (Epstein
& Rosen, 1984; Werhane, 1985). At-will employment is justified because no one has a right
to a government job; as such, employment is a privilege. Mandating employment security
diminishes managerial authority and the right to do what is best. Any abuses arising from
discretion can be controlled by formal procedures (in the form of internal auditors), informal
norms (employee pressures), and the operations of the free market (Epstein & Rosen, 1984).

Savvy managers, in fact, would refrain from unjust adverse actions because arbitrary and
capricious actions impair the organization's reputation, damage morale, lead to high quit
rates, and impede recruitment. Thoughtlessly exercising management proprietary rights and
prerogatives is clearly unwise. Since wrongful personnel actions and discharges diminish
returns on investments in training and development, they are costly and infrequent. The
at-will doctrine, then, actually serves to deter employer abuse. In addition, legislation exists
to protect the rights of employees from unfair dismissal (e.g., civil rights laws, whistleblower
protection). The concerns of Lord Acton, in short, are considerably circumscribed in modern
times.

At bottom, then, each party is at liberty to terminate a relationship should either one fail
to live up to expectations: Workers can quit at will, employers can fire at will. It follows that
fairness and *mutual respect* are accorded to each. Both parties are negotiators who attempt
to arrive at employment arrangements that advance their interests. As a matter of autonomy
and simple justice, once such commitments are freely made, the working conditions and
responsibilities apply to the partners. The market assures fair treatment; as long as employees
are paid for past work, they have been fully compensated and thus have no claim on future
employment (McCall, 2003). Abuses can occur, but sensible protections exist, and the deficiencies of job tenure outweigh the benefits.

In Opposition to At-Will Employment. Skeptics, following Lord Acton, are apprehensive
about the exercise of power. Employers are in a dominant position over employees because
they own the means of production without which the employee could not make a living. It is
evident that the employee needs the employer more than vice versa, jeopardizing *autonomy*.
Because of the asymmetric power relationship and the resulting inequality in resources
favoring employers, job security is a prerequisite to level the playing field (Gertz, 2008).

While acknowledging wrongful discharge legislation, critics point out that there are
numerous ways to terminate someone that are not protected by law. The at-will doctrine, in

effect, furnishes near-absolute power to managers to discharge a worker for any or no reason not contrary to the limited exceptions provided by statute. Because most people need work to survive, "there is a sense in which (they) are forced to work" (Bowie, 2005, 70). Genuine autonomy is impossible under such circumstances. Indeed, assuming that the market will deter abusive behavior overlooks the hundreds of thousands of employees annually whose contested terminations are found by arbitrators to be without cause (McCall, 2003). The very lack of power can also produce effects detrimental to both the individual and organization. As Werhane et al. (2004, 196) observe, the at-will creed "has, on numerous occasions, seemingly translated in a license for employers and employees to treat one another" unfairly.

The unbalanced nature of the doctrine violates basic *fairness* and *mutual respect*. Job loss can have serious economic and psychological repercussions for employees and their families, as well as exacerbate problems in the larger community (unemployment, poverty). Formal and informal pressures (internal auditors, coworker monitoring) and legal protections (civil rights, age discrimination, and whistleblowing laws) are often insufficient to deter abuse. Further, at-will employment is seen as part of a package of policies that includes outsourcing, privatization, and civil service reform—all of which enhances management rights at the expense of employees. Might does not make right. Instead, there is a duty to offer people meaningful work; to treat them as ends, not means; and to show each person respect.

In short, at-will advocates see a fair, symmetrical relationship, one that preserves the autonomy of each party. The balance of power is maintained not only by the employer's enlightened self-interest but also by wrongful discharge legislation. Any effort to unduly emphasize rule-based ethics at the expense of the rest of the ethics triad is thereby circumscribed. At-will protagonists, as free-market fundamentalists, believe that everyone should be at will so that mutually beneficial agreements can be struck with little or no outside interference. In contrast, defenders of the "just cause" standard see the one-sided power relationship leading to a lack of mutual respect and fairness and encouraging overreaching, detrimental practices. It follows, then, that the at-will creed must not be made universal, but rather job protections should be widely available. Attention now turns to the final point of the ethics triangle.

Virtue-Based Analysis

In virtue ethics, answers to the question of "What to do?" have little to do with results or rules, and everything to do with the kind of person one is. Personal character offers a third perspective by asking, "What would a person of integrity decide?" when assessing the ethical advisability of employment at will. Virtue theory stems from the classical writings of Aristotle (e.g., *The Nicomachean Ethics*) and the modern views of Alasdair MacIntyre (1984). As Geuras and Garofalo (2006, 59) note, the "theory considers an act to be good on the basis of the character trait or virtue that the act evidences." Virtuous conduct derives from a lifelong practice of self-discipline requiring commitment to ethical values.

Virtue ethics is enticing for policymakers because it is a more personal approach than cognitive ethics—decisions are informed not only by consequences and duties but also by the quality of one's character. What is right is that which nurtures individual excellence and contributes to collective well-being. While there is no one list of traits (the idea of virtue theory is to transcend procedures and rules by emphasizing one's moral being), characteristics such as trustworthiness, integrity, and prudence are integral to moral nobility.

In Support of At-Will Employment. Reformers believe that voluntary employer–employee relationships, unencumbered by regulations, promote *trustworthiness*. Employers trust that those hired will perform and employees trust that appropriate work opportunities will be provided. Legal requirements assume that trust cannot be assured, thereby damaging mutual expectations. Because an employer cannot exist without an employee (and vice versa), the at-will doctrine services both parties. A freedom of contract, laissez-faire approach is best to ensure trust.

Integrity, the synthesis of virtues, is the capacity to understand one's obligations and ensure moral soundness as a member of a larger community. By striving for integrity in work, employees will be secure in their positions. People are moral not because of rules but because of what they demand of themselves in character; externally imposed rules impair the development of authentic character. One's moral self grows from internal values; a person of integrity chafes at outside regulations in his relationships with others. The spirit of the at-will doctrine, then, enriches the association between the employer and employee.

Personal character, steeped in virtues, provides the disposition to take action. If moral rectitude directs one to the right end, then *prudence* (the ability to distinguish between right and wrong, and to act accordingly) directs one to the right means. The goal of individual freedom at work, in short, can be best pursued by employers and employees through the at-will principle.

In Opposition to At-Will Employment. Reintroducing the 19th-century at-will doctrine into government service reneges the social contract inherent in the merit system: job safeguards in exchange for modest compensation. Complementing legal protection in most workplaces is the existence of a "psychological contract," an understanding between an employee and employer that enhances loyalty and commitment (Berman & West, 2003; Niehoff & Paul, 2001; Rousseau, 1995; West, 2013). Because such a contract implies continued employment, the taking of such an entitlement is a betrayal of good faith. Having due process rights with orderly procedures (notice, opportunity to be heard, enforcement of rights) is an effective check on capricious behavior. When personnel know that they will be treated fairly, in brief, then *trustworthiness* in the employment relationship is fostered.

Without such protections, employment at will promotes a system in which *integrity* is difficult for employees to maintain. Even now, not only are civil servants unlikely to report fraud, waste, and abuse, but they may feel pressured to "go along to get along" (Gertz, 2008). A consequence of at-will employment is that staff will be increasingly reluctant to participate fully in decision-making or to "speak truth to power" by criticizing inefficient or unethical policies, or may even feel compelled to participate in dubious policies when confronted with job loss. Absolute power, manifest in at-will employment, can corrupt absolutely: It heightens the probability that such corruption will occur and that the public interest will be compromised. If employees are unlikely to report untoward behavior for fear of retribution, truth-telling, so critical to integrity, is devalued.

Prudent decision-making suggests a cautious approach to reform, thereby ensuring that proposed change will lead to desired improvements. As noted by Dobel (1998, 76), "Prudent judgment identifies salient moral aspects of a political situation which a leader has a moral obligation to attend to in making a decision." "Good judgment," he adds, "requires good information and a willingness to learn." However, many jurisdictions have seen the at-will doctrine as a seductive quick-fix to perceived problems. They have undertaken reform initiatives hastily and with little evidence demonstrating the efficacy of the change. They are victims of the "sin of superficial advice" (Meltsner, 2005, 412). Hastily adopting reform, for example, "amputation before diagnosis," results in misjudgments and dubious policies. Bowman, West, and Gertz (2006), for instance, note that the absence of reliable evidence, a distorted view of the business model, and ideological rigidity promoted radical reforms in Florida.

In a nutshell, at-will supporters argue that the mutual freedom to contract nurtures trust, regulations interfere with individual and collective integrity, and individual freedom creates prudence. Critics think the creed negates trust by breaking contracts, damages integrity by increasing fear, and undermines prudence by its panacea-like quality. Yet the strength of virtue theory (reliance on subjective assessment derived from personal character) is also its weakness: If at-will proponents and opponents believe that they are good, then it is not hard to believe that what they do is good.

SUMMARY AND CONCLUSION

Responsible policymakers develop virtues, respect rules, and consider results. The analytical decision-making process presented here is a conscious attempt to reconcile clashing values by highlighting an essential function of ethical management—developing different viewpoints, evaluating them, and producing a considered judgment. The approach offered is like a good map, presenting choices, not formula. Just as a map outlines a journey, the triad provides help in making the inevitable compromises, aiding skilled management of ethical ambiguity and independent thinking.

It is important to keep in mind potential pitfalls when just one school of thought is emphasized at the expense of the others. For example, the results approach may be problematic because it is difficult to anticipate all possible consequences and because it may lead to expedient action (thus, when choosing among appealing outcomes, rule-based ethics and virtue theory should also be applied). Similarly, rule-based ethics, if used alone, may lack compassion (Svara, 1997) when truth telling produces cold and inconsiderate behaviors (to compensate, benevolence in the virtue ethics might be applied). Last, the exclusive use of virtue theory is perplexing because of its intuitive and possibly self-serving nature (to be counterbalanced by utilizing the other two schools of thought). In short, an integrated approach helps to provide a defensible decision that takes into account results, rules, and virtues.

As part of NPM, the doctrine of employment at will has, after a long decline (Muhl, 2001), enjoyed a renaissance in recent years. As Schwab (2001) predicted, the principle of just cause protection against unfair dismissal would be eroded in the new century. Reformers believe that employees have no need of job security because modern civil rights and whistleblowing laws provide adequate protection and employers are generally honorable and rarely engage in egregious behavior.

Until a short time ago, one of the distinguishing features of public employment was the merit system and the neutral competence of the civil service, safeguarded from political pressures, cronyism, sycophancy, and corruption. The rise of at-will employment (and its functional equivalents such as hiring temporary employees) is seen by proponents as a way to reenergize the bureaucracy and by opponents as a return to the spoils system (Bowman, 2002; Bowman & West, 2006a). There are compelling, competing grounds found in the debate over civil service reform and at-will employment. The overall assessment of these contentions here will provide a synthesis, or at least a conclusion.

Result-based decision-making, as discussed earlier, evaluates at-will employment as it relates to productivity, flexibility, responsiveness, merit, and loyalty, and how these contribute to the greatest good. Stakeholders are benefited or harmed by employment at will. Elected officials benefit from the increased responsiveness of civil servants that eliminating job security is thought to produce. Managers, due to enhanced flexibility, are not required to deal with procedural requirements when undertaking adverse actions. However, career public employees, lacking tenure, fear losing their positions if they choose to serve the long-term public interest when it conflicts with short-term political advantage. More generally, the at-will doctrine encourages the treatment of personnel as means to organizational ends, as costs to be controlled rather than assets to be developed.

The largest stakeholder, however, is the citizenry. Reformers suggest that productivity will soar when government is run like a business. Yet there is little documentation adduced by reformers to substantiate this view, perhaps because available data suggest productivity, morale, and loyalty may be placed in jeopardy when employee protections are removed. Further, government can adopt proven business tools such as competitive pay and teamwork and still provide job safeguards. Such action is not inconsistent with the NPM emphasis and preserves the existing social contract with employees. A policymaker using result-based ethics may find some politically attractive at-will employment arguments, but the evidence suggests that the greatest good is served by neutral competence in the public service.

Rule-based imperatives, the second perspective, emphasize the need for principles such as autonomy, fairness/justice, and mutual respect. At-will supporters argue that the doctrine allows for freedom of contract. When the decision maker takes into account the asymmetrical nature of the employer–employee relationship, however, it is evident that personnel can easily be subject to intimidation and unjust actions that violate their autonomy and rob them of respect.

Virtue-based ethics relies on intuitive character traits such as trustworthiness, integrity, and prudence, said to be nurtured by the at-will doctrine according to reformers. Yet doubters believe that trust is compromised when rights are diminished, and adverse actions lacking just cause occur. Integrity suffers in a fear-filled environment. To the extent that reforms are rushed into place, with questionable grounds to support them, prudence is violated.

Each of the three approaches contains arguments for and against at-will employment. Taken separately, the creed may appear ethical at some points and unethical at others; as Aristotle admonished, one should not expect more precision from a subject matter than it can allow. On balance, however, it is difficult to see how an employment doctrine that permits harm without cause can be ethical from a results-, rule-, or virtue-based perspective. To have power is to be morally responsible for one's actions. An employment relationship with few reciprocal obligations in which the employer recognizes little obligation to the employee compromises the greatest good, duty, and personal integrity. In so doing, it needlessly places the hallmark of modern civil service—neutral competence—at risk. Because all power needs to be restrained, such concerns should inspire public employers to unambiguously reject the at-will doctrine:

> When others crucially depend on and expect continued participation in a cooperative enterprise, it appears patently unfair to abruptly end the relationship without notice and without good reason, an idea we reflect in our common moral assessments of contexts as varied as marriage, housing, and access to traditional routes of public passage

through private property. Thus . . . the power to terminate the relationship without due process . . . violates commonly held norms of fairness. . . . It is especially unfair when one party has the preponderance of power. (McCall, 2003, 166)

Since arbitrary behavior is not tolerated in other areas of management such as finance, it should not be accepted in employment relations. Lord Acton would agree.

***

Only they deserve power who justify its use daily.

—Dag Hammarskjold

NOTES

1. This chapter is adapted from Bowman and West (2007) with permission from Springer Science and Business Media. Parts of the background section are condensed from Bowman and West (2006b).
2. While other philosophies might be used to evaluate the ethics of at-will employment, these three schools of thought are dominant in the literature on administrative ethics (see Cooper, 1987; Frederickson & Ghere, 2005; Garofalo & Geuras, 1999; Geuras & Garofalo, 2006; Richter, Burke, & Doig, 1990).

DISCUSSION

1. Lord Acton's observation is one of the most well known in political history. Why?

2. People often hold strong views on employment at will. Identify the most convincing argument for the doctrine and the most compelling against it.

3. Can an at-will employee be terminated for having a cup of coffee or tea, wearing a long- or short-sleeve shirt, or smiling politely? Explain.

4. Following the January 6 insurrection at the capitol building in Washington, DC, some companies terminated employees for their participation. Discuss.

5. Are there other significant arguments in the at-will employment debate not included in the results, rules, and virtue trifocal analysis? To what extent, if any, does behavioral ethics (Chapter 7) shed light on the debate?

6. Contest this statement: The employment-at-will doctrine sees employees as commodities to be exploited and mistreated.

7. Are recent civil service reforms that include removal of tenure a harbinger of a neo-spoils system in government?

8. Critics of President Trump's October 2020 Schedule F executive order denounced it as "power grab" and claimed that whistleblowing would become much more unlikely. Discuss.

9. The chapter concluded that Lord Acton would endorse the view that arbitrary management behavior should not be tolerated. Discuss.

EXERCISES

1. A large majority of people in the American workforce, except most career civil servants, "work at will." Visit an employer and ask a manager about how the system operates in her organization. What legal protections exist against arbitrary adverse personal actions? Are they adequate?

2. Ask an employee who "works at will." Does he understand that he is vulnerable to termination for any or no reason not contrary of law?

REFERENCES

Aristotle. (1980). *The Nicomachean ethics* (D. Ross, Trans.). Oxford: Oxford University Press.

Ashford, S., Lee, C., & Bobko, P. (1989). Content, causes and consequences of job insecurity: A theory-based measure and substantive test. *Academy of Management Journal*, *32*, 803–829.

Bardwick, J. (1995). *Danger in the comfort zone*. New York: AMACOM.

Berman, E., Bowman, J., West, J., & Van Wart, M. (2022). *Human resource management in public service: Paradoxes, problems, and processes* (7th ed.). Thousand Oaks, CA: Sage.

Berman, E., & West, J. (2003). Psychological contracts in local government: A preliminary survey. *Review of Public Personnel Administration*, *23*, 267–285.

Bowie, N. (2005). Kantian ethical thought. In J. Budd & J. Scoville (Eds.), *The ethics of human resources and industrial relations* (pp. 61–88). Champaign, IL: Labor and Employment Relations Association.

Bowman, J. (2002). At-will employment in Florida: A naked formula to corrupt public service. *Working USA*, *6*, 90–102.

Bowman, J., & West, J. (2006a). Ending civil service protections in Florida government: Experiences in state agencies. *Review of Public Personnel Administration*, *26*, 139–157.

Bowman, J., & West, J. (2006b, March). *Removing employee protections: A "see no evil" approach to civil service reform*. Paper presented at the 2006 Western Political Science Association meeting, Albuquerque, NM.

Bowman, J., & West, J. (2007, August). Lord Acton and employment doctrines: Absolute power and the spread of at-will employment. *Journal of Business Ethics*, *74*(2).

Bowman, J., West, J., & Beck, M. (2010). *Achieving public service competencies: The professional edge*. Armonk, NY: M. E. Sharpe.

Bowman, J., West, J., & Gertz, S. (2006). Florida's service first: Radical reform in the sunshine state. In J. Kellough & L. Nigro (Eds.), *Civil service reform in the states* (pp. 145–170). New York: SUNY Press.

Burke, D., & Little, B. (2002–2003). At-will employment: Just let it go. *Journal of Individual Employment Rights*, *10*, 119–131.

Condrey, S., & Maranto, R. (Eds.). (2001). *Radical reform of the civil service*. New York: Lexington Books.

Cooper, T. (1987). Hierarchy, virtue, and the practice of public administration: A perspective for normative ethics. *Public Administration Review*, *47*, 320–328.

Dobel, P. (1998). Political prudence and the ethics of leadership. *Public Administration Review*, *58*, 74–81.

Epstein, R., & Rosen, S. (1984). In defense of contract at will. *University of Chicago Law Review*, *51*, 947–988.

Ferlie, E., Ashburner, L., & Pettigrew, A. (1996). *The new public management in action*. Oxford: Oxford University Press.

Florida Council of One Hundred. (2000). *Modernizing Florida's civil service system: Moving from protection to performance*. Tampa, FL: Author.

Frederickson, H. G. (1997). *The spirit of public administration*. San Francisco: Jossey-Bass.

Frederickson, H. G., & Ghere, R. K. (Eds.). (2005). *Ethics in public management*. Armonk, NY: M. E. Sharpe.

Freeman, R., & Medoff, J. (1984). *What do unions do?* New York: Basic Books.

Garofalo, D., & Geuras, D. (1999). *Ethics in the public service*. Washington, DC: Georgetown University Press.

Gertz, S. (2008). At-will employment: Origins, applications, exceptions, and expansions. *International Journal of Public Administration, 31*, 489–514.

Geuras, D., & Garofalo, C. (2006). *Practical ethics in public administration* (2nd ed.). Vienna, VA: Management Concepts.

Gore, A. (1993). *From red tape to results: Creating a government that works better and costs less: Report of the national performance review*. Darby, PA: DIANE.

Green, R., Golden, A., Forbis, R., Nelson, S., & Robinson, J. (2006). On the ethics of at-will employment relations in the public sector. *Public Integrity, 8*, 305–327.

Greenwood, M. (2001). The importance of stakeholders: According to business. *Business and Society Review, 106*, 29–50.

Greenwood, M. (2002). Ethics and HRM: A review and conceptual analysis. *Journal of Business Ethics, 36*, 261–278.

Guest, D. (1987). Human resource management and industrial relations. *Journal of Management Studies, 24*, 5–25.

Guest, D. (1998). Is the psychological contract worth taking seriously? *Journal of Organizational Behavior, 19*, 649–664.

Hays, S., & Sowa, J. (2006). A broader look at the "accountability" movement: Some grim realities in state civil service systems. *Review of Public Personnel Administration, 26*, 102–117.

Hegel, G. W. F. (1996). *Philosophy of right* (S. Dyde, Trans.). Amherst, NY: Prometheus Books. [Original work published 1821]

Herzberg, F. (1987). One more time: How do you motivate employees? *Harvard Business Review, 65*, 109–120.

Holger, R. (2004). *Employment relations in the United States*. Thousand Oaks, CA: Sage.

Howard, P. (2001, September 6). Demand accountability from public employees. *Miami Herald*, p. B7.

Hugh, S. (2001, May 25). Employment at will, an idea whose time has come—and gone. *Workforce*. Retrieved from www.workforce.com/apps/pbcs.dll/article?AID=/20010525/NEWS02/305259993&template=printarticle

Ichniowski, C. (1992). Human resource management and productive labor relations. In D. Lewin, O. S. Mitchell, & P. D. Sherer (Eds.), *Research frontiers in industrial relations and human resources* (pp. 239–272). Madison, WI: Industrial Relations Research Association.

Kant, I. (1959). *Foundations of the metaphysics of morals* (L. Beck, Trans.). Indianapolis, IN: Bobbs-Merrill. [Original work published 1785]

Kellough, J., & Nigro, L. (Eds.). (2006). *Civil service reform in the states*. Albany, NY: SUNY Press.

Kem, J. (2006). A pragmatic ethical decision making model for the army: The ethical triangle. *Unpublished manuscript*, U.S. Army Command and General Staff College, Fort Leavenworth, Kansas.

Kettl, D. (2020, October 29). Why merit matters. *Government Executive*. Retrieved from www. govexec.com/management/2020/10/why-merit-matters/169657/

Levine, D., & Tyson, L. (1990). Participation, productivity and the firm's environment. In A. Blinder (Ed.), *Paying for productivity* (pp. 183–236). Washington, DC: Brookings Institution.

Lim, V. (1996). Job security and its outcomes: Moderating effects of work-based and non-work-based social support. *Human Relations*, *49*, 171–194.

MacIntyre, A. C. (1984). *After virtue: A study in moral theory* (2nd ed.). South Bend, IN: University of Notre Dame Press.

Maitland, I. (1989). Rights in the workplace: A Nozickian argument. *Journal of Business Ethics*, *8*, 951–954.

McCall, J. (2003). A defense of just cause dismissal rules. *Business Ethics Quarterly*, *13*, 151–175.

McGregor, D. (1960). *The human side of enterprise*. New York: McGraw-Hill.

Meltsner, A. (2005). The seven deadly sins of policy analysts. In J. Shafritz, K. Layne, & C. Borick (Eds.), *Classics of public policy* (pp. 409–415). New York: Pearson/Longman.

Muhl, C. (2001). The employment at-will doctrine: Three major exceptions. *Monthly Labor Review*, *124*, 3–12.

Neal, J. (2020, October 23). White House drops an F-bomb on the career civil service. *Federal News Network*. Retrieved from https://federalnewsnetwork.com/commentary/2020/10/white-house-drops-an-f-bomb-on-the-career-civil-service/

Niehoff, B., & Paul, R. (2001). The just workplace: Developing and maintaining effective psychological contracts. *Review of Business*, *22*, 5–8.

O'Leary, R. (2006). *The ethics of dissent: Managing guerilla government*. Washington, DC: CQ Press.

Pfeffer, J. (1998). *The human equation*. Boston, MA: Harvard Business School Press.

Pollitt, C. (1990). *Managerialism in the public sector*. Cambridge: Basil-Blackwell.

Pollitt, C., & Bouckaert, G. (2004). *Public management reform: A comparative analysis* (2nd ed.). Oxford: Oxford University Press.

Reichheld, F. (1996). *The loyalty effect: The hidden force behind growth, profits, and lasting value*. Boston, MA: Harvard Business School Press.

Richter, W., Burke, F., & Doig, J. (1990). *Combating corruption/encouraging ethics: Sourcebook for PA ethics*. Washington, DC: American Society for Public Administration.

Rohr, J. A. (1988). *Ethics for bureaucrats* (2nd ed.). New York: Marcel Dekker.

Rousseau, D. (1995). *Psychological contracts in organizations: Understanding written and unwritten agreements*. Thousand Oaks, CA: Sage.

Salamon, L. M., & Elliott, O. V. (2002). *The tools of government: A guide to the new governance*. Oxford: Oxford University Press.

Schwab, S. (2001). Predicting the future of employment law: Reflecting or refracting market forces? *Indiana Law Journal*, *29*, 31–48.

Sherk, J. (2021, June 8). *Increasing accountability in the civil service*. Arlington,VA: America First Policy Institute.

Stone, K. (2004). *From widgets to digits: Employment regulation for the changing workplace*. Cambridge: Cambridge University Press.

Sulieman, E. (2003). *Dismantling democratic states*. Princeton, NJ: Princeton University Press.

Svara, J. (1997). The ethical triangle: Synthesizing the bases of administrative ethics. In J. Bowman (Ed.), *Public integrity Annual* (pp. 33–41). Lexington, KY: Council of State Governments.

Truss, C., & Gratton, L. (1997). Soft and hard models of human resource management: A reappraisal. *Journal of Management Studies*, *34*, 53–73.

Underhill, J., & Oman, R. (2006). A critical review of the sweeping federal civil service changes. *Review of Public Personnel Administration*, *27*, 401–420.

Wagner, E. (2020, October 26). Salary council chairman resigns in protest of Trump order politicizing federal workforce. *Government Executive*. Retrieved from www.govexec.com/management/2020/10/salary-council-chairman-resigns-protest-trump-order-politicizing-federal-workforce/169551/

Wagner, E. (2020, November 23). OMB reportedly designate 88% of its employees for schedule F. *Government Executive*. Retrieved from www.govexec.com/management/2020/11/omb-reportedly-designates-88-its-employees-schedule-f/170275/

Walters, J. (2002). *Life after civil service reform: The Texas, Georgia, and Florida experiences*. Arlington, VA: IBM Endowment for the Business of Government.

Werhane, P. (1985). *Persons, rights, and corporations*. Englewood Cliffs, NJ: Prentice Hall.

Werhane, P., Radin, T., & Bowie, N. (2004). *Employment and employee rights*. Malden, MA: Blackwell.

West, J. (2013). Employee-friendly policies and development benefits for millennials. In R. Sims & W. Sauser (Eds.), *Managing human resources from the millennial generation* (pp. 201–228). Charlotte, NC: Information Age Press.

West, J., & Bowman, J. (2004). Stakeholder analysis of civil service reform in Florida: A descriptive, instrumental, normative human resource management perspective. *State and Local Government Review*, *36*, 20–34.

14 To "Re-Hatch" Public Employees or Not?

The appointment power of the executive branch and subsequent character of public service has been the subject of controversy for years. Protagonists hold competing views on the appropriate administrative doctrine: the guardian model (a politically neutral, merit-based, impartial career bureaucracy) versus the politico model (a politically sensitive, patronage-based, partisan noncareer bureaucracy). The former construct reflects the Wilsonian dichotomy separating politics from administration, the hallmark of orthodox public administration. A component of this approach is the Hatch Act of 1939, a method to safeguard the principles of merit by insulating civil servants from political manipulation and protecting the public from partisan administration of law.

The latter model, based on business management practices, emphasizes managerial discretion and flexibility on one hand and employee performance and responsiveness on the other. Arguing that there is no merit in the merit system, (Ingraham, 2006; Condrey & Maranto, 2001), the NPM and contemporary civil service reform movements have introduced commercial values into public service, increased the number of political appointees, eroded civil service protections, and hollowed out many governmental agencies by privatizing their management functions (Bowman & West, 2007).

These initiatives to alter the nature of public employment paralleled a variety of significant developments at the dawn of the new century:

- The largest restructuring of the federal government in history, as well as significant changes in state public management, that place the concept of a public service career and an impartial civil service in jeopardy.
- Authorization to establish new personnel systems at the departments of Homeland Security and Defense, systems that expand managerial discretion and restrict employee rights.
- Institution of employment at-will in selected federal agencies, permitting adverse personnel actions for any or reason no contrary to law (see Chapter 13).
- Implementation of pay-for-performance techniques that potentially equate employee performance with political responsiveness.

DOI: 10.4324/9781003203148-18

- Claims that political loyalty overrides professional expertise in NASA global warming climate projections, Medicare prescription cost predictions, Central Intelligence Agency pre–Iraq War intelligence estimates, Federal Emergency Management Administration appointments and contracting, Food and Drug Administration (FDA) approvals, as well as similar, less well-known problems in agencies such as the IRS, the Forest Service, and the departments of Interior, Housing and Urban Development, and Education.
- Widespread allegations of patronage, cronyism, privatization and fraud, waste and abuse in the aftermath of Hurricane Katrina and post-invasion of Iraq.
- The Office of Special Counsel, an independent investigatory body responsible for enforcing the Hatch Act, recommended to the president in 2007 that the Administrator of the General Services of Administration be disciplined to the fullest extent of the law for asking department employees to "help our candidates" during a briefing at the agency held by a White House political strategist (similar meetings were convened at 20 other agencies).
- The FBI, the Central Intelligence Agency, the United States Army, and Justice Department involvement in controversial surveillance, extraordinary rendition, and alternative interrogation programs which were often developed against the advice of military and civilian professionals.
- Release of a 2007 executive order requiring that all new departmental regulations be subject to approval by an agency political appointee.
- Sudden classification of documents and removal of large amounts of information from public scrutiny by political appointees.
- The alleged "purge" of United States Attorneys in the Bush and Trump administrations (an office traditionally insulated from political pressure), and a wider politicization of the Justice Department in selection of career personnel.
- With the exceptions noted here, most other presidencies adhered to the law, while the last administration officials repeatedly ignored it, willfully failing to separate official duties and political activities in a Hatch Act "crime spree" (Clark, 2020, September 22; Rubin, 2020, August 26; Staff Report, 2020).
- Ongoing controversies about the integrity of the nation's electoral machinery including the activities of partisan election officials, restrictions on voter registration drives, the reliability of privately owned voting machines, the accuracy of voter registration rolls, and newly erected barriers to voting.

Under current law, Hatch Act provisions are not self-enforcing as the Office of Special Council can only make recommendations, which in the past would often result in administrative penalties.

Reorganizations, new personnel systems, loyalty versus expertise controversies, headline examples of civil service politicization, patronage and cronyism, and political appointee activities, in short, have heightened careerist-appointee tensions; such tensions impact employee professionalism, nonpartisan administration, and citizen confidence in government. In so doing, they highlight a defining issue in the post-9/11 era: the overall role of government and the nature of public service. Indeed, as these events suggest, there may be a failure to recognize that the government should be used to benefit all of the people, not one party. Given the unprecedented high number of complaints in recent years, an investigation revealed that 14 high-level Trump officials violated the law a total of 54 times plus another 22 officeholders under investigation for nearly 100 more transgressions. It found that "it's not simply the Hatch Act violations. Those are symptoms. The broader disease at play here is the intermingling of political and the national interest" (Staff Report Prepared for Senator Elizabeth Warren, 2020). Since anti-corruption legislation like the Act are intended to preserve a functioning democracy, the disregard of the law and politicization of nonpartisan government activities—with no official consequences—makes whistleblowing (Chapter 10) as important as ever.

This study examines the Hatch Act, as amended in 1993 to relax restrictions on political conduct, in light of these developments. It asks, "Is the law ethical?" To address this question, a tool is used that encompasses the complementarity of results-based utilitarian ethics, rule-based duty ethics, and virtue-based character ethics. The discussion begins with the importance of the problem, followed by its evolution and current status. After describing the method of analysis, the central section of the text evaluates the Hatch Act. The conclusion explores the implications of the findings.

BACKGROUND

Although the nation's founders seriously debated the grounds for employee recruitment by the new government, a century would pass before these concerns were resolved in the 1883 Pendleton Act and, later, the 1939 Hatch Act as amended. This section briefly traces the origins and effect of the latter legislation.

Since the 1880s, government has restricted employee political activity, thereby constraining executive ability to use partisan criteria in the management of the public workforce. Such regulation stems from the abuses of the 19th-century spoils system in which political leaders relied on governmental employees to financially support and work in political campaigns. The assassination of President Garfield by a disappointed office seeker, however, led to the passage of the Pendleton Act. It created a bipartisan Civil Service Commission, which in turn established the merit system and issued rules limiting civil servant political involvement. The law marked the beginning of the end of the spoils system and the eventual widespread adoption of merit criteria in public employment.

By the 1930s, however, the size of government dramatically expanded in response to the Great Depression and the number of unclassified appointments grew. Near the end of the decade a coalition of Republicans and anti-New Deal Democrats, led by Senator Carl Hatch (D-NM), passed the "Act to Prevent Pernicious Political Activities" to regulate the political conduct of federal personnel. In 1940, coverage was extended to state and local workers supported by federal funds. Most states also enacted "little" Hatch Acts, and many localities did the same with "littler" Hatch Acts, designed to limit the political behavior of their staff. Such limitations can be seen as a modern adaptation of the Framers' concerns about "faction" in government (Bloch, 2005) as Hatch Act-style legislation was the primary means to fortify the guardian model by circumscribing partisanship in bureaucracy. Indeed, until recently the politico model had been rejected in a series of court cases curtailing the use of patronage spoils on the grounds of impartial, ethical, and efficient public administration.[1]

The result was that for much of the 20th century, governmental employees were typically prohibited from being candidates for public office in partisan elections, campaigning in partisan elections, fund raising, holding political party office, and partisan voter registration activities. They could vote, express opinions, contribute money, display political signs, attend rallies, join parties, and assist in nonpartisan voter registration drives when off-duty. Violations of the law resulted in termination unless the Civil Service Commission (later the Merit Systems Protection Board) imposed a lesser penalty (minimum: 30-day suspension without pay). While considerable diversity exists among states and localities, restrictions were generally similar in nature to those at the federal level as they "proscribe employees from coercing other workers, using their official authority to affect election results, and engaging in partisan activities while on the job" (Snead, 2001: 262; see also Boyle, 1990: 257; Gely & Chandler, 2000).

Such regulations, supporters believed, would increase professionalism; reduce political manipulation, corruption, and favoritism; and maintain citizen faith in government. The fairness and efficiency of the administration of the nation's laws would thereby be assured. The risks of employee political participation, in short, warranted limitations on political rights. Critics argued that such claims were not sufficient to limit constitutional freedoms of speech and assembly of over one-sixth of the nation's workforce. Not only did government lose employees who wished not to have their rights negated but also society was denied the contributions that they could make. If political abuse was the danger, opponents pointed out, then appropriate penalties should be established rather than to deprive millions of citizen-employees their rights because they might be coerced.

Despite a variety of developments (court decisions and amendments noted subsequently, as well as a Congressional commission [U.S. Commission on the Political Activity of Governmental Personnel, 1967]), the "efficiency" argument to justify regulation of political activity prevailed. A significant public need was seen for an impartial civil service as the fundamental elements of the Hatch Act were retained for over half a century. The Supreme Court, however, left the door open to reform in *US Civil Service Commission v. National Association of Letter Carriers* (1973) when it stated that "Congress may wish to strike a different balance than it has" between employee and employer rights.

In subsequent years Congress sought to do just that. An amendment to the 1974 Federal Campaign Act, permitted state and local, but not federal, personnel covered by the Hatch Act to engage in partisan activities. Two years later, President Gerald Ford vetoed a bill expanding federal employee political rights. A similar bill was defeated in 1978, because it was thought to damage the prospects of President Jimmy Carter's omnibus Civil Service Reform Act.[2] The U.S. House passed a measure in 1987 and 1988 similar to the earlier bills, and in 1990 Congress approved reform legislation that was subsequently vetoed by President George H. W. Bush.

However, concerns that the quality of democracy was negatively affected in denying political rights of public servants ultimately triumphed. Amendments liberalizing the Hatch Act were signed into law in 1993; they relaxed off-duty prohibitions and strengthened on-the-job restrictions against political abuse. Thus, while restraints on partisan conduct remain, limits on political participation have largely been abandoned (Riccucci, 2006: 11). Supporters maintained that the change

- made the Act stronger because it outlawed all on-duty political activity,
- clarified confusing, contradictory aspects of the Hatch Act and civil service regulations,
- guaranteed nonpartisan administration because political coercion was prohibited.

(Gely & Chandler, 2000: 5)

It was argued that reform was necessary because the Act was obsolete and paternalistic. Instead, modern merit system principles shielded employees from partisan abuse and landmark court decisions (Roback, 1992) established that patronage practices do not serve a vital government interest.

Hatch Act defenders said that it was naïve to assume that the law was outdated. History had demonstrated the need for the law, as less restrictive measures proved inadequate. The civil service improved over the years precisely because the merit system and the Act worked. Sanctions in the Amendments would only apply to patent violations, while more subtle and effective forms of coercion left employees susceptible to political pressures. Accordingly, to relax protections was, at best, imprudent. Nothing had occurred since 1939, they argued, to suggest that reforming the law would do anything except to encourage unscrupulous, partisan behavior. Likewise, contemporary safeguards (e.g., just cause due process protections in cases of adverse personnel actions) may in theory restrict arbitrary management decisions; in fact, however, such cases must be heard individually—an expensive, time-consuming, uncertain process. To expect civil servants to file complaints when subject to potent, tacit sanctions is to expect uncommon courage.

The effect of the 1993 Amendments is ambiguous and a topic for future research. On the one hand, there appeared to be no negative results from earlier similar state reforms (Boyle, 1990: 285). Further, an examination of federal Hatch Act complaints and employee surveys before and after 1993, "suggests that the experience . . . has been generally positive" (Gely & Chandler, 2000: 5). On the other hand, later empirical work (Bloch, 2005: 21–22) finds that the effects are unclear but include an increase in the number of complaints about unlawful activity.

To summarize, modern public administration originated with the passage of the Pendleton Act and the merit system eventually would become pervasive in American government during the 20th century. In the name of impartial public service, the Hatch Act shielded personnel from partisan abuse and forbade them from engaging in political activities. The balance between employee political rights and the public's right to a nonpolitical bureaucracy shifted in 1993 when the Act was liberalized, largely "un-Hatching" federal employees. Since that time, the civil service reform movement has emerged and been successful in reducing career service protections and expanding the number of political appointees. The prohibitions against political activity in the 1993 Amendments,[3] as illustrated earlier, may not be sufficient (Maskell, 2007).

METHOD

This chapter provides an initial conceptual, normative qualitative ethical analysis of the Hatch Act derived from extant literature.[4] This is useful because the effects of the 1993 Amendments are uncertain, and the shift from the guardian model to the politico model, and the controversies that it has spawned, continues.[5]

As described in Chapter 7, various frameworks may shed light on the problem under study, but one is particularly useful because its comprehensive scope reduces the chances of an incomplete, flawed judgment. This tool, the ethics triangle or triad (Svara, 1997; Figure 14.1), recognizes the complementarity and interdependence of the imperatives in three schools of thought based on

- expected results of an action (consequentialism or teleology),
- application of pertinent rules (duty ethics or deontology), and
- personal integrity or character (virtue ethics).

FIGURE **14.1**   **Ethics Triangle**

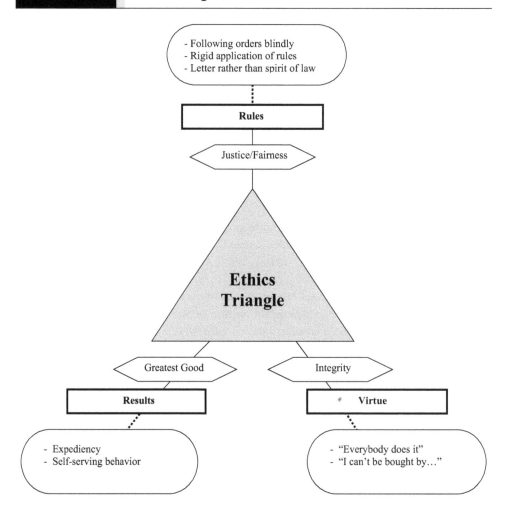

Key: Examples of non-ethical or unethical behavior or attitudes resulting from narrow application of the approach as shown at the outer edges of the diagram.

Each point of the triangle provides a lens to clarify and reframe different aspects of an assessment. Employing "Ockham's Razor"[6] to cut to the essence of an argument, three queries can be posed. When considering the results part of the triangle, the question is, "Which policy produces the greatest good for the greatest number?" In contemplating the rules angle, the issue is, "Would I want everyone else to make the same decision that I did?" From the virtue ethics vantage point, one might ask, "What would a person of integrity do?" A narrow, overreaching application of a single approach at the outer reaches of the triangle, at the expense of the other approaches, holds considerable dangers— namely, expediency (results-based ethics), rigid rule application (rule-based ethics), and self-justification (virtue-based ethics). Given the shortcomings of the individual points of the triangle, it is evident that this eclectic technique can be helpful.

Although the synthesis developed from triangulation analysis may not provide definitive solutions, it offers guidance by teasing out the underlying logic by which decisions are justified. Individual ethical theories may lead to different evaluations of the Hatch Act, but these differences must be assessed, not overlooked. The Act will be analyzed next using the three perspectives represented in the ethics triangle.

FINDINGS

Results-Based Analysis

In consequentialism, the best policy results in "the greatest good for the greatest number." What is right is that which creates the largest amount of human happiness with the least harm. This school of thought is associated with John Stuart Mill's ideas that "Decisions are judged by their consequences depending on the results to be maximized" (Frederickson, 1997, 167–168). A similar emphasis is found in Georg W. F. Hegel's writings where he articulates the principle, "judge an act by its consequences, and make them the standard of what is right and good" (1821, 113). This approach is useful for public administrators seeking the common good for the majority of citizens. Accordingly, consideration of a policy to re-Hatch civil servants examines affirmative and negative arguments on the grounds of (1) efficiency, (2) merit, (3) responsibility, and (4) public trust.

In Support of "Re-Hatching" Employees. Proponents view Hatch-like restrictions as a way to enhance the *efficiency* of the public service. Political partisanship is heightened with the 1993 relaxation of constraints on active participation in political management or partisan campaigns, and that this can negatively affect relationships between coworkers as well as between subordinates and superiors. Partisan-based decision-making can lead to "group think," allow politics to interfere with the delivery of services, and impede productivity when vulnerable employees fear job loss. To ensure efficiency and political neutrality, workers need protection from being coerced to vote or to participate politically against their will by superiors (Gely & Chandler, 2000), just as the public needs protection from government personnel using their position to aid partisan candidates or causes (Ley, 2000). In short, civil servants must be more concerned with public duty than with party politics. Their charge is to administer government impartially without respect to the political party in power or the policies of Administration champions.

Limitations on political activities make it more likely that decisions will be based on *merit* rather than political affiliation. A stable, merit-based career bureaucracy helps ensure that institutional knowledge be will accumulated and be maintained over the years (Heclo, 1977; also see an insightful interview with Helco in Pfiffner, 2007). If partisan considerations trump merit criteria in public management, personnel will lose confidence in their superiors. A politicized public service likely affects retention and recruitment because it discourages present and future employees who are not politically motivated.

Policies restricting politicization, in contrast, serve to enhance morale and provide protection against political abuse, which if unchecked can lead to bitterness and resentment among employees. Such measures help to ensure that staff are *responsible* for advancing public service or "good government" goals and thereby responsive to the general interest. Indeed, the Hatch Act has been referred to as "a first cousin of the ethics laws" (Brown, 1996: 20). *Trust* is, accordingly, enhanced when the citizenry is assured that civil servants are primarily concerned with civic well-being rather than partisan advantage.

In Opposition to "Re-Hatching" Employees. The original Hatch restrictions were paternalistic and infringed upon the constitutional rights of civil servants. The costs of such laws are borne by employees, while purported and speculative benefits accrue to the diffuse public, which remain oblivious to its effects. They are a form of political control, restricting the ability of personnel from becoming politically involved. Reinstituting such restrictions is likely to swell membership in employee organizations, which often emphasize protection over performance, thereby impeding *efficiency*. Maintaining looser restrictions, in contrast, could improve effectiveness of government and the efficiency of civil servants by increasing accountability and responsiveness to the public (Johnson & Libecap, 1995). Tighter controls will lead to morale problems, job dissatisfaction, and staff turnover (Brown, 1996; Pearson & Castle, 1990, 1991; Snead, 2001).

There are ample *merit* system protections and legal requirements already in place (e.g., "just cause" dismissal procedures, grievance arbitration, union protection, and federal legislation) to avoid abuses of partisan administration or political patronage. Unfortunate consequences can occur when these personnel, with their intimate knowledge of government, become "political eunuchs" with circumscribed participation rights (Boyle, 1991; Snead, 2001).

Re-Hatching employees would interfere with free expression, which must be weighed against the requirements for orderly management of governmental staff. Constitutional rights under the First, Ninth and Tenth Amendments and due process guarantees under the Fifth Amendment are at issue. Restricting these rights is unwarranted to counter the supposed evil of political partisanship by classified personnel. Earlier Hatch Act restrictions were applied across the board to all covered employees, with no distinction regarding the nature of the work or position involved. This clearly disregards important job-related distinctions that deserve consideration. For example, Justice Reed argued, in *United Public Workers of America v. Mitchell* (1973), that sweeping prohibitions on political activity by all types of public employees is substituting a hatchet where a scalpel is needed (LEXSEE 330 U.S. 75: 20). "Re-Hatching," in short, means that they become, once again, second-class citizens denied the opportunity to fully engage in democratic freedoms.

To ensure that civil servants are *responsible* to their political and managerial superiors, leaders need the flexibility to act, unfettered by burdensome restrictions more appropriate to an earlier era. As long as officials are elected on a partisan basis, complete political neutrality is impossible. Public *trust* is increased when corporate-style bottom line standards are met. Accomplishing policy and management goals is problematic if leaders are hampered by restrictions that limit their leverage over employees. Absent such leverage, it is more difficult to serve the citizenry and earn its confidence.

Summary. In results-based ethics, only consequences matter. "Re-Hatching" seeks the greatest good by: emphasizing expected results from restrictions on political activities to enhance efficiency, securing merit-based decision-making, holding personnel responsible for meeting citizen needs, and increasing employee and citizen trust. Without such regulations, the result will be increasing politicization of the public service and return to the abuses associated with the patronage era. In contrast, it can be maintained that cumbersome Hatch-type requirements reduce efficiency by overprotective regulations that undercut employee citizenship rights, ignore meritorious performance, and poorly serve the public interest. Such constraints limit leaders' flexibility and reduce citizen trust because they make it harder to meet performance standards. Because over-emphasis on any single point on the ethics triangle may put a proposed policy at risk, attention now shifts to another approach.

Rule-Based Analysis

Rule-based decision-making provides a different lens for evaluating government restrictions on political activities of public employees. Certain actions are inherently right (e.g., promise keeping) or wrong (e.g., inflicting harm), irrespective of their predicted consequences. This approach is useful for administrators who are obligated to follow the principles found in the Constitution, court cases, and laws and regulations (Rohr, 1988). Principle- or rule-based ethics is closely identified with Immanuel Kant's categorical imperative and Thomas Hobbes' social contract theory. Kant's imperative is to "act as if the maxim of your action was to become a universal law of nature" (1785, 17), which in turn is rooted in the belief that humans are capable of rational thought and self-governance; people, it follows, should be treated as ends, not means. Hobbes claims that natural law, by which he means a combination of all human experiences and competencies, yields a shared understanding of right and wrong (Kem, 2006). What is right is what conforms to moral rules; one must see one's duty and do it. In deciding what rule to apply, the person asks, "Would I want everyone else to make the decision I did?" Here the emphasis is on principles such as fairness and the commonweal in examining competing positions on whether to re-Hatch personnel.

In Support of "Re-Hatching" Employees. Advocates of restraints put primary emphasis on procedural and substantive *fairness*. Limits on partisan involvement serve to simultaneously protect personnel from unfair treatment based on political pressures and avoid capricious actions, which further partisan interests at the expense of the *commonweal* (Roback, 1992). Procedural due process is preserved with rules specifying permitted and prohibited forms of political participation. This insulates civil servants from inappropriate, illegal, or unethical pressures to advance the interests of a partisan cause, thereby enabling them to maintain objectivity and political neutrality in conducting the public's business. It also reassures the citizenry that the law will be equitably administered and that services will be delivered fairly, without consideration of political advantage.

However the 1993 anti-abuse provisions (8) punish only the most obvious forms of coercion, and have been inadequate to detect less patent forms of intimidation and coercion (Segal, 1998; Bloch, 2005; Moffit, 1993; Webster & Castle, 1988). When vetoing the attempt to reform the Hatch Act in 1990, President George H. W. Bush (echoing President Gerald R. Ford's 1976 veto message) stated, "The more subtle forms of coercion are almost impossible to regulate, especially when they arise in a climate in which the unspoken assumption is that political conformity is the route to achievement and security" (cited in Moffit, 1993: 10). "Re-Hatching" legislation would address this problem, as well as those related to recent technological and workplace changes (e.g., increased use of e-mail to campaign, and political activity while telecommuting) (Bloch, 2005).

It is not surprising, therefore, that representatives from a variety of good government and other groups opposed the 1993 Amendments, including the Federal Bar Association, Common Cause, the Public Service Research Council, the National Right to Work Committee, the National Academy of Public Administration, the U.S. Chamber of Commerce, the International Personnel Management Association, the National Taxpayers Union and the American Bar Association.

In Opposition to "Re-Hatching" Employees. "Re-Hatching" is neither *fair* nor necessary. Prior to the 1993 amendments, requirements were overly broad, vague and ambiguous (Segal, 1998) making it difficult to distinguish permissible from impermissible involvement in political affairs (Snead, 2001; Thompson, 1994). Furthermore, little was done to educate civil servants regarding their political rights both before and after the passage of the amendments (Robb, 2004a, 2004b). This led to claims that such restrictions have a "chilling effect," prompting employees to shy away from political involvement (e.g., Thurber, 1993a, 1993b). Others support this view, pointing to state-level findings, which show employees in jurisdictions with strict regulations to be less active politically (Snead, 2001).

In addition, there are important differences between conditions today and those at the time the original Hatch Act was passed. Indeed, President Bill Clinton opined in 1993 that because of changing conditions there was no justification for "the continued muzzling of millions of American citizens" (White House briefing, October 6, 1993). This theme was echoed at the time by representatives of groups lobbying to "unchain" federal employees, including the American Federation of State, County and Municipal Employees, the National Treasury Employees Union, the American Civil Liberties Union, and the International Association of Firefighters.

Private sector workers, many doing similar work to that of public employees, especially as a result of privatization, are allowed the full range of citizenship participation rights, yet their governmental counterparts are stripped of the same opportunities to participate. Further, Justice Black wrote in *United Public Workers of America v. Mitchell* (1973), that restrictions suppressing political activities of federal and state employees "hardly seem consistent with our system of equal justice to all" because government would be unfairly muzzling "millions of good citizens because a few bad citizens might engage in coercion," thereby reducing their liberty to "less than a shadow of its substance." (LEXSEE 330 U.S. 75: 26). The same inconsistency and double standard is present between "Hatched" and "Un-Hatched" employees (Thurber, 1993b). Moreover, "re-Hatching" would lead to similarly inconsistent applications of the law, especially when efforts overlook the role of public sector unions. In short, the *commonweal* is served by treating all employees in a like manner.

Summary. In brief, Hatch-like provisions result in greater fairness for both employees and citizens by clarifying expectations and establishing safeguards to avoid abusive practices that harm civil servants and undermine public confidence. Such restrictions provide a check on political leadership while enabling the equitable allocation of resources and delivery of services. In contrast, the vague statutory language of the original law, and an insufficient understanding of its provisions, rendered the legislation both impractical and counterproductive. Re-Hatching employees unnecessarily reintroduces these problems. Relying exclusively on rule-based analysis may provide inadequate guidance and inflexibility, so attention now focuses on the third approach, virtue theory.

Virtue-Based Analysis

In virtue ethics, answers to the question of "What to do?" have little to do with results or rules and everything to do with the kind of person one is. Personal character offers a third perspective when assessing the ethical advisability of re-Hatching employees. It asks questions such as, "What would a person of integrity decide?" or "Does the proposed decision improve my character and my community?" Virtue theory stems from the classical writings of Aristotle (1980) and the modern views of Alasdair MacIntyre (1984). As Gueras and Garofalo (2006, 59) note, the "theory considers an act to be good on the basis of the character trait or virtue that the act evidences." Virtuous conduct derives from a lifelong practice of self-discipline requiring commitment to ethical values.

Virtue ethics is compelling for public administrators because it is a more personal approach than cognitive ethics—that is, decisions are informed not only by consequences and duties but also by the quality of one's character. What is right is that which nurtures individual excellence and contributes to collective well-being. While no definitive list of traits exists (virtue theory avoids formulaic thinking and emphasizes, instead, one's moral identity), characteristics such as (1) integrity, (2) accountability, and (3) prudence are integral to moral nobility.

In Support of "Re-Hatching" Employees. The career civil service, without adequate protection, is clearly vulnerable to political manipulation. This is as apparent now, as it was in 1939, with reports of scandals including coercion of personnel and misuse of authority for political gain. Hatch-like restrictions show concern for the welfare of public servants, protect them from duress, and preserve their independence. In doing so, such legal limits help ensure *integrity* among those in public service, promote *accountability* to voters and taxpayers, foster a feeling of independence free from pressure under the law, and spur devotion to public purposes rather than political masters. Impartiality is a core value in civil service, one that requires vigilance to guarantee, and that will tarnish the reputation of an independent and nonpartisan civil service if it is compromised (Moffit, 1993). In government, public perceptions are crucial, and the "appearance of impropriety" standard is quite real. Citizens need the reassurance found in the Hatch Act and other statutes that services are administered impartially (Brown, 1996; Magness, 1987; Webster & Castle, 1988).

Limits on partisan involvement of civil servants are designed to simultaneously show respect for citizens and for employees by signaling that the first loyalty of public servants is to the state and its purposes. Such protections enable personnel to exercise *prudent* discretion in advising officials and implementing public programs. Rather than put their *integrity* at risk by making them vulnerable to undue political or administrative pressures, such provisions enable them to speak truth to power without fear of unjustified retribution.

In Opposition to "Re-Hatching" Employees. The separation between politics and administration is deeply ingrained in the civil service. Merit principles are widely recognized as useful imperatives, ethics codes reinforce these principles, and merit system structures are designed to implement these principles. Statutory law and common law protections exist, often buttressed by union contracts (Snead, 2001). These various elements, then, create overlapping requirements that adequately protect civil servants. Rather than elaborate, complex regulations that are inequitably enforced and seldom understood, a more fruitful area of emphasis would be to stress the nurturing of *integrity* among employees via training and development programs

Reinstituting policies that have long since outlived their usefulness is unnecessary, *imprudent*, and counterproductive without compelling evidence of abuse or wrongdoing associated with the 1993 Amendments (Gely & Chandler, 2000; Bloch, 2005; Moffit, 1993). Indeed, many citizens have negative views of government workers as "unresponsive to their demands, unproductive, and unaccountable" (Johnson & Libecap, 1995, 793). The flexibility provided by the 1993 amendments helps to insure that government workers are responsive to the will of the people as determined by electoral results. Indeed, to have political *account-ability*, elected leaders need to be able to expect that public servants are loyal to the current administration's values and purposes.

Summary. In brief, restoring Hatch-like policies will enhance the integrity and profession-alism of employees while simultaneously improving accountability by focusing attention on the general public interest. Alternatively, it can be argued that adequate protections already exist to avoid or correct abusive practices that may occur. Cultivating personal integrity is preferable to heavy-handed regulation and regards a return to questionable past policies as imprudent. Yet, virtue theory's strength—subjective judgments inferred from personal character—is also its shortcoming: If supporters and opponents of Hatch Act restrictions perceive they are good, then it is not implausible for them to think that what they do is good.

SUMMARY AND CONCLUSION

Responsible policymakers, by definition, are obligated to develop virtues, respect rules, and consider results. The ethics triad cannot produce a final, perfect decision for all seasons. Instead a conscious attempt to reconcile conflicting values highlights a key function of deci-sion-making: generating alternative viewpoints, systemically evaluating them, and crafting a considered judgment. The triangle enables the management of ethical ambiguity and pro-vides help in making the inevitable compromises. When choices are guided by benevolence, creativity, and an ethic of compromise and social integration—a moral tenet of democ-racy—there is at least the satisfaction that the problem has been fully examined and that the decision can be rationally defended.

Until recently, one of the distinguishing features of modern public employment (as rep-resented by the 1939 Hatch Act) was the merit system and the neutral competence of the civil service safeguarded from political pressures, cronyism, sycophancy and corruption. The Act's Amendments, which are consistent with NPM and current civil service reforms, is seen by proponents as a way to reenergize the bureaucracy. Employees have little need of restrictions because modern law provides adequate protection and employers are generally honorable and normally do not engage in egregious behavior. The Amendments are viewed by opponents as a first step to the return of the spoils system, a step that needlessly places one of the finest civil service systems in the world at risk. These risks are heightened today, as evidence mounts documenting politicization of the civil service, increasing the angst of those who have concerns about the adequacy of legal protections or the intentions and actions of elected officials and their appointees. For ready reference, the summaries provided here are shown in tabular form (Table 14.1). The overall assessment of these contentions, using the ethics triad, follows.

Result-based decision-making, as discussed earlier, evaluates the potential re-Hatching of employees based on efficiency, merit, responsibility and trust, and how these factors contribute to the greatest good. The 1993 Amendments were passed, in part, because it was believed that relaxed limitations would yield productivity increases when government is run like a business. Civil service laws and regulations, including Hatch-like constraints, do not serve the public interest; instead they protect employees from performance standards. However efficiency, merit, responsibility, and trust are jeopardized when loose restrictions encourage politicization of the public service.

TABLE 14.1	"Re-Hatching" Employees: Results, Rules, and Virtue Ethics Pro and Con Positions	
	In Support of Re-Hatching	**In Opposition to Re-Hatching**
Results	Seek the greatest good by emphasizing expected results from restrictions on political activities to enhance efficiency, maintaining merit-based decision-making, holding personnel responsible for meeting citizen needs, and increasing employee and citizen trust. Without regulations, the result increases politicization of the public service and returns to the abuses associated with the patronage era.	Cumbersome Hatch-type requirements reduce efficiency by overprotective regulations that undercut employee citizenship rights, ignore meritorious performance, and poorly serve the public interest. Constraints limit leaders' flexibility and reduce citizen trust because they make it harder to meet performance standards.
Rules	Regulations provide greater fairness for both employees and citizens by clarifying expectations and establishing safeguards to avoid abusive practices that harm civil servants and undermine public confidence. Restrictions secure a check on political leadership while enabling the equitable allocation of resources and delivery of services.	Vague statutory language of the original law, and an insufficient understanding of its provisions, rendered the legislation both impractical and counterproductive. Re-Hatching employees unnecessarily reintroduces these problems.
Virtues	Reinstituting such policies will enhance the integrity and professionalism of employees, while simultaneously improving accountability by focusing attention on the general public interest.	Adequate protections already exist to avoid or correct abusive practices that may occur. Cultivating personal integrity is preferable to heavy-handed regulation and a return to questionable past policies as imprudent.

What then is the greatest good for the greatest number? It can be argued that the 1993 elimination of off-the-job regulations made citizen-public employees whole; the restoration of the constitutional rights to a significant portion of the nation's workforce rights seemed to be the best thing to do. Yet removing protections is fraught with untoward consequences for the nation as demonstrated by the history of the spoils system and across-the-board deterioration of civil service safeguards in recent times. Political neutrality in conducting the public's business protects not only civil servants but also citizens. A policymaker using result-based ethics may find some politically attractive arguments to support liberalization of restrictions, but the greatest good for the country as a whole is served by neutral competence in governmental service.

Rule-based imperatives, the second aspect of the triangle, emphasize the need for principles such as fairness. Advocates of the 1993 Amendments argued that the constraints were vague and nebulous, had a chilling effect on democratic participation and, as noted, unfairly limited citizenship rights. Supporters of Hatch-style legislation maintained that on-the-job anti-abuse provisions in the Amendments, while welcome, are inherently inadequate to address subtle, powerful activities at work.

In the name of fairness, then, how does the rule, "what is good for one is good for all," apply? The conclusion for those in favor of the Amendments is that all employees should be treated equally because there are few if any differences between the public and private sectors of the economy; because there are no restrictions on business employees there should be none on public personnel. In contrast, fairness could be best achieved in today's multiple-sector public service by treating—and adequately safeguarding—all personnel in a like manner regardless of whether they are employed in government, business, or the nonprofit sector. A decision maker using rule-based ethics has a duty to avoid harm, a duty arguably best fulfilled by neutral competence in public service that nurtures "what is good for one is good for all" citizens regardless of party.

Virtue-based ethics relies on personal traits (e.g., integrity, accountability, prudence) when seeking improvement in character and community. Supporters of the revised Hatch Act argued that other protections were sufficient to ensure the nobility of civil servants and the public service and, in any case, developing individual integrity is preferable to paternalist regulation. Reinstating limitations on political activity, however, reinforces professionalism and guards against threats to the administration of democracy. How, then, is virtue ethics best served? Integrity is nurtured by placing responsibility on the individual, and by so doing the community will be improved as well. Others believe, however, that individual integrity and accountability is enhanced when supported by the community and its rules. Humans become fully human and flourish through others. Prudence, following James Madison's "if men were angels" admonition, demands that personal virtue be buttressed by the polity. A focus on virtue ethics suggests that it is best achieved when the individual and the community work to nurture one another.

Each of the angles of the ethics triangle contains contending arguments for and against the re-Hatching of employees. Taken separately, either position may appear ethical at some points and unethical at others. The triangle, it follows, offer choices, not formula; it informs, but does not eliminate, the need for judgment; it does not weigh the relative weight of each argument. Yet when choices are guided by benevolence, creativity, and an ethic of compromise—a moral tenet of democracy—there is at least the satisfaction that the problem have been fully examined and that the result can be rationally defended. As Aristotle admonished, one should not expect more precision from the subject matter than it can allow; morality is not mathematics.

On balance the Hatch Act Amendments of 1993 permit harm without cause by undermining the greatest good for the greatest number, fairness and duty, and the role of the community in reinforcing personal integrity. There is a need to reconsider the balance between civil servants' interest in engaging in partisan political activity and the goal of government to promote efficiency and neutrality.[7] The changing nature of the public service—as a consequence of the initiatives of the NPM and radical civil service reform movements—make it essential to recall the critical national interests that are served by the Hatch-like restrictions. These are well articulated in the 1973 *Letter Carriers* case:

> First, federal employees "should administer the law in accordance with the will of Congress, rather than in accordance with their own will or the will of a political party." Second, employees should not 'appear to the public" to be making politically influenced decisions, "if confidence in the system of representative Government is not to be eroded. . . ." Third, employees "should not be employed to build a powerful, invincible, and perhaps corrupt political machine.' Finally, employees should be free "from express or tacit invitation to vote in a certain way or perform political chores in order to curry favor with their superiors rather than to act out their own beliefs."
>
> (Magness, 1987, 1509)

In the end, "public office is a public trust; . . . political authority is to be exercised in service of the entire community, and should not degenerate into an instrument of partisan abuse or coercion" (Moffit, 1993, 6).

The shift from the guardian model to the politico model calls into question the fundamental underpinning of the merit system, selection based on technical competence, retention premised on performance, and impartial administration of duties. While the 1993 Amendments broaden and clarify public employee speech rights and the right to run for office, the looser restrictions on political activities make possible the increasing politicization of the public service. That politicization, led by political appointees, has yet to provoke reform. Instead, it has led to incompetent administration and headline scandal, "which is often blamed on 'bureaucrats' or government generally, thereby tarring the career service and all those in public service . . . with the same brush. All of this steadily and insidiously erodes public confidence . . . and our ability to govern ourselves" (Murray & Wamsley, 2007, 200). In light of the events noted at the outset of this chapter, and the ensuing ethical analysis of the amended Hatch Act, perhaps Norman Cousins was correct in saying that "History is a vast warning system." It is prudent, thus, to consider the "re-Hatching" of governmental personnel which may be part of President Joe Biden's effort to restore confidence in government and the public service.

NOTES

1. The key decision was *Rutan et al. v. Republican Party of Illinois et al.* (1990), which found that personnel actions could not be based on party affiliation absent a vital government interest. Important prior Supreme Court rulings include *Elrod v. Burns* (1976) and *Branti v. Finkel* (1980). The judiciary has also rejected arguments that the Hatch Act was unconstitutional, violated states' rights, or was excessively vague (Lee, 1993: 23, 216); the most significant case was *US Civil Service Commission v. National Association of Letter Carriers* (1973). This chapter is adapted from Bowman and West (2009b) with permission from Wiley Periodicals LLC.
2. This legislation included the establishment of the Senior Executive Service and mandated that 10 percent of its positions be open to political appointees, an early indication of the change from the guardian to the politico model.
3. The 1993 Amendments added a new section strengthening the penalties of anti-abuse sections of the statute, criminalizing intimidation and the coercing or threatening of a federal worker to become involved—or refrain from involvement—in political activity. A primary purpose was to provide "a deterrent to those who might abuse their official position" and a protection "to ensure impartial, evenhanded conduct" (Segal, 1998: 3; H.R. Rep. No. 103–16, at 34.).
4. As noted, the approach used here focuses on ethical considerations, in part, because such concerns can be overlooked or submerged into other decision-making criteria. Thus, there is no attempt to assess whether or not political support presently exists to "re-Hatch" public servants or if such an action is the only, or even the best, solution to current problems like those listed at the outset.
5. This work, as part of a larger study, relies on the extant literature, notably that published since 1993; state-level empirical data have been collected (see Bowman & West, 2009a).
6. Use the simplest possible explanation of a problem, and only make it more complex when absolutely necessary. Adding qualifications, explanations may make a position less elegant, less convincing, and less correct.
7. Further empirical research is needed to identify workplace issues created by the 1993 Amendments such as conflict of interest for both the employee and the agency, divided loyalties for personnel seeking office, or the creation of a hostile work environment because of increased political activity. Results from such studies would buttress, modify, or refute the finding from this qualitative analysis regarding whether the negative concerns created by the Amendments outweigh the additional rights granted to employees.

DISCUSSION

1. Compare the differences between at-will employees (Chapter 13) and career service governmental personnel. Identify the advantages and drawbacks of each policy. This chapter is adapted from Bowman and West (2009b) with permission from Wiley Periodicals LLC.

2. The Hatch Act prohibits federal civil servants from engaging in political activity on federal property while on duty or using government property such as vehicles or computers. These rules apply to officials when working at home and participating in Zoom meetings. Why are these restrictions important, if they are?

3. The Hatch Act is one of the predominant reform laws that lead to nonpartisan career civil service in the last century. To uphold the rule of law in light of recent flagrant and repeated violations, the Act should be enforced and/or amended; breaking the law is not a political difference. Discuss.

4. Referring to Chapter 7, to what extent do selected tenets of behavioral ethics shed light on the re-Hatching debate?

EXERCISE

1. Identify an agency or jurisdiction that is covered by either the federal Hatch Act or a state "little" Hatch Act. Were any public employees disciplined for violating the law?

REFERENCES

Aristotle. (1980). *The Nicomachean Ethics* (D. Ross, Trans.). Oxford: Oxford University Press.

Bloch, S. J. (2005, Winter). The judgment of history: Faction, political machines, and the Hatch Act. *University of Pennsylvania Journal of Labor & Employment Law, 7,* 225–277.

Bowman, J., & West, J. (eds.) (2007). *American public service: Radical reform and the merit system.* Boca Raton, FL. Taylor and Francis.

Bowman, J., & West, J. (2009b). To 're-Hatch' public employees or not? An ethical analysis of the relaxation of restrictions on political activities in civil service. *Public Administration Review, 69*(1), 52–62.

Bowman, J., & West, J. (2009a). State 'little' Hatch Acts: The state of the nation. *Review of Public Personnel Administration, 29*(1), 20–40.

Boyle, L. L. (1990–1991). Reforming civil service reform: Should the federal government continue to regulate state and local government employees? *Journal of Law and Politics, 7,* 243–287.

Brown, G. (1996). The constitution as an obstacle to government ethics—Reformist legislation after national treasury employees union. *William and Mary Law Review, 37,* 979–1043.

Clark, K. (2020, September 22). Viewpoint: We need an investigation of Hatch Act crimes at the republican convention. *Government Executive.* Retrieved from www.govexec.com/oversight/2020/09/viewpoint-we-need-investigation-hatch-act-crimes-republican-national-convention/168662/

Condrey, S., & Maranto, R. (eds.) (2001). *Radical reform in the civil service.* New York: Lexington Books.

Frederickson, H. G. (1997). *The spirit of public administration* (pp. 167–168). San Francisco: Jossey-Bass.

Gely, R., & Chandler, T. D. (2000, Fall). Restricting public employees' political activities: Good government or partisan politics. *Houston Law Review*, *37*, 775–822.

Gueras, D., & Garofalo, C. (2006). *Practical ethics in public administration* (2nd ed.). Vienna, VA: Management Concepts.

Heclo, H. (1977). *Government of strangers: Executive politics in Washington*. Washington, DC: Brookings Institution.

Hegel, G. (1996 [1821]). *Philosophy of right* (S. Dyde, Trans., p. 113). Amherst, NY: Prometheus Books (originally published in 1821).

Ingraham, P. W. (2006). *the foundation of merit: Public service in American democracy*. Baltimore, MD: Johns Hopkins University Press.

Johnson, R., & Libecap, G. (1995). Courts, a protected bureaucracy, and reinventing government. *Arizona Law Review*, *3*, 791–823.

Kant, I. (1785). *Foundations of the metaphysics of morals* (L. Beck, Trans. 1959). Indianapolis, IN: Bobbs-Merrill Company (originally published in 1785).

Kem, J. (2006). *A pragmatic ethical decision making model for the army: The ethical triangle*. Unpublished paper from the U.S. Army Command and General Staff College at Fort Leavenworth, Kansas.

Lee, R. (1993). *Public personnel systems* (3rd ed.). Gaitherburg, MD: Aspen Publishers.

LEXSEE 330 U.S. 75. United Public Workers of America (C.I.O.) et al., v. Mitchell et al., No. 20, Supreme Court of the United States 330 U.S. 75; 67 S. Ct. 556; 91 L. Ed. 754; 1947 U.S. Lexis 2960.

Ley, J. (2000). U.S. government integrity system and ethics. *Issues of Democracy. IIP Electronic Journals*, *5*(2), 32–38.

MacIntyre, A. C. (1984). *After virtue: A study in moral theory* (2nd ed.). South Bend, IN: University of Notre Dame Press.

Magness, W. (1987). Un-hatching federal employee political endorsements. *University of Pennsylvania Law Review*, *134*, 1497–1529. Retrieved September 1, 2006 from LexisNexis.

Maskell, J. (2007, March 26). *Meetings, conferences as "political activities in a federal office, and the Hatch Act considerations*. Washington, DC: Congressional Research Service.

Moffit, R. (1993). Gutting the Hatch Act: Congress's plan to re-politicize the civil service. *Issue Bulletin #180*. Retrieved June 23, 2006 from www.heritage.org/Research/PoliticalPhilosophy/IB180.cfm

Murray, W. L., & Wamsley, G. L. (2007). A modest proposal regarding political appointees. In Ali Farazmand (Ed.), *Strategic public personnel administration* (pp. 99–126). Westport, CT: Praeger.

Pearson, W. M., & Castle, D. S. (1990). Political activity among state executives: The effect of Hatch Act repeal. *Public Personnel Management*, *19*(4), 399–409.

Pearson, W. M., & Castle, D. S. (1991). Liberalizing restrictions on political activities of state employees: Perceptions of high-level state executives. *American Review of Public Administration*, *21*(2), 91–105.

Pfiffner, J. P. (2007). The institutionalist: A conversation with Hugh Helco. *Public Administration Review*, *67*(3), 418–423.

Riccucci, N. (ed.) (2006). *Public personnel management: Current concerns, future challenges* (4th ed.). New York: Pearson, Longman.

Roback, T. H. (1992). Patronage, merit, and the bill of rights: Evolution and current trends in public employment. *Public Administration Quarterly*, *16*(3), 326–343.

Robb, K. (2004a, October 4). Few agencies give refresher courses on Hatch Act. *Federal Times*

Robb, K. (2004b, October 4). Hatch Act: As political activism rises, so do violations, prosecutions. *Federal Times*, p. 1, 8.

Rohr, J. A. (1988). *Ethics for bureaucrats* (2nd ed.). New York: Marcel Dekker.

Rubin, J. (2020, August 26). The RNC is on a Hatch Act crime spree. *Washington Post*. Retrieved from www.washingtonpost.com/opinions/2020/08/26/rnc-is-hatch-act-crime-spree/

Segal, L. (1998). Can we fight the new Tammany Hall?: Difficulties of prosecuting political patronage and suggestions for reform. *Rutgers Law Review*, *5*, 507–562.

Snead, J. D. (2001). An Inquiry into the chilling effects of stringent little Hatch Act prohibitions. *Review of Public Personnel Administration*, *21*(4), 259–283.

Staff Report Prepared for Senator Elizabeth Warren. (2020, October). Lawlessness and disorder: The corrupt Trump administration has made a mockery of the Hatch act. *Boston Globe*. Retrieved from www.boston.com/wpcontent/uploads/2020/10/Hatch-Act-Violations-by-Trump-Administration-Final.pdf

Svara, J. (1997). The ethical triangle: Synthesizing the bases of administrative ethics. In James S. Bowman (Eds.), *Public integrity annual* (pp. 33–41). Lexington, KY: Council of State Governments.

Thompson, J. (1994). Social workers and politics: Beyond the Hatch Act. *Social Work*, *39*(4), 457–465.

Thurber, K. T, Jr. (1993a). Big, little, littler: synthesizing hatch act-based political activity legislation research. *Review of Public Personnel Administration*, *13*(1), 39–51.

Thurber, K. T., Jr. (1993b). Revising the Hatch Act: A practitioner perspective. *The Public Manager: The New Bureaucrat*, *22*(1), 43–47.

United Public Workers v. Mitchell, 330 U.S. 75 (1947) (Black, J. dissenting).

United States Commission on the Political Activities of Governmental Employees. (1967). *A commission report*. Washington, DC: Government Printing Office.

Webster, J. B., & Castle, J. (1988). The Hatch Act: Should it be repealed or reformed? *Government Union Review*, *9*(1), 25–52.

PART V

Future History

15 Choices and Strategies for the Years Ahead

It's an unnerving thought that we may be living the universe's supreme achievement and its worst nightmare simultaneously.

—Bill Bryson

Parts I–IV of the book have asked questions more than they have provided answers. Since it is better to know some of the questions than all the answers, the intent was to offer frameworks to raise important concerns. There is not a rule for everything; the core of ethical behavior is to learn how to act when no rule exists. Even when there is a standard, there may not be an unambiguous way to decide how to act on it. All an ethics text can do is leave readers with an understanding that they are moral agents; that they discern as much about honor as about rules; and that their choices in the public, private, and nonprofit workplace are between moral grandeur and decay, between civilization and barbarism. The key to praiseworthy action is knowing how to handle free will to expand ethical and reduce unethical behavior. This final chapter illustrates how to proceed by

- comprehending moral grandeur using four transcendental dimensions of life,
- recognizing moral decay and confronting it by understanding ignominious behavior,
- understanding how the American response to the next global emergency may signify moral grandeur or decay,
- developing guidelines to expand exemplary conduct in the future, and
- reinforcing the nature of the ethical professional.

MORAL GRANDEUR

Each day provides its own gifts.

—Marcus Aurelius

If Aristotle Ran General Motors by Tom Morris (1997) is not really about the Greek philosopher or one of the nation's largest corporations. But the title does effectively convey the symbolism of each—what might happen if four foundations of the human experience were used to run a modern

DOI: 10.4324/9781003203148-20

organization? The book urges conscious recognition of the philosophical elements that enrich life. The four components are intellectual (truth), aesthetic (beauty), moral (goodness), and spiritual (unity) in character. These constituent dimensions produce individual and organizational excellence, and permit human flourishing so as to make the world a better place.[1]

Truth—disturbing or comforting—is the basis of all relationships. One must be true to self and in interactions with others. Believing in something is not the same as knowing something; fabrication is not fact. As philosopher Soren Kierkegaard observed, "There are two ways to be fooled. One is to believe what isn't true; the other is to refuse to believe what is." There is no greater source of waste than speculation, gossip, and rumor that arise in the absence of veracity. Nothing inspires people more than the truth.

Despite its elemental significance, "The simplest truths," Frederick Douglass observed, "often meet with sternest resistance and are slowest in getting general acceptance." Indeed, in today's polarized political culture, fact-checks matter only at the margins, as fact-checking has only a minimal effect when findings oppose existing beliefs (Marietta, 2019, May 3; also review Chapter 7 on the limits and biases of human cognition). Arthur Schopenhauer instead argued that all truth must pass through three stages: "[F]irst it is ridiculed, second it is violently opposed, and third it is accepted as being self-evident." The classic example of the process of accepting a new reality is the earth-as-the-center-of-the-universe theory. For centuries, people were reluctant to abandon their beliefs about the nature of reality. Yet humanity cannot thrive without challenging ideas; without truth, progress perishes. Openness to transcendence is what distinguishes the disciplined process of inquiry and dialogue, a dynamic conversation that tests old conclusions and develops new ones (Palmer, 2007, 106, 109).

The world is too dangerous for anything except the truth. "Post-truth politics"—when feelings and emotions trump objective facts—reveals a profound contempt for democratic life by eroding the cognitive ability to distinguish veracity from falsehood (see Kavanagh & Rich, 2014, on truth erosion causes). Truth is succinct, balanced, and accountable; ultimately, truth speaks for itself. To govern is to choose; citizens must be up to the task of discernment. Engaging in evidence-based deliberations and embracing democratic norms are minimum standard for governance. The problem with truth is that people are afraid of it, and it is easier to lie. Liars attempt to deceive not only themselves but also others; in the process, reality becomes increasingly distorted, so that decisions are corrupted.

It is better, then, to deal with an ugly truth—to live authentically and responsibly—than to be mollified by a beautiful lie. Truth can set, and keep, you free—but only if there is the moral courage to use it (Chapter 5). "If you tell the truth," writes Charles Gordon, "you have infinite power supporting you; but if not, you have infinite power against you." It takes seconds to be honest and costs nothing. One of the beauties of truth is that it does not require many words to speak it. A lie takes time and effort, and costs everything when exposed. It is better, it follows, to admit mistakes before someone else exaggerates them.[2]

While essential, truth is not sufficient for fulfillment, since humans are not mere intellects; truth is not only a philosophical concept, it has an aesthetic quality as well. People must have something attractive to motivate them—beauty. There is nothing, it has been said, that makes its way more directly to the soul than beauty. Like the need for truth, the experience of beauty is universal. Beauty, in fact, is the result of truth. The "beauty of beauty" is all around us. The aesthetic dimension includes not only external observational beauty (as in a sunset) but also internal performance beauty (e.g., excellent work); both are a "thing of beauty," a masterpiece, a way to evoke the best in people.

Ralph Waldo Emerson says it best: "We ascribe beauty to that which is simple; which has no superfluous parts; which exactly answers its end; which stands related to all things; which is the mean of many extremes." Beauty liberates, refreshes, inspires, and thereby nurtures well-being. "Everybody needs beauty," John Muir wrote, "as well as bread, place to play in and pray in, where nature may heal and give strength to body and soul." Human flourishing releases great energy. In contrast, ugliness depresses the spirit. Badly done work is rarely rewarding. If people are to do a good job, they must feel they have a good job, career, or better, a higher calling (see below).

Doing true, beautiful work, however, is incomplete, Morris (1997) argues. That which is beautiful is not always good but that which is good is always beautiful. Leaders must be convinced of the essential goodness of what they are doing. Unethical work can be done with exquisite deception, just as data can be manipulated well but fraudulently. Goodness might be considered a special kind of truth and beauty—it is how humanity values itself. Standing for truth and beauty is to live with integrity. Paradoxically, humans are the only species capable of ethical awareness and, therefore, also capable of ignoring that awareness. Yet doing the right thing can be inconvenient, but doing it is often an indication that it is the right thing to do. People are at their finest when engaged in a worthy task, one in which they can make a genuine difference, doing a job that the world needs done and one that they want to do. True goodness is attained through fidelity to a worthwhile purpose. It is better to suffer for doing good than for doing wrong.

As John Wesley writes in *Rules for Doing Good*, "Do all the good you can, in all the ways that you can, to all the people you can, in every place you can, at all the times you can, as long as you can." For the administrator, service to the public is the place to start. Doing right things right includes both effectiveness (doing the right thing) and efficiency (doing things right). To paraphrase Socrates, the source of good is knowledge and the source of evil is ignorance.

Truth, beauty, and goodness are still not enough, as humans must feel they are a part of something greater than themselves. Not content with knowing what they are doing, they must also know why they are working. Matters of spirit are intertwined with truth, beauty, goodness—the worth of the person and the community to which he or she belongs. What is needed is a sense of the majesty of creation and the ability to be respectful in its presence. The Athenian Oath from ancient Greece, taken by all 17-year-old citizens, captures the idea of truth, beauty, goodness, and community of the human spirit:

> We will ever strive for the ideals and sacred things of the city, both alone and with many;
> we will unceasingly seek to quicken the sense of public duty;
> we will revere and obey the city's laws;
> we will transmit this city not only not less but greater, better and more beautiful than it was transmitted to us.[3]

This oath constitutes a public spirit, ethic, and mission that are neither liberal nor conservative, neither Republican nor Democratic. Respecting the common welfare is less a method to make a decision and more a question to pose during the decision process to guide policymaking. A polity without a foundation in veracity, brilliance, morality, and meaning is one that has lost its way.

If Aristotle ran General Motors, he would foster integrity throughout the company by nourishing a culture based on the four transcendental values—truth, beauty, goodness, and unity. The body politic can do a world of good by restoring a sense of dignity reflected in these values. Living the ethical life centered on them benefits the individual and the organization. Practiced well, ethics distinguishes between the necessary and the secondary and the useful and the wasteful. Everyone in the organization must understand their role as a moral agent, believing anything worth doing is worth doing well. Transforming the organization—internalizing and institutionalizing the four dimensions of quality—is anyone and everyone's responsibility but one that must be assumed by leaders (Morris, 1997). The keys to excellence lie before us; if things go wrong, do not go with them. Ethics is far more about creating strength than it is about avoiding trouble. "The difference between what we do and what we are capable of doing," Gandhi believed, "would suffice to solve most of the world's problems."

In fact, public service can be seen not simply as a job (a way to earn a living) or a career (a means for advancement) but as a calling (finding one's true place in the world). Philosophers have long proposed that well-being is the doorway to personal flourishing, to come alive to the true meaning found in pursuits that command conviction and commitment in civic service. More than an employee, you are a public servant, a high calling indeed. "The only way to achieve success," Aristotle observed, "is to express yourself completely in service to society."

> Politics practiced well is the noblest of professions. No other arena requires as much wisdom, tenacity, foresight, and empathy. No other field places such stress on conversation and persuasion. The English word "idiot" comes from the ancient Greek word for the person who is uninterested in politics but capable only of running his or her own private life.
>
> (Brooks, 2017, August 1)

Public service is a means of preserving democracy, considered by many to be one of humankind's greatest achievements. Calling—that wonder from antiquity—gives voice by discerning purpose in what one does in government (see Bowman, 2011–2012; Perry, 2020). Service is something to be honored, not demeaned. The sustained demonization of government—a profoundly antidemocratic movement aimed at delegitimizing the American system—may prove to be unsustainable. At least in the long run, the service orientation of the millennial generation suggests that the public service is being revalued (Perry & Buckwalter, 2012) and that the moral duty of politics is to appeal to our best instincts rather than our worst. In these times, nonetheless, it might be a mistake to believe that history is linear, moving gradually forward from past to present to a progressive, honorable future. Yet patriotism and integrity are what draw people to public service. Every employee who takes an "oath of office swears to protect the Constitution from all enemies, foreign and domestic. Rarely have those words echoed with more resonance than right now" (McEldowney, 2018, January 26). There can be little doubt that the most compelling foreign and domestic enemy in the years ahead is a future pandemic which is sure to inexorably come, silently and deadly (Exhibit 15.1)

EXHIBIT 15.1	**Masking Health-Care Employees and the General Public: Symbolic of America's Corona Virus Response**

"Personnel is policy." Management adage

As the 2019–2020 pandemic loomed, the national stockpile of N95 masks—essential to protect health-care workers—contained less than 1 percent of 3.5 billion face coverings needed in a pandemic. As a result, when the pathogen erupted, many employees reused N95 respirators designed for single use; others made do with less effective facial safeguards. These personnel accounted for 11 percent of all coronavirus cases; hundreds died, almost certainly a gross underestimate, making these jobs the most dangerous in the country.

Whistleblower Dr. Rick Bright, former director of the federal Biomedical Advanced Research and Development Authority, testified in 2020 that frontline health-care personnel were put in danger, not because of a lack of insight into the mask shortage, but because of an "unconscionable" refusal to fix it. He was removed from office after refusing to promote hydroxychloroquine, which the FDA later cautioned against using for COVID-19.

Globalization heightened the risk to the mask supply, as production had shifted to overseas factories. Offshoring left the United States dependent on an international supply chain that seized up when producing countries hoarded protection equipment for domestic use. Bright stated that "We were forced to procure the supplies from other countries without the right quality standards," as imported N95 devices were often only 30 percent effective.

In a symptom of broader disarray, Health and Human Services (HHS) top executives could not accurately gauge the need. In Senate testimony on February 25, 2020, Secretary Alex Azar cited an administration estimate of needing "possibly as many as 300 million masks for health care workers." Days later that number had grown more than tenfold. HHS assistant secretary Robert Kadlec told senators that America "would need 3.5 billion N95 respirators." It wasn't until nearly two months after senior officials like Bright first raised the issue that HHS signed deals for 600 million masks over the next 18 months far short of the need. The president, without evidence, claimed the shortage on hospital staff pilfering the facial protective gear and falsely blamed doctors for over-counting deaths because they get more money for COVID-19 cases.

Bright called the administration's failure to invest in masks indifference, but National Nurses United called it "willful negligence. . . . We can't even say they failed, because that would imply they tried." The compelling maxim "personnel is policy" was never more evident.

Logistical concerns about protecting public health employees were reflected in the use of face coverings among the general populace. Initially, officials discouraged masking partly because of the need to conserve personal protective equipment for medical personnel. In addition, conducting quality research during a pandemic is difficult as experts do not fully understand the novel coronavirus or know what to anticipate. Uncertainty is characteristic of scientific research as preliminary results may be suggestive, not conclusive: Hypotheses are tested based on what is believed at the time; some are not supported, so better hypotheses are tried as evidence accumulates (Wegman, 2020).

However, the World Health Organization examined 172 studies and concluded that widespread mask-wearing is a proven way to reduce virus transmission (Taylor, 2020; see also Tufekci, 2020; Lerner, Folkers, & Fauci, 2020, on why randomized clinical trials are impossible and unnecessary during a pandemic). The medical community is virtually unanimous that if people don them, wash their hands, practice social distancing, avoid large crowds, and get tested, it is possible to manage both the disease and economic recovery. In fact, the Director of the Centers for Disease Control and Prevention has stated that if everyone wore a mask the virus would be contained in four to six weeks (Bleifuss, 2020).

Although not without controversy, masking is commonplace in other nations as a matter of "health citizenship"—the responsible act of personal protection and civic hygiene, a basic duty of citizenship in a democracy. As one decision maker stated, "I wear a mask to protect you. You wear a mask to protect me." Mask mandates, for instance, are not First Amendment violations because face covering does not prohibit speech and, more broadly, constitutional provisions are not absolute. The exercise of rights must not endanger others and legal rights are subject to governmental authority to protect public welfare. So long as facial protection rules are reasonable and impartially enforced, they are likely to survive court challenge. This remains true for infected people who are asymptomatic silent spreaders of the virus (Mandavilli, 2020, December 8).

Yet instead of respiratory etiquette as a show of solidarity with others, it inflamed anti-government sentiment, provoking defiance, denial, misinformation, and conspiracy theories to the point that the president believed that to wear a mask was to show disapproval of him. Politicized as an infringement on personal rights—as well as an attempt to scare people, doubt masculinity, slow the economic restoration, and endanger reelection prospects—it quickly became evident that protection against the apolitical virus was not immune to political manipulation. Oddly, the rage against masks demonstrated that protests are the most intense when the inconvenience is the most trivial.

Nonetheless, COVID-19 is not a political controversy or public relations problem. It is a public health emergency that requires people to respond accordingly. Physicians are just one component of the clinical care team (Dreifuss, 2020); they depend upon nurses, paramedics, intensive care technicians, respiratory therapists, radiology technicians, social workers, pharmacists, and citizens to use best practice so that hospitals are not overwhelmed. As one commentator pointed out, "refusing to wear a mask is like driving drunk" (Kristof, 2020).

Writing in *Science* magazine, Prather, Wang, and Schooley (2020) conclude, "For society to resume, measures . . . must be implemented, including universal masking . . . as masks provide a critical barrier, reducing the number of infectious viruses in exhaled breath" (1422, 1424). As a reflection of the public's respect for science, 71 percent of Americans support mandatory face coverings, including a majority of Republicans (Neguyen, 2020). Mouth-to-nose "lockdowns" is more sustainable than stay-at-home lockdowns. Yes, mask-wearing is inconvenient and pandemic fatigue is real, but it must be recognized that the silent, deadly virus does not get frustrated or tired. Unless nearly all people wear simple, cheap, and effective face covers, the grim reality is that infections, hospitalizations, and deaths continue to rise. Indeed, it is evident that earlier policy interventions would have avoided tens of thousands of deaths.

There is no doubt that the viral scourge is a "wicked problem," one that is extraordinarily difficult with no clear definition or solution. With the worst health and employment outcomes in the developed world, it is imperative that America stop repeating the same mistakes, self-correct, and build a stronger nation to face the next crisis. Instead, 2020 saw not only inadequate efforts to slow the contagion but also high officials promoting its spread by mocking guidelines to get it under control. Importantly, global warming is likely to usher in a new pandemic, and having people behave responsibly to climate change is apt to be much harder than getting them to fulfill their moral obligations on COVID-19. In a time era when partisan enmity has disrupted civic culture, appealing to a basic sense of decency and expecting everyone to do the right thing are not sufficient.

While it may be too early to develop lessons from the current contagion, one starting point is to investigate why it happened and how to prevent it from happening again (a useful place to start is the well-documented study by Fallows, 2020; more broadly, consider

Schwartz, 2020). As part of any such effort, the logistical task is to organize the manufacturing sector to prepare for the next crisis by creating a virtual warehouse of electronic designs for emergency equipment, mapping supply chains and anticipating shortages, and developing a network of manufacturing experts to share best practices (Brown & Rassey, 2020, October 5). In the meantime, corona virus deaths in the United States surpassed those from. World Wars I and II (combined) and counting (see Wright, 2021; also consult Schechtman & Simon, 2021 May 27 on incomplete and fragmented data reporting systems that likely result in undercounts of cases).

Source: The first one-third of the narrative is adapted from Dickenson, 2020; also consult the references cited thereafter found at the end of this chapter as well as Berman et al. (in press).

Discussion Questions

1. "Personnel is policy," according to the epigram at the outset of this exhibit. Why? Do you agree?

2. Masking is used as a symbol to help understand the American response to the pathogen spread. Identify some other symbols that might provide additional insights.

3. Scientists know that masks limit corona contagion, but it is not possible for randomized clinical trials to prove that. Read Tufekci's (2020, November 6) op-ed, summarize her claims, and defend your conclusion.

4. As you read this book, have any official investigations into the pandemic been published? What lessons were drawn from these inquiries? Is the world ready for the next contagion?

MORAL DECAY

The best way to rob a bank is to own one.

—William K. Black

Internalizing the transcendental values into one's professional life is a challenging goal. Leaders in the public, private, and not-for-profit spheres all too frequently fail to rise to the task. While violent crimes have declined in the last decade, government—and particularly corporate—fraud, waste, and abuse have increased markedly (Chapter 9). The dollar amounts are substantial, and the types of untoward behavior have multiplied with the opportunities provided by the Internet (e.g., identity theft). This is at a time when the FBI's white-collar crime unit has been cut back to emphasize the real, if more remote, threat of terrorism. To understand the nature of this problem, two issues are discussed here: (1) the nature of corporate, government, and nonprofit sector crime and (2) strategies managers can use to combat it.

The Nature of White-Collar Crime

The Enron Era in the early years of the new century followed a robust anti-corruption program during the Savings and Loan scandal in the late 1980s in which 5,000 bankers served time. While some executives during that Era were prosecuted, just 18 went to prison. Since then alleged and proven corruption has declined as the Justice Department turned "felonies into misdemeanors, misdemeanors into torts and torts into regulatory offenses" (Hobbes, 2020, February 10; Taub, 2020) as society has been increasingly indifferent to white-collar crime.

In the wake of the 2008–2009 Great Recession, not a single senior official from a prominent bank went to jail. Corrupt behavior has largely been normalized to the point that the last decade has been called "The Golden Age of White Collar Crime" as fewer and fewer executives were investigated, prosecuted, penalized, and sentenced.

> In January 2019, white collar prosecutions fell to their lowest level since researchers started tracking them. . . . (Most) cases are against low-level con artists. . . . Since 2015, criminal penalties . . . have fallen from $3.6 billion to roughly $110 *million*.
>
> (emphasis added; Hobbes, 2020, February 10; see also Eisinger, 2018, August 24 and White Collar Crime, 2021.)

White-collar criminals in organizations inflict far more damage on society than all street crime combined (Chapter 9): They cost "victims an estimated $300 billion to $800 billion per year," while blue-collar crime cost approximately $16 billion (Taub, 2020). It is hard to avoid the conclusion that many people believe that white-collar crime does not really matter. In the meantime, street crime is treated as felonies and white-collar transgressions as misdemeanors.

Corporate. As the *Corporate Crime Reporter* ("Twenty Things," 2007) states, "[W]hether in bodies or injuries or dollars lost, corporate crime and violence wins by a landslide." While neither the FBI nor the U.S. Department of Justice keeps statistics on white-collar crime, what is known includes the following:

- Business crime is often "silent violence" as a result of criminal negligence involving occupational diseases, pollution, contaminated foods, hazardous consumer products, and hospital malpractice—yet deaths attributed to negligence are seldom prosecuted as homicides.
- Corporate violators are the only criminal class that lobbies and influences business laws to ensure that no legislation imposes criminal sanctions on knowing and willful violations of law.
- White-collar crime is under-prosecuted by a factor of approximately 100 (stated differently, prosecutors are underfunded by the same factor).
- Notorious corporate criminals, in sweetheart deals, do not plead guilty; instead, they (a) agree not to violate the law again (a deferred prosecution agreement), (b) consent to pay a fine and promise to change their conduct in exchange for no criminal record (a non-prosecution agreement), or (c) identify a unit of the firm that has no assets—or even a defunct entity—to plead guilty, leaving the organization as a whole innocent (Office of US Senator Elizabeth Warren, 2016).
- There are very few career prosecutors of corporate crime, as many see their jobs as a stepping stone to defending corporations.
- Having de facto immunity, not one executive responsible for fraud during the 2007–2008 metastasizing financial crisis, and became exceptionally wealthy as a result, was required to pay back the fraud proceeds or was imprisoned (for a different, if strained view, see Bourtin, 2017, November 3).

- The market does not take most corporate prosecutions seriously because when settled, the stock prices go up. There is no serious consequence to company reputation, and business practices remain largely intact.

In short, corporate malfeasance is a compelling problem with significant effects on society but is unlikely to be prosecuted due to lack of resources, business-friendly statutes, and case settlements that protect companies from serious consequences of wrongdoing (Coffee, 2020).

Government. Institutional crime, as discussed in Chapter 9, is hardly unknown in the public arena. Corruption cases dominate headlines across the nation. The Washington Blog lists 70 bullet points cataloguing instances of public sector fraud, waste, and abuse (see How Corrupt is the American Government, 2016).

Government corruption is a concern not only at the national level but at the state and local levels as well. The Coalition for Integrity (2018) published an index, States With Anti-Corruption Measures for Public officials (S.W.A.M.P). The comparative scorecard revealed the lack of clear, consistent laws and regulations governing ethics and transparency in state executive and legislative branches. Index items refer to the independence and scope of ethics agencies and their powers, disclosure requirements for gifts to officials and client disclosure by legislators. It also included transparency of funding sources for independent campaign expenditures. Table 15.1 provides the ranking and state-by-state S.W.A.M.P. index using a scale of 0–100, with 100 representing a perfect score. Key findings include

- no state received a score of 100 and none were in the top 20 percentile,
- most states scored 60 or below (e.g., New York was tied with Massachusetts and Illinois, each ranked 22),
- the highest ranked were Washington (78), Rhode Island (75), and California (75),
- the lowest ranked were New Mexico (36) and North Dakota (0); both voted in 2018 to create independent ethics agencies,
- the highest scoring states have laws and regulations that reflect best practice efforts to advance ethical frameworks and transparency.

Given the weakness of state laws and regulations, it is not surprising that corruption is widespread. States have been ranked from most to least corrupt using a variety of measures, including

- the absolute number of officials convicted in federal court on corruption (New York is highest; Enten, 2015),
- the number of public corruption convictions per 10,000 inhabitants (District of Columbia is highest; McCarthy, 2020),
- federal corruption convictions of state officials (Florida is highest; Wilcox & Krassner, 2012),
- per capita corruption convictions (Louisiana is highest; Enten, 2015), perceptions of state political reporters toward government (Kentucky is highest; Dincer & Johnston, 2014), and
- state anti-corruption laws (Washington in one study; Coalition for Integrity, 2018; and Alaska in another, Qiu, Zubak-Skees, & Lincoln, 2018).

| TABLE 15.1 | The U.S. States and DC with Anti-corruption Measures for Public Officials (S.W.A.M.P.) Index and Ranking | |

States	S.W.A.M.P. Index (%)	Rank
Washington	78	1
California	75	2.5
Rhode Island	75	2.5
Kentucky	74	4
DC	72	5.5
Kansas	72	5.5
Alaska	69	7
New Hampshire	67	8
Arkansas	66	9
South Carolina	65	10
Florida	64	11.5
Hawaii	64	11.5
West Virginia	63	13
Texas	62	14
Ohio	61	15
Nebraska	60	16
New Jersey	59	17
Missouri	58	18
Colorado	57	19.5
Wisconsin	57	19.5
Maryland	56	22
Massachusetts	56	22
New York	56	22
Illinois	55	24.5
Oregon	55	24.5
Montana	54	25.5
Nevada	54	25.5
Pennsylvania	51	28
Delaware	50	29.5
Tennessee	50	29.5
Louisiana	48	31.5
Maine	48	31.5
Minnesota	46	33
Connecticut	44	34
North Carolina	42	35.5
Oklahoma	42	35.5
Georgia	40	38
Iowa	40	38
Mississippi	40	38
Vermont	37	40
New Mexico	36	41
Alabama	35	42.5
Virginia	35	42.5
South Dakota	34	44
Utah	31	45
Arizona	28	47
Indiana	28	47
Michigan	28	47
Idaho	16	49
Wyoming	12	50
North Dakota	0	51

Source: Coalition for Integrity, 2018.

In the latter study, only three states scored a higher grade than a D+ (Alaska C, California, and Connecticut C–) and 11 flunked. Clearly, there are different ways to measure corruption, and findings can point in different directions, but results are not encouraging.

Focusing on a study using one of these measures—a ranking of states based on the number of public corruption convictions between 2000 and 2010 (Table 15.2)—shows Florida led the nation in federal corruption convictions of state officials over the past decade, ranking first among states five times between 1999 and 2010. The state's reputation has been tarnished, with adverse impacts on its economy and ability to attract new jobs. Furthermore, a *Forbes* ranking of America's Most Miserable Cities in 2012, which used corruption as a key factor, shows three Florida cities ranked (1) Miami, (4) West Palm Beach, and (11) Fort Lauderdale.

Such disturbing statistics spurred reformers to create Integrity Florida, a nonpartisan, nonprofit research institute with a mission to promote governmental integrity and expose improbity. This good-government group proposed a roadmap for reform that includes four steps to help citizens track and hold public officials accountable: (1) put all campaign finance data online in an electronic, searchable downloadable form; (2) place all lobbying expenditures online; (3) deposit all government expenditures online; and (4) digitize financial disclosure information (Perry, 2012). Most of these suggestions were adopted by the Florida Commission on Ethics in their legislative agenda and were passed by the state legislature. Like any reforms, they will be only as good as their enforcement. The group is seeking to (a) create a corruption hotline, (b) institute tougher penalties for violations, (c) strengthen the independence of inspector generals, (d) fortify whistleblower protections, (e) convene ethics reform coalitions throughout the state, and (f) empower the state ethics commission to begin its own investigations and have the authority to collect the fines that it imposes (Kennedy, 2012; Krassner, 2013).

Palm Beach County, Florida, provides a closer look at the history of profligacy and reform. At one time, the county had the national reputation as the "capital of corruption." This was based on scandalous behavior by city and county officials that led to the ouster of four county commissioners over a four-year period, three of whom were sentenced to prison. In the aftermath, sweeping reforms were passed, including a local ethics code, a county ethics enforcement agency with a budget of $476,000 and staff of five, and appointment of a county inspector general to investigate fraud and mismanagement (Wallman, 2012a, 2012b). The changes were modeled in part after those in Miami-Dade County, which has had a Commission on Ethics and Public Trust (see Exhibit 2.2) and an Office of Inspector General since 1998. As of August 2012, the Palm Beach County Ethics Commission had vetted almost 100 alleged ethics violations, administered some punishments, and offered advisory opinions in 225 cases. The commission holds televised monthly meetings. The county's Internet home page contains a prominent message for citizens to "Report! Waste Fraud or Abuse."

Nonprofits. Governments at the national, state, and local levels outsource many functions to community-based nonprofits; however, it is estimated that more than 10 percent are insolvent (even higher in human services) and nearly half have limited cash on hand or access to credit (Kaplan, 2017; MacIntosh, 2017). With cuts in federal discretionary spending, not-for-profits feel the hit and have difficulty using fundraising or volunteers as ways to balance declining government payments. Accordingly, as nonprofits face growing financial insecurity, the number of stories reporting on scandals is increasing. The examples are plen-

| TABLE 15.2 | State Public Corruption Convictions, 2000–2010 |

State	Total Convictions
Florida	781
California	753
Texas	741
New York	670
Pennsylvania	593
Ohio	551
Illinois	541
New Jersey	457
Virginia	442
Louisiana	407
Washington, DC*	383
Kentucky	306
Alabama	285
Puerto Rico*	269
Tennessee	269
Michigan	256
Georgia	228
Maryland	228
Massachusetts	214
Mississippi	201
Missouri	196
North Carolina	193
Arizona	183
Indiana	151
Oklahoma	142
Wisconsin	126
Connecticut	108
Washington	101
Colorado	98
Arkansas	95
Guam*	95
West Virginia	78
Montana	75
Minnesota	70
South Carolina	66
Alaska	64
South Dakota	61
North Dakota	57
Iowa	53
New Mexico	52
Delaware	47
Hawaii	46
Kansas	43
Virgin Islands*	42
Nevada	41
Oregon	41
Utah	40
Maine	39
Idaho	28
Rhode Island	28
Nebraska	26
New Hampshire	18
Vermont	17
Wyoming	17

Note: * Nonstate jurisdictions.
Source: Adapted from Wilcox and Krassner (2012).

tiful. The Breast Cancer Relief Fund raised large sums of money ($64 million) yet a paltry 2 percent was given to hospitals and cancer victims. Similarly, Kids Wish Network purports to raise money to help sick children and their families; however, in reality only three cents to the dollar actually go to helping kids (Kandt, 2016).

It is not surprising that confidence in the ethics of charities dropped precipitously following disclosures that the Red Cross had redirected gifts intended for the victims of the September 11, 2001, attacks to other purposes. The image of nonprofits had been besmirched earlier when the CEO of United Way was convicted of 25 counts of illegal conduct in 1992, including using United Way funds for his personal benefit and for inter-state transportation of fraudulently obtained money. In 1997, the president of Adelphi University was fired. He not only was arbitrary and capricious in dealing with those who opposed his initiatives but also engaged in lavish spending at a time when he was the second-highest paid university president (just behind Harvard) in the country. While the wrongdoing was not as egregious as that found in businesses like Enron and Goldman Sachs, such behaviors contradicted the "serving society" objective that has long been part of the identity of not-for-profits.

If nonprofits are to be seen as the ethical sector of society, Doug White (2010) suggests, they need to shift their thinking away from money-making and growth, cease paying exorbitant salaries to their top executives, focus less on next quarter's financial balance sheet and more on mid- to long-range goals they seek to accomplish, and avoid public relations gimmicks while reemphasizing their mission and purpose. Surveys find that the public ranks the ethical behavior of nonprofits ahead of either business or government.

However, according to an Ethics Resource Center (2007) survey, "[I]ntegrity in the nonprofit sector is eroding" and "misconduct is on the rise—especially financial fraud." In part, this is attributable to boards that fail to set clear ethical standards. A poll by Paul Light (2008) also reported skepticism regarding charitable performance, concluding that "confidence has not risen significantly since it hit bottom in 2003." Furthermore, fraud is costly—approximately $40 billion per year is stolen from charities by their employees, as an estimated 6 percent of their revenue is lost to fraud annually (White, 2010, 31).

The *Washington Post* analyzed IRS 990 forms of 1,000 large nonprofits in 2013 and found what was termed "outrageous, egregious, large-scale corruption within organizations," specifically an "'astounding' number that had serious financial irregularities" (Fine, 2013). Another study of corruption in U.S. nonprofit organizations between 2008 and 2011 (Archambeault, Webber, & Greenlee, 2015) examined 115 incidents of detected fraud and reported three key findings. First, the primary perpetrators of wrongdoing were operational or financial executives (e.g., president, CEO, executive director, treasurer, CFO), followed by accounting, finance, and other employees. Second, most instances of wrongdoing involved insiders victimizing the organization through check or credit card schemes, theft of assets through other means, or theft of cash or deposits. The wrongdoing also victimizes the public and defrauds contributors (e.g., using funds for other than intended purposes). Further, it involves improperly claiming loans, grants, or government funds, and other fraudulent activity. Third, the majority of settings in which nonprofit wrongdoing was uncovered was in health and human service organizations (Archambeault et al., 2015).

The effects of institutional crime in all three economic sectors include poor employee morale, difficulty in recruitment and retention of personnel, lowered trust in organizations, heightened fear among stakeholders, waste, and intervention by stockholders, legislators, and boards of directors. The result is the death of accountability, justice, and deterrence. While regulators are underfunded and marginalized, newspapers no longer fund in-depth investigations and corporate compliance units seldom question profit centers.

While few expect the historically low white-collar crime prosecutions to increase (Chayes, 2020), over 170 good-government groups have recommended that the new administration undertake specific actions to enhance transparency, ethics requirements, disclosure rules as well as to restore the rule of law (Buble, 2020, November 11; for more details, see Bauer & Goldsmith, 2020, and Rosenzweiz & Kannan, 2020, September 7). Candidate Biden also proposed a Commission on Federal Ethics to oversee and enforce relevant laws and rules. Finally, Biden promised to seek change in the past administration's policies that have critical ethical implications: the pandemic and the World Health Organization, Obamacare, global warming and the Paris Agreement, an economic rescue package, tax reform, as well as a return to civility and evidence-based decision-making. Whether or not the Biden administration, like the Obama and Trump administrations before it, fails to make a genuine difference remains to be seen: the president has reassured Wall Street that it would not be demonized, vowing that nothing would fundamentally change for corporate leaders (Wilkins, 2020, October 18).

There are easy legislative fixes (e.g., better IRS and Justice Department funding), which are nonetheless difficult to pass, but the hard part is shifting the political culture to demand change. In the meantime, white-collar crime continues unabated in all three sectors while resources to combat it decline. To encourage reform, the only thing that consistently worked in the past is credible warnings from government agencies, close regulatory surveillance, and harsh punishments of individual offenders (Benson & Simpson, 2014).

Confronting White-Collar Crime

Richard Nielsen (1987) examines a wide variety of strategies managers can employ when confronted with white-collar crime. In an analysis of ten cases, he discusses the advantages and disadvantages of not thinking about the problem, going along to get along, voicing protest, conscientious objection, leaving, several forms of whistleblowing, sabotage, and building consensus for change (Table 15.3).

While refusal to think about a problem or going along to avoid trouble will not produce change, the remaining approaches can be used to arrest decay in organizational ethics. Nielsen (1987) advocates the last strategy—negotiating and creating consensus for reform—because it provides the opportunity to discover more about the situation through diverse points of view. However, negotiation may not be effective when there is insufficient time, others are not interested, and the case circumstances are win-lose, not win-win. When negotiation is not possible, Nielsen recommends either secretly threatening to blow the whistle or administrative sabotage. For the first option, the organization is provided time to improve and avoids negative publicity. If reform is not forthcoming, then blowing the whistle may produce the desired effect. For the second option, sabotage—surreptitiously making a change that deters unethical behavior—may be effective. It is, however, ethically dubious, especially if more open and honest alternatives have not been tried.

As this work has shown, it is seldom ethically sufficient to say, "I had no choice," which, in effect, relinquishes ethical autonomy. Instead, Nielsen (1987, 318) writes, "[T]here are realistic alternative responses to consider and compare, that there are situational factors that

TABLE 15.3	Reacting to Ethical Issues in Organizational Management: Advantages and Disadvantages

Strategy	Advantages	Disadvantages
1. *Not thinking about it* Identifying so closely with the organization that United Fruit officials helped overthrow the government of Guatemala	Protect careers	No policy change Thoughtlessness
2. *Going along to get along* A contract negotiated the sale of equipment to the Navy involving kickbacks	Protect one's career	Thinking about, and cooperating with, dubious practices. No policy change
3. *Protesting* A salesman objects to the sale of unsafe products	Do the right thing	Putting career at risk
4. Conscientious objection A pharmaceutical researcher objects to the false advertising claims, refusing to have his name used in press releases or press conferences regarding the product	Set an honorable example	Not regarded as a team player
5. *Leaving* A drug company executive resigns after refusing to test a suspect drug on infants and the elderly	Courage of convictions Signal to firm that it will lose good people	Someone else will cooperate Prevents learning and change
6. *Secretly blowing the whistle* An executive of an electric company writes an anonymous letter to the Justice Department alleging bid-rigging among electrical contractors	Positive impact on problem Avoid retaliation	Sneaky behavior May be exposed by company investigation— unless whistleblower lies. Distrust
7. *Publicly blowing the whistle* A high-level public manager and former business CEO reveals underbidding and cost overruns by Lockheed to Congress and the press	Positive effect on problem Regarded as hero	Dissenter vilified Others discouraged from similar behavior Damages reputation of all agency and contractor employees
8. Secretly threatening to blow the whistle An insurance salesperson anonymously writes a letter to the sales manager threatening to send the state insurance commission a copy of unethical sales instructions	Change behavior Protect identity	No dialogue on problem Prevents injured parties from seeking remedies
9. Sabotage Instead of following an unethical and illegal order, a local social welfare manager creates a paperwork trail to funding agencies that undermined and delayed the order	Positive effect Protect identity	No dialogue to solve problem Retaliation if exposed. Is sabotage ethical?
10. *Negotiating and building a consensus for change* Concerned that cutting costs would undercut pollution control requirements and that closing the mill would impact the community, a division director negotiates a plan to extend the cost reduction targets to permit gradual improvements in pollution control and productivity that permitted the mill to remain open	Individual efforts can gain support from others Satisfaction in constructive solution	Ineffective when many benefit from existing situation Difficult process. Some situations are win-lose

Source: Adapted from Nielsen (1987).

can influence the decision, and that we do need to think about these issues and choose." Thus, there is genuine value in a contingency approach to decision-making in an effort to do the right thing at the right time and place. Not all battles are worth fighting; those that are should be big enough to matter and small enough to win.[4] To summarize this discussion of moral grandeur and decay, Machiavelli's *Discourses* posited a contest between order and disorder where in *virtu* (valor, civic duty) produces effectiveness and peace, while *ozio* (decadence and selfishness) spawns indolence and war. States must strive for the spirit of virtue: remember, while there is much that is bad in the world, there is more that is good. U.S. Supreme Court justice Louis Brandeis's sage observation is apropos: "[M]ost of the things worth doing in the world had been declared impossible before they were done."

NEW CHALLENGES: THERE IS A DAWN IN EVERY DARKNESS

Continued discovery will produce increasing sophistication in existing technologies, as well as the advent of revolutionary technologies beyond imagination. Current and new scientific advances will bring novel challenges to ethics. Already, surveillance technology in the form of drones is raising concerns in the United States (Case Study 15.1).

Yet the utility of ethics is that ancient methods can be adapted and applied to unprecedented situations. Dueling, foot binding, slavery, "honor killings," and female genital mutilation were once widely accepted but are now rejected by most people. Ethics, then, has matured and will continue developing to make sense of the modern world (Appiah, 2011; Shermer, 2015). Industrial meat production, the prison system, institutionalization and isolation of the elderly, and environmental abuse are increasingly subject to evolving views of morality. The ethics triad (Chapter 7) will guide future decision makers, linked to their colleagues present and past by a commitment to the public good.

Let it be said that the human condition is deep and dark and bright and beautiful; savagery and nobility coexist. Every saint has a past, every sinner a future (Cole-Whitaker, 2001). As Martin Keogh believes:

> If you look at the science about what is happening on earth and aren't pessimistic, you don't understand the data. But if you meet the people who are working to restore this earth and the lives of the poor and you aren't optimistic, you haven't got a pulse.

America begins not with a place but with an ideal; its people are imperfect creatures who aspire to be better than they are. Politics is not about perfection but the art of the possible. Historically, the American experiment has been predicated upon good faith, trust, reasoned opposition, free and fair elections, bipartisan compromise, respect for public service, and commitment to democratic values. In the end, the health of the republic depends upon the virtue of public servants to uphold not only the constitution but also the unwritten constitution, the norms and customs that form the foundation of democracy. As Lincoln's Secretary of State William Seward believed, "There was always just enough virtue in this republic to save it."

Yet today self-governance confronts a profound peril as the country has experienced a degree of calamity—impeachable conduct, pandemic denialism, economic collapse, social justice protests, floods, droughts, extreme heat waves, firestorms and hurricanes, voter suppression, incitement to violence, violation of campaign finance laws, FBI warnings of Russian interference in elections, controversial presidential tax returns, October surprises (the death of Justice Ginsberg, a panned presidential debate, virus infection of the president), the 2020 elections, the January 6, 2021 insurrection—that compromises the well-being of citizens, political institutions, and democracy itself. The political order, absent reform, is not self-sustaining.

If this was not enough, there is a stark divergence between the best of American traditions and the reality of governing. The unprecedented assault on the principles, norms, and purpose of democratic government included obstruction of justice, contempt of Congress, abuse of power, acceptance of emoluments, distain for the electoral process, disregard of science, contempt for apolitical career service, and indifference to corruption. These developments have compromised not only routine government functions but also the capacity to deal with emergencies like pandemics.

The quality of government is less in its laws, customs, and traditions than in the willingness to comply with those standards in the name of power-sharing, the rule of law, and stability. Remarkably, knowing that there are few consequences, perpetrators do not deny these unethical and illegal actions. Instead, "not only do they not care, they're *pleased*" as they take pride in such violations and invite corruption (Leonardt, 2019, December 8; Waldman, 2020, October 1; original emphasis). Stated differently, constitutional rights do not exist unless they are practiced. The founders assumed that officials would govern in good faith and that honorable people would set aside partisan differences to keep the machinery of the republic operating.

As proof of belief in the legitimacy of popular sovereignty and self-government, will brave men and women respond to threats to a free society? Will they embrace the 1975 Declaration of Interdependence (www.interdependence.org/about/overview-mission/declaration-of-interdependence/) to honor and compliment the Declaration of Independence? Enlightened leaders understand that reality-based solutions to today's crises require both vigorous American government and vibrant international cooperation to deal with the existential threats confronting humankind (Zakaria, 2020). These dangers include not only the climate crisis but also the plant and animal mass extinction tragedy as well as the plastic waste calamity. The essential task for the next decade is to create a civic renaissance, a lively dialogue about the creation of virtuous life and a just society, a demonstration that—despite its flaws—democracy remains the best form of government.

GUIDELINES FOR ETHICAL CONDUCT

There is no greater glory than to work for the public's good.

—Edmund Burke

In an effort to encourage exemplary action, three guidelines are offered. The first advises learning to differentiate two types of rationality—functional (a focus on means or "how to") and substantive (an emphasis on goals or "why"). An exclusive stress on doing things right—functional rationality—can become the dominant moral code for some professionals, instead of ensuring that right things—substantive rationality—are pursued. While both forms of rationality are important, they should not be confused. As Einstein observed, "The perfection of means and the confusion of ends characterizes our age." Conservative commentator David Brooks (2012) argues that today's elite lacks a self-conscious leadership ethos. The language of success has overwhelmed the language of meaning. "They have no sense that they are guardians of institutions the world depends upon" (see also Zakaria, 2017, August 18). Divorced from ethics, leadership has been reduced to management technique and public relations.

Kohlberg's theory of moral development is useful in clarifying the role of reason in human thinking. At the individual level, his taxonomy (Chapter 4) seeks to explain why people reason the way they do and defines increasingly sophisticated types of reasoning. At the organizational level, the developmental, "high-road" commitment approach to ethics can foster honorable behavior in a manner absent from the punitive, "low-road" compliance strategy (Chapter 8; also examine Eisen, 2021; Mazzucato, 2021). The substantive form of rationality counsels that there is never a wrong time to do the right thing.

The second guideline, to borrow a leaf from environmentalists, is to "think globally, act locally." While one might be discouraged by events beyond one's control, this should not affect what can be done in one's own life. "We can't do everything for everyone everywhere," Richard L. Evans observed, "but we can do something for someone somewhere." As Gandhi said, "Be the change you want to see in the world." And he likely would chuckle in agreement at the observation, "If you think you're too small to make a change, try getting in bed with a mosquito."

Kemal Dervis (2020) emphasizes that "there is an overwhelming consensus among scientists that this decade will be the last window for humanity to change (its) current trajectory." The decisions made in the next ten years will affect the future for decades to come. Joe Biden's "build back better" strategy offers the prospect of a sustainable future—"one that escapes a 20th century growth model based on fossil fuel dependence and degradation of the natural capital and ecosystem services (to) deliver a net zero carbon economy by 2050" (Bahattacharya, 2020). Political contingencies may be incalculable, but the longer it takes to comprehend the scale of the tragedy, the worse it will get and its solutions will be more difficult. The crisis is a call to conscience that will test humanity's resolve and reveal the true state of humankind's character (consult Exercise 2 at the end of this chapter).

CASE STUDY 15.1

Applying Rational and Philosophical Ethics Approaches: Drones in Domestic Law Enforcement

Sheriff Alonzo Griffith of Metropolitan County Government in a northeastern state was intrigued by the idea of using drones, smaller and less expensive versions of the aircraft used in military operations in Afghanistan, Iraq, and Iran. His interest was piqued last year when he learned that they could see through walls, use software for facial recognition, and intercept calls and emails, all with little regulation. He envisioned drones helping to find missing children or marijuana fields, detect wildfires, report accidents such as highway pileups or hazardous material spills, or track dangerous suspects. Yet he was aware that surveillance drones raise controversial issues of privacy. He learned many citizen groups strongly oppose their domestic use. Sheriff Griffith told his staff to arrange the purchase of two unmanned remote control aircraft as a law enforcement tool. Now, he is torn about the order, wondering if this was the ethically correct action. He decided to use the ethics triad to think carefully about the decision before acting.

Results-Based Analysis. Griffith started by considering the results of the pending purchase. He is confident that drones would serve the "greater good" and that law enforcement capabilities would increase with the new aircraft. He believes using drones is a more efficient, effective, and safer way to respond to critical situations. The Federal Aviation Administration (FAA) estimates 10,000 civilian drones will be in use in the United States within five years. Griffith thinks these numbers will continue to increase rapidly. He does not want his department to become obsolete. He considers drones preferable to manned helicopters. Plus, they cost less (approximately $36,009–$250,000 for a drone versus $3 million for a helicopter and crew).

Griffith also knows that drones will be perceived by some as a threat to civil rights and liberties. Lawyers and media commentary will likely bemoan this initiative as another step toward a surveillance society and warn about "Big Brother" spying on citizens in an Orwellian police state. Law enforcement offices in Miami, Houston, Metro Nashville, and Seattle have purchased drones, generating controversy and the attention of state policymakers (Seattle officials subsequently canceled their order). Smaller cities, including Montgomery, Texas, and Gadsden, Alabama, have had similar experiences with backlash. Griffith is aware that aroused citizenry could threaten his career and job security. Protest groups are already planning demonstrations throughout the United States; he would like not to be host to such an event.

Rule-Based Analysis. He is also mindful of rules and principles as he mulls over his decision. While laws and rules on domestic drones including FAA guidelines are in their infancy, Griffith has read about increased legislative and administrative rulemaking activity bound to result in stricter regulation. He believes that oversight, privacy safeguards, transparency, and public input regarding the purpose and intended use of drones are appropriate. He is also aware that drones carrying infrared cameras with facial recognition capability, heat sensors, GPS, and automated license plate readers pose First Amendment risks (chilling the right to anonymity and association); if misused, Fourth Amendment rights (to be secure against unreasonable search and seizure) are threatened as well. Citizens' "reasonable expectation of privacy" could be compromised without restrictions on data storage and dissemination. He recalls the controversy over whole body imaging technology as a screening tool at airports. Similar problems could surface over drones, especially if monitoring by drones is done clandestinely. Public safety issues could also surface when drones operate alongside of commercial or private planes.

Virtue-Based Analysis. Sheriff Griffith is also concerned about virtue theory—does the purchase of drones make me and my community better? Citizen confidence is crucial and public trust has declined recently. If he were to announce the use of drones without first adequately preparing and involving the populace, he likely would be subject to criticism that would further erode trust. In light of these considerations, he would rather "be right slower than wrong faster." He feels it is important to take his time and engage citizens in an open conversation about the pros and cons of using drones before making a final decision.

Griffith cares about his community and the welfare of others. He wants to make a decision that is in the best interest of those in his jurisdiction. If he opts to purchase the drone, it will be after prudent deliberation and due diligence. He intends to listen to the concerns of those who may oppose aerial surveillance, weighing their concerns and arguments carefully. He plans to clearly communicate his rationale regarding the advisability of taking advantage of this technology. He recognizes the need to balance law enforcement's obligation to protect the society from major disruptions against an individual's right to be secure in their person and household effects.

Behavioral Ethics-Based Analysis. Behavioral ethics research cautions about easily overlooked tendencies such as bounded rationality, issue framing, overoptimism, ethical fading, and confirmation bias. Griffith's enthusiasm for drones may rest in the efficiency, effectiveness, and cost-saving benefits for law enforcement, which may be the way he understands (frames) and assesses the issue. In the process, his infatuation with this new technology may desensitize him to the potential ethical downside of this development with its threat to citizen privacy (ethical fading). As with anything new, there are unknowns that impede rational decision-making—problems cannot always be anticipated; nevertheless, in the exuberance of the moment, Griffith may be overly optimistic about the benefits of drones. As he learns about them, he needs to be alert to confirmation bias—gathering information to reinforce existing beliefs.

***

The last guideline is one that was suggested early in the book—aim for the middle ground between naïve idealism and cynical pessimism, because of the very real dangers at either extreme; the former should not let the perfect become the enemy of the good, the latter should not let discouragement surrender to wrongdoing. Compromise is a moral virtue in a democracy. Any time the lion and lamb can be brought to the table—it is a worthy thing to do. The maelstrom of crises today is compelling people to see the past—and the future—in a new light and can be used to create a better world.

Using such guidelines—or developing better ones—should assist in knowing what to do and whether one is making a positive difference in people's lives. Life consists not in holding good cards, someone once observed, but in playing those you hold well. "Nobody who ever gave his best," according to legendary Chicago Bears coach George Halas, "regretted it." In fact, the classical definition—and vow—of a professional is leadership in technical and ethical competence (Bowman, West, & Beck, 2010). Public servants, accordingly, must not only do technical things right but also do ethically right things. The ability to contemplate, enhance, and act on ethical situations is the essence of service to the people. The guidelines will aid in this pursuit.

There are many ways of being ethical. In the end, it is up to each person to figure out who he or she is and who he or she is not. There is only one way in which one can endure inhumanity to man, and that is to try in one's own life to exemplify man's humanity to man. Man is a promise that he must not break. "Real generosity toward the future," Albert Camus observed, "consists in giving all to what is present." The cases discussed in the chapters here happened to people just like you—except most were not as prepared to deal with the dilemmas as you will be, having read this book and appreciated the ethical obligations of public life.

Since the world is seldom simple and clear-cut, the purpose of ethics is to encourage thinking about difficult matters. The human mind may not be readily equipped to ask, much less answer, important questions; crushing rocks with a feather duster is no easy task. But ethics expands the imagination and helps appreciate the extent of human ignorance, the first step to reduce it. As an exercise in self-realization, the book has sought not only to better understand who you are already but also to reconsider some of your most fundamental beliefs. Struggle and uncertainty are part of ethics, as they are part of life, and this is what makes it hard, intriguing, magnificent, and so full of possibility and promise. There is no time like the present to set higher standards. Striving to live by ethical guidelines, as difficult as it may be, is the best way to lead a life worth living. As Madeline Bridge observes, "Give the world the best you have, and the best will come to you."

Our ending is your beginning in expanding and enhancing individual and institutional responsibilities in public service ethics. As this book attests, people care deeply about ethics. It has tried to give readers resources to address dilemmas for themselves based on their own values. Despite the excrescence of decay, there is also the ethical exuberance of grandeur. No one can do everything, but everyone can do something to create a more honorable world. "When do any of us," asked Texas congresswoman Barbara Jordan, "ever do enough?"

***

The test of our progress is not whether we add more to the abundance of those who have much; it is whether we provide enough for those who have too little.

—Franklin D. Roosevelt

NOTES

1. This section is based on, and expanded from, the authors' work in Berman et al. (2022).
2. In a prescient observation, Charles Blow (2012) believed that the 2012 presidential election was a moment that "truth and lies lost their honor and stigma, respectively," that facts are fungible and disinformation acceptable, and that dishonesty exposed by fact checking is unremarkable and ignored.
3. As inscribed in the foyer at the Maxwell School of Citizenship and Public Affairs, Syracuse University.
4. Mark Twain once observed, "We go to heaven for the climate and we go to hell for the company." Exploring the strategies above may be useful when confronting decay and might reduce the number of the hell bound (!).

DISCUSSION

1. Identify trends that illustrate grandeur and decay in moral life.

2. The creation of national parks, frequently known as America's best idea, is an example of making an ethical decision that moved society forward. Discuss.

3. "Corporate corruption in recent years is not just a corporate failure but also a failure of governmental oversight gutted by deregulation." Comment.

4. Using the ethics triad (Chapter 7), discuss the best way to approach the pandemic—should policymakers seek the greatest good for the greatest number, what is good for one is good for all, and/or what action will improve character and community?

5. Discuss the ethical issues involved in deciding who receives the COVID-19 vaccine.

6. Comment on these two events:

   (a) Early in the outbreak, the U.S. Postal Service drafted an announcement that its nationwide delivery system could provide every household with masks, starting with the most impacted areas. The White House scrapped the idea and sent masks to companies, health-care facilities, and community organizations.

   (b) After the corona virus was known to be in America, the federal government shipped large quantities of protective equipment to China.

7. "The greater danger is not that our aim is too high and we miss it, but that we aim too low and we reach it"—Michelangelo. Discuss.

8. Add to, or subtract from, the guidelines for exemplary behavior.

9. Will the past bury the future, or will the future bury the past?

10. "To the question of your life, you are the only answer. To the problems of your life, you are the only solution"—Jo Coudert. Discuss in the context of moral grandeur and decay.

11. Of what does humanity consist? Risen apes, fallen angels, or something else?

12. Former high CIA officials as well as a Republican senior Justice Department officeholder expressed concern about the security of state secrets: classified information could be a "profit center" for the heavily indebted Donald Trump (Papenfass, 2020, November 27). By the time you read this claim, is there any evidence to support it?

13. Given that much of the general public sees political controversies as "inside baseball" (esoteric, technical in character), it is political elites who preserve—or destroy—democracy. Discuss.

14. While bringing about political change is a challenge, it is remarkable that the January 6, 2021 attack on the capitol did not create a bipartisan coalition to defend democracy. Speculate why that was the case.

15. Consider these insights:

    "It is what it is, but it will become what you make it."—Anonymous

    "Don't judge each day by the harvest you reap, but by the seeds you plant."—Robert Louis Stevenson

    "Knowledge is the source of good and ignorance is the source of evil."—Socrates

    "My concern is not whether God is on our side. My greatest concern is to be on God's side."—Abraham Lincoln

    "There can be no final truth in ethics any more than in physics until the last man has had his experience and said his last."—William James

    "Every gun that is made, every warship launched, every rocket fired signifies, in the final sense, a theft from those who hunger and are fed, those who are cold and are not clothed."—Dwight E. Eisenhower

    "Those who stand for nothing will fall for anything."—Alexander Hamilton

    "I hate quotations."—Anonymous

EXERCISES

1. A recent study attempted to assess the efficacy of oaths of office by using Morris's intellectual, aesthetic, moral, and spiritual transcendental values that define excellence. The analysis concluded by offering recommendations to reinforce the current significance of oaths that were once a venerable bond between citizens and government (Bowman & West, 2020. doi:10.1177/0095399719890836). Review this work and provide a critique for discussion.

2. Using the ethics triad (Chapter 7), discuss the best way to approach the pandemic—should policymakers seek the greatest good for the greatest number, what is good for one is good for all, or what action will improve character and community?

3. Consult the COVID Tracking Project https://covidtracking.com/ and report to the class the most significant developments on the site.

4. Watch "Totally under Control" (2020, October; www.imdb.com/title/tt13065386/media-viewer/rm3629424897, two hours). Health experts reveal the truth behind the government's pandemic response in this documentary. It includes a stark contrast between South Korea and the United States, both of which discovered their initial COVID-19 cases on the same day.

   State the thesis of the film in one sentence, identify several supporting subtheses, describe the methodology used to fortify claims, articulate the conclusion, and provide a 1–2 page critique.

5. The huge electronic Climate Clock that counts down the time left to the world is modeled after the National Debt Clock, also in New York City. Using data from the United Nations Intergovernmental Panel on Climate Change, it shows the earth's deadline. Consult https://climateclock.world for what has been called "the most important number in the world." Based on what you found, report to the class whether or not global warming has reached the point of no return. Keep in mind W. Edwards Deming's observation: "It is not necessary to change. Survival is not mandatory."

6. Ethical self-assessments are readily found on the Internet:

   > www.ethics.va.gov/ELSA.pdf
   > www.ache.org/newclub/career/ethself.cfm
   > www.walkthetalk.com/media/solution_finder/pdf/how_ethical_am_i.pdf
   > https://goodmenproject.com

   Such tools can be helpful to identify areas of moral strength and vulnerability, and to provide opportunities for reflection. They are intended for personal use and should not be used to evaluate others; they generally avoid scoring schemes because ethical conduct neither can nor should be quantified.

7. Consider these challenges for self-development created by Rich Gee (http://richgee.com):

   - Explain where you are now to your earlier self (talking to your past self produces insights into what might have been done differently; this not only may help you in the future but also will demonstrate that you can handle anything that life throws at you).
   - Look back from your future (imagine where you want to be and what advice he or she might give you; with a lucid view of your goals, you can take concrete steps to achieve them).

8. Create an actual plan for developing your ethical effectiveness, for "it is today that we create the world of the future" (Eleanor Roosevelt). It should contain three components:

   Assessment
   Gather feedback about yourself and your decisions by taking ethics self-evaluation questionnaires, establishing a mentor relationship with a person whom you respect, and asking friends, colleagues, and family about your behavior.

   Challenges
   Identify opportunities to further augment your skills by volunteering for organizational tasks, leading committees, taking advantage of training activities, forming clubs, writing op-ed essays for the local newspaper, and so forth.

   Support
   Discuss your concerns with peers, have an ongoing ethics reading program for yourself, or locate support groups that nurture leadership in your community.

Provide examples, ethical theories, personal behaviors, and references (journal/checklists, course readings, news events) to substantiate each of the aforementioned components. Include goals, tools, actions, and deadlines for each (Johnson, 2017). Identify strengths and weaknesses in the plan and strategies to address weaknesses. Appendix 15.1 offers a student example of this assignment.

REFERENCES

Appiah, K. (2011). *The honor code: How moral revolutions happen*. New York: Norton.

Archambeault, D., Webber, S., & Greenlee, J. (2015). Fraud and corruption in U.S. nonprofit entities. *Nonprofit and Voluntary Sector Quarterly*. Retrieved from http://journals.sagepub.com.access.library.miami.edu/doi/full/10.1177/0899764014555987

Bahattacharya, A. (2020). Rebooting the climate agenda: What should the priorities be? In B. Coulibaly, K. Dervis, H. Kharsas, & Z. Qureshi (Eds.), *Reimagining the global economy: Building back better in a post-COVID-19 world* (pp. 32–37). Washington, DC: Brookings Institution.

Bauer, B., & Goldsmith, J. (2020). *After Trump: Reconstructing the presidency*. Washington, DC: Lawfare Institute and Brookings Institution.

Benson, M., & Simpson, S. (2014). *Understanding white-collar crime: An opportunity perspective*. New York: Routledge.

Berman, E., Bowman, J., West, J., & Van Wart, M. (in press). *Human resource management in public service: Paradoxes, processes, and problems* (7th ed.). Thousand Oaks, CA: Sage.

Bleifuss, J. (2020, August 24). Stop blaming individuals for the spread of Covid and start blaming the government response. *In These Times*. Retrieved from https://inthesetimes.com/article/trump-covid-19-mask-mandate

Blow, C. (2012, November 1). Liberty to lie. *New York Times*. Retrieved from http://campaignstops.blogs.nytimes.com/2012/11/01/liberty-to-lie/

Bourtin, N. (2017, November 3). Five myths about white collar crime. *Washington Post*. Retrieved from www.washingtonpost.com/outlook/five-myths/five-myths-about-white-collar-crime/2017/11/03/5793fb3a-be6e-11e7-97d9-bdab5a0ab381_story.html

Bowman, J. (2011–2012). Public service as a calling: Reflections, retreat, revival, resolve. *Journal of Workplace Rights*, *16*, 47–61.

Bowman, J., and West, J. (2020). Pointless or powerful: The case for oaths of office. *Administration & Society*, *52*(8), 1147–1169.

Bowman, J., West, J., & Beck, M. (2010). *Competencies in public service: The professional edge* (2nd ed.). Armonk, NY: M. E. Sharpe.

Brooks, D. (2012, July 13). Why our elites stink. *New York Times*. Retrieved from www.nytimes.com/2012/07/13/opinion/brooks-why-our-elites-stink.html?_r=0

Brooks, D. (2017, August 1). Before manliness lost its virtue. *The New York Times*. Retrieved from: www.nytimes.com/2017/08/01/opinion/scaramucci-mccain-masculinity-white-house.html

Brown, C., & Rassey, L. (2020, October 5). We have the manufacturing might to fight COVID-19. *Government Executive*. Retrieved from www.govexec.com/management/2020/10/we-have-manufacturing-might-fight-covid-19/169010/Retrieved from www.govexec.com/management/2020/10/we-have-manufacturing-might-fight-covid-19/169010/

Buble, C. (2020, November 11). Over 170 groups call for Biden administration to take up ethics reforms immediately. *Government Executive*. Retrieved from www.govexec.com/management/2020/11/over-170-groups-call-biden-administration-take-ethics-reforms-immediately/169971/

Chayes, S. (2020). *On corruption in America and what is at stake*. New York: Knopf.

Coalition for Integrity. (2018). *Five Thirty Eight*. Retrieved from https://swamp.coalitionforintegrity.org/

Coffee, J. (2020). *Corporate crime and punishment: The crisis in underenforcement*. San Francisco: Berrett-Koehler.

Cole-Whitaker, T. (2001). *Every saint has a past, every sinner a future*. New York: Tarcher.

Dervis, K. (2020, January 9). When climate activism and nationalism collide. *Brookings Op Ed*. Retrieved from www.brookings.edu/opinions/when-climate-activism-and-nationalism-collide/

Dickenson, T. (2020, June 11). The unmasking of America. *Rolling Stone*. Retrieved from www.rollingstone.com/politics/politics-features/n95-masks-trump-covid19-coronavirus-health-care-workers-ppe-1013132/

Dincer, O., & Johnston, M. (2014, December 1). *Measuring illegal and legal corruption in American states: Some results from the corruption in America survey*. Retrieved from https://ethics.harvard.edu/blog/measuring-illegal-and-legal-corruption-american-states-some-results-safra

Dreifuss, B. (2020, June 26). Can't you wear a mask for the sake of health care workers? *New York Times*. Retrieved from www.nytimes.com/2020/06/26/opinion/coronavirus-arizona-hospitals.html

Eisen, N. Ed. (2021). *If its broke, fix it: Restoring federal government ethics and the rule of law*. Washington, DC: Brooking.

Eisinger, J. (2018, August 24). Why Manafort and Cohen thought they'd get away with it. *New York Times*. Retrieved from www.nytimes.com/2018/08/24/sunday-review/manafort-cohen-mueller-white-collar-crime.htmlEnten, H. (2015). Ranking the states from most to least corrupt. *Five Thirty Eight*. Retrieved from https://fivethirtyeight.com/features/ranking-the-states-from-most-to-least-corrupt/

Ethics Resource Center. (2007). *National nonprofit ethics survey: An inside view of nonprofit sector ethics*. Retrieved from www.ethics.org/files/u5/ERC_s_National_Nonprofit_Ethics_Survey.pdf

Fallows, J. (2020, June 30). The three weeks that changed everything. *The Atlantic*. Retrieved from www.theatlantic.com/politics/archive/2020/06/how-white-house-coronavirus-response-went-wrong/613591/

Fine, A. (2013, November 1). *Everyday nonprofit corruption*. Retrieved from https://allisonfine.com/2013/11/01/regular-nonprofit-corruption/

Hobbes, M. (2020, February 10). The golden age of white collar crime. *Huffington Post*. Retrieved from https://www.huffpost.com/highline/article/white-collar-crime

How corrupt is the American government? (2016, January 5). Retrieved from www.washingtonsblog.com/2016/01/corrupt-american-government.html

Johnson, C. (2017). *Meeting the ethical challenges of leadership: Casting light or shadow* (6th ed.). Thousand Oaks, CA: Sage.

Kandt, H. (2016, November 18). *Nonprofit corruption and why society needs to care*. Retrieved from www.linkedin.com/pulse/nonprofit-corruption-why-society-needs-care-hannah-kandt

Kaplan, L. (2017, March 31). *5 ways to fix dysfunctional government contracting*. Retrieved from https://nonprofitquarterly.org/2017/03/31/5-ways-fix-dysfunctional-government-contracting/

Kavanagh, J., & Rich, M. (2014). *Truth decay: An initial exploration of the diminishing role of fact and analysis in American public life*. Los Angeles: RAND Corporation.

Kennedy, J. (2012, June 6). Florida tops in public corruption, changes needed, watchdog says. *Palm Beach Post*. Retrieved from www.postonpolitics.com/2012/6/florida-tops-in-public-corruption-changes-needed

Krassner, D. (2013, September 9). Urgent reform needed for Florida's future. *Tallahassee Democrat*, p. 5A.

Kristof, N. (2020, July 2). Refusing to wear a mask is like driving drunk. *New York Times*. Retrieved from www.nytimes.com/2020/07/01/opinion/coronavirus-face-masks.html

Leonardt, D. (2019, December 8). Eight counts of impeachment that Trump deserves. *New York Times*. Retrieved from www.nytimes.com/2019/12/08/opinion/donald-trump-impeachment.html

Lerner, A., Folkers, G., & Fauci, A. (2020). Preventing the spread of SARS-CoV-2 with masks and other "Low-tech" interventions. *JAMA—Journal of the American Medical Association, 324*(19). https://doi.org/10.1001/jama.2020.21946

Light, P. (2008). *How Americans view charities: A report on charitable confidence*. Washington, DC: Brookings Institution.

MacIntosh, J. (2017, March 30) *How the mayor can save nonprofits hired by the city*. Retrieved from www.crainsnewyork.com/article/20170330/OPINION/170329881/how-the-mayor-can-save-nonprofits-hired-by-the-city

Mandavilli, A. (2020, December 8). Here's why vaccinated people need to wear a mask. *New York Times*, Retrieved from www.nytimes.com/2020/12/08/world/heres-why-vaccinated-people-still-need-to-wear-a-mask.html

Marietta, M. (2019, May 3). Fact-checking is effective where it counts. *Psychology Today*. Retrieved from www.psychologytoday.com/us/blog/inconvenient-facts/201905/fact-checking-is-ineffective-where-it-counts

Mazzucato, M. (2021). *Mission economy: A moonshot guide to changing capitalism*. New York: HarperCollins.

McCarthy, N. (2020, February 19). The most corrupt states in America. *Forbes*. Retrieved from www.forbes.com/sites/niallmccarthy/2020/02/19/the-most-corrupt-states-in-america-infographic/?sh=4db3c7172101

McEldowney, N. (2018, January 26). How to work for a president who loathes the civil service. *Washington Post*. Retrieved from www.washingtonpost.com/outlook/how-to-work-for-a-president-who-hates-the-civil-service/2018/01/26/34dbe95c-0204–11e8-bb03–722769 454f82_story.html?utm_term=.1beb1 1803b27

Morris, T. (1997). *If Aristotle ran General Motors*. New York: Holt.

Neguyen, H. (2020, July 10). How do masks make voters feel? *YouGov*. Retrieved from https://today.yougov.com/topics/politics/articles-reports/2020/07/10/how-do-masks-make-voters-feel

Nielsen, R. (1987). What can managers do about unethical management? *Journal of Business Ethics, 6*, 309–320.

Office of US Senator Elizabeth Warren. (2016). *Rigged justice: How weak enforcement lets corporate offenders off easily*. Washington, DC: US Senate.

Palmer, P. (2007). *The courage to teach: Exploring the inner landscape of a teacher's life* (10th anniversary ed.). San Francisco: Jossey-Bass.

Papenfass, M. (2020, November 27). Security experts fear state secrets won't be safe with indebted Donald Trump. *HuffPost Canada*. Retrieved from www.huffingtonpost.ca/entry/state-secrets-trump-international-businesses_n_5fc19706c5b6e4b1ea4b59be?guccounter=1&guce_referrer=aHR0cHM6Ly93d3cuYmluZy5jb20vbmV3cy9zZWFyY2g_cT0uK1NlY3VyaXR5 5K0V4cGVydHMRmVhcitTdGF0ZS

Perry, J. (2020). *Managing organizations to sustain passion for public service*. Cambridge University Press.

Perry, J., & Buckwalter, N. (2012). The public service of the future. *Public Administration Review, 70*(suppl. 1), S238–S245.

Perry, M. (2012, May 29). Florida's newest good government group wants to clean up state ethics. *CLTampaBay Loaf*. Retrieved from http://cltampa.com/dailyloaf/archieves/2012/05/29/floridas-newest-good-government-group

Prather, K., Wang, C., & Schooley, R. (2020, June 26). Reducing transmission of SARS-CoV-2. *Science, 328*(6498), 1422–1424.

Qiu, Y., Ziubek-Skees, C., & Lincoln, E. (2018, February 2). How does your state rank for integrity? *Center for Public Integrity*. Retrieved from https://publicintegrity.org/politics/state-politics/state-integrity-investigation/how-does-your-state-rank-for-integrity/

Rosenzweiz, P., & Kannan, V. (2020, September 7). Repairing the rule of law: An agenda for post-Trump reform. *Law Fare*. Retrieved from www.lawfareblog.com/repairing-rule-law-agenda-post-trump-reform

Schechtman, K., & Simon, S. (2021, May 27). America's entire understanding of the pandemic was shaped by messy data. *Government Executive*. Retrieved from https://www.govexec.com/management/2021/05/americas-entire-understanding-pandemic-was-shaped-messy-data/174323/

Schwartz, M. (ed.) (2020). *The ethics of pandemics*. Tonawanda, NY: Broadview Press.

Shermer, M. (2015). *The moral arc: How science makes us better people*. New York: St. Martin's Griffin.

Taub, J. (2020). *Big dirty money: The shocking injustice and unseen cost of white collar crime*. New York: Viking.

Taylor, A. (2020, June 25). How the split over face masks sums up America's chaotic coronavirus response. *Washington Post*. Retrieved from www.washingtonpost.com/world/2020/06/25/face-masks-america-divided/

Tufekci, Z. (2020, November 6). On masks and clinical trials, Rand Paul's tweeting is just plain wrong. *New York Times*. Retrieved from www.nytimes.com/2020/11/06/opinion/sunday/coronavirus-masks.html

Twenty things you should know about corporate crime. (2007, June 12). *Corporate Crime Reporter*. Retrieved from http://corporatecrimereporter.com/twenty061207.htm

Waldman, P. (2020, October 1). Trump has turned the entire government into a subsidiary of his campaign. *Washington Post*. Retrieved from www.washingtonpost.com/opinions/2020/10/01/trump-has-turned-entire-government-into-subsidiary-his-campaign/

Wallman, B. (2012a, August 8). No ethics investigations from corruption watchdog. *Sun Sentinel*. Retrieved from www.sun-sentinel.com/news/palm-beach/fl-inspector-general-20120805

Wallman, B. (2012b, August 7). Palm's reputation of corruption on way out, reformers say. *Sun Sentinel*. Retrieved from www.sun-sentinel.com/news/palm-beach/fl-inspector-general -performance-palm

Wegman, J. (2020, July 2). Seriously, just wear your mask. *New York Times*. Retrieved from www.nytimes.com/2020/07/02/opinion/coronavirus-masks.html

White, D. (2010). *The nonprofit challenge: Integrating ethics into the purpose and promise of our nation's charities*. New York: Palgrave Macmillan.

White Collar Crime (2012). Syracuse, New York: TRAC Report Service, Syracuse University.

Wilcox, B., & Krassner, D. (2012). Corruption risk report: Florida ethics laws. *Integrity Florida*. Retrieved from www.integrityfl.org/corruption-risk-report-florida-ethics-laws-3/

Wilkins, B. (2020, October 18). AOC and other top progressive urge Biden—if Elected—to deny K Street, Wall Street Exes top cabinet posts. *Naked Capitalism*. Retrieved from www.nakedcapitalism.com/2020/10/aoc-and-other-top-progressives-urge-biden-if-elected-to-deny-k-street-wall-street-execs-top-cabinet-posts.html

Wright, L. (2021). *The Plague year: America in the time of Covid*. New York: Knopf.

Zakaria, F. (2017, August 18). The mealy-mouthed cowardice of America's elites after Charlottesville. *Washington Post*. Retrieved from www.washingtonpost.com/opinions/the-mealy-mouthed-cowardice-of-americas-elites-after-charlottesville/2017/08/17/48913872-8396–11e7-b359–15a3617c767b_story.html?utm_term=.a4604acbfc65

Zakaria, F. (2020). *Ten lessons for a post-pandemic world*. New York: Norton.

Appendix 15.1
Sample Graduate Student Action Plan

The readings have made me aware of the potential ethical possibilities and pitfalls faced in the course of a career. One way to capitalize on the possibilities and avoid pitfalls is to expand my ethical capacity by creating an "action plan." My plan has four goals: Two have deadlines, and two are ongoing goals. I have also identified the tools I intend to use to achieve these goals. The last section discusses the overall development components of the plan.

Goals

1. Create a mission statement and identify the principles that are critical for ethical decision-making: one month out from today.

   The readings examine several decision-making methods. I realize this is important as both a professional and an individual to identify the tenets that are most significant for me. This would be the first step toward leading a principle-based life. These principles will also provide me with a way to assess my decisions on a continuing basis.

   Tools: I will read Stephen Covey, *First Things First* and *Principle-Centered Leadership*, as well as Tom Morris's book discussed in this chapter; continue journal writing; do research into servant leadership; engage in ongoing discussions with my mentor and my spouse to develop and update the mission statement I prepared at the beginning of this class to nurture, per Morris, the intellectual, aesthetic, moral and spiritual dimensions of my life.

2. Investigate the potential hurdles for continuing study: two months out.

   My studies and past experiences offer an opportunity to grasp the complications and ethical issues faced by professional administrators. Understanding and recognizing the challenges to be confronted in the future creates awareness of potential problems. I intend to pursue another degree next year and would like to understand and recognize the dilemmas that characterize that field.

   Tools: I will investigate the typical duties and responsibilities in obtaining another degree and examine ethical cases found in that area. I will talk to students and professors about the ethical issues that one would encounter in these situations.

3. Because an ethical administrator always does his/her best work for all projects, I will continue to improve my professional capabilities: ongoing.

It is my responsibility to always perform my best; it simply is not acceptable to perform below my personal standards. Although this goal might be seen as problematic, it is extremely important if one wants to retain the trust of his/her supervisors and my own self-confidence. In addition to maintaining the established standards, I should continue to enhance my skill set and capabilities.

Tools: Maintain professional certification, through continuing educational activities. Complete the Ethics Self-Assessment (2017) retrieved from www.ache.org/newclub/career/ethself.cfm), Ethics Quiz (2017) retrieved from https://icma.org/documents/ethics-quiz, as well as Integrity and Work Ethics Test (2020) retrieved from www.psychologytoday.com/us/tests/career/integrity-and-work-ethics-test. Look for opportunities to learn new skills or improve existing skills.

4. Assess my ethical capacity on a regular basis and change the action plan based on the new challenges and needs: ongoing.

    Like any other plan, this one is only as good as long as it is used. Therefore, it is key to constantly refer to it and make changes as needed. I will place the plan near my office calendar so it cannot be overlooked. Once a week, on Sunday evening, I will review the decisions I made and match them with my ethical action plan to check my progress. As part of this, I will benefit from the answers to the self-assessment here as well as feedback from mentors, my spouse, and friends.

    Tools: Weekly review and revision.

Developmental Components

In addition to the aforementioned goals, the plan includes the following elements.

Assessment. This allows an individual to recognize the gaps between the current performance and the aspirations in the action plan. I will use a multipronged approach to assess my performance on a regular basis: self-assessment, peer assessment, and supervisory assessment.

My new employer requires the supervisors to evaluate all the employees on a quarterly basis. During the next evaluation cycle, I will request my supervisor to add ethical decision-making to the evaluation criteria and request his feedback on my performance. I will suggest that ethics be a regular agenda item at staff meetings. Agenda items could include guest speakers, a review of the agency's code of conduct, and examination of ethical dimensions of major decisions under consideration by the department.

Challenges. I am a member of my local American Society for Public Administration chapter and, in the next few months, I will initiate new activities for our chapter and will expand my leadership capabilities and organization skills. I will continue to improve my academic standing by participating in conferences and will work on publishing an article in a professional publication.

Prior to the start date of my new job with the state government, I will write a plan to improve my ethicality, with particular attention to the blind sports, vulnerabilities, and irrational tendencies revealed by the behavioral sciences. I will also examine the state ethics code and determine if my department has more specific, complementary documents.

Support. I will request the support of my mentor in writing the mission statement and request her feedback on the other activities as they relate to this plan. I will start ethical discussions with my peers and provide support when needed.

Tentative Concluding Thoughts (to be regularly updated).

Responding thoughtfully to ethical dilemmas is crucial in order to reflect public values and have a meaningful career. Self-assessments have and will help me to understand my strengths and weaknesses. I am shaping my goals to move forward and marshaling resources to assist me in developing ethical capacity. I should be able to effectively discipline myself to become more ethical in my thoughts and actions. I commit to dealing with habits such as procrastination, time management, and distractions; my checklist, journal, and mentor will help to ensure that poor habits are replaced by good ones.

Index

Note: Page numbers in *italics* refer to figures and those in **bold** refer to tables.

Milton Keynes UK
Ingram Content Group UK Ltd.
UKHW031828300823
427791UK00010B/69